THE
LOCH

FRAN DORRICOTT

avon.

Published by AVON
A division of HarperCollins*Publishers* Ltd
1 London Bridge Street
London SE1 9GF

www.harpercollins.co.uk

HarperCollins*Publishers*
Macken House,
39/40 Mayor Street Upper,
Dublin 1
D01 C9W8
Ireland

A Paperback Original 2023
1

First published in Great Britain by HarperCollins*Publishers* 2023

ISBN: 978-0-00-844936-0

Typeset in Sabon Lt Std by Palimpsest Book Production Limited,
Falkirk, Stirlingshire

Printed and bound in the UK using 100% Renewable Electricity
at CPI Group (UK) Ltd

MIX
Paper | Supporting
responsible forestry
FSC™ C007454

This book is produced from independently certified FSC™ paper
to ensure responsible forest management.

For more information visit: www.harpercollins.co.uk/green

For Xena
I did not realise how brightly you shone until my
world went dark.

And for Tom
I finally managed to write a book without
spoiling the plot for you. Enjoy!

Prologue

Then

Mist hangs low over the shores of Loch Aven. Golden dawn light warms the tops of the trees but touches little else. Paul used to like it this way, endlessly quiet with only the gentle lapping of water and the distant trill of birds in the trees. Today is different. Instead of the sounds of nature muffling the world, there is the endless echo of footsteps; hoarse, sleepless voices calling; his world collapsing.

Paul has no proof that the loch has anything to do with it – with what has happened to his niece, or the other girl – but there is no proof that it hasn't either. It's why they have ended up here again, another small, exhausted search party fanning through the trees on yet another shore of this endless blasted lake.

The loch has always drawn folks to it, like the pull of its currents must be magnetic to the population of Blackhills. Paul himself remembers that same pull, that tugging in his gut that drew him and his brother here with their friends weekend after weekend, that drove them to light fires on its shores, to litter their cans amongst the rubble of their revelry – until the guilt made them clean it up.

There has always been something sort of . . . unworldly about this place.

It makes sense to him that his niece would have come here. Her first day back in the village, before even a visit to her parents. It's exactly what he might have done. He has no proof, of course, that she came here. None of them do. But they're grasping at straws, because where else could his best girl be?

He can't stop picturing the way he last saw her, her mane of hair flying behind her as she marched purposefully straight through the village, on a mission too important for her to hear him when he called her name. Although he hadn't tried especially hard. After all, he'd thought he would be seeing her later, after she'd been to her parents. After she'd reacquainted herself with village life. Would he have done anything differently if he'd known it would be the last time he'd see her? Would he have run after her?

No. He wouldn't have caught her.

There's no use thinking like that, though. He *didn't* know. Her coming back was supposed to be the beginning again, not the end. A smoothing out of tension between her and her dad, not . . . an unravelling.

Paul isn't sure what would be worse now: never finding out what happened to his niece, or having his darkest fears confirmed. He told Mary to stay at home this morning and she stayed, he thinks, because she didn't know what was worse either. Robert and his wife, Gwyn, are with the police again, going over and over everything as though that will solve anything. Paul is glad he doesn't have to be there. He doesn't know what he might think, who he might blame – what he might say out loud.

One thing Paul has realised is that Rebecca isn't the little girl who used to come and sit on his lap behind the counter so she could sort the pennies into piles of ten; she isn't the same young woman who only a year ago set out to travel the world, to become the best version of herself. The truth is none of them know her as well as they thought – and that's enough to break his heart.

A shout rips through the general cacophony of human noise, the crack of twigs and clap of warming hands.

'Hey!'

Paul pauses. Since they began half an hour ago, Rebecca's friend Joshua has not been far away, marching purposefully along the water's edge – but he's not there now. Paul swivels in his tracks and notices Joshua's dark head as he bends low over the water. A shiver of fear turns his bowels to water.

He breaks into a run. A couple of the others have noticed, too, from where they are spread through the treeline, and Paul hears what might be the thunder of feet coming to join them, or might just be the thunder of his heart. He feels sick.

Janie's brother, John, skids into him as they both reach Joshua's side together. He's panting, his speckled forehead slick with sweat.

'No,' he says. 'Oh, God.'

Joshua shifts out of the way and Paul sees he's holding a long stick, crooked at the end, and he's been using it to prod at something in the water.

'What is it? Please . . .' comes a breathless plea. Lucy is behind him now, her hands clasped in front of her in a kind of prayer. Her blonde hair is swept back in its usual chignon, but strands have escaped and she looks wild – as wild as Paul feels.

'It's not . . .' Joshua's voice trembles. 'But . . .'

But.

He is still holding the stick. At its crooked end is something dark, soaked with the water of the loch.

Paul peers closer. It's a piece of clothing. Something thick and heavy, embroidered with flowers. He recognises it. It's the proof, then. He was right. It's . . .

'It's hers,' he says.

SATURDAY

Eleanor

Loch House is waiting for us. We approach it from the road – a single dirt track, mud clumping to our already filthy shoes – and it appears between the trees like a mirage. A warm, dry, *gorgeous* mirage.

From the booking information, I'd been expecting something smaller, a cabin overlooking the lake, but this is something else entirely. It's huge, grand in a way that makes even the trees around it seem small. At the front there is a peaked roof above a covered square porch, tendrils of ivy snaking up past the wide windows and crawling along silver stone.

Michaela lets out a whooping sound, triumphant, and I can't help the grin that sneaks across my face as Clio shakes her head.

'See?' Michaela crows, doing a little dance that makes her rucksack bounce awkwardly on her back. 'I told you it wasn't far down this road. Didn't I tell you?'

Clio rolls her eyes, smiling good-naturedly. 'Yes,' she says.

'You told us. I still would have preferred to drive the whole way though, my feet are soaking.'

'We have been in the car for *hours*. Excuse me for wanting to stretch my legs! And hey, at least I'm not making you camp in this hideous weather any more.' Michaela sticks out her tongue childishly. I gaze up at the clouds, which are still dark and swollen with rain.

'We still would be if El hadn't managed to get us a refund on the pitch deposit.' Clio points out.

'Oh, hey,' I say, fighting a laugh. 'Don't drag me into this.'

Michaela always uses me to prove her points, even though it winds Clio up – she has done ever since the first week we met, freshers at uni thrust together to live in the same small, dark flat.

'You've been thoroughly dragged already,' Clio says to me. 'Through a hedge, by the looks of things.' She reaches up to tidy my damp hair, which has become windswept on the short walk from the car. The booking instructions weren't very clear and the road looked so narrow from the car that we'd decided to park about half a mile away, but really we probably could have managed to drive down the lane without getting stuck in the muck.

I pull my attention away from the beautiful grey stone house ahead, its black roof slick and shiny and its windows reflecting the solid mass of thunder clouds overhead. Cool air snakes at my back. The rain has stopped momentarily, but the air tastes thick with the promise of more.

Secretly, I'm glad Clio got her way this weekend; I didn't fancy the idea of camping in gale-force winds any more than she did. The weather's been so bad that there are yellow flood warnings, but it took until this morning for us to convince Michaela that maybe camping was a bad idea. She's a creature of the outdoors: hiking, climbing, travelling the world at the drop of a hat. I'm definitely more of a home bird.

'Besides,' Michaela goes on, 'the whole point of coming up here was getting to be in nature, right? Well, we're in nature. And isn't it gorgeous?' She spins on the spot, still triumphant.

'No, you're right, Kay, this place is absolutely stunning.' I gesture at the house and the trees, the short stretch of road between us and the house ahead littered with pine needles and the flame of fallen autumn leaves glittering beneath raindrops. 'It's worth the walk, and the rain. I actually can't believe it was available.'

Michaela preens, doing a terrible job of appearing modest. 'Guess I'm just a genius.'

'Or we got very lucky,' I suggest, mostly to wind her up.

'Lucky?' Clio snorts. The longer side of her cropped dark hair sways as she shifts so her own backpack sits more comfortably, another, smaller, leopard-print handbag slung over one shoulder. I think she's packed half her wardrobe for the weekend, and she might be wearing the other half right now, layered as she is in a T-shirt, shirt, hoodie and jacket. It's colder up here than back home, but it's not *that* cold. 'You call this luck? We're only here because we got *un*lucky and there was literally no other choice.'

'Psh,' Michaela brushes her off. 'Like I said: we're not camping. You can thank the storm for that, and you can thank whatever deity you believe in for this place instead. Isn't this, like, some kind of miracle as far as you're concerned?'

'Come on,' I nudge. 'I can't wait to get inside. I'm freezing and somewhere in there is a cup of tea with my name on it – with water from an actual, honest to God kettle.'

Plus, and I don't say this because it sounds weird even in my head, there's a strange feeling in the air out here. It's not bad – not really – but I've got this overwhelming urge to get into the house so that I can see the water, which I know is lapping at the dock of this rented property on the other side.

Clio nods gratefully and even Michaela seems happy enough to give up on her celebrations in favour of some warmth. The sky looks like it's going to open up again any moment and the rain is likely to be torrential when it does.

It takes longer than I thought it might to reach the house. The trees crowd close to the porch, giving the path a sheltered, tunnel-like feel, drawing us towards Loch House. I meant what I said about a cup of tea – it's genuinely a luxury I didn't think we'd get this weekend. I thought we'd be boiling all our water over a stove and eating beans out of a can.

'Wow,' Michaela remarks. 'Okay, I'll say it again. This place is great. I'm almost mad we didn't book it from the start. And it's closer to the village than the campsite was.'

There's a lockbox on the outer wall of the porch, grimy with dust and damp, and Michaela lifts her phone screen up to get the number right. It's gloomy here in the shadow of the house, the tall trees not doing much to help. The sun, hidden behind clouds and pines, feels like it hardly exists at all.

We manage to get into the lockbox after only a minute, Clio sagging against the damp wall with her giant rucksack hanging off one shoulder. When Michaela gets the key in the lock and turns it, there's a loud *snick* and the three of us cheer.

'Thank *God*,' Clio groans. 'I hope this place has a bathtub.'

'Oh my lord, Clio. I didn't exactly make you walk miles to get here. It's a good job we didn't camp. I can see that I'd definitely have killed you by the end of the weekend.'

We all laugh. To be honest, camping was a bad idea from the start, but it was *Michaela's* idea – one that she's been going on about in some capacity or other for near enough five years. She's been having such a rough time recently that Clio and I finally agreed to go along with it. It was an escape, and it was cheap, and that was all we cared about.

Besides, I haven't had many proper holidays since I started at my job two years ago; counselling adoptive families is rewarding, but I am definitely overdue the kind of break where I'm *not* glued to my phone.

Camping would have been the perfect switch-off, but I'm *very* glad we found Loch House instead.

'I was so looking forward to a campfire though,' Michaela says wistfully as she steps back to let me inside first.

I go ahead, ushered into what feels like another world.

'*Oh*,' Clio says.

The porch leads straight into a huge open space, a wood-panelled kitchen-diner on the right with a lovely old-fashioned stove and central island, and ahead is the lounge, which has a high ceiling, two cosy-looking sofas and a large stone fireplace complete with log burner, and – best of all – two sliding glass doors that look out over the decking and the lake beyond.

We rush forward, dumping our bags haphazardly on the floor in an attempt to get closer to the glass. The sky looks like a bruised apple, green and brown and grey, and the

11

first new drops of falling rain prickle the surface of the lake at the end of a long dock.

'This is incredible.' I turn to Michaela, almost reluctant to draw my eyes from the expanse of water, the rolling hills in the distance bordered with more pines, thick and dark and taller than you'd think possible. There is a mist that seems to cling to everything, sitting on top of the water at the edges like a shroud. 'And you said it just had like . . . open availability?'

Michaela's dark eyes are wide as she takes in the view. 'Yeah. I know, right? It's wild. Literally the only place for miles and I'm not sure anybody's booked it for the rest of the year. We could stay all week if we wanted.' She waggles her eyebrows suggestively, though I think she's only half joking.

Clio frowns. 'You didn't tell me that this morning,' she says. 'Doesn't that seem . . . a bit dodgy to you?'

'What? Why?' Michaela gestures around. The house is a little dusty but has a sort of rustic charm, woven throws on the sofas and an old, worn rug in front of the fireplace. 'We're in the middle of nowhere. I don't think it's that strange. We got lucky there was anywhere available at all, otherwise we'd have ended up in some stupid-expensive hotel somewhere random.' She grits her teeth and shakes her head as though it's the worst thing she can imagine. I suppose, given the new uncertainty about her job, it's not surprising that she might suddenly decide that any additional cost is one expense too far. I can't really blame her, I'm not exactly rolling in it myself, and I know Clio doesn't make loads from her storytelling gig, even though she's amazing at it. I think she's probably undercharging.

'It's probably just too out of the way,' I agree. 'It's not

like the village – Blackhills, right? It's not as if it's a massive tourist spot. My parents took me all over Scotland and Wales when I was growing up and there were always places like this that somehow just seemed to thrive despite never getting much attention.'

'But the loch,' Clio says. 'Surely people come for the loch. Why else would they have this big house just sat here?'

'I'm sure they do,' I say. 'In the summer. I suspect most people tend to go somewhere warmer this late in the year.'

This makes Clio pull a face in Michaela's direction and we all laugh again. Clio had wanted, desperately, to fly somewhere hot – and had been pushing for a summer holiday months ago, but Michaela hadn't been able to get the time off. Being a lawyer, it turned out, meant making some sacrifices. And now Michaela didn't have the money, and she'd had her heart set on camping, so a break in the UK had suddenly been on the table.

I'm not about to complain. It's been over four years since we graduated, and I thought it might be good to remember the things that had brought us together in the first place – cheap wine, uncomfortable beds and late nights talking about nothing much at all. As Michaela said: it would be fun.

'Sorry,' Michaela jokes. 'I didn't realise you were as dead set against a cosy house as you were the tent.'

'The tent,' Clio groans. 'Oh God, don't remind me. I was so stressed. I had *dreams*.'

'*You* were stressed?' Michaela says.

We've been skirting around the topic of Michaela's failure to be kept on after the training contract that was *supposed* to turn into a permanent role at the law firm she's worked at for the last two years, and it's starting to get uncomfortable.

13

I don't know how much Michaela wants to talk about it. Normally, she'd bitch and moan and get it out of her system, and then she'd have a plan and feel unconquerable once more. I was expecting it for the whole drive up from Durham, and I think Clio was too. Instead, Michaela talked about everything *but* her job, asking Clio about the story-telling, begging for tales about awkward parents who booked Clio for their parties, bugging me about how my parents were doing, whether I'd made any progress on finding my birth family – something I've been working on for months this time around. I usually get frustrated and bin it off after hitting the same brick wall, but this time I'm still going, though I've had no luck and I told her that.

Every time there was a lull in the conversation, I waited for her to bring it up, to tell us what happened. You don't just get let go from a training contract for no reason. But she still hasn't said anything and I don't want to pry.

I leave Clio and Michaela to bicker and wander back into the lounge proper. The way the half-light hits the sliding glass doors through the pine needles creates weaving shadows that look like long fingers, grasping. The place has an untouched feel to it, compounded by the old magazines scattered on the small rough-hewn coffee table and the creased spines of the paperback books on the bookcase. It's clean and very tidy, but it feels . . . unloved, I guess. Even though somebody clearly put a lot of effort into making it nice once upon a time. I want to fill it with our laughter, light the fire and make it warm and festive.

I grab my bag and haul it up the creaking wooden stairs. Everything is panelled in the same dark wood and it makes the place feel homey and yet somehow eerie too. Everything echoes. I can hear the sounds of Michaela and Clio talking downstairs as Michaela starts to empty the seemingly endless snacks from her bag; I can hear the crinkle of crisp packets and the dull shake of the sugar container, and I send up a silent prayer of thanks for both of them. It's good to be here, just the three of us, and the rain and the water and the trees.

Upstairs, there are three large bedrooms with double beds and a family bathroom, all clean and neat with neutral-tone decor accented with random items in green plaid: blankets, cushions, even the towels in the small linen cupboard. The back two bedrooms look out over the water, which is churning under the heavy rain. The weather app on my phone says the worst of the storm will pass soon – at least until tomorrow – but the temperature is set to drop below zero. Typical.

I dump my bags in the smaller bedroom at the back of the house, knowing Clio will want the one that looks out over the trees and the road at the front and Michaela deserves the biggest bedroom of the three, and then unpack a few bits – not that I brought much with me, just corded sweaters and comfortable jeans, a pair of leather boots with a fur trim which I'm glad for, and some slippers, which I pop on now. I send a quick text to my parents to let them know we arrived safely, though the signal here isn't very good and I have to stand by the window, holding my phone up high, waiting for it to send. Mum sends back a photo of her very wet garden in Leicester, which also takes an age to download.

By the time I eventually make it back downstairs, Michaela and Clio have emptied out the food stash and have put the kettle on, but there's a hollowness now that wasn't there before, their jokes and laughter a little muted. They're sat together on one of the sofas, Clio's legs draped across Michaela's lap, and they're staring out of the big glass doors. The mist that had been floating at the edges of the lake has rolled further across, even in the minutes since I last checked, and the whole surface of the lake is swathed in it. I suppress the delicious little shiver that worms its way up my spine.

The water is so still I find it eerie, yet somehow I can't bring myself to look away. It's at once beautiful and haunting, mesmerising in its promise of murky depths filled with who knows what. My heart beats faster, a flutter of emotion that might be longing or excitement or something else entirely.

'It's making me think of stories,' Clio says distantly and her voice startles me. It's a phrase I've heard before, countless times over the years I've known her. It means the situation, the weather, the way the stars have aligned, have made her remember one of the many stories she read while studying for her folklore degree, or one that she tells now when she's working. Normally, she frames it as a joke. *That cat's making me think of stories – you know the one about the fox with the two tails, the one that can divine the future? Wouldn't that be cool?* But today Clio doesn't follow it up until I prompt her.

'Which?' I ask.

Michaela blinks, shaking her head as though coming out of a trance. 'Weird. I was so focused on those trees in the distance, my eyes started to see double. Sort of like seeing a ghost.'

'Which stories?' I repeat.

Clio looks up at me and grins. 'The one about the beautiful brown-haired best friend who really fancies making me a cup of tea right now?'

'Cheeky!' Michaela cackles and jabs her thumb into the flesh of Clio's calf, causing her to scream and tumble away. I roll my eyes.

'Fine,' I grumble. '*Fine*. I'll make your tea, but only because you called me beautiful.'

'Maybe she was talking to me.' Michaela drags herself off the sofa and stretches like a cat. She wanders over to the fireplace, picking at various carved wooden ornaments – a stag's head with antlers made of polished brass, a bird of some kind, and what looks like it might be a snake or a lake monster captured in individual little loops that are meant to look as if the rest of its body are submerged in water, or in this case the mantel.

I reboil the water in the kettle and set out three mugs from a cupboard above. There's loose-leaf tea in a jar, but I opt for the teabags we brought with us since I'm not sure how long it's been there.

'What's the plan for the rest of the day?' Clio asks. She's stood by the doors again, fiddling with the locking mechanism until they slide open with a soft *swushh*, letting in a rush of October air.

'Watch those. The booking info says if they slam you need the key to get them open again.'

'It's okay,' Clio says. 'They're pretty stiff.'

'Anyway, back to the village, I think. I want to have a proper look around.' Michaela says this in a tone I *know* she learned on the job. She's a lawyer through and through, regardless of her shitty firm letting her go. This tone leaves absolutely no room for argument.

Clio, who has a history of whining until she gets her way, tries anyway. 'Are you *kidding* me? I thought we were done with the walking today.'

'You've hardly walked at all! It won't kill you to walk back to the car.'

'Ugh, that's what you think. These delicate bones simply can't take it. And we'll have to walk around the *whole* village and I know what you're like, so we'll be there hours and hours and I'm tired!'

'You're always tired,' I say kindly.

'Yes.' Clio nods sagely. 'I am, as the internet says, *bisexual and tired*.'

'I don't think that's actually how the saying goes.'

'Hey, have you guys seen this?'

When I turn around, teaspoon in hand, Michaela is kneeling on the floor by the coffee table. There's a big book spread out before her, with creamy pages that fall open at Michaela's touch.

'Nope,' Clio says. 'What?'

'Guest book,' Michaela replies. 'I think. Last entry is dated . . .' She peers closer, as if the ink is hard to read. 'Kinda faded. Is that a *nine*?'

'Let me see.' Clio walks across and leans over Michaela's shoulder, scooping the longer side of her hair behind her ear.

'Is it?' I drop the spoon in the sink and carry the mugs of tea over to the coffee table so I can join them. The book is quite small, around the size of a regular hardback, not the usual textbook size I've seen for guest books, and each page is printed with a spray of pine trees across the bottom. 'Oh my God. The *nineties*?'

Clio backs away, holding her hands up. 'Nah, Kay, you did not bring me to a place that's not had guests since, like, before we were born.'

'Hey, you're the one who didn't want to go camping.'

'We don't know there haven't been other guests,' I point out. 'Maybe they have a digital guest book now. Maybe people just never fill it out, or it's a keepsake or something. Where did you even find it?'

Clio doesn't look convinced. She glares at the book with her green eyes narrowed as if she might set it on fire by willpower alone. While she's definitely hamming it up, I can't deny there's something strange about it. The book, and the unloved little house, and the eerie mist on the lake.

'Oh what does it matter,' Michaela says. 'There's heat, running water and beds, what more could we want?' She pauses, then turns to me. 'There *are* beds, right?'

'Yes,' I laugh. 'There are beds. Or, two at least. I didn't check Clio's room. Probably she'll have to sleep on the floor. I hear it's good for your posture.'

The girls grab their mugs of tea and carry them back to the sofa, along with a pack of Jammie Dodgers. The door is still open a crack and the damp air blusters in. I stand right in the gap and suck in the fresh scents. The dock and the decking connecting it to the house look slippery with the rain. I glance down at my slippers and make a mental note to only head down there in proper shoes, and to encourage Michaela and Clio to do the same. The last thing we want is somebody falling in.

Eleanor

Michaela leads the way down the path that takes us back toward where we parked the car. We're quicker than we were this morning, less burdened by our heavy bags and with the comforting knowledge that we'll have somewhere warm and dry to return to later buoying our steps.

The chill in the air is refreshing now that we're not so wound up from the length of the drive, tiredness making everything feel heavy. All three of us had a little nap after the tea and biscuits and we're raring to go. Well, raring might be an overstatement, but I for one am enjoying the feel of the breeze on my cheeks and the soft dampness in the air, tinged with woodsmoke and the soft undercurrent of fresh water. We left Durham so early this morning that it's not even lunchtime yet and we have until Tuesday to take it all in, to unwind and—

'Why, exactly, are we heading to the village again when we have everything we need for the rest of the day in the house?' Clio interrupts my thoughts, striding alongside us as if she hasn't been lagging down the path so far. She's doing the voice she does when she's intentionally winding Michaela up, but for once Kay doesn't notice; her brown eyes look bright and her cheeks are flushed, and I realise how badly she needs this break.

'I want to have a look around,' Michaela says. 'There's hardly any information online about what sort of stuff there is in the village, but maybe there are some nice kitschy shops – or a really cosy pub. We could get a pint, some lunch. Oh, *lunch* . . .' She presses her hand to her chest dramatically. Food is Michaela's love language.

'Okay. Point taken. I am actually getting hungry,' Clio concedes.

'And we do need supplies for later, unless you want to live on roadside garage milk, tea, crisps and Clio's stale Pop Tarts,' I remind them.

The car is just up ahead, tucked off the road. We all clamber in eagerly and Michaela wastes no time cranking up the heat. 'I guess we've still got beans and bread and snacks, but we have a whole kitchen to use now. Wouldn't it be nice to buy something more . . . appetising?'

'I'll have you know I practically *live* on beans on toast for, I dunno, maybe a week out of every month,' Clio points out.

That doesn't surprise me. In fact, I'd go so far as to say it would surprise me if that *wasn't* true. Clio's an absolutely appalling chef. Her last partner, Bobby, did almost all of the cooking – and the cleaning, and the laundry, and the errands . . . I'm not surprised the relationship only lasted two months.

'Yes, well,' I say, 'not to be the mum friend, but I am thinking we could stretch the budget just a tiny bit more and incorporate some form of green vegetable with dinner tonight. And wine.'

'Ooh yes,' says Michaela. 'Wine.'

With the prospect of alcohol and snacks before us, we set off back into the village. Blackhills doesn't feel as far away now we know where we're going. The track that leads to the house, and to the loch, soon feeds into a larger road and then we're right in the thick of Blackhills. *Population 961.* I bet everybody knows everybody else's business around here.

The village seems to centre around one main road, lined on both sides with shops and amenities. It's small enough to be quaint but feels lived in, not like those tiny hamlets you usually find in the middle of nowhere. Benches are dotted along the low walls that separate the pavement from the buildings perched a little higher away from the road, festooned with flowers of all colours.

We drive past a church at one end of the road, its green graveyard verdant and damp, then past a school and towards what looks like a village hall, its large windows ornately leaded. Michaela spots a small square car park in front of a segmented bank of shops, opposite a pharmacy. Everything here seems to be hewn from the same rough silver stone, reflecting the weak sun. Bunting flutters between lamp posts, worn but still cheerful.

We pile out into the chilly air, Michaela battling a shiny new umbrella while Clio grins as she spots a small bookshop not far from the car park. There's a window filled with cute children's titles and she practically presses her nose against the glass to get a better look before Michaela grabs her arm and drags her onward.

'You absolutely do not need any more second-hand books.'

'Why not? They might have good ones. You know I'm still looking for that copy of the 1983—'

'*Neverending Story*. Yes, we know.'

Clio got into collecting antique children's books after she broke up with Heather, which was a much more serious affair than the Bobby break-up. They'd dated right the way through university, although we all said Heather wasn't good for Clio – and she openly admitted it, too. They broke up about a year ago, when Heather decided to take a job down in London, and Clio refused to go with her. Clio said she was relieved that they'd finally acknowledged it wasn't working, but she was incredibly down for months, and has only just started to get back to her childishly enthusiastic self.

Thinking about Clio's break-up with Heather makes me think about Charlotte. I still haven't told my parents that it's over, and whenever Clio or Michaela have tried to talk about it, I've shut them down. It's been two months and I'm still not even getting close to being over it. So maybe I can understand Kay not wanting to talk about the job thing . . .

'You do know you can buy that book online, right?' I offer gently, not wanting to burst Clio's bubble. 'I checked and it's available on—'

'I know, it's just not the same.' Clio tucks her hair behind one ear and moves to button up her jacket, which is bulky over her hoodie and shirt. 'Ooh! Thrift shop!'

Before I know it, we're tumbling out of the cold into a tiny boutique containing more mannequins than people.

The woman behind the counter to our left looks up, her golden brows arching in surprise. 'Uh, hello.' Her welcome is accented and hesitant.

I glance at the others, but Clio is already halfway across the shop searching through a display of bracelets and

Michaela has found a stash of scarves not unlike the silk one she's very stylishly draped around her own throat today.

'Hi,' I say.

'You're not . . . part of that group of campers I keep hearing about, are you?' she asks.

Clio lets out a squark of laughter. 'Not on your life,' she replies.

'Campers?' Michaela asks.

'Oh,' the woman says. 'No, never mind. I just . . . mistook you for somebody else.'

We browse for a few minutes, oohing and aahing over various bits of clothing and jewellery. The prices are great and Michaela purchases one of the scarves – a pretty teal one with a swirling grey pattern, gossamer thin and useful for nothing except looking gorgeous, which, against Michaela's brown skin, it really does.

'Don't you already have one that colour?' Clio says. 'I'm sure you have one in your bag—'

'That's for my hair. This one isn't. Justifiable purchase, thank you very much. Anyway, who made you the queen of sensible buying?'

I browse the back of the shop where there is a row of printed graphic T-shirts. There's one with a smiling bee on it which says *Don't worry, Bee happy* across the front, the font made of little black lines charting the flight of a bumble bee. It's the sort of thing Charlotte would have cackled at and then insist I buy. She insisted on a lot of things.

Michaela catches my gaze. 'Come on,' she says. 'Let's go. There are lots of other places to look before we eat.'

I hurry to join the two of them at the door, Michaela grabbing my hand as the dinging of the little bell above the door announces our exit. We lurch back out into the cool air and I'm grateful for the soothing sensation on my burning cheeks.

'I wonder what she meant about us being campers,' Clio says. 'Do I give off an outdoorsy vibe?'

'Not sure. I guess they just don't get a lot of tourists around here.' I shrug.

'Clearly not,' Clio replies wryly. 'Did you see the way she looked at us? Like, she definitely thought we were gonna steal stuff.'

'Weird,' Michaela determines, linking arms with mine as the three of us forge our way up the main street. 'Maybe she's just bored.'

'It *is* very quiet,' I say. 'I'd have thought it might be busier – I thought it was school holidays in October.'

'Maybe it's different in Scotland?' Clio suggests.

'Nah, it's probably the sort of place where everybody goes away during the breaks. Maybe they're all camping and they got stuck somewhere with all that awful rain.'

Clio grimaces, and I know she's picturing what would have happened if *we* had been the ones to get stuck. She's been bad enough since we got here, moaning about the phone signal at the house and how cold she is.

It reminds me of the week we moved into our off-campus shared flat in second year, when we didn't have power for two days. Michaela's mum lived in Durham, though Kay had chosen not to stay at home while she studied, so she let us all shower and cook at her house and we only really went back to our place to sleep, but Clio still spent pretty much every waking moment complaining about the lack of Wi-Fi at the flat – until Michaela threatened to unearth her fan-fiction account and start reading it aloud, which shut her up pronto.

Blackhills is a cute village, though, which more than makes up for Loch House's lack of signal. Everything feels well cared for, pretty and tidy. Even the moss on the walls looks like it's been grown there on purpose, giving it that rustic faerie vibe. There's something about the whole place that feels very homey.

We pass a small barbers complete with spinning red and white stripes, a cafe with empty outdoor tables, a rose-pink awning and a misspelled sign, which Michaela makes fun of, and a small convenience store wrapped around a street corner, two girls on bikes hanging around outside while they wait for a friend. There is a post office right ahead, sandwiched between an independent clothes shop and a Chinese takeaway. Clio's eyes practically bug out of her head at the mere promise of food before Michaela pulls her away, gesturing down another street where there's a very obvious pub.

'Please can we eat now?' Clio begs. 'I am *starving*.'

'You ate literally a whole packet of biscuits!'

'El had some.'

'I had two,' I correct.

'See?' Clio says. '*Some*.'

A sudden, sharp gust of rain-scented wind blunders down the main street and right through the seams of my jacket. I shove my hands deep into my pockets, shivering. I knew it would be colder up here than back home but this is the sort of wind that cuts through you. I wish I'd brought my thicker coat.

Michaela gives an exaggerated sigh, but then slings her arm around Clio's shoulders and manoeuvres her body in the direction of the pub. Clio claps. I follow along with my hands still in my pockets, secretly glad. My stomach is churning, whether from the motorway services coffee or the lack of sleep, but I'm sure a solid meal will help.

Inside the pub, we're greeted by the comfortable, welcoming smell of a roast dinner and freshly poured beer. It's an old building, papered walls hung with genuine-looking paintings and an actual fireplace with a crackling fire. Michaela makes a pleased sound in her throat and Clio whistles.

'Nice.'

'See,' Michaela says. 'Told you Blackhills was *the* place.'

'No, you absolutely didn't say anything of the sort.'

It's busy in here, but not crowded for a Saturday afternoon. A few people glance up at us, and a few more pairs of eyes follow us as we settle in at a table to the left and Clio and Michaela begin poring over the menu. It doesn't take us long to decide what we're having and Clio and Michaela both head to the bar while I stay at the table.

There's a gentle hum of chatter and it lulls me as I wait. I'm more tired than I thought. I rest my head back and glance around, taking in the rustic decor, the general ambiance. The lighting is low and the grey sky outside doesn't help. I have a feeling that the weather forecast is wrong and it's going to start pelting it down again at any moment.

The patrons around me chat amongst themselves, across tables and groups seemingly indiscriminate. I bet many of them have known each other for years. On the way in I saw a table full of teens playing Jenga over by the fireplace, and just beyond is a low bookcase filled with old children's games – Frustration and Monopoly and the one with all the sticks you have to pull out of a yellow jar without the plastic monkeys falling down. I can't see any of it now because of the pillar that blocks the table from this angle but I make a mental note to suggest we have a proper look later. Clio will love them.

This makes me think of Charlotte again, how she always hated Clio's childishness, Michaela's bossiness. There's no reason for me to think of her now we're here, except that we'd planned a Scottish holiday once, right before we broke up. I don't even miss her, so I'm not sure why I've thought about her twice today already.

When the others return carrying a tray with pints of beer and glasses of water, Michaela slumps into her seat and lets out a big breath. 'Well, that was strange.'

'What?' I ask.

'The guy behind the bar was so odd,' Clio says. 'Really intense.'

'Intense, how?'

'He just seemed really taken aback,' Michaela remarks. 'Asked if we were tourists, wanted to know where we were headed. When I said we were staying here, he looked surprised.'

'Yeah, and this big burly bloke muttered something about the place being overrun with *disaster tourists* and stormed off. Looked like he'd blown a gasket.' Clio turns to Michaela. 'What did you say to set him off?'

'Oh, I was just . . . asking about something I read online.' She shrugs. 'I don't think he was mad at *me* specifically.'

'They clearly never get anybody from out of town sticking around,' Clio says. 'Which is like, weird, y'know? Because it's such a cute place.'

'I guess it's not really on the way to anywhere else though,' I suggest. I take a big mouthful of beer, but my stomach churns harder so I grab the water instead. 'You don't pass through if you're just casually heading north. You've got to want to come here.'

'I guess.' Clio rests her elbows on the table. 'They also said something about a group of campers getting stuck out of town somewhere, though, which explains what that woman was on about before.'

'Because of the weather?' I ask.

'Yeah,' Michaela says. 'I don't know if they're stuck or lost or what, but apparently people are getting ready to go help.'

'I guess that's why it's quiet around here,' Clio adds. 'Maybe we should offer to help them too.' She guffaws as though she's said something hilarious. Michaela pulls a face and Clio amends, 'I'm *not* serious. What made you pick here, anyway, Kay? Did you just stick a pin in a map?'

'Oh.' Michaela glances up from her phone before placing it face-down on the table. 'Uh, I was just looking at the lochs and trying to find somewhere really pretty for us to camp. A few places were solidly booked and then I found that Bear Saviour Camp Ground and it looked perfect because of the lake and the great hiking . . . And then obviously with the weather . . . I just googled for the closest accommodation to the site.'

'And there was Loch House,' I say. Like a miracle.

We settle into a comfortable silence as we wait for our food, Michaela playing with a napkin from the cutlery bucket on the table, lost in thought, and Clio and I watching as a couple of teens enter and head towards the table by the fire to the sound of cheering from their friends.

There's a lot to like about this place. It feels worn in and comfortable, like an old pair of shoes. A man and his wife order drinks at the bar, another man clapping the first on the shoulder as he passes as if they're old acquaintances; somebody else puts money into a slot machine and the cheery jingle of music rings through the pub.

Suddenly Clio's gaze snaps up and she sits up like a dog at the table, and seconds later I catch a whiff of food: steak and burgers and a vegetarian lasagne that looks really good.

The server is an older woman, probably in her fifties, with a knot of fiery red hair and glasses. She places the food down plate by plate, her expression carefully guarded, and when she's checked that we're all set, she pauses by the table, elbows akimbo.

'Uh . . .' Clio says.

'Is there . . . anything else?' I prompt.

The woman shrugs and makes to shake her head and then she lets out an amused little laugh. 'Sorry,' she says. 'Sorry. I just . . . Did you say you're staying at Loch House? Tim said something about Rob getting shirty at the bar after mention of those walkers getting stuck.'

'Ye-es,' Michaela replies hesitantly. 'Why?'

'Oh, nothing.' The server glances back over her shoulder, as if waiting for somebody to come and rescue her. And when nobody appears and the rest of the patrons in hearing distance are pointedly looking away, she adds, 'Just wanted to make sure you folks weren't here to hike too.'

'Why? Do campers make a habit of getting themselves into trouble around here?' Clio jokes. She looks from Michaela to me.

The server gives a small laugh that doesn't quiet meet her eyes. 'I hope not,' she says. 'Anyway, enjoy your food!'

Rebecca

Then

This isn't how it is supposed to happen. It should happen in a coffee shop or a restaurant, when Rebecca is with her friends, wearing make-up and a nice dress, with a glass of wine in her hand. It should happen when she is feeling bright and fresh, when she's had a full night's sleep and is capable of being charming. It should not happen when it's raining and the floor is still wet and squeaky from the mop; it should not happen when Rebecca is tired, when she is not expecting it.

But it does happen. It happens at eleven in the morning on a Saturday, right before the lunch rush. It happens when she is behind the counter at her parents' farm shop, her apron dusted with flour from the freshly baked bread and the remnants of chocolate icing on the end of her plait. She has bags under her eyes because she stayed up far too late reading and she's already spilled two coffees on herself, one so hot it left a small smear of red skin on her hand. She feels mussed and grubby.

At first, she isn't sure if he even remembers her. It's been a long time since they've crossed paths in such close proximity. He's been in the shop before, though rarely when she works, and somehow she's never served him. She's certainly not been this close to him, just a counter and a pen between them, in maybe five years.

He's older than she remembers him; his hair is already beginning to grey at the temples and his build is thicker, especially across his shoulders. Thirty-five looks good on him. Perhaps it's because there's more to him now, something in his expression that isn't just cheerful enthusiasm. He looks, Rebecca thinks, as if he's had a bad day.

He never looks like that.

But when he smiles at her, his teeth are *exactly* as white and straight as she remembers. His blue eyes crinkle at the corners, and that's just like she remembers too. The old familiar feeling of butterflies in her belly swamps her, pauses her in mid-action, one hand on the counter and a smile frozen in place.

'Rebecca,' he says. And he seems genuinely pleased to see her. '*Wow*. You look really well. I thought you worked at the cinema – how long have you been here?'

'Hi.' She's breathless with how nice it feels to be acknowledged by him. 'I've been here a couple of years now. I started helping out while Mum took some time off and it sort of stuck. I don't normally work weekends though. How are you?'

'I'm good,' he replies. 'I'm great.' His smile grows wider and she realises he's holding one of her mother's handmade cheese and onion quiches and a box of salted caramel truffles. 'I'm better now.'

'You will be after a box of truffles,' she says.

'Oh, these aren't for me.' He puts the quiche and the

34

chocolates down on the counter and taps his flat stomach. 'I've got to be careful these days.'

'Don't be silly,' Rebecca says without thinking. 'You're perfect already.'

Any other time, there might be an awkward silence. It's not the kind of thing you say to a man who is basically a stranger now. It's not the kind of thing Rebecca says to anybody at all. But his grin only grows wider and he lets out a genuine laugh.

'You always did have a way with words. Are you still writing for that – it was a travel magazine, right?'

Rebecca is somehow both surprised that he remembers and filled with the warm glow that she must have made as much of an impression on him as he did on her.

'It was a journal,' she corrects. 'Of places I always wanted to go.'

'And you're still working on it?'

'Yes. Sort of. I still want to travel a lot, maybe for six months or a year. As long as I can, really. I've been saying it for ages but I swear I'm going to go soon. I'm making plans. Saving up. There are so many places I want to go, it's hard to choose where to start.'

'Plans.' He nods agreeably and she swells with pride. He always seemed so clever, so untouchable in his intelligence. A lot of time has passed and it's not like that now. Now she feels like she could have something to offer to him. It's as if something has shifted. It's different, somehow, than just seeing him across the street, or with tables and cafe patrons between them.

Or maybe it's just that this time was always meant to be different. Maybe today *they* are different.

'Very sensible,' he continues. 'You can't just dive straight in with these kinds of things.' His words are layered with meaning, and Rebecca thinks she knows exactly what he's not saying. She wants to dive straight in. She wants to spend all day talking to him. But there's Mr Arnold behind him and he's waiting to pay.

She rings up the quiche and the chocolates, adding a discount to both in a moment of wild disobedience. Her parents will probably notice, but he's a good man, well-known in the village and well-liked too, so they'll probably let it slide. Call it a loyalty scheme.

When she hands the chocolates back to him, his fingers brush hers, just a small gesture that means nothing and somehow everything to her. Even if she doesn't see him again for another year or two, she could live off this inter-action forever, a schoolgirl crush made real. She knows it's not the same. She's an adult now, and it felt like he never noticed her before, although clearly he did.

In any case, he has definitely noticed her now.

'It's been so nice seeing you properly,' he says. 'When are you off on these travels then?'

Mr Arnold shifts impatiently but Rebecca ignores him.

'I'm still saving at the moment. I'm a good chunk of the way there, but I want a buffer, in case I decide not to come back here afterwards. In case I need a bit extra while I look for another job.' She pauses. 'Maybe next year. But . . . I said that last year too. My mum, uh, wasn't very well a while back and I just . . . Haven't got around to going yet. Like I said, there always seems to be something making me stick around.'

She's surprised at her own honesty. She hasn't even told her parents about not coming home yet, though it's the absolute truth. She's been saving non-stop since she left school, torn between splurging all of her money on one epic trip, or using some for a deposit for a house. Both options scare her – as does her dad's probable reaction to both of them after how tense he's been the last couple of years – which is why she's still here, stuck in town and working in the shop. It's been easier, while her mum has been poorly, to just keep pushing it aside. And before that too.

But when she says it aloud to *him*, it all seems so conquerable. Why couldn't she just travel, and then figure out the rest later? Why does having her own freedom mean she's not a good daughter?

He nods again, scooping up the chocolates and quiche in its cardboard tray and cradling it as if it's very precious to him. 'I'm sorry about your mum, I did hear she wasn't well. But, now she's on the mend, you've got time to plan again. And when you go, I bet you'll do it properly, find all these hidden places and write about them and get famous. That seems exactly right.' He winks. 'Thank you for this.' He's noticed the discount but he doesn't say it outright, and she doesn't either.

'I write poetry too,' she blurts as he starts to leave. She's not sure what makes her tell him, except that she can't let him leave without an opening. Fair enough if he doesn't take it – and she knows he probably won't. He shouldn't. She doesn't even really want him to. He never, ever would have before. But she can't just let him leave without *something*, some sense of what this meeting has made her feel, the future she had forgotten to be excited about made gold again by his enthusiasm. 'I read it at events sometimes, at Bernie's. It's the new cafe on—'

'I know Bernie's,' he says.

He doesn't acknowledge the poetry, the reading. He doesn't ask her when. And when he says goodbye, it's with a kind of haze there that wasn't there before.

She doesn't have time to dwell on it though, because there is Mr Arnold with his basket full to bursting and his grunted, ''Bout time.' She pastes a different kind of smile on her face and pretends nothing ever happened.

But long after Rebecca's last customer of the day, she thinks about whether she overstepped, whether even friendship would be inappropriate. He's so much older than her, and really she barely knows him. Then she remembers the way he's always made her feel, like she could do anything, be anyone, and she knows she made the right choice. She's put the ball in his court.

Now it's up to him.

Eleanor

'What on earth was that about?' Clio asks. She turns to me. 'I know the weather is rotten, but those campers aren't exactly in *loads* of danger, right? Why's everybody acting like we're making their lives harder? People must come here just to hang out sometimes, surely.'

Michaela glances down at her burger, loaded with onion rings and a pile of fries, and her brows crease deep.

'I wonder if they've had trouble in the past,' I suggest. 'You know, with people staying at the Loch House and going hiking and getting stuck. There are a lot of hills around. Didn't you say it was popular with walkers?' I turn to Kay.

'Yeah, there are loads of really popular routes, though most of them start in Blackdale or further afield *because* of the hills. I bet a lot of people go climbing up there though, the real adrenaline junkies.'

'*Let's go to a tiny Scottish village nobody has ever heard of*, she said,' Clio scoffs through a mouthful of lasagne. '*It'll be fun*, she said.' She pauses to take a bite of garlic bread and then frowns too. 'I still think it's weird that the house we're staying in has no bookings, though. Like, is there something wrong with it?'

'I'm sure it doesn't mean anything,' I say in Michaela's defence because she's got a mouthful of fries. 'We're in the middle of nowhere. It's fine.'

'That's not what your face says.' Clio scoops another spoonful of lasagne into her mouth and yelps when she hits a hot spurt of cheese.

'Dude, take it easy!' Michaela begins to saw her burger in half, delving in.

I stare at my plate of steak and wish, now, that I'd ordered something else.

We settle into a comfortable quiet, eating until we grow full and then allowing our conversation to turn back to our normal topics. Clio is explaining the latest book she's been reading – a collection of Grimm short stories she's read before – and narrating one of the stories with gusto. I really don't think she charges people enough, she's very, *very* good at it.

'There's one about this nixie who captures a brother and a sister and keeps them trapped in her well. She makes them do awful jobs, like chopping trees with a dull axe, and feeds them only dumplings that are just about as hard as rocks. They wait one day until she's at church – if you can believe that – and then run away. There's a whole bunch of things they do to try to keep her off their tails, but the only thing that works is throwing a mirror behind them, which turns into this like . . . it's like, a sheet of ice and it's so slippery that the nixie can't pass without breaking it, so she has to go back and get her axe. I was thinking about it earlier when we sat looking over the loch, how it feels sometimes like the water is a big mirror. Only I wonder what it really reflects.'

Michaela nods and agrees in all of the right places, but I can tell that she's distracted. She sits with her chin resting on one hand, her phone still face-down on the table. We had agreed before we came to try to go phone-free, but the way she's actively *not* checking it is even more distracting than if she'd been glued to it all morning. She clutched it in both hands for the entire portion of the journey up here where I was driving.

'It's a Saturday,' I say gently. 'You can put that away.'

Michaela glances down at her phone, startled. 'What?'

'If you're waiting to hear something from the firm, it probably won't be today.'

Clio says nothing, but her silence is sympathetic. Michaela doesn't meet either of our eyes.

'No, it's not . . . I'm not waiting for anything.' Michaela slides her phone into her pocket. She looks as if she's considering saying something and then thinks better of it. When she sighs, it's big and full of the weight of the world.

'Did Marcel tell you why he let you go?' Clio asks. The words come out all in one go, as if she's been holding them in for days.

Michaela lets out a mirthless laugh. 'It's a long story.' Her tone grows sharp as she speaks and she has to visibly rein herself in. She flattens her hands against the table and I can tell there's something else she's not saying.

It would make sense if the training contract had been shorter, or if the industry had so many newly trained lawyers flitting between jobs. But Michaela expected – was led to believe – a job at the end of this two-year training contract would be the norm. I'm not surprised she's upset that it hasn't worked out.

I wait for her to go on, the silence growing long, punctuated only by the teenagers as they put away their games and leave in a horde. Fresh rain lashes the windows of the pub, streams of it running down the glass. So much for the weather forecast. There's a draught here, away from the fire. I wait a moment more, but Michaela only takes a big swallow of the last of her beer and shrugs. It feels, already, like the moment to ask her about it has passed. Still, there's the rest of the weekend. There's no use forcing it now; Michaela will talk when she's good and ready, and I doubt anything Clio or I say would make her do otherwise.

'My mum and dad said hi earlier, by the way,' I say. I show Michaela the photo Mum sent of her garden. 'She said something official-looking arrived in the post too, and I told her to open it, but it was just a letter from my GP.'

'Did you think it was to do with the adoption stuff?' Clio asks.

'Yeah, I'm still trying to get my hands on all the documents, but it's a right pain. You'd think with me having been left at a police station, there might be *fewer* hoops to jump through, but the red tape is an absolute nightmare. That's why I gave up last time, though I guess I didn't really try very hard.'

I've always known I was adopted – my parents were very open about that right from the start – but it wasn't until I hit my mid-teens that I started thinking about my birth family, about what it might be like to find out where I come from. It started out as a niggle, just on my birthday and at Christmas. I'd search a bit, hit a wall, and give up.

42

Recently the niggle has been more of a thorn in my side, always there, just beneath the surface.

Michaela puts down her burger and wipes her hands on a napkin. 'If you could find out what happened, even if you knew it was sad or not a good story, would you still want to?'

Kay has asked me variations on this before, and the answer is always the same.

'God, yes.' My heart swells at the thought, and even though I talk about it all the time, I can feel my skin start to hum with excitement. 'It's not about the story, though I guess it would be nice to meet any family I've got. My parents are my *parents*, you know? It's not like I have this whole big missing piece. My life is great and I don't need anything else. It's just . . . I'd love to know *details*. Where I'm from, what happened. Why I ended up at the police station. No judgement, just . . . facts, I guess.'

'Is that . . .' Michaela trails off.

'Is that what?'

'Is that why you and Charlotte broke up?' Her expression is half grimace, as though she was afraid to ask. Unlike Clio, who'd just blurted the same thing out on the phone a few weeks ago.

'Yeah.' I shrug. It's easier to pretend it doesn't bother me now, rather than the way I cried when Clio asked, big snotty tears I'm still embarrassed about. 'I mean, it wasn't the only reason, obviously. But she definitely didn't like it. She said it was "unhealthy to focus so much on the past and not enough on our present".' I laugh to show I'm okay with it, but I can tell both of them don't believe me. Charlotte was so controlling about everything in my life, and for over a year I made excuses for her. But this, the adoption and finding out where I come from, it was something I couldn't budge on. 'Anyway, we are *not* here to talk about me. Stop deflecting!' I say, stuffing food into my mouth.

Michaela holds her hands up in mock surrender, but still refuses to say any more about the job situation. I sigh.

'Oh, hey,' Clio says suddenly. 'Look at the poster. They have a quiz on this afternoon! Do you guys want to stay and play?' She glances dubiously towards the rain-lashed window. Michaela follows suit.

'I did want to get back to the house before it got dark, but this could be fun, yeah. Maybe the rain will slow down again too,' Michaela suggests, somewhat optimistically. 'I'm frustrated that I won't be able to get as much hiking in as I'd wanted. I just love being outside this time of year.'

'I don't,' Clio grumbles. 'Bloody freezing. Indoor quizzes are much safer too, much less chance of falling down a ravine or twisting your ankle in the mud. You heard what that waitress said. She doesn't want us going out and getting in trouble like those other people.'

'Clearly you learned everything you know about the outdoors from a TV screen.' Michaela laughs. 'The weather will be fine in a day or two, so at least I should be able to get some kind of walking in before we leave.'

'Whatever.' Clio waves her hand lazily. 'Anyway, are we staying to play? It starts soon.'

'I'm game,' I say. 'Ha. Get it?'

Clio groans.

We gather our things and move to the table that the teenagers have vacated. It's warmer here away from the window, tucked in an alcove by the fire. I've got my back to two or three tables and a great view of the slot machine, but it's comfortable and cosy, and I rest my shoulder against the pillar.

A member of staff comes around and takes away plates and glasses from all of the tables, while another collects a cash fee for entering the quiz, one per team, and hands out the quiz sheets. There's a couple sitting just behind me, though I can't really see them now I'm sitting down with the pillar between us, and a group of three older women drinking large beers on another table just to my right.

Michaela wanders back to the bar to order us more drinks and Clio excuses herself. It takes me a moment before I realise she's gone to the bathroom or the bar, not outside for a cigarette – she's finally quit and it looks like this time it's holding up.

The woman at the table sort of behind ours – I can just about see her if I lean forward – stares at me for a moment before glancing at the man she's with, though I can't see his reaction. The group of older ladies are staring too. I shift awkwardly in my seat.

Clio isn't so good at avoiding them, though, and when she comes back through with her hands still damp, rubbing her palms on her jeans, one of the women, white pearls around her neck and a cluster of silver rings on her fingers, waves at her. And when that doesn't stop her, she makes to get up.

Clio pauses. She looks at me, and then at the women, then back at me. I'm sure my face is as blank as my brain because I'm completely frozen. What is with these small towns that makes everybody so odd? They're all so friendly, which I love, but also just a little bit strange sometimes. I've been to plenty of places like Blackhills over the years with Mum and Dad – camping and caravanning was always

45

how we spent our summers, much to my distaste – and I know I have one of those faces, sort of soft and neighbourly, but this is beyond even that.

'You're tourists,' says the woman in pearls excitedly. She has styled her dark hair in a severe bob that makes her age very difficult to pinpoint. 'Are you girls staying here in Blackhills?'

Clio's guard goes up. I can see it because I know her, the way her shoulders lift ever so slightly towards her ears, the way her smile tightens, but to anybody else, I'm sure she just looks the same. The women certainly don't seem to notice.

'Yeah, fancied a change of scenery,' Clio says. 'Is that *so* strange?'

'Oh no, we love tourists.' This from another of the women, smaller than her friend. Visibly older, maybe in her sixties. 'We just haven't had this much excitement in years. First with those walkers and now with you young things.'

'News travels fast, huh,' Clio remarks.

'Oh, don't take it the wrong way,' the woman says. 'Blackhills is lovely. It's nice to have guests. And you've timed it perfectly, these quizzes are great! Every Saturday like clockwork and we've raised thousands for charity, you know. What better way to spend a few rainy hours?'

Clio looks to the bar, where Michaela is still waiting to get served. 'My friend over there was really excited about being able to have some time outdoors, but the weather does seem to have other ideas.'

'More's the pity,' the woman clucks. 'I was just saying to Margaret, wasn't I, Marge? We used to have hikers around here all the time, but it's been a while since we've had any. When I was young, we were *always* out and about. I guess it's an old Scots thing, being so outdoorsy.'

'Well, that rules me out,' Clio jokes, a little more relaxed now. 'My dad was Italian. My people like sleeping in the sun. Can't say the same for El, though.' Clio nods in my direction.

'Oh, are your folks from around here?' the woman called Margaret asks.

I laugh. 'No idea,' I say brightly. At the blank look on their faces, I elaborate – the same story and phrasing I've used since I was a teenager. Sometimes it feels worn, and I guess it is in places, a tale stitched together from only the parts that don't hurt. 'I was adopted as a kid. My parents couldn't have kids – my mum's a teacher and adores them – so they got lucky, and ended up with me! I've got no idea where I'm from originally, but I'd love to think it was some place like Blackhills. It's so charming here, and everybody always seems so friendly in small towns.'

'Oh. Well, who knows!' says Margaret's friend, a little too cheerfully. 'You look like you could have some Scot in you – doesn't she, Barbara? If you dyed your hair. Mind you, the dark hair's not *not* Scottish. In fact, there are a few families around here who are basically *famous* for their lovely thick, dark hair . . .'

I smile along, though I'm not really listening any more. It always unsettles people, the way I talk about myself. It started off as a defence mechanism, I'm sure, but it quickly felt better to be open about it. It makes *me* feel better, even if other people don't like it. So I'm used to the nervous babbling when I brush it off as though it doesn't matter.

The truth is, of *course* it matters. But I've done the time feeling sorry for myself, the part where I spent my childhood ignoring it, wishing my parents had never told me I was adopted as though that would make the truth go away. I've done the weeks as a teenager moping when my dad first

47

drove me from Leicester to the police station in Durham where I was found, the day I first saw Queen's Campus in Durham, sure I wanted to study at the university but finding my throat thick with tears as the thought that one, or both, of my parents might once have lived nearby, been to parties and bought drinks in the same bars where I drank with Clio and Kay so many years later.

I've done the feeling sad part. Now, mostly, I'm just glad. For my parents, for their trust and faith in who I am – and who I can still be to them, regardless of my start in life – and for Clio, who taught me once, in a tiny student bedroom, how to tell my story without letting myself get sad.

Clio hovers beside me now. The man from the table behind ours, with his blue jacket and swathe of dark hair, has disappeared, but his wife with her 'casual' updo that is not casual in the slightest is still in earshot. As we talk, she leaves her jacket on the chair and disappears to the bar, like she can't wait to get away from us.

'Anyway, it's nice to have people admiring nature instead of getting up to God knows what, all maudlin,' mutters the third woman. 'Give Blackhills the admiration she deserves, instead of dragging us through the mud. Right?'

'Oh will you stop going on about that,' Barbara says. 'Your grandson has a lot to answer for, showing you those *podbreaks* or *radiocasts* or whatever they're called.'

Clio and I exchange raised eyebrows.

'What podcast?' Clio asks as she finally sinks into her seat.

'Ignore them,' says Margaret tightly. 'That's just village stories aired like dirty old laundry.'

Eleanor

Clio opens her mouth to ask a question – I can see it in her face – but I guide her attention towards the quiz sheet in front of us, drawing a big circle around the bit that says *Team Name*. If we get started talking about stories, we will never hear the end of it.

We busy ourselves choosing a team name while Michaela is gone. Clio suggests *Gossip Girls*, which she thinks is funny ('Because we love listening to old lady gossip, get it?'), but which I don't.

'Well, what would you choose?' Clio demands.

'Something clever,' I say.

'Like what?'

'I don't know. A pun or something. Aren't they supposed to be high art?'

The man at the table behind ours laughs. I hadn't noticed him return while I was examining the quiz sheet but his laugh is warm and genial and directed, I think, at us. His wife is still missing, but he's rolled up his sleeves and looks like he's about to get serious. I can't see his face very well because I've still half got my back to him and it's too awkward to move in the cramped space.

'What?' Clio says, turning to him. 'What's *your* team name then?'

I can just make out the gesture of him pointing at his paper – but there's no way I can see what it says from here.

'Me?' he asks Clio.

'Yes, you.'

'We're *A Novel Idea*.' He sounds proud, as if he's been waiting for somebody to ask. I can just imagine him puffing his chest out. I feel rude sitting here with my back to him, with a pillar between us. I try to swivel, but it doesn't matter which way I sit, the damn pillar is still in the way.

'Oh God,' Clio groans. 'Who came up with that?'

'I did,' he says. 'My wife wanted us to be *Agatha Quiztie*, but I said it implied we expected to tie and I think we're going to win this week.'

'You've never won this quiz in twenty-five years!' yells Margaret from the other table, and Barbara cackles. It's clear they've all had a few drinks now and are starting to relax a bit more. 'Some head teacher you are.'

'Oh, you're a teacher?' Clio asks. I can tell from the way she's shifted in her seat that she's looking at him in a different light. She loves to pick thinking battles with people, especially if she can start spouting stuff about ancient folklore.

'Yep. Run the whole school and everything.' I still can't see his face but I can hear the playful smile in his voice.

Clio rolls her eyes, which is her favourite thing to do when she's secretly amused.

'You girls are here for the weekend, right?' he asks. The three older women are now talking between themselves and I shift forward in my seat again.

'Jesus, does everybody know that?' I ask. 'By the way, I'm not being rude, I'm just wedged into this corner,' I clarify, speaking to the pillar.

'Oh, it's all right,' he says. 'That's the, uh – well, they call it the snogging corner for a reason.'

Clio bursts out laughing and I feel my cheeks go pink.

'Jesus,' I say again.

'No, not even Jesus can see you there.' The man chuckles and it's a warm, low sound. 'Sorry. God, that sounded very suggestive, didn't it? Let me start again.' He clears his throat and leans forward to shake Clio's hand, and waves around the corner of the pillar, which cracks Clio up again. 'I'm Matthew. I live here. I'm not weird, I promise. If you girls need anything while you're here, just give one of us a yell – it's nice to have some tourists here again.'

'Thanks. We're especially interested in things we can do around here that don't involve walking,' Clio says.

'Ah, yeah. You heard about the campers,' Matthew says, not unkindly but with a hint of rebuke. 'Any gossip a bit lively around here travels like wildfire. Stories are our currency—'

I can see Clio gearing up to launch into one of her *stories are the lifeblood of human community* speeches, so I tap the table to get her attention. Poor Matthew really won't know what hit him if I let her get started.

'No, okay?' I warn her, laughing. 'I've got a good team name. What about *Prose Before Hoes?*'

There's an interruption as Matthew's wife comes back from the bar. I can just about see her as she leans in and whispers in his ear, her hands moving animatedly. He grumbles something in return and then she leaves again, taking her jacket with her. He doesn't return to our conversation, and after a minute he gets up to leave too, heading

51

away along the back wall so I only catch sight of the back of his coat. I wonder if maybe his wife mistook Clio's friendliness for flirting – because, admittedly, there isn't much of a difference between the two – but I don't feel guilty. It was nice to just . . . have fun? Charlotte would never have talked to strangers like Clio just has, she was always so uptight about things, and I forgot how refreshing it can be to relax.

'Jesus,' Michaela mutters as she finally returns with our drinks. 'Talk about a slower pace of life. If I lived here, I'd be dead in no time!'

Clio snorts. 'Did you meet a fit guy at the bar?'

'You're one to talk, I saw you getting chummy with the townsfolk. Apparently those three –' she gestures at Barbara, Margaret and their friend – 'are on some committee, and those guys –' she motions at the table where the couple were – 'are some kind of superheroes around here. They do loads of charity work and own half the village or something.'

'How did you learn all of that while you were waiting for booze?'

'Different server at the bar this time. He was really chatty, kept trying to tell me who everybody was. The man who was sat at that table is the local head teacher or something. His wife's some high-flyer, owns a bunch of businesses. All in the family, or something. They're a real power couple. I spoke to her at the bar, one of those intimidating but very cool types, y'know?'

'Yeah, he told us he was a teacher – right around the time Clio went all academic heart-eyes over him.'

'I definitely don't think his wife liked us talking to him,' Clio says, ignoring my teasing. 'But he was nice. He basically said he'd help out if we needed anything.'

'Now that I'm thinking about it, she did look a bit offended when we were joking about how I might be Scottish. Like I might sully the gene pool or something. I couldn't see his reaction though, bloody pillar.' I take a mouthful of my glass of water and tap the wall.

'Well, one good thing did come of my overlong chat with good barman Tim,' Michaela adds brightly.

'Tim? You got his *name*?' Clio flutters her eyelashes and then cranes to see if she can spot said server. Michaela has been notoriously single for pretty much the entire time I've known her, except for one short month of very bad dates in the first year of uni, and I'm starting to suspect she likes it that way most of the time. 'Is he hot? How old is he?'

'He's not hot,' Michaela says firmly. 'And anyway, that's not the point. Apparently, if we want somewhere to pick up supplies for the rest of the weekend, the best place – he says – is the farm shop. It's open late on a Saturday.'

'A farm shop?' Clio crinkles her nose.

'Oh, that sounds amazing,' I say. 'I bet they'll have fresh bread and really nice cakes and stuff. And if it's open late that means we can go to the shop after the quiz.'

'Agreed.' Michaela nods. 'And when we get back, I want to go back to this podcast I'm listening to. There's an extended episode that I found a link to that I think you'll like—' She stops.

'An episode I'll like because . . .?' I prompt.

Michaela pulls a face I can't read, almost guilty. 'Uh . . . Well, I'll . . .' Her mind is obviously scaling to find a different path, but for once it seems like her lawyer brain has drawn a blank and she just stares at me with panic.

'Spit it out,' Clio says.

'There's an episode about . . . the loch,' Michaela blurts.

'It's part of a sort of . . . thing I've been working on. A project. Or, no, not a project. Just a thing.'

'About "the loch". As in . . . this loch? *Loch Aven* loch?' I ask.

Michaela tries to pull it back but has the good grace to at least look sheepish. 'I was going to tell you,' she says. 'I *am*—'

'I *knew* there was a reason you picked this place,' Clio says. 'Nobody finds a village like this by just stabbing a map.'

Clio's right. Michaela is spontaneous, but it's usually a cultivated kind of spontaneity. If she found this place by putting a pin in a map, then it's more than likely she knew exactly where she was aiming the pin.

'Well, I *could* have found it like that,' Michaela argues.

'Does it matter where she found it?' I ask. 'Whether it was some rando podcast or a defunct Thomas Cook advert, we're still here and we're going to have a nice weekend.'

Clio shrugs.

Before any of us have time to say anything else, there's the *clink-clink-clink* sound of a spoon against a glass, followed by the tinny echo of a cheap microphone. 'Welcome to Saturday Night Quizzers! Annnnd can I have your team names please?'

'Oh, *Prose Before Hoes*,' Michaela says, pointing at my scribbled joke. 'Nice.'

Clio pouts.

The quiz is one of the best ones I've taken part in for years, although that's more because of my lack of socialisation than the quality of the questions. The atmosphere of the pub shifts, growing warmer and more welcoming as everybody forgets that we're outsiders – actually, I'm pretty sure they just forget we exist full stop, and that's fine with me.

By the time the quiz finishes, the noise level has gone up by about fifty per cent and the bar is much busier. A table full of teens is where most of the shouting is coming from as one of them attempts to adjust answers on their quiz sheet while somebody else is still marking it.

We end up ranking somewhere in the middle of the leaderboard. Michaela isn't as on form as she normally is with these sorts of things and drops the ball on several questions she probably ought to know the answers to. She's so busy being nosy at everybody around us.

It's my turn to head to the bar, so I leave Michaela and Clio squabbling good-naturedly over whether Rome or New York City is further north – Clio is convinced she isn't wrong after the quiz question about whether Paris or New York is furthest north, when in fact she very much was wrong on *both* counts – and wheedle my way towards the less crowded end, where a few regulars are propping up the bar.

I order our drinks from the server who brought us our food earlier and she puts them through the till without any chatter. To my right, there are a couple of older men, one still wearing his jacket and the other who is several pints deep.

'Did you see Robert earlier?' says the man in the jacket.

The other man mutters something into his drink.

'He was meant to stop by and pick up the keys.'

'Here you go, love,' the server says to me, sliding across the two bottles of beer.

'. . . he left. Stormed off in a right old huff,' the first man is saying. Then he catches my gaze and goes silent.

The server also goes quiet. Perhaps they're talking about the man Clio upset earlier.

'I'll take the keys over to the shop instead then,' the man in the jacket grumbles, leaving without another glance in my direction.

I shift from one foot to the other, waiting for Michaela's designated driver-friendly lemonade.

The server senses my discomfort. 'Don't mind that lot,' she says. 'Robert Kelly has been offended by just about everything for decades. He's just mad those campers went and got stuck and now he's got to go looking for them with a bum knee.'

Eleanor

I head back to the table with a sour taste in my mouth. The place is thinning out slowly, returning to that slightly hollow state it was in when we first arrived. Busy, but not as busy as you'd expect for a Saturday evening. I wonder if it's to do with those campers, and whether they're okay.

Nobody has given us many details, but they can't be in actual danger, can they? More likely they're just trapped by flood water and they are having trouble being found because of bad signal. It's obviously got the village in a bit of an uproar though and I feel suddenly guilty for even being here.

'You look like you've seen a ghost,' Clio says as I sit down with the drinks. She takes a big swig from her beer bottle. 'In fact, it reminds of me of a story—'

'Actually, I'm not really in the mood,' I say. 'Sorry.'

'Oh.' Clio blinks, but she isn't offended for long. She sometimes reminds me of a puppy. 'I wonder how long they've been doing those quizzes for. I bet they make quite a bit of charity money if they do one every week.'

'You okay?' Michaela asks me.

'Yeah. I . . . I just got this really weird vibe at the bar. Not a big deal, just . . .' I stop.

'What?' Clio asks.

'Just – do you get the feeling that there's something people are skirting around? Like they're worried to talk about it?'

Michaela frowns. 'What do you mean?'

'I don't know,' I say, a little frustrated. 'Everybody's just very on edge.' The beer prickles my tongue, metallic and sharp. 'Anyway, shall we finish these drinks and find this farm shop, then?'

Clio sips at her beer and watches a member of staff who's appeared, this one pretty and alternative-looking, which is exactly Clio's type. She doesn't think I can see her, but as we finish up and lazily grab our coats, I make sure to give Clio a huge wink as she tries, and fails, to flirt with her on the way out.

We're out of the pub and a few yards down the street, rain once again speckling our skin and hair, when Michaela freezes.

'What is it?' I ask.

'Shit. My umbrella.' She pulls a face and spins to duck back inside.

Clio turns to me, hardly even waiting until Michaela closes the door behind her before she leans in urgently. 'Don't you think it's weird that she decided to come here because of some podcast episode about a lake?' Clio asks. I'd already forgotten about it.

'Not really, no.' I shrug. 'Kay likes a challenge. Maybe she's decided to try her hand at writing stories and she's going to give you a run for your money.'

Clio seems to think about this for a second instead of just laughing it off like I expect her to. 'I guess it's not that weird. I just . . . didn't peg her for the nature documentary podcast kind, that's all.'

'Maybe she's trying new things,' I suggest. 'She's been a bit . . . down, lately. All this stuff with the job.' Although this is the biggest hiccup Michaela has had in a long time, it's really not that strange. I remember when she got her first bad grade on an assignment and instead of immediately deciding if she wanted to resubmit it, she spent a week learning how to play the ukulele. She copes with setbacks by learning new things.

'Yeah, I guess.' Clio takes a pack of gum from her pocket and pops a piece into her mouth. 'I don't expect her to be totally normal, but usually she just—'

'Rants about it a bit, learns to play another instrument, and then feels better.' I shrug. 'I don't know. I'm in two minds. On the one hand, she seems okay, distracted enough. But on the other hand – is that reaction healthy? I genuinely think I'd be more visibly upset if something like this happened to me,' I say.

I consider the children I work with, and the parents, how even the smallest change in routine can make you feel unmoored, never mind anything bigger. Most of the people I work with are feeling overwhelmed and that can make even the smaller things weighing them down feel giant. Michaela is smart and capable enough that I'm sure she will find another firm to take her on, but it probably feels like everything she's been working towards is coming crashing in at once.

'Maybe she's just building up to the mother of all rants.' I say. 'Likely, once we've had a few glasses of wine tonight.

We'll be wishing she'd go back to being moody and listening to podcasts.'

Clio nods. 'I know. You're right. I just worry that she's putting herself under so much pressure to do everything perfectly. She always makes herself feel bad even when things are still going well, so I'm worried she feels worse about this than she's saying.'

'And now you sound like me,' I tease.

'Definitely can't have that!' Clio gives me a little shove, playful, and I'm still rubbing my arm very overdramatically when Michaela steps back into the street with her umbrella hanging loose between her fingers. There's an expression on her face that I can't pinpoint; I'm not sure if it's confusion, or if she's upset.

'Are you okay?' I step closer as she starts to open her umbrella and then she stops.

'Did barman Tim just hit on you?' Clio smiles, oblivious to the strange tilt to Michaela's head.

'No, it's fine,' she says. 'I just overheard the staff talking about the house.'

'Loch House?' I ask.

'Did it win an award? Was it on *Homes Under the Hammer*?' Clio is dripping with judgement.

'They were just saying that it's weird we're staying there.' Michaela looks a bit shaken. 'You were right, before. About the guest book. Apparently *nobody* ever stays there.'

Rebecca

Then

It is perfect.

Not all of the time, of course. It is not perfect when they are apart; when they have to go back to their separate lives and pretend that the world hasn't changed for both of them. Rebecca can't stand it sometimes, how she's supposed to just act like nothing has happened, like her whole future hasn't condensed to the shape of his jaw while he's drinking his coffee, the sharp point of his nose under the stars as he kisses her, the way she craves the feel of his hand resting comfortably on the back of her neck. Sometimes when they are apart, it is agony, and that is not perfect.

But then, when they are together, like tonight, when the outside world seems to slow and all that's left is the sky and the trees and the snow outside the window, roaring like static, when it is just him and Rebecca – then it is perfect. And it all feels worth the pain.

On nights like this, she can pretend that they met in another place, a country far from here, where their histories don't matter. In this fantasy, Rebecca dreams that her mum never got sick, that she wasn't afraid to leave. She dreams that all her adventuring is done, that she left school five years ago and travelled the world, maybe published a book or started a small business all on her own – and then she met him and her world began all over again.

Tonight is one of those perfect nights where she can almost forget that fantasy isn't true. In fact, tonight is the most perfect it has ever been. They have the house to themselves for the whole weekend. It is a Friday evening in December and dark has fallen so early that the village feels a million miles away. All around them is the silence of nature, a peace that soothes Rebecca right to her very core.

They lie together on the floor, rugs and blankets and cushions creating a fort around them, firelight playing over their bare skin. He entwines his fingers in hers, holding her hand to his chest and playing with the ring that she always wears on her index finger. He swirls the silver band around and around carelessly, his mind far away from here.

'Are you sure we can have the whole weekend?' Rebecca asks. She doesn't want to ask, as though she might summon bad luck by verbalising it, but she also has to be sure. She can't let her hopes rise like a balloon only to be dashed tomorrow morning when he rushes home without her.

'All weekend,' he murmurs. He doesn't open his eyes, but his lips curve into a smile and it's the kind of smile Rebecca might die for, so open and soft. It makes her feel like he understands her more than anybody ever has. Like he always has. 'She's staying with some friends in Malven, so we might even have a bit longer, but I'll need to make sure I get the house tidy before she's home.'

He means *his* home, Rebecca knows. The one he shares with his wife. She hates to think of it that way, but it's the truth. Hiding from it won't make the eventuality hurt any less, but she finds herself avoiding it whenever she can. She doesn't like to think of his other life, the one he lives without her, in the same way she doesn't like to think of her other life any more – the one she always planned to have: travelling, studying, getting out of the village. He has muddied that water now whether or not he wanted to.

'Good,' she says. 'That's good. A whole weekend.'

This is the first time they've had so long together. Normally, it's snatches of time here and there – an evening stolen under the guise of him going for a run, a lunch break in his car, an afternoon driving to the far side of the loch where nobody might see them together. It always feels dangerous. Rebecca wonders, sometimes, if that is part of the appeal, but tonight she realises it isn't at all. She would simply do anything if it meant spending time with him.

She knows it's wrong. As far as anybody else might be concerned, she's the *other woman*. She's stealing him, isn't she? He isn't hers, has never been hers. Yet he's brighter when he's with her. He's full of joy. And she knows he has never done this before, because sometimes he's so *bad* at it. And that means something, doesn't it?

When they're together, they talk about books and movies; he teaches her things about Shakespeare and Hawthorne, Melville and Christie. They tell stories and jokes and create a whole world to live in that isn't this tiny village where everybody has known them since birth and where nothing ever changes.

'One day we'll go to Paris together,' he says tonight, his eyes still closed and his hair ruffled. He waits for a beat, listening for the telltale shortening of her breath, the excitement he knows he'll get from such a comment, then he opens one eye, cat-like. 'And Rome. We can go to Vienna, or . . . no – we need to go somewhere cold, so we can stay in an igloo and see the Northern Lights surrounded by snow.'

'There's snow here,' Rebecca says.

He rolls onto his side so that their noses are nearly touching. His eyes are dark in the firelight and she studies the day-old stubble on his jaw, the early silvering threads at his temples. She commits it all to memory, feeling a little unsettled by his words.

She doesn't like this conversation. If they talk about the future, they have to admit that what they're doing can't last. This weekend, tonight, is perfect – but she doesn't want it to end. What if they're only here now because it's the last time? What if, for him, this is a last hurrah? What if, when it's over, they have to try to go back to how it was before, just a gentle spark of something between them, not acted on – never acted on – because this was a mistake and he was just feeling penned in by his wife, his marriage? What if none of this is real to him?

Rebecca stops the spiral as fast as she can, because that reality burns.

'It's not the same,' he says, oblivious. 'I mean proper snow. Deep and utterly fucking freezing.' He snuggles closer, pulling her body towards his. Their bare skin touches and it's like lightning, like it always is, and she lets out a breath, because, God, she doesn't want this to end.

'We can't though.' Rebecca closes her eyes and inhales the scent of him. The words hurt, and she wishes they were anything but the truth. 'We can't just disappear for a holiday together.'

'Why not?' He lets out a barking laugh as Rebecca frowns. 'You know why.'

'Don't talk about things like they'll always be the same,' he admonishes. 'Time is a construct, and in the words of the great Marcus Aurelius, "change is nature's delight".'

'Wasn't he talking about loss? "Loss is nothing else but change . . . " Right?' Any other time she would be proud of herself for knowing this, but not now. Not when the words mean losing him.

'He's talking about loss and gain,' he says. He struggles to sit a little more upright on the piles of pillows and tugs Rebecca onto his chest, running his fingers through her hair with such familiarity and ownership she feels it in her bones like a secret language. 'Equilibrium. There will always be change; nothing stays the same. And so, in that way, everything stays the same,' he concludes with a mischievous smile.

'This is too heavy for four glasses of wine.' Rebecca laughs and it comes out throaty and rich. She wonders how she looks to him right now, her black hair free of its braid and trailing across his shoulder, her pale skin tinted in shades of umber and orange by the fire. Does he think of his wife when he sees her – his angelic, graceful wife, who will always have more poise and refinement than Rebecca could even dream of?

'All I'm saying is, never say never,' he says, chuckling along with her.

Rebecca can't help it. A flutter of hope stirs inside her. 'Do you think we really could go to Paris one day?'

'I don't see why not.'

Rebecca falls silent. She loves the feeling of his skin pressed to hers, the stubble that grazes her shoulder and his fingers in her hair. If she had known even six months ago that she might fall so hard for him, that their friendship would tumble so quickly into – *this* . . . would she have stopped it in its tracks? Or had she hoped for this from the very beginning?

Everybody has always called her *nice*. Kind. Lovely. She is the soft one, the gentle one. Her parents never despaired about her, motivated as she was in her studies and then her saving. Her dad just expected her to start working at the shop when her mum got sick, and she never complained. She stuck it out and she dreamed and she saved, because wasn't she too afraid to leave anyway? She'd already put it off under the guise of not feeling *ready* by that point. Uncle Paul always said she could do it, but she's realising now that she never really believed him.

Rebecca hasn't told her parents yet how much her plans have changed, how she's thinking about using her savings to put a deposit down on her own flat here in the village instead of plane tickets around the world because at least then she would have her own space – space she could share with him. She knows her dad would be happy enough if she told him she was staying in the village, but what would he say if he knew why?

She remembers an incident when she was maybe twelve or thirteen. Simon, a boy in her class, had been flirting with her for a few weeks and for her birthday he sent her flowers. Her dad had been suspicious enough when they arrived, but when he read the card with its little lewd quote he'd erupted, marched round to Simon's house with Uncle Paul and the two of them had it out with Simon and his dad. She suspected Uncle Paul, who always seemed so much softer to her, hadn't been the one to throw the first punch that day, though she's no doubt it didn't take much encouragement for him to join in.

The quote, Rebecca later learned, was from *Much Ado About Nothing*. Really it was no wonder she'd never been popular with many of the boys.

It's funny how six months of this secret romance have made the decision so concrete in her mind, and not in the direction she, or her family, would have predicted. She'd thought her dad hated the idea of her travelling, but somehow, she knows he will hate this even more if he ever learns why she's changed her mind. He wanted her to help her mother, to be the good little daughter, but she knows he has also always wanted *more* for her – that he expected her to go away to university, then come home and make something of herself. She has always been too nice to lie and say she wasn't sure which of those things she actually wanted.

But these last six months have made her realise that being nice doesn't mean she can't lie. And maybe right now lying is better anyway. Dad doesn't have to know about any of this. Not yet.

'We'd have to tell people,' she says. 'They'd find out, if we went away somewhere together. It wouldn't be like this. Paris isn't exactly our back garden.'

He guides her chin with his fingertips, drawing her head off his chest so that he can look directly into her eyes. This is how she knows he means what he is about to say. This is how she knows this weekend really is perfect.

'Then it's simple,' he says. 'We'll have to tell them.'

Rebecca's stomach lurches and she's not sure if it's the exciting prospect of finally getting to live openly, or if it's the fear of what her dad and Uncle Paul might do.

Eleanor

'What do you mean nobody?' Clio stands a little straighter, always ready for a story.

'I mean, like, the house has been empty for years. Nobody ever stays there any more. When they noticed me standing there, they stopped talking, so I didn't hear anything else.'

Clio pulls out her phone, a half-grin on her face, as if she can't decide whether to treat this seriously or make fun. She goes with the latter. 'What shall I google, do you think? I wonder if there's some delicious secret. Maybe the house is haunted – maybe the whole *village* is haunted.'

'Come on,' I admonish. 'It doesn't have to be some whole big mystery to solve.' Clio is *obsessed* with morbid stories, so no doubt she's hoping somebody died in the house or something. Her flat is decorated with all things gothic, black lace and creepy paintings on the walls, so this would be just her vibe.

Mind you, Michaela is just as bad sometimes, with her true crime shows on Netflix. Both of them tease me about how I studied psychology, and went into counselling, and I still have no taste for gossip – but that's exactly *why* I have no taste for it.

Growing up, I was always the kid who had to explain the gossip herself. When people asked why I didn't look like my parents, who are both tall and ruddy with sandy-blonde hair, I was always the one who had to say, 'Yes, I know, it's very funny, but I *am* actually adopted.' At some point, it started to hurt less, but I'd much rather spend my energy now helping people to feel better than gossiping about why they feel less okay in the first place.

'So the owner never advertises the house,' I go on, brushing off Clio's ghost theory, 'or Blackhills has a reputation locally as being full of assholes. We're here, we're staying in a perfectly nice house, and now we're going to ignore barman Tim and head to the farm shop, right? To buy cheese and bread and wine and other tasty things?'

'Yeah, but I can google while we walk,' Clio says, holding her hand over her screen to try to keep the rain off.

'No, you can't.' I loop one hand through her arm and the other through Michaela's and together we start heading down the street. Clio reluctantly slides her phone into her pocket.

'I bet it's something sad and boring like the tourism dried up due to some new road and that's why nobody ever stays at Loch House any more. I wish there was a better story though,' Clio says wistfully. 'Like maybe the house was built by a man for his new bride and then he went fishing or something and promised he'd be back, but he never came back so she just wasted away waiting for him and now it's haunted and everybody who stays there either disappears into the loch or is, like, driven mad by the ghost.'

'Clio, what the actual fuck is wrong with you?' Michaela asks, not unkindly.

'It's just a suggestion. Anyway,' she barrels on, 'more likely it's because idiot campers keep wandering off into the woods during ferocious storms and getting stuck, so the owner is just like "Nah, fuck this", which, y'know, is fair.'

We've reached the end of the street now and we come to a stop. The rain has eased off and the lights from the buildings reflect off the shining cobbles. It looks like something out of a watercolour painting and I wish, suddenly, that a photograph on my phone would capture its beauty.

'Where are we going then?' I ask. 'Which way?'

'Well, I don't know.' Clio sticks her tongue out. 'Because *you* won't let me walk and google at the same time.'

We find the farm shop with surprisingly little problem – still open, as promised – and load up on bread, cheese and wine, some breakfast bits for tomorrow, and even a tray of home-made chilli con carne that we can warm through for dinner, not that any of us are actually hungry yet. The shop is big with a huge variety of things, from gourmet sausage rolls to ready-made picnic hampers complete with Prosecco. It's busier than I expected too, one member of staff serving the three or four people in line and another man stacking a selection of gin bottles onto a shelf at the back.

After we're done I find, strangely, that I'm excited to go back to Loch House. I want to see what the water looks like at sunset, especially now that the rain has cleared again and the clouds are sparse and fluffy, though still tinged with an ominous black, as if they've been dipped in ink. I imagine that it will be very cosy inside as the temperature dips; we can light the fire and have a drink and just relax, and when Michaela is ready for her rant about the training contract, we will be there for her.

We drive all the way up the track this time, slowly to avoid getting stuck in the long stretches of thick mud, and park in the shadow of Loch House. It's even darker out here than back in the village, no street lights to brighten the black sway of the trees. We pile back into the house without ceremony, arms full of food and drink. Michaela insisted on buying a six-pack of little cupcakes and I can see Clio eyeing them before we even get in the door.

The house is dim and absolutely freezing. I hadn't noticed this morning, but it's as if the walls retain the cool lake air. Michaela dumps her spoils on the counter before rushing to build a fire in the burner. Clio picks at one of the cupcakes as I put the chilli in the fridge and open a bottle of wine to pour a glass for each of us. It's not even six o'clock yet, but it feels much later, because so little daylight filters through the dense forest that grows around us.

I turn on all of the lamps and then head to the doors that look out over the loch. The way the water sits still and dark like mirrored glass is eerie, reminding me of Clio's story earlier about the creature who couldn't cross the lake that turned into a mirror, and there are still roils of pale mist clinging to its edges which doesn't help with the overall atmosphere. I rub my hands on my arms, trying to shake the chill.

'So, this podcast you were on about,' Clio asks. 'Why is this loch on it?'

'Well, there are always stories about bodies of water, aren't there?' Michaela asks without a beat, her answer so smooth this time, it feels rehearsed. She's on her haunches, still trying to get the fire to light. The wood is dry and crackles and spits, but there's a lot of smoke. It hangs in the air like the mist on the loch. 'El, can you open the doors a sec?'

I turn the lock and let in a rush of cold air so that the smoke can escape.

'Yeah,' Clio says, 'but why is the podcast talking about this one?' She finishes her mouthful and then takes a big swallow from her glass of wine. 'Is it folklore? Would I like to listen to it?'

'Probably,' I say drily. 'If it's morbid.'

I turn back to the open doors, watching as a large dark bird swoops overhead. I bet my parents would know what kind it is, but I can't even guess. I've always felt a bit of an outsider with stuff like that. Both Mum and Dad are really into the outdoors – nature and climbing and walking; they can name just about any bird or small animal you might see in the British countryside and my dad can even imitate a few of their calls. But not me. I love being outside, and love being with them, but the second you tell me what kind of bird is in a tree, it's like the name falls right out of my head. I can never even remember the difference between crows and ravens, and one time I confused a pigeon for a seagull.

'You're not wrong there.' Clio shrugs like she doesn't find this at all worrying. 'To be fair, I've always been fascinated by stories about, like, oceans and rivers and stuff. Historically, I think people created these fantasies to explain away natural phenomena. Like if people had a habit of drowning in a particular part of the river because it gets suddenly deep or the current is unpredictable, it makes sense to create stories of monsters to keep children away from that stretch. You know, mermaids and kelpies and sirens and whatnot.'

'The Loch Ness monster,' Michaela quips.

'You're joking, but yeah exactly.' Clio brings her glass around to the sofa and perches on its arm. Finally, the fire is going properly, enough air circulating so that it's no longer as smoky in here.

I pull the doors to slightly and move back towards the sofa, reaching for my own glass of wine. I take a long swallow, letting it unknot the muscles that are still bunched from the hours in the car this morning. I'm so tired, I feel like I could sleep again already, but I suspect we'll be up late tonight, as we always are on our first night together. It's been this way since we all moved into our separate flats after uni, which seemed like the pinnacle of adult decision-making when we were fresh graduates with three very different career trajectories but now seems like we were kids playing dress-up. Clio can hardly feed herself half the time and Michaela's been so involved with work that we've hardly seen her; I don't like being so distant from them.

Last time we had a weekend together, Clio crashed at my flat after a disaster date with a girl she'd barely spoken to online before meeting and we'd stayed up until nearly four in the morning just chatting. That's easy to do with Clio; she's so full of life that you forget that you're tired or lonely or sad. The same goes for Michaela too, though she pretends to be the responsible one.

'Maybe you *would* like the podcast,' Michaela says. She's looking at me as she says it, almost as if she's gauging my response, which feels weird, but she's been acting kind of weird all day, so I let it slide. 'I'll send you the link at some point . . . or maybe we can listen together.'

'Yeah maybe. Anyway,' Clio says, 'I bet whatever the stories are, people around here have heard them too. It's probably why they're so stand-offish with strangers. All it takes is a rumour to spread, or gossip or old wives' tales, and before you know it, the whole village avoids the loch.'

'Is it bad that I'm kind of glad that everybody seems wound up about those poor people getting trapped out there by the weather? I was starting to think it was *us* everybody had a problem with,' Michaela says. 'Like maybe my shit luck had rubbed off.'

'It's not shit luck,' Clio counters. 'I don't believe in luck.'

'That's a lie. You absolutely do.' I've finished my glass of wine already and Clio's not far behind. We crowd onto the sofa with Michaela and I wrap the blanket over my legs.

Clio laughs. 'Okay, I believe in luck. But I don't believe this thing with your training contract is luck,' she corrects herself. 'I think there's something else going on.'

Michaela draws her knees up on the other end of the sofa so she can fit her feet under the blanket with me. They're like blocks of ice.

I shriek. 'Dude, you're actually *freezing*. Did you get touched by a *ghost*?'

'I've not been warm since we got here,' Michaela says.

'Don't change the subject,' Clio says. She's on a mission now. '*Is* there something else going on that you want to tell us?'

Eleanor

Michaela doesn't speak right away.

'About work,' I elaborate. 'There's more to losing the job than you were saying earlier, right? Clio and I both agree—'

Michaela sags, something like relief there. Whether it's relief that we're finally asking so she doesn't have to come right out with it, or simply just relief to get it off her chest, I'm not sure.

'There *was* . . . something that happened. At work. I didn't really want to talk about it because I don't want it to be a big deal.'

'Something?' Clio drains the dregs of her glass and gets up to pour us both more. Michaela is still on her first glass, but I can see that it's already loosened her up because she rubs her hand over her face and when she pulls it back, her brown eyes are heavy-lidded.

'Something other than the training contract ending?' I ask. 'Something that *caused* the training contract to end?'

Worry slithers up my spine. Suddenly, Michaela's cagey

behaviour makes more sense. She *has* been hiding something – and if she hasn't told us, it must have upset her.

'It's *not* a big deal. Or it *shouldn't* have been a big deal . . . No, actually that's not true.' She sighs. 'God, hang on. Okay, what happened shouldn't have been a big deal because I shouldn't have let it become a problem. But I did, so now I'm in this mess, and I'm dealing with it – I am – but I don't want to think about it all the time, so I'm keeping myself distracted.'

Clio brings back two full glasses and hands one to me wordlessly.

'What happened?' I lay a hand on Michaela's knee and her whole leg is cold. I shift the blanket so she can have more of it and she smiles gratefully.

'It's going to sound so childish when I say it aloud.'

'Go on,' Clio prompts. 'You'll feel better if you say it.'

'You mean *you'll* feel better if she says it,' I joke.

Clio laughs, but Michaela only smiles.

'There's a guy I work with. Dan—'

'Dan the *gym man*?' Clio gasps.

'Yes, Dan the gym man.' Michaela pauses. 'This is why I didn't say anything. It's so . . . unlike me. But anyway, we . . . we were seeing each other for a while.'

'Kay!' Clio squeals, completely oblivious to Michaela's tone in her excitement. 'Oh my God, I thought you'd *never*—'

'"Were"?' I cut her off quickly. 'It didn't work out?'

Michaela bites her lip. It's clear this is hard for her. 'No. It . . . It was really bad actually. I thought I could . . . I know you're only teasing when you ask me when I'm going to settle down or, like, even date somebody, and I really did try. I guess it just turns out that relationships, having to think about other people all the time, it's not for me. I

78

don't know if it's the sex or the romance or what, but I don't like it. I prefer it just being me, y'know? But Dan got super invested. Like, scary invested. I should never have messed around with him. It's frowned upon at the best of times, isn't it? Working with somebody you're dating, or dating somebody you're working with?' She sighs. 'But he wouldn't let it go. It was just supposed to be fun and he got weird, planning our wedding after like two months, refusing to listen if I had to rearrange our plans, turning up at my place uninvited.'

'Oh, dude,' Clio says softly.

My stomach churns. I feel anger and sadness all crumpled in one soggy emotion. I want to hug Kay and I want to punch Dan's lights out.

'I'm sorry,' I say. It's all I can manage.

'It was really messy,' she confesses. Her eyes are glassy, as if she's trying not to cry. 'Like *really* messy. I felt sick all the time and he kept trying to get back together, even after I stopped talking to him. I stayed the night at Clio's a couple of months ago and went home the next morning before work and Dan was already outside my flat, waiting to ask if he could drive me to work. I snapped and yelled at him to leave me alone. And I guess I should have handled the whole thing differently before because he stopped bothering me after that. But I just . . . I couldn't keep working with him. I couldn't keep seeing him every day. It started to affect my work and Marcel noticed.'

'He asked you about it?' I say.

'Yep. The whole thing came out and Marcel said he thought it might be awkward going forward if we couldn't be professional about it. Dan was being normal again by then. He apologised and said he didn't mean for it to come off as creepy, he was upset, but it made me so uncomfortable. And, look, I *tried*. For weeks, I tried. But I just can't be there with him pretending nothing happened.'

She blinks hard. No tears spill. She shrugs her shoulders and the shield goes back up again, the sad expression replaced by sheer pragmatism.

'So . . . *you* decided to leave? To end the contract?' I ask.

'It was up in a couple of weeks anyway. Marcel said they would have kept me on, but . . . Dan is staying. So I decided to leave. It's unconventional, but it *does* happen. With a good reference from Marcel, I should be able to find somewhere else, another firm to take me on.'

'Kay, you can't pretend to be fine about this,' I say. The sick feeling is still swirling in my belly. Michaela has worked *so* hard over the last two years – it's not fair. 'You must have all sorts of emotions. You can't just do what you always do and act like you don't feel anything. Maybe we should talk about it—'

'You don't need to psychoanalyse me,' she snaps. She looks immediately apologetic. 'Look,' she goes on more calmly, 'I know you process things by talking, but I process by thinking and *doing*. I was upset when it happened, but I'm better now I'm out of there. I genuinely am. Crying won't solve anything, so I just want to get on with things, you know?'

If this had happened to anybody else, I'd think they were lying about being okay, but now Michaela's silence over the last few weeks makes sense. I'd assumed she was angry about not being kept on, but, true to form, she's been plotting and planning. That's Michaela all over.

Still, I can't help the rip-roar of emotions pushing and

pulling inside me. I'm so angry for her that it hurts. Dan's behaviour was totally out of line and I desperately want to hit him. Not that I ever actually condone physical violence, but in this case . . .

'So this is a strategically timed holiday,' I say, reining in my anger. Michaela is right: it won't do anybody any good. 'We thought you wanted to come here so you could rant and rave. But you're looking for a distraction, aren't you?'

'I was fully expecting you to get absolutely wasted tonight and cry about everything,' Clio says conspiratorially. 'And then you'd ask me for advice and, like, I am *not* useful when it comes to career advice. I literally tell stories for a living.'

'I do not *ever* drunk-cry.' Michaela's expression hovers somewhere between amused and offended.

'I thought you might this time.' Clio's brows are knit with sympathetic concern, her green eyes bright. 'I thought maybe this would be the thing to finally make you lose your shit and it'd be my turn to give you advice. And I'd obviously be terrible at it.'

'Well, I give pretty good advice, not that either of you two ever take it,' I point out.

'I know it seems backwards, but this is me taking control,' Michaela says emphatically. 'If I start fresh, then it's my future. Does it suck? Yes, it absolutely does. Am I angry? Oh yeah. Is it my own fault? Nope. But Marcel will give me a good recommendation, and honestly I don't know how long I'd have stayed at a firm with such little room for growth anyway. Maybe I just need a totally fresh start at a bigger firm. So, yeah, coming here is somewhat for me, but . . .' She pauses.

Clio and I glance at each other.

'But what?'

'Well, I'm not exactly only here for a distraction for me . . . there's something in it for you too, El.'

'Me?' My heart thumps. For a second, I think she's talking about Charlotte and I feel a rush of confused thoughts tumbling through my head. Why on earth am I hoping it's something to do with her? 'I don't need a distraction.'

'It's not *distraction* for you. It's . . .' Michaela looks almost nervous. She glances between me and Clio and then down at her phone, which is dark. 'I don't really want to tell you until I've got a few more pieces in place because it's potentially a really big deal for you.'

'What is it?' I push, curiosity making me unsettled. 'You know I love surprises, but—'

'It's not a surprise,' she says quickly. 'And it's not a secret or anything, but I just want to make sure all my mental leaps make sense before I tell you exactly. I needed to be here to work some stuff out, so I thought we could all come together and tomorrow I'll tell you. If that's okay?'

'If it's not a surprise, is it still a good thing?' I ask.

Michaela hesitates before answering. 'Well, yes . . . and also no. But it will be something you will appreciate, if I'm right.'

'Is it to do with Charlotte?' I blurt. I'm not sure what I'm hoping for, but Michaela talking about her messy break-up with Dan has made me think of her again. I *miss* her, I realise. Even though she was no good for me. Even though I knew that. 'She's not here, is she?'

Panic overtakes me, until Michaela shakes her head fast. 'No, no. It's nothing to do with her.'

I slump in my seat.

'Dude, I thought you were over her,' Clio says. 'No

judgement or anything, but you're not still talking to her, are you?'

'Oh God, please tell me you're not,' Michaela echoes – with exactly the same amount of judgement Clio claims not to be passing.

'No!' I exclaim. 'I mean. We text sometimes—'

'Eleanor,' Clio groans. 'Dude.'

'Wait a second,' I say, my brain scrambling for a diversion. 'Kay, you said you need a fresh start at a bigger firm – I thought you said you didn't want to work at any of the others in Durham.'

'Ah. Well, you know. With my mum moving down south last year, I had a thought today that maybe it wouldn't be so hard to—'

'Kay!' Clio squeaks. 'You are *not* thinking of abandoning us!' She swings her wine glass dangerously and both Michaela and I reach out as if we might be able to catch it. But there's no harm done. 'I know Joy is literally the best, and we all miss our Durham mum, but you can't just skip out on us. Right?' She turns to me.

'We all agreed to stay together,' I add. 'Wait – that's not why we're here, is it? You're not scoping it out for a move?' My palms sweat.

'No! It's got nothing to do with this trip. And look, I haven't even really *thought* about it yet. I'm just considering my options out loud,' Michaela says over us.

'Well, please don't go,' Clio begs. 'Puh-lease. If you go, we all go.'

'Okay, it was a stupid idea anyway.' Michaela laughs and some of the tension flows out of my shoulders. When Joy left Durham, I worried Kay would want to go too. She and Clio are as much my family as my parents are and I'm genuinely not sure what I'd do without either of them. It's bad enough that I only get to see my parents twice a month. Their original plan had been that eventually they would move to Durham from Leicester so they could be closer to me after I decided to stay there once I graduated – closer to where we thought I might be from too, since I was found as a baby in that police station in Durham – but Dad's work situation has been sticky the last few years, so he's not been able to action that plan yet.

'Let's get the chilli on the stove,' I say, mostly to change the subject back to lighter things. 'If we don't cook it soon, I might be too drunk to eat it.'

'Man,' Michaela says, her gaze drawn to the dark windows. 'I hope those campers are okay. I've been thinking about them all day. If they're stuck somewhere because of the rain, they must be scared.'

'Mhmm,' Clio agrees. 'Maybe they found a cave or something and they're hiding out.'

Michaela looks dubious. 'I wonder if we should offer to help search for them. If they're lost, I mean.'

'What use would we be?' I laugh it off, but I have to admit I feel a stirring of something in my belly for those poor people. I don't know anything about them but, honestly, having seen how thick those trees are on the other side of the loch, I know enough to be nervous for them.

'Maybe we could leave the lights on down here tonight,' Michaela suggests. 'If they're higher in the hills and lost, they might be able to see them.'

Clio scoffs at the idea.

'What?' Michaela says. 'It might help!'

'Yeah, it might also bring strangers right to our door,

while we're alone in the middle of freakin' nowhere. No, thank you.' She shudders.

'Good point,' I say, finding after our conversation about Dan acting so weird after Michaela broke up with him that I like that thought even less than the thought of strangers stuck in the woods somewhere. At least it sounds like there's a group of the campers out there together. I'm sure they will be fine.

After we've eaten, we settle back in front of the fire, hopping between so many topics, it's sometimes hard to keep up. We joke about Blackhills some more, and Clio tells us a spooky story about a lake monster with eyes like black marbles who devours virgins – and Michaela laughs and says it figures she'd be the only one to get eaten alive by a fictional story. We talk about Dan, about the way Michaela didn't like how over the top he was, about how he was always pushing her beyond what felt comfortable, and Clio predictably offers to beat him up. We talk about Charlotte too, though I push away from the topic as much as I can, feeling intensely uncomfortable after the realisation of how much I miss her – and how much I know I shouldn't.

Then we end up full circle back with Michaela, and the more we talk, the more it's clear to me that she really *doesn't* want to move down to Devon to live closer to her mum, she's just exploring her options. For a future. I understand the feeling lately, to want to do *more*. University already seems like it was so long ago. It's easy to fall into a pattern of life that feels hollow sometimes, and I wonder if Michaela's comment about starting fresh is the same sort of crisis of confidence that led me to start searching for my birth family. The need to feel like there's something more than – all of this.

Clio seems less convinced than I am about Michaela's willingness to stay living nearby and offers more and more outlandish reasons for her not to go, from the price of a pint down south right up to the supposed undesirability of southern men.

Somehow, it's late. I'm not sure what time exactly, but it must be at least three in the morning and all of us are exhausted from the long drive and the several bottles of wine we've managed to consume between us – though I've definitely had more than my fair share. My limbs feel heavy and I almost imagine them pressed under the weight of a body of lake water until I snap myself from those morbid thoughts, laughing them off with determination.

Michaela yawns and stretches. 'Look,' she says. 'I'm sorry I didn't tell you guys about Dan before. It wasn't that I wanted to keep it a secret, I just . . . got bogged down in it. I thought I was coping until I wasn't and then I was just so deep that I needed to get out of the mess by myself. I *am* okay, and being here with you guys is helping. And I have time to think things through. But for now I've heard more than enough of Clio's horror stories. Let's go to bed. I'm exhausted.'

Clio finger-combs her hair and sighs. She turns to me. 'Coming?'

'You guys go up,' I say. 'I'll make sure the fire burns out properly first.'

The others argue with me half-heartedly but soon traipse up the creaking stairs. I hear the way their chatter dries up as they work through their routines in the bathroom, so familiar I could chart the pattern of them in my sleep even though it's been a few years since the three of us lived together. I listen for the rush of water in the pipes and then the *snick-snick* of two doors closing.

I sit on the sofa, staring at the black doors, the glass reflecting my face like a pale, haunted oval. I try not to think of Clio's stories as I hear the shuffle of feet overhead, the distant lapping of water against the dock. I don't normally get creeped out in new places, but there's something about the atmosphere here that's different. With the water out there with its fathomless depths, it's like the darkness isn't empty like normal – it feels full, but of what, I'm not sure.

Eleanor

I switch out all but one lamp and return to the sofa, revelling in the quiet. I love the girls, but I've been living alone since Charlotte left and I'd forgotten how hard it can be to be switched on all of the time. Especially with Clio and Michaela, who both have so much life in them. My job means I spend a lot of time *switched on*, always considering other people's emotions and ways to connect with them. Even when it's out of hours and I'm off the clock I always hesitate about turning my phone off.

I don't mind any of that – I find real joy in helping parents and children to get the best out of their adoptions in a way that I know would have helped me once upon a time – but sometimes I wonder how much of my existence is reactive, what I might have been like if I hadn't started my known life outside a police station. Maybe I would have been a bookworm like Clio, or a teacher like my mum. I don't think I could have ever done anything like law – I'm not committed enough – but I do like helping people, so who knows. And that's the thing, it's the not knowing that gets me down sometimes. If only I knew where I came from, I might have a better idea of where I'm going.

The doors are still open a little and the air that comes through is very cold, but it feels nice now that the fire has warmed the lounge right through. It reminds me of holidays with my parents growing up, how we'd take the caravan all over the country and stop at a different site each night. Mum and Dad would always sit in a pair of camp chairs just outside the van, a careful fire going to keep them warm, and I'd sit by the door, wrapped in a duvet, listening to the stories Dad would tell. Like Clio, he's good at telling stories.

The towering pines outside the house make the night feel exceptionally dark, but the sky I can see is speckled with stars. The water reflects a sliver of silver moon that I can't see from in here. It's somehow less eerie at night than it was at twilight, with the mist curling and the shadows growing long; it feels like this is how it's supposed to be. As if this is how this place is experienced best. Quiet and peaceful. It feels surprisingly like home.

Suddenly I want the sensation of cold air on my cheeks, want to press my feet against the wooden decking and feel the way it vibrates when I walk. I want to tilt my chin towards the sky and drink in the darkness, which is so unlike the watercolour dark back home, light pollution turning everything vaguely sepia.

But I resist the urge to go outside, remembering my thoughts earlier about slipping. Without Clio and Michaela to distract me, or I suppose because of them in the first place, I'm thinking about Clio's stories again. Fairy tales about monsters, kidnapped children and evil water creatures. A thought strikes me, out of the blue, as my mind drifts towards the podcast Michaela talked about earlier . . . I wonder if anybody has ever fallen into Loch Aven, if that is why she glazed over when Clio asked. Real stories about real people, lured into the dark water, tumbling head-first to their deaths.

I bet it's a podcast about unexplained historical mysteries, Victorian ghosts and lake monsters, and that's why she didn't elaborate. She probably didn't want to creep me out. The thought chills me even as I laugh at myself.

My thoughts turn then to Michaela's 'reason' for us coming here. It's not unlike her to be a little cagey – like I said, she's mastered a kind of cultivated spontaneity over the years – but it's the way she phrased it that sticks in my mind. She said it was something that I would appreciate. Not Clio, me. But try as I might, I can't think of anything. Besides, it's too late now to do much other than sleep.

I get up briskly, filling my movements with urgency as I lock the sliding doors and turn out the remaining lamp. The fire is nothing more than white ash in the burner now, though I give it a good prod before I sleep to make sure.

The stairs creak as I climb them and I hold onto the bannister tightly. The wood is grainy under my fingers, grooves worn by strangers' hands. Why would such a lovely place as this be empty all this time? It's remote, but isn't that what all of the Instagram influencers want to take photos of? Or am I totally out of touch? Probably. Probably they want the skyscrapers of Dubai, not the backwoods of Scotland.

I grab my night things from my rucksack quickly. Although the house has felt very much like home since we got here, I've freaked myself out to the point of ridicule and every shadow seems to twist.

The bathroom is cold. Actually, the whole of this floor

is freezing, and I shiver a little as I brush my teeth and dress in warm flannel pyjamas it's normally too warm for in my house. Charlotte always complained that I keep the heating too high, but I can't stand being cold, not like when I was a kid in the van with my parents, where I would deal with it just to be a part of whatever they were part of, the campfires and the late-night stories. Dad teases me about it still, about how I'd always make myself act like the cold didn't bother me and how they thought that was sweet. Dad says my determination to overcome the aversion is proof that I'm a Cranford through and through, DNA or not.

If any of the adopted parents I counsel said the same thing to their children in front of me now, I'm not sure what I'd say. As an adult, it seems kind of insensitive, but when I was a kid, it was the kind of compliment I lived for, this knowledge that I *belonged*. Fortunately, it's never come up.

When I finally climb into bed, it takes me an age to fall asleep. I'm exhausted, but I can't settle, my thoughts creeping. I think of Michaela and Dan, worried that she didn't tell us about what happened because she was worried we would judge her for dating somebody at work, or worse, that we might think Dan's behaviour was her fault. I roll over and try to think of her plans for the future instead, but the idea of her leaving Clio and me, no matter how unlikely that seemed earlier, just feels wrong. I thought the three of us would be having our weekly Tuesday dinner for the rest of our lives, and the idea that it might not be so permanent makes it feel like the ground is shifting underfoot.

When I eventually do sleep, it's lightly, punctuated by strange dreams. I know I am dreaming, the kind of lucid dreams I've had on and off since I was a child. I am approaching Loch House, but from the back, where the loch glistens in the sun. It's an angle I've never seen, but I can picture it, clear as the water of the loch itself, the grey stone and the flat roof above the decking. I turn my back to the house and wander down to the water; the wooden boards underfoot are cracked and dry and the heat of the sun through them scorches my bare soles. I see the faint ripples on the water, fish swimming under the surface, and the skin on my shoulders hums with the heat of the sun. I sit on the edge of the dock and dangle my legs into the water, right up to the knee. Even in my dreams, the water is shockingly cold and I grit my teeth, the feeling so vivid I begin to wonder if I'm really awake and everything else in my life has been a dream.

I get the sense that I'm not myself. I don't know who I am, but it's not me, not Eleanor the adoption counsellor, single and quiet and motherly. Not Eleanor who lost the girlfriend she knows wasn't good for her but who is lonely all the same. Not Eleanor Cranford, daughter of George and Bev. I'm a different me, a universe apart.

I peer into the water and my face wavers, half mine and half not. The sky begins to cloud over and the water grows murky and dark. My reflection wavers again, again, the surface of the loch undulating as something whispers within. There is a shape beneath the water, something pale and twisting. Dark eyes where my eyes were, lips where mine should be.

I am frozen in place, hands locked under my knees and feet in the water. I want to pull them back, to run, but I don't. I can't. I stare at the body in the water. Flashes of white skin, slick and covered in seaweed; a coil of long, dark hair, tangling upwards to break the surface. And then the face becomes clearer, so close to the surface now, I can see every awful detail. It is a woman, but also it is not.

Her head breaks the surface and her lips are wet and pink, and smiling, a hint of webbed fingers. 'Swim,' she says, her voice like shadows. '*Swim*.'

The fear inside me is as icy as the water of the lake and I'm finally able to pull my feet away, to scramble back onto the dock. It is like a shattering, time becoming unstuck. The woman – the creature – floats in place, hardy moving as I stumble away. Her eyes are black from corner to corner and she's strangely beautiful.

A part deep within me whispers treacherous things. *Swim*, it says. *SWIM*.

The fear in me grows and, just as the woman begins to swim for the dock, I run.

SUNDAY

Eleanor

I wake with my head pounding and lips that are cracked and sore. I grope for the bedside table and a glass of water before realising that I'm not at home. The hangover – from three (or was it four?) more glasses of wine – thuds directly behind my eyes. I rub the sleep from them and lie in the dimness for a while.

The curtains are thin and they let in the drab morning light. I forgot to charge my phone last night so I'm not sure what time it is, but it's no longer dark out. The sun is locked behind a low haze, not quite clouds but not mist either; it makes it seem like twilight.

I dig out my cosmetics bag and dry-swallow two pain-killers, flopping back on the bed until they kick in.

Once the pain subsides, I realise I slept pretty well despite my dreams. I can't remember everything, only snatches of the creature's face and the fear of being lured, but it's all left me feeling slightly unmoored. I debate staying in bed a while longer since it doesn't sound like Michaela or Clio are awake yet, but my brain is buzzing with thoughts, so instead I get up, wash and dress and am downstairs in half an hour with the kettle on while my phone charges.

I make a half-hearted attempt at lighting the fire, but when the pieces of paper just fizzle out without the wood catching, I leave it and go to stand by the doors instead. They draw me to them whenever I'm in here, like a magnet. I'm not sure if it's the lake or the pines or that flat expanse of sky that feels so close to the tops of the trees I could touch it, but this morning I give into my urge and carry my tea out onto the decking.

It's colder this morning than it was yesterday, but the sky is blue now, the haze faded to wisps of tiny white clouds. There's no hint yet of the rain that's predicted for later.

I don't intend to leave the flat decking outside the doors, don't intend to pick my way carefully down the length of dock that goes out into the water. It happens anyway.

The steam from my mug of tea reminds me of the mist on the water the day before. There's no mist this morning and up close the water is green and brown, like mottled glass. I think of my dreams, of the strange water demon. Clio's stories clearly got into my head, kelpies and mermaids and other creatures from the deep. There's obviously nothing there, not even fish that I can see, but I don't stand too close.

I stay out there until I can barely move with the cold. I should have put a coat on, because my sweater isn't thick enough – I'm fairly sure no sweater in the world would be – but I wasn't *intending* to stay—

'Yo!'

I spin, slipping slightly on the still-damp wood of the dock, and my stomach does a little panicked wobble as lukewarm tea splashes over my fingers. Clio's voice is husky with sleep and she carries a mug of her own. She lopes casually down to join me, dressed in a pair of baggy dungarees and the brightest yellow plaid shirt I've ever seen.

'Morning. You look like a ray of sunshine,' I say.

Clio preens. 'I know. I do my best.'

'How did you sleep?'

'Actually really great. That bed is so comfortable, it was like sleeping on a cloud. I guess there's some benefit to hardly anybody ever staying here, huh? I bet those mattresses haven't been used in two decades.' She grins, sipping her tea. 'How about you?'

I think of my dreams, the way I woke feeling like I was half-drowned despite never ending up beneath the water in my sleep. 'Fine,' I say. 'Been awake a while though. What time is it?'

Clio shrugs, carelessly, then sighs, big and contented, and turns to survey the view. The water stretches a long way, but the trees on the opposite bank are so tall, it feels like they're practically within touching distance. The illusion is one of tightness, almost claustrophobia, except when you look up and see that clear, empty sky. It feels like the loch is the centre of the universe.

'This place is actually really, really cool,' Clio says in a stage whisper. 'But please don't tell Kay. She'll be insufferable.'

'She already knows.' I gesture at the water and then back at the house, which stands big and proud behind us. It looks different in the sun, windows shining and crystalline fragments in the silver stone glittering. I imagine what it must be like here in the summer, deckchairs overlooking the water and the thick scent of barbecue smoke on the air, and I wonder again why more people don't seem to know about this gem.

'Yeah, yeah.' Clio drains her mug in one inhuman swallow and glances back over her shoulder. 'Where *is* she anyway?'

'Still in bed, I think.' My tea is long cold, so I move to pour the dregs into the water, but that feels wrong somehow. I stop myself.

'Don't blame her, to be honest.' Clio stoops to place her mug on the dock and then follows it down, careless of the damp wood, so that she is sitting cross-legged, so close to the water she could touch it. 'I bet she's exhausted. It sounds like she's had a rough few weeks.'

'I know.' I don't sit, mostly because I'm not sure if my frozen joints will let me – but also a little because of my dreams, the distant thought of hands snaking around my ankle. 'I'm sad she didn't come to us when it happened.'

Clio thinks about this for a second. 'I'm not,' she says eventually. 'I mean, I get it. She probably thought we'd meddle and she wanted to sort things through on her own. She's very . . .'

'Independent,' I offer.

'I was going to say bull-headed, but yes. Independent works too.' Clio rests her elbows on her knees and props her chin on her steepled fingers as she gazes out over the water.

Although I've been out here for what feels like hours, I find myself seeing it through new eyes again with Clio here, every rush of the breeze through the trees, every ripple of the water. I feel like I've known this place my whole life and I'm just now sharing it with friends.

'Remember when she decided she was going to learn to roller-skate?' Clio continues. 'And she bought those beat-up old boots off eBay and took them out every day for two months and literally *never* told us where she was going – and I had to follow her that night to figure it out? It's a bit like that.'

'Maybe. I just think we could have helped her out,' I say. 'Made her feel less alone.'

'I know. But she would have come to us if she needed us. I think the best thing we can do right now is just be here for her and try to help her make the right choices, ones that will work for her.'

Clio giving *me* advice feels weird, but I crack a smile. Maybe after all this time, I'm finally rubbing off on her a bit.

'What do you think she's got planned for you today?' she asks, changing tack.

'I honestly have no idea. She said it wasn't a surprise. Maybe she's got some activity planned?' I shift position to hide the new wariness in my voice. Last night I was mostly curious but this morning, probably because of my stupid dreams, I feel mostly nervous about it.

'God, I hope it's not walking. I hate walking,' Clio mutters. 'Dude,' she says then, looking up at me. There's mild alarm in her voice and I jump.

'What?'

'Are you all right? Your lips have gone blue. Let's go back inside.'

It's only then that I glance down at my hands and realise my fingers are blue too, just like the dead skin of the monster in my dreams.

Inside, we make breakfast with the pastries and jam we bought yesterday. Clio and I sit on the sofa, curled up with the blanket over our knees. Michaela's still asleep, which takes me back to our student days when she was rarely up before noon. She obviously needs the rest. I've got a book with me, but I don't even open it, instead losing myself to the feeling of the house warming my bones, food in my belly and a hot cup of tea in my hands. It feels good.

Clio scrolls endlessly on her phone, moaning about the lack of good signal, but doing her best to watch stupid saved videos from YouTube or TikTok, the gentle huff of her laughter punctuating the tinny audio from her ancient iPhone. Eventually she gives up with the videos and opens a game she can play without internet. I don't even mind that she's breaking our phone ban.

'This is nice,' I say sleepily. 'I've got to be honest, I don't fancy the idea of walking around Blackhills today. Or, God forbid, going on one of Michaela's epic hikes. I just want to relax.'

'Mhmm,' Clio agrees, equally sleepy, although she's not been awake half as long as me. 'I know what you mean. This place is like a big cushy pillow. I'd love to spend today sleeping and we can go shopping tomorrow. I feel like I need a holiday after the drive yesterday. I still wish we could have flown.'

'Maybe Kay will sleep long enough that all we can manage today is a pub lunch.' I visibly cross my fingers and it looks like a joke, but I'm really not joking at all. Although I thought I slept okay enough, the cold wind off the lake this morning has made me feel like I've run a marathon.

I don't know how long it is before I fall asleep, my tea abandoned on a side table and a second blanket wrapped around my knees. This time, I don't dream, just surrender myself to the blackness of unconsciousness. I float, somewhere between waking and sleeping, my body cushioned by the warmth of the blanket and Clio's legs pressed close.

When I wake, it's with a start, heart hammering and mouth dry. Blearily I peer around, taking in Clio's form sleeping beside me. The sun seems surprisingly low and I realise I still have literally zero idea what time it is.

I slide gently from between the blankets, shivering as the cool air hits me. We haven't lit the fire, but we probably should if we're going to hang around here for the rest of the day.

I pad to the counter where my phone has been charging since I got up. I click the screen on, expecting to see the time as around eleven or twelve. My stomach drops strangely as I realise it's actually two forty-five.

'Clio,' I say. And then less gently, '*Clio*.'

'Huh?' She sits up groggily, running a hand over her face. 'Damn, must have fallen asleep.'

'Have you seen Michaela yet?'

Clio shakes her head, eyes still glazed.

I leave her to wake up, climbing the stairs a couple at a time. Their creaking is the soundtrack as I think back to last night. Michaela was drunk, but not *silly* drunk. There's no way she should still be asleep now.

I check the bathroom first as it's on the way, but it's empty. And then I head for Michaela's room. The door is cracked open and I push it wide.

'Is she awake yet?' Clio calls from the bottom of the stairs.

'No.' I stop short, breath coming in startled puffs as my eyes scan the room anxiously. 'I mean, she's not here – she's gone.'

Rebecca

Then

Loch Aven is never more beautiful than it is in the early summer, green moss on grey stone, sunlight glinting off the water and the air abuzz with insects. Rebecca and Janie walk together along the south shore, where they spent so much of their youth lighting illicit bonfires and drinking cheap vodka and beer. Rebecca inhales, drawing in that damp, musty smell that reminds her of home.

'You've been quiet this morning,' Janie says.

Janie is lagging a little behind, her shorter legs forcing her to choose a slightly different path over the stones they're currently picking their way over. The water is low today, exposing the brittle, sandy world beneath it that rarely sees the sun. They're meant to be collecting stones for an art project Janie is working on, though they've done less collecting than they have general complaining about life, work, the weather, the news – just about everything. Although perhaps today Janie has done more of the complaining than usual.

'I don't feel quiet,' Rebecca replies. She turns and shrugs.

The sun is warm on her bare arms. Her flat canvas shoes aren't really appropriate for this kind of scavenging and they're already wet; she'll have to be careful not to fall and twist her ankle. 'I've just been listening.'

'That's my job,' Janie jokes. She catches up to the spot where Rebecca has paused and together they look out over the water. The trees stand tall on the other side, but it feels like a million miles away from where they are over here, sun and sand and the soft breeze bringing the sounds of distant birdcalls. 'Sarah and I have both been worried about you.'

Rebecca makes to carry on, but Janie reaches out and lays a hand on her arm. It's a shock, Rebecca realises, to be touched by anybody other than *him*. It's been so long since she's seen Janie, she almost forgot how tactile she is. How loving, even without words. Rebecca once thought that was just how Janie was, because it is how she has always been around Rebecca, soft touches and gentle words – but she's realised that there was more to it than that. Not that Rebecca cares, of course. Janie is just *Janie*. They'll always be friends. But the touch reminds Rebecca of how different they both are, how they want different things. She's just not sure Janie could ever understand.

'You've not said anything about the summer either,' Janie prompts. 'I thought you were planning to jet off to, like, New York or Florence or somewhere.'

'China,' Rebecca corrects with a small smile. 'I was going to go to China.'

'Right. Whatever.' Janie shoots her a smile to mirror her own. 'I thought you said last year that you wanted to go this summer. You know, now your mum's better. May? June?'

106

'June.'

'And?'

Rebecca feels an unfamiliar slithering anger, coiling like a snake ready to strike. It's not fair to lash out at Janie – she doesn't know. She doesn't know anything. She doesn't know how Rebecca can't think of things that way any more; she can't think about travelling alone, she can't think of travelling away from him *full stop*. All of the plans she had . . . They've paled beside the secret language she now speaks, the world full of colours she can't even describe to anybody else.

'And – I changed my mind.' It has been changed, she knows, since the moment he came into the shop last summer.

Rebecca begins to walk, but Janie's hand grips around her arm harder and it throws her off balance. She stumbles off the rock she's currently balanced on and lands fully in the water, right up to her ankle. It's shockingly cold, even now, and she lets out a yelp, dragging herself back onto the rock.

Janie looks mortified. In the old days, they would have just laughed. That kind of belly-clutching, raw laughter, the kind that swallows everything. Now, it feels like Rebecca has a bubble of helium in her chest and it hurts.

Janie's love for Rebecca has grown in her absence and it fills the space between them – space Rebecca longs to fill with the truth about why she has been so distant, why her life has changed course. It's like a barrier neither of them can quite cross.

'Shit,' Rebecca mutters.

'I'm sorry—'

'It's not a big deal, okay? Don't pull that face, you'll make me feel awful.'

Too late. Janie's cherubic features have morphed into an almost cartoon sadness, her big blue eyes wide and her soft mouth turned down. Combined with her fine blonde hair, she looks like a child.

'Janie, I mean it,' Rebecca insists. 'It's not a big deal. It'll dry.'

They start heading back towards the bank, Rebecca squelching along. It should be funny. Why does nothing seem funny any more? Only when she's with him . . .

'Why did you change your mind . . .?' Janie asks. It's tentative, as though she hardly dares say it.

'About travelling?' she says. She knows it's what Janie means but half of her wishes her friend meant something else.

'Yeah.'

'I just . . .' A thousand answers swirl around like her mind is a snow globe. She can't say most of them. *Because of him. Because everything seems foolish now. Because I don't want to go alone.* 'I need more time,' she settles on. 'You know. Money and stuff.'

'But you've been working so much. Surely you have enough saved by now?'

'I . . . Yeah, not yet.'

'Oh.' Janie stops for a second to pick up a particularly shiny blue stone. She rubs the dirt off it with her thumb and holds it up to the light. It's run through with pale marble-like veins. For some reason, it makes Rebecca think of her future, of the map she thought she'd laid out for herself only to find herself still here.

'Janie,' she blurts before she can stop herself.

'Hmm?'

'If . . . No, never mind.' She can't say it. It's too big.

'If what?' Janie pockets the stone and turns, her attention full on Rebecca, and it's like the sun shining between clouds, nearly too bright. Rebecca blinks.

'How do you know if . . . you're a bad person?'

Janie's face splits into a smile. 'You're not a bad person, Bec,' she says. 'I know you.'

'But how do you *know*?' Rebecca presses, unconvinced.

Janie shakes her head vehemently. 'You haven't got a bad bone in your body.'

'But what if I did?'

'You *don't*.'

'And if I did?' Rebecca insists. 'What then?'

'Bec, what's got into you?' Janie asks. 'Is something going on?'

Rebecca opens her mouth and she wants so badly to tell somebody. Anybody. Janie is gentle and she wouldn't judge her – would she? Would her love for Rebecca make her kind, or would it make her angry?

And if she did judge her – enough to tell someone else – it's not just Rebecca's reputation on the line. There's her whole family – and him too. Blackhills is so small . . . Rebecca can't risk it. She can't lose everything just because she's lonely. She's allowed herself to become so isolated, and it's getting harder to keep up with all the secrecy. And it's not fair to lay that pressure at Janie's door.

'It's nothing. I'm just . . . I worry I'll disappoint my family if I don't get on with things.'

Janie's face softens with sympathy as Rebecca goes on.

'I already didn't go to uni like planned and now Mum's better it just feels so obvious that I'm stuck. Dad keeps telling me I'm better than all of this. Sometimes I feel like I'm letting him down. Especially since he wanted me to stay here in the first place, so I'm sure he expects more from me. I feel like I'm grinding my gears half the time, waiting for my life to start.'

Rebecca hadn't realised until the words came that this is true, too. She is lonely and happy and excited and scared and so, so worried about disappointment and it all just feels too much sometimes. How *does* she know she's not a bad person? She's responsible, almost directly, for a fracture in another family. She could ruin *his* life, and his wife's. And yet she still can't stop herself.

'The only way you could let your family down is by not being yourself,' Janie says firmly. 'Just be the same lovely, sweet Rebecca you've always been and you'll be fine.' She gives her what she must think is a reassuring grin and Rebecca smiles weakly back.

Because how does she explain that she doesn't think she *is* that Rebecca any more?

Eleanor

'What do you mean she's *gone*?'

Clio's footsteps follow mine up the stairs, a steady *creak creak creak* until she's at the top, eyes scrunched against the golden slant of light that cuts through the window of my bedroom spilling into the hallway.

'She's not in there,' I say. 'See for yourself.'

Clio joins me and I gesture into the room, the curtains open, the bed made. Dust motes swirl. Together we step in, as though we might conjure her just by both being present. But there's nobody here, just folded pyjamas and her rucksack against one wall, her phone lead plugged in but no phone attached.

'This is just like her,' Clio mutters. 'Wandering off by herself.'

'I guess she woke up while we were napping,' I say hesitantly. 'Maybe she's outside.'

We traipse back down the stairs, neither of us saying anything. Clio's right. For anybody else, this sort of behaviour might be rude – disappearing for hours on end during a relaxing weekend *with friends* – but for Michaela it's totally normal. She's such a free spirit that we've often teased her about how at odds it seems sometimes with her lawyer self, all rules and regulations. But Michaela believes half the challenge in the law is finding the right path to take, the same as in life.

'Her boots aren't here,' I point out.

We open the sliding doors and head outside, though I'm sure we would have noticed the squeak of them rolling back if Michaela had gone out that way while we were sat right there, even if we were dozing.

'She must have been in bed earlier though, right?' Clio asks. 'Otherwise when did she leave?'

I shrug, stepping ahead of Clio. I tell myself I'm not worried at all, because this is Michaela. But that's not entirely true. This isn't the same as disappearing randomly during a sleepover at home, and we're not students any more. It's not like when we were all living together and could read the rhythms and patterns in each other's behaviour; we're in the middle of nowhere, in a strange place, by ourselves.

'Did she text you at all?' I ask. There are no new notifications on my phone, but again – not unusual.

Clio shakes her head. 'I'll try calling. She'll turn up eventually.'

We walk down towards the dock, where the water laps rhythmically. She's clearly not down here but for some reason I want to be close to the soothing calm of the water. I'm *not* worried. It's *not* weird. There's no way she's got herself into any trouble when there's basically nowhere around here to go. Except . . . Hiking. And falling into the loch. And, God – any number of other things.

Clio's phone rings and rings on speakerphone.

'Maybe she went into the village without us,' Clio suggests. 'She probably heard us earlier saying we didn't want to go.'

Clio is completely calm, which I have to admit I find reassuring given the way my heart is pounding.

'You're right,' I say, convincing myself. 'She probably had, like, a whole day of shopping planned and then she overheard us and thought we were being a bit ungrateful. Or she doesn't really care and just thought she'd go while we were sleeping. But, either way, she's gone by herself. Without telling us.'

In place of the initial pang of worry is a wave of annoyance. If she was going to wander off, the least she could do was leave a note.

'Maybe she went up into the hills without us,' I plough on. 'She said she was worried about those campers, but I didn't think she genuinely meant we should go and help.'

Clio shrugs and shoves her phone back in her pocket. 'I guess. She'll be fine—'

'Or maybe,' I continue breathlessly, trying to ignore the panic that's building inside me once more, 'she's just out walking and thinking.' It could be that she's taking time for herself, to process the stuff that happened with Dan – but the idea of Michaela out there, hiking alone, in *any* capacity fills me with a low-key sort of dread. Especially if she's thinking about what happened with Dan.

'I wonder if it could be to do with whatever she had planned for you,' Clio suggests instead.

'Maybe.' I like that idea the least of all of them. If she's out there somewhere walking around creating some kind of . . . treasure hunt? And if she falls into the loch? That's on me. 'I hope not. I like surprises, but only if they're nice.'

'She said it wasn't a surprise.' Clio waggles her finger. 'Just because she's not left a note doesn't mean she's not been planning it. Remember when she disappeared to Prague for the weekend?'

'Yeah, but she texted us, then.'

'She was in Prague, dude,' Clio says. 'Of *course* she texted us. Come on, you're normally the one telling me off for being too excitable.'

A loose strand of my dark hair sticks to my cheek and I sweep it away quickly. On second thoughts, I pull a hair tie from my wrist and twist my hair into a plait to keep it off my face.

'I just wish she'd answer her phone at least,' I say. 'I don't like not knowing where she is.'

'There's not very good coverage. If she's walking around the loch, or on one of those hikes that goes into the hills, maybe the trees are causing a problem. I'm sure she'll be back later. She's probably not even been gone that long.'

We turn back and head into the house. It's so quiet inside. I wonder if Michaela was even here when we were napping. We haven't seen her since last night. There's no way of knowing when she left.

I cross to the back of the house and peer out of the door. 'Well, she didn't take the car,' I say.

'Maybe she was too hung-over to drive,' Clio points out, 'and she didn't want to wake us up.'

'What if she *did* go to try to help those campers, though? What if she gets stuck herself?' I press, unable to hold back on my worries now.

'Dude, can you chill?' Clio blows out a breath. 'This is Michaela we're talking about. She's more than capable.'

I know I'm being ridiculous, but, after the dreams I had . . . I just can't shake the feeling that something is wrong.

But I'm meant to be the voice of reason. If Clio isn't worried, then that means I absolutely shouldn't be either.

I sigh, sinking onto the sofa. 'You're right,' I say. 'So what do we do now? Just sit around and wait here for her like widows waiting for soldiers to come home from the war?'

'Well, yeah.' Clio gives a silly little wave and I let out a frustrated snort, surprising myself. 'There's not exactly much else we can do, unless she lets us know where she's gone. No point taking the car anywhere if she's hiking in the bloody forest. And if she's gone to the village she'll be back in a couple of hours at the most. I can't imagine anything staying open past four on a Sunday.'

I stare at the fireplace and the remains of last night's fire and my shoddy attempts at making one this morning.

'Okay fine,' I say eventually. But I still feel unsettled. It's like hovering in this weird limbo state, knowing that everything is *probably* fine, not wanting to jinx it by thinking it too much, but also knowing that there's a very slight possibility that everything is *not* fine.

Another wave of worried anger hits me and I'm so irritated with Michaela for deciding that heading out by herself in the middle of fucking nowhere is a good idea that I can't sit still. I go to the kettle to boil the water, but the sound is too loud and I snap it right back off again. I wander to the fridge, open it and stare inside, but my stomach churns uncomfortably, so I close it without grabbing anything.

'El,' Clio says. '*Chill*.'

'I am chilled,' I snap. Then a wave of regret hits me. 'Sorry. I just had the most fucked-up dreams last night,' I say. 'Really, really odd. And I woke up feeling so strange. It's been bugging me all day.' I pause. 'I dreamed about the loch.'

Most people hate other people talking about their dreams. Everybody loves to narrate their own dreams to their friends, their family, but most recipients of the stories always look like their eyes are about to roll back in their heads. That's not Clio, though. The second you start talking about dreams, she's like a dog alerted by the presence of snacks.

'What about the loch?' she asks.

'I dreamed about creatures.' It sounds totally ridiculous in the light of day and this is a relief. 'Well, one creature, but it felt like there might be more somewhere under the surface. She came up with this milky white skin and eyes that were black the whole way through. Hair tangled like seaweed. She was weirdly beautiful though and I had this strange urge to—'

'To get into the water?' Clio raises an eyebrow.

'Yeah. Let me guess, that makes you think of stories?'

'Boy, does it.' Clio snorts. 'I don't know what it is, but there are always the grimmest folktales about, like, the ocean, lakes, even puddles of rainwater. With lakes, it's usually kelpies specifically. They're these shape-shifting spirits that live in the lochs of Scotland. They often appear as horses first, or black horse-like creatures anyway, but they're capable of shifting into human form.'

Although I know it's silly, I find myself shivering.

'Did she have hooves?' Clio asks.

'I didn't see. She was under the water, swimming. She wanted me to get into the water with her.'

Clio smirks, always the happiest when she can make fun

116

of me. 'Girl, you're bewitched. Loch Aven has got you in her sights.'

'Oh leave off,' I grumble. 'I don't know why I said anything.'

'Because, deep down, you absolutely love hearing about this shit. You always pretend you don't, but I saw the way your ears pricked when Michaela mentioned that bloody podcast yesterday.' Clio lets out a cackle. 'Anyway, the stories about kelpies have some variations that say if you see them in their horse form without any tack, then you might be able to harness one with a halter inscribed with a cross. Then you could, like, get it to do all your heavy lifting.'

'What heavy lifting do I do?' I ask. 'I'm not a farmer.'

Clio shrugs. 'I dunno. Guess I'd find it useful whenever I go on holiday. Could get it to lug my suitcase down the stairs for me, maybe carry it to the airport too.'

'You'd still have to pay for extra baggage.'

'I'd have a *kelpie*,' Clio says. 'In this imaginary scenario, I don't have to pay for excess fucking baggage.'

'What if you can't catch it though?' I ask. 'I mean, what if you don't have a bridle or harness or whatever? Do they just leave you alone if you leave them alone kind of thing?'

'No.' Clio shakes her head. 'They drown you.'

'Oh,' I mutter. 'Great.'

'I mean, you can totally kill them. I'm pretty sure it's the same as the whole werewolf thing and you can kill them with a silver bullet.'

'And this makes me feel better, how . . .?' I can't help the annoyance in my voice. I know all of this is just Clio having fun or blowing off steam or whatever and normally I don't mind listening to her make-believe tales, but today it's grating.

'You didn't ask me to make you feel better. You just asked

me about kelpies.' Clio laughs again. She's looking out of the windows, over towards the other side of the lake where the water is cast in patchy shadows from the trees as the sun continues its slow stretch overhead. The sky is still mostly clear, but there are a few more mottled rainclouds gathering than there were this morning. I'm not entirely sure what we'll do if Michaela doesn't reappear before the weather turns.

'Should we text Joy?' I ask. There's a group chat Michaela started when we were at uni, sometime during our first semester when the three of us already knew we'd be friends for life; it's just the three of us and her mum. Some weeks, I talk to Joy more than my own parents, which makes sense because when she was living in Durham she'd invite us round for Sunday dinner most weeks too. She's become like our second mother – or, in Clio's case, her first mother, since her own mum hasn't spoken to her since she decided to stay in Durham after graduation.

'About Kay wandering off? Nah. She'll just give us an earful about her *wayward daughter* and then ask us if we need any cookies posting or something.'

'Well, okay, but shall we try ringing Michaela again?' I ask. 'I don't even know if she was listening when I read her the forecast yesterday. If she's out there with nothing but a light jacket, she's going to freeze and then Joy will have my head.'

Clio picks her phone out of her pocket and hits the favourites menu before dialling the number. I can hear the empty echo of the dial tone through her crappy speakers. Ringing, and ringing, and ringing. Clio shakes her head just as the call hits the voicemail.

The person you have dialled is not available. Please leave a message after the tone.

'No, but seriously now, how long do we have to wait before we start to worry about her?' I ask. I don't know anything about this sort of thing. Michaela is the true crime nut. All I ever do is read romances; I don't know how this stuff works in the real world.

'Hours yet.' Clio shrugs.

'But say . . . Say she doesn't come back. Say she's fallen down and hurt herself or lost her phone and got stuck or something. Does it have to be, like, twenty-four hours before we can report her missing? Or is that just an American TV thing?' It's meant as an almost-joke, but I realise as the words come out that I actually mean it.

'Eleanor,' Clio says gently, as if she's trying to calm a spooked horse.

I take a breath and try to dial it back. 'No, I know,' I say. 'I know I'm overreacting. Sorry.'

'Would it make you feel better if we went out and looked for her?' Clio asks. Her expression has shifted now, from exasperation to mild concern. Maybe my nerves are rubbing off on her – or maybe she's just worried I'll have a melt-down again if she doesn't try to help. I don't know what's got into me, the voice in my head is usually very reliable, but a sense of relief flushes through me as I realise that that's exactly what I want. I don't want to just sit here, not when I feel like there's something we're missing. I'd rather overreact but be doing *something* than wait around hoping Michaela will waltz back in.

'Yes,' I say breathlessly. 'I'm sure she's fine, but I'm so antsy. Maybe some fresh air would do me good. We can leave her a note – like she should have left us, y'know – and maybe go out and check the area around here.'

'Around the loch?' Clio's eyebrows dip into a frown. She

119

knows why I'm suggesting it. And I think it's telling that she doesn't say it aloud, as if she doesn't want to believe me when I say there is a reason – however small – to be concerned.

'Yeah. Just in case.'

We stand for a moment, both of us completely still.

But I have to say it. I have to acknowledge what I am afraid of. Maybe it will sound silly. I want it to sound silly. For Clio to brush me off again. 'In case she fell in,' I say, trying to infuse my voice with the idea that this is a joke. That Clio is right to be mildly annoyed instead of worried – the way I would normally feel when Michaela pulls one of her stunts.

The problem is, I think I've jinxed us. Because when I say it aloud, it doesn't sound silly at all. And from the way her face pales, I'm pretty sure Clio doesn't think so either.

Eleanor

Every minute that passes, I swear the air gets colder. Clio
is ahead right now, picking her way between the thick trees
that grow all around the house and along the banks of the
loch, sometimes right up to the sandy dirt, and plumes of
silver-tinted air puff above her head as she breathes. I reassure myself that my lungs are tight with the cold, and not
with the anxiety starting to swirl inside me.

'Michaelaaaa,' Clio sing-songs, her voice intentionally
light. 'C'mon, dude. This is not funny.' She turns to me. 'Is
this making you feel better or worse?'

I can't bring myself to answer. I walk mutely, my phone
clutched in my hand and my eyes scanning the opposite
shore – or as much of it as I can see, anyway. The trees are
so thick on both shores that it makes for a difficult view;
the water reflects what little sunlight there is, low and bright,
and the shadows stretch and tug with the wind. Three times
now, I've sworn I've seen something moving across on the
other bank, some dark shape that might have been a person
or an animal – or a creature from my nightmares, if I'm

being really honest about where my mind is at – and three times, there's been nothing but trees. I tell myself that we're just out for a nice walk. That Michaela will laugh so hard she cries when she finds out she made Clio *willingly* go hiking. It doesn't help.

'It's no good,' I say. We've been out here for over an hour, looping back and forth around the property, skimming the banks and the area around them, popping back into the house every now and then to check she hasn't magically reappeared. This is the farthest we've come; this time, we've walked the curve of the loch and I can see the house from here, the dock that stretches into the water. It's so isolated, sitting there between the trees as if it might be a mirage, just like I thought when I first saw it yesterday.

'You're telling me. I could have been sitting down this whole time,' Clio moans.

'Clio,' I say. 'Please. I'm really worried.'

She blows out a breath. 'I know you are,' she consoles me. 'But this is Michaela. She's *fine*. I bet she did go and try to help those campers, bloody do-gooder.'

I try to find a sense of that feeling again, clutching to the belief that we'll head back to the house after our search and this time Michaela will be there and everything will be fine. Because Loch House is a home – it must have been, once, settled in a place like this, a slice of solitude that somebody built with love and ambition – and bad things simply cannot happen there. But the feeling doesn't fill me with warmth as it should.

Clio shields her hand against the weak rays of sun that are shining directly into her eyes, but I can tell from the hunch of her shoulders that she's not just scowling because it's bright. The hems of her dungarees are studded with dirty sand and she buries her hands in her pockets, chewing furiously on a piece of nicotine gum.

I feel a wave of guilt for making her come out here and deal with my irrationality. Perhaps this is because of Charlotte – indirectly. When we were together, I second-guessed myself all the time, tiptoed around her moods and panicked whenever I upset her. She was my first long-term relationship and I got so focused on trying to make everything perfect that I didn't stop to actually consider if it was what we both wanted.

I used to think I was well-adjusted, that the adoption and my search for my parents hadn't affected me much at all, but now, standing here on the shore of this lake, fresh panic making my stomach twist, I'm thinking maybe I'm more neurotic than I thought.

'We should probably head back to the house,' I say.

Clio shifts her gaze to the house, scanning the dock. The wind is still and the water does not even ripple. We could be the only people in these woods for miles in every direction but the road that leads to Blackhills. Or we could be surrounded by people and, in the thick of the trees, we might never see them at all. I'm not sure which of those is worse.

I begin picking my way back along the shore, this time walking on the sand itself, away from the trees that crowd at my side. The house soon drops out of sight, lost amidst more trees and a curve of the loch.

I'm trying not to let my thoughts run wild. I know what I'd say to the parents I counsel. I'd tell them to take a deep breath, that their concerns are valid but are they helpful? But it's easier said than done and my brain is crowded now by what might come next.

First the waiting. Then the worrying. And then – God

123

forbid – the police, if she doesn't come back soon. They'll ask us questions about Kay's mental health, her behaviour leading up to this morning, and I know I've got to resist the urge to rake over the last twenty-four hours for every morsel of emotional truth before I start to question everything Michaela said to us last night.

I feel like my thoughts are falling over each other as I try to sift them, to order the outcomes from most likely to least.

Most likely: we get back to Loch House and Michaela is there with her feet up, fire going, and a smirk on her face that will make me so angry, I'll see red. Mud on her boots from hiking through the woods looking for lost people, or a box of biscuits from the farm shop, ready to announce whatever plans she has for me.

Least likely: we get back and we wait and she's still not there, and then we have to wait and worry some more, and eventually we will have to report her missing. Which is stupid. She is *fine*.

It isn't that I think it's going to happen like that. It's the least likely option for a reason. And Clio is convinced that I'm being silly, which I want so badly to be true.

The thing that scares me is that it's an option at all.

By the time we reach the house again, the temperature feels like it must be nearing zero degrees, and, sure enough, I check my phone and it's not far off, though the weather app looks like it hasn't updated itself in a couple of hours due to the signal. If Michaela is out there somewhere, I hope she's wearing layers.

Clio and I both linger on the dock for longer than we should. I don't want to go inside and find Michaela still gone, and Clio is probably craving a cigarette after all that walking.

'There's a story about bright lights under the water,' Clio says. She points at a spot far ahead where a ball of sunlight reflects strangely on the water, a perfect circle that could be a light bulb under the surface. 'I tell it sometimes when I do the horror folk tale storytelling package. I guess it probably comes from those fish with the lights on their head or something like that, but it basically says that if you see the light, you should blink three times rapidly.'

'And if you don't?' I don't know why I always ask Clio to elaborate, but I can never help myself. I hate unfinished stories.

'The spirits under the water use the lights to draw you into the depths,' Clio says. 'I'm not sure exactly what the original tale says they do with you once they've got you, but the way I tell it is that you learn to breathe under the water. Maybe in the original they make you into servants of the Deep Ones. Or maybe I'm conflating stories.'

We stand on the dock for a minute longer. We can both already tell from here that Loch House is empty. The lights are off and the lounge looks dim through the glass doors. There's an air of abandonment about it. It's a feeling more than anything, but I know it's the truth.

I reorder my list of likelihoods.

We head up towards the house, looping through the narrow track between the wall and the trees that tower overhead to bring us back to the porch, using that entrance instead of the doors overlooking the loch because we made sure to lock them from the inside with the security bolt since we couldn't find a key. Clio unlocks the door with stiff fingers but hangs back to let me enter first.

Of course, the house is empty. We had the only key and Michaela wasn't waiting outside. It feels almost as if we are entering for the first time again, like some kind of do-over without Michaela. Almost like she never existed.

It's freezing in here without the fire burning and it feels dim and untouched.

Clio does a circuit of the whole house, while I plug my phone in and try Michaela's number again – to no avail.

'She's not here. Nothing has changed; she's not been back,' Clio says.

'I'm going to ring Joy,' I say, but I remain frozen by the outlet where my phone is charging, my gaze glued to the still waters of the loch. There's mist there again now, the late-afternoon sun not touching its edges.

Clio sinks onto the sofa, tucking her hands beneath her knees. 'And worry her?'

'So you admit she'll be worried.' My pulse quickens.

'Well, yeah, if you talk to her when you're in a flap.' Clio shrugs. 'You're so determined to panic—'

'Okay, fine. Maybe I'll give it another hour and then try. Kay's been gone *all day* though. We don't even know what time she left. And this weekend was her idea – aren't we supposed to be spending time together?'

I'm vacillating between anger and concern, the anger only worsened by Clio's blasé attitude, as if it's totally unreasonable of me to be worried. Eventually, I cave and try to call Joy anyway, in case she knows what Michaela was planning for me today, but the signal is so bad in the house that the call cuts out after a few rings. A text pops through about twenty minutes later, just a few lines that are probably meant to accompany a photo.

Enjoy your weekend. Remember what you girls always tell me. Blood pressure low = happiness high!

'Typical Joy.' Clio smiles. 'She's right though. We're meant to be relaxing. Why *are* you so wound up about all of this?' She narrows her green eyes at me. 'Normally you'd just be going on about the psychology behind Michaela's lack of concern for herself in the wake of caring for others or some bullshit. This isn't *half* as bad as the time she disappeared after Carnage – you remember that awful freshers pub crawl? You were fine about that.'

'Oh, God,' I say, remembering. But that was a long time ago, when we'd only known each other a week and a half. Making silly decisions as a teenager is hardly the same as doing it like seven years later, though. 'Didn't she go home with some random girl who was throwing up and end up taking her to A&E?'

'Yeah, but then she couldn't remember which dorm we were living in because it had only been like, two days, so she slept in the foyer of the Arts building because it was the only one you didn't need a pass to get into.'

I rub my hands over my face. 'And somehow they let her decide to become a lawyer,' I say, finding a strange laughter bubbling in my chest. It's a relief, actually. 'I don't know why I'm so wound up. I think . . . I think maybe it's because of Charlotte.'

Clio's face shifts. 'Why?'

'I . . . I don't know. I just . . . I used to get so worried about everything when we were together, like I would disappoint her or whatever. And now I feel like it's rubbed off onto everything.' I shrug, trying to hide the way it makes me feel. Like maybe *I* was the problem in our relationship, not Charlotte's possessiveness. 'But there's something weird

127

about this,' I add quickly. 'Michaela hasn't pulled a stunt like this for ages.'

'Yeah, but, dude, she just lost her job *and* ended a relationship, and neither in the best way. I'm kinda not surprised. Look, we know what she's like. Whatever it was she wanted to tell you today will have completely consumed her. It's a coping mechanism.'

'I know. I know you're right.' I find myself chuckling again.

Clio smiles and this time it feels more relaxed.

But still, every time there's a lull in our conversation, every time Clio's phone pings – which is more often than mine – the notification isn't from Michaela. None of her social media has had any activity that we can tell, but that's not unusual. She's not really that into Instagram like Clio, though she's been posting a bit more often recently, and she says Twitter is a cesspit she'd never venture into. Facebook is about the only thing she still uses and even that's only to post pictures of the breakfast for dinner she sometimes makes herself when she's just got in from work.

The sun sinks lower and still there's no sign of her. Clio lights the fire, out of necessity rather than anything else. It's freezing in the house, our noses and fingers icy. I put the kettle on and make us both a drink, but the whole time, I can't help staring at the extra mug on the counter, the sugar Michaela takes and the way she teases Clio about her *alternative milk obsession*.

This really isn't funny any more.

Where the fuck is she?

'Maybe we should go into the village,' Clio says. She's staring out across the loch with a cheeky expression on her face. It feels later than it is now that the temperature has dipped. 'You know, we can ask if anybody has seen her. Go to the pub. Maybe find that teacher guy again – Matthew . . .'

'Pretty sure he was married, Clio.'

'Hey, I didn't say *flirt* with him.' She snorts a laugh. 'Well, okay. I meant it. But there's no harm in flirting, even if he's way too old for me.'

The fact that even Clio is getting antsy now is worrying me even more, though likely she's more motivated by the fact that we have no food in the house for dinner and she's hungry.

'I don't know.'

'Come on,' Clio admonishes. 'Where's your sense of adventure? Pre-Charlotte Eleanor would have been all over this. Let's go, get dinner and a few drinks, and if Michaela turns up that's a bonus. And if we bump into *Matthew*, that's an even bigger bonus.' She nudges me when I don't crack a smile. 'Or, y'know, we can ask him if there's anywhere she might likely be. If we can work out what it was she wanted to tell you today we might stand a better chance of figuring out what kind of confirmation she needed beforehand. If she's doing research, maybe she needed a better signal. She might not have even left the house until just before we woke up at three so, like, it's not even that long if she's down an internet hole.'

It's no use. Everything Clio says to try to convince me this is all fine is only making me more worried. Why would Michaela do any of this without some warning, at least – especially if it's research to benefit me somehow? It doesn't make any sense.

No, what makes more sense are the thoughts swirling with every passing minute. Like, what if Michaela left the house this morning to take in the sights while we were asleep, to inhale the frosty morning air by the water, to feel at one with nature? Just like I had done. And what if something happened to her? What if she lost her footing on the slippery surface of the dock? What if she fell? *What if she drowned?*

'I think . . .' I say hesitantly. Clear my throat. 'You don't have to come with me, but I think we should go to the police.'

Eleanor

We take the car into Blackhills and park in the same place we parked yesterday. It's not yet late enough for the sun to have set, but the air has a definite autumn chill. A few families are out walking, a couple with children who seem particularly buoyant, perhaps excited that there's a school holiday. I remember as a kid most of my friends hated Sundays because they heralded the start of another school week, but I always loved them. I loved my parents, but school gave me a place to be myself – not in relation to my parents – at least until everybody found out I was adopted and started asking if I had weird powers like Matilda.

Blackhills feels livelier today than it did yesterday, but there's still a strange absence of people. Almost like everybody over the age of thirty just upped and left. I wonder how many villagers are out trying to help find those campers – or perhaps they've already found them and they're all celebrating in the pub, Michaela included. She's still not answering her phone though, so I doubt it.

Clio and I walk in silence, Google Maps directing us to the nearest police station. She's not happy about it; I can tell by the slope of her shoulders and the way she stomps her feet that she thinks I'm being silly, but she's agreed to let me do this.

The police station is a small, squat building at the far end of the village, tucked down several winding, cobbled side streets with overhanging roofs. Everything seems to be hewn from the same grey stone, which catches the daylight when there is an abundance of it, but which in the twilight looks dull and prison-like.

It's not even a proper police station. Its sign says *Blackhills Community Police Office* and up close we see that it's basically just a house with a large wooden door and windows on either side, all bordered in the same shade of post office red. Opposite is a relatively large, empty structure that looks like it might once have been a B&B, though there's no signage now, only shadows of dirt on the stone where a sign once hung. The streets are empty here and it feels like we could have travelled back in time but for my mobile phone clenched in my hand.

Clio glances at me and I know what she's thinking. It doesn't look like much. But then, the village is small. They're hardly going to need a proper station and multiple police officers. They probably don't even have a whole team. We're lucky they have this, probably a hangover from a time when the village got more attention, or the nearest other town was miles and miles away. We duck inside out of the spitting rain.

The building is unsurprisingly empty, the floor squeaking under our wet shoes, the décor possibly from any time after the eighties, everything beige and plastic. There are a few old newspaper articles on the walls in frames, and signs about parking fines. Behind a boxy desk sits a woman, flipping through a magazine idly, her hair the colour of autumn leaves. She startles and shoves the magazine away hastily, then plasters a smile on her face to take our details.

We wait for a few minutes and are then ushered through to another room, where a man in a dark suit takes the same details again. He's maybe in his forties, dark-haired and dark-eyed, and his accent is thick enough that I struggle to understand what he's saying. I give him a run-down of everything as calmly as I can and, to his credit, despite the look of mild disinterest on his face, he listens.

'When was the last time you saw her?' It's the first real question he's asked us.

'Last night,' I say. 'We went to bed late. It was definitely the early hours. I'm not sure exactly what time. It might have been around two-ish though. Maybe three.'

Clio nods her agreement, though her scepticism is visible on her face.

The man scribbles the information down, but his whole attitude is relaxed. He leans back in his chair, one elbow on the desk in front of him, the picture of nonchalance. 'And you said this isn't entirely unusual.' His tone is gentle but his posture doesn't change. He's clearly not worried about Michaela at all. I know I should find this reassuring, but it only makes me more grumpy.

'It would be normal at home,' I say. 'But we're not at home.'

'That being said, it's not unusual generally,' the officer rephrases. 'She's an adventurer. She's young and fit, yes? You mentioned that she was excited to be here, wanted to be outdoors for a change of scenery. That she likes to hike.'

'I don't like that she isn't answering her phone,' I point out.

'The signal around here is pa—'

'She's been gone for *hours*,' I say.

'Okay, look.' The police office sits upright and folds his hands on the desk. 'As far as I see it, there are a few likely explanations. The first is, as you said, your friend is a keen outdoorswoman. There are a lot of old trails in the area around Blackhills. They don't get as much use as they used to and the paths aren't exactly straight lines. They're difficult to navigate if you don't know where you're going, circular loops around the loch cutting back towards the road. So it's possible that she's lost.'

I start to open my mouth, but the officer talks over me.

'Which brings me to the second option. We've got a bit of a sticky situation going on right now. Neighbouring towns around here share resources, you understand, and there is a group of hobby hikers who've managed to get themselves split off from a friend thanks to all that rain. The signal up in the hills is awful, so we've not been able to locate them yet, largely because of a small landslide that happened near their last-known location.'

I shoot a glance at Clio, who leans forward, suddenly intent, the longer side of her hair falling forward and she tucks it behind her ear.

'I don't tell you this to panic you,' the officer continues swiftly. 'In fact, quite the opposite. We've got teams of people out in the woods and the hills as we speak, so if your friend *has* got herself disorientated, I'm sure we'll find her.'

'We know about the campers,' Clio says. 'Everybody's

been talking about it. Michaela was worried they were hurt.'

'It's quite the local event.' The officer's expression doesn't shift, but there is gentle humour in his voice. 'Locals get stuck up in the hills all the time, but it's the first time in years we've had it happen to campers, and they didn't have the proper equipment.'

'If you *didn't* have this going on, would you be able to do more for Kay?' I ask. The firmness of my voice shocks me, and Clio looks taken aback. 'Sorry, I just mean . . . Is what's going on going to cause problems if Michaela doesn't turn up?' It's all well and good if Michaela is lost out in the woods somewhere, but what if she's somewhere else?

'There is another option,' the police officer says, not answering my question directly, 'which is that your friend was worried about the situation, as you've said, and decided to help. Is that the sort of thing she might do?'

'No,' I say defensively at the exact same moment that Clio says, '*Yes*.'

The officer looks between us and then steeples his fingers. 'Well then, I wouldn't worry about her just yet.'

'See,' Clio says to me, gentle but firm. 'That's what I said.'

'Well, when *should* we worry?' I push, exasperation making me breathless. I feel like nobody is listening to me, least of all Clio. 'When she's been gone overnight? I don't like the idea of her out there with limited signal and "looping paths". What if she's lost and your "teams" don't find her?' All these spooky tales about creatures in the water and monsters in the woods have been getting to me and I can feel my voice getting shrill. I try to dial it back. 'I don't even know if she has a map with her, whether she's got something proper—'

'Or if she was just out walking and relying on that podcast she was listening to for, like, navigation,' Clio finishes thoughtfully. 'Yeah, okay, I am a bit worried about that too.'

'A podcast?' The officer shifts. 'You mean something about the area?'

'Yeah, uh,' Clio says. 'Michaela listens to all sorts, but she mentioned one had a bit about the loch, I think?'

'It was one of the reasons she wanted to come here apparently,' I say. 'We don't know what it was about though.'

I must be imagining the way the officer's demeanour changes when we mention the podcast. It's like we've got his full attention now, whereas before he was half-interested at best.

'Your friend came here because of a podcast about the loch? Did she tell you anything about it, where she was listening to it, or why?'

'I assume it was Spotify or something.' Clio shrugs and glances at me, a question mark in her gaze.

'Why?' I ask.

'No reason. We just don't get many folks talking about us here in Blackhills any more.' The officer shifts again, this time angling himself away from us to make another note on his paper. I can't read it before he closes the notebook. 'In any case,' he says, 'I genuinely wouldn't be too worried just yet. There's still daylight left – you might even find your friend is back wherever it is you're staying by the time you leave here. You're on the loch itself, right?'

'Yeah, Loch House.'

The officer starts to open his mouth, but Clio cuts him

off. 'We know nobody's stayed there in ages. Everybody in the pub seemed to delight in the fact. Do you *all* know about that place around here?'

'Blackhills is very community-minded. Most of us spent some summer fling camped out on the dock outside. It's sort of a local legacy.' The officer rolls his shoulders. 'Look, I understand you're worried about your friend, but it sounds to me like there are plenty of reasonable explanations, none of which necessarily have to have us worrying just yet. The whole village is out in force anyway, so it's unlikely she'll get herself into any trouble out there.'

'What about if she doesn't come back tonight?' I push. Clio seems relaxed again now, but I'm not ready to let this go. 'What if she slipped and fell somewhere? What if she's stranded? You mentioned a landslide – does that kind of thing happen often? The rain—'

'This is all very nebulous at the moment. I'll alert the teams to keep an eye out for her on the trails, and if she's still not around by tomorrow morning, then we'll discuss further options. As you said, she might well not have left the house until this afternoon anyway, so she's not been gone long. We can file the report, and I've got your details. I'll give you my card and you can ring me if anything changes. For now, I think it would be for the best if you both headed back to the house. In cases like these, especially around here, there's usually a very good explanation and it's not worth the panic.'

Clio looks at me and nods. I don't like this. I don't like it at *all*. But the officer is right. If Michaela didn't start out until after lunchtime then it's only been a few hours. And if I tell him about the other stuff, about Michaela's job and her messy break-up with Dan, about whatever she was talking about last night that I would *appreciate*, and how she hasn't seemed quite like herself . . . will that spur him to action or would he just write her off as 'troubled'? I don't know how any of this works.

This weekend has thrown me through a loop; I'm not used to being the one needing to be consoled or soothed. Normally that's my job. I feel so out of control. It scares me.

Rebecca

Then

Rebecca doesn't make a habit of stopping at the cafe after work any more. Sometimes it's because she's seeing him – early evening is the best time for both of them most nights because he can tell people that he's going to the gym in Blackdale after work and it's the time of day that Rebecca often used to go for a run.

It's a Saturday though, and Rebecca never sees him on a Saturday. It's been the rule for as long as they've been doing . . . whatever this is. She doesn't like to think of it as an affair; that sounds torrid, as though they're doing something wrong. It doesn't feel like anything is wrong except the world conspiring against them. She doesn't like the phrase *lover* either, or fling, or romance. She still hasn't decided what word she *does* like.

She ends up in the cafe on this particular Saturday for the simple reason that she can't remember what she did without him. She'd started getting dressed for her 'run' after the early shift at work, her mind whirling through all of the things she was going to tell him, and because she doesn't often work Saturdays – instead she usually spends the day writing, long journal entries, or occasionally seeing Janie, though that's become fraught recently – she was halfway out the door before she realised what day it was.

By that time, it was too late, though. Her dad was home – her uncle and her mum always work the late together on a Monday and a Saturday, so Dad saw her leave – and if she'd turned around to go back, he'd know something was suspicious. He already knows something is up. Twice in the last month he's asked her if she's okay, and she's not sure if she's imagining it but he always seems to be watching her now, asking her where she's going. She can't remember him ever caring so much before.

So Rebecca did actually run about half a mile. She even considered heading out to the loch, doing her old loop just to keep up pretences, but by the time she reached the Lane, with its array of shops, she couldn't be bothered. She's lost interest in a lot of things lately, and she was never particularly good at running anyway.

The sky is crisp and blue and everything feels fresh and bright. Rebecca squints as she cuts across the Lane, searching the big window of the cafe to see who's working tonight. The angle is wrong though and the sun catches like a firework. She stands for a moment, briefly allowing herself to imagine a future where she no longer has to worry who she might talk to, what she might be tempted to say, before she decides to risk it.

It isn't until she gets inside that she realises her mistake. Tiffany is behind the counter, which is fine. They've not spoken much, except to be polite, since Tiffany's brother, Alec, threw up in Rebecca's shoes at a party when they were fourteen. But over by the table where they keep the packets of sugar and ketchup and mayonnaise is . . . Sarah.

Damn.

Rebecca has nothing against Sarah. Actually, that's not true. Sarah is the worst gossip of anybody Rebecca has ever met, but they used to spend a lot of time together in school. The two of them and sweet Janie, and a group of silly little boys. They're all still friends in the way of people who once knew each other too well, and this more than anything is what Rebecca dislikes about Sarah. She knows she still sees Janie sometimes, more often probably than Janie sees her now, and that rankles her too, even though the distance building between her and Janie is her own fault.

And, as easy as that, Rebecca's mind drifts back to *him*. He is so unlike those boys she used to spend so much time with. He's so mature and gracious and clever; she can't believe she ever thought she would end up with one of them. In her head, travelling the world always brought her back here to settle down like her mum and dad. Now . . . She pictures all of the places she'll go with him, the monuments they'll see, the late dinners they'll eat, the stage shows and operas and galleries they'll experience. That's what she really wanted all along. Now she realises why she spent so long holding back, as if the universe was saying to her *Wait*, even though she never, ever expected this would happen.

Rebecca wants to leave, to turn right around and walk away, but she knows that will only make Sarah gossip. Instead she unclips her Walkman from her waist and orders a hot chocolate from the counter. It's dead in here tonight, only half an hour until closing. It's still light out, but they've got the fairy lights in the window, a tacky little disco ball on the counter and a lava lamp plugged in at the back where they make the coffees, so it feels kind of unearthly in here.

Rebecca's gaze strays to the world outside the window. The street is mostly empty, just a couple of people she recognises vaguely cutting across the Lane in a diagonal path – probably headed for the pub.

Her eyes follow one couple without really realising she's doing it; she can only see the back of them, both dressed in dark jackets, his with a collar turned up. The woman with him has her arm wrapped around his elbow and they lean together as they walk. The way he alters his pace to match hers . . . for some reason, it makes Rebecca's heart seize.

'Earth to Rebecca.' Sarah is tapping on her forehead with her index finger like she's trying to dial through her skull. 'Are you in there?'

'Oh, hi Sarah.' Rebecca picks up her hot chocolate with its less than generous three mini marshmallows and takes a sip, her attention still half on the couple outside. They've stopped for a moment, the woman rooting around for something in her handbag. Her golden hair catches the light.

'I was beginning to think you were away somewhere far better than here.' Sarah waggles her eyebrows suggestively at Tiffany. 'Where were you? Or, is it *who were you with?*'

'Somewhere far better than here,' Rebecca says quickly. The three of them laugh.

It's only when the man outside turns to the side, his face in profile, that Rebecca pays attention to him. Perhaps she knew it all along and her head has been carefully guarding her heart. Perhaps she knew and simply refused to see it – but now she has seen his face, she can't deny it. It's *him*, his hair swept back in that careless style she loves, the almost-arrogance in his stance that has always made him irresistible, even before she knew why she wanted him.

And the woman – the woman he gazes at with such soft fondness, his expression so like the one he wears around Rebecca – his wife. It hits Rebecca like a punch to the gut. She *knows* that it shouldn't come as a surprise to see them together. It shouldn't hurt her. But the idea this is the reason he is unavailable every Saturday? It brings sharp tears to her eyes.

'Oh.'

Rebecca snaps to attention at the sound of Sarah's sigh. She is also staring out of the window, her eyes fixed on the same point. Rebecca feels a strange swelling emotion. Pleasure? Pride? She hasn't forgotten the way Sarah has always mooned after the man who chose *her*, who chooses her every day – except today. The feeling sours.

'Who are you looking at?' Tiffany peers to get a better view of the window and when she sees the couple, walking away now, him laughing at something she has said, she rolls her eyes. 'Oh lord,' she grumbles. 'Why do you have *such* a thing for him? I don't get it, Sarah. He's not even that good-looking. And he's *married*.'

'It's not a "thing",' Sarah snaps. Rebecca tries to drag her gaze away from the window, but she has to watch him walk away, has to examine the slope of his shoulders and the sick feeling inside her until he's totally out of sight. 'I don't have the time for any of that mooning rubbish. I know he's married – but a girl can look, can't she?' Sarah's face shifts as she says this, a sharp kind of jealousy pinching her features. Her voice, too, is shrill and high. And she's staring at Rebecca, something burning in her eyes. Rebecca blinks slowly, a nonsense idea forming. The idea that maybe Sarah has seen the way Rebecca looks at him and . . .

No, Sarah doesn't know anything about their relationship. She's projecting. Sarah always fancied him, would always reference him when the girls were fresh out of school and talk would turn to the kinds of men they wanted to marry. It's a small village and the options are kind of limited. Secretly, back then, Rebecca thought Sarah was silly.

Tiffany shrugs and goes back to wiping down the counter and the tables, lifting the chairs up on top. Rebecca stands at the counter so she doesn't make any more work for anybody and sips her drink in silence while Sarah fiddles with the settings on the radio.

'Are you all right?'

Rebecca jumps. 'Hmm?'

'Are you all right?' Sarah repeats. Her auburn hair is loose from its bun, frizzy from the heat of working with the coffee machine all day, but her eyes are bright with curiosity.

'Sure,' Rebecca says. 'Why wouldn't I be?'

'Oh.' Tiffany's voice pipes up from the other side of the empty cafe. 'Awkward.'

'What?' Rebecca says.

'Nothing.' Sarah shrugs. 'But you . . . missed my birthday. You said you'd come.'

'Oh, no!' Rebecca's face floods with embarrassment. What date is it? The thirteenth. 'Oh, Sarah, I'm so sorry. I've been so swamped recently—'

'Yeah, Janie said you were busy. I thought maybe you'd booked tickets to fly out somewhere or something, that's all.'

'No, I'm sorry. God. I'm not going anywhere yet. My

mum . . .' It's the same excuse she's been trotting out now for years. Why do people still believe in her? 'Can I make it up to you? We could grab dinner . . .' But even as she says that, Rebecca's brain is supplying her with all of the days she *can't* do. Evening plans with him that have been made by necessity, timings altered to fit around his work commitments, the parts of the job he always has to take home, evenings and weekends consumed like wildfire. All the plans, except Saturdays of course. The hurt swells in her chest again, so vicious it makes her breathless.

Sarah must see the hesitation on Rebecca's face because she shrugs a little coldly. 'It's fine,' she says. 'It doesn't matter. We had a good time. Josh was asking where you were though.'

Rebecca resists the urge to cringe. Josh – speckle-faced and always smelling faintly of the fish that he sells on the market. She can't believe she used to like him. 'Oh, uh. Tell him I'm sorry too?' She abandons the chocolate dregs in her mug on the counter, no longer caring if she's making a mess for them to clean. 'I'd better go, but – thanks.'

'I don't think sorry will cut it,' Sarah jokes. But there's an edge to her voice, as if it's loaded with something more. There is jealousy there, something pointed.

And Rebecca wonders again – how much could Sarah have guessed?

Rebecca doesn't go straight home.

Seeing him with his wife, and the conversation with Sarah – well, it's shaken her up more than she'd like to admit. It isn't as if she didn't know he was still spending time with his wife. It isn't as if she's totally naive about how all of this works. She knows that just because they have whatever

145

they have doesn't mean that real life just stops. He's never done this before with *anybody*, obviously, which is a comfort to Rebecca when she's having her dark days where she worries and pines, thinking this isn't going to work out. She doesn't have many dark days, but Saturdays often hit her hard, the reminder that he still has his other life and he has to keep up pretences.

But . . . seeing them together still hurts. For some reason, she always hoped his rigid refusal to meet her on a Saturday was more to do with preparing for work the next week, or that he was genuinely going to the gym or something. Anything that didn't involve his wife.

And even if a part of her knew that this was happening, seeing it is something else. She can still feel a phantom of that sensation inside her, the feeling of having the stuffing pulled out, her guts pummelled by strong fists. She feels sick.

It might be naive, but Rebecca assumed that the fact that he has never done this before with anybody means it's special, and if it's special then he can't love his wife. Now . . . the way he looked at her . . . she wonders if that is true.

She takes the long way home, skirting the shores of the loch. The banks are slippery, water pooling in crags, grass and sand both slick, so she has to be careful. She slows down to an amble and takes breath after pine-scented breath, inhales so deep it feels like her lungs are on fire.

By the time she gets home, it's dark out. The front door is unlocked and she slips in quietly, hoping to make it upstairs for a shower before anybody sees her. She doesn't feel in the mood for talking—

'You've been gone ages.'

Rebecca pauses with her trainers dangling from her fingers, caught like a rabbit in a trap. Her dad stands in the doorway between the kitchen and the hallway, hands on his hips in a classic display of parental disappointment.

'Oh, yeah. I had to go slow by the water, it's wet.'

'Hmph. I was about to send out the cavalry.' Dad doesn't move. He doesn't invite her into the kitchen for a cup of tea like he would have once. The space between them feels like it's full of static, a barrier between who they had been before, the relationship they shared, and whatever this is now. She feels the same way with Uncle Paul, unable to talk about the things going on in her life, because they won't understand. And that hurts because she was always so close to both of them, and now sometimes the thought that they might find out why she's been 'throwing her life away' – their words – scares her.

'I'm going to go and have a—'

'Is there something you're not telling me, Bec?'

Rebecca pauses halfway to the stairs. She turns, her heart in her mouth. 'What do you mean? Obviously there's a whole lot of things I'm not telling you, I'm not a child.'

'Don't get smart with me,' he says. It's bordering on snappish. Rebecca is shocked. They haven't always seen eye to eye, but he's never snapped at her in her life.

'I'm not getting smart. I'm—'

'You are,' he insists. 'You think you're being clever. I don't like it. All this sass. I said to your mother—'

'I'm not being sassy!' Rebecca resists the urge to throw her hands up but only barely. The look of shock on her father's face is enough to wind her up again; he looks like she's just slapped him. 'I'm sorry,' she mumbles quickly. 'I just mean . . . I don't know what *you* mean.'

147

He's watching her carefully now, staring at her as if she's a stranger, a puzzle to unpick like one of his cryptic crosswords. She blanches under the weight of his stare.

'You've been acting differently lately,' he says, each word landing hard in the quiet of the hall, and harder still in the disquiet of her mind. 'I'm worried about you. All this pressure with your mum. You're letting it get to you, I can see it.'

Rebecca wants to sag with relief. He doesn't know exactly, then. But then guilt slithers in and she realises that this isn't a good thing. Dad thinks she's worrying about her mum, and she's not. Not any more, not really. She's been so wrapped up in *him*.

'You don't need to worry about me, Dad,' she says. 'I'm twenty-five years old, I can look after myself.'

'Really?' Dad shakes his head. 'I used to believe that. Now I'm not convinced.'

'What? Why?' Rebecca's skin prickles, the ancient desire to please burning inside her. His disappointment stings.

'You used to be so organised. So dedicated. I know you put a lot of stuff on hold to stay here, but Paul says you're not even focused at work when you're on shift with him any more. And you haven't made any new plans in months.'

'I've been planning,' she says defensively. It doesn't matter that these aren't the kinds of plans she could ever share with him, or that they're so different to the ones she once had. They should be enough to prove that she's capable of looking after herself. 'I don't tell you everything, but I have lots of plans. Besides, I always got the feeling that you didn't really want me to go anywhere anyway.'

'Oh come on, Bec. That's not fair. Of course I don't want you to leave, I'm your dad. But I want what's best for you.' He says it, but the words sound hollow. She had a similar conversation with Uncle Paul only last week which left a sour taste in her mouth, the way he'd pushed up against the counter and said, 'You're floundering, kid.'

Sweat runs between her shoulder blades and she resists the urge to shiver.

'Well, yeah, but Mum—' she tries again.

'No, this isn't just to do with your mum. You were fine when she was sick, held up like a rock. What's happening with you lately?' Dad narrows his eyes and she flinches. 'You're not focused at work, you're letting your laundry build up. Your mother had to wash all of your pots in scalding water because you left them so long. You've not seen any friends in weeks, you're *always* out exercising.'

'I . . . I've just been really busy.'

'Sure,' Dad says. 'Busy. You seem busy. But you've stopped talking about any of it. I thought you were planning to head abroad this summer? I thought you were going to make something of yourself now everything is back to normal.'

Silence.

'Ouch,' Rebecca says quietly. It feels like he's cracked open her ribs and scooped her heart out. He's right, though. She did have plans. So many plans she was scared to go through with any of them. But she doesn't like the way he's said it, disappointment turning his eyes dark.

'I'm sorry, Bec, but it has to be said. You're not yourself. And if I find out it's all because of some *lad* . . .'

Rebecca is surprised by the sudden vehemence in her father's voice. She always knew that dating would be difficult, that he would never stop seeing her as a child, but this reaction is extreme. The relief she felt before evaporates. 'There isn't any lad,' she insists. And it's only half a lie.

149

Her father shifts in the doorway, his hulking frame blocking out the dim lamps of the kitchen, and she feels trapped, her throat tight. Suddenly it's too warm in here and she longs to be back out on the shores of the loch, where the air is fresh and clear.

'There'd better not be,' he warns. 'I won't let you throw your life away, Rebecca. I won't.'

And Rebecca feels it all pressing in on her, too much pressure she can hardly breathe, and her dad – this is the first time he's ever actually scared her. What will happen if he ever finds out?

Eleanor

Once we're back out on the street, it feels like the air has been sucked out of the world. It's freezing and getting dark, the clouds overhead thick and black. It's been hours since Clio and I ate, but we don't even discuss the subject of dinner. Instead, we pile straight into the car and do as the officer said: head back to the house.

'Do you really think I *am* overreacting?' I ask as we drive.

Clio shifts awkwardly and doesn't answer.

'Clio?'

'I . . .' She sighs. 'Dude, I think I wound you up with those stories, didn't I? I genuinely bet Kay is having the fucking time of her life. And she'll be at the house pissing herself laughing when she finds out we went to the police.'

Maybe Clio is right. Maybe *everybody* is right. I just can't shake the bad feeling that's been following me since this morning. Since last night. No – since we got here. I don't like it one bit.

When we get to the house, there's still no sign of Michaela, though I'm past the point of expecting things to go right. We bundle through into the lounge, dumping our coats unceremoniously across the back of the sofa. Clio lights the fire and I put the kettle on. It's after six now. Michaela's been gone for something like four hours – at least. Maybe more. I wish we knew when she'd actually left. Before long, it will be dark.

'Step fretting,' Clio says.

'Ugh. I'm trying. I'm trying to work out what on *earth* she could have up her sleeve that I would *appreciate*.' I try to mimic Michaela's tone yesterday, but it comes out sounding snotty.

'I dunno. Maybe it's some kind of massage therapy thing,' Clio says. 'You know, you were saying you were super tense in the car.'

'Why would she have to leave the house to sort that out? Why wouldn't she tell us about it?'

Clio continues to fiddle with the fire in the log burner. 'Okay, so not that. Oh my God – maybe she's trying to set you up with somebody she met on the internet. Maybe it's some rich countess who owns a bunch of land, or, like, some incredibly fit woman who seems too good to be true, so Kay has to investigate first.' Her eyes sparkle with excitement.

I feel a hum of it in my own chest momentarily. 'No, that's stupid,' I brush her off.

'Is it? You were saying about how you fancied something long-distance next.'

'Clio, Michaela hasn't been hunting for a long-distance wife for me, for God's sake.'

'How do you know?' She laughs and the sound is full of promise. I want very badly to believe it's something so

152

ridiculous. 'It would explain why she didn't want to tell you, get your hopes up.'

'Is that *all* you can come up with?' I ask.

'No.' Clio tucks the longer side of her hair behind her ear with an impatient gesture, just as the logs she's arranged tumble down into the grate. 'I definitely have other theories,' she adds playfully.

The more I think about it though, I know I'm right. There *was* something weird about Michaela yesterday, and I don't think it's got anything to do with Dan or the job or any of that. It was like she wanted to tell me what she was up to but felt nervous about it. It must mean whatever she's planning is big. But big how? What might require this kind of secrecy?

If she'd done something like this at home, would I be worried? No, I don't think so. But here, the mist rolling on the water and the trees crowding close like this? It all feels very ominous.

Fucking Clio and her fucking stories.

We trade ideas back and forth for hours, Clio's stupid suggestions punctuated by my sheer disbelief, the crackle and pop of the fire and the distant lapping of the water outside, the sounds wrapping around us like snowy static on an old TV screen.

It's dark outside now, but at least it's not raining. The temperature must have plateaued because with the fire going, it's getting warm in here. My sweater starts to feel scratchy against the sweaty prickle of my skin; my socks feel too tight; my hands are dry and cracked. Everything feels too heavy.

'What do you want to do about tonight?' I ask Clio after

the ideas have run dry. She's scrolling on her phone, but the videos won't load.

She clicks her phone off and looks up at me, her green eyes glittering like malachite in the firelight. For a second – just one solitary second – the flames dance and her eyes look nearly black, her skin pale, and I'm reminded of the creature from my dream. But then the malachite glitter is back and I blink furiously.

'What do you mean?' she asks.

'Are we both going to stay down here in case she comes back? Do we leave the door unlocked? Do we go up to bed?' I am trying not to show how afraid I am. It's been at least eight hours now since we know she definitely left the house. Might be longer than that. I wish we knew if she'd been here this morning. 'You don't think she's had some mega thought about her career and rushed back home, do you?'

Clio just stares at me.

'What?' I ask.

'Really?' she says. 'That's the conclusion you've come to? Michaela has taken herself *home*, without the car and without her stuff or letting us know she was leaving, because she wants to sort her job out?'

'No,' I say stupidly. But for all of the semi-plausible theories I've come up with, this is the only one that doesn't scare me.

'You're trying to make up stories.' Clio shakes her head. 'I know I'm always going on about the power of positive storytelling, but Jesus, El.'

'What, you're the only one allowed to tell stories?' I grumble.

Clio lets out a huff of laughter. 'I'm the only one who tells them *well*,' she corrects. 'More likely . . . okay, the

154

most likely, imaginary scenario is that she went out trying to help those poor sods who got stuck and she got lost. Her phone is dead, but she's probably found somewhere warm to hole up. Maybe some nice receptionist has made her a big mug of coffee, or a Horse's Neck with her favourite brandy, and they're offering to let her hang around in the lobby. She can't call us because she doesn't know our numbers off by heart, but she's gone into the bar to wait for her phone to charge.' Clio starts to relax into the telling and I find I can picture it too. 'I bet she's bumped into some really hot Scottish lord, super buff, with this country estate and a vintage Rolls-Royce, and she's so enamoured with him that she's totally lost track of the time. Her phone is charged by now, but she's smitten. He's not even super into the physical thing. He wants to talk to her *intellectually* and she's losing her mind over it.'

'What is your obsession with Scottish lords and ladies?' I joke. 'Do you have some weird fetish I don't know anything about?'

She swats at me playfully.

'I don't know, maybe she's in Blackhills somewhere,' I suggest, warming to the idea of Michaela hiding out some-where. 'In a really cosy bar, sat in some booth with a guy who is totally in love with her – like love at first sight type love – and she's trying to decide how to tell us she's moving to Scotland and getting married at the end of the month. Screw being a lawyer, he's rich and she won't need to work ever again. That makes more sense than your idea that she's been online dating for *me*. And maybe he's so rich, we could both move up here as well, and maybe he runs a charity and I could do some pro bono counselling and he'll set me up with a little yearly income for the trouble.'

By the time we run out of scenarios to joke about, it's gone midnight. I can feel the tiredness creeping up on me, all of the stress of the afternoon crowding my brain, but I do feel better after playing all of these harmless scenarios out. Clio has her head resting on the back of the sofa, her eyes open and staring at the shadows that play across the ceiling from the flames in the burner. We're going to exhaust our ready supply of firewood at this rate, and I don't fancy going out to find more.

I'm holding my phone in one hand and my empty mug in another when a buzz startles me. I glance at Clio and then down at my phone in alarm.

'What?' Clio blurts. 'What is it?'

MONDAY

Eleanor

'Is it her?' Clio snatches the phone from my hand before I have chance to take a look. She swipes straight into the message. For a second her brows furrow and she stares at the screen.

'What did she say?' I push.

'She's . . . fine?' Clio blinks up at me, triumphant. 'She said she's *fine*. I told you!'

I snatch the phone back, gripping it so hard my fingers hurt. There it is, a text from Michaela right there in black and white and green. Relief makes my head spin.

Hey. Sorry for silence. I've been helpful today, but got turned around out here. Totally lost. Walked miles! Weather not great. Okay though, just got bad signal. Low battery too. Don't worry.

I stab the contact details and try to call her immediately. The call goes straight to voicemail.

'Fuck's sake,' I mutter. 'We missed her.'

'She's *fine*,' Clio reaffirms. 'I told you. The policeman told you. *Don't worry*.'

Although I know I should feel satisfied, I'm still uneasy. 'I can't get through now.'

'Her battery will be dead. Or she'll have turned the phone off because it's low. Oh, I wonder if she found those walkers and they're all at some hotel licking their wounds.'

'We could have gone to get her if she'd told us where she was.' I throw my phone down, barely resisting the urge to scream into a cushion in frustration. For a lawyer, sometimes Michaela isn't very smart.

'Well, she didn't, but it's fine! She can just be Queen of Bad Choices for the weekend. The award goes to Michaela Jones.' Clio makes fake cheering noises inside her cupped hand.

'So, now what?' I mutter. 'We just . . . go to bed? We still have no idea where she is.'

Clio's frenetic energy slowly dries up as her adrenaline drops. I can feel my own heartbeat, still slamming hard against the wall of my chest. I'm not sure now whether it's anger or fear that's churning in my belly.

She shrugs. 'We should probably at least try to sleep,' she says. 'Unless you have a better idea.'

The worst thing is, I have no ideas at all.

I hardly sleep. I'm thinking about what we'll have to do in the morning. Text the police to call off the search. But only after Michaela is back, when she's safely where I can see her.

When I do finally sleep, I'm plagued by the same dreams as last night, hands reaching from beneath the black surface of the loch, threatening to drag me down into its depths.

But I also dream of Michaela lost in the woods near the water, skeletal branches catching on the scarf that covers her hair, tearing at her clothes. She races, a blur that becomes faceless, limbless, encapsulated in motion, so all I can see is movement. She is running from something. Something with hooves. Something that wants her.

I want to run to her, to rush to her aid, though God knows what I would do when I reached her side. But I can't move. I am planted in the sand at the shore of the loch, invisible roots holding me to this spot, so all I can do is scream.

And Clio – where is Clio? She is nowhere, yet her voice is everywhere, echoing inside my ears.

I wake long before dawn and lie silently in this bed that isn't mine. Outside, the weather is calm, all of the rain of the last days gone so that all that is left is an overcast sky that slowly lightens to the colour of gunmetal. The walls in the bedroom I'm sleeping in are unadorned, white and clean, except in one place where it looks like a picture once hung beside the door. I can only see it as the morning light slowly creeps up the wall. I don't know why, but this makes me think of my parents, of the little house they sold after I moved out, with walls bare like these.

I check my phone. There are no further updates from Michaela, but I have two texts from Mum I probably only received now because of the awful signal – there's no way she sent them at four o'clock. The first is a picture that won't load, probably of whatever my dad cooked for dinner – he's been super into his cooking since I left home and in the last seven years, he's got himself to *MasterChef* level, all small fancy portions that drive Mum crazy.

The second text is just, *Hope you're having a nice time, Eleanor Cranford!!*

I smile. That started as a way to reassure me when I was

little, the way they'd use my full name – their name – all the time, to prove I was one of them. It's a nice gesture, and they think it helps, though I'd never tell them that sometimes it made me feel worse. I don't look like either of them after all, with their brown and gold hair, their ruddy outdoorsy tans. No matter how much time I spend in the sun, I will always be pale and dark-haired. Sometimes it feels to me like I'm living a lie, pretending to be completely full and happy when there will always be a part of me that questions who I am deep down inside.

That's what this house feels like. It feels as though it was once a home, but it's long since been left to its own devices, and now we are here and it is having to decide: is it empty or full? There's an energy here that comes from a long abandonment. I've seen the evidence of the long-ago gatherings the locals mentioned to have happened here, scars on the wood of the decking from cigarettes being put out on its surface, a single old beer can forgotten down the path that loops round from where the car is parked. It feels, in the dim morning light, as if the house is cradling us against the world outside, against the weather and the water of the loch. As if it wants to protect us.

Yet, this morning the house feels quiet around me. Too quiet. And fresh worry begins to prickle under my skin.

Climbing out of bed, I feel like my body has aged a year overnight. I ache all over and my head is throbbing. I get dressed in a clean pair of jeans and a long sweater, tying my hair back in a braid, which I don't normally bother with. I can't face the thought of having to deal with it today.

By the time I make it downstairs, Clio is awake too, which is unusual.

162

'Michaela's still not in her room,' Clio says.

My stomach sinks. It's only now that I realise how readily I'd been willing to believe that everything would be normal again this morning. 'She's still not back?'

'No.' Clio shakes her head, handing me a cup of tea. 'I'm sure she's fine, just not back yet. Are you okay? You look like you hardly slept.' I see the bags under Clio's eyes and I'm convinced she slept less than I did.

'I kept jumping at every little sound,' I say. 'I swore at one point I heard the door open, and another time I was convinced Kay was knocking at the windows trying to get in.' I don't tell Clio that I also dreamed about Dan, stalking Michaela, threatening to hurt her if she didn't go back to him. In the light of day it feels silly, but the dreams sit heavy in my mind all the same. I rub my hand over my face and inhale the steam from my tea. 'I assume you haven't heard from her again yet.'

'Nope.' Clio's rubbing her hands together over and over, filled with nervous energy. 'Fucking great time I picked to quit smoking. She's really winding me up now.'

'I'm still mad she didn't tell us where she was,' I say. 'We literally have a car. We could have gone to pick her up. It's all very well telling us she was fine last night, but what about this morning?'

'Just furthers my "hot Scottish lord" fantasy,' Clio jokes, but it sounds brittle. I don't laugh. 'I'm sure she'll have an easier time of getting a taxi back this morning,' she adds solemnly.

'And if she doesn't turn up?' I ask. 'How long do we wait?'

Clio's face remains static. 'I don't know.'

* * *

Time stretches. The sun has broken through the patch of cloud that appeared earlier, but it's still freezing and the water looks darker than before, almost as if all of the rain has churned the silt up and left it murky and black.

Clio is sat with her knees drawn underneath her chin, holding her phone loosely in one hand. She's been that way for the last hour, barely even lifting her head. There's no energy for jokes.

'This is getting ridiculous now,' I say firmly. 'You were right yesterday, maybe we should go to the pub and find that guy again.'

'I was half joking about that,' she says. 'What good will he do?'

'You said yourself: he knows the village. We can ask him if he's seen anybody from the search parties or had an update about the campers at least. And if we don't find him, we can ask *somebody*.'

'Okay,' Clio says. Her response takes me aback.

'What, no argument?'

'Nope.' She shrugs.

I'm already tossing my half-drunk tea aside and shoving my feet into my boots. 'Well, there's a first for everything.'

Rebecca

Then

This isn't how it is supposed to happen. It *shouldn't* have happened – not yet.

Rebecca stands in her parents' bathroom, puce towels and white porcelain, frosted glass protecting her breaking heart. It's not easy to know what she will do now; she feels like a ghost of her former self. She knows what the old Rebecca would do, but she isn't that person any more.

The one thing she knows is this can't carry on. The lying, the sneaking around, she has always done that *with* him. Because of him. But she can't do it any more. Not after this.

They have plans to see each other later at the house because his wife is having dinner with friends. Rebecca checks her watch and realises she will need to hurry if she doesn't want to be late – he really does hate when she's late.

She wipes her hands over her face, dislodging the remaining tears, and then she tidies the mess she's made in the bathroom and gets herself ready, cleaning her teeth and tugging on his favourite little white dress with a pair of thin tights and flat shoes she knows he'll hate, but she loves how comfortable they are. She braids her hair and sprays the special perfume that she's bought especially for when they spend time together. It is subtle and floral and reminds her of summer fields, of day trips with her parents and hikes on the paths around the loch.

Her *parents*. It's the same thought she's had before but magnified now. They will be so disappointed in her if they ever find out about this. Rebecca's only hope is that he will finally make the decision she needs him to, to step up and hurry with the planning. If they're going to be together, it needs to happen now. And if his wife is as unhappy with him as he has told Rebecca she is, then maybe Rebecca can talk some sense into him. It's what his wife deserves. Independence, freedom. Why would anybody like her choose to stay when there is so much more out there?

The truth is, he is the reason both of them stay. But his wife is so much older than Rebecca and so much more accomplished. They have no children. He says they've been together since they were practically kids, and it's nothing more than a close friendship now. If that's true, then he is literally the *only* thing keeping his wife here, chained to this village. Well, that and the businesses she inherited from her parents, but she could take her skills and do that sort of thing anywhere, right? Rebecca can't imagine why anybody would want to stay in this place – except for him.

Rebecca hurries out of the back door so that her parents don't see her leave. Her dad in particular. Things haven't been the same since their talk; he's convinced now that something is going on. She doesn't like the way he looks at her. Calculating. It scares her.

She manages to get out unseen and drives her old beat-up

car to the house. It's nearly dark but not quite, that half-light that makes everything look like its haunted by ghosts of the day. The weather is awful tonight, heavy rain that slams into the windscreen and blurs her view even with the wipers on full. She drives slow, slower than normal perhaps.

By the time she pulls up to the house, he is already there. He's been there long enough to light the fire and get it roaring and he's poured both of them glasses of dark red wine, fruity and acidic. Her stomach churns at the scent she catches even from the other side of the room.

'I thought we said nine,' he says as she enters. 'I'll have to get back soon.'

She's dripping rainwater on the floor from her leather jacket – the one he bought her – so she shucks it off and hangs it on the back of a chair to dry.

'Sorry,' she says. 'I couldn't get away. My parents—'

'There always seems to be some kind of excuse,' he says. It's a little snide, a tone he doesn't often use on her. He's stood by the fire and hasn't lit many of the lamps, so she can't see his face very well, but she can see the way he's twisting his wedding ring around and around on his finger. Maybe he and his wife have fought. Maybe he finally told her about them and that's why he's being awful. Maybe this means she won't have to be the one to bring it up tonight.

A delayed zing of fear floods her. If he's this upset, it can't have gone well. What does that mean for their future?

'That's not true.'

'I'm starting to think that you don't want to spend time with me any more.' He turns and Rebecca's stomach swoops. His expression is dark and she can tell, instantly, that he's already had a glass or two. It must have been a bad fight, whatever it was about.

'Oh, please don't say that,' she beseeches. 'It's just hard, all this sneaking around. I don't want to keep feeling like we're going to get caught every time we so much as exchange a glance in public. It's exhausting trying to keep track of it all.'

'Exhausting?' he scoffs. 'All you have to do is go to work and have dinner with your parents and then slip out the back door. You're young – what are they going to say about it? What do you have to keep track of? It's me who should be exhausted.'

Rebecca can see his rising frustration, but she can feel it inside herself too, like a wild horse in her chest trying to break free. This is not how she wanted tonight to go. She crosses to him, her soft shoes squeaking on the wooden floorboards until she reaches the rug in front of the fire. He is still wearing his suit from work, the grey one that she loves, with a rose satin tie she hasn't seen before. 'Baby,' she says gently. 'You know it's not that simple. People expect things of me, just the same as they do you.'

'Expectation is the death of serenity,' he intones. It's something he's said before, but it's never hit quite as hard as it does now. 'What do you want me to do? To tell you that it's okay if you want to stop doing this? I can't. I don't know what I would do. I love you. I've never loved anybody the way I love you. It makes me *feral*.'

'No,' Rebecca says. 'Of course not.' The thought sits heavy inside her, that he would think she would want to end things just because it got difficult, because the shine wore off. She loves him. She can't keep doing this, especially with the secret she's carrying, but she still wants him. 'I want to tell you s—'

'If you can't do this any more, you need to tell me. Right

now. I can't keep being the only one sustaining this.' His expression is dark.

'That's not—'

'It's exactly what's happening,' he cuts her off.

She tries reaching for him, to lay a hand on his sleeve, but he shrugs her off and marches away from the mantel. He grabs the bottle of wine and pours himself another glass.

'I can't lose you, but I can't just switch all the other stuff off either. I've got my job, the expectation that comes with it. I can't make all of this go away.'

Panic blooms in her chest. 'I never said—'

'You don't have to say it!' he explodes. He slams the wine glass down hard enough that the stem snaps, ruby liquid sloshing over the side, dripping onto the floorboards. Rebecca jumps.

'What's gotten into you tonight?' she pleads. She wants to hit rewind, to dial back to the beginning of this evening and salvage this conversation. 'Why are you being like this?'

'I'm just so tired of always feeling like I'm the only one taking this seriously,' he snaps. 'The time we get together is so little, so precious, and you can't even get here on time.'

'Is this really all because I'm a bit late?' Rebecca says. 'You're worried I'm . . . leaving you? Because of that?' All hopes that his anger might stem from having had the conversation with his wife about her die inside her, withering under a new frost. 'I had to drive slowly because of the rain.'

'It's not just about this time,' he ploughs on. 'It's all of the times. It's happening again and again. I'm starting to feel like you're just not committed any more and I don't want to make you do this.'

'I was late *once* before, and that was because I had to

169

lock up at work. My parents . . .' Rebecca sighs. 'It won't be like this forever, right? You keep telling me that. *It won't be forever.*'

He looks, in this moment, like she's slapped him. As if, finally, he has seen what she's been trying to say, all of those times she asked him if he meant it when he talked about their future adventures. But now she sees it clearly just as he does. All these months, they've been talking at cross purposes. All of those moments when he would hold her hand, create scenarios for their future – they were his fantasy. While she's been building a picture of their life together, he's been creating a fabrication, just another story. 'No.'

'No?' She crosses to him again and now he doesn't push her away. He stands, letting her get so close, she can smell the wine on his breath, the cologne he put on this morning as familiar as her own name. 'No it won't be forever, or no—'

'I can't,' he says. This is softer than before. He reaches out to her, takes her hand in his. His palms are warm and so large they envelop her hand, her fingers, warming the ice from her bones. And yet . . .

'You . . . can't.' Her voice is so frail it could break.

They have been having two conversations. The realisation is a stone in her gut, dragging her down. She doesn't know how she wanted tonight to happen, but she did not expect this. It's all happening too fast. She wanted tonight to be the start of something for them, but it's beginning to feel like the end.

'I'm sorry. I'm sorry I snapped. I'm . . . I know you want me to tell you I'll leave her,' he says. 'I know you want the two of us to ride off into the sunset. I know the things that I have promised you, and God . . . I'm so afraid that you're going to leave me – it makes me sick just thinking about it – but I can't do it. I can't do it to *her*.'

'To your wife,' Rebecca says. Her tone is cold and she is surprised to hear it. It doesn't sound like her own voice at all. 'You are afraid that I am going to leave you because you refuse to leave her. Is that right?' There is a roaring in her ears, her blood pounding hard. She did not expect this. She knew it wouldn't be easy, she knew there would be roadblocks. She knew that they would have to be careful, that the timing of everything was awful, but she had thought if they could just work out a plan that it might be okay.

She was wrong.

'It's not as black and white as all that,' he says. He's the one pleading now. He won't let go of her hand, his grip so firm that it starts to feel like a trap. 'You knew what the situation was when we started this. You knew about her, about me. You knew what this would look like. You know what she's like.'

'You promised me it wouldn't be forever,' Rebecca repeats. 'You told me that and I believed you. And now you're worried that you've, what, oversold it? Jesus.' She yanks on her hand but he holds it tight. 'No,' she snaps. 'Let me go.'

The wounded look on his face is new, but it reminds her so much of all the other times, the way he would look when he was planning their imaginary life together, the reality hiding just beneath the surface, that it makes her feel nauseous. He knew, the whole time he *knew*, that it was all a lie. She was stupid to believe him.

She yanks her hand again and he finally lets go.

'How long did you think this would go on?' she demands.

'I didn't . . . It's not like that. You make it sound like I

171

had this all planned from the start. You were the one who invited me to your poetry reading. You started this.'

'Yes,' Rebecca admits. 'I did. I'm not innocent in this, but you lied to me. You made me think there was more to this than just some silly little fling. We could have carried on, pretending there wasn't a spark, but we didn't. We could have just been friends.' She doesn't know if that is true, but she wants badly to believe that. 'I put my whole life on hold for you.'

'And I didn't risk things too?' he asks. She knows that it would be pointless to try to talk to him now. His reputation is always, *always* going to be more important than anything she has to say.

The realisation is a jolt that feels like an ice bath, a new future unfurling ahead of her. It doesn't matter how much she loves him, she will always be second fiddle to his wife. The world they have built for themselves. And how can she ever compete with *her*? The woman is a superstar, a businesswoman with her finger in all of the pies, and beautiful to boot. What hope does Rebecca have?

'You know what?' she says angrily, finally letting all of the frustration show in the simmer of her words. 'I didn't want to have this conversation tonight. In fact, I would have been happy to never have it as long as there was just a glimmer of hope that one day things would change. But you're right about one thing: you can't do this to your wife. And you can't do this to me any more either.'

He starts to speak, but she doesn't let him.

Instead she marches for the door, her voice cutting over his. 'But I'll tell you now, and this is the truth. This – me hoping you would leave your fucking *wife* – was not the reason I was late.'

Eleanor

I make Clio drive us into the village because I'm not feeling at all confident about my ability to control the car, given how my whole body feels like it's running on caffeine and literally nothing else – actually, that's not far from the truth. Clio's been muttering about her desperation for a cigarette since we left the house, but so far she's still furiously chewing her gum as if she might start a fire with her jaw.

We park in the same place again, spilling out into the street without a proper plan. It's only once I start marching down the street, Clio trailing just a little way behind me, that I realise I really am intending to just retrace our steps from the other day. What else can I do?

There's the little boutique where Michaela bought her scarf, and we head inside without hesitating. Well, I do. Clio stands outside holding her phone and for a second I feel a trill of nervous excitement. Maybe she's heard from Kay again? But then she's joining me and her phone is back in her pocket.

'No?' I ask, so softly the words are barely audible even to me, and Clio just shakes her head.

The woman behind the counter is a different one today. She's younger than the other lady, probably only in her late twenties, with a messy knot of blonde hair, very casually beautiful. I see Clio clock her, even despite the situation – she's exactly Clio's type, if I'm being honest – but then Clio seems to realise what she's doing because she looks horrified at herself.

'Hi,' the young woman says, a smile that's more generous than any other we've received since arriving in Blackhills on her lips. 'You must be the tourists my aunt was telling me about.'

Her accent isn't as strong as some of the others we've heard either. I wonder if she's been to university, perhaps somewhere outside Scotland even. I wonder what it must be like to work in a family business like this, but the thought is only fleeting before my mind jumps back to Michaela and why we're here.

'Everybody seems to know about us,' Clio mutters. 'It's like some kind of whisper game.'

'We don't get—'

'Many tourists,' I cut her off. 'Yes, we've heard. Listen, I'm really sorry to be rude, but I have to ask: is your aunt around?'

'No, she's meeting with a supplier today. She'll be back tomorrow, though. Why? Is there a problem? She said you bought something.'

Clio glances at me.

I open my mouth to speak, but nothing comes out. How can I just say it?

I wet my lips and try again. 'We came here with a friend,

but she's – well . . . Yesterday. She's . . . She went out and said not to worry, we thought maybe she's looking for those people that got stuck in the woods or whatever, but she should be back and—'

'She's gone missing,' Clio blurts.

The silence is so thick, it suffocates the air from my lungs.

The woman behind the counter looks like she's not sure whether we're joking, whether she should laugh, though I'm not sure why anybody would make a joke out of something like this.

I dig my phone out of my pocket and pull up a picture of the three of us we took in the car on Saturday. I zoom in on Kay's face and show it to the woman, whose expression remains wary.

'That's our friend,' I say in what I hope is a 'this is not a joke' tone. 'Michaela. She's been gone since yesterday. We're trying to find out if anybody has seen her, or if you know who else was out helping the police locate those campers yesterday? She's probably with them and it's probably fine, but . . .' I don't finish that thought.

The woman looks at the picture on my phone. Looks at me. Then back at my phone.

'She was listening to a podcast,' I say, latching onto the only thing I know about the loch. 'About the area. Maybe you've heard it?'

Now the woman's expression morphs into something unreadable, the humour dropping away. She moves back, then, away from the counter and my phone.

'She's not answering her phone now,' Clio adds. 'We think it died and she's been out there since yesterday. It was cold last night.'

The woman's gaze rests on me and she doesn't look away. Just sort of studies me for a second. Then she shakes her head. 'I'm sorry,' she says. Her tone is clipped, almost as if she's trying to get us to leave. 'No. I've not seen her, but I've not been around much. I'm only back from studying for my masters for reading week. I'll ask my aunt for you.'

'Are you sure?' Clio pushes. She's pulling up another photo on her own phone, one of Michaela in a different outfit but wearing a fashionable scarf over her dark hair and a tan-coloured coat she favours.

But the woman doesn't even look at it as she answers. 'I'm sure. I'm sorry I can't help you. I'll talk to my aunt.'

We get a similar reaction in the bank and the corner shop we passed on the way to the pub. When we reach the farm shop, we're greeted by the same two members of staff who were here on Saturday, but the older of the two, a greying man in his fifties or sixties who was stacking shelves last time we were here, excuses himself before we have chance to ask him if he's seen Michaela.

His colleague, a much younger boy, probably in his late teens, with braces and a shock of ginger hair, watches the older man retreat before leaning over the counter. He's got his eye on Clio, I think, but she doesn't seem to notice.

'Paul's not great with . . . uh, with anybody but the regulars. Sorry about that. I'm Marc. How can I help?'

'Our friend is missing,' Clio says, cutting right through my waffling. She gestures to me and back to herself. 'Her name is Michaela. We've not seen her since yesterday, well, actually since Saturday night, but she probably left yesterday morning. She went for a hike, but we're not sure if she

176

came into the village beforehand or anything. She might have been out in the woods.'

Clio holds up her phone so the boy can have a look at her photo. He barely glances at it.

'You're not from that other group who got lost north of Blackdale, are you?' He tilts his head curiously.

'No, but Michaela might have gone out there to try to be helpful,' I suggest. 'We've got no idea.'

The more often I say it, the more ridiculous it sounds and I'm angry that I let Clio and that police officer convince me yesterday that I was overreacting. I should have mentioned the break-up with Dan. If he was creepy when she stopped seeing him, even if he was fine when she quit, how do we know he isn't holding a grudge?

I stop myself. Now I really am overreacting.

'I've not seen her,' Marc says. 'I doubt she's actually, uh, missing though. Right?' He glances between us, a flush creeping up his neck. When neither of us answer, he blunders on. 'I wasn't working yesterday, but we can, uh, check the CCTV or something?'

'Thank you,' Clio says quickly. 'Yes, that would be really helpful. We would be grateful if you could. We're not having much luck so far, but she's got to be around here somewhere. Don't guess she could have got far without a car.'

'Well, I doubt we'll have any more luck than anybody else,' the boy says quickly, already seeming to regret his offer. He looks over his shoulder towards the back, where we can hear the older colleague shifting stock around. 'The video machine is old and I'm not even sure we'll get a good angle to tell who's coming in and out . . .' He shifts awkwardly and scratches his arm.

'Do you . . . want us to leave you a phone number?' I prompt. 'You could text us.'

'Oh sure,' says the boy. 'Sure. That'll do fine.'

We scribble both our phone numbers down onto a bit of receipt paper and make it back out onto the street before Clio grabs my arm. It looks like she's about to erupt, so I guide her away from the brightly lit shopfront, fairy lights strung up in the window to illuminate their special prices for gourmet sausages this week.

'Ugh,' Clio fumes. 'Is it really so hard to just give us a straightforward answer or be helpful for the sake of being helpful? Why do people start acting like they've seen a ghost whenever we open our mouths?'

'I don't think they're being intentionally difficult,' I soothe, although actually this is exactly what I think. Every single person we've spoken to about Michaela has been stand-offish or downright cold with us, almost as if word has spread about us overnight. I wonder if it's me, my attitude. I do feel like I'm maybe being a bit short, but not outright rude. 'I guess they just don't like the fact that the whole town is out looking for those other people and now we're here too saying our friend's missing. Probably too much excitement.' It feels better, somehow, to be back in my mothering role again. Now I've got Clio on side, understanding that this *is* serious, I feel more in control. And then I feel guilty for even thinking that.

It feels like the day is escaping us. Very soon, it will be twenty-four hours since Michaela might have disappeared. It's already been that long if you count from bedtime Saturday night and that feels wrong, so stupidly wrong, that we *have* to make more progress with this. There's no choice.

'Let's try the pub now,' I say, trying to infuse my voice with fresh purpose and energy. 'They'll be open now. Maybe somebody's seen her.'

We hurry through Blackhills' grey streets to get out of the cold, rubbing our hands together as we step in through the narrow door of the pub. It's much quieter today, despite us having seen a lot more families out in the village thanks to the school holidays, the space down the stretch of windows completely unoccupied, and only one table near the fireplace with people seated at it. The bar has a few older people scattered along its length, two men and a woman stood at one end and a group of younger students at the other. Only a few of the tables are set for food service.

'What can I get you?' the barmaid says. Her back is to us and she doesn't turn right away – but when she does, she pauses immediately. It's the same woman from Saturday, her glasses strung round her neck on a chain and her hair today in a vague approximation of a beehive.

'We want to ask if you've seen—' Clio starts.

I nudge her and she looks at me. I shake my head minutely.

'I'll have a latte please,' I say.

'Oh, uh. Diet Coke please,' Clio adds.

The woman heads down to the other end of the bar and begins to make the drinks while the card machine loads for our payment.

'I thought we were going to ask here as well?' Clio asks quietly.

'I just wonder if we should take our time. Everybody has been so funny with us. Maybe if we ease into it, they won't go straight to being unhelpful? We don't want them thinking we're accusing anybody of anything. I don't know.'

179

I can't really explain it other than instinct. Maybe it's years of psychology, of listening to the words people don't say as much as the ones they do, but something is holding my hand here, guiding me down this path.

Clio stares at me for a moment and then she nods. 'Fine. But if we don't get anywhere, I'm gonna just start accusing people of conspiracy.'

When the barmaid returns with our drinks, I force Clio to stand with me at the bar. I heap sugar into my cup, more out of something to do with my hands than because I actually want it, and I listen as the barmaid returns to the other member of staff stood nearby. I wonder if this was the guy from the other day, Michaela's 'Barman Tim', but if it is, he's not as gossipy today. In fact, it feels like the whole pub is on tenterhooks, waiting for us to either say something or to leave.

'Can I . . . get you anything else?' the barmaid asks after it becomes apparent that we're not just going to disappear to some table in the corner so people can whisper about us.

Clio looks at me and I nod.

'Well actually,' she says. 'We were hoping you might be able to help.'

From the expression on the woman's face, it's clear that my strategy to get them to feel at all at ease has not helped in the slightest, but she raises an eyebrow, her gaze on mine.

'I can try.'

'Our friend,' Clio says. The woman continues to look at me, breaking off only to shoot a glance somewhere behind me, maybe towards the door. 'The one we came in with on Saturday. We wondered if you'd seen her.'

'You don't know where she is?' The barmaid's lips narrow

180

into a thin line and her gaze now darts between the two of us.

Clio explains briefly as I scan the other patrons. I'm pretty sure they're all listening to us, though half of them are pretending they're not.

'So we've not seen her since Saturday night,' Clio concludes.

The male colleague shifts from one foot to the other, obviously listening to our conversation. He goes still when Clio looks at him.

'I hope—' he murmurs.

'Well, that's really not good.' The barmaid speaks over him. 'And you're sure she's not just around the village? Might seem small, but there's lots of nooks and crannies to get lost in.'

'That's why we're here,' Clio says. 'Just in case.'

'You hope what?' I say to the young man.

He startles, as though he didn't expect me to hear him. His eyes are wide and very dark brown, giving him the look of a rabbit caught in a car's headlamps.

'I was just going to say . . .' He pauses, cringing. 'It sounds stupid now.'

'Tell us anyway,' Clio says. She looks much bigger than her five foot frame, the way she's leaning on the bar. I feel a brief burst of gratitude for her. I'm glad I'm not on my own.

The door opens and somebody steps inside, immediately stalling when they notice the energy in the room.

The guy behind the bar hesitates.

The barmaid starts to speak again, but Clio holds up her hands. 'No, if you know something, if you've seen her or if she said something to you, you've got to tell us. I don't care if she told you not to.'

'It's not that,' he blusters. He's glancing about in a panic, but everybody else in earshot is avoiding his gaze so studiously you'd think they were watching a man dig his own grave. 'It's just . . .'

'Just what?'

'I was just going to say that I hope it's not happening again.'

Eleanor

My blood runs cold, the barman's words slithering down my spine like ice. Clio opens and closes her mouth like a fish, clearly lost for words. I stare at the barmaid, but she's grabbed a rag and is wiping down the surface of the clean bar as if it's smeared in mayonnaise or something, even though there's nothing there.

'What do you mean you *hope it's not happening again*?' I demand.

'I've put my foot in it,' he says. 'I . . . It's just . . .'

'Oh leave it, Tim,' the barmaid snaps. 'For God's sake, just give over. You sound like a fool.'

He shrinks back. 'Well, it's just that everybody is probably thinking it—'

'What does he mean?' I ask the barmaid.

She sighs. There's a cough from somewhere behind us and I know we're the centre of attention right now, the eyes of everybody in here probably glued to us like we've got targets on our backs, but I've never been less concerned about that in my life.

The man who entered crosses hesitantly to a table where a blonde woman sits and I wonder distantly if he is the friendly teacher from the other night. I never got a proper look at him, nor him me because of that stupid pillar, but I'm almost certain this woman is his wife. The man looks at Clio, then catches my gaze and an expression of recognition passes across his face; he looks almost shocked.

'It's nothing,' the barmaid says, drawing my attention back to her. She holds up her hands when I open my mouth to argue that it's absolutely *not nothing*, and continues, 'It's nothing to do with this. Tim's just referring to a local . . . ah, story. History. Something that happened a long time ago.'

'And?' Clio pushes. 'What happened?'

'Years and years ago – when I was a kid – these women disappeared around here,' the guy says breathlessly, almost as if he's glad to say it aloud. The barmaid rolls her eyes. 'Three of them.'

The silence is so loud, it feels like my ears might pop.

'What?' I demand.

'Uh, yeah. They were all from around here. Blackhills and Blackdale. I just . . . Sorry. I know that's an awful thing to bring up when you're looking for your friend. I thought you knew and that's why you were here. I got that vibe from you all on Saturday, especially her. We get people asking about it sometimes, though less now than when I was a kid. We used to have all these tourists coming and snooping around, and after that stupid podcast, I thought maybe it was—'

'What did you mean that you hoped it isn't happening again?' Clio repeats my question. 'Why did you *say* that?'

'He reads too much,' the barmaid answers, turning away. 'Watches too many of those stupid CSI shows.'

'Beth—'

'No, for God's sake, Tim.' She turns back to us, the rag still in her hand. She's waving it around like a peace flag. 'Look, he shouldn't have said anything. We're not used to having people in Blackhills that don't know the history. Even the odd tourist over the years only seems to want to prod and poke at it like some kind of scab. Everybody here either remembers it or was brought up talking about it. It's just local legend now.'

'What happened?' I ask. 'To these women? Why would you mention them *now*?'

'It's just that you're staying at the Loch House,' Tim stumbles. 'Right? Nobody ever goes there any more because it's so close to the water. Too risky. Everybody always says those girls were probably hanging out by Loch House before they disappeared.'

'What, did they drown or something?' Clio has pushed the sleeves of her shirt up aggressively and she looks like she's ready to deck him right in the jaw.

He notices it too and he steps back a little, bumping into the register awkwardly.

'We don't know. Nobody knows. But I guess everybody assumed so,' Beth says. She reaches up unconsciously to straighten her rock-solid hairdo. 'I think the police couldn't figure it out, but everybody thought that must be what happened. The ground is so uneven up there, all those paths into the hills with no real footholds, and so steep.'

'There was never any evidence that they drowned.' This interjection comes from the man I'm fairly sure is the teacher – Matthew. He's speaking to Clio as if he knows her. His wife is gone now and he looks a little too spooked to be reassuring. He's tall and broad, grey hair and kind eyes. Up

185

close, I'd peg him in maybe his early sixties. As he talks his gaze keeps straying to me and I wonder if I look as scared as I feel. 'All sorts of stories went round after. All the students in town gossiped because everybody knew them, but what's frustrating is they could easily have just upped and left. I hate how this whole village has been stained by what happened. I'm sure the loch has nothing to do with your friend.'

'Yeah, there was no evidence at all,' Tim agrees. 'My dad thinks they had some sort of pact to leave, or some sordid secret they were protecting. They had all been at school together or something, so they definitely knew each other.'

'So why do people think they drowned?' Clio pushes.

I want to ask questions as well, but my brain is occupied instead by the stupid creature from my nightmares. I picture those awful hands reaching up to snag unaware women, pulling them down into the depths.

'It's the most likely scenario really,' Beth says. 'There was a lot of rain that year, so the loch was really awful, and the currents are rotten at the best of times. The girls all came from either here or other towns nearby, easy access to the water, and before it happened it was the sort of place a lot of youngsters went to pass the time. You know.' She drops the rag to the bar. 'You've got to ignore Tim.'

'I didn't mean to freak you guys out,' he says earnestly. 'I just read a lot of folklore. There are stories about these monsters that come once every decade – or maybe it was twenty-five years? I can't remember. But I was thinking about it when you said your friend was missing and I should have kept my mouth shut. I'm sorry.'

Clio turns to me, and now it's not anger or annoyance on her face. It's not even directed at the rest of them. It's genuine worry, perhaps the most I've seen since we realised Michaela was missing. As if she's only now realised how dangerous it might be here, the water so close to the house. Like it was . . . not a game, before, but not real, somehow. It would be so easy to fall in if Michaela wasn't being careful. 'How do we know Michaela didn't drown?' she says softly. 'She's been missing for twenty-four hours.'

'Is this why everybody is being so weird with us?' I ask, ignoring Clio because I don't have the answer. I turn to Beth and Tim. 'You thought we were here to dig around into these missing women?'

'For a while, the news was big. It drew people here. Morbid folks,' Beth says with resignation. 'That's why we're still . . . wary.'

There's something in her manner that still feels like she's not telling me the whole story, but I have no idea why.

'Does *everybody* know about this?' I'm thinking about the way that pretty much everybody has reacted to us while we've been here, and it's all starting to make sense. There's such folklore and superstition surrounding the loch that people can't seem to see past it. Maybe that's why Michaela wanted to come here. She's always been into her true crime. God, maybe this was what she wanted to talk to me about – though why she'd think I would be interested in any of that is beyond me.

I turn around and catch the teacher's eye again. He's watching me with concern etched into his features.

'I'm sure your friend is fine,' he says gently. 'There's no reason to think otherwise.'

'If she was fine, she would be back by now,' I grind out.

'If she wasn't fine, I'm sure you'd know,' he says, almost as if he's trying to convince himself.

'You said she might be helping the police search,' Beth comments. 'That lot are prone to being blown into the nearest pub. Are you sure she's not just with them?'

'No, we're not sure. But we're *worried*.' I don't understand what about that is so hard to understand.

Matthew is still watching me. He seems . . . shaken. I wonder if he knew the girls that went missing. In a village this size, I bet everybody did. Perhaps he has a daughter who knew them, or a cousin or a friend.

'Not to be rude,' Clio says, 'but we're really not here to go round in circles like this. You're all talking about missing girls and lake monsters, but our friend is the reason we came in here today, not some tragedy from years ago. We want to know if anybody has seen Michaela. Or, I guess, if there's somewhere specific she might have walked.' She turns to me as if she's just realised the same thing I have. I bet the podcast Michaela mentioned was a true crime one. *That's* how she found this place. For fuck's sake – that's the most Michaela thing I've ever heard. 'If she knew the stories before she came,' Clio goes on, 'where might she go? She went out there by herself. Can we show you her picture?'

Matthew waits patiently as Clio opens her phone and pulls up the photograph she's been showing everybody, Michaela smiling like always. He looks at the photo and then at me as I pass Clio's phone to Tim, and then to Beth. Next, another man at the bar who looks like somebody official, his dark hair swept back with oil. All of them are shaking their heads. They look stricken, as if it's only just hit them. This isn't just some story, a piece of gossip, Michaela is a real person who might be in danger.

'Are you sure she didn't just . . . go home?' Beth asks.

'Wouldn't be the first gal to take a dislike to the countryside in favour of home.'

'She didn't just *go home*,' I snap.

'I wish I could help,' Matthew says. 'But try not to worry—'

'I'm even *more* worried after all these stories about your stupid loch.' Clio pauses. 'No offence.'

'Oh, none taken,' Beth says. 'I don't much like the stupid loch either.' This is the first humour we've seen from her, but rather than annoying me, or upsetting me, I find that it helps me to relax a bit. I lean against the bar, feeling my tiredness rise like a wave.

'Those girls that disappeared,' Clio asks. 'You said they all went to school together. Were they friends?'

'Yeah, I think at least one of them had moved away, but that's not that unusual.' Beth leans on the bar. 'It's not like there's no movement,' she says. 'People *do* move around a bit. But even nearby, the towns are small and most people know somebody who knows somebody who knows somebody.'

'Yeah, my dad's from Blackdale,' Tim pipes up. 'Moved here when he was six but still has friends there. Lots of families marry between the two, I guess, but Blackdale's a lot bigger.'

'I bet a lot of your kids have parents who work in Blackdale,' Beth says, gesturing to Matthew.

He startles, in a world of his own, then nods. 'Oh, yeah. Half the kids in school have parents who commute. And my wife does loads of charity work in local towns too.'

'I don't remember exactly how they were all friendly,' Beth muses. 'I only knew one of them. Her parents still own the farm shop, though the uncle does most of the running of it now. Her dad's the man you upset at the bar the other day.'

'The one who stormed off?'

'Yeah, he's not been right since they went missing.'

'We met the uncle too,' Clio blurts. Beth raises an eyebrow. 'Well, we saw him. We spoke to the other guy.'

'Oh, that'll be my brother, Marc,' Tim says, proudly. 'He's worked there for a year or so. We're twins. Non-identical.'

'I'm sorry,' I cut in. This is all too much, and none of it is helping. 'I really am not trying to be rude or anything, but I've got to ask again. Are you sure none of you have seen Michaela since Saturday? Did she say anything to either of you when she came back for her umbrella after the quiz? Any suggestion of somewhere she might go, something she had planned? Did she talk to anybody?'

'I don't even remember her coming back in.' Beth shakes her head.

I can't help the tears that prickle behind my eyes. Clio still has Michaela's picture up on her phone and she keeps touching the screen every few seconds so the light doesn't dim.

'For fuck's sake,' Clio mutters.

'I'm sorry, loves,' Beth says. Her tone is warm, but there's still an element of distance there, almost a reticence. I'm not sure if it's because we don't belong here, or if they simply have no idea how to help, but everybody is the same, holding us at arm's length as though what happened to Michaela might be contagious. But with three women having gone missing in the past, and now Michaela as well, maybe it's too late.

Eleanor

There's nothing for it but to sit and wait. Beth and Tim insist that we stay a while, and other than traipsing around the whole village some more, or heading back to Loch House, there isn't anything else we can do. This thought itself pains me more than I'd like to admit, so I usher Clio towards a table – about as far away from the one we sat at on Saturday as possible – and order us both another drink, though I opt for a decaf tea because I'm not sure I can handle any more caffeine on an empty stomach without losing control of my hands.

'This is such a mess,' Clio says. She rests her head in her hands and massages her scalp, mussing her short hair. The humour we both found in our stories last night is well and truly gone now, but I'm surprised to find this comforts me.

'I keep thinking it's a dream,' I agree. 'I hope that any minute now we'll wake up and it'll be yesterday morning and Michaela will be in the house begging us to go shopping with her. And then we'll come here and have another lunch and it'll be awful and amazing and then she'll want to go on a fucking *walk*—' I stop myself.

Clio flinches.

'Do you really think, after she texted us, she could have . . .' She stops, picks at a cuticle. 'She's a good swimmer.'

'She's an excellent swimmer.'

'How do lochs even work? Aren't there rivers involved or something?' She shakes her head. 'God, I keep picturing everything that could have happened. And I'm not sure what's worse, the idea that she could have ended up in the loch or that there's another alt—'

I cut her off with a stare that's so icy I even surprise myself. If Michaela stays gone, we will, at some point, be forced to ask the question: is she hurt? Right now, though, I can't face it. Maybe that makes me a coward, but I know what my limits are.

Clio pulls her phone out and starts to type furiously into it. I watch her face as she slowly gets more and more frustrated.

'What?' I ask.

'I'm trying to google about the girls that disappeared or whatever, but there's hardly any information. You'd think it would be super obvious, but all I'm getting is like *black hills South Dakota*, totally different place.'

'Did you try Scotland?'

'Have you got any idea how many girls have ever gone missing in Scotland?' Clio mutters. 'Friggin' impossible. I need more information. All I'm getting is some American horror TV show.'

'There must be something,' I say. 'Maybe you're just not looking in the right place. What's that podcast that Michaela was listening to – can we find that?'

'And how exactly am I supposed to find one true crime podcast in a sea of thousands? We don't even know what platform it was on, and she said it was only an episode. I've tried searching for Loch Aven, but nothing is coming up.'

'I don't know anything about podcasts,' I say. I've never paid any attention to them, but now I'm thinking about it, the police officer seemed cagey when we mentioned it, and people around town have been too. I doubt any of them would entertain us asking for details. It makes me think about the man who stormed out of the pub on Saturday, the father of one of the missing girls. He probably thought the podcast was why we were here and got angry about it – which I guess might not be entirely unfair. I wish I could ask Michaela what the hell she was thinking with all of this.

When Beth brings the tea and Clio's soda and lime from the bar, she also comes bearing two plates of sandwiches, fish fingers between thick slices of white bread, chips and tartar sauce.

'I didn't know if you two were hungry, but . . .' She places the plates down.

'That's really kind of you,' I say, even though the sight of food turns my stomach. I haven't eaten since breakfast yesterday, but my body wants food less than anything on the planet. Clio looks the same, her skin taking on a green tint, although she does eat fish.

Beth leaves the food without another word and we sit for a moment, both of us in silence, before Clio eventually forces herself to pick up a chip. I peck at my own meal, my phone sitting right beside the plate, its blank screen taunting me.

The people who were in here when we arrived have all emptied out one by one, and a group of men in their twenties and thirties have stumbled in. One of them clocks us and nudges the others until they all fall quiet. Beth swoops straight over to them and I know without having to listen that they're talking about us.

I'm paralysed, barely even able to keep eating. I'll have to call Joy, but I'm putting it off because I don't want to scare her. I know we only received Michaela's text message last night, but I haven't laid eyes on her in over twenty-four hours and that's just wrong.

'I'm on my break – do you mind if I sit with you?'

Tim appears so suddenly that I jump.

Clio waves her hand in a lazy gesture that probably only I know is forced.

Tim sits in one of the empty chairs, resting his elbows on the table awkwardly. Up close, he really is young, probably only just old enough to be working here, and I think I can see the similarities between his face and the boy from the farm shop.

'I really am sorry if I upset you earlier,' he says. For a second, I wonder if Beth has put him up to this, but I can't see why she would. Besides, his expression seems genuine enough.

Clio snorts.

'It does explain the way everybody's been acting,' I say. 'But what made you think of it?'

'I don't know.' Tim shrugs. 'I grew up hearing the stories. You guys just reminded me of them on Saturday, three young women, about your age. I often think about it. It's so tragic, y'know? Young people, just like us, dyin' or disappearing like that. Nothing else bad has ever happened

194

here. We have the lowest crime rate in all of Scotland, probably.'

'Yeah, that you know of,' Clio mutters.

'No, I'm not kidding,' he says earnestly. 'Nothing bad *ever* happens. Like, we don't even really have road traffic accidents or house fires or any of that. It's like the whole village is cushioned by this one horrible thing that did happen, and as far as anybody knows, nothing actually happened in Blackhills itself. I was morbidly obsessed with it as a kid, and you like . . . reminded me of one of the girls. She was really pretty.' He's looking at me as he says it, a flush on his cheeks. 'Anyway, Marc and me would go up to the loch and root around, pretending we were looking for *evidence*. But then Marc nearly fell in and we didn't go back.'

I flatten my hands against the table so I won't check my phone again out of nervous habit; I'm not used to having the volume turned up loud, and my notifications pinging keeps sending me into a frenzy, even though it's just junk emails.

When neither Clio or I speak, Tim goes on, nervously filling the silence, 'I don't know what came first though: the superstition or the disappearances. Nobody round here goes to the loch any more. I do remember this one story my big brother told Marc and me when I was a kid. About the time he went to Loch Aven. It was after dark with some mates, drinking and smoking and the like.' He mimes the act of lighting up. 'Think he said there was a big group of them, boys and girls. Y'know. They were down by the water, made a campfire of sorts, just chilling and what have you. He said one of his mates properly pelted away from the water, just randomly out of the blue. Legged it right back

195

to the road, over a mile. Don't think they could get a straight word out of him – he was pissed as a newt – but he kept going on about some shadow. A shadow with horns or hooves or some shit. I remember being really frightened, but my brother told me it was all bollocks – excuse me. It was all rubbish.'

'And people think it's *haunted* or something?' Clio asks. I've never seen her look less impressed with somebody else's storytelling though I'm not sure if it's his style she doesn't like or simply what he's saying.

'Nah, not haunted. I dunno, I just think people like, get themselves all tied up about it. The water and what lives under it. I saw this meme once—'

'I'm gonna stop you there,' Clio says, a little unkindly. 'I don't need a teenager explaining a meme to me, thanks.'

Tim has the good grace not to blush again, but he does look at me, almost silently asking whether he should leave us to it. I wonder how I've yet again ended up in control when I feel like all I'm doing is drowning under all this.

'I think we should get back out there,' I say. 'I want to have another scout around before we head back to the house and it's getting late.'

Clio taps her phone screen and it lights up, a photo of the three of us that's been her background since last Christmas beneath the clock ticking over yet another minute. Whatever we think about all of this, it's plain as day: something isn't right.

Janie

Then

Janie likes to think that people can talk to her about everything. She was always the girl at school who knew everybody's secrets, like a mother they could trust, instead of one who would scold or shout at them. She's always been proud of it, a skill she's cultivated over many years. When her parents separated and she moved to Blackdale with her dad, and her younger brother John stayed with their mother, she relied on it, gathering secrets from both of her parents like other children might have collected shiny stones.

And it's served her well as an adult too. She knows she isn't much to look at, small and birdlike, with fine hair that isn't blonde or brown but some mousy shade in between; her kindness is what people cherish, her calmness, her ability to listen. It's why she's surprised, then, that Rebecca comes out of the blue.

They've been friends for years, even after Janie moved away. They progressed from a childhood of playdates to meetings at the library, and then to those evenings on Loch Aven. Janie, Rebecca, Sarah, Josh, Magnus and Tommy, a ragtag bunch, laughter and screaming into the darkness, frozen feet in the marbled depths of the water with a campfire burning at their backs.

Rebecca used to be her best friend, though it doesn't always feel like it now. She thought Rebecca could tell her anything, even despite the distance growing between them. She realises, fairly quickly on this cold day in early February, that she was wrong.

It happens in that magic hour between day and night, when everything is gold-slanted and speckled with dust motes. Janie isn't working this weekend, which she supposes is lucky. Although she might come to change her mind about that. She's sat on her sofa drinking a cup of tea and contemplating whether she has time to get some knitting done before her crooked little house – the one she inherited when her father died – gets too cold. She doesn't like to pay for the heating after the end of January, though this cold snap might make her rethink that.

There's a knock at the door that startles her. Nobody uses the knocker any more, not since she had the new doorbell installed, and even as she gets to her feet, her brain is whirring, a suspicion forming. There's only one person she knows who knocks like that – two sharp knocks, a pause, another knock.

When she opens the door, she's already gone through half a dozen possibilities. The house is right on the outskirts of Blackdale, so far out it's inconvenient, and people don't stop by accidentally. She's trying to come up with an excuse for why she doesn't want to join the others tonight, even as she considers how long it's been since she heard that particular knock at her door; she thought they'd grown out of that, hadn't they?

But there is Rebecca.

And she isn't dressed for the outdoors in her usual jeans and parka. She's wearing a hoodie, her jacket slung over one arm and a duffel bag in the other. Her face is pale, her eyes red-rimmed, and suddenly Janie's brain kicks into another gear.

'Jesus,' she says. 'Come on. Let me put the kettle on.'

Rebecca brings her meagre belongings into the house, eyes flicking around the once-familiar space.

Janie sets to in the kitchen, refilling the kettle and pouring out a fresh mug of the loose-leaf tea she favours. Rebecca takes the mug reluctantly, a brief hesitation flitting across her face that Janie can't read – but instead of elaborating, like she might have when they were younger, Rebecca sinks into the sofa in silence.

'What do you need?' Janie asks gently. She moves her knitting to the coffee table and sits in the armchair nearest the dark fireplace. 'Do you want to talk? Or do you want quiet?'

Rebecca says nothing, only cries.

Janie thinks this must be her answer, so she settles back, tucking her feet up. She can wait. She can mind her own business. It hurts her to see Rebecca like this, but she knows pestering won't help. Still, she's used to people opening up to her. It shouldn't feel like a punishment, but tonight it does.

Half an hour passes in near silence. Slowly, Rebecca's tears start to ebb and she reaches up and lets out a sigh that is filled with so much frustration, sorrow, that Janie has to resist the urge to reach out to her. She does not look pretty when she cries, and yet somehow that endears her to Janie even more.

Rebecca shifts slightly, her gaze searching, and Janie senses her opening. It's subtle, like the tiniest snag on a woollen jumper, but she knows it's the right time to pull.

'I didn't think I was going to see you again,' Janie says lightly. 'Word around town is that you're finally off on that big adventure you told me you weren't ready for last year. I was so pleased. Of course, by "around town", I mean I popped to Blackhills last week to the florist Dad liked, you know, for his grave, and your dad was in there talking to Mr Philips about how you were finally going travelling—' Janie realises immediately this is the wrong thing to say.

Rebecca's eyes grow wide like a spooked horse and she pulls her knees to her chest in alarm.

Janie holds up her hands. This isn't the Rebecca she knows. She has always been so quietly confident in her dreams, even if they never came to much; the old Rebecca would never flinch.

'My dad can't know I'm here,' Rebecca blurts. 'If he finds out I'm not . . .' She doesn't finish that thought.

Janie catches the meaning in it. She remembers Rebecca's dad. A big, broad man with hands like dinner plates. Quick to anger. He always scared her. He was stricter than most of the parents she knew, always wanting to know where they were going, and God forbid Rebecca missed curfew by even a minute. He wasn't one to talk much about his feelings but you always knew when he was disappointed.

Janie remembers one time, years ago, when they were both eighteen and Rebecca had that job at the cinema, he'd gone in to meet both of them for lunch and Janie had arrived just after him. Rebecca was on the refreshment stand and a group of lads were messing around at the till, cat-calling the girls and throwing popcorn, aiming for their cleavage. Janie sort of laughed along – Rebecca didn't really seem that bothered and the boys were just having a laugh.

But Mr Kelly didn't find it funny. He lost his temper, went up like match paper, and he didn't calm down until he'd successfully had all but one of the boys kicked out for harassment. Rebecca had been mortified, obviously. She apologised the whole way through the stilted lunch while her dad brooded silently over his sandwich. Janie had made an excuse to leave early, discomfort driving her away, and when Rebecca's mum got sick and Rebecca started working at the family shop, Janie wasn't surprised.

'Well, I certainly won't tell him,' Janie swears. 'You know my lips are sealed tight as a tomb.'

Rebecca lets out a whoosh of a breath. 'Sorry. I . . .'

'Why *are* you here?' Janie asks tentatively. 'I don't want to pry, but . . . I'm assuming you didn't just stop by for a cup of tea.'

'I don't really have anywhere else to go.' Rebecca shrugs. She lowers her feet and reaches for the mug she'd left on the coffee table, though the tea is likely cold by now. 'I just needed to get away.'

'From Blackhills?'

'From everything.' Rebecca stares at the mug in her hands. Her cuticles aren't tidy like normal. Janie thinks she must have been picking them. 'I really messed up, Janie.'

Janie wants to reassure her, to tell her that it can't be so bad – but the truth is, Rebecca is here. She is here without warning, with a duffel bag and her face the colour of spoiled milk under all those tears. And Janie thinks back to last summer, to their conversation on the loch when she had seemed so unlike herself. So, it is bad.

'What happened? Is it money trouble? Did you . . .' Janie

runs out of ideas fast. Rebecca has always been a romantic sort of girl: she likes books and movies and dreams of travelling the world. But she never takes risks in the real world, mostly keeps to herself. What sort of trouble could she have got herself into that would bring her to Janie's door?

'No. I . . .' Rebecca blows another sigh. 'God. It sounds so sordid when I try to say it. I . . . got involved with somebody.'

'Romantically?' Janie suggests. Her heart sinks, despite everything she has told herself about her feelings for Rebecca. They are old, though, buried deep, wrapped like roots around her bones, and they won't let go.

'Yes.'

'More?' Janie presses, though she doesn't want to hear it.

'Yes.' Rebecca sighs and it's as if she's releasing years of pain. 'Oh Janie, I thought . . . I thought everything was going to be different than this. He's older than me – married.'

'Jesus,' Janie says. A small fire of anger begins to smoulder in her chest. Not at Rebecca – well, not entirely. 'A married one? How long's it been going on for?'

'Ages. A year and a half. I thought that – he made me believe . . . I thought he was going to leave his wife.' Rebecca looks so small, so fragile.

Janie's mind is running a mile a minute, her brain flying through the possibilities. She lands on another fact hard, though. This is why Rebecca is here. Her dad is old-fashioned, and has strong opinions about marriage; he'd never jive with this kind of thing, especially if the man is older. Blackhills is small and affairs like this drive rifts through communities. She tries to silence the little trill of fear in her, the one that questions what Robert Kelly might do if he knew Rebecca was here.

'Does *anybody* know you're here?' Janie asks.

Rebecca shakes her head. 'I stayed in a hotel last night, miles away, and hitchhiked back up here today. Everybody thinks I left Blackhills. They think I'm travelling like I always said.'

'You're sure?'

Rebecca's lips thin as she presses them together. Fear bands between the two of them. 'I didn't mean to drag you into this,' she says. 'I'm sorry. It's . . . I . . .'

Janie gets the feeling that there is something else, something Rebecca isn't telling her. But no matter how hard she tries, the girl won't budge. Yes, she's sure nobody knows she's here. No, she doesn't need to see a doctor or a psychiatrist or anybody else. Yes, she's got money – at least enough for now.

It's long grown dark by the time Janie leads Rebecca to her spare bedroom. She's changed things up since they last spent time here – way over a year ago now. It's only in the light of what Janie's learned that she realises how distant Rebecca has been with her for months. A year. She'd put it down to them growing apart, working and dreaming and evolving into their adult lives. A twisted, shameful part deep inside her wondered if it was because of her – because Rebecca knew how she feels about her. Sickness roils in her belly.

But Rebecca is different tonight than Janie has ever seen her. She's nervous, that much Janie can see. The weight of an unpredictable future pushes down on her. But she's brighter than she has been for months too, a flinty piece of determination deep inside her reflecting the light.

'You can stay as long as you need to,' Janie says. She tries to sound reassuring, but she knows there's an edge to it. 'But I can't afford to support you as well as myself.'

203

'I know that,' Rebecca says quickly. 'I have savings. You won't even know I'm here.'

'You'll be here a while?' Once upon a time she would have wanted Rebecca to stay as long as possible, but things are different now. She doesn't exactly want this any more but Janie knows she could never turn her away.

'A little while, yeah. If you'll have me. I . . . I don't have much choice. It's not forever. Just until I work out exactly what I want, you know? I can't go back. Not yet. Not until . . .'

'Right. Just – if there's something you're not telling me, Bec . . . You need to tell me. We need to talk about it all, get it all out in the open. I need to know what happened so I can help you through this. Okay?'

She's much shorter than Rebecca is, used to being the one people look down on, but today she makes herself stand as tall as she can. Rebecca slouches in her oversized hoodie, wrapping her arms tight around herself.

'Yeah,' Rebecca says. 'I mean . . . No. I'll . . . Okay.' The walls are going back up again. Janie can see it in real time, how Rebecca's eyes dim, how she grips tighter onto her duffel bag, fingertips whitening as if she's planning to flee again any second.

'Bec, please,' Janie says. 'You know how much I care about you. Whatever else there is, you can tell me. I won't judge you.'

Rebecca flinches again, as if she's only now realising what she is doing. A sacrifice she has already made. Then she looks up, her eyes growing clear once more. Her bottom lip trembles, but only once, shame flaming on her cheeks.

Janie's heart aches, sadness squeezing it tight. But . . . the treacherous part of her feels something else too.

Somehow she is *glad* – because Rebecca has come back to her. Because Janie can finally, finally be what she needs.

'It's okay. You can tell me,' she repeats. 'Whatever it is, I'm sure it's not insurmountable. I can help you through this. If you just need time to lick your wounds, that's fine. If you want to stay until you're ready to travel, that's fine too. It's *okay*.'

'Janie,' Rebecca whispers, and Janie feels a lump form in her throat. She can sense it before it happens, the whole future she dreamed about but never dared act on slipping away. All it takes is two words. 'I'm pregnant.'

Eleanor

Despite our intentions, we don't head straight back to the house. Instead, we do another round of the village, starting near the car and checking all of the shops and alleys we pass as though Michaela might just suddenly appear. Then we loop back to the main square where the bunting between lamp posts looks less festive than it did only days ago. Everything feels barren, the wind colder and the sky darker. I want to pass comment to Clio, but she looks lost in her own thoughts and I know stating the obvious won't change things. It's not the village's fault; the difference is not in Blackhills but in us.

Michaela's text message of reassurance, which had seemed like a blessing last night, now feels like a curse. It has been nearly two days since we last saw her. And a solid day and a half since we suspect she was last in the house. I know I should take comfort in the fact that she said she was fine and we shouldn't worry, that she was out there being helpful – probably with those bloody lost campers – but I don't. Because if she's so fine, where the fuck is she?

By the time we finally get back into the car and drive the short distance to Loch House, the sky is already darkening, leaving us in that awful in-between that is neither day nor night, where everything looks haunted.

'You agree that I'm not overreacting now, right?' I ask, my whole body coiled taut like a spring.

Clio scowls.

'What if they've found those campers, or some of them? What if they've stopped searching, and she's not with them, and they've forgotten to look for Kay?' I ask.

Clio's scowl deepens, but she doesn't have an answer.

The track that leads up to Loch House is awful in the dark. It's bumpy and uneven at the best of times, but with only our headlamps and the last remaining light of the day to guide us, it's slow work, trees seeming to jump out of nowhere. I wish I'd driven because all Clio does is slam the brakes on and curse excessively and my heart hammers in my throat.

It's a relief, almost, to reach the house, looming in the dimness. The windows are dark, but the grey stone reflects what's left of the daylight, giving the feeling once again that I'm looking at some kind of mirage. I half expect to blink and find it gone, replaced by nothing but trees upon trees and, eventually, maybe, a view of the water.

Earlier, when we left, we made sure to leave the door key in the hide-a-key, at the front door where we got it from when we arrived, just in case. I open it with trepidation and feel only a numb kind of resignation when I find the key exactly where I put it. No Michaela. No hope that she's been here, unless she learned how to walk through walls. Wryly, I think Clio probably has a story like this.

The house echoes. We traipse through in silence, almost

208

as if to talk would be to disturb what little peace there is here in the twilight. Clio snaps on every single lamp, blaring the room to life in a riot of different colours, light dancing with the fringes from some of the shades that look older than the ones my mum has in her house.

I focus my attention on the fire. Clio would be better at it, I'm sure, but right now I'm craving something that might take up all of my brainpower. I don't want to be inside my own mind, which is buzzing with countless thoughts and fears, or inside my body, where my stomach is churning from the little food I ate.

I crouch low, gathering an armful of skinny twigs and placing them one by one into a tower in the grate on top of a fire lighter and kindling, just as my dad showed me. I build the perfect pile, measuring the distance between them evenly, making sure there's room to stick my match. It feels like architecture, like art. I get the sudden, overwhelming urge to call my parents.

Would they even know what to do? Would they panic or would they stay calm in the face of tragedy as they always have? I'm reminded of the day I went to them to tell them I wanted to start digging into my heritage. It was a question I think they'd known was coming for years – they'd always been incredibly open with me about my adoption – and instead of hurt, all I saw was a question. Tactics.

'What do you want us to do to help you?' Dad asked.

Always 'what do you want us to do to help?', never 'this is the way things should be done'.

I've spent my whole life praising them for their parenting skills, the things they have taught me about how to handle myself. But now I'm facing down the barrel of an impossible situation, a situation I never thought I'd have to experience, and it turns out I'm not like them at all. I don't have the ability to prise apart this weekend and work out a plan, to be as tactical as a war counsel. All I feel is panic and it's clouding everything, like the shroud of mist on the surface of the loch.

'Dude, if you glare at those logs any harder, you'll set them alight with your mind alone,' Clio mutters. It's the sort of thing my mum would say, right before telling me to stop squinting. Clio's nothing like my mum though, perched on the sofa behind me, wearing a hoodie with a layer of fluff inside the hood that looks incredibly warm. She's got her hands stuffed in the front pocket, and I know she's still holding her phone like a talisman.

'I was just thinking about my mum,' I say.

'Your *mum* mum? Or your bio mum?'

'Nah, my *mum* mum.' My nose is freezing and I rub at it before striking a match, trying to get the firelighter to catch. 'Just like . . . I was thinking I should call, to see what I – what *we* should do now. Because I have no fucking idea. And it makes me feel so helpless, you know? But . . . yeah, I guess, I can't help thinking about my bio mum too.'

'How so . . .?'

'I just wonder if this kind of panic is how she felt, overwhelmed and emotional.' The thought hits me square in the gut. 'I mean, if I was her, in some sort of impossible situation like she must have been, I guess I would have left me at a police station too.' I've never considered it like this before.

'You're getting all morbid,' Clio points out. 'That's my job. Dude, the firelighter—' she urges.

'Oh shit.' I push the errant cube back under the pile of

sticks it's rolled out of, cursing my inability to even do this one thing right. Then I catch myself. Isn't this exactly what I tell my clients not to do? I'm catastrophising. 'All I'm saying is, I think I get it more now than I ever have before. The kind of worry I'm feeling right now is making it so impossible to understand what we should do. My head is in ten thousand places at once. Should we look for her? Should we stay here in case she comes back? Should we go somewhere with more signal, or go to the police again? If she hadn't texted, we would have, but . . . Yeah. I think I understand why my mother thought the police station was the best place for me, because I couldn't look after a kid right now. Could you? Is that a weird thing for me to say? Not to make this all about me, or anything.'

Clio laughs, but the sound is very strained, sort of like she doesn't know how to react. 'Oh, make it about you,' she says lightly. 'Make it about me too, if you want. I can't stand all of this waiting around. It feels like we're waiting for the other shoe to drop, like any minute either Michaela is going to come waltzing in and I'm going to kill her or—' Clio stops. 'Sorry, that's actually not funny. Jesus, doesn't it make you realise how many things a day you say that are totally fucking insensitive?'

'I knew what you meant.'

'Anyway, yeah. It just feels like perpetual twilight, fully just in the in-between.' She starts to sing the theme for *The Twilight Zone*, which is probably supposed to make me laugh, but it only makes me feel worse.

'I feel so guilty,' I say.

'Why?'

'I don't know. Because – it was my idea to actually have a weekend away in the first place. Michaela just wanted to go out for dinner to start with and I convinced her that time away would be a good thing. And then she got it in her head and she probably only heard this place mentioned on that podcast and decided to come here because of *me*.'

'It *was* a good thing. It *is*.' Clio pops a piece of gum in her mouth. I turn back to the fireplace, where two of the firelighters have gone out without doing much more than blackening the logs on top. 'You didn't make this happen. How could you know?'

'How do we know I didn't?' I push. The words build in me along with my frustration. My chest is tight with panic that just won't abate and my ears are ringing with an impending anxiety attack, the likes of which I haven't had since I was a kid. 'We don't know why she's gone. I've been assuming that Michaela's text about being helpful meant she was helping those campers, but what if it's to do with whatever she wanted me to appreciate? What if she was trying to be helpful to me, because of Charlotte or something?'

'We don't know any of that. You can't just make these assumptions—'

'Well, at least I'm trying to come up with ideas. You hardly seem like you care!'

My words echo in Clio's silence.

'Dude,' she says. Her face is stricken, suddenly pale. A surge of guilt flares and I cover my eyes with my hands. 'That was . . . *a lot*.' Her voice is thick.

'Oh God. I know. I'm sorry.'

'You've got to put smaller kindling underneath and leave the heavy logs until it's already alight,' she says quietly.

I get up and wander over to the kitchen area where there is still a lamp she hasn't turned on. I can't look at her, not right now. I feel like I'm just falling apart over this and it's wrong. I've spent my whole adult life making a living out of being the well-adjusted one, but this weekend is pushing me over the edge.

Gathering myself, I turn my attention back to the fire and try implementing Clio's advice. I take my time removing the larger logs with the provided fireproof glove, restructure my work of art and set the kindling alight. Sure enough, this time the flames take hold and soon I can place the bigger logs on top.

I'm so focused that I don't understand what's happened right away. All I know is one minute Clio is there, fiddling with a lampshade she's knocked crooked as if righting it is the most important thing in the world, and the next second she's gone.

'Clio?'

I rock back on my heels, scanning the room. It's empty, but the doors that lead out to the dock are open and a frigid draught nips at my bare skin. I grab my jacket from where I slung it over the back of the sofa earlier and wander to the doors.

The light plays havoc with my eyes, shadows stretching as I search the growing darkness. When I spot Clio, she's already halfway towards the dock, marching with purpose. My heart thuds and I launch after her, through the open doors and across slick blades of grass and then slicker wooden steps, already primed with frost.

'Clio, wait—' I call.

She doesn't slow down, just keeps going with that straight set to her shoulders, her short legs making impossibly long strides.

'I'm sorry. I shouldn't have said that. I'm just so scared

that something bad happened to Kay and I feel so useless being here where we don't know anybody and can't get any help . . .' I trail off as Clio comes to a stop. She's right at the water's edge now, her toes curled over the end of the dock. The water laps loudly, furrowed by the same wind that chills me to my core.

For a moment the lapping is the only sound and it seems to stretch and stretch into the murky darkness. And then Clio leans forward.

I break into a jog, still careful of the dock underfoot and the way my feet slide across the wood. My heart pounds. Clio whirls and I can see the water. And something *in* the water.

'What is it?' I gasp.

Clio lets out a startled cry.

'It's Kay's scarf.'

Eleanor

We fish the scarf from the loch gingerly. Clio holds onto the back of my shirt as I lean in and grab it. The water is a shock, freezing my fingers, numbing my whole hand as I claw the material away from the grasping darkness. It feels impossibly heavy, considering it's only made of some kind of gauzy silk.

'It's the one she bought in the village,' Clio murmurs. 'Isn't it? The one she got on Saturday?'

'I . . . I think so,' I say, almost too afraid to admit it.

Clio is spaced out, her eyes bugging wide, and I can see the way they shine even in the dark. 'Fuck,' she says. 'FUCK.'

'It doesn't mean anything. It doesn't . . .' I scramble back to my feet, but the weight of the scarf in my hands feels like irrefutable proof, although I don't know of what. Does it mean she fell? Or did she just lose it?

'I feel sick,' Clio groans. 'Oh God—'

'Look,' I say as calmly as I can manage. My whole body is trembling with adrenaline, but my voice is surprisingly steady. 'I know it seems bad, but it doesn't mean anything.

Maybe she lost it yesterday and the current brought it here. Or . . .' The reasons I have seem stupid. 'Maybe she fell in and floated—'

'Floated *where*, Eleanor?' Clio snaps. Then, 'Sorry. Sorry. I just . . . How is this possibly a good thing?'

'I didn't say it was a good thing. But it doesn't necessarily mean she's hurt.' My heart is like a jackhammer. The material of the scarf feels like slime in my hands, like murky water weeds, and I have to resist the urge to drop it back in.

'This is bad, El. I thought . . .'

I'm still holding the scarf, its weight pulling me down, down, feeling like a lodestone dragging me into the depths. I wish we could pretend we never saw it, which is ridiculous. I want to hold it so tight that I never let go.

'I know,' I say. 'But the text message . . .? She said she was okay. She said not to worry.'

'It's been an entire day since she sent that. She *said* the weather was bad. What if she was heading back here while we were out today and she fell in? How would we know?'

Now it's my turn to be the one who keeps her cool. I have no choice. We can't both lose it. 'One of us needs to go to the police,' I say. 'Now. Tonight. We have to show them the scarf.'

'What do you mean *one of us*?' Her face is grey with panic.

'We can't both go. Somebody needs to stay here.'

'What? Why?' Clio's eyes are still wide and – I think – filled with tears.

'What if she's here somewhere?' I ask. 'What if she only just dropped it?'

'Eleanor, no, it's too dark out here. It's too *dangerous*.'

I reach out with one free hand, grasping for Clio's warm fingers. She wraps both of her hands around mine and I swear I can feel the pounding of her pulse, the panic that rushes through both of us. But I know that this makes sense. There's no point both of us going to police. 'I'll stay here,' I say emphatically. 'I'm wearing my good trainers. I won't go close to the water. I'll just check. If she fell, she might have banged her head. She might not even be *in* the water. There's that patch of beach over there—'

Clio spins unsteadily and starts to walk back towards the house, her teeth chattering. The falling night has brought with it another wave of coldness, so cold it feels like it might snow. I don't remember expecting temperatures this low and it feels, somehow, like Loch Aven is taunting us.

I grip the scarf tight and hurry – carefully – to follow Clio indoors.

'It makes sense,' I say.

'I don't want to go by myself. I don't want you to stay here by *yourself*.'

The lights of the lounge hurt my eyes after the stillness of the lake and I blink a handful of times before I can see the scarf without a blur of glitter dancing in my eyes. It's definitely Kay's scarf, beautiful, although it's been stained dark by the water and there are pieces of bracken stuck to it, a twig too.

'Clio, you've got to get a grip.' I carry the scarf to the sink and lay it on the small draining board. 'This is about doing what's best for Michaela.'

'How do you know what's best?' Clio cries.

I turn and realise she's fully shaking now, her whole body trembling. I leave the scarf where it is and rush to her, folding her in my arms. I can feel the vibration of her worry deep inside me as she shakes. I hold her until she calms down.

'Okay?' I whisper.

She pulls back and lets out a jagged sigh. 'Sorry. Yes.'

'Will you be okay driving?' I ask.

She nods.

'Do you want to call the police first? You have the number he gave you in your phone, right?' I go back to the draining board to pick up the scarf, seized by the overwhelming urge to check it for blood, but there's nothing on it except the murky water and the dirt and the twigs.

Clio says nothing.

I turn and she's stood holding her phone, a confused look on her face. She glances up and her gaze is a question mark.

'What?' I prompt.

Clio holds her phone up. I'm too far away to see, so I move closer. It looks like a photo. Of the loch?

I'm still trying to work out what exactly I'm looking at when Clio says, 'She posted that today.'

'Who?' I grab Clio's phone. 'What?'

It is a photograph on Instagram. Taken during the day, grey sky just visible over the tops of the towering pine trees, the water dark and glassy. It is definitely this lake, Loch Aven, viewed from somewhere close to Loch House.

And it was posted by Michaela half an hour ago.

Eleanor

'What?' I breathe. 'I don't . . . I don't understand. How did she post it? Why? Is it a photo she took on Saturday?'

Clio shrugs. 'I've been checking her socials, just in case. I don't know.'

I scroll down. The caption, no hashtags, reads simply: *This place is bliss. How lucky am I?*

Clio snatches her phone back and navigates to Facebook, but there are no new posts on Michaela's profile.

I dig my own phone out of my pocket and pull up my call history, clicking Michaela's name from the list, though I only have one bar of signal. It rings. And rings.

'She's still not answering.'

'This doesn't make any fucking sense,' Clio grunts.

'Maybe it was scheduled?'

'Can you even schedule to Insta? I didn't think you could.' Clio is pacing now and I can feel the same urge building in me. It's an urge to run, to not stop running until I'm back home in my bed where hopefully everything will start to make some goddamn sense.

'I don't know.'

'What do we do about the police now?' Clio asks. 'If we take them the scarf and they see this post . . . They'll just think she buggered off and left us.'

'You've still got to go,' I say. 'I don't care. We have to tell them.'

'Call her mum again.' Maybe you'll get through this time.

'What's Joy going to do? She's in bloody Devon!'

'Call *your* mum then,' Clio says wildly. She's run her hands through her hair so many times that the shorter side is standing up of its own free will. 'Call somebody.'

None of this makes any sense at all. It feels like I'm going crazy. It feels like every time Charlotte would tell me something wasn't true, even though I knew it was.

'Is it genuinely possible she *has* just . . . dumped us? That she lied in her text when she said she was lost and she's just somewhere else?' Saying the words sounds ridiculous, but what about the rest of this situation isn't ridiculous?

'What do you mean?' Clio pauses mid-stride.

'I mean . . . She listened to that podcast. She said she had some things to sort out before she told us what she had planned. Maybe she knew about those missing girls,' I say. 'Maybe she heard about them and . . . I don't know. Decided to do her own podcast?'

'You're supposed to be the fucking psychologist and *that* is where you've landed?' Clio frowns. 'Michaela wouldn't do that. And where the hell would she even go if she's meant to be *investigating* the loch? She didn't even take the car.' Clio's voice is inching higher and louder with every second. It looks like she's about to explode. And she's right: I'm just clutching at straws.

'Okay, how would you explain the picture then?' I ask.

'It's more likely that she found a way to schedule it than that she's friend-dumping us, that much I do know.' Clio opens her phone and looks at the post again. 'It's definitely taken from this angle, on the dock. Or maybe – just to the right, you know, where the bank is?'

'So, it could have been taken today then? Earlier, while we were out?' My brain begins to whir. The whole weekend has turned into a blur of hours, cold weather and rain, but might Michaela have been around the house today? Could she have fallen into the water after posting it?

'I guess. You can't really see what the weather is doing, only that it's daytime. There were patches of the day on Saturday where it didn't rain. She could have taken it then.'

I rub my hands over my face. 'Okay,' I say. 'We're not getting anywhere. You need to go, drive to the police station and see if somebody is there. Maybe they'll spot something we missed. Tell them about the text message too.'

Clio does as I ask, reluctantly but quickly. She takes the scarf from the counter carefully, almost as if she's carrying a carton of eggs, and holds the car keys tight so they don't jangle.

'It's going to be okay,' I say firmly, with more belief than I feel.

Clio looks at me, her green eyes dark and what's left of the firelight creating hollows in her cheekbones. I realise that this might be the longest I've known Clio to ever go without cracking a joke.

'Is it?' she asks.

With Clio gone, Loch House takes on a haunted quality. I don't hang around for longer than it takes to put a bigger coat on over my jacket and tighten my shoelaces, and then

221

I head outside. Dark has well and truly fallen now. Two days since we last saw Kay. I don't know where the hours have gone but I'd give almost anything to get them – and Michaela – back.

I walk with my phone torch pointed at the ground. Everything is different in the dark, even the blades of grass seem sharper. I take my time, placing each foot carefully in case I do something stupid like roll my ankle, stopping every few steps to scan around with the torch.

I don't really know what I'm looking for, what I'm hoping to find, but there is nothing but dirt and grass and water. Shock spikes through me as a flapping sound bursts through the quiet and I catch whatever it is – a bat, I think – with my light. It throws me off balance and my stomach drops as my foot slips, sand and dirt skidding. The bouncing light catches on a patch of dark water and for a second – one long, hideous second – I think it's Michaela's body, floating on the surface.

Algae, I realise. Not hair and a dark jacket. Just algae.

I stop, panting. Brief relief makes me sick, followed by a fresh, slamming fear. This is no good. I don't know what I was thinking. Even if Michaela is out here, I'm hardly going to find her in the dark.

I hurry back to the house, kicking aside an old beer can with a rattle that echoes in my bones.

Back inside, the fire is burning low, so I add another log, poking it until the flames flare, then I add two more. It hisses and spits, like my temper. I take a deep breath and slowly sink onto the sofa. This place felt like home to me when I first arrived, but now it feels claustrophobic, like a prison. Just this one room, those bloody glass doors, and, outside, the loch pressing against my consciousness like a wall.

The minutes tick past. I open and close Instagram, scrolling through apps which won't load. I finally get Michaela's profile up again and load the picture after several failed attempts. There are still no comments, but there are twelve likes. I screenshot the picture and the caption.

It's long past dinnertime when Clio returns. I'm sitting on the floor in front of the fire when I hear the roar of the car engine and then long minutes of silence stretch. When she finally comes in through the door, her hair is ruffled, tears still streaking her cheeks.

'What did they say?' I blurt.

Outside, the wind is picking up. I can hear it rushing through the trees the way you can hear the ocean inside of a seashell.

'They asked me,' Clio says coolly, 'if Michaela is a fan of practical jokes.'

'What? Are you kidding?'

'Nope.' She slams herself down onto the sofa and kicks her shoes off angrily. 'They asked me if I was *sure* she wasn't trying to mess with us. Because the fact that she's posted on Instagram means she must be fine as it's unlikely it's a scheduled post.'

'And did you tell them Michaela isn't like that?' I demand. Anger burns hot in my belly, hot like the fire licking at my back. 'Did you show them the scarf?'

'Yup. They took it, said they'll look into it.' Clio's face is a mix of anger and sadness, the same feelings warring inside me right now. 'They said they will keep looking, but there's nothing yet that indicates Kay is in any trouble. It's just a lost scarf.'

Horror curdles beneath all my anger.

'And,' Clio goes on, 'get this: somebody matching Kay's

223

description was seen in the village yesterday when the search parties went out for the campers.'

'*When?*'

'Morning,' Clio says. She shrugs angrily. 'They didn't give me details, just said somebody in one of the groups helping the police said they thought maybe they saw her – but I don't know. And all that proves is she was in the village yesterday morning, if it even proves that, because what if they were thinking about Saturday instead? And, frankly, it's not yesterday I'm worried about any more. She's had two days since Saturday to . . . I dunno. To get hurt? Lost?'

I don't know what to say. If Michaela was in the village, could she have been trying to help those campers and then . . . what? Wandered off? Decided to go somewhere else? All her stuff is here.

But if the police aren't worried . . . does that mean we're still overreacting? *Could* Michaela be playing a joke on us?

I don't know any more.

'So now what?' Clio interrupts my thoughts.

I wrap my arms around my knees. 'I guess we wait.'

At some point, Clio opens one of the bottles of wine we had left over from Saturday night and comes to me holding two huge mugs filled to the brim with it. I take mine hesitantly, but after the first sip, I find that I'm craving something – anything – that might knead the tension from my muscles. I've forgotten what it feels like to not be scared, and somehow, suddenly, the wine seems like a great idea.

We don't laugh and joke as we would normally, but the wine helps to mellow some of the panic that's been hanging in the air. Clio bundles her legs up in the blankets and closes her eyes. I sit and watch the flames as they dance and roll.

My thoughts tumble towards the day I first met Michaela and Clio. We'd moved into the on-campus flat before anybody else and the whole place was dead silent, except for us and laughter – which was easy right from the start.

Clio was so unprepared she hadn't even brought bed linen with her, and our first conversation included her asking if she could borrow a set of mine. Michaela had already got her room set up when I arrived, posters of Paris and New York on the walls and stacks of hefty books. She had deferred a year to figure out what she wanted to do and had spent the last ten months working to save money towards her fees for the law degree, her mum bursting with pride.

Michaela was so confident and collected. Clio was the free spirit, driven by stories. I was the serious, determined one; I knew that I wanted to study psychology, to go into adoption counselling, driven by some childish need to understand my own childhood. It had seemed so easy, then. And now here we are.

Clio and I drink until there is no wine left and we are bone-tired with worry. I've run my battery down twice trying to get back onto Facebook or Instagram. I'm still trying to load them again while I brush my teeth and wash my face, every action feeling pointless and somehow so important that I do it correctly, that I change nothing about our normal routine. Not that anything feels normal any more.

We were supposed to be going home tomorrow. We'll have to choose if we're going to stay here a while and find out if we can extend our stay. Maybe if we can work out where the photograph was taken, we can find a trail to follow Michaela's steps.

My thoughts swirl like the water down the plughole. I comb my hair and tie it back and I meet Clio as I'm coming out of the bathroom. She's wearing her pyjamas and a hoodie, and it's only then that I realise how cold it is upstairs. Every time I move, it feels a little like icy hands are tracing my spine.

I head back down to the lounge one more time to make sure the fire is totally extinguished and switch out the lamps, plunging the room into darkness. I pull up the screenshot of the Instagram post, hoping maybe I will see something we've missed. A hint. A clue. But there's nothing. Nothing except that one picture and that stupid, stupid caption that seems worse, somehow, imprinted as it is in the blue glare from my screen.

How lucky am I?

TUESDAY

Eleanor

I'm tired enough that I manage to get a couple of hours sleep, but when I wake, it feels like I was hardly unconscious at all. My thoughts are crowded with images of Michaela, her body floating in Loch Aven like some kind of modern-day Ophelia, or surrounded by others too, women whose faces my mind refuses to complete so they are left blank and staring, black eyes and long, wicked mouths.

I am numb with worry. I know I should be asking questions, about Michaela, about those other women, about this town and the loch and *everything*, but for once in my life I am completely without curiosity – or, no, that's not true. I am so filled with fear I am paralysed by it.

When I finally drag myself downstairs at just after eight, Clio isn't awake yet. We've got no food in the house except for a single stale croissant, but I don't want it anyway. My stomach is churning, but when I wretch over the toilet, all that comes up is bile stained with wine. I wipe my mouth and make a cup of tea.

'Jesus, you look like you slept less than I did.' Clio pads

downstairs dressed in baggy high-waisted jeans and a knitted sweater. Her dark hair looks greasy, but she's tucked the longer side that brushes her jaw behind her ear and she rubs at her nose sleepily.

We set about making another tea, which feels ridiculous, but I know we'll need the fortification for the day ahead, and when we're done, Clio lets out a sigh that's so full of everything I've been feeling that tears prick behind my eyes.

'Oh, don't start,' Clio says, not unkindly. 'If you start, I'll start.'

'There must be more we can do to figure this out,' I murmur, wiping my eyes. 'Michaela is out there somewhere and I'm fast reaching the point where I don't care what the reason is, I just want to know *where she is*. I want her to be safe, I want her to be okay, but none of this makes any sense. It's been two days, Clio. Two fucking days. If everything was totally fine with her, surely she'd be back by now. What if she's having some kind of breakdown?'

Or worse. I don't say that.

Clio slumps against the counter in the kitchenette, defeated.

'I need to go back to the police,' I say. 'Maybe I can be firm with them. They've got to take this seriously. What if . . . somebody stole Michaela's phone?' This is one of the many thoughts that have plagued me overnight. What if her phone was stolen, what if Dan followed us here and him and Michaela are hiding away in a little hotel somewhere having a seriously ill-advised meet-up, what if Michaela didn't *want* Dan to follow her? What if, what if?

Clio is silent, but I can tell the suggestion that she wasn't firm enough with the police last night rankles her. I know what Clio is like, though. As soon as they mentioned that somebody had seen Michaela in the village on Sunday, she would have backed down, because, at the end of the day and despite her childish obstinance, she always prefers it when somebody else takes the lead.

'I think I should go this morning,' I affirm, 'and you can stay here. I've been thinking we should go through Michaela's things, see if there's anything that might give us an idea where she is. Maybe she made a note of the name of that podcast? I'd feel better if we could find it and have a listen.'

'I don't want to split up again,' she says.

'Why?'

'Because I don't feel *safe*, El.' She's working her jaw, trying to figure out how to express the same feeling I can sense brewing in my bones. The sense that if Michaela *didn't* go wherever she went willingly, didn't take that photograph yesterday, then somebody else might be responsible for both. 'I don't like that we're totally isolated out here,' she says. 'And the police don't even seem to care.'

'That's not true. They're just busy—'

'It feels like it!' Clio runs her hands through her hair and storms towards the doors looking out over the loch. 'For god's sake, El. I'm not trying to fight with you. I'm just freaking myself out.' She turns back and I see the horror on her face. 'Young women are the prey in so, so many stories. We get lured into woods or conned into magic bargains; we get sold and we get trampled and we get *killed*. And I know they're just stories, I really do, but, fuck . . . There's truth in them, too.'

The word *killed* makes my blood run cold. It is a dark, nasty word. But as much as I understand where Clio is coming from, none of this changes my mind. There are two

231

of us and we can cover twice as much ground if we split up again today. We need to get to the bottom of this.

'I won't be long,' I say. 'I promise.'

I don't have much more luck with the police than Clio did. The text message and the Instagram post together are damning evidence that Michaela is probably just doing what young people do: making poor decisions. I sit in front of the same police officer as before, whose expression is dark – he looks like he might have slept less than I have – and listen as he explains, patiently, how one hiker has been found in the woods and had to be rushed to the hospital due to exposure. Another has a broken ankle.

'Is this supposed to make me feel any better?' I demand, anger simmering barely below the surface. My eyes are scratchy and I'm *this* close to losing my temper. 'Your incompetence – and your lack of resources – isn't exactly filling me with hope right now. We heard about those missing girls all those years ago. What makes you think that something similar hasn't happened to Michaela?'

'Those were local girls,' the officer says coldly. 'As far as I understand it, there was no evidence of foul play then, either. Sometimes when people disappear around here, they don't want to be found.'

'Is that what you're suggesting happened to Kay?'

'Based on what your other friend showed me last night, it looks very much like she's just out and about enjoying herself without you both.' His tone is matter of fact, but it still stings.

'She wouldn't do that! Why won't you listen to me?'

'You said,' he begins, checking his notes, 'that she does, in fact, have a history of this sort of behaviour.'

232

'Not like this!' I explode. 'Don't you understand? We're worried because she hasn't been acting like herself. She's . . .' I start to mention the training contract, the job, Dan and the break-up, then hesitate, but if it could help us to figure out where she's gone . . . 'She's been having a rough time lately,' I say, dialling my voice back down to a normal level. 'She lost a job – well, no . . . Sort of. Her job prospects have changed. When she told us, she seemed . . . Not unbothered, but like she had other things she was thinking about.'

'Things like what?' he says, his voice still verging on bored. Perhaps he is trying to make me feel better.

'Like – I don't know. But she was distracted. And she just went through a break-up. It got messy. I don't know all of the details but her ex was acting a bit weird for a while, not quite stalking her but . . . She said he's fine now, only a bit awkward, but she didn't even seem especially bothered by any of that either. '

The officer shifts in his seat, his curly hair flopping across his forehead. His expression softens as I calm down. 'Look,' he says. 'I don't know your friend like you do, obviously. But if it walks like a duck and quacks like a duck, maybe it's just a duck? If she didn't seem that bothered about losing her job, or breaking up with this ex, or whatever it is that's going on, and now she's here letting her hair down, maybe she's just trying to find herself. She wouldn't be posting on social media if she was in any kind of trouble, would she?'

'No,' I acquiesce. 'But—'

'I'm not saying we're not taking this seriously. We've got people out in the woods right now,' he goes on. 'And we've got boats on the loch too. If your pal so much as stumbles into our search area, we'll know about it. All I'm saying is there's every chance she's just taking some time for herself. Don't you think?'

I try to argue again, but it's clear I'm going to get nowhere new. He can't change my mind, though. He might not think there's anything to worry about but I know he's wrong.

By the time I leave the station, I have no idea what time it is and my phone battery is already running low. I've been cycling through app after app, half praying Michaela will have posted again and half praying that she won't have so the police will have to take us seriously. Even after this latest conversation, I'm not entirely convinced that they think Michaela is in any danger at all. There's this feeling hovering over all of it, like *Not yet*. And I don't know what it will take before they start to believe that this is beyond her usual independent quests for fun, that she *can't* be safe, that something is going on here and whatever it is isn't good.

The sickness rises in my throat again, bile stinging, and I realise that caffeine and not very much food is a poor combination. It doesn't matter that I'm not hungry; I can't help Michaela if I fall down and faint in the middle of the street. So instead of heading back to the car straight away, I walk the short distance along the main street until I come to a coffee shop. We passed it on Saturday – and I remember Michaela pointing out the misspelled sign in the window and Clio laughing.

I duck in out of the cold air. Though it feels a bit warmer than it did first thing this morning, my fingers are still numb and my stomach feels as if it's been filled with lead. I wander to the counter in a daze. I'm thinking about the police officer, how I can't even remember his name, how I'm not sure I gave him *all* of the details. I'm picking apart our conversation, dissecting every piece of it.

Logically, I know this is ridiculous. I'm usually fairly confident about my ability to be objective – after all, I spent years in private therapy paid for by my parents so I could be impartial, about myself and my history. I learnt all of the tricks, how to make my mind quiet and focus on the things I could control. But all of a sudden it feels like I'm the same self-conscious kid I was once, who couldn't get over the fact that her mother abandoned her, who couldn't distance herself from the deep, wrenching loneliness and feelings of unbelonging long enough to see the nervousness and anxiety for what it was.

Now it feels like my anxiety, once pushed down to a deep dark cave in my chest, is back and in overdrive. Who gave me the right to become a counsellor to help other people? I can't even help myself when something goes wrong, never mind helping Michaela.

How am I supposed to help *her* when I can't even be sure I've given enough information to the police? Maybe I should have pushed harder. Maybe we shouldn't have told them about the Instagram post.

I'm so deep in my spiral that I don't notice the woman behind the counter. When I finally hear her, it looks as if she's already spoken a couple of times – and there are now people behind me in the queue. Guiltily, I scoot forward, pulling my scarf down from over my chin. I place my order with the young, blonde barista, asking for the first thing that comes to mind. I pay, though I can hardly remember what I've ordered by the time I'm done. I need, as Michaela would put it, to calm the fuck down.

I head to the end of the bar to wait for my coffee in its

cardboard to-go cup and whatever toastie I've somehow ended up ordering, and I've just pulled my phone out to text Clio – belatedly wondering if I should get her something, and also desperately hopeful that she's managed to find something that might be a clue to Michaela's whereabouts – when a second barista sweeps out of a back room holding a thick slab of chocolate cake. She stops dead in her tracks when she sees me.

'Oh my god,' she says, clapping her free hand to her chest in a joking gesture of fright. 'Jesus. You look just like her. You made me jump.'

She makes to move away, but I shift into her path.

'Sorry, what?'

She blinks. 'Oh, nothing.' She's thinking about leaving again, the cake probably on its way to somebody who is patiently waiting – but she stops. 'It's just that you look *so similar* to somebody I used to know. Must be a doppelgänger thing. Ha. Kind of uncanny.'

This woman doesn't treat me the same as the other people here. She laughs and it's a warm and inviting sound, and strangely it makes me want to cry. It makes me feel more like myself again. There is, I realise, something to her accent that's different too. Perhaps once upon a time she didn't belong here either.

'Who do I look like?' I ask.

'She used to live in Blackhills,' the woman says. 'A long time ago, when I first moved here, back when I worked at the library on the weekends. Are you sure you're not Scottish?' She smiles. 'Might have some Scots blood in you somewhere.'

She must notice the next wave of panic that sweeps through me, the way my skin goes clammy and I start to

236

breathe heavy and fast, because she cocks her head, shifting the plate of cake to her other hand.

'Are you all right?' she asks. 'You look a bit . . . peaky.'

I massage my forehead, a headache brewing, sickness churning. My chest hurts. But she's given me an idea, so I ignore the question.

'The library,' I ask. 'Where is it?'

Eleanor

The library isn't far away – like everything in Blackhills – but I take the car so I can leave it right outside. I stop in the car park for long enough to inhale the toastie, texting Clio again in case she missed the last one if the signal dipped out. I still feel sick, but the headache is wearing off. With a numbness that often comes only from distance, I realise that that was my first panic attack in over twelve years.

The library is somehow more imposing than the police station. It's an old building, like they all seem to be around here, made from the same grey stone with the same peaked black roof. It's got big round windows, postered with drawings done by children of all ages, and an old-school revolving door that reminds me of the library my parents used to take me to as a kid. The first story I ever remember connecting with was Roald Dahl's *Matilda*, about the girl who loved to read and had special abilities, whose family hated her so much she made a different life for herself. And who had found a loving family in an unlikely place. I was envious of her sometimes, and comforted by her the rest.

Big-headed, perhaps, but I liked to think that I had special abilities too. I was, as my parents always said, very *sensitive*. I was good at reading people, at connecting with them. It felt like a superpower.

I'm wishing for that old confidence as I stride into the library and head straight for the check-out desk, where a librarian is sat fiddling with a clunky old computer. She is perhaps in her early fifties, auburn hair cut short and curled around her ears. Her face is morphed in a deep frown, her lips puckered in distaste as she smacks the side of the computer.

'Goddammit,' she mutters. 'Think I must have magnets in my fingers for the amount of bloody use this thing is.' She glances up. 'Oh. Hello.'

'Hi.' I look around. To the left, there are the book stacks, more than I'd have thought would fit in here from the front of the building. To the right, there is a small table and a collection of mismatched chairs, plus a beanbag which is currently in use by a young mother breastfeeding one child while the other browses the lower shelves.

'Can I help you?' the librarian prompts. 'This isn't the tourist information.'

'I didn't think you had any tourist information.'

'We don't,' she says drily, a ghost of a smile on her lips. 'What can I do you for? Need some light reading to stave off village boredom?'

'How does everybody know I'm not from here just by looking at me?' I mutter.

The librarian barks a laugh and this seems genuine enough. 'You've got a city air,' she says, weighing me up. There's something in her expression I can't read, a wistful sort of sadness.

I'm sure I look a state, my hair greasy, my clothes crumpled. I haven't changed my jumper in two days because this is the warmest one I brought with me, but I've been sweating. I shift uncomfortably.

'You look expensive.' She sniffs exaggeratedly, and then laughs again. 'Oh, I'm only pulling your leg. My sister, Beth, works at the pub. Word travels fast round here. Besides, pretty sure I recognise everybody around here by face or by feature.' She pauses for a second as she says that, then shrugs. 'Anyway, folks around here could do well to read more and gossip less, but what can you do?'

'Right,' I say.

'Anyway, what *can* I do for you if you're not here to find a book? Not that you can check anything out without a library card anyway—'

'I don't want to check anything out. I was wondering if you might have any old newspaper archives here? Just for the local paper, or something like that.'

'Whatever do you want those for?' The librarian raises an eyebrow, suddenly serious. 'Musty old papers, a glam girl like you?'

'I want to look at . . . what happened here. With those girls going missing. Your sister told us about what happened, sort of. I would like more details and I can't find anything online because I don't know what I'm looking for.' This sounds stupid when I say it out loud. It occurs to me I could have played this whole thing differently. I could have tried asking for names, details, so I'd know what to search for – but she'd probably have clammed up as fast as everybody else. I start again, softer this time. 'You've probably heard, but my friend who we came here with – we can't find her. Some people suggested she was helping find those

241

campers, but . . . Well. I'm not so sure. And she was listening to some sort of podcast before, and I wonder if it was something to do with Blackhills' history. And if it was . . . We just . . .' I trail off. 'I don't know.'

'I did hear about that,' the librarian says. She shakes her head. 'You must be worried sick.'

'We are,' I say breathlessly. It's the first time it feels like anybody has acknowledged how awful this is for Clio and me. Even if Michaela is fine – she *is* fine – this whole experience is scooping me out.

'Not sure you'll find anything remotely useful, but you're welcome to knock yourself out with the papers – we don't have anything fancy, just boxes of 'em in the back. They take up far, far too much space, but I haven't the heart to throw anything away. My dad used to run the local newspaper and me ma ran this library, so we kept . . . pretty much everything. Come on.'

She heaves herself off her chair and shuffles off with surprising speed. I hurry to catch up, stepping around the stacks and breathing in the old book smell that will always remind me of my mum and her library of teaching books, storybooks. It reminds me of *home*. I find myself getting choked up again, overwhelmed with homesickness for my childhood, but I blink hard to park the tears, furious at myself, and Michaela, and this stupid little village in the middle of fucking nowhere.

We go through one door and the librarian points me down a narrow corridor. There's a toilet to the left, a staffroom to the right, and then a door with a big metal handle at the end.

'That one.' She points. 'The light switch is on the right. Take all the time you want, just put them back in the right boxes when you're done.'

The door closes behind her as she goes and the electric lights flicker overhead. The corridor seems to stretch endlessly, narrowing every second I look at it. Instinctively, I pull my phone from my pocket and check my messages, hoping to hear from Clio. If she's found something useful in Michaela's bags, some note or clue or *anything*, then I won't even have to be here any more.

But there isn't *any* signal in here.

'For God's sake,' I mutter, moving forward. I'm committed now, though I have no idea what I'm even hoping to find. No sense going back until I've at least tried to look.

The door at the end of the corridor is unlocked and I find the light switch exactly where the librarian said it would be. The room trembles to life, wan and silver-toned under the strip lights overhead. It feels like a concrete bunker, pale brick walls painted white, a grey carpet that has seen better years, and it's lined with shelves – the huge metal kind that always make me think of industrial warehouses.

And on the shelves are boxes. There must be a hundred here. They're all dated, marked with labels and, thankfully, in meticulous order. There aren't just boxes for the local paper, either. On closer inspection, I find a few marked *Council Meetings: MINUTES, 1998–2008* and another with a faded label reading *Blackhills Fundraisers: M & L Webster co-chair*. I skip past these and head further into the shelves, counting back the years. I don't really know how far I'm going – twenty-odd years is a lot of years to cover.

I pick a box at random, knowing only that whatever happened was around twenty-five years ago – so probably the early nineties – and skim through the newspapers, which are well-preserved, although their ink is beginning to fade.

243

I'm thinking that whatever I'm looking for will probably be front-page news, so I sort through the box quickly and then move onto the next one, month by month, working my way back in time. It's like a time capsule for village life in Scotland formatted into a weekly Sunday newspaper.

The sound of the heating through the vents lulls me as I search and I feel myself start to relax a little bit, half my brain fixating on the panic attack of earlier, searching my body for new aches and pains, tightness in my shoulders and the muscles of my chest; the other half is scanning front page after front page: a new local charity drive called *Saturday Night Quizzers* at the pub raises £1,346; a hit-and-run kills two people and injures a third; a storm is so bad it knocks the power out for days . . .

I'm starting to think I might have missed something, perhaps I should have started in the mid-eighties, when a headline catches my eye.

It only takes a second – just one second – and then I'm back in full-scale panic mode again. This time it's different, though.

I scan the headline again.

Search for Missing Blackhills Women Continues

There, right in the centre of the page, are three photographs, all lined up in a row. Three young women, one petite and blonde, the other with fiery curls, and the third . . . The third one stops me in my tracks.

Mid-twenties, she has long dark hair, straight as a pin, and a fine aquiline nose. Her eyes are pale, and so is her skin. In the photograph, she is smiling, although there's something reserved about the expression, something intelligent and shy at the same time.

It isn't the headline that has upset me. Or even the

collection of photos, these three young women who disappeared and haunted this village forever. It's not the first or
the second woman, though I know I'll remember their faces.

It's *her*. The third woman.

Because the face that's staring right at me from this
twenty-five-year-old newspaper is so familiar it might as
well be my own.

Janie

Then

Janie has been replaying the first day Rebecca came to stay with her over and over in her mind since Rebecca disappeared. It's hard to focus, especially with the baby taking up most of her time – she still thinks of the girl as *the baby* even though she has a name, all because they both spent so long calling her that after she was born.

Janie still isn't very good with her. She's not a baby person. This surprised her. She thought she would be great at it. Janie's spent so many years being a people person that she sort of expected that raising a kid would be like second nature – but, actually, Janie has realised she doesn't like children at all. Not even this baby, who in the end brought Rebecca back to her in a way neither of them expected.

But when the baby cries, it hurts her, physically almost, and after several months of so little sleep, her eyeballs feel like sandpaper. She was already losing the will and that was before the unthinkable happened.

And now Rebecca is gone.

At first, Janie was worried sick. She paced and cried. She thought about calling the police, but she couldn't do it. Instead, she spoke to Rebecca's mother, making sure she knew that Rebecca had been coming to see her that day. Janie never knew the details of Rebecca's plan, only that she wanted to talk to her mum. To let her know she was 'back in Scotland'.

They'd argued about it that morning. Rebecca had been in such a strange mood for two or three days, grating Janie's nerves and pacing like a cat in heat.

'For God's sake, Bec,' Janie had snapped. 'What's got into you?'

'Cabin fever,' Rebecca had said.

It was the sort of conversation they'd had before, about how Rebecca could only stay hiding out in Janie's little house for so long before she would deplete all of her savings, before there would be nothing left to do except either move on or go home. But Janie had started to believe – how stupid it was – that maybe they could just carry on like this forever.

This time was different, though. Janie could see it in the way Rebecca's expression shifted, flitting between anger and frustration and a deep, painful longing that sent a spike right through Janie's heart.

'I can't keep doing this, Janie,' she'd said. 'I hate that I'm such a burden to you.'

'You're not a burden.' Janie had hated herself for not being able to admit it even after all of this, that hiding out here with Rebecca and the baby had been wonderful, yes, but really damn hard too. Janie had put everything on the line for her, Rebecca knew that, and still Janie didn't regret it.

'Janie, I *can't*. This isn't going to work forever. I'm sorry – I know.' She'd put down the fresh bottle she'd made for the baby and turned around. 'I need to go and see my mum.'

Janie had wanted to ask about Rebecca's dad, but she had learned not to do that. And now . . . she's gone. All of this is hard, so hard, when nobody knows about the baby. Nobody knows that Rebecca has been living here in Blackdale for nearly a year. Everything is based on lies. When Rebecca went into labour, Janie drove her miles and miles, so she could have her baby in the anonymity of a city. Janie has been in charge of shopping, driving to towns she's never had cause to visit before, just to buy baby supplies where nobody will see her. It's all so *dishonest*.

She knows she should tell people. The police, especially. But somebody has already reported Bec missing, either her uncle or her mum, and the baby is Rebecca's secret. And it *is* a secret. One she's not sure anybody is ready to hear. Rebecca still has a reputation in Blackhills, among their friends and their friends' families. She is the golden girl, bright and sweet and ambitious. She is not the sort of person who has a baby because of an affair. With a married man, no less. She is not the sort of person who runs off to live with her best friend – her friend who's so hopelessly fucking in love with her that she will keep whatever secrets she wants her to.

Janie doubts telling anybody would help anyway. They have an idea of Rebecca in their heads, and now it doesn't matter what Janie or anybody else says, that won't change. If Rebecca doesn't turn up . . . well, that will be different.

At first, the hours after Rebecca's disappearance had trickled by. Long, painful hours, the baby on one hip and her phone pressed between her neck and her chin. Twelve hours gone. Twenty-four. Thirty-six. Now she has to think in days not hours, and she still has to feed the baby. She's called in sick to work. She's even dropped the baby off with a childminder who doesn't know them once or twice – something Rebecca would kill her for if she was here – so she can spend another hour or two, or three, walking the lengths of Loch Aven.

She knows Rebecca went there. Rebecca *always* goes there. She might have been planning to see her mum, but Janie knows the loch would have called to her. Whenever things get too much for Rebecca, whenever she regrets the choices she's made, the loch is there to listen. Not Janie any more, though she's made her peace with that. Janie knows Rebecca sneaks out at night sometimes, borrows Janie's car and takes it to the loch. She comes back smelling of damp lakeside air, mud in her hems and bark under her fingernails, her voice ragged from crying.

For long months, Janie has consoled herself. She might not have Rebecca's voice any more, but she has her presence, and while it might not last, it will be – *has* to be – enough. Turns out she had just buried her anger deep. At Rebecca, yes, but at *him* too.

The baby hasn't been asleep very long. Janie should sit and make another list. Of other places Rebecca might go. It's pointless, though, because Janie knows Rebecca wouldn't lie about planning to go to Blackhills that day. She was definitely going to see her mum, at least, and probably her Uncle Paul. Janie knows she's always been very close to him.

Janie suspects she was going to tell them about the baby.

Every time this thought passes through her, she feels a

chill. A proper bone-deep chill. It was so easy to fall into a routine with Rebecca and the kid, easier than she'd ever thought it would be to settle into a new kind of normal when she agreed to let Rebecca stay. It was easy, honestly, to forget that there was a world outside. Rebecca learned to keep to herself, and the baby kept both of them busy enough that they didn't need much else. Janie thought Rebecca was content. She was obviously wrong.

Things have been bubbling away for some time now, a quiet sort of resentment building between the two of them. This wasn't the sort of life either of them had planned: just the two of them and her daughter, together in this tiny house, wasting days and weeks and years while they try to figure out what future they actually want.

And now Rebecca is gone.

Janie's thoughts play and play on that first day Rebecca came. How nervous she'd seemed. In the months since, Janie has put that down to embarrassment. Rebecca had found it hard enough to talk about the affair without talking about the baby too. Now though . . . Now Janie is starting to wonder if Rebecca wasn't maybe . . . afraid.

The question is, what was she afraid of? The future she saw unravelling before her, lonely and full of hidden traps, or something – someone – else?

Janie makes another cup of tea she probably won't drink, barely making a sound as she pads around in threadbare slippers so she doesn't wake the kid. Her eyes are so tired that they're swollen and she presses cool hands to them, trying to push down the sick feeling of worry that surges whenever the baby is asleep, whenever she has minutes to kill, whenever her mind starts to wander and she feels like she's not doing *enough*.

She closes her eyes and tries not to picture all of the places Rebecca might be: in a ditch somewhere, lying with her lovely dark hair all matted, or worse, dragged into the depths of the grimy waters of the loch. She'd rather think that Rebecca has simply had enough and abandoned them, walked into the woods and walked and walked and not stopped until she got somewhere far, far away. But Janie knows that whatever was going on inside Rebecca's head, she wouldn't do that. She loves the baby with all of herself; Janie has seen that since the moment she was born, and sensed it before even that. As unnatural a caregiver as Janie is, Rebecca has been the opposite, taking to motherhood as though it was what she was made for.

Besides, it's been four days now. If Rebecca was safe, well, she would have at least told Janie where she was, of that much she's sure.

A knock at the door startles her, sends her heart to clanging in her chest. It's *her* knock. Rebecca's. Tap tap – tap.

Janie hurtles to her feet, dragging the door open with a swinging arc that surprises both herself and the person on the other side.

She stops. It's not Rebecca.

'I've come for the child.' There's a man standing in the doorway. It's been years since she last saw him. She hadn't thought she would ever see him at her door. Janie had forgotten how tall he's always been. He towers over her now, although she hasn't grown much since back then. Panic and confusion engulf her in one. Why is he here?

She doesn't mean to, but without realising it she's stepped away from the door and suddenly he's there, still towering, taking up the space in her lounge so she can hardly breathe.

This isn't right. This is *her* space. He doesn't belong here. What does he want?

'What are you doing here?' she demands with an unfamiliar fire rising to smother her fear. Realisation dawns and the anger grows. 'Do you know where Rebecca is?'

'No,' he says calmly. 'You're her friend. Shouldn't *you* know? You know her better than I do.'

'She came to see you, didn't she?' Janie feels a dangerous storm brewing inside her. Rebecca's daughter is upstairs. Janie knows that whatever happens, she has to protect her. If she can just get rid of him – then she can think.

'She told you that?' he demands. There's something in his eyes.

'She didn't have to.'

'She didn't come,' he says. But he says it with an urgency that they both know means he's lying. He's a bad liar.

'Then where is she?' Janie pushes. 'You must have scared her. Made her run.' Even as she says this, she knows it can't be true. Rebecca would never leave without saying anything; she would never *ever* go without her daughter, the child she fought so hard for. The secret she kept. Janie stops. 'Wait.' It hits her like a punch to the gut, all of the breath whooshing out of her so she can't even think. 'If she didn't come to see you – how do you know about her daughter? Nobody knows but me—'

He moves before she can even process the blur, his hand connecting with her throat and pushing back – back against the wall. There's a thud that might be her head, but she's too focused on her breath, on trying to catch it. Stars spin across her vision, her brain fogging.

Dimly, she's aware that she's struggling, but he doesn't let up. He doesn't let go. She tries to claw at him, but she can only get his sleeve, his soft jumper slippery under her fingers. She wants to scream. She wants to but she can't.

Rebecca, she thinks. *I'm sorry I didn't protect you enough – I'm sorry you didn't feel like you could talk to me when it counted – I'm sorry.*

The last sound she hears is the baby, waking from her nap alone.

Eleanor

I stare at the newspaper. It takes me minutes before I can even lift this particular one out of the box I found it in and when I do, my hands recoil from the paper. I don't want to read it any more. I no longer want clues. Instead, I have the strongest urge to run.

The face that stares at me from the line-up of photographs is so similar to mine and I don't know how to feel about it, the emotions a mix of confusion and rage.

Her chin is longer, I think. My nose might be shorter. It is like looking into a mirror, but the mirror is one made of Clio's faerie glass. It isn't right.

My stomach wobbles and I wonder, absurdly, if I might be sick.

How is this possible? I've heard of doppelgängers. I read a story once about two women who looked so similar they decided to swap lives, just to see if anybody else might notice. This, though . . . This is something else. It's not as if we have the same features exactly – more as if the same artist drew us at different points in his career.

I never thought it possible I could come from anywhere but Durham, because that was where I was abandoned. But . . . is it possible we could be related somehow? A cousin or an aunt?

I don't actually have any idea where my parents came from.

I don't know where *I* came from.

I know my mother gave me up, abandoned me outside a police station like an unwanted gift. For many years, I've quietly assumed she might be dead. I thought she and my father were probably students who met at university, or maybe my dad was a businessman who she had no meaningful connection with, just a one-night stand.

Everything I thought I knew – how much of that is a fiction of my own creation? How much is based in truth?

I stare at the photograph again and a horrifying feeling unfurls in my chest, slimy and dark. She looks *so* much like me . . . Could this woman – this woman who nobody has seen for twenty-five years – be my *mother*?

I think back to Saturday night. To whatever Michaela had said I would 'appreciate'. How she said she had things she needed to check out. Is it so much of a stretch to wonder if she had seen a photograph of this woman's face after hearing about her on that podcast? What if *this* is why we are here?

Rage and disbelief swirl inside me. Why didn't she tell me? Did she want to make sure first? Is *that* why we're here? A reconnaissance mission of Michaela's creation?

Suddenly the world tilts again. Perhaps when Michaela texted and said she was being helpful she didn't mean she was looking for those campers, after all. What if she was trying to help me?

I pull the newspaper into my lap and read the front page, careful to keep my eyes just south of the photographs. Three women, all missing. The first – Rebecca – disappeared after reportedly visiting Blackhills after having been away for some time. She had been travelling abroad for a year or so and had not returned home to visit her parents since then. An unnamed source close to the family reported that she was back in Scotland and had been supposedly coming home for a visit and was even spotted in the village that day by her own uncle, but she never made it to her family home.

Those who knew her said that once she arrived in the area, it was likely she had headed for the loch before anything else, as she so often did when she lived here because it was her comfort, *her place*. Her uncle said that when he had seen Rebecca, she had seemed distracted, and that he tried calling to her, but she did not hear him. He assumed she was heading towards her parents' house, but later claimed it 'very likely' that she might have gone to the lake first – and perhaps fell into its icy depths . . .

I shiver. I'm cold enough that my hands shake, although I don't know how much of that is from shock or adrenaline. There is no mention in the article of her having a child, or a sibling. In fact, the details on Rebecca herself are scant, the focus on the other two women who went missing shortly after. I dump this newspaper aside after taking a snap of the cover on my phone, and then move backwards again.

I'm working with a renewed sense of purpose now, though it's not the purpose I had before. I ignore everything that doesn't catch my attention, flicking through each one in case there are other mentions of Rebecca. I'm only searching for her.

The next few issues of the newspaper are jumbled, some from months ahead slid in here as though somebody has been in this box before, ferreting for these scraps of information just as I am.

I find two more full articles in the end, plus a small snippet early on that references requests that if anybody spoke to Rebecca, or saw her in the village on the day she came home, could they let her parents know. I read the other articles carefully, once again attempting to glean information about her from them. *Rebecca*.

There is another photograph. In this one, she is smiling at the camera, this time without a hint of reservation; her dark hair is tucked back with a plastic headband that makes her look young and bright and charming. She is rosy-cheeked, her lips tinted pink and her blue eyes bright. She looks the way you might picture an angel, kindness and warmth evident in the easy way she sits for the photo, the curve of her lips.

I feel a rush of emotion that I can't name.

Am I making this up? Am I jumping to conclusions because of the last few days, the strangeness here in this town? Is it because I feel so unsettled, so lost and unlike myself, out of control and afraid? Or is it as plain as I can see – a biological connection that seems at once impossible and somehow . . . true?

There is little more information in this article than the last. I pause when I read one thing, though. Rebecca had worked here in the village up until she left to travel the world – in the farm shop owned by her parents. The name of the shop is the same one Michaela, Clio and I visited. The man who worked there, who left so quickly when Clio and I went in to ask about Michaela . . . Was that her father, or her uncle? And now I'm thinking about it – though maybe I'm making it up – the way he left so quickly: it was like he couldn't bear to look at me.

Another shiver wracks me and I have to tuck my hands under my armpits for a minute to try to warm them up. I glance around, slowly coming back to my senses. I have no idea how long I've been here. I pull my phone out again to check, but I can't even remember what time I got to the library, never mind how long I've been in this windowless room. There's still nothing from Clio, but there's also no signal.

I sift through a couple more of the newspapers but find only the same small-town rubbish I've been searching through for an age. I go back through to the articles about the other missing girls, the blonde and the redhead, and take photos of everything, then store the newspapers away carefully, almost as if I'm handling dynamite. My head spins and it's all I can do to just maintain my composure.

I want to ring my parents, but I know that won't help. I had a closed adoption so they won't know any more than I do, and I haven't even told them about Michaela yet. God, everything has just spiralled totally out of control.

I want to ring somebody. Anybody. I've got a desperate urge to post on social media, to ring the police or the adoption agency, to just ask the question a thousand times into the void, because I feel like knowing this, or *thinking* I know this, is somehow worse than not knowing ever was.

As I duck back through the door and down the long, narrow corridor, my head spins and spins. I don't think I can face the librarian. When she looked at me before, with that mixture of confusion and pity – what did she see?

The question I keep coming back to is this: am I making

it all up? I want to find answers. I have *always* wanted to find answers. Perhaps the uncertainty of the last few days is making me grasp at the impossible, straws that only barely resemble straws. But I return again and again to the way Michaela hardly seemed bothered about losing her job – the job she has fought to be the best at for the last two years. The way that she brushed off what must have been a very traumatic break-up for her. And I realise what I think I already knew, deep down: it's not that she wasn't bothered. I was right before when I said that this was a distraction – but more than that, it was *hyperfocus*. A way to occupy herself. By helping me do the thing that she knew I'd always wanted. To find where I came from, to find my family. But if she succeeded, if she found the truth, where is she now?

The librarian – should I find her? Demand to know more about Rebecca and those other girls? Do I tell her what I've found and what I suspect? Do I do the absolutely unhinged and unload the most life-changing information I've ever possibly seen, albeit am unable to confirm, to a complete and total stranger?

I couldn't even if I wanted to. My mouth won't work and my head hurts.

So instead, I run.

Eleanor

Somehow I make it into the car without passing out, though I can feel another panic attack rising and rising in my chest with the violence of a storm. I grip hold of the steering wheel and breathe through my nose until I think I can open my eyes without being sick. Then I take my phone out of my pocket and I click straight to the photos I took of the articles, pretending to myself that I'm checking they are legible, so Clio can read them – but knowing deep down it's because I want to see the picture again. And when I do, there's no denying the connection, the familiarity, I feel.

I can't keep this to myself.

I try Clio's phone, but the signal at the house must still be dire because it goes straight to voicemail. So I do the only other thing I can and ring my mum.

'Darling!' She answers on the third ring and the sound of her voice is at once so familiar and so foreign to my ears that I well up. 'I wasn't expecting to hear from you until later. Are you guys back already?'

Now I really do cry. I burst into tears that are so awful

I can hear my mum panicking over the speakerphone and it takes me a minute to rein them in, to drive them back to something manageable so I can speak through the onslaught.

'Oh my God,' I pant. 'I'm sorry.'

'What happened? Are you all right?' Her voice is soothing, always calm in the face of a crisis.

'No,' I blurt. 'No, I'm all right, but everything isn't okay. Michaela . . .' I don't even know how to say it, so I just plough on. 'Michaela isn't here. We don't know where she is. She's been gone since Sunday morning and I was trying to keep everything under control, but I don't know what to do—'

'Whoa, honey. Whoa. Slow down. Start from the beginning. I can't hear you very well, you keep breaking up. Tell me everything.'

And I do. I tell her about arriving here on Saturday and the way everybody we met was so stand-offish, I tell her about Michaela disappearing Sunday morning, how we didn't notice she was gone, how she isn't answering her phone. I tell her about the text and the social media post, about the scarf on the loch, and about the missing Blackhills girls from decades ago and finally, finally, I land at the library.

'I came here to try to find some clues. I don't know. I realised I didn't have details, you know? About what happened before? I thought if there was any connection to those missing girls, if Michaela was following this stupid podcast or whatever, or if anybody *thought* there was a connection to those missing girls . . .' I pause.

My mother waits and I can hear her breathing, and I know that my dad is probably there too because there's the tinny echo of the phone at the other end being on speaker and I know I just have to take the plunge.

'Do you . . . Do you think it's possible that *this* is where I'm from? I mean . . . Like, biologically? Originally?'

The silence stretches, taut like elastic. I resist the urge to cry again but only barely.

'What do you mean?' This comes from my dad, and I feel only hollow at the vindication of how well I know both of them.

'I mean that I found photographs. Of those missing girls. And one of them . . . God, she looks so much like me. Michaela said . . . She had something she wanted to talk about. I thought it was to do with her *job*. But what if she found out about this woman? Saw the photograph I did? What if that's why we're here – is it possible?'

'Well . . .' Dad says. He is hesitant.

'It's obviously possible,' Mum murmurs. She's gone so quiet I can hardly hear her. 'We don't know. We don't know anything at all except that you were left at a police station in Durham. A foundling—'

'So I could be from here.' I pause and the silence stretches long. I know it sounds crazy. 'Did you know why Michaela chose here? She didn't . . . text you or anything?'

'No.' Dad's responses are curt, but I know it's not because he's angry; he's thinking. 'No, nothing like that.'

'Maybe she wasn't sure,' I say. 'She said she had things she wanted to check before she told me about this thing she'd been working on. I assumed, I guess, that it was a kind of project. You know how she gets when she's upset. But . . . I don't know. I don't know.' I bang my hands against the edge of the steering wheel in frustration as my phone rocks in my lap.

'Do you think . . .'

'Will you know . . .'

I can hear the indecision in their voices, both of my parents quelling that urge to soothe me, to brush off my concerns or to tell me I'm being silly. And the fact that neither of them will say that means it could be true. But how will I ever know?

'Can you send us the photo?' Mum asks hesitantly.

'Yes. It might take a while; the signal—'

'Have you been to the police about Kay?' Dad cuts in. 'I didn't hear that bit. Your mother . . . What? Oh, right.' Mum speaks across him, so everything is jumbled as she catches him up and he makes a grunt, then another. 'Well, you've done everything you can, sweetheart. I don't know what more you can do. Do you want us to come and get you?'

'Dad,' I say, 'how will that solve anything?'

'We can . . . We could help.'

'How?' I ask. I know he's just trying to be supportive, but now I'm itching to move, to head back to Loch House and tell Clio what I've discovered, to hope she's found something too. Maybe she's been trying to text me all this time. To call me. Maybe Michaela is even there, right now.

The thought momentarily warms me, even if it is wishful thinking.

'Well, I don't know. I could talk to the police. I could . . .' He trails off.

'Better to let them do their job,' Mum says. 'They know what they're doing. Real life isn't like TV. I bet they've got loads of people out looking for her.'

'They definitely have people out there, but there were these campers who got stuck while hiking or something –

264

close by. They must share resources because I swear they've been pretty unhelpful until now.'

'Stretched thin,' Dad says.

'Exactly. And they're looking, I know they are, but what if . . .' I stop, but it's clear what I was about to say. *What if it's too late?* It's Tuesday. Michaela disappeared on Sunday. That's two entire days where the police's attention has been split. We thought she was fine – but what if she wasn't?'

'I'm sure they are doing the very best they can,' Mum says. 'Have you rung her mum? Is there anywhere else she might go? If she's, I don't know, *investigating*, are there any cities nearby she might have gone to, for records or something?'

'I have the car.'

'Well. What if she got a taxi?'

I know Mum is trying to be rational about this, but I'm suddenly overwhelmed again by all of the things I do not know. Things I haven't even thought to do. Michaela is the crime nut, not me. I don't even remember the police officer's name. I start to cry again and Dad makes soothing noises until I can breathe again.

'Okay,' I say. The fight rushes out of me and I'm exhausted. 'I guess . . . I guess I'll go back to the house and see how Clio is getting on. There's virtually no signal there and I've got the car, so I'm not sure if she would have been able to text me if she found anything. Must be all those hills and trees and stuff, obviously the house is in the valley . . .'

'Yes, that sounds like a good idea. And you'll feel better if you're together.' Dad pauses again and there is the murmur of indistinct voices. When he comes back to the phone, I hear the emotion in his voice, tight and deep and so *him* that I want to cry all over again. 'Don't worry about the photo,' he says. 'We'll have a look.'

'Yes,' Mum agrees.

'I just . . . El, I don't want you to get your hopes up. You know, this girl might be a distant relative, or, I suppose, a close one. But she might . . . She might not. Right? And until we know for sure, I don't want you getting—'

Mum cuts across him. 'If it's true, we'll support you. You know that.'

'Thanks,' I say softly. 'I know.'

As I hang up the phone, I let the tears fall again. Their support means the world, as it always has, but how do I find the words to explain to them that it's not just about proof? I've wanted all my life to know where I came from – not because I'm not happy with who I am, or who my parents are, but because I just have this burning need to *know*. It's all very well Dad telling me not to get my hopes up, but what about my fears? What about my insecurities? They taught me to be level-headed, but right now that's hard; my emotions feel like somebody dropped a Mentos mint into a bottle of Coke and shook it up.

And it's not just that I want to know who I am. Now there are more questions too. I want to know if Rebecca is my mother – and the longer I sit here staring at her photograph, the more questions I have. Why did she give me up for adoption? Or rather, why did she abandon me at a police station in a different fucking country? Why did she want me so far away from her that she did that?

I want to know what happened to her.

I sit for long enough that my vision stops blurring, check my phone once more and send the photo to my parents, and then put the car into gear and drive back to Loch House.

Although it's only late afternoon, it feels like it's getting dark already. There are grey clouds overhead that hang low like a ceiling of night pushing down, and the first specks of rain prickle the windscreen as I pull under the foliage on the track that leads to the house.

I drive slowly, careful of the slick leaves under the car's wheels, and when I pull up, the rain is falling in earnest. I clamber out and head for the house, slipping my shoes off as I step inside. It's freezing in here, though there's ash in the fireplace like Clio must have lit a fire earlier to ward off the chill. It's been extinguished a while.

It isn't just cold, though. It's icy. The doors to the decking are open, the curtains at the edges billowing in the fresh breeze. I walk over and shut them, warding off a fresh shiver.

'Clio, I'm back!'

I wander through the lounge-cum-kitchen and find evidence of Clio's search scattered beside the coffee table. Michaela's bag is down here, all of her clothes and her jewellery, toiletries, spread out across the floor, almost as if Clio was cataloguing it all. There's a phone charger, two more scarves set to one side, a loose piece of paper with the booking information for Loch House on it, and a notepad.

There's no real order to any of it. It might have been neat when she started, but now everything is a jumbled mess, bits of paper blown by the breeze, an empty crisp packet and one of the sachets of sweeteners Michaela keeps in her bag by the doors.

'Clio?'

I turn for the stairs and climb up them two at a time. I'm out of breath before I reach the top, half out of a desire to blurt it all out, to tell her about the library and the photographs, and half because of the panic attacks and my general lack of fitness.

I search in Michaela's bedroom first, but there's no sign of Clio beyond the obvious evidence that she was in here gathering up Kay's things. I try the bathroom next, but it's empty. Then Clio's room, and then, finally, mine.

They are all as empty as the day we arrived.

I run down the stairs, breathless for real, hand gripping so tight on the handrail that I nearly catapult myself to the bottom instead of guiding myself safely down. I skid into the lounge again, searching as though I wasn't here just moments ago.

'Clio?' There's an edge to my voice. A panic that's creeping in to strangle me.

I jam my feet into my shoes, the backs of my trainers crushed under my heels, and stumble out through the double doors. The rain lashes on my face, heavier and colder than only minutes ago. The lake roils underneath it. But it's no use. I can't see her.

Clio is gone.

Eleanor

I stand in the rain for what seems like minutes, unable to unfreeze my brain for long enough to assess the situation. When I finally move, it's out of necessity. Although the rain isn't heavy, I'm already soaked. I force my limbs to obey and carry me back indoors before my teeth start to chatter. Then I stand, dripping, on the mat. I fumble for my phone, scrolling through my apps. Nothing. In fact, I notice that the message to my parents hasn't even sent. I try to breathe for a second, to gather myself. A spark of inspiration strikes and I reboot my phone, waiting for long seconds as the screen goes blank and then waiting again as it loads once more. The little white logo feels like it's been scored into the backs of my eyelids.

'Come on,' I mutter. 'Come *on.*'

It does, eventually, turn back on. The screen feels very bright, but more importantly there is a bar of signal where before there were only four little dots. I navigate back to my messages and feel dizzy with sudden relief when I see a message from Clio that wasn't there before.

Just heading out to have a scoot around. Stay there and I'll be back.

That's it. There's nothing else, no indication that she was making any progress with Michaela's things, still scattered on the floor.

I stand for a moment, my brain processing, and then it's necessity that moves me again; I head up to my bedroom to change into dry clothes, towelling my hair and wrapping myself in another sweater. I'm still feeling dizzy, a maelstrom of emotions inside me. There's the relief that Clio is okay, swamped again by frustration at the lack of progress with Michaela's whereabouts and confusion about the photograph I found.

When I finally start to warm up, I head back down to the lounge to wait for Clio. I make tea and set up camp on the floor in front of Michaela's stuff. There's her rucksack, which has been practically turned inside out in Clio's determination to find something, all of the pockets emptied and the contents scattered. I paw through her make-up bag, toiletries, her clothes, a book, a notebook and pen.

Michaela is such an efficient packer that it's impossible to tell if any of her stuff is missing. There aren't many clothes, only a pair of leggings, three pairs of socks of varying thickness, some underwear, two tops and a sweater. I wrack my brains trying to think if there is anything else she might have brought with her and taken when she left, but her pyjamas are still on the bed upstairs and so all that I'm sure about is that her scarf is gone. I don't know if there's anything missing from her bag; I don't know what she brought with her to start with. I root through her toiletries looking for any evidence that the bag might have contained anything that's not there now, but the bag is pretty full already.

Did she think, when she left the house on Sunday, that she would be gone for over two days? Panic builds inside me again and I breathe through it, returning my focus to my phone. I spend the next few minutes trying to find the best spot for signal. If I sit right beside the doors it's too cold, though the signal is the best there; if I stand in the kitchen the connection to any data is tenuous at best, but it's better than on the sofa. So I lean against the counter and I type every single combination of words into the search bar I can think of, hoping Google might be helpful now I have more information.

Missing girls Blackhills.

Disappearance Blackhills.

Missing women, Scottish villages.

Rebecca Kelly, Janie Howell, Sarah McNeil missing, Blackhills.

Considering the way people around here have talked about, or not talked about, the disappearances, I would have thought there would be more information, but all I find are approximations of the newspaper articles I found at the library, and even then, I can't find all of them.

I loop back to the photos I took on my phone, zooming in so I can read the articles I skimmed over earlier. I try to ignore the photos, but it's hard.

One day Rebecca Kelly was here, visiting the village after time away, witnessed briefly by her uncle, who assumed she was on her way to her family home – but later suggested she might have been on her way to the loch, her place of solace. Then, with the blink of an eye, she was gone. Over the next couple of days, a police search was mounted. The whole village came out in force to find this girl, who, according to the first article, was 'so sweet', 'just the nicest girl'.

Rebecca's parents were besides themselves. Her dad retreated from the public eye, and when he appeared for an interview, the journalist noted that he looked 'haggard' with loss.

Only days later, Janie – blonde-haired and dependable – disappeared too. Janie had been an old childhood friend of Rebecca's, and the two of them had often been seen on the banks of the loch as teens. Rumour around town, and in the press, had it that Janie may have been concerned for her friend – and that it was likely that she had returned to the paths the two of them had once frequented to search for Rebecca. And so, the story went, that the loch had claimed Janie, just as it must have done Rebecca.

The searches continued, aided by local villagers. The Saturday Night Quizzers, who were more used to charity drives than search parties, turned their powers of organisation to acquiring help from folks from the neighbouring towns, fire officers – including the Blackdale Fire Chief – and farmers, teachers and local business owners, along with an army of teens and young women who had known Rebecca at school.

And among these women was Sarah, another old friend of Rebecca and Janie's. I remember her face from the photographs I saw in the library. I swipe back and look again. Red-headed, with a shrewd look about her olive eyes. The last article of the three says she helped by getting in touch with national news outlets, attempting to make people outside Scotland aware of the disappearances. There wasn't much uptake, as far as I can tell from my searches. Especially when it came to light how little evidence there was: no foul play, no suspicious activity, just nature and the universe conspiring against them.

And then, just like that, Sarah disappeared too. Another victim claimed by the waters. Or, as the national news claimed, another young girl who'd had enough of rural living and fled in favour of the big city.

From the little extra I can find on Google, it looks like the searches for the three women continued for several weeks with decreasing frequency and attendance until there was just a small group of villagers who would hike the shores of Loch Aven on the weekends, hoping to find some evidence of them. Until that, too, stopped.

I find little else except a few anonymous blog posts from the early 2000s where the author broke down what happened into days and times, reaffirming what I've already read – but it's clear to me that even this blogger, no doubt like the folks in Blackhills, seems to think it was a case of a mishandled police investigation into a terrible accident.

If the police had reacted more firmly to Rebecca's disappearance, if Janie hadn't felt she had no choice but to search for her missing friend by herself, then perhaps she would not have succumbed to the same fate. And if the search parties had been organised by the police instead of by locals whose only experience was in charity planning, then perhaps Sarah would not have succumbed to it either.

My stomach churns, my mind turning over with it. I have so many questions I'm desperate to answer, Michaela still at the forefront of my mind, but Rebecca Kelly worming her way in too. If she is – *was* – related to me in some way . . . How? Could she be my mother? Is it possible she might have had a child before returning to Blackhills? And if so, when and where did that happen?

There are still no references to any family members other than the mother, father and uncle – so it's unlikely she had a sibling who had a child. Perhaps her uncle is the connection? Or, I think, slamming my phone face-down on the counter with a surge of anger, maybe I'm just making things up and this has nothing at all to do with me.

I march back to Michaela's things, picking through them, searching with renewed vigour – or perhaps it's manic frustration. Every minute that passes is another since Michaela left. I can't face the thought of another night without her. We're supposed to be going *home*. I don't know what time our check-out was supposed to be, but nobody has come to kick us out. I can't even process what might happen if they did.

I grab Michaela's notebook and leaf through the pages. Maybe there are notes in here that hint at what she knew, where she might have gone for more information. But there's nothing, just a recipe for a soup that uses cucumber and mint; a shopping list for a totally different set of ingredients; an email address that looks like it belongs to a law firm; and a list of seemingly random names I don't recognise, written in three different colours of ink: *Gwyneth, Paul-John, Robert, Joshua, Bethan, Lucy . . .*

Laughter bubbles up in my throat, hysterical and totally inappropriate. I feel like I'm losing my mind, all of Clio's folk stories rotting my brain from the inside out. I realise with a kind of distance that this frightens me itself, the calmness with which I have come to this conclusion – but it feels like I am *cursed*. Like ever since I stepped foot in this place, something has been following me, draining my energy, haunting my dreams – corrupting everything I touch.

I know it's ridiculous, but it feels like the truth.

On the next page of the notebook, I find words that don't immediately make sense to my delirious brain. *Mythify: Crime Tales*. Underneath, there are two names: Bonnie MacKenzie and guest host Lydia Oxen. I stare at them for a moment before realisation dawns. It's the name of the podcast.

Eleanor

I pull up Google first – because I have never in my life listened to a podcast – and typing *Mythify podcast* is a jackpot right away. The first link takes me right to it, opening an app I didn't even know I had. There are lists of episode titles and I feel a moment of panic as I stare at the nonsensical names: *Jack Robey, The Superstore, Sister Death, Eclipse But Not Vampires*, until I reach the end. And there it is. *The Loch*.

I have to hold in the screech of excitement – and nerves and fear and everything in between – which threatens to burst out of me. I turn, starting to speak to Clio without thinking, and then the memory that she's not back yet slams into me.

I load up the podcast and turn up the volume on my phone – only to get endless buffering. I curse, close the app and head to stand next to the open doors. It's freezing in here now, the rain pelting down and splashing up my legs. I hope Clio has a jacket.

When I reload the podcast, it works better but won't buffer properly and keeps breaking up. I try again and press play, getting a sweep of dramatic instrumental music and then a young American voice introducing herself as Bonnie, host of *Mythify*. I scrub forward impatiently, and there's a heart-stopping moment when it refuses to load, and then I'm rewarded with the stop-start of two different voices, the second also young but Scottish.

'. . .we don't talk about it, but it's like everybody knows. I don't remember anybody telling me, but I grew up just . . . knowing. Like I knew that's why Paul Kelly and his brother have this super weird relationship, because there was tension after Robert's daughter went.'

'Did he think Paul had something to do with it?'

'Dunno. Think they both thought the other one had something to do with it. Or, not really, I don't know. Paul saw her that day, you know. He said he didn't speak to her, but I'm not sure Robert believed him. But it's not like he'd lie about it. And Paul said something once about not knowing if she ever made it to her parents' house. They only have Robert's word he never actually saw her. I think it's just normal tension though. It's a small village: you know everybody and everybody knows you, so, like . . . it's super awkward when families have these rifts and fall out because you're married to half the village and the other half want you dead.' The girl laughs nervously. 'Actually, can you cut that? My boyfriend works with Paul and I don't want to get him in any trouble.'

There is an awkward silence, and suddenly I understand why barman Tim had been upset about the podcast when he mentioned it – and probably server Beth too. I can't imagine Paul Kelly would have been happy knowing Marc's girlfriend was gossiping about his still-missing niece online, and Tim would probably have been worried about his brother losing his job, especially when I recall how proud he was to announce that Marc worked at the farm shop.

'Anyway, there's a lot of implicit stuff I knew. Like, you don't go by the water because you might drown. There's rumours that Janie – you know, the second girl – was in *love* with Rebecca, and Sarah was a proper gossip so she found out, and some people even think maybe Sarah got into a fight with the other two over it and they drowned accidentally, but that's ridiculous. The other story is this whole Ophelia narrative where they think it was some kind of suicide pact. It's kind of romantic – and stupid.' She snorts. 'I've actually only ever been down that end of Loch Aven once because everybody knows you don't go hang out on the decking outside the big house, even if somebody invites you to smoke a blunt, because you might slip—'

'This house,' Bonnie cuts in. 'Does anybody live there?'

'Nope, empty. It's been empty literally forever. No idea who owns it. Apparently a few groups of teens used to have parties outside it a lot, use the decking and the dock and jump into the water. Or have bonfires on the beach or whatever. Rebecca's friend group were the main lot, though. Our school janitor said he was friends with the girls – that's the most he's ever said about them – and that they used to go on weekends during the summer— Wait, actually he did say one more thing. He said that after everybody stopped hanging out at the house – this was actually before the girls disappeared because they stopped going there the summer before, or I think when Rebecca left Blackhills – Josh went there to smoke, you know, and he thought he saw somebody, maybe Rebecca, *in* the house. So, like, somebody owns it, they just don't live in it. But he was probably wrong about it being Rebecca anyway, he said, because nobody even had

279

keys and she was such a perfect girl she wouldn't have broken in. So it was probably somebody else – the owner maybe, he said they were acting like they owned the place. I think in the old old days the owner used to rent it out to holidayers, but literally nobody has stayed there since the girls went—'

The track stops abruptly and my heart slams in my throat. The big house. They're obviously talking about Loch House, right? I try to scrub the episode forward, but the signal has dropped again and there's nothing. I can't even get the previous bit to load.

I throw my phone down in frustration. Is it possible that Rebecca Kelly was in this house, once upon a time? That nobody has been here since? No, there must have been guests in the meantime, surely.

A strange feeling swoops over me. A certainty that is based on nothing but gut belief. Rebecca was here before she went travelling – and what if she had been here more than once? Maybe she knew the owner? Could it have something to do with her disappearance, and possibly her death . . .?

A fresh determination seizes me. I pull the patio doors to and search the house room by room, looking under beds, underneath pillows and inside pillowcases, in the wardrobes and even shining my phone flashlight down the sink in the bathroom. I check floorboards for evidence of hidden cavities, pull the basket of cleaning supplies out from underneath the kitchen sink. I have no idea what I'm searching for, except that I know I'm looking for *something*. Anything out of the ordinary.

The problem is, the entire house is completely ordinary. The bed linen was clearly fresh when we arrived, the towels neatly folded. There's nothing in the cupboards except for tea and coffee with labels from the farm shop – hardly a coincidence, given that it's so local – peeling at the corner, and nothing left in the fridge except milk. My stomach lets out a pained rumble and I ignore it.

It's only when it rumbles again that another thought occurs to me. I check my phone. I have no new notifications, no messages or even anything from Twitter. Nothing from my parents, either. I loop back to the main section of my messages and check the time stamp on Clio's message.

It's been *two hours* since she texted me. Or, since I received the text – and, worryingly, that is not the same thing.

I read the message again, something bugging me. I read it twice more. And then I scroll up to her last message to me before this and I realise what it is.

Clio never, ever uses capital letters in her texts to me. Not even with autocorrect. You wouldn't think it for a folklore grad, but Clio loves the evolution of internet language, spends all of her time working out how to create the maximum impact from her words, and has landed on 'no capital letters makes me look cool', which I've always respected even if I could never pull it off myself.

The text she sent me today is perfectly punctuated, capital letters and full stops. Alarm bells begin at the back of my mind, growing louder by the second. I don't want to think it. At first, I close the text app and take a second to slow my thoughts, to make sure I'm not overreacting. Maybe I'm imagining things.

But I'm sure I'm not.

I don't think Clio wrote this text message. But if she didn't . . . who did?

Eleanor

I am shaky and sick with panic. I don't know what else to do, but I know I can't stay here without doing *anything*, so I grab my coat and dart back out to the car. It's stopped raining and the afternoon is quickly turning into early evening. Very soon, it will be three full days since I last saw Michaela . . . And now Clio is missing too.

I speed down the lane, faster than I should, but I don't care. I am familiar with the road now and I park in the same spot in the village. Distantly, I note that I'm starting to think of this as *my* slot, right between a broken pay-and-display machine and a brick wall.

I get out of the car and stand in the car park for what seems like an age, trying and trying to get my brain to kick into gear. When I finally get myself moving, I almost run, hurrying along the same route I took this morning – was it only this morning? – to reach the police office. Inside, I'm passed from pillar to post until I'm installed in the same small room as earlier, table bolted down, lukewarm cup of coffee in front of me that I have no intention of drinking, and the same tired police officer before me.

'My other friend has gone too.'

'Gone?'

'She went out – apparently – but she's not back. Just like Michaela. I got a text message from her. Look.' I fumble for my phone. 'It's not like her normal texts.' I shake the phone.

He reads the message and a frown creeps across his features – perhaps the most genuine reaction I've had from him thus far. 'When did you see her last?'

'This morning. We split up. I came here, then went to the library to do research. She was supposed to stay at the house in case Michaela turned up. She was looking for clues. I found the podcast Michaela was listening to, it's about the girls. What if Clio . . .' I ramble on and on, until I'm totally out of words. Tears are fresh on my cheeks, though I don't remember the point at which I started crying, and the police officer's frown is deeper still.

'Okay,' he says.

And then it's like everything happens all at once. He gets fresh coffee for both of us – which I still don't intend to drink – and a tape recorder is suddenly on the table. Another police officer, a woman with a nose like a beak and pretty red hair, stands by as the officer asks me to repeat everything again for the record. Clio's disappearance is like the key that unlocks the whole thing.

After I've butchered my own explanation, the male officer patiently reiterates to his colleague how Michaela was seen in the village on Sunday morning, but how none of the teams have seen her since. How during the locating of the campers – who are all accounted for now, and have been

284

interviewed along with the locals – they searched the woods and the loch for signs of Michaela's presence. How the team in Blackdale repeated the efforts. Things that have been bubbling along for the last two days without my knowledge. I feel very overwhelmed – and very stupid.

But then the questions begin to make me uncomfortable.

'Did the three of you have a falling out on Saturday evening?' the female officer asks.

'No.'

'You said Michaela was upset, but not as upset as you would have thought.' The male officer's expression is blank, showing no hint of what he's thinking.

'She was. She lost her job, and broke up with an asshole, and she was embarrassed and upset, but her focus was split. I'm not sure exactly, but she was definitely interested in something, some project, and I think it was to do with the podcast—'

'You are referring here to the *Mythify* podcast, yes?'

'There's an episode on Loch Aven, and those girls that disappeared. Rebecca . . .' I pause as I say her name, but can't bring myself to voice my suspicions about her. About me. 'And Janie and Sarah.'

The officer narrows his eyes. 'And you think that the podcast has something to do with your friend's disappearance?'

'I know everybody thinks they drowned, but what if they didn't? I don't know, but why else would she have been so distracted?'

The two officers exchange a glance and my stomach twists. I'm hot and angry. It feels like they're judging me.

'Did Clio say anything before she left the house today?' the female officer asks. From the way the man defers to her I suspect she's probably his senior, but when I respond I talk only to him.

'No . . . I don't know, because I wasn't there. She left while I was in the village.'

'Would she have any reason to leave?'

'No, I don't think so. Not unless she thought she saw Michaela or . . . I don't know. Maybe she got scared by something?'

'Did you and Clio have any words this morning?'

'What? No! Nothing like that. Don't turn this around on me.'

'It's my job to ask these questions,' the female officer says. The man says nothing, just watches me carefully. 'It's just routine.'

The male officer takes a sip from his coffee. I notice that his shirt is rumpled under the arms, and it looks like he hasn't shaved today. Distantly, I realise that for him this isn't a normal week either, and then I feel guilty and overwhelmed again.

'Please,' I say. 'I don't care about anything except finding my friends.'

The female officer makes a note in a little book and exchanges another glance with her colleague. I expect this to be it, for the questions to end and for them to shoo me away so they can get back to work, but instead after they're done, I'm left in the little room for long minutes waiting.

And then another thought swallows my focus: what if they actually do think I had something to do with Michaela and Clio going missing?

I finally get out of the station what seems like an hour later. I've lost all track of time, but it's getting dark, the air wet and cold like the lick of a draught directly on my skin. I

286

stalk away from the police office with barely concealed fury burning in my limbs, my blood. My heart pounds.

As I walk, I do the familiar checks on my phone. No new messages from Michaela – or Clio. No calls, or texts. I try Michaela's number first and it goes straight to voicemail. Switched off. I try Clio's next and it rings and rings before I finally get her voicemail.

Next, I scroll through my favourites and dial Joy's number. She picks up on the third ring.

'Ellie! How's my favourite psychologist?'

'Joy,' I blurt.

'What's wrong, sweetie? You sound upset.'

My chest aches and suddenly I'm crying again, big gulping sobs. It takes me a few attempts to get the words out while Joy makes confused noises, starts to ask questions, but I don't even have the sense to wait and listen. I launch into a full speech, explaining about Michaela's disappearance, the podcast, the campers and the landslide in the rain. Joy listens without interruption. 'It's been days, Joy. The police are involved and everything. I didn't want to worry you, but . . . now Clio's gone as well. Please tell me you've heard from one of them. Please.'

'Clio texted me this morning,' Joy says quietly. 'Early.'

'Did she tell you about Kay? Have you heard from her?'

'No.' The silence feels full, but I think Joy is simply processing rather than being angry.

'Clio's been gone since this afternoon,' I say. 'Or, no. Earlier. But not *early*.'

'Where has she gone?'

'I don't know! I don't know where either of them are. They've both left me and I don't know what's going on. There's all this stuff in my head about some girls who went missing in this stupid village years ago and I'm worried that I'm somehow connected to it all and Michaela had a plan and . . .' Silence on the line. 'Joy?'

Joy says nothing.

'Joy,' I repeat. 'Did you know? Did Michaela tell you this was why we were coming here? Did you *know*?'

'I . . .' Joy trails off, her voice distant. Then she sighs. 'She did say, yes. She told me that she wasn't sure. Actually, she was—'

'I've seen the photo,' I say. 'The one that's in the newspapers. I googled after and found it online too. That girl looks just like me.'

'I've seen the picture,' Joy says. 'Michaela said the same thing when she saw it. That's why she started to wonder. And the timing of it . . .'

'And you didn't say anything?' I spit. Anger temporarily smothers the fear. I know I'll regret lashing out because it makes me sick to think of fighting with Joy, but I can't help it. 'Did everybody know but me?'

'No, no,' Joy says quickly. 'No, Michaela just said she wanted to talk it through with me to make sure she wasn't being insensitive. And I said maybe she was, but that you'd probably want to know. And you'd want to be there. Right?'

I am so angry I can't find words.

'Was I right about that?' she asks.

'No.'

She is right, though. If Michaela was here, if she'd come back on Sunday afternoon with her concrete proof, or more information, or sources, or anything like that . . . If she'd sat me down and told me what she suspected to be true – I would have been grateful. Angry, yes. Upset, too. But *still* grateful. But now . . .?

'Do you know where she went?'

'No, only that she was going to speak to somebody. She said she'd met somebody who offered to help her – to get proof.'

I pull my jacket tighter around my shoulders as a cold gust of wind knocks through me. It feels like a punch, leaving me breathless. 'She said that?'

'Yes.' Joy starts to ask a question, but I cut her off. I can't talk any more right now. If I do, I'll explode and I don't want to say anything I'll regret. I end the call and send a quick text that I'll keep her updated. That definitely is insensitive, but I can't do anything else.

Panic overwhelms me as my mind flits back to Michaela's notebook and the list of names. I'd drifted past them without thinking, but they were in three different ink colours – as if the list had been added to more than once. I remember seeing that and thinking it was odd, but not understanding why.

Now a fresh question threatens to capsize me again: could one of those names be the person Michaela was supposed to meet on Sunday? And more importantly: did she ever meet them?

Eleanor

I've been walking for the duration of my conversation with Joy without paying attention to where I'm going, and with a jolt I realise I've come to stand outside the farm shop.

The same farm shop where Rebecca worked – the one owned by her family.

I march inside with my lungs tight, anxiety swirling deep in the pit of me. The younger guy, Marc – Tim's twin – isn't here today. In fact, when I first enter, I don't spot anybody at all. It's an assault of gentle yellow light, the smell of fresh bread and something heartier, spiced meat and pastry perhaps.

I glance around, taking in the surroundings with new eyes. Was this how it looked when Rebecca worked here? Did she spend her days behind that counter waiting for a future she would never get to experience? I stop my thoughts before they stray too far. It scares me to think that I have some connection to this place.

And another question forms, slowly. So slowly I daren't acknowledge it at first. If Michaela thought I belonged here, if she was asking questions . . . What if she asked the wrong person, and that's why she's gone?

Panic overwhelms me and I turn to leave, but before I can make it to the door, a voice stops me.

'Can I help?'

It's the same man I met very briefly the other day, before he disappeared into the back. I take him in carefully. I'd guess he's probably in his sixties, his hair grey but still threaded with black, dark like mine. His eyes are blue, shrewd.

When I turn around and he sees my face, I can see his body language change and he starts to move away.

'We're actually getting ready to close soon—'

'Sorry, wait,' I blurt.

He pauses, suspicion taut in the lines of him. He glances around as if he's searching for somebody who might be able to help him, but instead of making me nervous, it fills me with fire. I roll my shoulders back and walk closer.

'I'd like to talk to you about . . . Rebecca.' Her name has an immediate effect on the man in front of me, who visibly recoils.

'What do you want with her?' he says. 'I didn't take you for some kind of disaster tourist. Weren't you here about your friend the other day?' His accent is strong and his voice is gruff.

'I . . . Look. I've got no idea how to even say this, but I didn't know anything about Rebecca until I came here. I saw her picture.'

'And?' He doesn't move.

'Are you Paul?' I ask. 'I was told her uncle works—'

'I'm Paul,' he cuts me off.

'I heard . . . I heard you saw her. The day she went

292

missing. I'm not . . . I'm not a "disaster tourist", I swear. I'm not here to bother you. It's just . . . my friend. She was asking questions about the . . . about what happened. And . . .' I stop. I don't know how to say it, so I don't, but there must be something in my expression that he can read as plain as day.

For a moment, Paul doesn't move, doesn't say anything. His gaze drifts towards the open door behind me, the rain pouring outside. The glass of the windows is flecked with it and the sky is growing darker by the second.

'Hang on,' he says. 'I won't do this while anybody can just walk in.'

He crosses behind me and closes the door, flipping the sign to closed, although it's still a few minutes off closing time. A distant part of my brain trills that I should be afraid. Maybe I am, but I'm so numb from the confusion, the constant panic, that I don't react.

'I don't talk about it,' he says. 'Not usually. But you . . . Anyway, yes. I did see Rebecca that day. I was here, in the shop. I saw her pass the window. At first, I didn't think it was her because she looked different, I don't know how – just different. But I went out and looked and then I was sure. I called after her. She didn't turn around, but that wasn't that unusual. I figured she'd go see her dad and then come back and see me.'

'Why?'

'She'd have wanted to get it over with,' he says. 'And then after, she'd come here and rant. Or at least that's what she used to do. Lots of ranting. But only to me – because I always said that was okay.'

'I saw her picture,' I say again softly. 'She looked . . . just like me.'

Paul blinks slowly, as though he's trying to temper his reaction, and shrugs. The studied, casual air makes me wonder how many other people in the village have thought the thing I have just said aloud. That woman in the cafe. The other one who stared at me in the boutique. How many of them saw my face and felt they were looking at a ghost?

'You see it too, right?' I say.

Paul glances behind himself, at the door, and walks away from it towards the safety of the counter, where he's less visible from the street.

'Is that why you're here?' he says, suddenly cold. 'You want to latch onto some poor grieving family—'

'No!' I exclaim. 'I didn't even know. But my friend . . .'

God, this all sounds absolutely mental. I start to cry and I can't stop it, it's like a wave crashing over me so heavy and angry that I'm crushed beneath its weight.

I can't bring myself to say what I fear, what I somehow *long* to be true. But the way he looks at me . . . It's strange. As if he's cataloguing my features, a thousand questions bursting like fireworks behind his eyes.

'You look nothing like her,' he says. 'You're not even remotely as tall. And your chin . . .' He stops, his expression softening.

'Is that all you can say?' I ask. 'That she was taller than me?'

'There's nothing in it,' he mutters, as if to himself. 'Just a coincidence. You're a stranger.'

'I'm a stranger with no family,' I say without thinking. It's a shock to repeat the words that have been living in my head since I saw the photograph. I went looking for answers about Michaela and there was nothing, and now it feels like everything is going at a million miles an hour in the wrong direction. 'I'm a *foundling*.'

Again, Paul blinks slowly, his gaze firmly rooted to the counter in front of him so he can avoid looking at me.

'So I want to know about her,' I push. 'I'm not joking around. I didn't know anything about her, or what happened – before I came here. But you've got to admit this is really damn weird. Right?'

'What good does it do, you snooping around here? Asking questions?' Paul snaps. The loose skin on his neck quivers. 'We don't know you. *I* don't know you. A thousand girls probably look like my niece, but it doesn't matter anyway because Rebecca is *dead*.'

'How do you know?' I demand. The tears are still falling and my voice is thick, so it's hard to speak. I can feel anger rising again, but I don't tamp it down. 'If nobody ever found her? Or her friends? How do you know they didn't just run off together?' There's desperation in my voice, a desperation I didn't know was there, buried beneath so many questions I feel like I'm drowning. 'Couldn't she be alive? She might be—'

'Girl, when I tell you that you need to let this drop you should listen to me.' Now he's looking at me, his steely gaze fixed right on mine.

'Why?' I ask. 'Are you so afraid that maybe Rebecca had . . . a life outside this village? That she had . . . that she had a daughter?' Hysterical laughter builds in my throat and I swallow it down. Even saying it aloud sounds like something out of a nightmare. A dream. I don't even know any more.

'I don't know anything about any daughter,' Paul says, his tone steely, 'but I know enough about the Kellys to know you don't want any part in us. I don't care if you look like her – you don't belong here. You and your friends. So if I were you, I'd get gone.'

'In case you hadn't noticed, I'm *trying*! But my friends aren't here. I don't know where they are – either of them, now. And all I have as a lead is a bloody photograph of a girl who looks just like me. Can you blame me for coming here and asking questions? Is it really that unreasonable to expect that somebody gives me a straight answer? Especially a man who should have loved her.'

Paul blanches. '*I* loved her,' he says fiercely.

'But somebody else didn't?' Static buzzes in my ears.

'Who knows!' Paul throws his hands up. 'For God's sake, don't you understand? Nobody knows *anything*. One day Rebecca was here and then she was off in the big wide world having fun.' He sighs. 'You know what? Maybe you are her kid, because you're a dreamer just like her. But that is all I know. She was here, then she was gone. And then she was here – and gone again, this time for good. Could she have had a daughter? Sure, she could have. Not when she lived here, but afterwards. Could she have made enemies?' He shakes his head. 'The day Rebecca left Blackhills was the day I stopped knowing that girl. But, of course, if you talk to her father, it started before that. She'd always been such an angel—'

'Are you saying that her behaviour changed?' I ask. I know I'm latching onto everything, but I can't help it. 'Before she left, I mean.'

'Her dad said so. He got real suspicious right before she left the village. He thought she was seeing some lad, that she was wasting her potential. He told her she was getting secretive, that she was always busy and always tired, and out exercising too damn much. I said it wasn't a surprise, on account of her mother having been sick – you know, Rebecca stayed here instead of travelling for years because Gwyn wasn't well. She worked in the shop and she took on responsibilities that no child should have to bear. And maybe that made her secretive with him when she finally decided it was time to leave. But Robert swears blind it wasn't that. He makes up these stories about a boy because it makes him feel better. He's still old-fashioned even now, and has the temper of a . . .' Paul stops himself again. It's as if every sentence is something he desperately wants to say, and also desperately wants to keep in.

I know I should stop, but I can't let it go. 'You don't trust your brother—'

'Look, it's no good you digging up the past. Things haven't been good here since Rebecca died. Rob . . . He was never the same. His temper is understandable. I won't speak ill of a man who lost his daughter because there's no proof of *anything*. You won't find what you're looking for here, even if there's truth in it.'

I want to lash out, to smash things – even though I've never been that sort of person. But hell, if this is my family, who knows what sort of person I really am? I want to call my parents and make them talk to him. I want answers, I want truth. But . . . I'm not going to get it like this.

I take a deep breath, trying to steady the quivering feeling in my belly. 'I—'

'I told you.' Paul cuts me off before I can begin. The shutters are back down now, his blue eyes dull as he glances once more towards the door. 'I know nothing. Now, we're closed. You need to leave.'

Eleanor

I stumble back out into the street, power-walking until I'm as far away from the shop as I can get. My sides burn with a stitch and bile is churning in my empty stomach. What the fuck was that? The idea that I might be related to him fills me with a dread that feels like quicksilver in my veins. It makes me want to wash my hands.

The things he said about his brother, about him being old-fashioned, about how he's never been the same . . . What if Rebecca was pregnant before she left the village – and what if her father found out? There's so little information in the articles I've read that I don't know if I'm making wild, imaginative leaps, but . . . It isn't so far-fetched a thought, is it? That Rebecca's dad might have known about a baby . . . About *me*?

I stop myself. No, I'm taking it too far. I don't even have any proof that Rebecca had a child, never mind proof that I'm in some way connected to all of this. If Michaela was here, I could ask her – she'd talk some sense into me. And Clio, too. But they're not, which is why I'm on this wild

299

goose chase. I need to find them and then we need to get the hell out of here.

I fumble in my pocket for my phone and check, but no. Nothing.

I look up and realise I have no idea where I am. I've been walking for some time, just deep in thought. And now – *fuck*.

I scan the street, searching for something to latch onto. Is that the same barbers we passed before? Or is it the cafe that I'm thinking of, both with their striped awnings and fairy lights in the window?

'Hey, girl. Hey.'

The man standing in front of me holds his hands up as if I'm a spooked horse that needs calming. He takes a step back.

'There,' he says. 'Eleanor.'

'Oh god, I'm sorry.' I stare at his face for a few seconds before I place it. Matthew, the head teacher, from the pub. The one with the kind eyes and the square jaw that reminds me of my father.

I wish my dad was here. I wish I'd told my parents to come and help me after all, because I can't do this. And the thought is so sharp that I nearly burst into tears again.

'Are you all right?' He takes a hesitant step forward, leaning in and giving me a small smile. 'You look . . . frightened.'

'I am frightened. It sounds ridiculous. But I'm terrified. I'm on my own and I don't know what to do,' I blurt.

'Are you still looking for your friend? Is she okay?'

'Yes – but not just that. Clio – she's gone now, too.' The tears start up again and I squeeze my eyes tight to stop them.

'Gone?' the man asks. His eyebrows crease and for the first time it feels like somebody is actually listening to me.

'Yes, *gone*,' I repeat, exasperation making me hiss. 'She just disappeared. She said she was going to look around some more. Maybe she's out there, by the loch somewhere now, hurt. I didn't go and search for her. There's so much ground to cover. I don't know where she went and I'm scared to go looking by myself. She texted me hours ago saying she would be back soon, but I don't think she sent the message. Or maybe she did. The police are definitely worried now and that should make me feel better, but it doesn't at all. And I know this sounds literally made up, but I listened to this podcast, the one Michaela was listening to, and there's all this stuff about what happened with those missing girls and I have this awful, *awful* feeling that I'm . . . connected?' I let out a hysterical laugh, because if I don't laugh, I'll cry. 'I found articles and photographs. I'm so afraid that Michaela and Clio are missing because of *me*. That's why we're here. It's happening again and it's all because of *me*.' I'm aware that I'm not making much sense, but I can't stop the word vomit.

The man stands and listens, concern etched into his features.

'And now I'm rambling like I've been drinking all day and I swear – I swear I'm sober as a judge. I'm sorry for dumping this on you – you don't know me.' I'm crying now whether I like it or not, big, embarrassed sobs.

The man hovers awkwardly, waiting for me to finish. He doesn't rush me, doesn't tell me I'm being crazy, and that only makes me more afraid.

'Listen,' he says. His voice is soft and warm, his accent sounding so different to how Paul's did in the farm shop

301

that it makes me want to cry all over again, but I take a deep breath. 'I know you don't know me, but I am a friend. I don't know how much you know about the girls who disappeared back then, but I can tell you that you don't want to get involved in it. Whatever happened back then, it's probably risky for you to go digging now. I don't want anything bad to happen to you. If your other friend is . . . If she's . . . not here too, that's definitely cause for concern. Why don't you go back to the house? I can come to you, if you want – so you're not on your own. But I just . . . I think it might be best if you go back there. I'll let Lucy – my wife – know where I am – and then I'll come and make sure you're okay.'

I take another shuddering breath. He's watching me, his expression a mixture of kindness and maybe pity too. But also fear. He's afraid – for me. And that scares me even more. Maybe, hopefully, I'm imagining it.

But Michaela and Clio are both gone. What's to stop me being next?

A realisation hits me, and it seems so ridiculous and somehow I can't believe I missed it before: Michaela spoke about listening to that damn podcast while we were in the pub on Saturday. She might have even asked people about it at the bar. Anybody could have heard her and known why Michaela was here. How many people did she ask about Rebecca, trying to figure out the potential connection between us?

How many people did she anger?

'Go back to the house,' Matthew repeats. And this time I know that the fear in his voice isn't imagined. 'Lock the doors. I'll come to you.'

Eleanor

I don't stop to consider if what Matthew suggests is the right idea. I daren't pause long enough to examine the tremor in his voice or the expression on his face.

I know where I am now, enough sense left in me to turn the panic to cold, hard steel. I have to go. I have to get myself to familiar ground and contemplate my options. I can't think about anything else.

I leave Matthew behind, glad to be away from everybody in this damn village. If I'm on my own, then there's only myself to trust. An old, dormant part inside of me claws its way free; the part of myself that as a young girl wanted to wall herself off from those who claimed to love her now, because, at some point, once upon a time, somebody else gave her up. I've fought so long to be the woman my adopted parents raised – confident, brave, casually vulnerable – that this dark, hidden part of me felt, as a child, like it might have been a phantom. But it isn't. It's there and it drives me onwards, desperation for safety and silence over-riding all else.

I run with my breath coming in grey puffs, a stitch forming in my side. Embarrassment wars with fear as a woman with greying hair in a cafe stares at me as I sprint across the road. I must have looked to Matthew like I'd totally lost control of myself. I *did* lose control – but is it unexpected?

I shake off the thoughts and focus on the only thing I can do: putting one foot in front of the other.

I find the car and drive back to Loch House faster than I should. This time I don't have any hope when I pull up the long driveway. I've stopped expecting to see Michaela, or even Clio, waiting for me. And I'm right. The house is as still and empty as it always is.

I do what Matthew suggested, locking all of the doors and even the window in Clio's bedroom that she left on the latch. I shiver. The whole house is frigid, echoing with abandonment. I remember distantly when I thought that this place would have once made a good home; now all I can see is the fear it's brought to me, and I wonder if it's not only the loch that is haunted by Rebecca, Janie and Sarah's disappearances, but the house too.

This thought brings on another wave of fear and I have to stop and breathe slowly through my nose, one arm on the wall to steady myself.

I check my phone again and again, although it's on its loudest setting. Nothing new from Clio.

Should I go to the water and search for her?

I glance out of the window, taking in the view from Clio's bedroom, the way the trees sway at the back of the house, the track into the village mostly hidden. The sky is growing steadily darker. I rub my arms. No, I won't leave the house to go out there alone. I won't.

I head back downstairs, to the piles of Michaela's belongings that I left scattered where Clio had abandoned them. It's the notebook I'm looking for. When I spot it, I leaf through several pages at the front, finding shopping lists in Michaela's sloping handwriting, a doodle of a rabbit drawn in red ink, another of a kitten curled up asleep in green.

Tears swell in my throat and I swallow hard.

I flip further, finding the page with the podcast title, the list of names. *Gwyneth, Paul-John, Robert, Joshua—*

Paul-John. Is that Rebecca's uncle Paul? And Robert – her father? Why did Michaela have this list of names? Were they people she wanted to talk to about Rebecca . . . or are they people she was suspicious of?

A fresh wave of fear slams into me. Who knew why Michaela was really here? Who did she tell?

On the next page is a list of locations that mean nothing. Two look like residential addresses, one in Blackhills and the other in Blackdale. Then there's the name of the farm shop owned by Rebecca's family, then a name that looks like it belongs to a church. I resist the urge to rip out the page and screw it up for all of the good that the knowledge does me.

I sit back on my heels.

'Think, Eleanor,' I demand. '*Think*.'

But there are no thoughts that help me. In the end, it doesn't matter why Michaela brought us here – what matters is what happened once she was here. And I don't know anything.

Through the wild static of my thoughts, I slowly, slowly begin to circle back to the farm shop. To Paul Kelly. Rebecca's uncle. If Rebecca fell into the loch, that is one thing. An accident that can be explained away by lack of caution – despite Janie's apparent insistence that Rebecca knew the shores of the loch like the back of her hand.

But if not . . . That leaves two other options. The first is that she went to the loch by herself before going to see her parents, like Paul claims she might have. Perhaps she was startled by something, or someone, and she fell in, her body swept away by the currents. Or perhaps I'm making the same assumptions as everybody else in the village, the assumption that Rebecca somehow ended up in the loch.

Which leads me to the second option: maybe she was attacked. It might have been an attack by a stranger with no more logic than that she was young and beautiful and they wanted to hurt her.

But, no, if it was an attack, given the size of Blackhills, what's the likelihood of something random like that? What is the likelihood that there was even a stranger here to start with? A tourist? Maybe more likely back then – but surely somebody would have seen something. Remembered *something*.

So, if it wasn't a stranger . . . maybe Rebecca came back to Blackhills and somebody wasn't happy about it. Perhaps somebody preferred it better when she wasn't here. This has me circling back to Paul again. To the way he spoke about his brother. *He's still old-fashioned even now, and has the temper of a . . .*

No. That doesn't bear thinking about. Rebecca's father wouldn't have hurt her, surely. Even if he was angry with her. Even if he wished she had made more of her life. Even if . . . even if he found out she had a baby.

I'm clutching at straws again.

In a fit of rage, I throw Michaela's notebook off my lap, watching it with satisfaction as it skids across the floor, scattering two other pieces of loose paper and Kay's tooth-paste, coming to rest underneath the log burner. I almost laugh at myself. If the parents I counsel could see me now, they'd never come back.

This more than anything is the thing that spurs me on. I stumble to my feet unsteadily, scooping up a couple of the loose sheets of paper and stuffing them in my back pocket. I'm hungry and tired, but the fear is still so sharp that I feel nauseous. Outside, the sun has set and the glass is dark, reflecting the single lamp that I've turned on in the lounge.

I don't know what to do. I spin once, twice, eyes searching for anything that might help. Nothing. I can't just sit here and wait for something to happen. I climb the stairs and go into Clio's room again. Her bed is a mess, clothes scattered across it, two books, an empty mug on the bedside table and more clothes on the floor. I shift stuff aside with my feet, then get down on my hands and knees and root through it all, pushing aside fabric and bottles of lotion until my fingers reach the cold wooden boards.

A frustrated cry builds in my throat. There must be something. There must be *something* useful here. Did Clio tell anybody about Michaela going missing? I try to think hard.

Only the people here in Blackhills. The bank and the boutique, the pub and the farm shop. I can't remember seeing anybody specific who made me worry. I can't remember *anything*.

I throw more of Clio's stuff aside, finding her duffel bag and pawing through it. Medication, a pack of Rennies, two pens, a pack of nicotine gum that's been half demolished, another full pack beneath it.

I sit cross-legged on the floor, digging Michaela's scrappy papers from my pocket and throwing them down, trying to resist the urge to cry again. I feel so useless. This is a waste of time. The police are my only option now.

And if they can't find Clio and Kay? What then? The thought of a life without them is so empty, so awful, that I feel my body grow numb with dread.

This can't be it.

It's so dark outside now that the dim light from the bedside lamp up here casts shadows that are long and skinny; they look like grasping fingers at the end of fat hands, reaching for me.

I can't stay up here by myself. The sound of the wind in the trees is like the whistle of a distant train, haunting and vibrating something deep in my soul.

Back downstairs, I head for the log burner again, getting on my hands and knees to pull out the notebook and the rest of the scattered bits of paper I threw there earlier. My hand brushes something that's a little sharp, like the corner of a cereal box. I pull my fingers back from the floorboard and examine them, but there's no splinter, no cut. I roll down lower, leaning on my forearm and angling myself out of the way of the lamp for a better look.

It seems like a piece of paper, trapped beneath the floorboards, just the very tip peeking out. I try at first with my fingertips, but my nails are too short. I can't get enough leverage to get it out. It might be something of Michaela's, but I'm not sure.

I root through Michaela's toiletries, pleased with myself when I find a pair of tweezers. I know it's probably not important, but it feels like it, in this moment. It's progress – only towards what is unclear.

I get back down on my knees and attack the bit of paper with renewed vigour, but it's caught on something or angled weirdly. I can't tug it in case it rips, so I have prise it out gently, millimetre by millimetre.

From this position, it looks blank, but when I finally force it free, I realise it's thicker than paper. The top corner is faded, almost white, but the rest—

I stop, my stomach flipping nervously, a fresh dread whipping through me.

It's a photograph. Two people stand together in front of Loch Aven. The sun glitters off the water, and there is the dock that I've come to recognise by the jut of its wooden planks over the green-blue lake.

One person I recognise right away. Her dark hair is long and braided back off her face, her pale skin catching the sun so she seems to glow. She is the one holding the camera, her body twisted so she can turn the disposable box towards the two of them.

The other person in the picture is a man. He is older than her, his hair shot through at the temples with silver. He has his arm around her and the two of them smile, an expression so similar you'd think they'd rehearsed it.

'No,' I whisper. 'It can't be.'

But it *is*.

It's Matthew.

Matthew

Then

This isn't how it was supposed to happen. None of this is how he pictured it; none of it is good or right. But – it is what it is, and there's little he can do about it now except for try to control as much of the damage as possible.

He loads Janie Howell's body into the boot of his car by the light of a sickle moon, barely even worth its presence in the sky. He does it with a detachedness that scares him; he notes without interest how small Janie looks, even now. He remembers her as a teenager, how she and Rebecca had been thick as thieves but good as gold. They were model students, no chatter or gossip, just hard work and bright ideas. He remembers the way Janie always looked at Rebecca, as if the sun shone out of her, but he doesn't remember much else.

Rebecca, obviously, left more of an impression, but he still feels a pang of sadness as he covers Janie's body with the blanket he keeps in the car for picnics with Lucy.

He waits in the house until it is time to leave. The child – *his* child, God that takes some saying – consumes all of his attention. Not because she is demanding, or because he is shocked to find how much she looks like her – like his Rebecca. It's simply that he cannot stop staring at her. Her perfect, chubby little fingers, the way she grunts as she kicks her legs in the air.

He did not realise how much he wanted to see himself echoed in another person until this moment. Lucy has never wanted children, and – he thought – neither did he. But seeing the girl changes things. Ever since what happened with Rebecca at the house . . . He hasn't been able to admit to himself how badly he wanted parts of this life, the life he's fucked up beyond words.

He never intended for that to happen, either. She sent him a message a week before, just a sheet of paper taped to his car. There was no note, only a drawing of the house on it in simple lines, accompanied by a number. The time. It was a shock to see it, honestly. A year of no contact, just her travelling the world, off forgetting about him, he thought – and then that?

He knew what it meant. She wanted to meet him. She was back. And . . . Well, a part of him wasn't happy about it. He had never meant to fall into the situation with Rebecca. It had been like a magnetism, a force outside of his control. He *loves* Lucy. Still. He loves her with all of his wicked heart.

Is it possible to love two people? Matthew had always believed that couldn't be true. But that was before he stumbled upon Rebecca that day. He still doesn't know what changed, or why it happened. When he was her teacher, he'd always just thought Rebecca was nice. Friendly. He knew there was something special about her, but it wasn't something *for him*. He wasn't attracted to her, nothing like that at all.

312

But that day in the farm shop, her standing behind the counter with flour on her apron and chocolate in her hair . . . it was like the sun had come between clouds. He finally *saw* her. And there was something in her that spoke to something in him – a picture of a life not lived, a life that he wanted, suddenly, so badly he could think of nothing else.

He doesn't know what happened, but that day, almost in one second, he went from loving Lucy, *only* Lucy, to loving Rebecca too. And the love was so different. With Lucy, he always felt cool, comfortable and controlled. With Rebecca, it was as if his world had been set alight, everything was heat and fire. Excitement, energy. Anger sometimes, too. That was new. Rebecca somehow dialled his feelings up to *max*; it's the only explanation he has, and even then he knows it's no good.

And the thought that Rebecca was back in Blackhills, after the way they parted . . . it made his blood run cold. She would, he realised, tell Lucy if it came to it. With Blackhills behind her, what would stop her? So – why did she want to meet him?

He spent three hours agonising over it. Should he see her? If he didn't, would she tell everybody what had passed between them in some fit of petty revenge? Would she ask for money, to buy her silence?

If he *did* go, would he be able to control himself around her or would it be like it always had been? Inevitable.

In the end, the risk of Rebecca telling anybody about them was too great. Lucy didn't deserve the shame of it. Her family owns half of Blackhills, sure, but that only means she has further to fall. She's spent her life trying to live up to the legacy her parents left, and Matthew always swore he would help her. Even when they were teens, newly dating with their whole lives ahead of them, Matthew promised he would help Lucy be as great as she could be. Because, boy, could she be great. He wouldn't let himself be part of her destruction.

Because if Lucy ever finds out, it *will* destroy her.

So he drove out to the house on the loch. It's been in his family for generations but so far back everybody has forgotten it's his – even Lucy. Matthew had never bothered with it until Rebecca. Well, that's not true, but the last time had only been for spring and partway into the summer, when he was new to teaching and overwhelmed by it all. He would come and sit sometimes, early in the morning before work, watch the sun rise over the loch and dream of another life. He'd tidy up the remnants of the gatherings from the night before – kids, no doubt, using the banks as their private party space – and think about how he might be able to keep this secret prize, this house, all to himself.

With Rebecca, it was different from the beginning. He wanted to *share* Loch House with her. They tidied it up together, filled it with nice furniture, rugs. Some of it was stuff Lucy didn't want any more, but Matthew didn't tell Rebecca that part, obviously. They made it into a retreat, a haven – a home.

Driving back there after a year away still felt a little like coming home, although he had that sick feeling in his belly, the one that warned he was making a mistake. He'd only just managed to get back to normal with Lucy, Saturday nights at the pub quiz aside. What if Rebecca ruined that equilibrium again?

By the time he arrived at the house, he was so riled up that he wasn't even pleased to see her – though he had to admit she looked beautiful. She was waiting for him in her usual spot, right down on the deck where the wooden dock juts out over the water and it feels like the loch is cocooning every part of you.

She looked older than when he last saw her, surprisingly so. There were creases at her eyes which weren't there before, on her forehead too, but overall the effect was one of maturity. She turned when she heard his footsteps on the dock and while she didn't smile, she did look pleased that he had come.

'I wasn't sure if I'd ever see you again after last time,' Matthew said. He tried to make sure his tone was even, but it crept through anyway, that old warmth. Though maybe the heat now was less love and something closer to fire.

'No, I wasn't sure either.'

She was dressed in a baggy pair of jeans, her hair pulled back tight in one of her signature braids. Her stance was solid, almost as if she was expecting to have to fight her own body to stay. He knew what that was like, his own knees locked, although all he wanted was to run back to his car and drive away. And yet . . .

'You look good,' he said.

'Thanks.' Rebecca shifted her gaze to the water, where flies hovered just over its surface. There was no other sound, not even the wind in the trees. Still. Silent.

'I missed you,' he said. And there, the slip. He knew it was coming. The magnetism was different this time, but God, she still drove him crazy. There was just something about her that felt like a part of him; as if their souls were connected on some level so deep it was inescapable.

She didn't speak right away. This was different, too.

315

Before, she would have repeated the phrase even if she hadn't meant it – though, of course, she would have meant it. Now she tilted her head, the muscles in her jaw clenching.

'I have something to tell you,' she said.

And that was when he knew. This wasn't like before. It could never be like before. And not only because he didn't want it to be. Because it *couldn't* be. He didn't want to hear the words; whatever she had to say, he could see it in the expression on her face, that things had changed. Coming here had been a mistake.

'Rebecca, I—'

'No, you need to hear me out. I came today because I have missed you too. God, I've missed you so much. I love you, and I want to be a part of your life. But it's not just that. When I left – before . . . Fuck.' She rubbed her hands over her face, scrubbing away at her fear until she could get her words out.

He waited.

'Matthew, I had a baby.'

'Excuse me?' This wasn't what he had expected her to say. In fact, it was so far outside of what he had expected that he stood, entirely stunned, his mouth open.

'A baby. Our baby.' She sighed and it was like the flood-gates opened and there was the emotion he had been expecting when he'd arrived. Her face morphed, a brightness there that had been locked away. When she spoke, it was as if a weight had lifted – a secret finally revealed. 'She's gorgeous. The most precious baby. She—'

'Rebecca. I don't believe this.'

'I'm not lying,' she said.

'No,' he snapped. 'That isn't what I'm saying. Fucking hell. You had a *child* and you didn't tell me?' There was a

316

rage in him now. That burning love, lust, whatever it was, shifting and growing into bright hot anger, just like before. He couldn't control it. 'You kept that from me for a *year*? How could you?'

'I tried to tell you!' Rebecca said. Her eyes grew wide and she took a small step back. And that only made him angrier. She was *afraid* of him. Well, she wasn't afraid of him before, when she spent months lying and hiding and—

That was where she had been, when she was away. Not travelling. Having their fucking baby.

'You tried to tell me?' he scoffed. 'And, what . . .'

'You told me flat out that you'd never leave your wife. What was I supposed to do with *that* information, Matthew?' She was angry too, and it was more unfamiliar to him than anything else. Mild, gentle Rebecca, finally growing a backbone.

'That's hardly the point.' He could remember that day vividly. She'd been late to meet him and he had been so afraid of losing her that he'd erupted – and then he'd lost her anyway. For a year he fought to forget, to move on, and now she was back to tell him *this*?

'That's entirely the bloody point,' Rebecca says hotly. 'What, did you expect that I'd just wait around forever? With a baby? Did you expect me to get rid . . .?' She couldn't even finish the thought and Matthew realised that he probably would have, actually. And he wasn't sure how to feel about that except more rage.

'So you want me to leave my wife now,' he said. 'Is that it? You want me to drop everything and run back to you because you couldn't be bothered to take a pill?' He couldn't stop the bitterness in his voice.

'Are you kidding me?' Rebecca's expression was careful

317

but her tone was sharp. She was no longer the meek dreamer he once knew.

'No, are you kidding *me*? Rebecca, I can't understand how you could keep something like this from me! And then just . . . drop back in here like you haven't ruined my entire fucking life. What do you want from me?'

'I wanted you to want her!' she screamed. 'I wanted you to want her, and to want me. I came here because I missed you and I wanted you to be a part of my life. Our daughter's life. Is that such an awful thing to want? I thought . . . Actually, I don't know what I thought. I *dreamed*, naively, that you might want to love her – but I was wrong.'

'You have no right,' he warned. She was backing away again, her feet perilously close to the edge of the dock. He followed her. He wanted to grab her, to shake some sense into her. 'You can't just make these decisions for people. You never even asked me if I wanted to keep the kid.'

'No, I didn't. I didn't because you wouldn't even let me tell you about her. All you cared about was your own life: career, wife, a quick roll in the sack but *make sure you're on time*. For God's sake, Matthew. Isn't it too late for that now?'

'Too late?' he barked, bitter laughter clawing in his throat. 'Of course it's too late. It's always too goddamn late. I've missed months of her life! How could you do that? You didn't even give me the *choice*.'

'I don't have to be here,' she said. 'I don't have to listen to this.'

'You'll stay here and talk to me. Explain it to me. Explain the logic that went through your head when you decided to lie – it *is* a lie. Regardless of what I would have wanted in the beginning, when you decided to keep that kid, you should have told me. Given me the chance to decide what I wanted. She's still my child, Rebecca. Jesus. I want to meet her. We're going to figure this out—'

'No.' Rebecca took another step back. 'You know what? I don't want to. I thought coming here was the right thing. I thought telling you was the *right thing*. But Janie's right. I can do it without you. I've changed my mind. You're so angry, Matthew. You're not the man I thought you were, and you have no right to our daughter's life—'

That was the thing that did it. The final push. He hadn't meant for it to happen, but those words . . . they were the fire under him to push him forwards.

He reached out for Rebecca. He wasn't sure what he was planning to do. Hold her, knock some sense into her. Just wrap her in his arms and scream until she listened.

But she was afraid. She yanked her arm away from him, the fear burning in her eyes. She stepped back.

And then she was in the water.

He tried – God, he tried. But the cold was shocking and Rebecca must have hit her head because she was there one second and then she was gone, tugged under by the currents that lurked beneath the surface, clawing, grasping hands pulling her down.

Even thinking about it now, sitting with his daughter at his feet in the car seat he found, Janie's house echoing around him, he can't quite believe it happened at all. It was an accident. But . . .

The baby shifts in her sleep, suckling noises the only sound in the silence.

He can't sit here any longer. The sun will be up in a couple of hours and he needs to make sure that he does what needs to be done before it's light enough to see.

So he grabs the child and heads out to the car. He leaves Janie's house dark but has the forethought to make sure he puts her trainers in a bag, along with a light jacket she might have worn if she was going walking. Those things, just casually lying around in her house – the things he might need to rely on when people wonder where she has gone.

Perhaps it will be easy to lie. He can seed the idea that Janie was out looking for Rebecca. Everybody knows they were friends; it's how he knew where to look. The two were always out by the water together – before Rebecca left. He can suggest that she didn't think the police were doing enough. Which is laughable, because they *are* trying. He knows because he and Lucy have been out in the search parties, Lucy's concern palpable and Matthew's well-faked. They've used the Saturday Night Quizzers charity to raise money, to organise searches; Matthew makes sure he always heads the ones around the loch, though the presence of the dark water unsettles him.

He's learning that the affair with Rebecca has taught him a lot of skills. Lying is one of them. He's not proud of it, but he knows it will save him.

He drives to the loch with the baby buckled safely in the back of the car. He's surprised to realise that babies don't come easily to him. He thought after decades of teaching that children would eventually make sense – especially his own daughter. Which is a ridiculous thought, isn't it? Since when have children ever made sense? And yet there is something about her that draws him in, some softness, a kernel of delight deep in his chest.

He parks in his usual spot at the side of Loch House and carries Janie's body to the water. He's grateful that she is so light, almost elfin, because otherwise this would be much harder. The sadness he felt earlier is gone, even being back here by the water's edge, feeling Rebecca's ghost pushing at the corners of his consciousness. In its place is that fog of detachment, plans running through his head.

The baby can't stay. As much as he wants to know her – wants to discover if she will always look so much like Rebecca, with her dark hair and wide blue eyes, pale skin, the soft scent that reminds him of milky tea and sweet biscuits – he can't. Lucy doesn't want children, and even if she did, he could never ask this of her. The child would be a reminder, constant and burning with resentment. And her presence would prompt too many questions.

No, now Rebecca is gone, the child needs to be gone too.

Once Janie's body is in the water – pulled to its depths as easily as Rebecca was – Matthew comes up with a plan. He has money. A separate savings account he's been quietly adding to for years. He's not really sure why, except he always thought maybe it would be nice to surprise Lucy one day, to prove that he's just as capable as she is. A retirement trip, maybe. A cruise. She's so driven, so smart and financially responsible; he just wanted to prove he could do it too.

Now, though . . . Well, he can draw as much of it out as he can. He's got some blank envelopes in the car from the last charity collection he and Lucy did. And then he'll drive – away from Blackhills, away from Scotland even. He's planning to choose a city. Maybe Newcastle or Durham. High traffic. And he'll leave the baby with the police. He doesn't want her mixed up in all of this, but he doesn't want her hurt, either. None of this is her fault.

It turns out that the drive is the hardest part. His mind

wanders constantly and he has to stop twice to be sick. This reaction surprises him only so far as he's not been sick in years and the feeling is unexpected. At first, he thinks maybe it's the lack of food and the two coffees from the service garage where he stopped for petrol, but it isn't. It's the thought of all of this.

He can't let it win. So he swills his mouth out and he gets back into the car, and when the baby starts to cry, he lets her suckle on formula milk from the same service garage and he burps her, all while making sure he holds her as little as possible, looks at her as little as possible.

And when it comes time to leave her, he makes sure to wipe down the car seat with antibacterial wipes, tucks the money into the envelope using a piece of tissue wrapped over his fingers. He doesn't kiss the child, doesn't even say goodbye.

He can't. Because now he has to go home and pretend that she doesn't exist. That's the second most important thing.

The first: she, and Lucy, and, well, everybody – none of them can ever know what he has done.

Eleanor

'No,' I say again. No, this can't be right. This can't be the Matthew I've met this weekend – the Matthew who was so kind to me today, who told me to come home and make sure I was safe. Who told me to lock the doors as if he was concerned for my wellbeing, as if he wanted me to feel secure. Matthew, who spoke about Rebecca as if he had hardly known her.

And yet, here he is in this photograph, gazing into Rebecca's eyes as if he has never seen anything more beautiful in his life, as if the very sun is shining just for the two of them.

I find myself searching his expression, examining the shape of his eyes, the long dip of his nose, how his jaw is a little square – just like mine. Could he . . . Is it possible that this is the man? That this is my father?

The bulb in the lamp goes out with a pop and I jump, letting out a shriek. My heart slams in my chest and my whole body begins to tremble. I drop the photograph, and scramble back up the stairs, towards the lamps and away from that brittle darkness, searching for the sheets of paper I abandoned, searching for one I saw earlier.

I stare at the paper in disbelief. How could I not have noticed this earlier? It's the booking details for Loch House. The address and the location and . . . the owner. Right there, next to the booking information.

Matthew Ferguson.

A sound outside startles me. I drop the paper and run for the window. Outside, I can hear the rumbling of an engine, but I can't see anything. No headlights, no car. Fresh fear rolls through me. The doors are locked, but if Matthew is here, if he's the owner, he'll probably have a key—

And then, without warning, the rest of the lights go out and the house plunges into frozen darkness.

Eleanor

I scramble to my feet in the pitch darkness. There isn't even a moon to see by tonight, thick clouds hanging heavy, and the whole house is dark as tar. The rumbling has stopped now. My heart is in my throat. For a second, I freeze, unable to force my thoughts into gear.

I strain hard, training my ears on downstairs. I can't hear anything except my own panicked breathing and the thud of my pulse. There's a distant scream of a bird.

But then I hear a sound that might be the gentle creak of the door. And then – unmistakable – footsteps.

I spring into movement, lowering myself into a crouch and kicking off my shoes without thinking. I grab hold of them and then sneak to the door, reaching blindly for the handle so I can swing it open as silently as possible.

The footsteps grow louder.

'Eleanor,' he calls.

It is him. It's Matthew. It shouldn't surprise me – at this point, nothing should surprise me – and yet I am surprised.

I'm surprised by the hollow echo in his voice, in the way it sounds even now like he *wants to help*.

He must know who I am, I realise. He must. He must have seen something in me the way Michaela did. I remember the way he looked the first time he saw my face – a shock I'd put down to worry about Michaela. Did he know Rebecca had a daughter? I want so badly to believe I'm making all of this up, but I can't. Panic surges inside me.

He must have known. He must never have expected this – but now he's come to tidy up one last loose end, the last remaining evidence of a two decades old mystery, a secret he has fought to keep.

'Eleanor! Come out. I don't want to hurt you.'

I keep silent, trying to breathe through my nose but finding it almost impossible. I can't focus on anything except the wild beating of my heart and the soft creak of my feet on the cold boards. My toes are already numb and I swear a fresh, icy breeze whips through as if Matthew has left the door open.

Maybe I can make a run for it. If he came through the front, maybe I can leave through the sliding doors. I might make it to the woods and if I do, then I can lose him. Like everybody has told me this weekend, there are so many winding, twisting paths. He can't possibly know *all* of them, and if I can get to the village, then it isn't far to the police station or the pub.

But then, will they believe me? Or will they choose to believe Matthew, a long-standing member of their community, the man who taught their children, whose wife apparently owns half of Blackhills and fills the rest of her time with charity work?

Fuck. *Fuck*.

I pick up my pace on the stairs, knowing if he catches me here, I'm doomed. There's not exactly any other way down. I hold my breath when I reach the bottom, peering around the bannister like a child. It's so dark that I can make out only snatches: faint light glinting off the counter in the kitchenette, the glass of the log burner, the shape of the sliding doors that lead to the outside.

Maybe it would be quicker to go out the main door, but the darkness of the path out there scares me. With a silent curse, I realise I don't have the car keys either, so I can't even run and hope I can get it started and pull away before he finds me.

Worse, though, I can't hear him any more.

The breath catches in the back of my throat and I freeze again, lungs burning, eyes straining into the ink black. Silence. Silence. And—

He's so close I can smell him.

'Eleanor.' He calls my name again. The sound of it rolling off his tongue makes me shiver. 'Eleanor. The power is out. I've come to make sure you're okay. Eleanor . . .?'

He walks past the bottom of the stairs towards the main door again. Now is my chance. I lose silence for speed, throwing myself off the bottom step and pelting for the double doors.

'Eleanor!'

Matthew is nothing but a thunder of footsteps behind me. I reach the doors and yank at them. My arm jars but nothing happens.

'Eleanor, you can't—'

'Let me out!' I scream. 'Let me *out*!'

I haul my entire body weight on the doors again, scrabbling at the lock. It shouldn't stick like this. It worked fine earlier. Oh God, has he locked me in somehow?

Matthew is there, right behind me.

I finally get the door open, the metal grating as I pull it back. I stumble out into the night as Matthew lets out a frustrated grunt. I manage to slide the door back into place, the lock clicking down as the door slams against the jamb with a satisfying *smack*. A joyous swooping balloons in my chest and I can see the water, hear it lapping.

I run. Fast and hard, legs like the jelly of a newborn calf's, but it doesn't matter. I'm *free*.

Until a bright, arcing wing of pain thrashes through my head as something heavy comes down on the back of my neck. It hurts so badly, I immediately think I'm going to be sick.

I stumble to my knees, vision wavering. My palms skid in the dirt. Oh God, is this what dying feels like? No. I can't. He can't have caught up with me. My knees are wet and my hands sing with the pain of landing hard on them and I want to get up, but I can't. My vision bucks again, stomach roiling.

Then, blackness.

Sarah

Then

Sarah returns to chaos.

Fresh off her first holiday abroad in three years, she'd been looking forward to showing off her very faint tan – as a redhead, she's never tanned well, but this time she's got more than just freckles – and catching up on the gossip from Tiffany, but her first shift back at the cafe is cancelled when Tiffany calls the landline.

'Tiff, what's up?'

'Haven't you heard yet?' Tiffany asks. She sounds breathless, as if she's just run to the phone. It's not even eight o' clock.

'Heard what? I only got back last night.'

'Rebecca Kelly,' says Tiffany emphatically. 'And now Janie, too.'

'What about them?'

'They're missing.' Tiffany doesn't wait for a reaction before ploughing on. 'Rebecca disappeared last week. She was meant to be back in Blackhills to visit her parents, but she never made it to their house. Somebody saw her –

her uncle, I think – but then she disappeared. People think she maybe fell in the loch, y'know how she was always there—'

'And *Janie*?' Sarah asks. The shock has left her numb. These girls . . . she's known them since they were all five years old. Her and Rebecca and Janie were best friends for years. And whatever distance has grown between her and Rebecca over the last couple of years, she would never, ever wish her harm. 'Wasn't Bec meant to be travelling?'

'I guess she came back. Janie's been banging on to anybody who'll listen that the police aren't looking hard enough and my theory is she was out looping the water looking for her. You know how she had a bee in her bonnet about Rebecca. God, what would possess her to go alone? John said he only went round to her house to ask her if she'd heard anything yet and Josh said—'

'So, what, people think Janie drowned too?' Sarah asks. It doesn't sit right with her. Those girls have spent their lives by the water.

'Don't know. Anyway, Martha says we're gonna close the cafe today so we can help search. I'll come pick you up on my way over.'

Over the next few days, Sarah's life spirals out of control. It isn't just her, though. The whole village is shaken. Search parties leave from the Lane at intervals throughout the day; police from Blackdale crawl through, stopping for coffee in the cafe, asking questions in the pub. It feels like Blackhills is suddenly the centre of the universe, and not in a good way.

She's seen Matthew – and his wife – out and about at all hours, co-ordinating search parties and making sure everybody is getting enough to eat and drink. She and her colleagues at the cafe have taken turns helping too, and Sarah always makes sure she's in the groups that circle the loch. Partly because she's convinced if Janie and Rebecca are anywhere, it's going to be there – and partly because Matthew looks dashing even when he's obviously not had much sleep. Sarah knows she shouldn't even *think* about how attractive he is, but she's never been able to help herself. She still remembers being his student, wishing madly he would notice her. Him and the art teacher, James Neilen.

There's something that bothers Sarah, though. It's driving her mad that she can't figure out exactly what it is. She thinks about it when she's in the shower, when she's bushing her teeth, when she's behind the counter at work and especially when she's cycling through the local radio stations hoping that there will be some news.

Rebecca wasn't *right* before she left Blackhills. That is the thought that Sarah keeps settling on. She was distant, forgetful. She thinks back to the day in the cafe over a year ago, when Sarah had called her out for missing her birthday. She'd meant it as a joke, but she got the sense at the time that Rebecca hadn't taken it that way. Janie always stuck up for her, saying, 'Oh you know, she's just got a lot on her plate with her mum,' even though it had been over a year since Gwyn finished her chemo. It felt a bit like an excuse – but, of course, then Sarah felt guilty about it.

That interaction in the cafe is what she's thinking about today as she wipes down the counter between customers and a Cher song comes on the radio. That day was the last time she saw Rebecca to talk to her. She saw her a few times about the village, but that was it, and then she was finally off on her travels. Sarah plays it over and over in her head.

She's fixating on how spooked Rebecca had seemed when Sarah had joked about her daydreaming. *Who were you with?* A joke. And yet, Rebecca *had* been looking, eyes fixed out the window. And that sigh, it had been full of something—

The bell above the door dings and in comes Matthew Ferguson. Sarah always gets a bit flustered when she sees him, her old schoolgirl crush making her shaky and silly. Even though they've been out together several times over the last week along with a bunch of other folks from the village, trawling the shore of the loch, tramping the fields on the other side of Blackhills, she still gives a startled smile.

'Two coffees with skimmed milk please, Sarah,' he says after the pleasantries are out of the way. He looks extra tired today, dark circles under his eyes and a couple of days' worth of stubble on his jaw.

'How are you holding up?' she asks as she pours the coffee and passes it to him. She wouldn't have dared even ask a personal question a few weeks ago, but she feels like she's getting to know him a bit now. He's been so worried about Rebecca and Janie. 'Is your wife out there again this morning?'

He nods distractedly. He's glancing at his watch, and then at the wall, and then stirring sugar in the coffee, all without looking at her. And there's something about the way he's standing that makes her think back, again, to that day last year. To the way Rebecca had been looking out the window . . . watching him.

Sarah had been too busy mooning that day to think much about it, but now – now she remembers another time at a charity dinner Lucy and Matthew hosted in the old cinema. A whole bunch of Matthew's ex-students had been there to support him, head teacher now, a world away from the fresh-faced teacher he'd been when they were at school.

Sarah remembers a brief moment, an encounter over a glass of wine, Rebecca staring wistfully across the crowded space. That time, when Sarah had asked her who she was looking at, Rebecca had been coy, smiling shyly and just shrugging. Josh was manning the little bar with Tiffany's brother and Rebecca's uncle Paul. Josh had not long been working at the school as a janitor and he'd gained a lot of muscle. He looked good. Sarah had thought that Rebecca was staring at him. At Josh.

Now Sarah realises something, and it's enough to make her breathless. Because maybe Rebecca hadn't been staring at Josh after all. The humming feeling she gets when she discovers a delicious piece of gossip is starting in her chest.

'*You* must be devastated about Rebecca,' Sarah says now. Offhand. Casual. She stops what she's doing to pick at her nail, keeping her face neutral. She's always had a nose for the truth, and now she's noticed she can't believe it took her so long. That, surely, is why Matthew is going out of his way to search for Rebecca. Why he looks so tired and so damn sad. He and Rebecca were *together*.

Matthew's gaze snaps to her face. 'What makes you say that?' he asks.

'Oh. You know.' Sarah shrugs, returning to her damp rag and the counter. 'You and Rebecca always got on, didn't you?'

She isn't sure, exactly, how she's expecting him to answer, but the blank expression on his face says it all.

'I'm just as devastated as everybody else should be,' he says firmly.

But Sarah knows that's not true at all.

Two days later, Sarah bumps into Matthew as she's closing up the cafe. Tiffany went home at just gone four because she had a doctor's appointment but forgot to tell Martha so she could build it into the rota. But it's been quiet and Sarah quite likes closing up by herself, where she can take her time and walk home slowly. She's just turning the final lock when Matthew rounds the corner.

'Sarah,' he says. His breath plumes in the air. They've been having another cold snap and the temperature has already dropped now the sun is sinking.

'Hi. Sorry – I've just closed up.'

'Oh, it's . . . I don't want a coffee. Listen.' He steps closer to her, almost uncomfortably so, but she doesn't back away. In fact, even after all of these years, his presence makes her feel flustered, warm and tingly. God, she's stupid. She bets he made Rebecca feel the same way, and wonders how far things went.

'Hmm?'

'I . . . I've been thinking about what you were saying the other day. About Rebecca.'

Sarah's focus shifts and she tries to make some sense of this. 'What do you mean?'

'I . . .' Matthew glances behind himself and when he looks back, his eyes are wide, nervous. 'Can we talk about it, please? Not here, though. I'll make it worth your time.'

'Oh.' Sarah's heart thumps. He probably thinks she's going to tell everybody. Maybe he's going to deny it all. Or maybe – a wild thought passes through her mind – maybe he's going to offer to pay her to keep her mouth shut. With Rebecca gone, it looks bad, and Matthew won't want people to think badly of him. Sarah doesn't think badly of him. How could she? In truth, she's a little jealous of Rebecca. What she wouldn't have given for a harmless little fling with him.

'Please?' Matthew says again. His expression is wounded, gentle. She can see how much it's costing him to ask. 'Can you come to the big house on the loch in about an hour? It'll be quiet there and we can have a proper chat. I want to explain.'

'Uh, sure. Okay. I guess.'

Sarah doesn't let herself think too much about it. If she does, she knows she'll decide against going. It's a stupid thing to do, probably. But part of her is curious and wants to be proved right. Maybe this is the reason that Rebecca left the village in the first place. Maybe it's the reason she's gone again. Sarah is half convinced that Rebecca isn't missing at all, that she's accepted a huge pay-off from Matthew, and she's probably taken Janie with her. Sarah always got a bit of a vibe from the two of them. And honestly, part of her wants to be proved wrong too. Matthew is too good to be caught up in all of this.

In the end, she can't resist. There are too many questions. And if nothing else, she wants the confirmation. Not that she'll *do* anything with it, but she loves to know. She's always been the same. When they were growing up, Janie was always the secret-keeper. Sarah was the secret-sharer. And she knows which one brought people more joy. Or, at least *amusement*. Besides, if there's money on the table, she's not above taking it.

* * *

Sarah heads to the old house on the loch an hour later. She hasn't even bothered to get changed after her shift, though she did throw on a lined jacket because it's even colder than it was this morning. It looks like it might start to rain and she hopes at least that Matthew can give her a lift home later because it's not exactly round the corner.

It's only as she draws up to the house that she starts to really, properly consider if this is a good idea. She hasn't been out here for years, not since she used to come with Josh and Magnus and Janie and Rebecca. She's never liked it out here anyway. There's something about the water that makes her uncomfortable, the darkness of it maybe, the way you never know how deep it is, or what might be lurking in its depths.

Matthew is already at the house when she arrives. He gets out of his car.

'I'm glad you came,' he says. He's had time to get changed and he's wearing a loose pair of joggers, so thin that Sarah can't help staring.

'It's fine.'

Matthew leads them straight to the door, which feels wrong to Sarah somehow. Nobody ever goes into the house – it's empty and has been forever. But then Matthew pulls out a key and she stops.

'Wait. *You* own this place?'

Matthew gives her a small smile. 'I know. Nobody ever remembers. But I wanted to show you – what we did. Come on in, I'll put some lights on.'

Sarah hesitates, but only for a second. She can't help but admit she's curious. Matthew locks the door behind her and leads her into a large living space, a kitchen and a lounge decorated in neutral tones. The view out of the glass door is lovely, what little she can see of it as the sun sets, all water and trees.

'Does somebody live here?' Sarah asks. She's shocked. It looks so different to how she remembers from when she and the boys would peer through the big glass doors. It had been empty then, and now it is not.

'No, not really. But maybe at some point I'll start renting it again. The house belonged to my great-uncle originally,' he says. 'They used it for holiday lets, or when family came to stay. That sort of thing.' He wanders to the mantelpiece and rubs a finger through the faint layer of dust. 'We did it up – Rebecca and me.'

Slowly, the pieces start to slot into place in Sarah's mind, the last year spinning out ahead of it. Matthew's new commitment to the charity work Lucy has been doing, setting up the canned goods drive, the new animal shelter in Blackdale – all of it Lucy's doing, but Matthew always there like a loyal dog.

Guilt, Sarah realises. *Guilt.*

'Does Lucy know about it?' But that isn't the only question. Does Lucy know about *Rebecca*? Sarah has seen her more times over the last few weeks than she has over several years before, directing search parties, mapping out which parts of the loch shores still need walking. Surely she must have seen it too, the way Rebecca looked at her husband? The way her husband looked back? If Sarah has noticed it . . .

'Lucy doesn't know anything at all,' Matthew says coldly. 'And that's the way it's going to stay.'

'Not about this house? Or even Rebecca?' She swallows. This is the part where she sees if he's angry, if he'll offer her anything for her silence. They've both gravitated towards the sliding doors now, Sarah with her back to the view of the water and Matthew's closeness suddenly uncomfortable. She waits and he only stares at her, his gaze calculating. So she forges forward. 'Does Lucy know that you cheated on her?'

Sarah knows, immediately, that she should have just left it alone. The look in his eyes is wild. Like a cornered animal. Fear zings through her. Her heart races and her palms sweat. She backs up until her shoulder blades press against the door, the glass so thin she can feel the icy wind off the water and it chills her to the bone. She always felt safe with Matthew. He was her *teacher*, for Christ's sake. This feeling, this fear, is entirely new – and it consumes her.

'Matthew,' she says, panic making her voice shake. 'I'm sorry. I shouldn't have joked. I won't say any—'

'Don't lie,' Matthew cuts her off. 'I know you, Sarah McNeil. I've known you since you were fifteen years old.'

'Why did you ask me to come then?' she yelps. 'If you didn't want to talk?'

'I wanted to know how much you knew. Because you can't keep a secret to save your life.'

The word choice is unfortunate, but Sarah only has a second to register it with horror before Matthew is coming at her. He's strong, but he's surprisingly fast too. And he was ready; she wasn't.

She shrieks and tries to dodge his hands, but they're so big and in seconds they have her by the throat. It's a practised swoop and she's back against the door, cold at her back, limbs tingling as the breath whooshes from her lungs. Surprise catches her. She thought he would be upset. Angry, even. But she didn't expect . . . this.

She lashes out, legs flailing, fingernails scrabbling. She

catches him off guard, a kick to the knee and then another to the groin. That gets her as far as the coffee table before he catches her and she goes down hard. He throws her like a child's toy, her body slamming into the table so hard that she hears the glass top shatter. She knows she could reach for something, a piece of it, cut him, but her head is exploding with pain and she can't see and—

He's on her, knee on her chest, hands around her neck.

'I can't have you telling anybody,' he pants. 'I can't have you ruining it all. For God's sake, Sarah, why couldn't you keep your damn mouth shut?'

He's heavy. So heavy. She can't breathe. Rebecca, Janie, was this how it was for them? All this time everybody thought they were missing, but no. Matthew got rid of them.

'*Matthew.*'

'No,' he grunts. 'No, I won't let you tell Lucy. It will kill her. Everything we've built.'

She can't fight any more.

'You won't steal our future. *Nothing* will steal our future.'

Matthew squeezes harder.

Matthew

Tuesday afternoon

He is cursed.

There is no other explanation for any of this. Perhaps the children who whisper silly, spooky stories on the playground are right. The lake is haunted, and at some point in his youth, the demon spirit of Loch Aven burrowed deep into his soul, and dug her claws into the most vulnerable part of him so he might never be free.

After Eleanor heads back to the house at his request, he stands in the street reeling. He hadn't expected to see her, wasn't prepared for the way it would make him feel. He has had his suspicions for two days – even if she hadn't looked so much like Rebecca, he might have guessed it. There is just something about her, some part of her nature that feels so familiar to him, it's like looking into a mirror. Only the mirror is warped and shows only the newness, the fresh blood and the sharp wounds he spent years trying to stitch.

But today, right now on the street . . . it has brought this half-truth, this suspicion, into the full light. He can't ignore it any more. The way Eleanor looked only minutes ago, that look of sheer panic, it is familiar to him in a way that cuts him deeper than anything else.

It's the same look Rebecca wore in that last second before she went into the loch.

The same look he sees imprinted behind his eyelids whenever he sleeps.

He told Eleanor – his daughter – to go back to the house, because what the hell else was he supposed to do? Now he has to work out a plan. God, he never wanted this for her. He never wanted her to get hurt.

More than that though, he never wanted her here in this rotten place. This place that ate up Rebecca and spat her out. This place that corrupted him from the inside out. Eleanor – God, even her name is noble – she deserves something so, so much more.

He stands in the street for long minutes after she is gone. The air whips down the Lane and his blood simmers in his veins. It's only the numbness in his hands that drives him back towards his car, and then, without thinking, towards home. *Home*.

He feels like an animal caught in a trap. Lucy was with him in the pub on Saturday. She must have seen Eleanor, even though he didn't. But would she notice? She had never cared for Rebecca one way or the other, only knowing her well enough to recognise her as one of the raven-haired Kelly clan. What would she care for another black-haired stranger?

When he pulls up on the driveway he shares with Lucy, he notices that she isn't home yet, which is strange. She is nearly always home by now on a Tuesday, even during the school holidays. They often have dinner together and spend the evening in the soft quiet reserved for long-married couples who have worked hard and grown used to each other's company.

He gets out of the car in a daze, his mind still whirring. He has to come up with a plan. He can't let Lucy find out about Eleanor. He can't let Eleanor find out about *him*. Can he? Jesus. This is all too much, it feels insurmountable. It feels, he thinks, like a thousand litres of loch water are crushing down on his chest, his bones turning to rubble inside him.

How will he survive it? He'll lose everything. And if they find out about Eleanor, how long before they start asking questions about Rebecca? About Janie and Sarah?

He isn't built for this. Not any more. Secrets make him feel feral, like a cat left too long to its own devices. He'd rather gnaw his own arm off than go to prison. And that's exactly where he's headed, even if he swears he isn't that person any more. Even if, well, it seemed justified at the time. Even that thought sickens him.

He cuts across the driveway and swings into the house the way he always does, dropping his keys on the front hall table and his jacket on the bannister.

'Lucy?' he calls. Just in case. Maybe she left her car at the pub. Sometimes she goes after work lately, probably letting off some steam. She's been trying to wrap up a few loose business ends so she can retire, but there's too much for him to understand and she's so stressed all of the time.

She's not here though. The house echoes at him.

He stalks through the hall and up the stairs, stripping off his jumper and shirt and throwing them in the hamper. The more he thinks about Eleanor, the more jumbled it all gets inside his head. What the fuck is he going to do?

He's got to get rid of her. Obviously. It's the only logical solution. But her friends . . . Her friends.

He stops. He's been so tied up in thoughts about the girl, about *his* girl, that he has barely thought about them at all. Perhaps he's listened to the narrative around town long enough that he's started to believe it. To believe that those girls fell into the loch, breathed their last breaths with lungs full of dark water.

But, Jesus, he knows that isn't what happened in the first place. Well, not in the manner they think it happened anyway. The water swallowed them, but that was only because of him. And he did not ever want to do that again.

He cuts to Lucy's side of the bed and throws his watch down – and it tumbles to the floor. With a muffled curse, he bends to scoop it up and discovers . . . what? A bag? It's not one he's seen before, and not something that Lucy would be caught dead with, leopard print and brown leather.

He pulls it out, dragging it from under the bed and onto the carpet with the thick, soft pile that Lucy insisted on and he's always hated. It feels like worms under his feet. He remembers when he used to be so offended by this stuff, by all the decisions she made without him, the way he always worried what she would think, and now he is glad for it. It's direction, and it means he has less time to feel guilty about everything. For the prison he's locked them both in.

He starts to push the bag back under the bed, but something stops him. Some instinct. The loch demon clawing inside him, wanting to be free. He unzips the corner, and then more. And then the whole thing in one satisfying rip.

There's a chapstick inside, a pack of tissues and a hair tie – and a phone that he doesn't recognise. Not even one of his wife's old ones, he doesn't think. The battery is dead.

Fear sweeps through him, along with the sudden urge to burn it all to the ground. Everything he touches turns to shit. This can't be happening.

What has she done?

And then, the next thought – he's got to get to Eleanor. This is going to destroy them all.

Eleanor

I come to groggily, pain lancing through my skull and down my neck into my shoulder. I open my eyes slowly, a wave of sickness threatening to capsize me, to drag me right down into the murky depths of Loch Aven, which teeters into view under my feet between wooden boards. A cold wind snaps and the clouds scud overhead, revealing a bright scrap of moon.

I groan.

'Oh good,' says a voice I can't place. 'You're awake.'

I shift, testing my body. I'm seated on something that doesn't feel very stable. It reminds me of a camping chair. I let my eyes follow the shape of my legs, the dock, and slowly – achingly slowly – draw them upwards. The sickness comes in another wave and I gag, but nothing comes.

A shape moves to my right, a wriggle, followed by two familiar grunting noises. I turn my head, taking in the outline of two figures, hunched in chairs similar to mine. Hands bound together at the wrists with dark climbing rope—

Another figure moves and a light flares to life, pale and eerily white. It illuminates the girls beside me, Clio and Michaela. Alive. *Alive.*

Michaela sits hunched lower than Clio, her dark eyes haunted in the sliver of moonlight. She has some kind of tape over her mouth, but otherwise she looks unhurt. Exhausted, but unharmed. Clio's eyes are wide and she flicks her gaze back and forth between me and Michaela.

I want to cry, relief threatening to swallow me even as fear drives the sickness in me still, but I don't have time to cry because my eyes are already following the light. It isn't on the dock but nearby, the kind of stake light my parents always used to take camping, jammed into the sandy grass of the shore. And in front of it, a figure. Stood completely still, watching me. Watching the moment of realisation as I see Clio and Michaela, the relief followed by the bone-wrenching panic.

Matthew?

No. It's a woman.

At first, I don't recognise her at all. But then she turns to the side and I catch her face in profile: smooth golden hair, small chin, perfect nose.

Matthew's *wife*.

'With a head wound like that, I thought it might be longer,' she says. Her tone is light, but I can tell that it contains a multitude of sins, not least a barely restrained fury. She steps further into the light of her camping lamp and I see that her hands aren't empty.

In one there is a rucksack. In the other – rocks.

'You,' I croak. My voice is as cracked as a dry riverbed.

'Yes,' she says calmly. 'Me. Little old Lucy. You put up quite the chase.' She bends to select another rock within the circle of unwavering silver light and drops it into the rucksack with a terrifying thud. 'Really. Very well done. And very clever locking the door behind you when you ran out; that's bought us some time for a chat before he can find a key, or get the front door open. Unless he decides to smash the window, but I don't know – he really likes original windows . . .'

'Please,' I say. I try to coat my tongue with spit, but there's nothing there. I glance at Michaela and Clio, fighting off another wave of sickness. '*Why?*' I beg. 'What are you planning?'

'What am I planning? You'll have to wait and see about that. I reckon we won't be much longer.'

Lucy picks up another rock and adds it to the rucksack. Her face is wild. She's totally consumed by this. She hefts the rucksack's weight in one hand, testing it, and then – apparently satisfied – she rips the stake light out of the ground in a spray of dirt.

She marches to the entrance of the dock and then heads towards the three of us. She stops about a foot away, planting the light carefully on the dock. It's so bright, it feels like sunlight and I wince.

'Up,' she says. She's at Michaela's side. She grabs her under the arm, with the confidence of somebody who has done this exact movement before.

Michaela doesn't fight her. From the exhaustion, the way she obeys without even a mumble through the gag, it's clear Michaela has done this dance before too.

Clio's eyes widen as Lucy kicks the chair away. And it's Clio she comes to next.

'Up,' Lucy demands.

Clio thinks about fighting her. I can see it in her eyes.

But unlike Michaela, she has a nasty bruise forming on her jaw, sickly blue in the light of the torch, and this seems to make her hesitate.

She stands, and Lucy kicks her chair away too.

Now she's next to me. I feel my limbs quiver even as I fight the fear. She can't hurt all three of us. Between us, we could take her – I'm sure of it. And yet, when Lucy barks a third and final command, '*Up*' – I stand.

'Lucy,' I whisper.

'Patience,' she says coldly.

She can barely bring herself to look at me. While she handled Michaela and Clio to get them to their feet, I notice that she doesn't touch me. She doesn't even stand close enough that I could touch her. She is watching Loch House with an intensity to her expression and I realise two things in quick succession:

1. She is waiting for somebody. Probably Matthew, still shut in Loch House.

2. She probably knows, if I'm right about Rebecca, if that photograph I found means anything at all, that Matthew could be my father.

The thoughts sweep through me with a speed that leaves me breathless, and my brain has only just finished formulating enough for me to begin to form a question when I hear a crash somewhere out of sight, followed by the rustle of undergrowth as something comes barrelling through the hedge near the house.

'Lucy, wait. Let's talk about this first, please!'

Matthew.

He skids to the end of the dock, panting. There's blood on his hand and a steely look in his eyes as they flick from his wife – to me.

Lucy springs to attention, throwing herself behind me, and I don't see so much as *feel* the press of something against my throat. Something cold and shining and sharp.

A knife.

Lucy has a knife to my throat.

Clio lets out a little wail and Michaela curses emphatically enough that I can make it out even through her bound lips.

Matthew freezes, his hands going up in panic. 'Lucy,' he warns. 'Lucy, what are you doing?'

Lucy is so close to me now that I can feel the warmth of her body at my back, smell the expensive perfume she must have applied this morning. Briefly, ridiculously, I imagine her spritzing it on in front of the mirror before packing a bag with a fucking *knife*.

I swallow carefully, but the knife presses tighter to my skin and I feel the first wince of pain before Lucy draws it back a little.

'What am I doing?' she breathes. 'What does it look like I'm doing?'

'Lucy—'

'No, Matthew. The only words you get to say right now are a fucking explanation.'

'For what?' he says. His voice is undercut with terror, making it tight and weak. 'What do you want me to say?'

'Did you honestly think I didn't know about her?' Lucy demands. I can feel the rage in the vibration of her, barely contained beneath the surface. One movement and she'll slit my throat. 'Do you think I'm stupid?'

'I only found out at the weekend—'

'Not about this one,' she seethes. 'Rebecca! Did you honestly think I would never find out?'

'I—'

'All those years of lying to me. All that I endured because of *you*. God forbid, Matthew. I knew about Rebecca from the beginning. I thought it was my *job* to just take it, because you were everything I had ever wanted. Did you honestly think I couldn't see? The way you looked at her? The way the two of you would disappear off in the middle of functions, after work, fucking in your goddamn car like animals? At first, I thought at least you'd have the decency to be discreet about it, but then, you had to play house too. And the nerve of it, after everything – to pay her off?'

I feel dizzy. Any relief I have at hearing my suspicions confirmed is swallowed by grief as Matthew's face grows pale, a lifetime of mistakes laid bare before him. 'The money . . .'

'Well, I *assumed* you were paying her off,' Lucy says. 'So I guess the joke's on me, huh? I knew about the bank account, Matt. I thought it was *sweet*. I thought it was going to be for us, money to retire with, and I thought *Isn't my husband thoughtful?* And then – the pay-off. Jesus Christ. That's what I thought was happening. I thought she disappeared and you were giving her money to keep her quiet. And I thought, well, all of that isn't so bad, at least she's gone. Let's get some good publicity for the charity out of it.'

Lucy laughs and the sound is bitter as lemons. It's enough to make me shiver.

Clio lets out another whimper and Lucy hisses at her, brandishing the knife. I gulp a breath but don't have time to move before the knife is back at my throat and Matthew winces, swaying forward. But Lucy isn't finished yet.

'You know, at first I was mostly just offended. No, that's not true. I was downright angry. But I thought – she's gone, it's done, what's the harm? And then the other girl disappeared. And the other. Friends of Rebecca's. And, I suppose that was harder to reconcile. But still, there was something left in me that trusted you, Matthew.'

'I—'

'I don't fucking know why. You're a cowardly piece of shit. What happened, huh? Did they find out about you and Rebecca? Did they threaten to tell me? I hoped – God, you know, I hoped you were paying them off too. I thought when that Sarah disappeared that it had to be true, because she was such a little snitch – you said. I bet you don't remember, but you said that once, when she was still a *kid*. And when she went, I thought . . . I thought, *yes, I'm right*. The three of them clubbed together and got you paying through the nose – and you know what?' She laughs again. 'I actually thought *good on them*. I wanted you to suffer. And I tried to give you a chance. I wanted you to tell me. I thought, well, if you were man enough to get yourself caught cheating, you could at least admit it to me. We promised to help each other through everything, didn't we? Or did those vows mean nothing to you? No, you didn't even have the balls to talk to me. And it drove me insane. I gave you opportunity after opportunity. I opened up the floor. I asked you if there was anything you wanted to tell me.'

'I couldn't. I didn't—' He's pleading, though his tone barely registers as I struggle to keep up, a whole lifetime of questions beginning to unravel.

'You didn't want to,' Lucy snaps. 'Exactly.'

'It's not that simple!' Matthew exclaims. 'I didn't mean for any of this to happen.'

Lucy moves the knife and it digs in again and I cry out.

Matthew stumbles backwards and the water laps and I want to scream.

'But that isn't actually what happened, is it?' she hisses. 'I *hoped* you were paying them off. For years I conned myself into believing it. I thought if they were dead, we'd have found them. But – I was wrong about that. Wasn't I?'

'No. I—'

I feel hollow. Sick. This can't be true – it can't be happening.

'Wasn't I, Matthew?' she pushes. 'I want you to admit it. Admit what happened. Why did you do it? Because you did something, didn't you? Something awful? I needed to see how you'd react, when it happened again. I needed to see and now I've seen it and I *know*. This is what guilty looks like.'

'I didn't mean to!' Matthew cries. 'I didn't want anybody to be hurt. It just happened. It was an *accident*.'

An accident. My stomach swoops. How can he say that? An accident is what you call knocking over a glass of wine, not killing somebody and effectively making your own daughter an orphan.

'I don't believe you!' Lucy shouts, blisteringly loud in my ear. 'Which one of them, exactly, was an accident? Because I know you. You pretend that you're all sunshine and roses, but there's a nasty streak inside you. And I don't care – you know that, I've loved you, been devoted to you, since we were fifteen years old. I would have *died* for you – but I do want you to take some fucking ownership.'

'All right!' he shouts. 'All right. I did it. I hurt them.' He covers his eyes with his hands. 'I genuinely didn't mean for – Rebecca. It was an accident. We fought and she fell. But then Janie . . . she *knew*. I could tell the second I saw her

354

that she knew. I don't know how, but she did. She freaked out. And Sarah – she figured it out. I couldn't let it ruin our lives . . . I couldn't lose you!'

There it is. The truth of what happened to Janie, to Sarah, and Rebecca – my *mum*.

'How could you?' I bleat. 'They trusted you!'

Matthew's face is stricken, his shoulders hunched. Anger washes over me, bitter and hot and absolutely useless. And then, as Matthew's face contorts, comes an unexpected wave of pity, which makes me sick. He doesn't deserve my pity. I don't want to give it.

For some reason, I think of Charlotte, of the way even her most awful attributes made me feel sorry for her. Only it wasn't real, that emotion. It was a reaction to the real feelings I was trying to bury. That anger. That fear of her lashing out.

Then I realise: Matthew's body language is so familiar to me because it has been mine. He is *afraid* of Lucy. After everything he has done . . . Rebecca, and Janie, and Sarah. The realisation that he is responsible for their deaths and even he is afraid of his wife, it punches the air out of me.

'I could have continued to pretend, you know,' Lucy continues. 'I'd have taken it to my grave because I . . . Lord, Matthew, I loved you. For better or worse and all of that shit. But then, this . . .' She can't find the word and the knife presses tighter again.

Tears squeeze between my eyelids and I realise Clio is crying too, the sound punctuated by the lapping of water against the dock. Michaela has inched closer to her and they stand tucked up against each other.

'Eleanor,' Matthew says slowly.

'Exactly. Did you hear her? In the pub, telling the world

about her adoption and her search for her bloody birth parents and, my God, *look at her*. If the rest of Blackhills doesn't put two and two together, there's not a brain between the lot of them. Jesus. It felt like being *slapped* with it. If what you did was because you couldn't lose me, well what about this?'

I want to scream. I want to run. They are talking about me as if I'm not even here, and this is as much a knife to my throat as the one in Lucy's hands. Anger and fear war inside me still, but I have to push both aside. I *have* to listen. This man, responsible for the deaths of three women . . . he is my father.

'Lucy, I'm sorry,' Matthew whispers. 'I didn't mean for this. I told you. I didn't mean for *any* of it. It was . . . an accident.'

'Nothing about this was an accident.' Lucy's voice is so tight it could snap. 'You made this happen, Matt. You carried on with Rebecca while you were married to me. And you were surprised by the fruits of it, like some kind of fool. Well, I wasn't surprised.'

'But why this?' Matthew begs. He's crying now, too. Anger simmers inside me, somewhere beneath the fear. Lucy hates me. She really hates me. And all Matthew can do is *stand there*. 'Why did you . . . take them?'

Lucy laughs. 'I didn't mean to,' she mimics. 'It was an accident.' Her laughter grows stringy. 'I told you: I wanted you to say something, Matt. I wanted you to tell me the truth. I thought, if I can't do it by love and attention and opportunity to speak, well, I'll do it by fear. Because you are a *coward*.'

Now the knife is really hurting me. Blood flows and I feel it sticky and hot in a trickle just below my collarbone.

I let out a noise that sounds like it can't be mine, so threaded with pain and panic. My whole body is shaking with adrenaline, heart pounding.

'Lucy, please, just let her go. We can talk about this. I can explain now. I'll admit everything – it's not too late. I'll do whatever you want. But if you go ahead with this – what then?'

'You think I haven't thought it through? Mister Philosophy asking me to consider my life choices?' She scoffs. 'I knew you'd care the most about *her*. That's why I saved her for last. I took *her* phone,' she gestures at Michaela with her free hand, 'so I knew that would buy us some time. I hoped you'd come around, panic enough about a copycat that you'd talk to me. Confess to me. But, as always, you were too up your own arse to even see what I was trying to do. So I took the other one, too.' She shrugs. 'But, you know, I'm past that now. I don't just want you to admit it to me – not any more. The time has passed. I'm done messing around.'

'Then what do you want?' Matthew begs.

'You're going to write me a note,' Lucy says. Each word is cold and filled with fury. 'You *are* going to admit it. Everything. You are going to tell *everybody* what you did. To me. To those poor girls. You tell them that you should have known better, that you – and your position of fucking authority – should have *done better*. And instead, when faced with what happened, you got rid of them. You threw those girls away as if they meant *nothing*.'

'I didn't . . .' Matthew tails off, a fresh wave of fear visible on his face.

'And then,' Lucy goes on, 'you're going to put on this rucksack. And you're going to jump in.'

357

Eleanor

'*No*.' Matthew gasps. 'You can't—'

'And once you're gone,' Lucy forges ahead, 'I will tell everybody you were going to hurt these lovely tourists. And that I saved them. And then I will show them your *suicide note*.'

'What?' I ask. Lucy swats me like a fly. This isn't right. There is so much to process but this can't be the answer. Why would more violence solve anything? Panic overtakes me. If Lucy's plan goes ahead then I won't even get the chance to ask Matthew *anything*. 'Please, don't.'

'The girls are confused,' Lucy continues determinedly. 'They have head injuries. Nobody needs to listen to them.'

'But—'

'Shut *up*, Matthew – I know people will believe me, because why wouldn't they?'

'Lucy,' Matthew weeps. 'Please. Isn't there another way?'

'No.'

There is a stalemate. A fresh gust of icy wind whips

down the length of the dock and Lucy leans against my back, pulling me tight against her. Her breath is so close to my ear that I'm not sure that death wouldn't be the best option right now. If Matthew does this . . . If he takes the rucksack . . . What's to stop Lucy killing us anyway? Almost better to take a knife to the throat than endure whatever else she might have planned.

Indecision wars on Matthew's face, shadowed half in silver by the camping light. He looks like a ghost.

Michaela starts to move and I see the thought on her face – I tap my thigh urgently, hope she can see the warning in my face. *No.* She freezes.

And then, finally, Matthew sags. It's as if all the years of secrets melt out of him and he's left, just him, a husk with nothing left to lose. My own pity surges again, and at its heels is the same anger as before. I hate that I want to know more. I hate that I *care*.

'Okay,' he says softly. 'I'll do it.'

'Correct answer. There's paper there, and a pen. Write something convincing, won't you?'

There's nothing left in him. He bends to where the paper flutters, tucked in the front pocket of the rucksack. Lucy removes the knife from my throat for just long enough to point it at him, but Matthew makes no attempt to do anything except grab the paper and the pen, and then he starts to write.

I realise I'm crying. I feel so helpless, so foolish. There must be something I can do, but what? It's like I'm about to lose everything, regardless of whether I wanted it. Clio lets out a breathless sound and Michaela leans against her again, trying to keep her still. I don't know what they're thinking, but God – please, let them stay where they are.

More than anything, it is fear that holds me still; fear for them, more than for me.

The silence is unbearable. Even the water seems to still, the loch holding its breath as Matthew stares at the paper for a moment, his jaw working. The knife glints in the camping light, shining directly into my eyes for a second so I get sunspots. I blink rapidly, trying desperately to see again.

Matthew is writing. He cradles the paper like a child, the pen darting across it.

'Faster,' Lucy hisses.

'Do you want a confession or an apology?' Matthew snaps.

Lucy lets out a huff that goes right into my ear and I wilt, trying to angle myself as far from her and the knife as possible. It doesn't work and she yanks the back of my hair – a fresh wave of sickening pain crunching through me and turning my legs to jelly.

'Enough,' Lucy demands. 'Enough now. Put the note down on the floor and leave the pen on top – that's it.'

Matthew does as she asks. The pen is a hefty silver thing and holds the paper despite the wind. Matthew straightens but doesn't move.

'The rucksack. Put it on,' Lucy orders.

There's a moment of hesitation, his expression shifting between fear and – something like compassion, or love, or somewhere in between. I notice it and my throat grows thick with tears. I don't want his compassion – do I? This is all too much.

He shakes his head and then reaches, slowly, for the rucksack. He moves with the wariness of a stray cat. The rucksack strains as he lifts it from the dock, his weight shifting to accommodate its bulk. Over his right shoulder, and then his left. Lucy's breaths in my ear are short and fast and Clio and Michaela's eyes are wide.

What can I do?

I want to run. If I shove Lucy hard enough maybe she'll fall backwards, but what's the chance she'd cut my throat on the way? It might be worth it, to save Clio and Kay. My mind is whirring a thousand miles a second. If I kicked her in the knee, what then?

But then, there's Matthew. He's killed before – and I can't even let myself think about that right now, about what that means, or how I feel – accident or not. Is Lucy really the dangerous one here?

I don't know what to do.

I watch with horror as Matthew moves, not towards the water but towards Clio and Michaela, a look of concentration driving him onward. Lucy doesn't have long to react, whipping the knife back with such speed that she catches my skin and I cry out.

She shoves me away as Matthew lunges for Michaela—

Only he doesn't ever reach her. Instead, he spins with surprising grace on the ball of his foot, dodging away at the last second so that it isn't my friends he collides with but Lucy. Clio screams and Michaela stumbles into her, and suddenly they're both scrambling away on the dock as Matthew brings Lucy crashing to her knees.

The knife skids out of her grasp, flying down the slick surface of the dock until it becomes wedged between two uneven boards. Matthew has Lucy by the shoulders and she's hissing and spitting at him, lashing out with knees and elbows.

I know I should do something. I should move. But I'm completely frozen, fear and anger still warring, pity buried deep, my whole body ringing with confusion.

Lucy kicks Matthew hard and he lets out an audible *oof*, but he doesn't stop. He scrambles after her, the rucksack weighing him down – but he is fast, still. He catches her around the waist. She kicks and screams, like an animal caught in a trap, but it's no use.

Matthew glances at me – our eyes meet and I see sorrow there, and something else, a feeling that punches me so hard it feels like a physical touch, breath whooshing from my lungs as my own sorrow echoes his. Longing and sadness, knowing that here is a whole story I will never get to hear flashing behind those eyes.

'I'm sorry,' he grunts.

And then he kicks off the edge of the dock, overbalancing towards the black water – Lucy still in his arms. I scream.

There is an almighty splash, freezing water droplets spraying us. The surface heaves and in the badly angled camping light, I can see a hand – a foot – another arc of water. More splashing as they kick hard against the water. But Matthew does not let go of his wife.

Seconds go by. Long, frozen seconds. My heart is in my throat and I feel like I am drowning too.

Nobody comes to the surface.

They're both gone.

Eleanor

'I didn't mean for any of this.'

Michaela stands shivering on the dock with her arms wrapped around herself. Clio is clinging to her, the discarded ropes in a tangle at their feet. I haven't moved from the water's edge, my eyes fixed on the same spot for what might be hours – or minutes.

'Don't say that,' I say softly.

'No, I mean, I thought this would help you. When I saw a photograph of her, of the . . . of your . . .' She stops and starts. We've discussed only a little, barely able to figure out between us what we know, what we assume. It's felt like walking on broken glass, too painful to speak. 'When I saw the photograph of Rebecca,' Michaela goes on, her voice a little stronger, 'I worked out the timeline and it just seemed too *right*. And I knew how badly you wanted to know. I didn't want it to be true in one sense, but you didn't stop talking about it, and about how you wanted to know even if it was a bad story, and I thought if I was right . . . You would appreciate me bringing you here so you could learn more.' She shakes her head. 'My mum said it was a bad idea and, God, she was right. I was so focused on this, and making myself feel better and being distracted, that I didn't stop to think if it was a total dick move. I was only trying to help.'

'I know,' I say.

Finally, I drag my gaze from the water. Michaela's forehead is furrowed with concern and she stands so awkwardly in Clio's arms that I have to go to her. I pull both of them against me and Clio sobs.

'I *know*. I don't want you to blame yourself, Kay,' I urge. 'Please. You couldn't have known – about any of this.'

'I should have said something sooner,' she whispers. 'I've been thinking about it . . . I've . . .' She stops.

'Did she hurt you?' I pull away. 'All that time. You must have been so frightened. *I'm* sorry—'

'No,' Michaela says quickly. 'Just once. She said we could talk about things. I met her on Saturday, at the bar in the pub. She overhead me mention the podcast to the barman while I was waiting for my drinks and we got chatting. I asked if she knew anything about Rebecca and her friends, and she said she would be happy to talk about it. I think she wanted to know what I knew. She took my phone number. And then later she texted and told me if I wanted to get a coffee in the morning, she would be available. So I went to meet her on Sunday before you guys got up.' Michaela lets out a bark of laughter that startles Clio's sniffling to silence. 'It was so stupid, but I thought . . . I wanted proof, you know? Before I confirmed anything. And Lucy seemed so . . . knowledgeable.

'We went to a cafe and she answered a bunch of my questions and it seemed fine, and then she asked me if I wanted to see some of the school year-group photos her husband had, of kids he'd taught. She said she probably had pictures of the girls in amongst those, because they were all the same age. And I thought maybe if I saw a picture of Rebecca Kelly as a teenager I would confirm something, I don't know. So I went back to her house with her . . . And she knocked me out. I woke up in some . . . garage? Or something? She came back to check on me, but she hardly said anything the whole time. It was . . . It was . . . awful. But I'm okay.'

'Liar,' Clio says kindly, her voice thick with tears and snot. She wipes her nose with her sweater sleeve.

Michaela nudges her gently. 'I'm just glad you're both okay. El . . . Your neck—'

'It's fine. I think it's stopped bleeding already.'

The three of us stand together, arms linked, at the edge of the water. I can't help thinking of Clio's stories, and of my dreams. The rocks will likely have done the job, but if they don't – I'm not sure if it's a comfort to think of a creature below the surface making sure they don't make it to shore or not.

My father? Because . . . even Lucy seemed to think that was true. How will I ever be able to prove it?

Rebecca – my mother? Gone long ago.

Those other women, other lives lost – because of me?

I look around. Loch House. This village. This history, all of this . . . How can this be *my* history? I've spent my whole life resigned to the fact that my mother's probable death would mean I'd never find out exactly where I was from. And now here it is, presented in piecemeal. An accident. Murder. A family left grieving – my family, Paul and Robert Kelly *right here* in the village. Secrets and lies and awful, awful guilt.

Why did I ever want to know where I was from? Why do I *still* want to know?

'We need to call somebody,' Michaela says, her voice calm, the wavering only minimal now. She sighs. 'The police, I mean. I assume one of you still has a phone.'

Clio shakes her head. 'Mine's gone. I think – into the water, earlier.' She lifts her hand to her jaw and rubs at it, as if remembering the altercation. 'She took it. Then threw it.'

'The only people I want to call right now are my parents,' I say.

Michaela looks at me and there's a ghost of a smile there. Clio shakes her head.

'I think my phone must be inside. I don't know.' Eleanor says.

It's only then that I look down. I see the note that Matthew left, tucked underneath that silver pen. The batteries on the camping light Lucy brought have run low, but there's still enough to see by. I bend on one knee and lift it gently – maybe I shouldn't; maybe the police will need it, but I can't help myself.

The handwriting is jarring in its unfamiliarity. Some part of me, I suppose, expected that I would feel some kind of kinship with it. A feeling of – what, love? Loss? Right now, I only feel dazed. The writing is scratchy, uneven from where Matthew had to lean on his palm to get the pen to bite.

But there it is, in black and white. Proof.

Something in Loch Aven has called to me since the day I arrived here, like a magnetic pull that thrums in my blood and haunts my dreams. This is my story. My heritage.

The loch devoured my mother and my father.

It will not have me.

My girl,

I've always believed Loch Aven had its claws in my soul, that I could blame it for the awful things I have done. I was wrong. The evil is all mine. I see that now.

The water claimed your mother as its first victim, but I am determined to be its last. Please – don't let this ruin you too.

Love,
Your father

Acknowledgements

The drafting of this book happened at a difficult time in my life and I am even more grateful than usual to all of the people who came together to help me see it through. I hope you'll agree that the book was worth the hard work in the end. As always, thank you to my wonderful, magnificent, powerhouse of an agent, Diana Beaumont, and to the whole team at Marjacq who make this job *so* much easier. Thank you, too, to the Avon team for creating such a fun, collaborative atmosphere, but especially to Lucy Frederick for your trust in me and my ability to tell this story.

For my family, who witnessed far more of my grousing during this draft than any other. Mum, thank you for never losing your temper when I was throwing a strop over characters not co-operating, and Steve for helping me out without me ever having to ask. Dad, your pep talks are always invaluable and cheer me up to no end.

Thank you to my wider family, friends, and bookseller colleagues. This book would never have been finished if it weren't for your collective warmth, flexibility and patience. I love you all dearly and feel so honoured to have such support.

Finally, I know you can't read, but I always owe a debt of gratitude to my furry family. Your love soothes and distracts me in equal measure, and I wouldn't have it any other way. Shadow, Xena, I miss you both more than words can say.

No one expected them to go there.

The question is: will any of them leave?

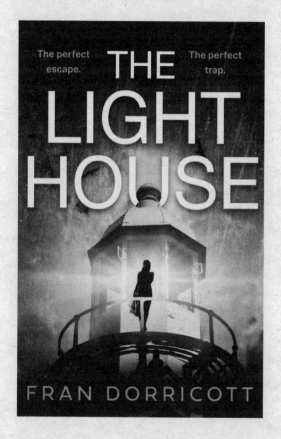

LET THE GAMES CONTINUE...

www.thehungergames.co.uk

Praise for

!) Business Classics

" explains the gist of books better than Tom Butler-Bowdon,
a   monstrates to great effect in *50 Business Classics*. He curates
   1 wisdom written by leading practitioners, such as Richard
Brar   oward Schultz, and Sheryl Sandberg, the most astute observers
(Pet   ucker, Jim Collins, and others), and master storytellers such as
Walt   acson and Ron Chernow. The revelations about the creation of
wea   he changing nature of work and employment, and the impact
of   nological advancements are timely, practical, and relevant."

Bruce   nstein, Managing Editor, *Leader to Leader*; Author, *Create Your
Future the Peter Drucker Way*

"Tea   management, I'm always looking for ways to distil knowledge
for t   nefit of my students. *50 Business Classics* provides an excellent
base   nagement history, mission and goal development, and ethics.
High   recommended as a tool for business and personal growth."

Lawre   e J. Danks, Assistant Professor of Business, Camden County
College, New Jersey, author of *Your Unfinished Life*

THE GREATEST BOOKS DISTILLED

by Tom Butler-Bowdon

The *50 Classics* series has sold over 350,000 copies

50 Business Classics

Your shortcut to the most important ideas on innovation, management, and strategy

Tom Butler-Bowdon

NICHOLAS BREALEY
PUBLISHING

London · Boston

First published in 2018 by Nicholas Brealey Publishing
An imprint of John Murray Press

An Hachette company

1

Copyright © Tom Butler-Bowdon 2018

British Library Cataloguing-in-Publication Data
A catalogue record for this book is available from the British Library.

ISBN 978 1 857 88675 7
eBook (UK) ISBN 978 1 473 68391 4
eBook (US) ISBN 978 1 473 68392 1

Typeset by Palimpsest Book Production Ltd, Falkirk, Stirlingshire

Printed and bound by Clays Ltd, St Ives plc

John Murray Press policy is to use papers that are natural, renewable
and recyclable products and made from wood grown in sustainable forests.
The logging and manufacturing processes are expected to conform
to the environmental regulations of the country of origin.

Nicholas Brealey Publishing
John Murray Press
Carmelite House
50 Victoria Embankment
London EC4Y 0DZ
Tel: 020 3122 6000

Nicholas Brealey Publishing
Hachette Book Group
Market Place Center, 53 State Street
Boston, MA 02109, USA
Tel: (617) 263 1834

www.nicholasbrealey.com
www.butler-bowdon.com

Contents

Introduction

"People always overestimate how complex business is. This isn't rocket science — we've chosen one of the world's most simple professions."
Jack Welch, former head of General Electric

50 Business Classics is a mix of intriguing theories, real-life examples, and salutary stories aimed at getting you thinking more deeply about business. From genuine historical classics that still carry meaning, to the best of recent writings, the aim is to pick out the most important ideas that can help you come up with a worthy idea, turn it into a business, and strategize your way to success.

Most business books contain only one or two major ideas; the rest of the pages simply fill out the argument with illustrations and examples. On the assumption that a single idea remembered is more powerful than a set of concepts and examples stored somewhere in your notebook or computer, I have tried to cut through the texts and capture the essence for you. Writing about expensive business degrees such as MBAs, the marketing thinker Seth Godin once wrote, "it's hard for me to understand why this is a better use of time and money than actual experience combined with a dedicated reading of 30 or 40 books." *50 Business Classics* does not claim to be an alternative to doing a comprehensive course of business study, but it may save you a lot of time trawling through many of the texts you feel you should have read, but haven't. Business may not be rocket science, but it is full of ideas, any one of which could transform how you do things or help you discover the next big thing. This book is a shortcut to those ideas.

Is business an art, a science, a discipline, or a practice? When, in the early twentieth century, business schools started springing up, and management emerged as a field of study in its own right, many claims were made that it could be "scientific." And yet, business did not become a science, or even a social science. One reason is that the main unit of analysis, the company, comes in billions of different shapes, sizes, and flavors, and with different people involved, so it is a bit of a stretch to generalize "laws" from one business to the next. Another is that companies exist in markets which are constantly changing: no sooner do you get a picture of what that market looks like than it is disrupted, disappears, or bifurcates into more specialized fields. Just as economists have found when looking at economies, anything that rides on human expectations and motivations is hard to pin down and properly analyze. Business is no different.

Though it can never be a proper science, business is at the same time something more than an art. "Practice" is the best word. There are some insights, practices, and ways of thinking which do seem to hold true across companies and markets, and it has been through the business literature that they have been identified and disseminated. A good business book is one that provides new ideas for how things can be done, using examples of successful execution that you can apply to your own organization. A great business book not only does this, but also fires the imagination, promising some kind of leap forward or breakthrough. The business book genre has sometimes been accused of being *too* inspirational, with not enough statistical foundation, but sometimes a bit of motivation is all we need to kick off some new enterprise which might change the world in some way, making people's lives easier, more productive, or more beautiful. Such noble intentions can make business a vocation as much as a career, because in striving to provide something of value we transform *ourselves* in the process.

A quick tour of the literature
The titles covered in this volume can be grouped according to three broad themes:

- Entrepreneurship & Innovation
- Management, Leadership & Effectivenesss
- Strategy & Marketing

Entrepreneurship & Innovation

Richard Branson   *Losing My Virginity*
Ron Chernow   *Titan: The Life of John D. Rockefeller Sr.*
Duncan Clark   *Alibaba: The House That Jack Ma Built*
Martin Ford   *Rise of the Robots*
Michael E. Gerber   *The E-Myth Revisited*
Conrad Hilton   *Be My Guest*
Ben Horowitz   *The Hard Thing About Hard Things*
Walter Isaacson   *Steve Jobs*
Guy Kawasaki   *The Art of the Start*
Stuart Kells   *Penguin and the Lane Brothers*

Phil Knight   *Shoe Dog*
Marc Levinson *The Box*
Eric Ries   *The Lean Startup*
Howard Schultz   *Pour Your Heart Into It*
Seema Singh   *Mythbreaker*
Brad Stone   *The Everything Store*
Peter Thiel   *Zero To One*
Donald Trump   *The Art of the Deal*
Ashlee Vance   *Elon Musk*

The "origin stories" of businesses—accounts of the early days of significant companies such as Virgin, Apple, Penguin, Tesla, Nike, Starbucks, Amazon, and Alibaba—may not be scientific, but they are often very inspiring. It is easy to look at a large corporation or chain of restaurants or hotels, or a successful online platform, and see its rise as having been inevitable. Usually it was anything but, and only unscientific grit, passion, luck, and faith pushed people forward after the initial enthusiasm, through frequent troubles, to achieve something they still believed in. One only has to read the stories of Nike's Phil Knight, Alibaba's Jack Ma, and Starbucks' Howard Schultz to appreciate what a white-knuckle ride business can be, even after a brand has become known. As venture capitalist Ben Horowitz points out in *The Hard Thing About Hard Things*, the world is full of good business ideas, but it is execution that ultimately matters. No one can understand what it is like to run a company until they are in that position, and his book looks at the psychological costs of leadership that few talk about.

Often it is only the size of the initial vision that keeps an entrepreneur going. In *Losing My Virginity*, Richard Branson notes how he has never gone into a business purely to make money; it has to change the way things are done in some way, and it has to be fun. Ashlee Vance's biography of Elon Musk reveals a person driven to change the world through electric cars and affordable space travel. As a character, Musk is uncannily like the late Steve Jobs in his intense demands on people to achieve almost impossible things. Both truly fit the description "visionary" in terms of their ability to shape the future and build entirely new products and even industries, not just reacting to what the rest of their peers are doing. Indeed, in *Zero To One*, PayPal founder and venture capitalist Peter Thiel bemoans what he sees as a trend away from vision and toward incrementalism or tinkering. What the world really needs is transformative products and whole new industries that can solve some of the biggest problems. Ironically, this can be achieved with seemingly mundane inventions. In *The Box*, Marc Levinson tells how the

3

invention of the shipping container had a huge impact on world trade, eliminating wastefulness in ports and linking up global supply chains as never before.

John D. Rockefeller's relentless push to dominate the oil industry has often been painted as an exercise in greed, but his efforts to standardize oil quality, making it safer and more uniform, paved the way for the automobile age. Neither should we lessen the achievements of retail innovators such as Amazon's Jeff Bezos. Amazon's masterstroke of having millions of user ratings of products helped make buying decisions more objective, while reducing prices and making purchasing safe. Jack Ma's Taobao and Tmall websites have done a similar thing for Chinese retail, which until Alibaba was characterized by an unappetizing combination of state-owned department stores, small shops, and street markets.

The *raison d'être* of every entrepreneur and innovator is surely to lift up humanity in some way while making a profit. There are few better examples than the Lane brothers' leap of faith to launch, in 1935, a new "Penguin" book series of top-flight writing at a tiny price. Suddenly, people on low incomes could afford to educate and elevate themselves, and for their part, the Lanes were able to get rich and create one of the first global media businesses.

If you are able to begin a new enterprise, you can save yourself a lot of wasted resources by reading great start-up books. Guy Kawasaki's *The Art of the Start* remains popular, as does Michael E. Gerber's reminder in *The E-Myth Revisited* to avoid getting overwhelmed by the nitty-gritty of running a business. Finally, Eric Ries' *The Lean Startup* articulates the incremental, iterative approach to innovation, which provides a reality check on ego-driven ideas that look good on paper but won't fly in reality. As all great entrepreneurs know, business success comes from a curious mix of blue sky thinking and a love of feedback and data.

Management & Leadership

P. T. Barnum   *The Art of Money-Getting*
Andrew Carnegie   *The Gospel of Wealth*
Alfred Chandler   *The Visible Hand*
W. Edwards Deming   *Out of the Crisis*
Peter Drucker   *The Effective Executive*
Roger Fisher, William Ury & Bruce Patton   *Getting To Yes*
Josh Kaufman   *The Personal MBA*
Terry Leahy   *Management in Ten Words*

Patrick Lencioni   *The Five Dysfunctions of a Team*
Stanley McChrystal   *Team of Teams*
Douglas McGregor   *The Human Side of Enterprise*
Tom Rath & Barry Conchie   *Strengths Based Leadership*
Sheryl Sandberg   *Lean In*
Eric Schmidt & Jonathan Rosenberg   *How Google Works*
Alice Schroeder   *The Snowball*
Peter Senge   *The Fifth Discipline*
Alfred P. Sloan   *My Years with General Motors*
Matthew Syed   *Black Box Thinking*
Frederick Winslow Taylor   *The Principles of Scientific Management*
Robert Townsend   *Up the Organization*
Jack Welch   *Jack: Straight from the Gut*
James P. Womack, Daniel T. Jones & Daniel Roos   *The Machine that Changed the World*

"Management" was only really invented in the early twentieth century, in France with the writings of mining engineer Henri Fayol and in the United States with Frederick Winslow Taylor's *The Principles of Scientific Management*. Taylor worked as a machinist in a steel plant, and saw at first hand the rank inefficiencies involved in the "craftsman" way of turning out goods. By standardizing every step of the manufacture of a good, it could be turned out a lot quicker and with higher quality. The massive efficiencies that Taylor unleashed enabled the modern world of cheap, mass-produced goods, of which Henry Ford's factories were a great example.

Once mass production became ubiquitous, what separated one firm from another, and one country from another, was the quality of the output. W. Edwards Deming studied systems of quality control and gave his insights to Japanese manufacturers at a time when American makers weren't interested. The story of the rise of Japan's quality-obsessed companies, which evolved the "lean" ethos and "just in time" methods made famous by Toyota, is well told in Womack et al.'s *The Machine that Changed the World*.

In a capitalism, it is accepted that the "invisible hand" of the market is what drives demand. Alfred Chandler argued instead that it is the *visible* hand of managerialism in the form of the modern industrial enterprise, with its legions of professional managers, that actually coordinates the activities of the economy and allocates its resources. There was no better example of this than General Motors, and Alfred Sloan's influential account of his three decades at its helm is an insight into how a huge corporation can stay responsive to changes in consumer tastes and needs.

INTRODUCTION

The hierarchical, command-and-control management system of big companies was challenged in Douglas McGregor's path-breaking *The Human Side of Enterprise*, which argued that employees would perform better, and be more fulfilled, if they were given more autonomy and responsibility. "Theory Y" companies understood that people were not just motivated by money, but by the desire for personal development and contribution. As Peter Senge writes in *The Fifth Discipline*, great companies are *communities* in which there is a genuine commitment to every member's potential being realized. Bob Townsend's success running Avis, he claimed, was due to following McGregor's principles, and McGregor's emphasis on teamwork is still being played out today. In the US military's efforts in Iraq, General Stanley McChrystal found that only a radical sharing of information and devolved power could create a force capable of defeating Al-Qaeda.

The goal of management, of an organization and of one's self, is effectiveness. Peter Drucker's *The Effective Executive* reminded us that an executive is paid not to "put out fires," but to make a few really important decisions that help define the organization and its purpose. The true executive is always more strategic than reactive. The executive must also work to their strengths, rather than trying to correct their weaknesses, which is a theme taken up more recently in Rath and Conchie's *Strengths Based Leadership*. The Gallup researchers tell us that leadership is an inevitability when people turbocharge their existing talents.

No organization can be truly effective, Sheryl Sandberg argues in *Lean In*, if it does not purposefully try to represent the population at large: if you don't, you end up with a one-dimensional workplace that is not fit to create products and services that cater to 100 percent of the population. Addressing a conference, Bill Gates was asked his best tip for business success. For a start, he said, you will never achieve your economic potential if one half of the population—the female half—with all its brains, talents, and different points of view, is cut out of the workforce.

If you can build a great business, then its effects can be greater and more long-lasting than you ever imagined. If you succeed financially, the mind naturally turns to the legacy you want to leave, your wider impact. The person who dies rich, as Andrew Carnegie put it, "dies disgraced." Carnegie's wealth funded hundreds of libraries and a foundation for peace. Warren Buffett's money will join together with the fortune of Bill Gates to help eradicate preventable diseases. Businesses do not exist within a vacuum, but are part of society. When we succeed, we show gratitude and give back to the community whose existence made it possible.

Strategy & Marketing

Clayton Christensen   *The Innovator's Dilemma*
Jim Collins   *Great by Choice*
John Kay   *Obliquity*
W. Chan Kim & Renée Mauborgne   *Blue Ocean Strategy*
Richard Koch & Greg Lockwood   *Simplify*
Theodore Levitt   *Marketing Myopia*
Geoffrey A. Moore   *Crossing the Chasm*
Al Ries & Jack Trout   *Positioning*
Simon Sinek   *Start With Why*

Strategy has its roots in warfare, but became applicable to the business world as companies grew larger and more complex, and had to make important choices about where to devote their resources. Strategy, in essence, is *focus*—becoming clear on the markets and avenues that you *won't* pursue, so that all your capabilities and intellectual fire power can be thrown at what you have identified as your company's strength. The great advantage of strategic focus is that it helps you to avoid competition. As Kim and Mauborgne argue in the strategy blockbuster *Blue Ocean Strategy*, the aim is to create a product or service that is so differentiated it creates a new category and "owns" that market.

In a similar vein, Richard Koch and Greg Lockwood's *Simplify: How the Best Businesses in the World Succeed*, argues that the great success stories in business, from Ford to Ikea to Google, were ones of radical simplification of price or product. Products that are suddenly made much cheaper than the competition, or which are much easier to use or a lot more advanced, sweep the market. Smart companies, to avoid being stuck in a mushy middle, choose one or the other. Michael Porter's *Competitive Strategy* (1980) argued that firms should choose either between cost leadership of product differentiation, but *Simplify* contains a myriad of contemporary examples, from Airbnb to Uber to Facebook, that make these concepts come alive for today's reader.

The challenge of getting strategy right is wonderfully expressed in Clayton Christensen's *The Innovator's Dilemma*, which shows how established companies can become a victim of their own success. They need to keep generating revenue from profitable products in order to cover all their fixed costs and make a profit, but in doing so they can fail to spot emerging technologies that at the start appear to have little commercial value. Smaller firms, because they have little to lose, start selling a basic version of the technology to a limited market, but as their product gets more advanced, the firm dominates the niche market, which grows and grows. By this time, it may be too late for the established players to make a name for themselves.

However, as Jim Collins observes in *Great by Choice*, many companies, from Intel to Genentech, have only become great through a *combination* of being open to the new and innovative, yet also being uncommonly disciplined when it comes to being able to deliver and sticking to financial targets. In achieving such a balancing act, it is crucial to be crystal clear on what your organization stands for. Simon Sinek's *Start With Why* provides inspiration for companies that have lost their way, and is must reading if you are in the process of starting one.

There is often a fine line between strategy and marketing, and in fact Al Ries and Jack Trout's seminal *Positioning* led to a new field of "strategic marketing," which helps firms attain clarity on how to position themselves, or a product or service, within a market. As the public will quickly equate your offering with an idea (e.g. Volvo = safety), awareness of this allows you to build marketing perceptions into the creation of a product from the start. Making a product without fully understanding its likely positioning in people's minds does not give marketing its due place within strategy.

Finally, British economist John Kay's *Obliquity* provides an original take on business strategy by noting that it is companies which *do not* put profits or shareholders first that tend to do best. The reason is that, when they have some great mission, it galvanizes and inspires all involved to achieve it, and the buying public appreciates the authenticity too. We can see right through organizations that exist only for themselves, feeling little responsibility for employees or the wider world.

About the list

Perhaps half the books on the main list can be classed as undeniable classics; other selections are more subjective choices that are underrated and deserve to be more widely read, or that articulate some important business idea extremely well. Equally, in considering the selections I was careful not to include books simply because they were known as "classics." The definition of a classic is surely something that remains relevant despite its age, and the business landscape is constantly changing.

John Brooks' *Business Adventures*, for instance, despite being recommended by Bill Gates and Warren Buffett, is a collection of journalistic stories of events in American business and finance in the 1960s that I did not find particularly relevant for today. Tom Peters' and Robert Waterman's *In Search of Excellence*, though a breakthrough business book in its time, uses examples of companies that either no longer exist or have totally changed in the ensuing period. If there was a recent edition, with updated examples, it would be included. Having said that, at the end of the book you will find an additional list of "50 More Classics," divided into the same categories outlined above, that includes these titles and more.

Final word

I hope this volume achieves its purpose of helping you discover business ideas, texts, and people you didn't know about before. It is said that "A little knowledge is a bad thing." This may be true for people who are happy with a little, but for most of us a taste of knowledge leaves us wanting more. Enjoy these commentaries, but don't hesitate to read the complete books which are discussed here. There is no substitute for having a physical book on your desk, or by your bedside, to remind you of its message.

Related books

As businesses operate within economies, it makes sense to educate yourself to a basic level about economics and capitalism. *50 Economics Classics* (2016) may help you toward that end.

50 Business Classics touches on the personal development side of business success, but if you would like to go deeper into this area you may enjoy *50 Success Classics* (2nd edition, 2017).

Reader bonus

As a thank-you for buying the book, allow me to send you two free commentaries. The first is on a standout title on effectiveness: *Deep Work: Rules for Focused Success in a Distracted World* (2016), by computer science professor and productivity expert Cal Newport; the second is on Katherine Graham's classic autobiography, *Personal History* (1998). Graham, played by Meryl Streep in the Spielberg film *The Post* (2017), was the first female editor of a major American newspaper. Just send an email to tombutlerbowdon@gmail.com with "Business Bonus" in the title bar and you'll be sent the bonus chapters.

The Art of Money Getting

"The foundation of success in life is good health: that is the substratum of fortune; it is also the basis of happiness. A person cannot accumulate a fortune very well when he is sick."

"We are all, no doubt, born for a wise purpose. There is as much diversity in our brains as in our countenances. Some are born natural mechanics, while some have great aversion to machinery . . . Unless a man enters upon the vocation intended for him by nature, and best suited to his peculiar genius, he cannot succeed."

"The possession of a perfect knowledge of your business is an absolute necessity in order to insure success."

In a nutshell

There are no shortcuts to wealth, aside from right vocation, good character, and perseverance—and don't forget to advertise.

In a similar vein

Andrew Carnegie *The Gospel of Wealth*
Ron Chernow *Titan: The Life of John D. Rockefeller Sr.*

CHAPTER 1

P. T. Barnum

P. T. Barnum was possibly the greatest showman who ever lived, famous for his circuses and museums of "curiosities." His shows transformed nineteenth-century commercial entertainment, and he was considered a master of promotion whose ideas are still studied by marketers today. Modern audiences have learned about Barnum's dramatic life through Hugh Jackman's brilliant portrayal in the film *The Greatest Showman* (2017).

Barnum's autobiography tells his colorful story, but it is *The Art of Money Getting, or Golden Rules for Making Money* that offers a recipe book for success in business. Consistent with a great marketer, the title is a slight exaggeration of the content. There are, in fact, no detailed ideas or techniques for getting rich. Instead, the author provides 20 rules for personal advance and the development of good character that, indirectly, will make a person's financial rise almost inevitable. Contrary to the image of Barnum as an over-the-top impresario, the book is actually a solid business ethics primer.

Health, wealth, and happiness

Barnum draws attention to something which is, on the face of it, obvious, yet is so often overlooked: you need to have good health in order to be successful. The pursuit of riches requires gusto, and poor health saps that. The successful person therefore, if they wish to remain so, ignores the laws of health at their peril.

Barnum, who once smoked ten to fifteen cigars a day, goes on the offensive against the "filthy weed" tobacco. Its effects on the taste buds closes the smoker off to the simple pleasures of life, like delicious fruit; all they can think of is their next wad to put under their tongue or puff. But he reserves his greatest attack for alcohol: "To make money, requires a clear brain. If the brain is muddled, and his judgment warped by intoxicating drinks, it is impossible for him to carry on business successfully. How many good opportunities have passed, never to return, while a man was sipping a 'social glass,' with his friend!"

Recalling the phrase, "wine is a mocker," Barnum notes the way alcohol initially flatters the drinker into feeling omnipotent, then drains them of vital energy. Apart from this is the sheer amount of time that is wasted by the drinker when they could be studying and developing real opportunities.

Choose the right career

Barnum notes at the beginning that, in a country like the United States, where there is "more land than people," money can be made by anyone who properly applies themselves. There is room for good people in any vocation. But you have to make sure you choose the *right* vocation.

Ahead of his time in emphasizing the importance of choosing a career that you love, Barnum goes as far as saying that selecting a vocation on the basis that it was "congenial to [your] tastes" was *the* surest way to success for a young person. We are all born for some purpose, he opines, and the fact of the extraordinary differences between us suggests that people were made to do some things and not others:

> *"Unless a man enters upon the vocation intended for him by nature, and best suited to his peculiar genius, he cannot succeed. I am glad to believe that the majority of persons do find their right vocation. Yet we see many who have mistaken their calling, from the blacksmith . . . to the clergyman. You will see, for instance, that extraordinary linguist the 'learned blacksmith,' who ought to have been a teacher of languages; and you may have seen lawyers, doctors and clergymen who were better fitted by nature for the anvil or the lapstone."*

. . . then the right location

Yet Barnum goes further than the now hackneyed exhortation to "do the work you love" in his even more practical tip about *where* you do it:

> *"You might conduct a hotel like clock-work, and provide satisfactorily for five hundred guests every day; yet, if you should locate your house in a small village where there is no railroad communication or public travel, the location would be your ruin."*

He refers to a man he met running a museum of curiosities in London. The gentleman was good at what he did, but was not attracting much custom. Barnum suggested he move to the United States where his show would find more enthusiastic audiences. The man duly did, working first for two years in Barnum's New York Museum and then establishing his own "traveling show business." Some years later, Barnum reported, the man was rich, "simply because he selected the right vocation and also secured the proper location."

Stick to your business, master your field

Too many people scatter their powers. Barnum notes that "A constant hammering on one nail will generally drive it home at last." When you are focused on one thing only, you will soon see ways that it can be improved and made more valuable. While it is tempting to have many irons in the fire, a lot of fortunes have passed people by because they cast themselves too wide and not deep.

No one succeeds, Barnum asserts, without knowing their field inside out. His reflection on nineteenth-century countrymen could be applied to people in any time and place:

"As a nation, Americans are too superficial—they are striving to get rich quickly, and do not generally do their business as substantially and thoroughly as they should, but whoever excels all others in his own line, if his habits are good and his integrity undoubted, cannot fail to secure abundant patronage, and the wealth that naturally follows."

"Be both cautious and bold"

The founding member of the Rothschild banking family had this as a maxim. At first glance a paradox, it simply means to be very careful in the making of your plans, but once made do not hold back on their execution.

Learn your own lessons

It may be convenient to be given or to borrow a load of money to start a business, but as Barnum notes, "Money is good for nothing unless you know the value of it by experience." John Jacob Astor noted that it was more difficult for him to make his first thousand dollars than it was to accrue all his succeeding millions. But the lessons learned in creating the initial capital—self-denial, industry, perseverance, and patience—were priceless. Even in Barnum's time most successful businesspeople were self-made, and the same is true today. Do not depend on or wait for other people's capital, particularly inheritances. If anything, this "easy money" will hold you back.

If it's good, tell people about it

You would expect the greatest showman of his time to advise promoting your wares, but what he says is just common sense:

"When you get an article which you know is going to please your customers, and that when they have tried it, they will feel they have got their money's worth, then let the fact be known that you have got it. Be careful to advertise it in some shape or other because it is evident that if a man has ever so good an article for sale, and nobody knows it, it will bring him no return."

Avoid the unlucky

Barnum mentions the Rothschild family's maxim, "Never have anything to do with an unlucky man or place." There is always a reason why a person is unlucky, even if they are honest or intelligent; it may not be evident, but there will always be some defect that has held them back from success.

Read a good newspaper

He who does not read newspapers, Barnum says, is "cut off from his species." Even in Barnum's time there was rapid daily advance in terms of technologies and changes to industries. To succeed in any field you have to know what is happening in it.

Final comments

Though the examples given are typical of the pen of a nineteenth-century American, with glowing mentions of the rich and famous of his day, *The Art of Money Getting* is remarkably relevant today for anyone wanting to make the most of their talents and chances in life.

Some of the points may seem obvious, but it does not hurt to be reminded of them, especially the idea that personal virtue is the foundation of wealth. Without honesty and reputation, fortunes can disappear overnight; with these things, an enterprise or a service can create prosperity for all involved. Barnum himself saw both "struggles and triumphs" in his career, but he never actually uttered the remark famously attributed to him, "There is a sucker born every minute" (it was a competitor). If this really had been his attitude, according to his own rules he would not have become so well established or wealthy. It should not be a surprise that the Rothschilds are mentioned twice in the book, a family who built a fortune not on "taking advantage," but on trust.

The Art of Money Getting is short because it was essentially a speech Barnum often gave on the speaker's circuit. It is in the public domain and can be downloaded free from the internet.

P. T. Barnum

Phineas Taylor Barnum was born in Bethel, Connecticut, in 1810, the oldest of five children. His father ran an inn and a store. Barnum displayed early business sense, and by 12 had done well from selling lottery tickets. However, at 15 his father died, and for the next few years he had to try his hand at a range of enterprises. One of his early ventures was a newspaper, the Herald of Freedom, *which attracted several libel suits.*

After moving to New York City in 1834, he discovered his calling in the "show business." He established a popular show whose main draw was Joice Heth, an ex-slave who was promoted as being 161 years old and the nurse to a baby George Washington. In 1841 he bought an existing museum that became Barnum's American Museum; its natural history exhibits, memorabilia, and oddities, including the midget General Tom Thumb and the Feejee Mermaid, entertained and educated millions. It burned to the ground in 1865. A new museum was built three years later, but was also razed by fire.

Barnum was 60 by the time he moved into the circus business. His Grand Traveling Museum, Menagerie, Caravan, and Circus (also known as the Greatest Show on Earth), which covered five acres, toured America. He is also remembered for bringing Swedish opera star Jenny Lind to the country. Despite paying her $1,000 a night, Barnum made a large profit on the tour.

In later years Barnum turned to politics, getting elected to the Connecticut legislature in 1865 and serving two terms, fighting unsuccessfully for a seat in Congress, and becoming mayor of Bridgeport, Connecticut in 1875. He died in 1891.

Barnum wrote several books, including The Life of P. T. Barnum: Written by Himself *(1854, with later revisions),* The Humbugs of the World *(1865), and* Struggles and Triumphs *(1869). He intentionally put his autobiography into the public domain, and by the end of the nineteenth century it was second only to the New Testament in terms of copies in print.*

1998

Losing My Virginity

"You're trying to create something that is original, that stands out from the crowd, that will last and, hopefully, serve some useful purpose. Above all, you want to create something you are proud of. That has always been my philosophy of business. I can honestly say that I have never gone into any business to make money."

"I may be a businessman, in that I set up and run companies for profit, but, when I try to plan ahead and dream up new products and new companies, I'm an idealist."

In a nutshell

Don't be afraid to be different. On entering any new field or an industry, aim to really shake it up and provide new value.

In a similar vein

Duncan Clark *Alibaba: The House That Jack Ma Built*
Conrad Hilton *Be My Guest*
Howard Schulz *Pour Your Heart Into It*
Ashlee Vance *Elon Musk*

CHAPTER 2

Richard Branson

E veryone knows who Richard Branson is: the entrepreneur famous for the Virgin brand name, the adventurer who has crossed oceans in a hot air balloon, and the philanthropist knighted by the Queen.

What most of us know about Branson comes from snippets on television and newspaper articles, but there is a reality behind the image that only a good autobiography reveals. There are hundreds of "how I did it" stories by well-known businesspeople, but *Losing My Virginity* is better than most. This is thanks to the rich material Branson has to draw from (he is an inveterate note taker and diarist, and his scribblings over a 25-year period enabled the book to be written), but also because he manages to avoid self-aggrandizement. If you are an aspiring entrepreneur, it is a great read. The message: being different is not an obstacle, but almost a requirement, in achieving business success.

"You will either go to prison or become a millionaire": 1

Born in 1950, Branson enjoyed a happy childhood, with parents who considered their children equals and who often set challenges to make them self-reliant. Though decidedly upper middle class, the family never had a great deal of money, and Branson's mother was always thinking up ways to earn extra income from cottage industries in the garage.

At the private school he attended, Stowe, Branson was considered a bit slow and lazy. He was, in fact, dyslexic and admits that by age 8 he still couldn't read and was hopeless in mathematics and sciences. On leaving school, his headmaster said to him, "You will either go to prison or become a millionaire."

Branson's first entrepreneurial success was a national magazine for students, which included interviews with Mick Jagger and John Lennon. He admits he did not go into it to make money, more as a fun enterprise. In fact, it did not make money, but was kept going with the help of his friends and a bit of advertising.

Branson's friends were obsessed with music, and he hit upon the idea of selling records cheaply through mail order, particularly ones that were not stocked in the high street stores. The business mushroomed, but a postal strike made him realize how vulnerable it all was. He began looking around for a retail space.

"You will either go to prison or become a millionaire": 2

The first Virgin record store, opened in 1971, became a hangout for young people, and was the first to cater exclusively for the youth market. Many more stores followed around Britain.

The early days of Virgin were anything but regular. The business was run not from office quarters but basements, church crypts, and houseboats, with plenty of hangers-on helping out, only some of whom were earning the standard Virgin salary of £20 a week. Branson never obeyed the business rule to not work with your friends; most of the Virgin inner circle for the first 15 years were people who had grown up with him. Though there were inevitably fallings out, this accidental management strategy was remarkably effective.

In an atmosphere of free love and plenty of drugs, someone had to be getting up early and worrying about paying the invoices and salaries, and Branson was unusual in his coterie for not indulging much, preferring instead "to have a great time and keep my wits about me." Behind the barefooted, long-haired hippy was a businessman who wanted to make a difference.

Though his chain of record stores was growing, with all the overheads Virgin was actually losing money. Branson accidentally fell upon a solution to the problems that would almost fulfill the bad part of his headmaster's prophecy. He began buying records wholesale, saying they were to be sold in Belgium, and thus escaping hefty UK domestic sales duties. After three trips taking the records across the English Channel to imaginary buyers, records which he then sold at great profit back in the Virgin stores, his activities were discovered by the Customs and Excise men. To escape jail he had to pay back three times the amount not paid in duties (£60,000 in 1971—a lot of money). Under tremendous pressure, he somehow met the payments from stores' earnings, but the experience burned him, and he resolved never to do anything close to illegal again. Barely 21, he was growing up fast.

Entering the big time: music

Fond of the idea of having his own record label whose acts could be promoted through the Virgin stores, Branson scraped together enough money to buy an old manor house in Oxfordshire, which was slowly converted into a recording studio.

The first act Virgin signed was an unusual choice. A young musician called Mike Oldfield had spent months perfecting a recording that had no vocals and lots of bells and other unusual instruments. This was a bizarre first choice for what was intended as a rock music label, but it paid off. Oldfield's *Tubular Bells* was one of the biggest selling albums of the 1970s, and it bankrolled Virgin's early years in the business. It later attracted The Sex Pistols, Culture Club, Phil Collins, The Human League, and other stars to its fold, and by the early eighties had become a major label. Branson had achieved his wish for a "vertically integrated" music company, in which the Virgin stores, including the famous Virgin Megastores, could promote the bands that Virgin Music had signed.

Entering the big time: airlines

With his focus on the music industry, Branson had never considered starting an airline. But when he received a proposal to establish a transatlantic service to compete with British Airways, he could not resist. Against the better judgment of his advisers, he called Boeing in Seattle and negotiated to lease a 747 for a year, "just to see" if the whole idea would work. Virgin Atlantic was soon a reality, aiming to satisfy the demand that Freddie Laker's Laker Airways had tapped before British Airways had forced it out of business.

Virgin Atlantic almost never got off the ground. On the inaugural flight, a flock of birds flew into one of the uninsured engines, ruining it at a cost of £600,000. This brought the company over its overdraft, and it came close to being bankrupted. Only an emergency recall of cash from Virgin's overseas operations got it through. Between 1984 and 1990 Virgin Atlantic remained tiny, however, with only a handful of planes.

The fuel price jump brought on by the first Gulf War was a major obstacle, as was the sudden loss of passengers after the events of September 11, 2001. Virgin also had to contend with a constant dirty tricks assault from British Airways, which saw Virgin as a threat that had to be crushed, whatever the means. As Branson's airline soaked up more and more cash, its bankers were losing patience, and he was led to a painful realization: either sell Virgin Music and keep Virgin Atlantic flying, or lose the airline and leave the Virgin brand name in tatters, not to mention losing thousands of people's livelihoods.

Again, in spite of the good advice of family and friends, Branson took the decision to sell Virgin Music, which he and his team had spent 20 years developing. It was a harrowing decision, particularly as he had just signed The Rolling Stones, marking the culmination of the label's rise. He had "lost his virginity," but the sale brought in £560 million, or $1 billion, and gave Branson the freedom to chart the course of the Virgin group of companies without bankers yapping at his heels. His share of the sale, he noted, gave him money "beyond his wildest dreams."

The Branson style

Branson notes that, no matter what people may tell you, there is no "recipe" for business success that can be applied to any field. There is, however, a Branson style of doing business that might be instructive for the aspiring entrepreneur.

Throughout the book Branson never comes across as exceptionally brainy. Rather, the secrets of his success could be boiled down to:

- Thinking big and taking calculated risks: "My interest in life comes from setting myself huge, apparently unachievable, challenges and trying to rise above them."
- Being less stressed than others by uncertainty.
- Trying to prove people wrong.
- Having the simple belief that "you can do it".

Branson's main criterion for entering a new market or industry is that it be fun. There has to be room to shake up stodgy markets and provide something new. Unfortunately, this often involves being the minnow trying to take on corporate whales.

During the war with BA, there were lots of rumors that Virgin Atlantic was about to go bankrupt. At one point it owed £55 million to banks, and Branson had to do a tremendous juggling act to keep things afloat. He notes at one point, "It sometimes seems to me that I have spent all my life trying to persuade bankers to extend their loans." Since the Virgin group has always reinvested profits back into the businesses, it has never had a cash cushion like established corporations, so there was always the danger of it running out. Every record deal Branson made seemed like putting the company on the line, and it was only in the mid nineties that the Virgin group could relax a little.

Branson's reflection on these difficult years provides good advice for anyone in business under financial pressure: "However tight things are, you still need to have the big picture at the forefront of your mind." Whenever he found himself in a tight spot and his advisers suggested shrinking back a little and playing it safe, was the point where he would actually go out on a limb.

Other insights include:

- He generally makes his mind up about people and new business proposals "within about 30 seconds." Though a business plan has to be good, he ultimately goes on gut instinct.

- He is not a fast talker or a great public speaker, and admits that it often takes him time to properly answer a question: "I hope that people will trust a slow, hesitant response more than a rapid, glib one."
- He hates criticizing people who work for him, and the lowest points of his working life have been when he has to let people go. He always tries to get someone else to do it instead.
- He admits many of his successes were not his own ideas (he did not even come up with the name "Virgin"). Despite the image of a lone entrepreneur, like any great company, Virgin was in fact built by a core of trusted managers and advisers.
- Virgin has no huge corporate headquarters, but buys houses in UK and American cities for staff to work from. Branson saw a lot of his two children when they were growing up because he literally worked from home. He and his wife Joan lived on a London houseboat well into their thirties.

Final comments

A significant portion of the book relates to Branson's various efforts to break world hot air ballooning and ocean powerboat records. Why has he felt compelled to go off on such adventures (which have brought him close to death several times), when he is already someone—with his wealth, success, and happy family—who "has it all"? His answer is simply that it adds another dimension to his existence and makes him feel alive.

One of the interesting parts is the soul-searching that came upon him on turning 40. Was he going to spend his life creating and building companies? Surely there was something more? For a time, he considered selling off his assets and going to university to study history. Today, however, he puts much of his non-work energies into philanthropy. Among his causes have been climate change, HIV Aids, African wildlife, and young entrepreneurship.

Yet it is through his companies that he has changed people's lives the most, constantly seeking ways to deliver new value to the public, whether through low cost flying, mobile phones, or cheaper credit cards. Virgin Galactic may become one of the first companies offering commercial passenger flights into space. This enterprise fulfills Branson's business criterion of only going into fields that are fun and exciting, yet where there is also money to be made.

The Gospel of Wealth

"This, then, is held to be the duty of the man of Wealth: First, to set an example of modest, unostentatious living, shunning display or arrogance; to provide moderately for the legitimate wants of those dependent upon him; and after doing so to consider all the surplus revenues which come to him simply as trust funds, which he is called upon to administer . . . in the manner which, in his judgment, is best calculated to produce the most beneficial results for the community . . . doing for them better than they would or could do for themselves."

"The man who dies rich thus dies disgraced."

In a nutshell

The wealth creator has a moral obligation to enrich the lives of others in whatever way they can.

In a similar vein

P. T. Barnum *The Art of Money Getting*
Ron Chernow *Titan: The Life of John D. Rockefeller Sr.*

CHAPTER 3

Andrew Carnegie

I t might be a nice difficulty, but it is a difficulty nonetheless: if you are incredibly rich, what will you do with all your money when you die?

When in 1901 he sold his huge iron and steel interests to financier John Pierpont Morgan, personally receiving over $225 million, Andrew Carnegie became the richest individual of his age. The son of a poor Scottish linen weaver, he was the classic American immigrant success story who, in addition to possessing great judgment and drive, also admitted he had been in the right place at the right time.

Carnegie's family had settled in Pittsburgh, then a cradle of America's industrial revolution, and as a young man he held jobs in the country's emerging telegraph and railroad industries. Later, as a captain of industry, he was sharply criticized for keeping wages low and hours long (the famous Homestead strike in 1892 at one of his plants resulted in the deaths of ten men), yet he also kept with him a European sense of the "public good," spending the last part of his life working out how to give his money away for the greatest benefit.

Carnegie's grandfather had been the first to establish a small lending library in Carnegie's native Dunfermline, Scotland, at a time when there were no public libraries. His family were far from well-off, but the love and respect for book knowledge made a permanent mark on young Andrew. Later, when he was rich, Carnegie's massive endowment of libraries were the obvious choice for his largesse.

One evening in 1868, aged 33, Carnegie wrote a memorandum to himself while living in the St Nicholas Hotel, New York. He began the memo with a goal: "Thirty three and an income of $50,000 per annum!" He would organize his business affairs so as to bring in the same sum annually, while spending the surplus on "benevolent purposes." Getting more philosophical, he wrote of his intention to retire at 35 and henceforth devote his life to reading and study. He did no such thing, but in these words, you have the seeds of his later philanthropy. Knowledge gained from reading and study represented real value; a good life was one that truly opened the mind. Money alone was worthless.

Though not very well-educated himself, like Benjamin Franklin Carnegie knew that "leaders are readers" and that wealth was created from deeper knowledge and better thinking. When his first donated library came to be built, he was asked for his coat of arms to put above the entrance. He didn't have one. Instead, he asked for a plaque portraying the sun and its rays and the words "Let there be light."

The Gospel of Wealth, as it became known after publication in Britain, was an essay originally published in the *North American Review*. It became famous across the Atlantic when former prime minister William Gladstone helped organize its publication in the *Pall Mall Gazette*. Even today its influence is out of all proportion to its length (a few thousand words).

Freedom, inequality, and wealth

Carnegie begins his essay by noting the huge differences in wealth in the modern world. Voicing a common view of his times, he argues that this great inequality is the natural way of the world, a demonstration of the self-evident principles of "survival of the fittest" and advancement of the best able. Luck certainly plays a part, he admits, in the fortunes of men, but in a free society the people of ability and ambition naturally prosper while others lag. All wealth comes from healthy individualism and the freedom to create and do. In a free country, we are free to make a million, and free to starve.

All this, according to Carnegie, was a given. But the big question facing a capitalist order was this: if the order leads to great wealth being concentrated into the hands of a few, what should be done with all the excess? Even though some people have been "born lucky" in terms of attributes, it is also true that whatever they create through enterprise cannot be achieved without the public's patronage. Therefore, he reasoned, great wealth ultimately belonged to the society that had helped created it.

What to do with it

Noting the obvious, that "you can't take it with you," Carnegie runs through the ways in which a rich person can get rid of their fortune. They can:

- Leave it to their family
- Bequeath it to the public on their death
- Dispense and distribute it during their lifetime

What was the point, he asked, in leaving all your money to your family? History shows that large fortunes are to their heirs more of a burden than a boon. Though some heirs turn out to be exemplary stewards of the family resources, without an incentive to work hard most children of the wealthy tend to lead mediocre lives, and some are destroyed by their money. Naturally, he comments, a magnate would want to leave their wife and daughters well provided for, but they should think hard about leaving much to their sons.

As a general rule, he noted, most fortunes are not passed on because of thoughts of the welfare of children, but because of family pride. But what use was pride when you were dead? Much better, he felt, to distribute your fortune during your lifetime, using the same imagination and diligence that you had displayed in creating it. This meant avoiding the typical philanthropist's path of simply giving it away to charity, but working actively yourself to ensure maximum social benefit for your bucks.

Where to spend it

According to Carnegie, it was a waste of money to give directly to those who had nothing, since they would fritter it away on "indulgence" and "excess." He sternly noted that "Neither the individual nor the race is improved by alms-giving." Resources should only go to those who could help themselves, and to worthwhile public projects that government did not have the funds to build.

In another, related essay, he listed some areas that were deserving of entrepreneurial largesse. They included universities, libraries, parks, museums and art galleries, hospitals, concert halls, swimming baths, and churches. He observed that wealth, "passing through the hands of the few, can be made a much more potent force for the elevation of our race than if it had been distributed in small sums to the people themselves." People on their own could not be trusted to make the best use of given money, but give them a noble institution or needed facility and they would use it to good ends. Carnegie became famous for his endowment of public libraries (close to 5,000 around the world) and funding of institutions devoted to peace (he pulled out all the stops to try to prevent World War One).

New York City already had been endowed with the Astor and Lenox libraries, which were combined to create (with further funds from Samuel J. Tilden) the famous New York City Public Library. Carnegie takes his hat off to other philanthropists in this mold, mentioning Tilden, Cooper, Pratt, Stanford (endower of Stanford University), and the Vanderbilt family, which built the university named after them while they were still in their financial prime.

Final comments

Wealthy people are always eager to find ways around the biblical line, "It is easier for a camel to go through the eye of a needle, than for a rich man to enter into the kingdom of God." Carnegie, however, did not dispute the warning, wryly noting that it "betokens serious difficulty for the rich." His own *Gospel*, he believed, expressed the full intent of Jesus's words, in its recognition that a person who dies rich, "dies disgraced."

Some have viewed Carnegie's attitude—that a great fortune given away wisely would do much more good to society than millions of "trifling amounts" given away to many—as paternalistic. Yet he honestly believed that individuals counted for little in relation to the progress of humanity overall. This included himself.

Software king Bill Gates and investor Warren Buffett, two of the richest individuals of our age, have both been influenced by *The Gospel of Wealth*. Their fortunes, joined in the one Bill and Melinda Gates foundation, represent by far the biggest endowment in history, now dispensing billions of dollars a year to worthwhile causes, mostly relating to health and education. Chuck Feeney, the duty-free billionaire behind Atlantic Philanthropies, was also inspired by the essay. In relation to big giving, Carnegie set the modern standard, and beyond the millions of lives enlightened by his libraries and other institutions, this is his even greater legacy.

Andrew Carnegie

Born in Scotland in 1835, Carnegie enjoyed his childhood in Dunfermline in the bosom of an extended family. His father moved the family to the United States when he was in his early teens. His first job, at 13, was in a cotton mill, followed by work as a telegraphist and a railroad clerk. He quickly rose through the ranks at the Pennsylvania Railroad Company before launching himself as an iron manufacturer in Pittsburgh.

When the Civil War erupted, he was asked to take charge of US government railways and telegraphs. He was a Republican and opposed slavery, and this provided an opportunity to serve the cause.

After selling his iron and steel works, Carnegie spent his retirement years at his beloved Skibo castle in Scotland. He died in Lenox, Massachusetts in 1919, the same year as industrialists Henry Clay Frick, Henry John Heinz, and William Woolworth. Carnegie's endowment was mainly for the building of public libraries throughout America and Britain, plus large gifts to universities. He also funded the Carnegie Endowment for International Peace.

A keen writer, his books include Triumphant Democracy *(1886),* Round the World *(1884),* The Empire of Business *(1902),* James Watt *(1905), and* Problems of To-day *(1907). He also inspired Napoleon Hill's research into successful American businessmen, which led to the writing* of Law of Success *(1928) and* Think and Grow Rich *(1937).*

1977

The Visible Hand

"Historians as well as economists have failed to consider the implications of the rise of modern business enterprise. They have studied the entrepreneurs who created modern business enterprise, but more in moral than in analytical terms. Their concerns has been more whether they were exploiters (robber barons) or creators (industrial statesmen). Historians have also been fascinated by the financiers who for brief periods allocated funds to transportation, communication, and some industrial enterprises and so appeared to have control over major sectors of the economy. But they have paid almost no notice at all to the managers who, because they carried out a basic new economic function, continued to play a far more central role in the operations of the American economy than did the robber barons, industrial statesmen, or financiers."

In a nutshell

Our civilization is as much managerial as it is capitalist.

In a similar vein

Ron Chernow *Titan: The Life of John D. Rockefeller Sr.*
Alfred P. Sloan *My Years with General Motors*
Frederick Winslow Taylor *The Principles of Scientific Management*

CHAPTER 4

Alfred Chandler

I n *The Visible Hand: The Managerial Revolution in American Business*, which won a Pulitzer Prize in 1978, Alfred Chandler describes the transformation of American business from millions of small, family-run firms to the age of big business. Any economic historian could have done this, but his more original assertion was that the modern business enterprise *took the place of* the market "in coordinating the activities of the economy and allocating its resources." In other words, he famously writes, the *visible* hand of management replaced what Adam Smith called the *invisible* hand of the market. The market generated the demand of goods and services, of course, but their supply increasingly became the domain of business enterprises with a modern bureaucratic structure that not only controlled present production and distribution, but looked ahead and shaped the future supply of goods and services. Thus dawned the age of "managerial capitalism"; the large business enterprise, run by professional managers, became the defining feature of American political economy—and all developed economies.

The shape of business changes

Chandler defines the modern business enterprise as having "many distinct operating units" that are "managed by a hierarchy of salaried executives." Each unit or division could in theory be run as its own enterprise. How different this was to the traditional shop, factory, or bank, which typically was at one location, providing a single product or service, and run by a single family or owner. Where once all managers had been owners, now a class of middle managers and executives arose often without any ownership stake, charged with organizing thousands of workers. If, once upon a time, a bank manager would have to find employment with another bank if he moved state, now he could get a transfer within the same company.

The small, family-run firm was constantly trimming production or investing depending on current prices and the winds of the market, to which it was totally exposed. The new, big, managerial firms, in contrast, were set up to cater to many markets across a whole region or even the nation at large. Because of their larger market share and often dominance in a particular product or service, they were less at the mercy of market forces. Their size meant that they could internalize and integrate functions which a small firm had to perform in the marketplace.

What is remarkable is the speed with which this transformation happened. Within just over a century, between the 1820s and 1940s, the American economy went from being an agrarian economy to an industrial, urban one; the landscape of American business was utterly changed. This took economists a long time to get used to, since economics was based on the assumption that production and distribution were managed by lots of small firms adjusting to the market; giant businesses such as Du Pont, General Motors, and Sears, Roebuck, geographically dispersed and performing many of their functions in house, called into question how economies actually worked. Indeed, when the big managerial corporations arose, economists dismissed them as an aberration borne of the desire for monopoly power. By their very nature, it was contended, these firms upset the sacred power of competition and the invisible hand, and went against the efficient allocation of resources. Meanwhile, historians had not been very interested in the large firm either, preferring instead to look at individuals and judge them "robber barons or industrial statesmen, that is, bad fellows or good fellows." Both economists and historians, Chandler contends, failed to see the big change that had swept modern political economy: the rise of management itself.

The managerial revolution

One reason for the success and spread of the modern business enterprise, Chandler says, is that its structures of management encouraged longevity. Whereas traditional firms were often wound up at the death of the owner, the big new firms did not depend on individuals. "Men came and went. The institution and its offices remained." Yet managers had an incentive to make good, long-term decisions because their careers depended on the success of the company. Indeed, Chandler argues, managers were *more* likely than owners (who simply wanted a regular dividend out of the firm to fund their lifestyles) to play a long game, favoring future growth over short-term profits.

The other crucial difference between large managerial enterprises and traditional firms was that jobs were filled according to talent and experience rather than family connections or capital. Until World War One, Chandler notes, the Du Pont family still managed the businesses it owned. Thereafter, its firms were run by professional managers, and only those De Ponts who were graduates of top engineering schools and had experience in the company were allowed to be managers.

Because it was worth firms' while to invest in their managers, the quality of management increased. The scion of a smaller family firm probably wouldn't get the same level of management training and experience that he or she would in a big firm, so "talent" was naturally drawn away from the old forms of business. Management schools arose, and management became a profession. As standards were upped, so the modern managerial corporation, based on scientific allocation of resources, quickly nudged aside firms run through the nous of a wise family member, or driven along by the greed of a financier.

Why it happened in the United States

Britain's industrial revolution, despite its impact on the world, was more technological than managerial, Chandler says. Founding families of enterprises, often backed by large banks, appointed capable overseers and foremen to run things, but a managerial class such as the one which arose in the United States between the 1820s and the 1940s, did not evolve to the same degree. Chandler's explanation for why the US became the home of managerial capitalism was simply the sheer size and nature of its home market. Already by 1900, this market was twice the size of Britain's, and by 1920 thrice as big. Moreover, it was growing much quicker than those of the major European nations, the US market being more homogeneous (incomes were more equal than in Europe, and social class was less important). Lastly, the newness of the United States as a social and political entity meant that ways of doing business were not set in stone, and new ideas in production, distribution, marketing, and management were quickly adopted along with technological innovations.

Increased coordination meant lower costs and higher productivity, and so higher profits compared to traditional ways of doing business. A big portion of the lower costs came through internalizing many transactions in the company. For a manufacturer, an army of permanent wage laborers saved on the costs of hiring and firing in the marketplace, internal divisions for sales, marketing and distribution reduced the costs of obtaining market information, and ownership of suppliers took the uncertainty out of production. Greater coordination of inputs and production meant more intensive use of plant, equipment, and labor.

Crucial to the transformation of American business were new technologies which allowed for much greater volumes of production of a single good and constantly expanding markets for these goods. Chandler argues that technology and new markets almost *required* the new form of business enterprise to come into being. Fast population growth and the spread of people across the US required both the ramping up of production and the administrative coordination of distribution of goods and services across territories and regions. And increasing per capita income meant people could afford the new mass-produced, standardized goods, including cloth, clothing, shoes, saddlery, groceries, confectionery, tobacco, furniture, pharmaceuticals, jewelry, and tableware. The sheer scale of production and economies of scale brought profits to the large industrial concerns, much of which was reinvested in new product lines and production capacity. Thus happened a virtuous circle of rising population and rising wages, while at the same time the cost of consumer goods dropped. These trends only reinforced the dominance of the big industrial players.

Perhaps the greatest benefit that expanding markets brought was coordination. After all, much greater administrative coordination was required to run a regional or transcontinental railroad network moving people and freight across large distances, compared to a network in just one state. If it was not very well run, losses quickly mounted.

Industrial behemoths from Standard Oil to Ford built their own sales and distribution networks, and succeeded in coordinating the flow of production from the sourcing of raw materials to point of sale to the consumer. Coordination was also necessary to manage a national telegraph system. When telegraphy began to be replaced by telephones, there was already a management system in place that could adapt to the new technology. In distribution and marketing, small commission merchants were pushed aside by large wholesalers, commodity dealers, and mass retailers. Despite legislation in various states to protect the small merchant, chain store and department store fortunes were made and families such as Wanamaker, Kresge (later K-Mart), Straus (of Macy's), and Woolworth became household names. The mass retailers, because they became such large operations, often became their own wholesalers, sourcing their own stock directly from suppliers. In finance, size also began to make sense. By expanding the number of branches and outlets, a bank could make more intensive use of the centralized head office operations that had already been set up.

In total contrast to traditional enterprises, the new large corporations in rail, steam, communication, energy, retailing, and banking were by their very nature expansionary, demonstrating a good blend of centralized policy development while letting regional offices have a free hand to respond to local conditions. The bigger they got, the more productive and more profitable they became, providing security for the phalanxes of middle and upper managers who ran them.

Managers rule

Yet as enterprises grew, there was pressure to sustain themselves and not to give up any market share to rival concerns. When management's efforts were directed into defensive measures, it is easy to understand how the result could be suboptimal for consumer and nation—for instance, the tangle of private railroads that existed in the nineteenth century, requiring passengers to get a variety of tickets, change trains, and so on. Standard Oil, which provided a public boon in standardizing fuel for lighting and transport, poured huge energy and money into ensuring that it had no competitors.

Chandler notes that there was plenty of public and government opposition to large-scale enterprise, which seemed to go against American values of freedom of opportunity for all, particularly the entrepreneurship of the small proprietor, factory owner, or farmer. The new class of executives, who seemed to have so much power over modern life, were accountable only to their bosses and shareholders, not the public or politicians, and public anger led to a framework of law to counteract it. Yet the backlash did little to stop the rise and rise of big business in America and around the world. Growing populations and the demand for goods and services made the "technology of management" as important as technology itself in satisfying this demand.

The size of relative affluence of the US domestic market made the development of mass production techniques almost a necessity, whereas in the smaller markets of Europe and Japan traditional structures of retailing, wholesaling, production, and management were not forced to change so quickly. Even when family firms combined to protect markets or supplies, the structures were more federal than central and did not require a cadre of professional managers. When they did employ managers, the family and their financiers retained control.

After World War Two, as markets grew and prosperity spread among societies, differences between Europe, Japan, and the US diminished. Managerial capitalism became the default for any country wishing to be economically powerful, and everywhere, Chandler notes, "the paraphernalia of professional management has appeared—the associations, the journals, the training schools, the consultants."

Final comments

One important factor in the story of modern business enterprise, Chandler reminds us, is stronger and bigger government. After the shocks of the Great Depression and World War Two, and with the intellectual revolution in Keynesian economics, governments were expected to act to maintain full employment and keep economic demand steady through state spending and monetary policy. The private sector, despite its power, had not been able to regulate demand, and it fell to government to ward off the threat of another depression. A mass production, mass distribution economy, it seemed, needed a correspondingly large government to keep things on an even keel.

This suggests that our civilization is not strictly a capitalist civilization, but a managerial one. Prices and markets provide crucial information on where resources are best allocated, just as Adam Smith said, but given the sheer size of the consumer base today, and the variety of products and services, huge coordination is required to feed, clothe, house, and entertain us. It is hard to imagine this being achieved without large corporations and their thousands of managers acting within a regulatory environment which protects their interests and which enforces contractual and intellectual property rights that are often the result of huge investments in research, design, and technology. As Joseph Schumpeter observed, the bigger the economy and society, the more such things are routinized and organized, and become no longer the job of the individual entrepreneur. In rich nations people retain a misty-eyed view of the entrepreneur and the quaint small proprietor, but in poorer parts of the world people wish for the greater sophistication and efficiency that come with professional management and large firms.

Alfred Chandler

Chandler was born in 1918 in Delaware. He studied at Harvard University and completed his Ph.D. in history there in 1952. He taught at MIT, Johns Hopkins University, and then Harvard, and began teaching at Harvard Business School in 1970. He died in 2007.

Chandler wrote widely on business strategy and business history, focusing on the early railroad business, the chemical and pharmaceutical industry, and the consumer electronic and computer industry. His classic Strategy *and* Structure *(1962) argued that firm structure must follow strategy. He wrote a biography of the industrialist Pierre du Pont, and one on his great-grandfather Henry Varnum Poor, a cofounder of Standard & Poor's. He also helped edit the letters and papers of presidents Theodore Roosevelt and Dwight Eisenhower. Funded by a grant from the Sloan Foundation,* The Visible Hand *was awarded Columbia University's Bancroft Prize as well as the Pulitzer.*

Chandler was not a blood relative of the Du Pont family, but was given his middle name, DuPont, because his great-grandmother had been brought up by them when her parents died. Chandler's other great-grandfather was an engineer who helped transform the Du Pont de Nemours Chemical Company into the DuPont corporation.

Titan: The Life of John D. Rockefeller Sr.

"As always, the greater the tumult, the cooler Rockefeller became, and a strange calm settled over him when his colleagues were most disconcerted . . . Like all revolutionaries, he saw himself as an instrument of a higher purpose, endowed with a visionary faith. He knew his actions would at first be resisted and misunderstood by the myopic crowd, but he believed that the force and truth of his ideas would triumph in the end."

"Something in the nature of J. D. Rockefeller had to occur in America, and it is all to the good of the world that he was tight-lipped, consistent and amazingly free from vulgar vanity, sensuality, and quarrelsomeness. His cold persistence and ruthlessness arouse something like horror, but for all that he was a forward-moving force, a constructive power."

H. G. Wells, The Work, Wealth and Happiness of Mankind

In a nutshell

Society's interests are best served by giant monopolies which provide quality and lower prices for the consumer.

In a similar vein

Andrew Carnegie *The Gospel of Wealth*
Alfred Chandler *The Visible Hand*
Walter Isaacson *Steve Jobs*
Peter Thiel *Zero To One*
Ashlee Vance *Elon Musk*

CHAPTER 5

Ron Chernow

When his publisher suggested he write a biography of John D. Rockefeller, Ron Chernow wasn't keen. Previous biographies had portrayed the magnate as "a gifted automaton at best, a malevolent machine at worst," and Chernow didn't want to spend years researching a man who, for all his wealth, was essentially uninteresting as a person.

But one day at the Rockefeller archives in New York, Chernow discovered in an unpublished set of interviews a more layered, intriguing character, whose life was "marked to an exceptional degree by silence, mystery, and evasion." Agreeing to write the first full-length biography since the 1950s, Chernow aimed to get beneath the folksy, wisecracking grandfatherly image of Rockefeller's later years, and expose the rapacious monopolist of the younger man. "This panorama of greed and guile should startle even the most jaundiced students of the Gilded Age," Chernow writes, and would show up previous hagiographies of Rockefeller.

Yet neither did Chernow simply want to do a hatchet job on his subject, as crusading journalist Ida Tarbell had done, or Henry Lloyd in his study of Standard Oil's practices, *Wealth Against Commonwealth*. The salient point about Rockefeller, what made him so interesting, Chernow says, is that "his good side was every bit as good as his bad side was bad." At the point where he was most vilified, he began focusing his considerable powers on philanthropy, giving away history's greatest fortune for the benefit of humankind.

Luck and judgment

John Davison Rockefeller was fortunate in the timing of his birth, 1839, which meant that he, along with Andrew Carnegie (1835), Jay Gould (1836), and J. Pierpont Morgan (1837), would come of age just as the post-Civil War industrial boom was about to get under way. It seemed a time of limitless possibility. He grew up a Baptist, then an evangelical church, in New York State, but his father William, a charismatic entrepreneur, forced the family to move several times in his childhood and adolescence. With William often away, John became the man of the house to his mother Eliza, with early responsibilities. William ended up boarding the family with his sister near Cleveland, Ohio, while he pursued an affair with a woman he would eventually marry. Chernow describes William as a "bigamist and snake-oil salesman" who went around the country selling patent medicines. For the rest of his life, John would go to great lengths to cover up his father's shenanigans. However, Ohio, with its oil fields, proved to be a fortuitous place for John to enter the adult world.

Although not a top student, John had a head for numbers, and had been nicknamed "the Deacon" by his classmates for his serious air and rectitude. His first job was as an assistant bookkeeper in a merchant's firm in Cleveland, and before long he had started his own merchant firm dealing in food and grain. In 1863 Rockefeller started investing in the emerging oil refining business. For the cost of setting up a shop, anyone could launch a crude refining operation producing kerosene, which was providing lantern light in houses and huts across America.

At only 25 he took a controlling interest in the biggest refinery in Cleveland, and married Cettie Spelman, the daughter of well-to-do, cultured parents. They were not keen on the match, as Rockefeller had little social standing, but he was persistent. Chernow notes that, "in love as in business, he had a longer time frame, a more settled will, than other people."

Rockefeller's business partners were often vexed by his strange blend of extreme frugality (inherited from his mother) and prodigality (from his father). This "tightfisted control of details and advocacy of unbridled expansion," Chernow writes, "daring in design, cautious in execution . . . was a formula he made his own throughout his career." When, for instance, his partners wanted to move more cautiously, he had no compunction borrowing as much as he could from banks in order to expand, so sure was he of his own judgment.

It could be so much more than this

In Rockefeller's day the oil industry was a wild frontier, with brothels, taverns, and gambling dens littering the fields, and everyone out to make a quick buck. His aim from the start was to tame it, rationalize it, and make it a respectable industry. He would "impose his iron rule on this lawless, godless business."

Relentlessly inquisitive and hungry for knowledge, his nickname in the oil fields was "the Sponge." What made Rockefeller different, Chernow argues, was that he did not simply think of his own operation, but developed a picture of the entire oil industry and its place in the modern economy. This involved planning far ahead and striking strategic partnerships so that he could dominate the industry. "The Standard Oil Company will some day refine all the oil and make all the barrels," he told a Cleveland businessman.

Rockefeller methodically set about buying up the 20 to 30 smaller refiners in Cleveland, and created a shell company that allowed collusion between a small group of major refiners and the railroads. At a time when there was an excess capacity and "suicidal" price wars on the railroads and in the refining business, creating a cartel seemed to Rockefeller to be the only thing to ensure the oil industry's future and allow it to advance. He and business partner Henry Flagler managed to secure preferential secret rates with the Erie and New York Central railroads to transport oil to the eastern seaboard. The railroads were willing to reduce their rates because it meant steady, large business that would reduce their costs and increase their profits, enabling them to compete against their arch rival, the Pennsylvania railroad. The cozy arrangement allowed Standard Oil to cement its position as a leading national refiner, because it had certainty about costs. Rockefeller would never see the move as corrupt, more a matter of logic. Why wouldn't the railroads give his company preferential rates, if it was giving them lots of business? Rockefeller wanted a massive, efficient, hi-tech industry, dominated by his company, and it was a goal that could not be achieved through conventional competition.

Arguably, he was proved right. The consolidation of the industry under Standard Oil, thanks to big investments in research and development, would allow it to increase quality and consistency of products while at the same time reduce prices for consumers by cutting the cost of refining in half. In Rockefeller's mind, only without the annoyance of competition could he make long-term investments in quality and efficiency; innovation was only possible through monopoly, and he was doing the public a service.

Too successful

As the company grew, however, it was faced with two possible nightmares: either new oil fields would be discovered, and the market would be swamped with oil, seeing a precipitous fall in prices; or no new oil would be found, and existing fields would simply dry up. In either case, much of Standard's investments in infrastructure and research would be a waste of money. Yet when Rockefeller's executives raised these possibilities, he would simply say, "The Lord will provide."

By 1891 he had bought up vast areas of land for crude oil production, not just refining, and controlled a quarter of American oil production. Yet as the company grew like an octopus, criticism increased. The ethic of American individualism in business was being hijacked by the dark motivations of big corporations like Standard Oil. Much of the public attack was justified. Rockefeller made sure that politics would not stand in the way of his ambitions, and though his public donations to political parties were stingy, in secret Standard Oil was not averse to "buying" politicians who were supportive of its interests.

The rise and dominance of Standard Oil taught the American public a lesson, Chernow observes: that if left totally unregulated, markets could end up being very *un*free. There is nothing natural about markets; there must be laws that prevent monopoly. We take this knowledge for granted now, but in the early, unregulated and largely untaxed days of American capitalism, it seemed like heresy. Rockefeller underestimated the power of the small business lobby, and could not stop the march toward antitrust (antimonopoly) legislation. In 1892 he had to reorganize the company to escape antitrust law, with compartmentalization into 20 different companies. But the law was weak, and the power of Standard Oil, now headquartered at 26 Broadway, New York, remained the same. With the economic depression of the 1890s, a populist anticapitalist groundswell made Rockefeller into a hated figure. The firm prospered anyway, with steady demand for illuminating oil and lubricants. It became so replete with cash that it no longer needed Wall Street banks, but became a sort of bank itself, financing its own growth to such an extent that no other company or trust could come near it, and charging low prices for oil products that no company could match.

By 1907, Standard Oil refined 87 percent of the nation's kerosene, had 90 percent of the domestic market, was the dominant world exporter of oil, and was *20 times* the size of its next competitor. In the same year, with the support of President Teddy Roosevelt, a multitude of antitrust cases were brought against Standard. Looming over Rockefeller was the possibility that he, now in his sixties, could go to jail. To reduce the risk, in a courtroom in Chicago he pretended to be a bumbling old man who couldn't remember much. The show didn't stop the Supreme Court, in 1911, handing down a judgment that Standard Oil be dismantled into 34 smaller companies, which now would compete with each other. But in the years after the breakup, shares in the new constituent companies soared in value. With the automobile age dawning, the boundless thirst for oil would make Rockefeller richer than ever.

To give a sense of just how vast Standard Oil's market power was at the time of the judgment, consider that its constituent companies would become each in their own right big corporate names with huge market shares: Standard Oil of New Jersey became Exxon, Standard Oil of New York became Mobil, Standard Oil of Indiana Amoco, and Standard Oil of California Chevron. Though "Standard Oil" as a name disappeared, Rockefeller's fingerprints would remain on millions of gas pumps and oil cans across the United States and the world.

Christ and capital

Tired out by the details of running Standard Oil, and facing Congressional hearings and court cases, not to mention bad press, Rockefeller had a kind of breakdown in 1890, staying away from the office for several months and developing alopecia, or hair loss. He was effectively retired from the business by age 55, but the public believed he was still in charge. Even after he had begun to give away his fortune, providing a massive endowment to establish the University of Chicago, he was vilified by popular heroes such as Upton Sinclair, who exposed the corrupt meat industry and now had Rockefeller in his sights, and the famous anarchist Emma Goldman. He led an ordered, secluded life on his estates, so as to avoid the possibility of confrontations with the public, or worse, terrorist attack or an assassin.

As America's richest man (his untaxed income for one year alone, 1902, was $58 million, or over a billion dollars in today's money), every day he received thousands of letters requesting money. He did his best to respond to genuine need, but came to the view that, with his wealth mounting, the only way to give responsibly would be in a large, systematic manner.

Even from his first job as an adolescent, Rockefeller was charitable, giving away 6–10 percent of his income to causes that took his fancy. Echoing Methodist John Wesley's call to make money, save it, and give a lot away, Rockefeller once said, "It has seemed as if I was favored and got increase because the Lord knew that I was going to turn around and give it back." This thinking, Chernow believes, is what gave Rockefeller extraordinary license to pursue his business life with gusto, free of scruples. The Calvinist idea of "calling" meant that any money gained from his work would be a sign of God's blessing.

His founding of the University of Chicago, and money to colleges for black Americans, though big moves, were just a foretaste of his later giving through the Rockefeller Foundation, created in 1913. Before its creation, philanthropy had largely been about rich men getting their names associated with pet institutions such as symphony orchestras or art museums, or funding schools or orphanages. The sheer size of the new foundation enabled Rockefeller to move beyond personal whim and invest in the creation of knowledge that could benefit humanity in the biggest way over the long run, focusing on medical research and education.

The Rockefeller millions found their way to some unlikely causes too. His daughter Edith Rockefeller McCormick, the first of the clan to rebel against the family's strict religious conformity, moved to Switzerland and became a supporter of psychologist Carl Jung and an analyst herself; she also funneled money to James Joyce during World War Two, while he had sought sanctuary in neutral Zurich. Abby Aldrich Rockefeller, wife of Rockefeller's son John, became the major benefactor of New York's Museum of Modern Art (MoMA). She somehow convinced her stuffy husband, who could not fathom his wife's liking for Picasso and Matisse, that they should have their nine-storey mansion (and the mansion of John D. Rockefeller) razed to the ground to make way for the museum. John D. Jr. had his own passions, pouring millions into the rehabilitation of colonial Williamsburg, and funding virtually the entire contents of The Cloisters museum of medieval artefacts in New York. John D.'s grandson, Nelson Rockefeller, was a four-time governor of New York, made three attempts to win the US presidency as a liberal Republican, and was vice president to Gerald R. Ford.

Final comments

Chernow was probably a bit too harsh on Rockefeller's business strategies. After all, every business aims to dominate its field, or at least be its leader—it's just that few are able to do so. Rockefeller achieved his aim of making the oil industry modern and efficient, ramping up quality and saving consumers money, not to mention employing legions of people. Without his rapacity in business, there would be no Rockefeller Foundation today.

For Rockefeller, the cutthroat competitiveness of the early oil industry was good for no one, and he saw his buying up of the industry's small players as a public service that was inevitable if the industry was ever to mature. An argument can be made that we are now again living in a rentier kind of capitalism, in which most of the gains go to giant monopolies or oligopolies of three or four giant companies in each field. The online world (think of the power of Google and Facebook), with its network effects and dominant platforms, is a good example. Yet as Peter Thiel argues in *Zero To One*, the public benefits of monopoly power can be significant, and even if there are choices, people often *want* to go with the product or service that everyone else is using. The great prize of business is not so much cornering the market, but setting the standard.

Ron Chernow

Born in 1949 in Brooklyn, New York, Chernow has degrees from Yale and Cambridge. He was a freelance journalist and worked at the progressive think-tank, Twentieth Century Fund, before becoming a full-time writer.

His other books include The House of Morgan: An American Banking Dynasty and the Rise of Modern Finance *(1990);* The Warburgs: The Twentieth Century Odyssey of a Remarkable Jewish Family *(1993);* Alexander Hamilton *(2004);* Washington: A Life *(2010), which won the Pulitzer Prize for Biography; and* Grant *(2017), a biography of Ulysses S. Grant.*

1997

The Innovator's Dilemma

"In their efforts to stay ahead by developing competitively superior products, many companies don't realize the speed at which they are moving up-market, over-satisfying the needs of their original customers as they race the competition toward higher-performance, higher-margin markets. In doing so, they create a vacuum at lower price points into which competitors employing disruptive technologies can enter."

"Companies whose investment processes demand quantification of market sizes and financial returns before they can enter a market get paralyzed or make serious mistakes when face with disruptive technologies. They demand market data when none exists and make judgments based on financial projections when neither revenues or costs can, in fact, be known."

In a nutshell

Bigger companies can fall into a trap in which it only makes sense to serve existing customers; but new customers and technologies are where the growth is.

In a similar vein

Jim Collins *Great by Choice*
Ben Horowitz *The Hard Thing About Hard Things*
Walter Isaacson *Steve Jobs*
Kim & Renée Mauborgne *Blue Ocean Strategy*
Geoffrey A. Moore *Crossing the Chasm*

CHAPTER 6

Clayton Christensen

U nlike many business school professors, Clayton Christensen actually worked in business before becoming a doctoral student at Harvard, where he researched the ideas that would become *The Innovator's Dilemma: When New Technologies Cause Great Firms to Fail.*

The book, which is often put in lists of the top five business books of the last 30 years, is "not about the failure of simply any company, but of *good* companies," Christensen writes, ones that are much admired, even considered innovative, yet that fail to stay ahead of changes in the market and technology. Sears, for instance, the American retailer, was for decades considered extremely well run, and pioneered catalog retailing, supply chain management, store brands, and credit card sales. Yet even when Christensen was writing in the 1990s, Sears had lost its way, missing the big trend to discount retailing fully exploited by Walmart, Kmart, and others, and failing to adjust to online retailing.

So many companies are considered to be very well managed at exactly the time, in hindsight, when they failed to see important trends that would upend their industry. Why? Christensen's research revealed that firms fail precisely *because* of their "good" management—that is, they listened to their customers and tried to provide them with what they wanted. Yet there are times when it is right *not* to listen to customers, and instead to pioneer new products for markets that barely yet exist. The innovator's dilemma is that the "logical, competent decisions of management that are critical to the success of their companies are also the reasons why they lose their positions of leadership." Firms must remain good managers of the existing business while at the same time making sure they give enough resources to disruptive technologies that, if not embraced, "ultimately could lead to their downfall."

The focus of Christensen's research was the computer disk-drive industry, which although now of only historical interest, was so fast-moving in its day that it allowed him to see how established players were frequently upended by industry upstarts. The book was an important influence on Apple's Steve Jobs, for one. But it also includes a range of fascinating case studies of industries including retail, earth excavation, steel milling, accounting software, and motorcycles, across which the same principles apply.

Disruptive and sustaining technologies

"Disruptive" technologies are ones that underperform or are worse than existing technologies, in conventional terms, but which do something that fringe or new customers value. Disruptive products are often cheaper, more basic, or easier to use. One example: the cheap, lesser powered off-road motorcycles exported to America by Japanese makers such as Honda and Yamaha in the 1970s, which paled in comparison with powerful, deluxe road bikes make by Harley-Davidson and BMW—and yet proved popular. A recent example: cloud computing data storage, which has given people a cheap alternative to buying expensive servers from firms such as IBM.

Big companies usually don't invest in disruptive products or services for the rational reason that there is "not much money in it." Demand is usually from the low end, less profitable part of the market. But by not investing at all, Christensen notes, they may have to watch as that tiny, low value market grows into something bigger—and by then it is too late.

Corporations prefer to invest in "sustaining" technologies, that is, ones that try to improve performance along parameters that existing customers in mainstream markets value. They are so focused on the customer that the best-performing companies "have well-developed systems for killing ideas that their customers don't want." But to really grow, they have to look to technologies and products that are *not* currently wanted, but which there may be a market for in the future.

The problem is that "Small markets don't solve the growth needs of large companies," Christensen writes. The bigger a company gets, the more revenue has to come in just to keep the juggernaut going, and going after a new technology that might bring in an extra 1 percent sales down the line doesn't make sense. In addition, big firms like to think of themselves as leaders in their field, creating the "best" products. To suddenly develop more basic, cheaper products seems like an affront to their pride. Most sizable companies are good at market research, planning, and execution. This works for the development of known technologies, and existing customers, but doesn't work for emerging or barely known technologies. After all, "Markets that don't exist can't be analysed," Christensen notes.

The management theory of "resource dependence" says that companies will only succeed by finding out and giving their customers exactly what they want and need. The idea draws on the theory of evolution and natural selection, in that the firm with the greatest adaptation to its commercial environment will flourish. It is the customer and market that determines where a firm's resources are spent, and managers' blue sky thinking is an indulgence that will lead to bankruptcy or irrelevance. In fact, the last two fates can eventuate when a firm is so focused on their customer that they fail to see the potential gains of emerging technologies.

Never saw it coming: established industries and upstarts

The first kinds of earth excavators were steam powered. The next generation powered their shovels via cables activated by gasoline-powered engines. Nearly all of the steam-powered excavator makers, including names such as Bucyrus, Thew, and Marion, transitioned to be makers of internal combustion engine excavators, including the later adoption of diesel engines.

But when hydraulic-powered excavation replaced cables, only a small handful of newer entrants, such as John Deere, Caterpillar, Ford, Liebherr, and Komatsu, became successful. Hydraulic excavators were not developed by the previous established players because the market for them at first seemed small. The first kinds of hydraulic digger, known as backhoes, were often just mounted on the back of tractors, for smaller jobs like digging for pipes and residential construction, and sold through tractor and implement dealers. This was in contrast to established excavator firms, which were making bigger and more powerful machines with wider shovels. Bucyrus tried to sell a smaller, hydraulic/cable hybrid digger, but its general excavation contractor customers didn't have much use for it. It was stuck with the wrong customer base. The new entrants, using only hydraulic technology, were, in contrast, focused only on customers who could see the benefits of it. In time, hydraulic technology was adopted across the board, and engineered into all forms of excavator, big and small.

Established makers failed not because they didn't invest in the new hydraulics technology, not because they were ignoring their customers, and not because management was asleep. In fact, having to cater to existing customers meant they did not have the attention or resources to devote to a "maybe" product that their client base didn't even want. It often seems to makes sense for a company to migrate from an existing customer base toward higher-value customers, ones that generate more profit. It is rare for a company to go down-market, Christensen notes, but this is often where the new markets lie. Established firms usually do not lack any technological edge over the upstarts. Rather, it is their inflexibility over strategy and cost structures that sees them lose out.

The problem is, firms selling disruptive technologies rarely sell only their cheaper, disruptive offering for long. In time they cannibalize the established market too. An example of this was the rise of "minimills," small steel mills that used scrap metal to produce "rebar" steel of marginal quality for a limited range of uses. Rebar was cheap to make, but it was a low-margin, competitive industry. This market was quite distinct from that served by the big, integrated steel mills that made high-quality steel for major manufacturers. However, after mastering the rebar market, minimill producers such as Nucor and Chaparral began making inroads into the next low-margin area of bars, rods, and angle irons. The main steel markers didn't mind, as it wasn't that profitable for them anyway. Then the minimills began making structural steel beams, taking this part of the market away from the big steel makers. Again, conventional steelmakers took this in their stride; their profits were high from producing high-quality flat-rolled steel for high-expectation makers of cans, cars, and appliances.

The focus on the high end of the steel industry made big makers such as Bethlehem Steel profitable, but even as this was happening the new approaches and technologies of the innovators were finding more customers. As the minimills continued to increase their market share, becoming more advanced, the legacy steelmakers were having to close plant after plant. Nucor, once a marginal outfit, became the market leader in US steel production.

Christensen's point: while it seems to go against the grain for a company to give up on its established business and embrace lower profit offerings, it is natural for a disruptive firm to move the other way—upward into established markets.

Embracing disruption

In part two of the book Christensen looks at the few companies that dealt with disruptive change well. Common to these firms was, firstly, that they looked beyond their existing customers to find ones that may be interested in the disruptive technology; and secondly, they created autonomous small units to go after these markets, units which were charged with failing early, often, and inexpensively in their search for customers of a disruptive technology. Christensen mentions how, in contrast to many other mainframe computer makers such as DEC, IBM had success in the first few years of the personal computer industry because it created a separate business in Florida, away from its New York base, which had freedom to develop its own machines, create its own supply chains, and set its own prices that suited the personal computer market, not IBM's own pricing traditions.

Because some emerging technologies are so new, firms are not even sure how products incorporating them will be used or viewed: "mutual discovery by customers and manufacturers . . . simply takes time." With its first handheld computer, the Newton, Apple tried to shorten this process through exhaustive market research before launching, trying to work out what people wanted. In the event, its handwriting recognition software was not up to scratch, wireless communication was then too expensive, and the market for the Newton's capabilities was not as big as was thought (it only sold 140,000 units in its first two years of launch, 1993 and 1994). What happened was that Apple was trying to launch a mass-market product in what was still a marginal market. Of course, years later the iPhone would demonstrate the power of handheld computing, and a massive ecosystem of app creation developed around it. Its potential was by then fully appreciated and fulfilled. The lesson: "Small markets cannot satisfy the near-term growth requirements of big organizations." *But*, if Apple had neglected handheld technology completely, it would never have set itself up for the iPhone's success.

We can see the same kind of dynamic today. Google's experimental "X" division is not tied to the success of its other businesses, but specifically charged with developing amazing new technologies. One of its first products, Google Glass, was a commercial flop. When buyers wore the glasses, people around felt they were being recorded. It was too intrusive to be popular. However, Google Glass is now being used by companies such as Boeing in its production teams. Clear uses for the product have only been found several years after initial release. "There is a big difference between the failure of an *idea* and the failure of a *firm*," Christensen observes. Most new businesses abandon their business strategies when their new product or service makes contact with the market, and they find out how people *actually* use them.

Christensen observes that if you enter a market in which there is an established technology, with enough resources and good management you can still do very well in it. There is no clear advantage in being the first mover, technologically. However, there are real advantages in being a first mover in a *disruptive* technology field. A disrupting company, free of legacy clients, is more willing to keep pouring resources into untried technologies and products, thereby sustaining their edge and increasing their share of the market. His conclusion: "creating new markets is significantly *less* risky and *more* rewarding than entering established markets against entrenched competition."

Final comments

Late in the book Christensen includes a prescient chapter on electric cars and their potential for disruption of the automobile industry. They had "the smell of a disruptive technology" in that mainstream car-makers doubted the demand for them. He warns that big American car-makers could miss the boat by catering only to their existing, profitable customers.

When Christensen was writing, range and acceleration for electric vehicles was so poor that it was difficult to imagine who would want them, and for what purpose. Give one to your teenager so that they could stay nearby and only drive slowly? As it turned out, battery technology improved at such a rate that one company, Tesla Inc., found a ready market for a very fast, luxury electric car for the well off and environmentally minded. This proves Christensen's point that just because there is no clear initial use or market for a technology, it doesn't mean it can be ignored or seen as a distraction to your main business. In fact, it is the people and companies who are fascinated by today's unknown, untried technologies that may own your industry tomorrow.

Clayton Christensen

Born in Salt Lake City, Utah, in 1952, into a family of eight children, Christensen gained a degree in economics from Brigham Young University before becoming a Rhodes Scholar at Oxford University, where he took an M. Phil in econometrics and economics, focused on developing countries.

Between 1979 and 1984 he worked as a management consultant in manufacturing strategy for Boston Consulting Group, taking a leave of absence in 1982/3 to be a transport adviser in the Reagan administration. In 1984 he helped launched CPS, a ceramics engineering firm, which had a public flotation just before the stock market crash of 1987. After the share price dropped from $12 to $2 and Christensen was ejected as its head, he enrolled at Harvard as a Ph.D. student. Christensen joined the faculty of Harvard Business School in 1992, and is the Kim B. Clark Professor of Business Administration.

His other books include The Innovator's Solution *(2003),* Disrupting Class: How Disruptive Innovation Will Change the Way the World Learns *(2008),* The Innovator's Prescription: A Disruptive Solution for Healthcare *(2008), and* Competing Against Luck: The Story of Innovation and Customer Choice *(2016).*

Alibaba: The House That Jack Ma Built

"Jack's fame stems from the story of how a Chinese company somehow got the better of Silicon Valley, an East beats West tale worthy of a Jin Yong novel. His continued success, though, is becoming a story of South versus North—of a company with roots in the entrepreneurial heartland of southern China testing the limits of the country's political masters in Beijing."

"More than 10 percent of retail purchases in China are made online, higher than the 7 percent in the States. Jack has likened e-commerce to a 'dessert' in the United States, whereas in China it is the 'main course.' Why? Shopping in China was never a pleasurable experience. Until the arrival of multinational companies . . . there were very few retailing chains or shopping malls. Most domestic retailers started as state-owned enterprises (SOEs). With access to a ready supply of financing, provided by local governments or state-owned banks, they tended to view shoppers as a mere inconvenience."

In a nutshell

Don't be cowed by the big players in your industry, or the people with top credentials. The main ingredients in business success are vision, patience, and agility.

In a similar vein

Walter Isaacson *Steve Jobs*
Brad Stone *The Everything Store*
Ashlee Vance *Elon Musk*

CHAPTER 7

Duncan Clark

"The communists just beat us at capitalism!" So said television wit Jon Stewart when, after its flotation on the New York Stock Exchange in 2014, Chinese firm Alibaba raised $25 billion. The IPO, which was for only 12 percent of the company, was the biggest on record, beating all previous American capital raisings.

With over 400 million people a year buying things from its e-commerce websites, Taobao.com and Tmall.com, Alibaba has helped turn China into a consumer country. But it is much more than an "Amazon of the East"; Alibaba had global ambitions from the start, and in the past five years has been fulfilling them fast.

In *Alibaba: The House That Jack Ma Built*, Duncan Clark tells the story of founder Jack Ma's remarkable rise from failed student to multibillionaire. Clark, who has lived in China since 1994, met Ma in 1999 when he was starting Alibaba in a sweaty apartment in Hangzhou. Clark became an adviser to Ma as he expanded internationally, and in 2003, when Alibaba was not doing that well, Clark was offered the chance to buy cheap shares in the company in return for his services. He declined. It proved to be "a $30 million mistake," Clark says in his introduction. Writing the book has been a "cathartic" experience, serving as a warning to anyone not to underestimate Ma's abilities and ambitions. Clark provides a gripping account of the Alibaba story, but also an education in Chinese political economy, culture, and geography that explains the rise of Alibaba's many competitors including Tencent, Baidu, and Sina over the past 15 years.

East meets West

In 1980, 12-year-old Ma Yun was keen to learn English and began hanging around the few foreigners who were visiting Hangzhou. One of them, Ken Morley from Newcastle, Australia, took a shine to the boy, and his sons Ken and David became fast friends. After the Morleys' return to Australia they and "Jack" Ma kept in touch through letters.

In the ensuing years Jack finished school and took the national *gaokao* exam to get into university. But he was terrible at maths, which brought his total score down. He did menial jobs while studying to take the *gaokao* again . . . and again. On the third try he got just enough points to get in to the very unprestigious Hangzhou Teachers College. In 1985 Morley jumped through a lot of diplomatic hoops in order for Jack to visit the family in Australia. The trip changed his life. Ma had been taught that China was the richest country in the world; now he knew it wasn't true. The Morleys paid some of Jack's living expenses to continue at college, and later Ken gave Ma money to buy his first apartment, with his new wife Cathy.

Clark notes the irony that Ken Morley, a socialist who had once stood for office as a candidate of the Australian Communist Party, became the mentor to a young man who would go on to embody Chinese capitalism. Ma would later repay the favor by donating $20 million for a scholarship program at the University of Newcastle.

China goes online

Zhejiang, in which Hangzhou is situated, is historically one of China's most entrepreneurial provinces. Following Deng Xiaoping's opening up of the Chinese economy from 1978, its inhabitants took Deng's statement, "You can be rich. You can help other people to be rich," to heart, and along with the Pearl River Delta and Beijing, the region has been an engine of China's economic rise.

After Ma graduated from college, he got a job teaching English and international trade at Hangzhou Institute of Electronic Engineering. Though he loved teaching, he was swept up in the fervor for business, and at 29 started a translation agency. It wasn't a success, and to pay the rent he traded in gifts, books, and flowers. In 1994 he made a trip to the United States, where for the first time he accessed the internet. It was a revelation, and he saw an opportunity to help millions of Chinese businesses export their goods to America and elsewhere. He enlisted friends and family to create China Pages, selling space on the directory to local businesses. Within a couple of years the Chinese government, fearing a technological gap between China and the West, had its state-owned telecoms companies establish the infrastructure for the internet, with help from US telecoms provider Sprint.

China Pages was never a commercial success, and when it was taken over by a subsidiary of a state company, Ma took a job in Beijing at the trade and economic ministry, overseeing the building of its website. He hated it and counted the days until he could leave and get back into business. "I couldn't realize my dreams as a public servant," he recalls. It was 1998, and Ma, now 35, watched other Chinese internet entrepreneurs run ahead of him. Inspired by Yahoo in America, these entrepreneurs (all of whom, unlike Ma, had been to top universities and were very tech-savvy) were setting up equivalent portals which could make the internet more accessible. Extricating himself from the government job, in 1999 Ma founded Alibaba, a name he took for its "open sesame" connotations. As a non-Chinese name it made the firm stand out, yet its meaning could be understood around the world. Having bought the Alibaba.com domain name from a Canadian for $4,000, he was properly in business.

In February 1999 there were only 2 million internet users in China. By the end of 2000 it was 17 million and rising fast. The government was making it easier and cheaper to connect to the internet, and the price of computers was falling. Ma figured that Chinese firms would want to be represented overseas, and his free website would help connect them to the world without having to go through slow-moving and officious state-owned trading institutions. Alibaba also had an advantage compared to start-ups from Shanghai or Beijing in that Hangzhou was located in the provinces, so rents and wages were cheap. Goldman Sachs and some smaller funds got interested in Alibaba, and Ma took funding of $5 million for half the company's equity. As internet fever gripped China, this was small money compared to the mountains of cash that internet portals Sohu, NetEase, and Sina were attracting.

Slaying the western giants

Alibaba had no clear business model, but Masayoshi Son, the Korean-Japanese founder of SoftBank who had become a billionaire through his investment in Yahoo, saw a lot in Ma and invested $20 million in Alibaba, in return for 30 percent. The investment allowed the firm to have a long-term horizon, and when the internet bubble burst in 2000, Alibaba was in a good place. It had spent only $5 million of its $25 million funding, and while many of China's e-commerce outfits bit the dust, Alibaba continued to expand, setting up offices in the US and Europe. The charismatic Ma became a drawcard for audiences, and as the new face of Chinese capitalism, was the subject of stories by *Forbes Global* and *The Economist*. Yet although Alibaba now had half a million business users, its revenues from giving Chinese companies an e-commerce presence were not even $1 million; the firm needed other sources of revenue.

Having established a business-to-business portal, Ma became more interested in launching a consumer e-commerce site in the manner of Amazon or eBay. Already EachNet, founded by the Harvard-educated Shao Yibo, was gunning to create the eBay of China. eBay itself noticed, and acquired the company for $180 million. But in the early 2000s there wasn't much trust among Chinese consumers to buy things online; credit cards were not common, and there was no online payment system to speak of. Ma felt that there was still plenty of scope for another player to enter the consumer e-commerce market and win. Half a dozen Alibaba staff worked in secret to launch a new consumer commerce website, Taobao.com (*taobao* means "hunting for treasure" in Mandarin). Masayoshi Son decided to pour $80 million into the new venture, which launched in May 2003.

At this point, eBay China didn't even consider Taobao a threat. It felt it could get away with increasing fees to sellers from 3 percent to 8 percent, but sellers were starting to rebel. There was a growing contrast between the imperious giant eBay and the friendly local start-up Taobao, which did not charge sellers or buyers commission. Clark notes that "in website design, culture matters." eBay's site looked foreign, while Taobao had the visual busyness of a typical Chinese market, and had a popular chat window allowing buyers and sellers to communicate directly and haggle over prices, in the Chinese way. In a fatal move, eBay decided to transfer the hosting of its Chinese site back to California. The migration put the site outside the "Great Firewall of China," and meant that it would be slower to load and attract the government's censors. eBay experienced a sudden drop in traffic, which was a boon to the local, nimble Taobao. Alibaba launched its own online payment system, Alipay, which soon eclipsed the eBay-owned PayPal, which had failed to catch on because of the many regulatory hurdles involved in a foreign payment system. By 2006, eBay in China had been reduced to a rump, while Alibaba's sites, combining the best elements of Amazon, eBay, and PayPal, reigned.

Yahoo had also wanted to "win" China, but its information portal model had been rendered redundant by Google's mastery of search in the mid 2000s. Yahoo's cofounder, Taiwanese-born Jerry Yang, wisely turned Yahoo's Chinese business over to Alibaba, having the company invest $1 billion in Alibaba in return for 40 percent equity. The money enabled a big expansion of Taobao and Alipay, and for the declining Yahoo it would prove to be its smartest bet. Google itself would depart China in 2010, after only four years, citing the regulatory barriers of being a foreign company, and the fundamental incompatibility of its search prowess and censorship. In the space of a few years, eBay, Yahoo, and Google had all been conquered and supplanted by Alibaba and other indigenous start-ups, including Tencent and Baidu. Western companies, Clark observes, learned the truth of a Chinese adage: "It is better to be a merchant than a missionary."

Alibaba now and tomorrow

Between 2006 and 2009, Taobao went from strength to strength, with sales on the platform rocketing from $2 billion to $30 billion. If Taobao is the online version of China's street markets, Alibaba's subsequent offering, Tmall, has the feel of a glitzy mall, Clark notes. Tmall makes money for Alibaba by charging commission on sales, and many big US retailers, including Nike, Costco, Macy's, and Amazon, are investing heavily to get into the mind of the Chinese consumer through the site. It is a smarter strategy than opening physical stores across China.

Explaining the success of Taobao and Tmall, Clark notes that whereas in the West, buying online is just another way to shop, in China it's a lifestyle. In the past, most shops were owned by state enterprises which treated shoppers with contempt. Privately owned retail chains had always been held back by the price of land, which the government keeps artificially high in order to extract the maximum rent. So when Alibaba's sites came along with their excellent 24/7 customer service, it changed everything. Along with service, simplicity, and transparency, Alibaba created something that was in short supply: trust. Its Alipay system is not just used to buy Alibaba goods, but to buy anything, anywhere, including cashless payments in shops and restaurants. Alipay's online bank, Yu'e Bao, which launched with much higher interest savings rates than the state-owned banks, now has massive deposits, shaking up the state banking system and making it one of the biggest money managers in the world. Ma has caused controversy by saying that China's banking system "shouldn't be up to monopoly and authority, but up to customers." Increasingly, Yu'e Bao is becoming a lender, and it can make good credit risks because it already has the account history of all its depositors through their spending habits in Alibaba's sites.

Jack Ma sees three areas of growth for Alibaba: cloud computing and Big Data, rural China, and globalization. Alibaba wants to mimic and overtake Amazon's success with its cloud computing and web services, and to make customers of the 700 million people in China who live outside the cities and who are not online. This focus could prove to be even more important than spreading overseas. But Alibaba is having real success with its original purpose of connecting buyers and sellers from different countries, through its AliExpress sites. Whereas originally Alibaba's goal was to help sell Chinese goods abroad, now its attention has shifted to helping companies in the US and Europe sell their wares into China, including luxury goods for the emerging Chinese middle class of 300 million-plus.

Alibaba is becoming a big investor in Chinese film, television, sports, and entertainment, providing online streaming of films through its TBO service on Tmall. Alibaba Pictures, based in Pasadena, California, has funded *Mission: Impossible – Rogue Nation* and other films. And in 2015, the company bought the famous Hong Kong daily, the *South China Morning Post*, quickly removing the paywall in order to give it a global readership. Critics said the purchase was aimed at pleasing the Chinese government by softening the paper's editorial line, but Ma insists that the purpose is to help the rest of the world understand China. Too many foreign journalists, he says, are unable to look beyond its political system to see the country's dynamism and increasingly innovative companies, which no longer just copy, but create.

All the same, Ma knows that the Chinese Communist Party still has plenty of antipathy to entrepreneurs. Clark notes the unexplained disappearance, in 2015, of Guo Guangchang, the "Warren Buffett of China." Though Guo reemerged, entrepreneurs and tycoons can never be sure what will displease the government. The Communist Party wants China to be dominant economically, but won't lose its grip on power and public order. Despite his vast wealth ($28 billion and counting) and fame, Ma has to tread very carefully, particularly if his firm starts to become dominant in areas traditionally the preserve of the state, including finance and the media. His outspokenness about the cost of China's industrial rise in terms of water quality, air pollution, adulterated food, and increasing rates of cancer may also be taken as an affront to state policy.

In Ma's mind, Alibaba and big private firms like it provide a necessary balance to state power, making people richer and happier through an increased ability to trade and buy. For its part, the Communist Party can be satisfied that China's increasing economic power is at least driven by Chinese firms, not merely by foreign firms investing in China.

Final comments

Ma learned from his battles with eBay and Yahoo never to be galled by a much bigger player. David could definitely beat Goliath. Now Alibaba has become Goliath, its challenge is to stay fast-footed and inventive, retaining its unique culture. Ma developed an "unpredictable yet nurturing" management style, Clark says, in the manner of his hero, a fictional swordsman called Feng Qingyang. Though everyone at Alibaba in its early years worked like a dog, Ma was very generous in doling out stock options (particularly to the first 18 employees, who included six women), to such an extent that his stake in Alibaba was constantly being reduced.

In 2009 Ma quietly set up a company which transferred ownership of Alipay from Alibaba to himself, for a payment of only $51 million. Investors Yahoo and Softbank were furious, as Alipay was worth at least $1 billion. Ma's reasoning was that to preserve Alipay, it needed to become a fully Chinese-owned company in the eyes of the law, particularly as it was now the biggest and most prominent payment system in China. The episode called into question Ma's reputation for transparency, but other entrepreneurs and investors could see why he had done it: whereas before he had had a very whittled-down financial stake in Alibaba, now there was a massive personal incentive to make Alibaba, and its payment system Alipay, an enduring success.

Though Tencent is the "king of mobile" in China, with its super-popular Wechat messaging app, and Baidu the default Chinese search engine, the Alibaba companies look set to continue dominating e-commerce, such is the trust in its name. If for any reason the Chinese state comes down on Alibaba, by this time it will probably have cemented its position in many other countries and markets, just as other global firms with a long-term view have done.

Duncan Clark

Born in the UK, Clark graduated from the London School of Economics in 1986 and began a career in banking, working in London and Hong Kong. After moving to China in 1994 and working for Morgan Stanley for four years, he started a consultancy, BDA China, which advises large investors, foreign governments, and corporations on the country's technology and retail sectors. Clark has chaired the British Chamber of Commerce in China, and for his work advising the UK government on China's digital economy was awarded an OBE (Officer of the Order of the British Empire). He has been a visiting scholar on entrepreneurship at Stanford University, and set up the China 2.0 conference series at Stanford's Graduate School of Business.

Despite not taking up the offer to earn shares in the early days of Alibaba, when the firm had its 2007 and 2014 IPOs Clark did get the opportunity to buy shares. He continues to invest in early stage companies in China and abroad, and is on the board of Bangkok Bank (China).

Great by Choice

"Our work began with the premise that most of what we face lies beyond our control, that life is uncertain and the future unknown . . . But if one company becomes great while another in similar circumstances and with comparable luck does not, the root cause of why one becomes great and the other does not simply cannot be circumstance or luck."

"The greatest leaders we've studied throughout all our research cared as much about values as victory, as much about purpose as profit, as much about being useful as being successful. Their drive and standards are ultimately internal, rising from somewhere deep inside."

"The best leaders we studied did not have a visionary ability to predict the future . . . They were not more risk taking, more bold, more visionary, and more creative than the comparisons. They were more disciplined, more empirical, and more paranoid."

"Innovation by itself turns out not to be the trump card we expected; more important is the ability to scale innovation, to blend creativity with discipline."

In a nutshell

The measure of a company is not how much it can expand in good times, but whether it is able to withstand downturns and crises and carve out a long-term future.

In a similar vein

Clayton Christensen *The Innovator's Dilemma*
John Kay *Obliquity*
Eric Ries *The Lean Startup*

CHAPTER 8

Jim Collins

I n 2001, Jim Collins was the author of two bestsellers, *Built To Last* (1994) and *Good To Great* (1999), which seemed to offer the last word on business success. Then came a deflated stock market, 9/11, war in Iraq, and other calamities. The go-go late 1990s gave way to geopolitical uncertainty, while constant technological change was shifting the ground under companies and society.

Collins and his team of researchers began thinking about change and how organizations react to it. When the world seems to be going to pot, he wondered, why do some companies seem to thrive regardless? Collins began a nine-year research project which involved identifying "10X" companies, those that had outperformed their industry indexes by at least 10 times over a minimum 15-year period. Southwest Airlines, for example, grew into a major, highly profitable airline in the years 1972 to 2002, despite fuel shocks, deregulation, labor strikes, recessions, and terrorism. The airline industry is historically a volatile, low margin one. How and why did Southwest beat the odds?

For each "great" company identified, Collins found a comparison company that had roughly similar opportunities in the same industry, in the same period, but which failed to beat the average, or was taken over. For example, Intel and AMD, Microsoft and Apple (during Apple's wilderness years until 2000), Southwest Airlines and Pacific Southwest Airlines, Stryker and United States Surgical Corporation (USSC).

Though not as popular as his earlier books, *Great By Choice: Uncertainty, Chaos, and Luck—Why Some Thrive Despite Them All* is arguably Collins' most fascinating. After all, any person or company can seem "great" when luck and circumstances are going their way. It's when the challenges hit that people and companies reveal their true grit.

Fanatical discipline

Collins begins the book with a vignette of the early twentieth-century race to the South Pole by Norwegian Roald Amundsen and Englishman Robert Scott. Amundsen was super-organized and disciplined, with a margin of safety built into everything he did. He stuck fanatically to completing a certain number of miles a day (13 to 20), even in atrocious weather, and even when the weather was good and he could have gone faster. Scott did the opposite, driving his men to do long distances in good weather, and staying in the tent in bad. Amundsen's approach meant a significantly higher daily mile rate. In the event, he won the race easily, and Scott perished on his return journey.

As Collins looked into 10X companies, the Amundsen–Scott comparison seemed salutary. He discusses the medical supplies and instruments company Stryker, which for 20 years under CEO John Brown held tightly to its aim of increasing net income by 20 percent a year. In a growing market Brown could have achieved higher growth rates some years, but believed that a steadier approach would mean a more sustainable company. Its competitor USSC was hyper-aggressive, aiming for higher growth, yet in the mid to late 1990s reduced demand and heightened competition walloped USSC's bottom line. By 1998 it had disappeared as a public company (acquired by Tyco) while Stryker continued its rise.

Collins observed a similar pattern with other companies. Ones that made aggressive growth their mission usually did worse, over the long term, than those which consistently hit clear performance markers year upon year. They made superhuman efforts in bad times to meet their targets, yet held back in good times with self-imposed limits. Southwest Airlines was profitable year after year because it believed that overextending one year could erode profitability the next. Only eight years after starting did it expand, tentatively, beyond the state of Texas, and it was 25 years after being founded before it expanded to the east coast. This self-discipline led to Southwest being one of the best investments in the period 1972 to 2002, despite all the downturns and shocks plaguing the airline industry.

The great benefit of "20-mile marching," as opposed to fast but erratic growth, is that it provides your company with a measure of control in an out of control environment. For instance, Intel's growth purposely followed Moore's law, seeking to double the complexity and power of its circuits every 18 months. As long as it was doing this, it felt, it could remain a player. While Intel was seeking high but consistent growth, AMD's aim to be No.1 in integrated circuits saw it grow at twice the rate of Intel in the first half of the 1980s, but from 1987 to 1995 it began to seriously lag behind Intel. Why? During the 1985–6 recession in the semiconductor industry, AMD, which had piled on huge debt to expand, lost serious ground to Intel and never quite recovered. Collins's point: when you run your company to the limits, an external shock will lay bare any weaknesses. In contrast, successful companies, because of their prudence and discipline, move ahead of competitors in times of instability.

For a decade and a half biotech firm Genentech was "the next big thing"—full of promise but an underperformer. It was only with the promotion of chief scientist Arthur Levinson to CEO, Collins notes, that the company finally gained some discipline, focusing only on areas where it could dominate, and seeking to grow steadily each year instead of, as Levinson put it, "2% in year one, two, three and four, and 92% in year five." When Genentech was able to combine its famed innovation with discipline, it blossomed.

Companies always searching for the next big thing, Collins observes, be it a drug that will transform its fortunes, a killer app, or a bestselling book, will probably remain searching. The really successful companies, through discipline and focus, simply work harder to make the most of what they already have. Or as Collins puts it, "the Next Big Thing just might be the Big Thing you already have."

Empirical creativity

Collins was shocked to discover something about very successful companies: often they weren't that innovative. Southwest Airlines, for instance, was a virtual carbon copy of Pacific Southwest Airlines, a Californian outfit that pioneered most of the features that Southwest became famous for, including point-to-point routes, fast plane turnaround times, and zany air stewards. Stryker outperformed USSC, Collins notes, by being *less* innovative, "never first to market, never last." CEO John Brown argued it was best to be always "one fad behind."

Collins's point, looking at many other companies' innovation records, is that the outperformers "innovated less than we would have expected relative to their industries and relative to their comparison cases; they were innovative *enough* to be successful but generally *not the most* innovative." There is a threshold of innovation which is low in some fields, such as aviation, and high in others, such as biotechnology, but once you are over it, other things matter more for success.

An example: Intel, by the admission of its own executives, was often behind competitors such as Texas Instruments, Motorola, and AMD in its chips. It was AMD that broke the 1,000-bit memory chip barrier in 1970, launching it successfully on the market months before Intel did. Yet within three years, thanks to its superiority in manufacturing, delivery, and scaling up, it was Intel's chip that dominated the market. Its motto, "Intel Delivers," reminded itself and the world that it wanted to be great at innovation, but just as great at engineering and the market. Semiconductor chips were, after all, not only about speed and power, but had to be sold at a reasonable price and be reliable. Intel CEO Andy Grove wanted his company to be the

McDonald's of the chip world. "Innovation by itself turns out not to be the trump card we expected," Collins writes. "More important is the ability to *scale* innovation, to blend creativity with discipline."

It turns out that a "bullets over cannonballs" approach is much more amendable to long-term success. By this Collins means making smaller bets on new ideas or technologies ("bullets"), either by creating a small in-house team to develop them and bring them to market, or acquiring a company that is already doing it. If nothing comes of it, it won't bring down the company, and yet if it does, it could be a source of future growth. Many companies made big early mistakes by firing off an uncalibrated "cannonball" (a big investment in an in-house idea, or an expensive acquisition) that almost brought down the firm. Be aware, Collins says, of "the danger of achieving good outcomes from bad processes." Getting lucky with big, risky bets just leads your company to make more such bets, most of which will not succeed. It is very easy to become a victim of early success, and of hubris; 10X companies remain creative and optimistic, but their paranoia about possible failure means that whatever final strategic decisions made are heavily researched.

Productive paranoia

The really successful companies Collins studied kept "irrationally large" margins of safety to prepare them for bad luck and events that would inevitably come their way. Compared to the median ratio of 87,000 companies analyzed in the *Journal of Financial Economics*, for instance, all kept 3 to 10 times the ratio of cash to assets. For instance, when 9/11 happened, Southwest Airlines had $1 billion of cash on hand, and the best credit rating in the airline industry.

The 10X companies got that way not by taking big risks, but by being risk averse. In a chaotic, fast-changing world, such self-discipline is crucial. When faced with poor results, successful companies don't assume that their principles are obsolete. Rather, they "first consider whether the enterprise has perhaps strayed from its recipe, or has forgone discipline and rigor in adhering to the recipe." Many companies fall for the idea that the only answer to their problems is a radical overhaul of how they work, but sometimes they have just lost sight of their core mission. "Just because your environment is rocked by dramatic change," Collins says, "does not mean that you should inflict radical change upon yourself." In fact, successful companies change *less* than other companies. They treat their core values and practices like a constitution that is amended only rarely and with gravity. For instance, in the mid 1990s, Bill Gates had a Damascene moment about the internet, and pivoted Microsoft's products toward it. Yet the company did not abandon any of its other core purposes and products, from Windows to Office, that had made it big in the first place.

Final comments

One of the novel aspects of *Great by Choice* is the research on the role of luck in corporate success. Great companies, Collins notes, have about the same amount of bad and good luck as other companies, but they do more with the good luck. In contrast, average companies squander good luck, do not seize opportunities, and blame bad luck for failing. Standout enterprises avoid at all costs a culture of blame or resignation, and know that it is only unusual discipline that leads to success.

Collins adds a final element that separates outperforming companies from also-rans. Not only are their leaders more ambitious, but it is a different kind of ambition, for fulfilling a wider purpose that goes beyond mere commercial advance. "The greatest leaders we've studied throughout all our research," Collins writes, "cared as much about values as victory, as much about purpose as profit, as much about being useful as being successful." The results of such good intentions are impossible to quantify, and yet they seemed to lift an organization above the norm. Perhaps it is because their gaze is lifted a bit higher, and more seems to be at stake, that the only way to bring about their aims is through unusual rigor and discipline. Collins heads one chapter with a quote from poet Ron Serino: "Freely chosen, discipline is absolute freedom."

Jim Collins

Born in 1958, Collins has a degree in mathematics and an MBA, both from Stanford University. After stints working for McKinsey and Hewlett-Packard he taught in Stanford's business school, and in 1995 set up an independent "management laboratory" to research corporate success. In 2012–3 he taught leadership courses at the United States Military Academy at West Point.

His other books include Built to Last: Successful Habits of Visionary Companies *(1994),* Good to Great: Why Some Companies Make the Leap... and Others Don't *(2001), and* How the Mighty Fall: And Why Some Companies Never Give In *(2009).*

Out of the Crisis

"Performance of management should be measured by potential to stay in business, to protect investment, to ensure future dividends and jobs through improvement of product and service for the future, not by the quarterly dividend."

"The supposition is prevalent the world over that there would be no problems in production or in service if only our production workers would do their jobs in the way that they were taught. Pleasant dreams. The workers are handicapped by the system, and the system belongs to management."

"You can install a new desk, or a new carpet, or a new dean, but not quality control. Anyone that proposes to 'install quality control' unfortunately has little knowledge about quality control. Improvement of quality and productivity, to be successful in any company, must be a learning process, year by year, top management leading the whole company."

In a nutshell

Quality is not the result of an individual worker, but must be part of a system.

In a similar vein

Alfred Chandler *The Visible Hand*
Jim Collins *Great by Choice*
Peter Senge *The Fifth Discipline*
Frederick Taylor *The Principles of Scientific Management*
James P. Womack, Daniel T. Jones & Daniel Roos *The Machine that Changed the World*

CHAPTER 9

W. Edwards Deming

I n 1947, Japan was full of bombed out cities, and what factories existed were producing shoddy things not fit for export. Hardly anyone in the West believed that within a couple of decades Japanese cars and electronics would become a symbol of quality. But through the 1950s W. Edwards Deming and another American, Joseph Juran, gave lectures and ran courses for Japanese engineers and managers in statistical methods to achieve quality control and productivity. Having lost the war, Japan was desperate to regain its pride. All the energy that was poured into military victory was now expressed in a determination to rise from the ashes as an industrial power.

The great irony of Deming's career: here was an American teaching the Japanese how to create quality products, which in due course began to overtake American ones (in cars, electronics, and other areas). While seen as a prophet in Japan (a portrait of Deming hung in the lobby of Toyota, along with those of the founders), he was mostly ignored in America. *Out of the Crisis* was a plea for his own country, whose industry had become bloated and wasteful, turning out defective products for a domestic market protected by tariffs, to discover the principles of quality, value, and pride in workmanship. His "14 points" of quality and productivity (the essence of which are discussed below) were eventually taken on board by American managers, and late in life he was seen as a seer—but perhaps too late.

Deming's work reminds us of the question, "What *is* quality?" In the classic book *Zen and the Art of Motorcycle Maintenance*, Robert Pirsig observed that quality is hard to define in a rational way, but we know it when we experience it. Quality is not simply "betterness," but the fact that thought has gone into something. It is the difference between someone who cares and someone who does not; between a machine or a service that can enrich our life, and one designed to fall apart so we have to buy another one. Deming was well aware that his ideas went beyond engineering and statistics to be a philosophy embracing both the potential of the individual and the fact that great organizations were a system that was greater than any one person. Toyota's famed "lean production" system (see Chapter 50), which has been copied by nearly all successful manufacturers around the world, is rooted in Deming's philosophy.

It's all management

The big failure in business, Deming argues, is the inability to plan for the future and imagine problems. "The basic cause of sickness in American industry," he writes, "and resulting unemployment is failure of top management to manage . . . The causes usually cited for failure of a company are costs of start-up, overruns on costs, depreciation of excess inventory, competition—anything but the actual cause, pure and simple bad management."

When Deming insists that "Management must declare a policy for the future, to stay in business and to provide jobs for their people, and more jobs," it is an almost European sensibility in terms of looking ahead a generation or more, in contrast to the usual American ethos of fast-moving, Schumpeterian "creative destruction" of old industries and businesses to make way for the new.

Deming's maxim was, "The consumer is the most important part of the production line." What do consumers want? Products that genuinely work, that last, and that are good value. This approach was rather different to that of American and European manufacturers in the postwar period, when demand for goods and services was so high that you could get away with mediocre production quality. However, as Japanese goods began to enter western markets in the 1970s, people could see the value and started buying them.

Postwar Japan, Deming notes, was a shell of a country, with negative net worth and devoid of the natural resources that many nations take for granted; it couldn't even support its own people in agriculture. It was known for poor quality consumer goods, and in order to survive and import food and materials, therefore, it had to make better-quality *things*. Luckily for Japan, "the wealth of a nation depends on its people, management, and government, more than on its natural resources," Deming writes. The Japanese "got" quality from the start, and would reap the benefits.

Quality and productivity: two sides of the same coin

The conventional view of American management was to ask, "Surely there is a point at which it costs too much to invest in higher quality, which means higher costs and a less competitive position?" The question, Deming said, "packs a mountain of understanding into a few choice words."

From 1950 onward, Japanese manufacturers poured resources into increasing quality, no matter what the apparent costs. Over the next three decades they raced ahead of American manufacturers who did not appreciate the virtuous circle of "improved quality leads to lower costs from less waste and faults."

The answer to Deming's frequent question, "Why is it that productivity increases as quality improves?" is that less reworking of defects means less waste, and the resources that would have gone into fixing problems now goes into making a better product or service. Lower costs mean you are more competitive, which creates more jobs and happier workers. Workers begin to feel control over their efforts, and pride in workmanship. Because the company is doing well, they feel secure in their jobs, and so start to think about the company and its sustainable future, not just what they are personally getting out of it. For their part, managers are not simply managing defects, but creating and refining *systems* in which defects cannot even occur.

To start, Deming writes, you create clear definitions of what is acceptable in terms of quality, and what is not. Only when you start to measure do you see clearly, and know what needs to be done to fix the issues. Deming mentions the Nashua copier company, which began using detailed statistical measurement of its production of carbonless paper, and through this was able to save costs on unnecessary chemicals and increase the stability and quality of the product. What you measure or track, you improve.

It is possible to progressively reduce the defect percentage until it is zero, because all defects can be traced back to their original source, whether it is an issue with incoming materials to the plant, machinery not working properly, or vagueness in terms of what is acceptable and what is not. Instead of just buying parts or raw materials or supplies of something from the cheapest vendor, quality should be the main determinant of who you work with. If you choose based on quality, you can develop a long-term relationship with the supplier in which your specifications get more detailed and they can come up with smart solutions based on what you need. That quality of such a relationship will feed through to the finished product.

New machines and gadgets, Deming liked to point out, aren't the magical answer to increasing productivity and quality. Unless there is a fully worked out system seamlessly blending man and machine, there will be as much wasted effort and downtime as before. "A company cannot buy its way into quality," Deming writes. At the time he was writing, computers were already playing a significant role in companies, but he warns that ever greater amounts of data, which just sits in computers with little real analysis, is not the answer. What matters is someone taking the data and showing exactly how and where quality variation is taking place in the product or service, and why. Unintended variation is the death of any product. The thing about consumers is that they don't usually complain, they just go to another provider. It may be months or years before you become fully aware that your quality isn't good enough. Reduce variation to nil, and productivity can suddenly go through the roof, with all the cost savings that entails, which can be passed on to the consumer.

It's the system, not the worker

Once, Deming got a stack of copies of one of his articles printed up. He soon discovered that one or two of the pages in the article were blank. The printer was furious with his staff for the mistake, somehow unwilling to see that the real issue was a problem of management: how the shop was organized to produce or not produce quality.

It's *always* about the system, Deming notes, not the worker. American managers thought that Quality Control Circles, in which workers provide information on production problems, were the answer to creating leaps in quality. But these circles sidestepped the fact that defects aren't just caused by particular workers, but by the design and specification of products, a lack of training, and poor machines. He disapproved strongly of individual performance evaluation, merit rating, and annual reviews, which was effectively management by fear. By its focus on the end product, the system glosses over problems with people and processes which doom products in the first place. There had to be understanding so that the system as a whole can be made better. Performance ratings had become all the rage, but Deming felt they had a corrosive effect. Instead, organizations had to focus on (a) better selection of people in the first place, and (b) deeply instilled leadership education. The only evaluations of people should be whether they are:

- "On the good side of the system" (clearly contributing a lot by objective measure)
- "On the bad side of the system" (it is management's job to help the individual)

In America, Deming notes, there was way too much mobility of labor and changes in management. With people in jobs for too short a time, and short-term time management horizons, it was hard to build anything substantial and long-lasting. People need stability and security of employment in order to fulfill their potential. He points out that the 80 Nobel prizewinners up to the time he was writing, "all had tenure, security . . . They were answerable only to themselves." By this he means they had responsibility for their work, and so only published what they were proud of. In the West, Japan's system of lifetime employment and promotion according to seniority has been much criticized, but it has many benefits. In contrast, the super-fluidity of the American labor market created a climate of "every man for himself." Working life becomes about getting raises, getting promotions, trying to please the boss. In such a climate, people are not predisposed to think of the good of the company, its long-term future, or even take pride in their work.

Quality in services

Even in the 1980s, 75 percent of American jobs were in service industries, from restaurants, hotels, and banks to insurance, journalism, religious ministry, construction, and communication. As that figure has only increased since, it is clear that the standard of living depends on quality and productivity in the service sector. Deming's ideas for increasing quality in service organizations included:

- Make everyone in the organization very clear on the new focus on service and purpose, and implement it through training. The perception of big corporations often comes down to the one person representing it, for example a truck driver or a call center operator.
- Drive out fear by breaking down communication barriers between management and labor. For example, making it clear that subordinates will be properly listened to by bosses.
- Break down barriers between divisions and departments.
- In place of slogans and posters to have workers "do better," make it clear what *management* is doing to help people do their job.
- Reorient expectations in favor of quality over quantity. Once the quality increases, the quantity can be ramped up.
- Train all workers in the analysis of numbers, so all can see whether standards are being met, and be able to act on it quickly.

It goes without saying that the key to every successful service is planning and design: "Once the plans are part way in place, it is too late to build quality into a product." Most of the experience of quality in a hotel, for instance, is already there on the day of opening, in the layout of the rooms, the plumbing, the lifts, the air conditioning. If any one of these are wrong, Deming notes, friendly staff won't make up for it.

Final comments

Deming was far-sighted in saying that American industry would not progress via restoration, but transformation. That is, not by making the existing things a bit better, but by imagining and building things from the ground up, with new processes and systems. This won't happen if executives are working only to meet dividend targets and chase short-term profits. Deming also believed that mergers, reorganizations, corporate takeovers, and buyouts were "a cancer" because fear of takeovers distracts a business from "constancy of purpose." Such "paper entrepreneurialism" is always a distraction from building a productive base. Managers, Deming says, "have a moral obligation to protect investment," knowing that their primary task is to run the company so that it lasts beyond the current generation.

It has been argued that Deming's ideas, emphasizing the team over the individual, the company over the boss, and a healthy, sustainable corporation that looked far into the future in order to maintain livelihoods, is anathema to the West's individualistic ways and short-term corporate culture, and at the same time particularly well suited to the Asian mindset of community over individual. Indeed, Deming was writing at a time when Japanese companies were in the ascendancy, their high-quality goods and lower prices striking fear into the minds of American manufacturers. Yet several salutary examples of poor practice in the book were from Japan, and today there are many Japanese corporate failures all arguably caused by poor transparency and leadership. Quality is not "American" or "Japanese," but is achieved company by company, system by system.

W. Edwards Deming

William Edwards Deming was born in Sioux City, Iowa, in 1903, and grew up on a farm in Wyoming. He obtained a degree in electrical engineering from the University of Wyoming, and later got his Ph.D. in mathematical physics from Yale University. He also spent a year, 1936, studying at University College, London.

After working for a time at Bell Telephones in a team devoted to quality control, followed by a stint in the US Department of Agriculture, in 1939 he became head statistician for the US Census, and during World War Two promoted statistics as a way to increase industrial production standards. As the war ended Deming took a position as professor of statistics at New York University, where he stayed until his death in 1993.

In 1947 Deming made his first visit to American-occupied Japan at the invitation of General MacArthur, to help design the 1951 census. During his time there he was asked by the Japanese Union of Scientists and Engineers to give talks on his statistical methods and management ideas. He told the Japanese that, if they instituted principles of quality control, they could soon up their game and in time be producing things of high quality that the world *actually wanted. The managers he spoke to included Akio Morita, founder of Sony.*

Throughout his career Deming consulted to private companies, and his work with Ford in Detroit has been credited with its resurgence during the 1980s as a profitable maker of well-built cars. In his last years he taught at Columbia Business School, where a center for competitiveness and productivity was created in his name. In 1987 he was awarded the National Medal of Technology by President Reagan. His other key book is The New Economics for Industry, Government, and Education *(1994).*

1967

The Effective Executive

"If the executive lets the flow of events determine what he does, what he works on and what he takes seriously, he will fritter himself away operating. He may be an excellent man. But he is certain to waste his knowledge and ability and to throw away what little effectiveness he might have achieved. What the executive needs are criteria which enable him to work on the truly important, that is on contribution and results, even though the criteria are not found in the flow of events."

"Executives who do not ask themselves: 'What can I contribute?' are not only likely to aim too low, they are likely to aim at the wrong things. Above all, they may define their contribution too narrowly."

In a nutshell

No one is born effective, just as no one is born a leader. Effectiveness depends on clarity of aims and the desire to contribute.

In a similar vein

Alfred Chandler *The Visible Hand*
Douglas McGregor *The Human Side of Enterprise*
Tom Rath & Barry Conchie *Strengths Based Leadership*
Peter Senge *The Fifth Discipline*
Robert Townsend *Up the Organization*

CHAPTER 10

Peter Drucker

U ntil a century ago, Peter Drucker notes, most people acquired positions and jobs based on rank or social standing. Whether working for the state, in a religious order, or in the military, "effectiveness" in the position mattered much less that who held it.

Today, we live in a society of organizations run on meritocratic lines. We have jobs in companies, government agencies or NGOs that constantly monitor performance and progress. Whatever initial advantages or disadvantages we had, it is whether we are effective in the job that matters. Yet Drucker shockingly asserts that people of high effectiveness "are conspicuous by their absence in executive jobs." There are plenty of brilliant people in the upper echelons, and some with real imagination. Some have vast knowledge of the industry or the sector. But many of these people are simply not very good at *getting the right things done*. In the same organization there will be plodders who are not as brilliant or creative or charismatic, *and yet* show a record of performance.

Effectiveness is not the same as working hard, or being intelligent, or having knowledge, Drucker says. It is about a set of practices and ways of thinking.

What an executive is for

In Drucker's time there had been surprisingly little attention given to effectiveness, for the simple reason that management was about the tiny fraction of people, whether it was in armies, hospitals, or firms, that gave the orders, and the mass who carried them out. Not many people had to actually think about whether something was working well, they just had to be efficient in their tasks.

Today's knowledge worker is paid to *think*, that is, to work out the thing that the organization should be doing, and put it into action. Some people are called "executives" simply because they have a lot of people "under" them, but a true executive is not dependent on position or their number of reports, Drucker says, but on whether they are delivering for the organization in some fundamental way—running a lab whose products are charting the direction for the firm's future, for instance, or seeing how the market is changing and coming up with an intelligent strategy.

One sometimes hears that a good manager "makes lots of decisions, and quickly," in response to what is happening. Drucker says this is a fallacy. The true executive is paid not to "put out fires," but to make a handful of really important decisions that help define the organization and its purpose. These decisions are made slowly and after much thought. The true executive is always more strategic than reactive.

There is no "effective personality," Drucker found in his consulting work with scores of organizations. Effective people had diverse temperaments, abilities, and interests. Some are garrulous extroverts, some quiet and scholarly; some fit the image of a "leader," others seem colorless and unassuming; some make calls with their gut, others go into agonies over every decision. The only thing they had in common was a set of practices which enabled them to get the right things done, involving the following areas.

Time

The effective executive knows exactly how their time is spent, and zealously guards the portion of their time that is truly theirs.

Effective people first work out where their time goes, because it is the resource in shortest supply. You can always obtain more capital or find the right people, but you can't "get" time from anywhere. "Nothing else distinguishes effective executives as much as their tender loving care of time," Drucker writes.

Most executives have to spend a lot of time doing things that don't add any real value, but are expected of them in their role. To do anything important, they have to carve out reasonably large chunks of time—six to eight hours for the first draft of a report, for instance—because if interrupted the train of thought is lost and one has to start all over again. It is not the same to devote 15 minutes to the report each day over a two-week period. Equally, you don't establish rapport with an underling by giving them 10 minutes here and there. An important relationship needs at least an hour at a time, in which can be discussed how the report sees their role within the organization, and what can be done to improve performance. Conversely, there are many tasks which seem to be the job of a senior executive, but in fact are peripheral and can be done by someone else. This is not a matter of "delegating," which implies getting someone to do *my* work, but rather saying, "Is this really my work in the first place? Am I needed personally?" Get younger staff to do a lot of the travel for the company, for instance—they will enjoy it and handle the tiredness more easily.

The effective executive is very aware of the 20 percent of her time that generates 80 percent of results, and guards that time zealously. Some executives work at home one day a week, others reserve calls and meetings for the afternoons, and so on. The important thing is that the day is not wasted on things that do not matter in the long term, and that the big, consequential matters that will shape your organization, and which require your brains and insight, get the attention they deserve. This, after all, is what you are paid for.

Contribution

Most executives, Drucker observes, are focused on their efforts, not their results. They think about what the organization owes them for the work they've done, and are very mindful of their status and authority. When asked how their position in the company is justified, they say, "I am in charge of a sales force of 300" or "I run the engineering division." This may be true, but the effective executive will be heard to say, "I am responsible for finding out what products the customer will want tomorrow." She is measuring her performance against a clear goal, not thinking about the power she wields. The effective executive is continually asking, "What contribution can I make?" They are not starting the day saying, "I will work 10 hours," but rather "I want to get X done."

The most common cause of executive failure is inability to adjust to the demands of a new job. But when an executive asks, "What can I contribute?" at the outset, he or she will zoom in on the one or two things where a big impact can be made, even if doing so will require them to learn new things or change their ways. A focus on results turns a manager away from their specialty to embrace the goals of the whole organization. To see them realized, they have to be focused on what results the organization is achieving in the world, for the customer, the client, or the patient. The title of their position matters little if the organization isn't achieving its stated purpose.

When an executive is focused on contribution, standards are automatically raised for all the people who work for him. They are constantly made aware of the higher goal and work toward it instead of being distracted by trivia. A focus on contribution stops the executive from living in a day-to-day swirl of reacting to events and crises. It is essential to creating great teams, because in the absence of a clear goal no one can pull together.

Strengths

When President Abraham Lincoln made General Grant the new commander-in-chief during the American Civil War, he was warned that Grant liked to drink. But Lincoln had not been looking for a teetotaler, rather someone who could win battles. The "well-rounded" generals he had appointed had been disappointing. He finally realized that what he needed was people with narrow but great strengths.

Focusing on the things that a person isn't good at, Drucker says, is "a misuse, if not abuse, of the human resource." The modern job appraisal is an opportunity to judge the weaknesses of a person, and so undermine relationships between superiors and staff. Yet if a person feels that their weaknesses are being overlooked, and their strengths noticed and cheered on, they will work their guts out for a boss. Executives who don't follow the rule book and fail to do appraisals, Drucker says, are doing the right thing.

The job of the executive is simple: pull together a team of people who do one thing "uncommonly well." Faced with a tax accountant who is great at what he does but terrible dealing with people, an effective executive will shield the accountant as much as possible from the public—there are other people in the organization who can do this well—and let him get on with his job.

Drucker advises only to promote the person who has demonstrated they are the best person for the job. It doesn't matter if that person is "too young" or "won't be acceptable to the people there," or that the appointment will break some internal rule like "never appoint someone without field experience." Conversely, you must ruthlessly get rid of anyone who doesn't perform, as it will corrupt the whole organization. No judgment is made on their person, only that they were not the right person for the role.

To be an effective executive you must build not only on the strengths of those beneath you, but on your boss's strengths. If her strength is numbers, make sure there is copious data to back up every recommendation you make. If she only makes a decision when in a room with the interested parties, don't write a long report she will never read, but be ready to sum up a position verbally in three points. Remember that if your boss succeeds, most likely you will too.

Concentration

Humans are good at a lot of things. We are a "multipurpose tool." But big things are accomplished when we concentrate the range of our knowledge and abilities on *one task*.

A new leader of an organization could go down the conventional route and do analysis which reveals a range of 'must dos' facing it. But it is not analysis that the new leader needs, rather courage—courage to zoom in on one priority or opportunity around which the whole organization will become oriented, and which if achieved will make the organization first in its field. The alternative is chasing after goals that other companies have already identified, and so becoming a mediocre bandwagon chaser.

Focusing on a single opportunity does not make the executive or leader inflexible. In fact, as soon as it is accomplished, the organization can quickly shift to another priority. The effective executive is always focused on the future, putting resources into the best performing areas and cutting off resources to things that belong to the past. Just as some laws have an automatic repeal unless they are continually able to prove their worth, the same should apply to the private sector. The effective executive institutes a "systematic sloughing off of the old." Just because your company pioneered a product, it doesn't mean it should always stay in the market. It may need to kill off a product or service in order to launch a new one.

Decisions

The effective executive spends a lot of time and effort on getting the few, fundamental decisions right, knowing that most other decisions are of less consequence and can be reversed.

The conventional wisdom on decision making is to "first find the facts." But one person's facts are different to another's. We can always find facts that suit our argument. It's best to start with an opinion, and then it can be tested by you and others to see if it holds water. A decision is a judgment, and all judgments are made under uncertainty. Therefore, it is wise to have alternatives at hand; sometimes effectiveness comes from abandoning a plan altogether in the light of reality. When Franklin Roosevelt came to office he wanted economic recovery through austerity. He had campaigned on a platform of economic orthodoxy, which meant fiscal prudence. But it soon became clear that this was a strategy that would work in normal bad times, but not in an emergency. He quickly shifted to a strategy of radical financial and political innovation, with the New Deal measures.

Conventional wisdom says that good decisions come from consensus. The opposite is true, Drucker says. Good decisions come as a result of competing positions which are fully worked out. In court, lawyers engage in "adversary proceedings" to drill down and get at the facts. An effective executive encourages his people to disagree strongly, and to allow their positions to be tested against reality. Only then can a right call be made. Many times, a decision almost "makes itself," as it arises out of what has become known.

A good alternative to making a decision is not to act at all. Often the effect of a decision is shock that causes too many negative effects. Therefore, Drucker says, we should act only if the benefits of the decision clearly outweigh the costs. But if a decision is made, we should never hedge or compromise.

Computers will not replace human decision making, Drucker says, because humans are much better at seeing the whole picture. Logic alone, which the computer is good at, cannot take in factors involving taste, opinion, values, and, crucially, relationships, that are all important in making good decisions. The computer can crunch the data, but only the executive can say what the data means for the organization.

Yet Drucker also foresaw that computing power would push decision making downwards, since more people would have access to data and information. Nevertheless, the abundance of information would still require judgment about how to use it. Paradoxically, more computing power requires more decisions to be made, by more people. Even if they are not in a suit and tie, organizations would have increasing proportions of their staff carrying out executive functions—that is, making intelligent decisions.

Final comments

Drucker is happy to admit that becoming an effective executive is not a world-shaking achievement, and that there are undoubtedly higher goals. All the same, society needs ever larger numbers of effective executives to run the organizations that make up modern life. If a nation wants to maintain its standard of living, it has to make its knowledge workers and executives not just educated, but effective. We will have to ensure that organizations flourish, for the economy's sake, and that people flourish, for their own and society's sake. The organization needs the individual, but because it still offers the best means to learn and fulfill our potential, the individual needs the organization too.

Peter Drucker

Born in Vienna in 1909, Drucker went to study in Germany after leaving school, obtaining a doctorate in public and international law at Frankfurt University. He worked as a journalist in London before moving to the United States in 1937, becoming an American citizen in 1943. From 1950 to 1971 he was a business professor at New York University, and in 1971 was appointed Clarke Professor of Social Science and Management at Claremont Graduate University in California, a position he kept until his death in 2005.

Drucker wrote 39 books and was also a columnist for the Wall Street Journal *from 1975 to 1995. His 1946 book* Concept of the Corporation, *based on a study of the inner workings of the General Motors Corporation, made him well known. Other titles include* The Practice of Management *(1954) and* Post-Capitalist Society *(1993).*

In 2002, in his nineties, Drucker was awarded the Presidential Medal of Freedom by George W. Bush.

Getting To Yes

"In short, the approach is to commit yourself to reaching a solution based on principle, not pressure. Concentrate on the merits of the problem, not the mettle of the parties. Be open to reason, but opposed to threats . . . The more you bring standards of fairness, efficiency, or scientific merit to bear on your particular problem, the more likely you are to produce a final package that is wise and fair

"A good negotiator rarely makes an important decision on the spot. The psychological pressure to be nice and to give in is too great. A little time and distance help disentangle the people from the problem."

"Few things facilitate a decision as much as precedent. Search for it. Look for a decision or statement that the other side may have made in a similar situation, and try to base a proposed agreement on it. This provides an objective standard for your request and makes it easier for them to go along."

"People think of negotiating power as being determined by resources like wealth, political connections, physical strength, friends, and military might. In fact, the relative negotiating power of two parties depends primarily upon how attractive to each is the option of not reaching agreement."

In a nutshell

The best negotiators focus on principles, not attempts to manipulate.

In a similar vein

Peter Drucker *The Effective Executive*
Patrick Lencioni *The Five Dysfunctions of a Team*

CHAPTER 11

Roger Fisher, William Ury & Bruce Patton

Many people are as afraid of negotiating as they are of public speaking. The ability to negotiate well may seem like a "dark art" practiced by diplomats, union officials, or salespeople, or a natural gift that we could never possess. In fact, we all negotiate for things every day, whether it involves the give and take with our spouse over how to spend the family budget, or trying to set homework rules for our teenager. As soon as we get to work, we are negotiating with bosses, colleagues, suppliers, and customers.

When *Getting To Yes: Negotiating an Agreement Without Giving In* was published over 35 years ago, "negotiation" was still a word that conjured up images of gun sieges, the threat of factory shutdowns, and international political crises. The book succeeded in normalizing the skills of negotiation to such an extent that they are part of the curriculum in law schools, business schools, and public administration courses around the world.

Though Fisher, a law professor, and Ury, an anthropologist, wrote the original 1981 book, the 1991 and 2011 editions have involved Bruce Patton, an international mediator. The three were founders, in 1979, of the Harvard Negotiation Project (part of Harvard's law school) which has developed the theory and practice of dispute resolution. The latest edition updates some of the examples in the book so that it is relevant to younger readers. If you want to learn "how to get to yes without going to war," it is worth studying.

Agreement in place of hierarchy
In the past, things got done through clear hierarchies. Some people gave orders, and others carried them out. But today, with more democratic organizational structures, the need for fast innovation, and the increasing role of contractors who are neither superiors nor reports, things are achieved through agreement, not imposition. This is true even of employees; few people these days blindly follow orders if they don't see

the rationale behind them, or if there is no "buy in" to the boss's outlook or philosophy.

The authors claim that a quiet revolution is under way in which "the pyramids of power are shifting into networks of negotiation." Indeed, they argue that the negotiation revolution is bringing more conflict, not less—but this is a good thing. Traditional hierarchical structures, including organizations and social groups including families, often bottle up conflict, and only when the structures get less rigid do the problems and issues come into the light. Think of a noisy and quarrelsome democracy compared to an authoritarian regime. "Strange as it may seem," the authors suggest, "the world needs *more* conflict, not less."

Negotiating on positions

The traditional form of negotiation is *positional bargaining*, in which each side takes a position—say, a seller and a buyer on what something is worth—and through making concessions a deal is finally made—or not. You start with an extreme price, knowing that it is unrealistic, and try to keep the other party in the dark about what price you will really accept. The problem with this kind of bargaining is that we become attached to our positions, and in order to "save face" negotiations can easily break down, create enmity, or result in a poor outcome. In most people's minds, "negotiation" conjures up images of adversarial exchanges in which one side gets what they want while the other has to give in.

Taking positions often uses a lot of time, because it takes time to find out what the other party's real position is. Dragging of feet, stonewalling, or threatening to walk out makes for time-consuming situations that boil down to a contest of wills. One side may feel so hard done by that they refuse to speak to the other again.

To avoid this kind of negotiation, people often go to the other extreme, trying to see adversaries as friends and offering too many concessions so that no negative feelings enter the frame, and relationships are not put at risk. But negotiations which prioritize the relationship over the outcome often result in a poor agreement. And when a soft negotiator meets a hard, positional one, the latter will invariably dominate and win.

Negotiating on principles

There is a better way. True negotiation, the authors argue, involves "a joint search for mutual gains and legitimate standards." Their concept of *principled negotiation*, developed through the Harvard Negotiation Project, focuses on the objective merits of a situation, not on how long one side is prepared to dig in their heels. Principled negotiation protects you "against those who would take advantage of your fairness." Unlike all other negotiation strategies, which depend for their success on the other side not knowing something you know, principled negotiation actually works better if both sides are doing it. There is no need for tricks, gambits, or posturing. Both parties are guided by the truth. This does not always result in a win–win situation, but fairness will have prevailed.

What is the difference between interests and positions? "Your position is something you have decided upon," the authors note. "Your interests are what caused you to decide." A skilled negotiator looks at what led the opponent to their positions—their desires, needs, fears, and concerns. Good solutions are only found by looking at these, beyond stated positions.

In the Six Day War of 1967, Egypt had attacked Israel. Israel fought back and took the entire Sinai Peninsula. Egypt was desperate to get it back, and entered negotiations with Israel at the Camp David Summit in 1978. No matter what proposals were put forward for Israel keeping some of what it had gained in its victory, Egypt insisted there would be no deal unless the Sinai was returned to it in full: it had, after all, been Egypt's since the time of the Pharaohs. For its part, Israel didn't want Egyptian tanks anywhere near its borders, ready to cross at any time. At Camp David, the US helped Egypt's Anwar Sadat and Israel's Menachim Begin arrive at a solution, taking into account each other's needs, desires, concerns, and fears: Egypt would get back the Sinai, but there would be a large demilitarized zone which allowed for Israel's security.

When you look closely at any conflict, the authors say, there are usually interests in common. For instance, in a landlord–tenant relationship, both want stability: the tenant wants a permanent address, and the landlord a stable tenant. Both want to keep the apartment in good condition: the tenant so they have a nice place to live; the landlord, so they can increase the value of the apartment. Both need a good relationship with each other: the tenant needs a landlord who will respect their privacy and do maintenance; the landlord needs a tenant who will pay the rent on time. When interests are shared, there is likely to be a long lease. Even when they differ, a focus on each other's interests (e.g. "I will keep maintenance requests to a minimum, if you don't raise the rent") can result in deals that satisfy everyone.

What's fair, what's right
To go into more detail, the alternative to positional bargaining, *negotiating on the merits*, involves:

Separating the people involved from the problem   Instead of seeing yourself and the other party as facing each other off, imagine you are side by side, attacking the problem. For the moment forget about your bottom line; instead ask, "What is at stake here for each of us?"

Be aware of the emotions of people on the other side of the table. Find out which things they are particular proud of or sensitive about, and phrase your proposals accordingly. Don't react to polemical speeches or angry outbursts, which may just be letting off steam or giving the chance to the negotiator to please his colleagues and seem tough.

It is hard to really listen to what the other side is saying if a negotiation (or a disagreement with a spouse) is emotionally charged, but we must try to do this if we are to find good solutions. Get them to explain their position, then repeat it out loud. Remember that understanding is not the same as agreeing.

Creating many options by which both sides can gain   Have a low-pressure session in which every possible option is imagined and considered. This increases the chance of creative solutions becoming apparent; coming to an actual agreement is saved for another session.

If you have a proposal you want to get agreement on, get the other side involved very early on so that they feel they have participated in it. Presenting something as a fait accompli often creates pushback or resentment. Go into a negotiation with "illustrated specifics." For example, a sports agent might begin with saying that his client, at this stage in his career, feels that $5 million a year would be a good reflection of what he believes he is worth, and a five-year contract would meet his need for job security. This gives the other side a good idea of what you are after, but at the same time it shows you have an open mind, you are not rigid. It's more important that you be explicit about your interests than your positions. "Two negotiators, each pushing hard for their interests," the authors note, "will often stimulate each other's creativity in thinking up mutually advantageous solutions."

Insisting that any outcome meets objective criteria   To avoid negotiations becoming a battle of wills in which the most stubborn person wins, insist that any agreement measure up to some independent standard, such as market value, expert opinion, custom, or law. This way, no party can be seen to "lose."

In negotiations for deep sea mining under the Law of the Sea, India proposed that mining companies pay an up-front fee of $60 million to host nations. The United States, home to many big mining companies, opposed it. There seemed no way to bridge the two views until it was discovered that researchers at the Massachusetts Institute of Technology had created a model for assessing the economics of deep-seabed mining. Both parties came to see that it was objective and useful. The result was that India agreed to settle for a much lower fee, which would not put off miners from drilling, while the US came to see that some fee was appropriate. If the parties had dug in their heels, it is unlikely any agreement would have been made. In the event, no side backed down, looked weak or lost face, but simply changed their position based on evidence.

People are "strongly influenced by their notions of legitimacy" the authors note. You should come up with solutions that are "fair, legal, honorable" if you want to appeal to all parties' sense of what is right. This also takes the personal out of negotiations.

What if . . . ?

It's all very well talking about objective standards, but what if the other side is much stronger than you?

Often, the authors suggest, power in terms of wealth, physical strength, or military or political might matters less than we think. More important is coming to the table with attractive alternatives to an agreement, so that you are happy to walk away if no deal is reached. If you have a best available alternative in your mind, you won't be so desperate in the negotiations and so will play with a stronger hand. Who has the power depends on which party has thought through the alternatives to reaching an agreement, and is happy with them. Don't ask, "Who's more powerful?" If you perceive that your side has the power, it will make you relax and not properly prepare for a negotiation. Equally, if you see yourself as weak, you may give up too easily.

What if the other side refuses to focus on the merits and plays a game of positions and attacking you? The natural response is to criticize and reject their position as being unreasonable, but all this does is make them defend it more, and be defensive about your position. The best response is "nego-tiation jujitsu," in which you do not try to block or reject their strength and personal attack, but instead assume that their position is indeed an honest attempt to meet the concerns of all sides. You ask, "What can we both do now to reach an agreement as quickly as possible?"

In negotiations, questions are actually more powerful than statements, because they allow all sides to really examine the principles and interests at stake in a non-defensive way. If the other side has made an unjustified assertion, one of the best responses you can make is to not respond. Silence tends to bring forth explanations and new suggestions.

If the other side plays a game of dirty tricks, threats, and unreasonable offers and demands, the key is to call out their behavior and say that you will take a break and decide whether it is worth continuing negotiations. This gives you a chance to avoid making a hasty but poor decision, but also allows them to reflect on their conduct and whether it is achieving the desired effect.

Beware of good cop–bad cop routines and staged fights among the other side which aim to manipulate you into accepting their terms. If you are seated in a lower chair with your back to an open door, instead of getting mad, ask, "What's the theory behind my being seated here?" If there is no good answer, request that tomorrow your opponent will be seated in the same chair. To make sure the other side knows that you know what they're doing, you can even say things like, "Shall we alternate spilling coffee on one another day by day?" Generally, making it clear that you are aware of the other side's games and ruses tends to dampen their effects, and brings the negotiation back to the issues.

Final comments

It is important that we begin any negotiations with a vision of the best possible outcome for all. With this in mind, it is easier to work backwards and work out the things that would need to be sorted or satisfied—for both sides—to make it happen. "The best rule of thumb is to be optimistic," the authors say. "Without wasting a lot of resources on hopeless causes, recognize that many things are worth trying for even if you may not succeed. The more you try for, the more you are likely to get. Studies of negotiation consistently show a strong correlation between aspiration and result. Within reason, it pays to think positively."

A good outcome for all is worth seeking given that you will, after all, need to keep working with the other side as the agreement is implemented, and may have to make future agreements. If they know that you only negotiate on principles, the next time you sit down with them things should be easier, both contractually and emotionally. Indeed, it is not necessary to even think of negotiation as adversarial. If your relationship with the other party is good and has developed over time, you will automatically be looking for mutual gain and will be happy to be influenced by them. "Your reputation for honesty and fair-dealing may be your single most important asset as a negotiator," the authors assert.

In a more populous and connected world, how we interact with each other matters ever more. The authors recall the words of poet Wallace Stevens: "After the final no there comes a yes and on that yes the future world depends."

Roger Fisher, William Ury & Bruce Patton

Fisher (1922–2012) was Samuel Williston Professor of Law at Harvard University, and the director of the Harvard Negotiation Project. As a young man he worked on the Marshall Plan for Europe's recovery, and after practicing as a lawyer joined the Harvard Law School faculty in 1958. He designed the process of negotiation at Camp David that led to the Egypt–Israel peace treaty, and was an adviser to both the US and Iranian governments on the release of hostages at the American embassy in Tehran. He worked to bring peace in El Salvador, and the parties working to create a new constitution for South Africa used his interests-bases negotiation process. Other books include Beyond Reason: Using Emotions As You Negotiate *(2005) and with Ury,* Getting Past No: Negotiating With Difficult People *(1992).*

Ury, cofounder of the Harvard Negotiation Project, was educated at Yale and Harvard, gaining a Ph.D. in social anthropology. He has worked as an international mediator in conflicts in Venezuela, Chechnya, the Middle East and Yugoslavia, and advised the American government on reducing the risks of a nuclear war starting via accident, mistake, miscalculation, or terrorism. With President Jimmy Carter he founded the International Negotiation Network to mediate in civil wars. Other books include The Power of a Positive No *(2007), and* Getting To Yes With Yourself *(2016).*

Patton is deputy director of the Harvard Negotiation Project, and from 1985 to 1999 was the Thaddeus R. Beal Lecturer on Law at Harvard Law School. He played key roles in international negotiation efforts including the process leading up to the dismantling of apartheid in South Africa, and talks between the United States and Iran during the 1980 hostage crisis. He is also the author, with Sheila Heen, of Difficult Conversations: How To Discuss What Matters Most *(1999).*

Rise of the Robots

"In Silicon Valley the phrase 'disruptive technology' is tossed around on a casual basis. No one doubts that technology has the power to devastate entire industries and upend specific sectors of the economy and jobs market. The question I will ask in this book is bigger: Can accelerating technology disrupt our entire system to the point where a fundamental restructuring may be required if prosperity is to continue?"

"So if automation eliminates a substantial fraction of the jobs the consumers rely on, or if wages are driven so low that very few people have significant discretionary income, then it is difficult to see how a modern mass-market economy could continue to thrive. Nearly all the major industries that form the backbones of Western economies (cars, financial services, consumer electronics, telecommunications services, healthcare, etc.) are geared toward markets consisting of millions of potential customers."

In a nutshell

Artificial intelligence and automation, as well as providing business possibilities, will transform the economic and political landscape.

In a similar vein

Frederick Winslow Taylor *The Principles of Scientific Management*
James P. Womack, Daniel T. Jones & Daniel Roos *The Machine that Changed the World*

CHAPTER 12

Martin Ford

Kurt Vonnegut's 1952 novel *Player Piano* depicted a society in which machines did nearly all the work, leaving most people with a meaningless existence. Vonnegut died in 2007, but he believed his vision was proving "more timely with each passing day."

Economists are usually dismissive of the effect of technology on jobs, and for good historical reasons. When agriculture became mechanized, millions of farm workers drifted to the cities and found work in new industries there. When automation and globalization in manufacturing took hold, growth in white-collar and service jobs took up the employment slack. Technological innovation and increasing productivity made workers more valuable, and so they were be paid more. In the decades after World War Two there was a perfect symbiosis between advancing technology and productivity, and job creation and increasing prosperity spread across the workforce.

The economists were right up until about the year 2000, futurist Martin Ford argues in *Rise of the Robots: Technology and the Threat of Mass Unemployment*, but the statistics show that from 2000 to 2010 in the United States, for instance, no new net jobs were created. Compare this to the decade 1970 to 1980, when there was a 27 percent increase in jobs, even in the midst of various economic crises. In short, 10 million jobs that should have been created in the US, were not. The reason, Ford argues, is that innovation in information technology is different. Yes, in the last 30 years there have been armies of people paid to program and manage computer systems, but on the whole computers have not made people more valuable—they have made them redundant. We can no longer think of machines as *tools* for workers; they are becoming the workers.

It's not just computational power on its own that will remove the need for many jobs, blue collar and white collar, but its combination with vast quantities of data, Ford argues. Given that algorithms can replace most human thinking and decision making, just acquiring more education and more skills will not necessarily be enough to make your future bright or protect you from your job becoming obsolete. For example, radiologists require years of training to be able to accurately interpret medical images, but armed with enough data and training, computers are already doing the job as well if not better than humans, and at a fraction of the cost. And consider that even in supposedly high-skilled analytical professions such as the law, medicine, science, even journalism, a surprising amount of the thinking is routine—not many jobs involve constant creativity.

Once the airplane, the telephone, the television, were invented, the world changed. Robotics and artificial intelligence are here to stay, Ford points out, and no amount of worker demonstrations, union organizing, or political policy will put the genie back in the bottle.

You can't stop this: first to go, the manufacturing and basic service jobs . . .

Everyone has heard of Moore's law (computing power doubles every 18 to 24 months), but few people really appreciate what it means. For instance, if the power of our cars had increased at the same rate as computer chips, we would now be driving them at a speed of 671 million miles per hour, or be able to get to Mars in five minutes.

Many robots can now see in three dimensions, like humans do, and so can perform increasingly sophisticated tasks that had defeated them for decades, such as doing multiple jobs and packing products into boxes. The code that powers most robotics, ROS or Robot Operating System, is free and open source. The existence of a common platform will allow for an explosion in innovation in the next few years. Robots once cost millions of dollars to develop and make; now there are kits you can buy for the price of a desktop computer.

The decreasing cost of robots has meant that the drastic decline in textile and clothing industry jobs in the US and UK has halted. It can make more economic sense to make clothes at home ("reshoring") instead of outsourcing production to poorer countries, combining skilled staff with machines. As a result, the industry is growing again. Benefits include reduced transportation costs and delivery times, and being able to closely oversee quality control. Yet as robots get increasingly sophisticated, Ford notes, even reshoring won't provide the jobs of the future, particularly as manufacturing now makes up less than 10 percent of the economy in the US and UK. But in countries such as China, where manufacturing accounts for a much larger component of the jobs market, advancing robotics will have big effects on the economy and society. For instance Foxconn, a maker of Apple devices, is planning to replace thousands of workers with robots. When it does, it won't have to contend with relentless criticism of its work practices, which led to multiple suicides at its plants. For its part, Apple and companies such as Nike, whose shoe making provides thousands of jobs in Indonesia, will naturally go for higher quality, lower costs, and the absence of sweatshop controversies that automation will bring. As this book is being written, Adidas is setting up "sewbot" machines that can churn out 800,000 shirts a day.

In richer countries, the really big effects of automation will be in service jobs, where most people are employed. It's often said that we will still need people to cut hair and flip hamburgers, but even the latter is under threat. A San Francisco company, Momentum Machines, has developed a robotic system that makes customizable gourmet burgers from scratch, and has plans to open its first store. Given that McDonald's employs 1.8 million people, and fast food jobs currently provide "a kind of private sector social safety net for workers with few other options," as Ford puts it, this is scary. McDonald's already has touch screen ordering in many of its restaurants—a sign of things to come. "Economists categorize fast food as part of the service sector," but Ford points out that "from a technical standpoint it is really closer to being a form of just-in-time manufacturing."

Online retailing is also a big destroyer of jobs. Blockbuster, the video rental chain, once had 9,000 stores and employed 60,000 people. Netflix performs the same function without all the staff, and without the real estate footprint with all its associated costs. The cost of sales assistants, checkout staff, warehouse staff, and managers once had to be factored in the price of things you bought in a department store or variety store. These jobs are increasingly being automated away, and the physical stores of the future may become little more than "scaled-up vending machines." It will mean much lower prices for goods, but this is only good if you still have a job, any job, to pay for them in the first place.

Any process that can be broken down into simple tasks or steps can be automated, and most new companies created now have labor-saving technologies built into them. Consider the tech giants Google and Facebook, whose ratio of market capitalization to number of employees dwarfs that of industrial-era companies. Just a few thousand highly selected people are needed; advances in software technology mean the rest of the work can be done by computers. In 2012 Google's profit was almost $14 billion, and it employed 38,000 people. In 1979, General Motors' profit was $11 billion (adjusted for inflation), but it employed *840,000* people.

To see where service industries may be headed, consider agriculture, which once employed half of all American adults. Today it requires less than 2 percent of the workforce, and the figure is falling. Already there are machines that can move up and down almond groves in California, shaking the trees so that the almonds drop to the ground, while another one collects them. The same thing is happening for oranges and tomatoes, bringing fantastic abundance through lower labor costs and better use of land and water, and changing the demand for immigrant labor. In countries such as Australia and Britain with aging populations that require immigrants to pick much of their crops, automation would solve many of their problems.

Yet if technology advances so much that the demand for labor falls, paradoxically companies may then be willing to employ more people, because the cost of labor remains low. There is a point where human labor can be more attractive than machines. So even when it seems that technology has not changed the labor market, in subtle ways it has. In the future, Ford suggests, plenty of people may still have jobs, but their wages will not increase because they are just not that valuable.

He gives the example of London black cab drivers, who acquire their licenses after an incredibly grueling test of memorized knowledge of the city's street layout, known as "the Knowledge." But GPS navigation makes this knowledge largely redundant, and taxi apps like Uber are quickly eating into the traditional black cab market. The only thing keeping up cab drivers' wages is regulation. And this is even before we start to think about the coming impact of driverless cars on the army of people currently employed to drive and deliver people and goods.

. . . then the middle-class ones

When the internet got going, it was seen as a great leveler, empowering anyone to blog, publish an e-book, develop an app, all at low cost and without education or training. It soon became clear, however, that the online world is a winner-take-all one, and all these "opportunities" are not going to replace the safe, stable, well-paying jobs that our parents or grandparents had.

Techno-optimists, Ford notes, tend to be in the high-earning bracket of the population, or own companies that benefit from the internet. One of them, Ray Kurzweil, likes saying that the average person is carrying around in their smartphone massive computing power compared to what was available a few decades ago. "Left unsaid," Ford writes, "was how the average person is supposed to leverage that technology into a liveable income . . . for the majority of people who lose middle-class jobs, access to a smartphone may offer little beyond the ability to play Angry Birds while waiting in the unemployment line."

The amount of data in the world is increasing at a rate similar to Moore's law—doubling every three years. The combination of "big data" with powerful analyzing software and algorithms means that many of the traditional white-collar jobs that involved a person collecting information, analyzing it, and presenting their report will disappear. Instead of layers of middle managers and teams of analysts, Ford suggests, there may just be "a single manager and powerful algorithm." But surely we will at least need people to write up the data in reports? Writing has been the preserve of university-educated people and seems the least likely area to be automated, yet every month the software is getting better, and lots of writing jobs may not exist in the future. Already many shorter sports and finance reports you read online are written by bots that process data. While hardly great writing, it is usually indistinguishable from what a person would produce. The CIA is using this kind of software to process its vast quantities of data into prose that people can understand.

Many other middle-class or service jobs are likely to disappear. The ability of firms to store all their data in the cloud (cheap, secure, external servers) is doing away with the need to employ the ubiquitous IT people to manage in-house computer systems and servers. There are lots of job losses to come in the financial industry, as algorithms replace traders and analysts, and millions of customer relations jobs will be vaporized by the application of incredibly smart natural language systems such as that deployed by IBM's "Watson" computer. In the future, talking to machines will become increasingly the norm. Lawyers and paralegals sift through mountains of paper and electronic documents in the process of "discovery" to find the ones that are important to the case. With all documents being put online, e-discovery software can do the same job quicker and more cheaply.

What about the idea that the jobs of the future, as Erik Brynjolfsson and Andrew McAfee have argued (in *The Second Machine Age*; see *50 Economics Classics*), will involve productive collaboration with machines? Such collaboration, Ford says, will probably be short-lived, since whenever a human works with a machine, it will be programmed to see what the human's contribution is, and work to replicate it or do it better. In short, "you are also training the software to ultimately replace you." In the jobs that do exist, Ford suggests, the human role will be "unrewarding or even dehumanizing."

As venture capitalist Marc Andreessen put it: "Software is eating the world." Starting salaries for new graduates are falling, at the same time that student debt is rising. Underemployment is everywhere, with graduates giving up trying to find professional work to work in cafés. This is true even for engineering and computer science graduates. Since 2000 there is just much less demand for what graduates offer. As things stand, it is pretty hard to see today's graduates enjoying the well-paid, reasonably fulfilling careers enjoyed by their parents. Education has many great personal and societal benefits, Ford notes, just don't expect it to be a ticket to prosperity as it once was.

Not just jobs are at risk, but capitalism as we know it

Henry Ford paid his workers the high wage of $5 a day, which meant they could afford to buy the cars they were making. The big risk with automation is that there won't be enough people with decent incomes around anymore to pay for all the things it produces. Workers consume, and when they are replaced by a machine, Ford notes, that machine does not buy anything. "Nearly all the major industries that form the backbones of Western economies (cars, financial services, consumer electronics, telecommunications services, healthcare, etc.)," he notes, "are geared toward markets consisting of millions of potential customers."

One rich person buying a very expensive car, or even owning a garage of expensive cars, will not make up for a thousand people buying normal-priced cars. Our economy rides on mass demand, from phones to mortgages to toothpaste, that comes from the existence of reasonable purchasing power across the broad middle of the economy. Take that purchasing power away, because there are no jobs, or because wages are driven lower and lower, and it calls into question the whole basis of modern capitalism. We could return to a nineteenth-century distribution of income in which there were a few very wealthy people who could afford to buy almost anything, including lots of servants, and the rest who live at a subsistence level. Ford calls this "techno-feudalism," calling to mind the 2013 film *Elysium* in which the world's rich retreat to a pristine world orbiting above the Earth, which is now filled with billions of poor living in a degraded environment.

Ford's preferred solution to the problem of hundreds of millions of people being unemployed or underemployed: a basic minimum income guarantee or "universal living wage." In the 1970s free-market economist Friedrich Hayek proposed it for people who, for one reason or another, are not able to make a living through the open market, and cannot depend on traditional family structures for sustenance. A society that had reached a certain level of wealth could afford this, he thought. Where those on the right today would view a guaranteed minimum income as a push to "equalize" society, and thus reduce freedoms, Hayek simply saw it as necessary in order to maintain society rather than see it fall apart. Ford believes that, rather than eroding a market system, ensuring that everyone has a certain basic income (thought not so high that it incentivizes people not to work at all) means they can participate in the economy as a consumer, and can take risks in terms of starting businesses or going back to education. The alternative is expansion of the traditional welfare state, which is a lot more expensive because there is constant means testing and administration, not to mention the stigma of being a recipient.

Ford prefers the phrase "citizen's dividend" to "guaranteed income," because "it captures the argument that everyone should have at least a minimal claim on a nation's overall economic prosperity." For instance, a lot of the funding that was poured into creating the internet, through the Defense Advanced Research Projects Agency (DARPA), came from the taxpayer. Grants to the National Science Foundation contributed to the research that resulted in Moore's law.

Ford addresses the argument that although jobs might be fewer and less well paid, automation will mean that the price of goods and services drops in tandem. In fact, in the sectors that have been resistant to automation, such as education, healthcare, and housing, costs have only risen, and will do so for the foreseeable future. What you get is people, on the wages they are getting, being unable to afford to rent or buy housing in the city where they've grown up, being unable to pay back student loans they incurred at university, and, if in the US, an inability to afford health insurance. If there is a long-term trend of stagnating or falling incomes and rising costs, you have a severe long-term attenuation of demand that no government "priming of the pump" or deficit spending will fix. This is why such measures in the years after the 2007–9 financial crisis did not spark the growth levels that normally follow recessions. Yes, stock markets (as of 2017) are riding high, but again this is indicative of a long-term trend: because corporations are saving a lot of money on labor, profits have risen, even if demand is not what it once was. What you arrive at is a kind of rentier economy in which the gains going to owners and investors increase, just as the percentage of national wealth going to workers declines—a picture already painted by Thomas Piketty in *Capital in the Twenty-First Century* (see *50 Economics Classics*).

Final comments

Is what Ford says about increasing income inequality true? Is the middle class really drying up? In the years since *The Rise of the Robots* was published, unemployment in the UK and US, for example, has dropped to the 4–5 percent range. Yet in the book he warns not to look at the numbers of people who still have a job, but at the quality of the jobs. How many, for instance, involve zero-hour contracts (when the employer has no obligation to give someone a certain number of hours of work in a week)? And how many hundreds of thousands of young people are working as baristas as they fruitlessly apply for professional and technical positions? He points to some startling numbers from the US Bureau of Labor Statistics, which tabulates the total number of hours worked each year in the American economy. In

1998, 194 billion hours were worked. In 2013, the number was . . . 194 billion. Yet in this time span, output (the amount of goods and services created) increased by 42 percent, thousands of new businesses were created, and the US population rose by 40 million.

"The unfortunate reality," Ford writes, "is that a great many people will do everything right—at least in terms of pursuing higher education and acquiring skills—and yet still fail to find a solid foothold in the new economy." What does success mean when, no matter what you do in terms of education and skills, it is not enough? Will the work of moral refinement or character actually do anything for you, if you are competing against a machine? A question running through the book, which Ford does not address or even attempt to answer, is: "How important to happiness is meaningful work?" John Maynard Keynes imagined a future in which the problem of production was to a large extent solved, so that people could enjoy the good things in life. Two things stand in the way of this: (1) the gains of technology are not necessarily spread across society, but in capitalism can be captured by a relative few; and (2) people soon tire of "good things" if they have not contributed in any meaningful way to society, or developed themselves through work.

Ford admits at the end of the book that it may be decades before his vision fully plays out, and in the meantime things may seem normal, incremental. This is often how it seems prior to revolutions.

Martin Ford

Ford has a degree in computer engineering from the University of Michigan, and a graduate degree in business from the Anderson School of Management at the University of California, Los Angeles. He writes for a range of publications and is a frequent speaker on the impacts of AI and automation. Rise of the Robots *won the 2015 Financial Times and McKinsey Book of the Year Award. Ford's previous book was* The Lights in the Tunnel: Automation, Accelerating Technology and the Economy of the Future *(2009).*

2001

The E-Myth Revisited

*"I don't believe your business to be the first order of business
on our agenda. You are."*

*"Human beings are capable of performing extraordinary
acts. Capable of going to the moon. Capable of creating
the computer. Capable of building a bomb that can
destroy us all. The least we should be able to do is
run a small business that works."*

*"A business that looks orderly says that while the world may
not work, some things can."*

In a nutshell

**The key to real prosperity in business is to work *on* your enterprise,
not in it.**

In a similar vein

Guy Kawasaki *The Art of the Start*
Eric Ries *The Lean Startup*
Frederick Winslow Taylor *The Principles of Scientific Management*

CHAPTER 13

Michael E. Gerber

*T*he *E-Myth* came out in 1985 and became an underground bestseller, with over a million copies sold. The initial edition became quite hard to get hold of, but Michael Gerber brought out a new one, *The E-Myth Revisited: Why Most Small Businesses Don't Work and What to Do About It*, containing revised material but with the same powerful messages, in 1995, which was itself updated in 2001.

Despite its age now, few people have done a better job of presenting the anatomy of a small business, including what people really do in them and what they really earn from all their efforts. Gerber learned from his consulting work that people in small businesses generally work far too much for the return they get. The "tyranny of routine" means that there is never time to take an objective overview of what they are doing. His book aimed to be a friend to those stuck in the quagmire.

The book proceeds partly through a running dialogue with a woman Gerber worked with, "Sarah," a pie-shop owner whose problems and challenges perfectly encapsulate those faced by most people going into business. Specifically, the book is a recipe for putting yourself back in control of your working hours—in short, to be able to work *on* your business, not in it. Never before have so many people entertained the idea of starting their own business. If this applies to you, before you take the leap, read this book.

Business as self-development

Gerber's surprising message is that going into business is as much about who you are and who you want to be as a person, as it is about the business itself. If you are disorganized or greedy, he says, or if your information about what is happening in your business is not good, your business will become a reflection of these things. If your business is to thrive, it will engage you in a process of constant personal development. For it to change, so will you.

Gerber quotes Aldous Huxley: "They intoxicate themselves with work so they won't see how they really are." If you start a business with full knowledge of what it means to you and why you are doing it, it can be a wonderful experience. Go in blindly, and it can be—as many discover—a nightmare.

The myth of the entrepreneur

The "e-myth," Gerber notes, is the belief that anyone who starts a small business is an entrepreneur. Yet entrepreneurs in the heroic sense of a Herculean wealth creator are actually quite rare. Most people simply want to create a job for themselves and stop working for a boss. Their thinking goes, "Why should my boss earn lots of money from what I am doing?

The problems begin because this person may know a lot about their specialty, but nothing about business itself. After the initial exhilaration of the start-up, they realize they have become the boss (of themselves), and are soon exhausted and demoralized. Knowing their specialty inside out has not prepared them to run a business—in fact, it becomes a liability, since they become unwilling to hand over the work reins to anyone else.

As Gerber puts it: "Suddenly the job he knew how to do so well becomes one job he knows how to do plus a dozen others he doesn't know how to do at all." He discovers he must become three people in one:

- The Technician—the person actually doing the work itself;
- The Manager—making sure everything is organized, pushing the Technician to ensure goals are met; and
- The Entrepreneur—the visionary or dreamer charting the overall direction of the company.

Each of these selves does battle with the other, and most people have a lopsided balance within them. The most common breakdown of someone who starts a small business is 10 percent entrepreneur, 20 percent manager, and 70 percent technician.

How things go wrong

The problem of the Technician is that he or she believes that the answer to every problem is to work harder. When Sarah's pie shop begins to come apart at the seams, she thinks that making more and better pies will sort things out—it won't.

What she needs is to step back and look at the business as a business. Gerber forces her to ask: "Is it a *system* that works irrespective of who is working in it?" Or is it just a place where a lady makes pies and tries to sell them? The familiar pattern of a Technician who has started a business, Gerber notes, is this: exhilaration, followed by terror, exhaustion, and despair. What they once loved most—their work—they begin to hate.

A small business in its infancy is easy to spot: The owner is doing everything or trying to do everything. They are the only person who *knows* how to do everything, after all. But with the business growing, they have to employ someone else. This is a relief; now they don't have to think about that aspect of the business they didn't like anyway (more often than not, it is doing "the books").

But at some point this person decides to leave, and the business is thrown into chaos again. The owner's answer is to do more, work harder—forget about any long-term goals, just get the product out the door! No one, you realize, can do the work like you do, so it must stay at a size so that you can do all the work.

This point, Gerber says, when an owner does not want to move out of their comfort zone of them being in control as the Technician, is possibly the most dangerous for a small business. Such a shrinking back is a tragedy. The owner's morale dips, and eventually the business dies because of its natural limits.

Taking the bolder route

It does not have to be this way. Gerber tells Sarah that "the purpose of going into business is to get free of a job so you can create jobs for other people." It is not to be "free of a boss," but rather to go further in your field than you could just working for yourself—to create something great out of your life's work that makes a difference, and which naturally requires more organization and resources. The key question, Sarah learns, is not how small her business could be, but how big it could naturally become with the right systems and organization in place.

The first thing to do if you take the bolder route, Gerber suggests, is to crystallize where you want to go with the business and *write this goal down*. He is amazed how few small businesses actually have written goals, yet "any plan is better than no plan." Without such a goal or plan, should we be surprised at the lack of direction, organization, and general panic that clouds the way most enterprises are run?

A mature company, he writes, *begins* differently than the rest. Most great companies set out with a vision of where they wanted to go. Tom Watson, the founder of IBM, is quoted as saying: "I realized that for IBM to become a great company, it had to act like a great company long before it ever became one." Watson had a template or vision and each day tried to fashion the company after it, however far-fetched it seemed. He had a picture in his mind how the company would look and be "when it was finally done."

The Technician's only model for his business is work, whereas for the Entrepreneur, the model is the business itself; the work is secondary. This paradox is summed up in Watson's remark, "Every day at IBM was a day devoted to business development, not doing business."

This again is Gerber's message: work *on* your business, not in it.

It's the system

Gerber mentions McDonald's as the perfect example of a business that "worked." The brilliance of the concept was a system that could be replicated thousands of times over. Though McDonald's founder Ray Kroc loved the food, he loved even more the beauty of the *system* that the original McDonald brothers had developed: its speed, simplicity, and order.

Most small businesses believe they will grow through hiring brilliant people—managers who can take the business to a new level. In fact, Gerber suggests, this is a hit and miss way of doing things. What you really need is idiot-proof systems and procedures that enable merely good people to do extraordinary things—ways of operating that guarantee a customer is satisfied, *not by individual people, but by the system itself.* This may seem a cold way of looking at it, but anyone who has been delighted by the way a hotel or a restaurant is run will understand the distinction. If you can build a great business around ordinary people, Gerber remarks, you don't have to worry about finding extraordinary ones.

Creating a world of order

You have to orchestrate, organize, and standardize your business down to the smallest details, because the only certainty in your business is that its staff will act unpredictably. With proper standards, systems, and accountability, you cut out that risk, and as a result the customer gets what they want all of the time. A business is like a machine that generates money. The more you standardize and refine the machine, the clearer its value will be.

You may say, I can't work out standards, I am a master craftsman in what I do! But Gerber responds: what does a master craftsman do when she has learned all there is to know? Passes it on to others. In fulfilling this duty, your skill can be multiplied many times. Orchestration through a business system leverages what you know. It is your mastery writ large.

Most people, Gerber notes, feel either a lack of purpose in their lives or a sense of isolation from others. A great business can fill both holes, giving a sense of camaraderie and order that would otherwise be missing. It brings more life, both to customers and employees, providing a "fixed point of reference"—an island of purposeful calm in an otherwise disorderly world.

Final comments

Gerber asks Sarah to imagine how her business would be run if it was the model for 5,000 exactly like it. Would the extension of her ideas and philosophy to such a grand scale mean she would have "sold out"? Or would she feel that it was the natural expression of a system she had lovingly built and that *deserved* to be replicated?

The success of *The E-Myth* partly owes to the fact that it coincided with the boom in business franchising. Gerber calls franchising the "turnkey revolution," in that it allows someone to buy the right to use a business system in which all they have to do (with some capital and a reasonable amount of work) is "turn the key" to get it going and become profitable. Franchising rests on the understanding that "The true product of a business is the business itself." However, though you can do very well buying a franchise, you can do even better by starting some kind of business system yourself—as Sarah begins to realize.

Gerber's book can get almost mystical at times, quoting the likes of Carlos Castaneda, Robert Assagioli, and Zen writers such as Robert Pirsig. Since Gerber is a self-confessed former poem-writing hippie, this is no surprise. What is surprising is his injection of a spiritual sensibility into what is essentially a business title, and this has been a key to the book's success. It is, given its subject, quite an addictive read, because it is ultimately about who you are and where you want to go in life, not about business. Echoing his first principle of business success, Gerber notes that "Great people have a vision of their lives that they practice emulating each and every day. They go to work on their lives, not just in their lives."

The E-Myth Revisited can be a bit self-promoting at times, but this should be forgiven in the context of its powerful messages. The chapter on marketing, which shows why it is so important to be clear on exactly what you are selling, is worth the price of the book alone.

Michael E. Gerber

Born in 1936, the California-based Gerber once sold encyclopedias for a living. He founded his company, E-Myth Worldwide, in 1977, eight years before writing The E-Myth. *It assists small businesses through its consulting and programs. Gerber is also a widely traveled keynote speaker. His other books include* The E-Myth Contractor *(2003),* E-Myth Mastery *(2007),* The E-Myth Real Estate Investor *(2015), and* Beyond The E-Myth *(2016).*

Be My Guest

"The type of dreaming that appeals to me has nothing to do with a reverie, an idle daydream. It isn't wishful thinking. Nor is it the type of revelation reserved for the great ones and rightly called vision. What I speak of is a brand of imaginative thinking backed by enthusiasm, vitality, expectation, to which all people aspire."

"I was twenty-three years old. I had been working for eleven years. So far I had earned a partnership in a store in the town in which I was born. But it was my father's store. A. H. Hilton & son. A. H. Hilton & Shadow? a small voice within me was questioning. Wasn't it time I formulated a dream of my own? I had an idea . . ."

In a nutshell

Thinking big is the basis of all great enterprises and fortunes.

In a similar vein

Richard Branson *Losing My Virginity*
Duncan Clark *Alibaba: The House That Jack Ma Built*
Howard Schultz *Pour Your Heart Into It*

CHAPTER 14

Conrad Hilton

These days Conrad Hilton is a historical figure, obscure to most people compared to his celebrity great-granddaughter, Paris. Indeed, how easy it is to forget that our prosperity often rests on the hard work and vision of our parents or grandparents.

Hilton's autobiography is also less celebrated than it should be. Most people come across it in their bedside drawer during a stay at a Hilton hotel. Yet it is one of the more engrossing of the hundreds of "how I did it" self-told business stories, to be enjoyed alongside titles such as Sam Walton's *Made in America*. And unlike most books of this type, Hilton actually wrote it himself.

Be My Guest is a fascinating window into the life of a frontier American family around the turn of the twentieth century and a gripping story of the creation of one of the world's biggest businesses, at a time when branded hotel chains were few and far between. It also happens to be a superb little motivation book on the importance of faith in your idea and thinking big.

Young Conrad

Conrad Hilton was born on Christmas Day, 1887. His father Gus was a Norwegian immigrant who made his living selling supplies to men working in the back blocks of New Mexico. From his store in the small town of San Antonio (not the Texas city), he eventually made enough money for the family to leave behind the dusty Southwest frontier. They moved to Long Beach, California, where it was hoped Mrs. Hilton could enjoy an easier life. But with a financial crash in 1907, Gus Hilton was caught holding a lot of stock no one would buy. The family reluctantly moved back to New Mexico and took a hard look at their assets. These included: a very large adobe house next to a main railway line; Mrs. Hilton's great cooking; and with several kids, plenty of helping hands. The Hiltons decided to turn their house into a hotel. With room and all meals only $2.50 a day, the business did well.

By the time he was 23, Conrad had been working for his father for 11 years. He was finally made a business partner, but he was eager to do something on his own. Not particularly interested in trading or hotels, he ran for the state legislature in Sante Fe, but his dream was to own a chain of banks. At 26, he had raised enough money to start his own. World War One intervened, however, and in 1917 he enlisted. He spent most of his service in France, but while on active duty back in the United States received the news his father had died in a car accident. Returning to New Mexico, his home town now seemed like "a toy town of adobe and wood surrounded by emptiness."

Looking for opportunities

Now in his early thirties, and having to sort through his father's financial affairs, Hilton took stock. He had savings of $5,011 and "big ideas," but was not sure what to do. A friend of his father's gave him some advice: "If you want to launch big ships, you have to go where the water is deep." So he went to Albuquerque, then only a town of 15,000 but quite cosmopolitan compared to where he had come from. He continued to pursue his dream of owning a chain of banks, but only met brick walls.

A dying man, another friend of his father's, instructed him to go to Texas, saying, "There you will make your fortune." So in 1920, now 33, Hilton moved to Cisco, where he looked around to buy a small bank. Again he got nowhere, and one day, exhausted by his efforts, he entered a small, very crowded hotel to find a room for the night. It occurred to him that this bustling, run-down hotel, the Mobley, might be a better proposition than owning a bank. He got talking to the owner, who despite his good turnover and margins was desperate to sell: this was a town crazed by the possibility of oil riches, and the owner, too, wanted to make his fortune in oil. The Mobley was the first of several "old dowagers" that Hilton would buy— decrepit properties, yet whose books were good and had room for potential.

Hilton now wanted to own a chain of hotels around Texas. He bought one, the Waldorf (not the famous Waldorf Astoria) in downtown Dallas. Included in the manager's library was a set of books by inspirational author Elbert Hubbard, *Little Journeys to the Homes of the Great*. Though already ambitious, Hilton's idea of what might be possible grew through the stories of financiers and entrepreneurs such as Meyer Rothschild, Andrew Carnegie, Stephen Girard, Peter Cooper, plus the great statesmen, artists, scientists, and philosophers.

He ran these shabby hotels for several years, but now wanted something more: his own "Hilton" hotel. The Hilton Hotel, Dallas, was a much bigger project than anything he had done before. He had to race against time to raise a million dollars, and in 1924 he broke ground on the site. After running out of money twice, in August 1925 the hotel finally opened.

Times good and bad

With his confidence high, Hilton got married and had two kids, Nick and Barron, in quick succession. By the time of his 41st birthday, he had nine hotels, including the new El Paso Hilton. Opened in the fall of 1929, and built at great expense, it seemed like the crown of a growing empire. Yet as Hilton ruefully records, "Nineteen days later the stock market crashed."

Looking back, Hilton marvels at how he got through the torturous years of the Depression. Many times it seemed as if he was about to go bankrupt, but then "something happened" (a family friend or business acquaintance would step in at the last minute to provide an injection of funds) that would enable him to keep going. Reflecting on his Catholic faith, he notes that in these years it seemed that it was "the only guilt-edged security" he owned. Meanwhile, the time, energy, and constant travel required to keep things afloat also meant time away from his wife and family, and it cost him his marriage.

Slow-cooked success

The book reveals a surprising fact: despite later becoming known as the founder of an international hotel chain, Hilton was almost 50 before he bought a hotel in a state outside Texas.

After acquiring the esteemed Sir Francis Drake, San Francisco, he bought the coveted Stevens Hotel in Chicago, the biggest in the world at the time, with 3,000 rooms. Then little known in the hotel industry, the sale took him six years to negotiate. On the challenges of financing and organizing such large purchases, Hilton notes: "If you are content with planting radish seeds you'll get radishes in a few weeks. When you start planting acorns, the full-fledged oak may take years. And I was beginning to learn what all gardeners know—patience."

Yet what seemed like slowness at the time had its benefits. By buying and operating all these other hotels before the Hilton franchise was properly established, it allowed him to truly master his industry and avoid risking the Hilton name. Hilton Hotels was incorporated by Hilton in 1946.

When he began expanding overseas, Hilton saw his chain of hotels as a way of expanding the American ideals of freedom and democracy. Providing people with a place to meet for business, he reasoned, was a good way of achieving "World peace through international trade and travel." During the Cold War, he writes, his intention was that his hotels show off "the fruits of the free world," and his properties became hubs for business and investment in developing countries.

The need for a dream

Hilton's life bears out the great observation made by David Schwartz in *The Magic of Thinking Big*: "Most people fail in life not because they aim too high and miss—but because they aim too low, and hit." In the depths of the Depression, deep in debt and with a court judgment against him and his clothes at the pawnbroker, Hilton had clipped out a picture of the newly completed Waldorf Astoria Hotel in New York. Later, when he had enough cash again to buy a desk, he put that picture under the desk's glass top. At that time, owning it seemed like a ridiculous fantasy, yet it was a recognition to himself that you had to have things to aim for.

He recalls that his mother's tip for success in life could be boiled down to one word: "Pray." His father's philosophy could be reduced to another: "Work." By the time he and his siblings had grown up, they had heard the "pray and work" mantra hundreds of times, yet his brother had noted, "There must be some other ingredient that goes in but I can't put my finger on it." Writing the book at age 70, Hilton recalled sitting in the ballroom of New York's legendary Waldorf Astoria—which he now owned—and wondering whether there was in fact anything to be added to his parents' wisdom. It was only then that it came to him: *You had to dream!*" He is quick to note that "nobody ever called me a dreamer," yet this was where, he believed, great things had to start.

> *"To accomplish big things I am convinced you must first dream big dreams. True, it must be in line with progress, human and divine, or you are wasting your prayer. It has to be backed by work and faith, or it has no hands and feet. Maybe there's even an element of luck mixed in. But I am sure now that, without this master plan, you have nothing."*

Final comments

The story of Hilton, who died age 91 in 1979, provides inspiration for anyone who does not yet know what they want to do, but who is hungry for a big opportunity. It suggests keeping our eyes and ears open, as the next chance meeting, purchase, or trip may be the turning point in your life, just as Hilton's discovery of the Mobley Hotel was for him. It does not matter if you have not yet found your life's mission, as long as you are in a state of readiness to seize it when it comes. Neither does it matter if you think opportunities have passed you by. Hilton was, after all, well into his thirties before his life really started in terms of setting his own course and moving out of his father's shadow, and 50 before he began to expand outside of Texas. He still had decades of life and work in him.

Today Hilton is a public company controlling over 5,000 hotels in 80 countries. The Conrad hotels are the most luxurious of the various levels of Hilton establishment.

The Hard Thing About Hard Things

"The Struggle is when you wonder why you started the company in the first place. The Struggle is when people ask you why you don't quit and you don't know the answer. The Struggle is when your employees think you are lying and you think they may be right."

"If there is one skill that stands out, it's the ability to focus and make the best move when there are no good moves. It's the moments where you feel most like hiding or dying that you can make the biggest difference as a CEO."

"If you want to build an important company, then at some point you have to scale. People in startup land often talk about the magic of how few people built the original Google or the original Facebook, but today's Google employs twenty thousand people and today's Facebook employs more than fifteen hundred people. So, if you want to do something that matters, then you are going to have to learn the black art of scaling a human organization."

In a nutshell

Nothing really prepares you for leading an organization and getting it through the inevitable crises.

In a similar vein

Jim Collins *Great by Choice*
Eric Ries *The Lean Startup*
Peter Schmidt & Jonathan Rosenberg *How Google Works*
Peter Thiel *Zero To One*

CHAPTER 15

Ben Horowitz

Every business and self-help book that Ben Horowitz had read had offered a simple solution, something that could be applied universally. Yet fluid, complex situations, by their nature, elude simple recipes. There are no recipes for all the really hard things in life, from running a successful company to having a happy marriage to becoming president.

It is easy to have a "big, audacious, hairy goal"; the hard part is making it happen. It is easy to hire great people; the hard bit is what to do when their demands increase and they get a sense of entitlement. It's not hard to dream big, either; "The hard thing is waking up in the middle of the night in a cold sweat when the dream turns into a nightmare." As a former CEO and now venture capitalist advising technology start-ups, the only thing Horowitz thought he could offer was some tips on what to do when your new company inevitably faces crises.

The Hard Thing About Hard Things: Building a Business When There Are No Easy Answers arose out of Horowitz's popular blog, when people started asking about the back story behind the ideas and advice he was giving. What provides an extra dimension is that the book is peppered with lyrics from Horowitz's favorite hip-hop artists. Their experience in "competing, making money, being misunderstood," he says, is no different to the difficulty entrepreneurs face in achieving success, coming up with new ideas, getting them heard, and creating a public identity from scratch.

Silicon Valley odyssey

While working at Lotus Development in the 1990s, Horowitz was shown Mosaic, the first kind of browser to access the internet. He was amazed, and instantly felt that the internet was the future. When he heard about a new company, Netscape, founded by Mosaic's 22-year-old inventor Marc Andreessen and the founder of Silicon Graphics, Jim Clark, he made sure he got a job there.

The historic 1995 Netscape IPO, a huge success that changed the business landscape, divided companies into "new economy" and "old economy." The firm would end up losing the browser battle to Microsoft, and Andreessen and Horowitz left Netscape/AOL to start the first cloud computing platform,

LoudCloud, in 1999, mostly to provide cheap server space for thousands of start-ups and with some bigger firms like Nike in the mix.

With Horowitz as a green CEO, LoudCloud grew fast with lots of capital at its disposal. Then came the dot.com crash. The firm began to run out of cash fast, and "I felt like I was going to die," Horowitz remembers. It raised some money, but sales of its services were plummeting. Would he lose all the investors' (including his mother's) money? Would he have to lay off the hundreds of great people that had been so carefully selected? Horowitz came up with the seemingly crazy idea to float the company on the stock market. Comparable firms were losing half their value, and they were planning an IPO! It was the worst possible time, but seemed the only way to raise money.

In the end, the IPO went through and LoudCloud staved off bankruptcy, but it was the most depressing time in Horowitz's working life. In the months following, despite the cash raised, he had to lay off lots of employees and anger investors with much lower revised earnings calls. The stock price fell from $6 to $2, and it lost its biggest customer, Atriax, that owed it $25 million. With the cloud business apparently doomed (apart from the Atriax loss, sales were not increasing enough to cover fixed costs and debt), Horowitz put together a secret team to develop LoudCloud's proprietary software so that it could become a sellable product. The shift from data storage to software perplexed investors and most employees, but Horowitz saw it as the only way out. A deal was made in which LoudCloud would sell nearly all of its business to data company EDS. All it retained was the proprietary software, which it leased back to EDS for $20 million a year, and it would operate under a new name, Opsware. But the rump of employees still left with the company were far from convinced, and the stock price dropped to 35 cents.

In the years following things improved, and Opsware became seen as the leader in its field. From a company that had become worth almost nothing, in 2007 Horowitz sold it to Hewlett-Packard for $1.6 billion. As he had given eight years of blood, sweat, and tears to the company and poured his heart into it, he felt terrible. Only later did he realize it was the best decision he had made. Aside from the money that set him and his family up for life, he had learned all the major lessons of being a founder and a CEO, lessons that would be highly valuable when, with Marc Andreessen, he established pioneering technology venture capital firm Andreessen Horowitz. Not many venture capitalists had actually run sizable companies, and he knew inside out the perilous psychological journey that goes with starting and scaling a technology company.

The struggle

Horowitz devotes more than a few pages to what he calls "the Struggle," the world that every company founder finds themselves in after their bright vision mixes with reality: your employees lose faith and start to leave, you stop believing your own spiel, the market has changed, the press are writing terrible stories, the analysts believe the company is walking dead. Why did you ever think it could work? Idiot.

Every entrepreneur goes through the Struggle, Horowitz says; the difference between people is how they respond. He only offers some pointers on how to get through it:

- Don't put it all on your shoulders. As founder or CEO, you feel like it is all up to you, and it is true that you feel it the most, but it is crucial not to keep the problems to yourself. Make it a shared struggle.
- There are always moves you can make, even if things seem desperate. Horowitz took a company public in the worst possible business climate, with uncertain revenues and business model. "There is always a move."
- "Play long enough and you might get lucky." The technology business is constantly changing, so if you can just stay in the game a bit longer things can suddenly work out for you.
- There is a cost to greatness, and what you are going through is it. "Remember that this is what separates the women from the girls. If you want to be great, this is the challenge. If you don't want to be great, then you never should have started a company."

As head of the company, Horowitz always felt a lot of pressure to be Mr. Positive and rally the troops. But he came to see that companies that try to cover up or stop the sharing of bad news are dangerously vulnerable. When everyone discovers how bad things are it is usually too late to do anything. It is always much better to face your fear of being seen a failure and lay out the true situation. When you do that, a funny thing happens: people respect your candor and get behind you, working day and night to get the firm back on track.

No matter how prominent, every company will go through periods when it faces an existential threat. In these times, it is tempting to make excuses or come up with new strategies to fool the competition or try to take on a whole new market by going up market or down market, but there are no silver bullets that will rescue your company in tough times, Horowitz says, only lead bullets. By this he means direct, ugly, full-on battles with your competitor, either by digging deep to make a better product, or through a sales onslaught, or both. When you or your people start to sound like excuse-making machines remember that in every company's life there will be a time when it must fight for its life. "If you find yourself running when you should be fighting," he remarks, "you need to ask yourself, 'If our company isn't good enough to win, then do we need to exist at all?'"

Can you take it: CEO psychology

Easily the most difficult skill he had to learn as CEO, Horowitz says, was "managing my own psychology"—in other words, avoiding psychological meltdown. You can get through a corporate career having minimized mistakes quite well, but when you are suddenly in charge of 1,000 or 10,000 people in a fast-changing market environment, things will frequently go wrong in a big way. This is psychologically very challenging for anyone who has always been a straight-A kind of performer. Every company will go through at least two to five "We're fucked, it's over" moments, and it's the CEO who feels it most deeply.

Horowitz's tips for coping: *"Get it out of your head and onto paper."* Putting a big move or decision into carefully chosen words will help you to see its rational merits, aside from your emotional position. *"Focus on the road, not the wall."* There are always a million things that can go wrong while you are CEO, but you have to focus on your goals. *"Don't quit."* When Horowitz quizzes other CEOs on how they got through tough times, the really good ones don't point to their great strategic moves or business prowess, they simply say, "I didn't quit." There will be times when you feel so bad, so stressed, so fearful, that you feel you have to leave, but it's nearly always the wrong thing to do. Having the courage to stay on and do something, even if things seem to be going down the tube, is what separates mediocre and great CEOs.

People still have the idea that great CEOs are born, not made, but Horowitz candidly tells of the multiple mistakes he made in every area before he found his feet. Even then he was often wracked by doubt over a decision. Not only is there nothing natural about heading an organization, you continually have to do things that go against the natural human wish to be liked. "Yet to be a good CEO, in order to be liked in the long run," he writes, "you must do many things that will upset people in the short run. Unnatural things."

Horowitz notes that the really big decisions he had to make were more about courage than intelligence, and it is courage (along with brilliance) that he looks for in start-up founders. With every hard, correct decision made, it makes you a bit more courageous. Conversely, easy but wrong decisions only make you more cowardly. The end result is either a cowardly company or a courageous company. "Over the past ten years, technological advances have dramatically lowered the financial bar for starting a new company," Horowitz writes, "but the courage bar for building a great company remains as high as it has ever been."

Build a good company

There are two reasons why people quit their jobs, Horowitz observes: (1) they "hated their manager," and were "appalled by the lack of guidance, career development, and feedback they were receiving"; and (2) "They weren't learning anything: The company wasn't investing resources in helping employees develop new skills."

A great training program addresses both, and will cover all practical knowledge about your company's products, but also the nuts-and-bolts management things such as team-building, negotiating, reviewing performance, interviewing, and finance.

Companies are short-sighted in believing that training is too expensive in terms of time or effort, but "being too busy to train," Horowitz says, "is the moral equivalent of being too hungry to eat." You can have a company with an amazing fit between its products and what the market wants, but when things go wrong, and they always do, a company with a weak organization or culture can fall apart quickly. When things go wrong in a company with a good organization and culture, it will be a lot more resilient. "Being a good company is an end in itself," Horowitz says. "If you do nothing else, build a good company." Always put people before products and profits.

Even the best companies go through crunch times when they have to lay people off. When doing so, be honest. You can say, "The company failed and in order to move forward, we will have to lose some excellent people." Employees can see that it is not personal, and they can appreciate that things don't go to plan. The person who hired must also be the person who fires. Don't leave it up to HR or "a more sadistic peer." How you lay people off will make your reputation in the industry. Invest in benefits and support to help them as best you can. How you treat the people who have to go is deeply significant for the ones who stay. They will only want to stay in a company that admits its mistakes and does what it can for the ones it let down.

How to scale

Every founder of a successful company faces the problem of how to shift it from a tight group of like-minded individuals with ill-defined roles, to an organization involving hundreds or thousands of people, some of whom you will never know. Imagine a start-up CEO, Horowitz says, who "has complete knowledge of everything in the company, makes all the decisions, needn't communicate with anyone, and is totally aligned with herself. As the company grows, things will only get worse in each dimension. On the other hand, if the company doesn't expand, then it will never be much of a company."

You have to "give ground grudgingly," even if you feel like you are losing control. The quandary is that you don't want to burden your growing company with too much organization, but neither do you want a meltdown as it grows too fast. You will have to spend time getting the organizational processes right, but it's worth it.

The right kind of ambition

Three traits that Horowitz and his colleagues look for when they interview start-up founders are: the ability to articulate a compelling vision that people will want to follow you for (think Steve Jobs); the ability to implement it; and having the right kind of ambition—that is, for the company, not for themselves. Technology companies usually hire for IQ, but if all of the hires are just out to gain for themselves, the company will go nowhere. In contrast, people who are constantly thinking about the company and where it is headed, will be inherently valuable.

What's not being done?

Most meetings are about what you and your team or company are doing, and fixing any problems. But you must also be constantly asking, "What am I not doing?", for example some important product, service, or deal that lies in the shadows and which needs bringing into the light. The other things might improve if you focus on them, but the thing that's *not* being done could transform the company.

Final comments

Not only does nothing prepare you for running a company, Horowitz says, but hardly any management books make the distinction between "peacetime CEO" and "wartime CEO." The kind of leader he was when things were going well was very different to the one he had to become to get his company through a crisis. The friendly, approachable, nurturing approach does not work when there are deep problems in an organization, or you have just lost a major client, or a new technology or a competitor is taking your business from under your feet. Such things require big, drastic moves that will shock the people and investors you have lovingly cultivated in peacetime, but ultimately the worth of any leader is in how they respond in the worst of times. Faced with terrible choices, the best become creative and insist that there is a way out that appears to defy reality.

The Hard Thing About Hard Things is an unusual business book. It combines peering into the soul of the CEO with pages and pages of details on how to run an organization. Much is known now about what works and doesn't work in organizations, and Horowitz's diligence in putting it into words is appreciated. As for the soul-of-the-CEO stuff, if you are ever thrust into a position of leadership, the book will help you not to feel so alone as you begin your white-knuckle ride.

Ben Horowitz

Born in 1966 in London, Horowitz grew up in Berkeley, California, famous for its left-wing politics. He was in the top math stream in high school, but as part of the football team was listening to Run DMC and getting into African-American culture. He has computer science degrees from Columbia University and UCLA. Andreessen Horowitz was founded in 2009 and has invested in over 300 companies including Skype, Facebook, Pinterest, Foursquare, and Twitter.

Steve Jobs

"His personality was reflected in the products he created. Just as the core of Apple's philosophy, from the original Macintosh in 1984 to the iPad a generation later, was the end-to-end integration of hardware and software, so too was the case with Steve Jobs: His passions, perfectionism, demons, desires, artistry, devilry, and obsession for control were integrally related to his approach to business and the products that resulted."

"For Jobs, belief in an integrated approach was a matter of righteousness . . . But in a world filled with junky devices, inscrutable error messages, and annoying interfaces, it led to astonishing products marked by beguiling user experiences. Using an Apple product could be as sublime as walking in one of the Zen gardens of Kyoto that Jobs loved, and neither experience was created by worshipping at the altar of openness or by letting a thousand flowers bloom. Sometimes it's nice to be in the hands of a control freak."

In a nutshell

Great products are about art as much as technology.

In a similar vein

Eric Schmidt & Jonathan Rosenberg *How Google Works*
Brad Stone *The Everything Store*
Ashlee Vance *Elon Musk*

CHAPTER 16

Walter Isaacson

When Steve Jobs contacted Walter Isaacson, whom he had known slightly since the 1980s, and suggested he write a biography of him, Isaacson said no. The *Time* feature writer had only written bios of the long dead—Benjamin Franklin and Albert Einstein—and Jobs's life and career was still clearly a work in progress.

Two things changed his mind: Jobs's wife Laurene told Isaacson that her husband had pancreatic cancer, and so wouldn't be around for ever; and the biographer's realization that Jobs's life had been played out at the intersection of technology and the humanities—much as Franklin's and Einstein's were.

Jobs's "passion for perfection," Isaacson says, "revolutionized six industries: personal computers, animated movies, music, phones, tablet computing, and digital publishing," to which could be added retail stores. Also, "on his second try," Jobs created a company infused with his thinking that would long outlive him.

To write his 600-page book, Isaacson would do over 40 interviews with his subject, and scores more with friends, relatives, colleagues, and enemies. Jobs had no input into, or censure of, what Isaacson wrote. The only thing he was adamant about was the cover. Jobs rejected the original version in favor of one that simply had Albert Watson's stark black-and-white photo, and an unobtrusive title/author line. Simplicity itself, just like an Apple product.

Where it started

One long-time colleague of Jobs, Del Yocam, theorized that Jobs's abandonment by his biological parents (at his birth, in 1955, by University of Wisconsin graduates Joanne Schieble and Abdulfattah Jandali) made him want to be an extreme controller of his environment, and that the products he brought into existence were like an extension of himself. Jobs's deep insecurity about his origins, combined with doting adoptive parents (Paul and Clara Jobs) and his extreme willfulness and intelligence as a child, made him feel like the world was a blank slate to make or remake. As Isaacson puts it, Jobs felt both "abandoned and chosen" at the same time, driven by demons and yet with a superiority complex that often made him insufferable.

Jobs grew up just south of Palo Alto, now the heart of Silicon Valley, in a new subdivision called Mountain View. The houses in the area were built by the developer Joseph Eichler, whose hallmark was simple, inexpensive, yet well-designed homes. The idea that something could be made for the masses yet be elegant and not cost too much, Jobs told Isaacson as they looked over the old house one day, would be the inspiration behind all Apple's products.

In high school Jobs dabbled in marijuana and LSD and read *King Lear*, *Moby-Dick*, Dylan Thomas and Plato. This deep interest in the humanities would make him different to people he started to hang out with, including super-geek Stephen Wozniak, who had spent his youth building calculators and intercom systems.

How it started

Leaving school in the early 1970s, Jobs was obsessed with Bob Dylan, existing on a fruitarian diet, spending time at a commune growing apples (yes, where the name came from) and getting deeply into eastern spirituality. He was not that keen on going to college, but his parents had pledged to his biological mother that he would, and he chose Reed College, a small, expensive liberal arts college in Portland, Oregon. At Reed, Jobs was deeply influenced by books like Ram Dass's *Be Here Now* and Shunryu Suzuki's *Zen Mind, Beginner's Mind* (see *50 Spiritual Classics*), and walked around campus barefoot. To save his parents money he dropped out and went traveling in India. Jobs later felt lucky that he was part of the tail end of Californian counterculture, a generation "raised by Zen, and also by LSD." What the drug did, he said, was show him a bigger picture, of "creating great things instead of making money, putting things back into the stream of history and of human consciousness as much as I could."

But while most hippies thought of computers as a tool for Big Brother, Jobs believed they were a tool for liberation. After a stint working at a new computer games company called Atari, he and friend Wozniak hatched the idea to build a "personal" computer, using Wozniak's brilliance at circuit design. Astonishingly, it was Wozniak who in 1975 created the first machine that, when you typed a character on a keyboard, it showed up as that letter on a screen. Wozniak would have been happy to give away his circuit designs and knowhow to the hobbyist tech community, but Jobs convinced him that they could build and sell their stuff. With an order from an electronics store, and the help of family and friends, the "Apple I" computer was put together in Jobs's parents' garage. All of them were sold, and they were in business.

It was the Apple II, though, a professional-looking machine with a hard case, developed with venture capitalist Mike Markkula's money, that turned a garage outfit into Apple Computer Inc. With the marketing brilliance of Regis McKenna, the Apple II would sell almost 6 million units over the next six years, launching the personal computer industry. In his emphasis on product focus, image, and packaging, Isaacson tells just how important Markkula was to Apple's development, particularly his idea that everything a company does must "impute" its value to the public. Jobs admitted his debt to Markkula in the way that the feel of Apple's products, and even their beautiful, tactile packaging, was designed to condition the user into loving them.

Going mainstream

Many have argued that Apple stole the screen look and layout of its computers from Xerox. Though Jobs and his team were very inspired by what they saw on a visit to Xerox's labs in 1979, the fact is that Xerox was doing nothing to commercialize its "graphical user interface" software. It took Jobs to see how revolutionary it was, Isaacson notes, and push the technology further, creating a much easier to use and cheaper mouse using a ball, and getting his team to produce the overlapping windows effect that we take for granted on our screens today. Xerox did finally release its Xerox Star in 1981, but it was very slow, and at $16,595 prohibitively expensive. Jobs believed Apple could produce something much better, at a fraction of the price. The result was the Macintosh (the McIntosh is a variety of apple), launched in 1984, with its famous Superbowl ad casting IBM as evil.

The Mac succeeded because it made it much easier for the general public to interact with computers. Jobs even made sure that it looked like a human face, to appear friendly. He believed the best products were self-contained "whole widgets" with the software and hardware inextricably bound together in one product, and he didn't want his products contaminated by programmers and hackers who could customize the product to their liking. Jobs had the Macintosh team think of themselves as artists, and even got each of the 45 engineers to have their signatures inscribed on the circuit board of every Mac shipped. His obsession with fonts annoyed the engineers, but for him this was as important as the hardware. He took the team to see an exhibition of Tiffany art at the Met museum in Manhattan. The message: it is possible to produce things of beauty for the mass market, and if the team was creating an object, why not make it beautiful? Andy Hertzfeld, who worked on the Mac, said: "The goal was never to beat the competition, or to make a lot of money. It was to do the greatest thing possible, or a little greater." Jobs's greatest achievement, Isaacson argues, was developing "no merely modest product advances based on focus groups, but whole new devices and services that consumers did not yet know they needed."

By the time Apple went public in 1980, the markets valued it at $1.79 billion. Three hundred people in the firm were made millionaires, and Jobs himself, at 25, was worth $256 million. While he watched Apple colleagues go out and buy mansions and yachts, he preferred well-designed or beautiful things, Isaacson notes, like Porsches, Bosch appliances and Ansel Adams prints. Jobs never traveled with an entourage or had household staff or security. True to his counterculture roots, he preferred to keep life simple.

Back to beautiful basics

After the high of the public offering, over the next decade Apple would increasingly lose market share in the personal computer market to IBM–PC clones running Microsoft software. Jobs worked uneasily with "grown-up" CEO John Sculley, but they had vastly different conceptions of the direction Apple should head in. By 1985 the mismatch came to a head and Jobs was forced to resign.

The story of Jobs's years after his ejection from Apple, and his building of two companies, NeXT (networked workstations) and Pixar (the animation studio), is a book in its own right. Brent Schlender's and Rick Tetzeli's *Becoming Steve Jobs* (see *50 Success Classics*, 2nd edition) covers these years in more detail than Isaacson. Suffice it to say that Apple had become focused on profit maximization, not great products, and predictably it fell into a financial heap.

Jobs returned to Apple in 1997 as an interim leader until the board found someone else, but under some pressure he became permanent. He had a growing family and enjoyed his time at Pixar; it was only his love of Apple, rather than corporate scheming, Isaacson says, that brought him back. He knew that the company had to be relaunched not just with new products (while terminating an array of unsuccessful ones) but by reminding people what Apple stood for. Lee Clow of advertising agency BBDO\Chiat\Day came up with a "Think Different" concept, Isaacson says, "to celebrate not what computers could do, but what creative people could do with computers." Its influential ad spoken by Richard Dreyfuss, and with images of Einstein, Gandhi, Picasso, Ansel Adams, the Dalai Lama, Martha Graham, and others, carried the tag line, "Because the people who are crazy enough to think they can change the world are the ones who do."

The partnership between Jobs and British designer Jonathan "Jony" Ive was crucial to the success of the new Apple. For both men, Jobs said, design did not mean the veneer of something, but "the fundamental soul of a man-made creation that ends up expressing itself in successive outer layers." The way something is manufactured is as important as how it looks and performs. The whole object had to be "pure and seamless," and it was this design sense—bringing art to technology—that would separate the iMac, iPod, iPhone, and the iPad from the rest of the computer market, turning Apple into the most valuable company in the world.

Jobs's name is listed along with those of other inventors for over 200 Apple patents. He was deeply involved in tiny details, such as the magnetic power connector for every iMac, that is so beautiful and satisfying to use. Another Jobs decree was that the iPod have no on–off button. It should just work as soon as a user pressed anything, and go dormant when it was not being used. This feature was later applied to all Apple devices. Ive pushed for the iPod to be "pure white," including the headphones, which looked revolutionary at the time, but Jobs supported him.

Jobs was never afraid of creating products that might cannibalize its existing ones, believing that if you didn't do so, other companies would. He knew that the iPhone, when it came out, would take away a lot of the market for the iPod, and that the iPad would cut deep into sales of iMacs, but this wasn't an issue for him as long as Apple was coming out with products that would create new markets.

Running Apple for the second time, Isaacson notes, Jobs was no longer a tempestuous visionary but a down-to-earth manager who remained passionate and pure about design and engineering quality, while at the same time being the hard-headed CEO who allowed manufacturing to be outsourced. His remaking of Apple was not just about products but building a great *company*. Jobs spent a lot of time finding the best talent, and got the different departments, from engineering to design to marketing, to work together so that new products were all of a piece, avoiding the usual division or silo company structure.

Art and magic

As well as creating iconic products, with the music download site iTunes Apple managed to create a "platform," the holy grail of big tech companies. Millions of users now trusted Apple with their credit card details and email addresses. Jobs oversaw the development of iTunes in the face of piracy. He loved artists and the music they made, and he believed in intellectual property. The record companies were good at creativity and bad at tech, he thought, while it was vice versa for the tech corporations. Jobs's time at Pixar taught him:

"Tech companies don't understand creativity. They don't appreciate intuitive thinking . . . I'm one of the few people who understands how producing technology requires intuition and creativity, and how producing something artistic takes real discipline."

Jobs loved a recording of the Beatles' making of *Strawberry Fields Forever*, which they did over the course of a few months. It took so many iterations to make it right, and provided the perfect analogy for the creative and engineering process at Apple: "It's a lot of work, but in the end it gets better, and soon it's like, 'Wow, how did they do that?!? Where are the screws?'" Jobs, who took great pleasure in lifting the veil on new products at launches, wanted to create art and magic.

He had always hated the idea of Apple products being sold alongside what he felt were lesser brands, like Dell, IBM, or Gateway, and by salespeople working on commission who cared nothing about the brand. Because computers were an infrequent, expensive purchase, people were happy to drive a few miles out of town to big, ugly electronics stores to get them. But he began thinking of Markkula's maxim that everything a great company does must "impute" its value. He convinced Apple's board to invest in the opening of stores that sold only Apple products in the very best main street or mall locations across America. If the company believed it was a bigger brand than Gap, for instance, the stores had to be bigger and smarter than a Gap store. Though Apple executive Ron Johnson developed a prototype store, Jobs was deeply involved and made all the final decisions, obsessing over the layout, the type of flooring used, and the signature staircases.

In 2017 there were 498 Apple stores, spread across America and the globe. Though they make up a fraction of Apple's total revenue, Isaacson notes, "by creating buzz and brand awareness they indirectly helped boost everything the company did."

Final comments

Jobs's Nietzschean "faith in the power of the will to bend reality," Isaacson suggests, is perhaps the mark of all great entrepreneurs. What is, is not good enough, and what could be, must be done. His Rasputin-like ability to hypnotize gave rise to the phrase, "reality distortion field," coined by Bud Tribble, an early Apple software developer. When in Jobs's presence, Tribble recalled, people would agree to ridiculous deadlines because he made them seem possible, or he would convince others of arguments that had no basis in fact. He would constantly dismiss the work of engineers and desires by saying, "This is shit." Some couldn't take it, but others felt the years they worked at Apple were the best of their lives. Despite Jobs's ferocity, his perfectionism made the most of their talents.

Andy Hertzfeld said of Jobs: "He thinks there are a few people who are special—people like Einstein and Gandhi and the gurus he met in India—and he's one of them." It's this side of Jobs, looking to the future of humanity, that made his former girlfriend Chrisann Brennan describe him as "an enlightened being" even if (particularly to her, after he denied he was the father of their child Lisa despite all the evidence) he could be supremely arrogant and cruel.

Jobs's intense desire to "make a dent on the universe" was partly to do with his premonition that he would not live a long life, so he had to work twice as fast as others to fulfil his desires. He traced his health problems to working 14-hour days at Pixar and Apple simultaneously, but when the cancer in his pancreas spread to his liver in 2004, it didn't help that, as a lifetime vegetarian or vegan, he insisted on natural cleansing diets and refused chemotherapy. For most of his life he had succeeded in creating his own reality, but could not prevail against death itself.

Walter Isaacson

Isaacson was born in 1952 in New Orleans. He studied history and literature at Harvard, and was a Rhodes Scholar at Oxford University, leaving with a PPE (Philosophy, Politics, and Economics) degree. His journalism career started with the Sunday Times *in London, and he was hired by* Time *in 1978. He became its editor in 1996. From 2001 to 2003 he was the CEO of CNN, before becoming president of the Aspen Institute, which is funded by various foundations to generate policy ideas and develop leaders. In 2017, he announced his departure in order to become a history professor at Tulane University in New Orleans.*

Isaacson's books include The Innovators: How a Group of Hackers, Geniuses, and Geeks Created the Digital Revolution *(2014),* Einstein: His Life and Universe *(2007),* Benjamin Franklin: An American Life *(2003),* Kissinger: A Biography *(1992), and* Leonardo da Vinci *(2017).*

The Personal MBA

"The vast majority of modern business practice requires little more than common sense, simple arithmetic, and knowledge of a few important ideas and principles."

"While management and leadership are important in the practice of business, they aren't the be-all and end-all of business education: without solid business knowledge, it's possible to organize and lead a group of people toward the accomplishment of the wrong objectives. Business is about the profitable creation and delivery of valuable offers to paying customers—management and leadership are simply a means to this end."

"Unless you work in an industry with unusually aggressive, competent, and well-funded competitors, you really don't have to worry about other people 'stealing' your idea. Ideas are cheap—what counts is the ability to translate an idea into reality."

In a nutshell

A few good books and practical experience will serve you just as well, or better, than going to business school.

In a similar vein

Ben Horowitz *The Hard Thing About Hard Things*
Eric Ries *The Lean Startup*

CHAPTER 17

Josh Kaufman

Every business book has some great new idea that claims to provide an answer, often defying the conventional wisdom taught in business schools. But if we are to judge these ideas properly, shouldn't we first be aware of the conventional wisdom, the core concepts of business practice?

This is the purpose of *The Personal MBA: A World-Class Business Education in a Single Volume*. Kaufman's book doesn't try to replicate the curricula of business schools, but rather presents 248 key business concepts in the clearest way possible.

Reading his book, Kaufman boldly says, will "put you in the top 1 percent of the population" who know how business really works. Perhaps, but at least you will become aware of the concepts that you hear others talking about, and he is right that "Having a common language to label and think about what you notice opens the door to major improvements." Of course there is no substitute for experience, but then many MBA students don't have much experience in the business world either, he notes.

"People always overestimate how complex business is," former General Electric head Jack Welch once said. "This isn't rocket science—we've chosen one of the world's most simple professions." Much of what Kaufman says is common sense, and if you already work in the business world you can skim over many of the chapters. At times the book seems little more than an expanded glossary of business terms. But if you are starting out, or work in the non-profit sector, it is an interesting primer that will make you think about the value of business school education.

MBAs: worth it?

In the movie *Good Will Hunting*, Matt Damon's character Will Hunting mocks Harvard student Clark for spending $150,000 on his education. He would have got the same benefit, Hunting opines, from paying a few dollars in late return fines at his local library.

There are over 12,000 new business books a year, not to mention millions of blog posts on business theory and practice. What Kaufman wanted to know was: What is really worth knowing? While still at university he started publishing his findings on his website. People were immediately interested, but traffic only exploded when blogger and writer Seth Godin linked to Kaufman's reading lists. Godin had previously written, "It's hard for me to understand why [getting an MBA] is a better use of my time and money than actual experience combined with a dedicated reading of 30 or 40 books."

In "The End of Business Schools? Less Success Than Meets the Eye" (*Academy of Management Learning and Education*, 2002), Jeffrey Pfeffer and Christina Fong reported their findings from a study which found "zero correlation" between having an Masters of Business Administration degree, or even doing very well in the MBA, and long-term career success (either in terms of salary or getting top jobs). The implication: What is taught in MBA programs is just not what is needed for succeeding in the real world of business. The fact is, Pfeffer said, "If you are good enough to get in, you obviously have enough talent to do well, regardless."

So what are business schools for? An MBA is a kind of "social proof" to employers that you are aware of certain concepts, that you are reasonably intelligent, and that you're not too much of a maverick. "Business schools don't *create* successful people," Kaufman writes, "They simply *accept* them, then take credit for their success." This doesn't mean that the schools them- selves are worth it. You can get the same education without mortgaging your life with loans that may take decades to pay off. And even if you can justify the costs of tuition by paying it off in a few years with higher wages, you have to account for the opportunity cost of foregoing actual experience in the business world while you spend two years on campus. What top business schools do, Kaufman admits, is increase access to top recruiting firms like Goldman Sachs, McKinsey, *Fortune* 500 firms, and investment banks. However, it is one thing to get hired by a top company. Within three to five years it is very clear that performance is the only thing that matters, and if you don't perform you are still saddled with sometimes colossal debts.

Business schools evolved, Kaufman notes, in a time when big business was king. This means that they can teach some pretty fancy stuff (models, statistics, etc.) and yet the student can come out of the experience without a basic idea of what's needed to start a business. The schools still teach outdated ideas like how to take over a company, load it with debt and seek fast expansion in order to sell it on to another buyer. Yet financial engineering is not what business is about; rather, it's about coming up with new products and services that improve people's lives. Business is a lot more fast-paced than it used to be. You learn fast on the job through constant iteration and innovation, and if you want new or inspiring ideas that your employer might not be providing, then there are plenty of books, blogs, and talks that will widen your perspective. Taking two years out of your life and spending a fortune may not be the smartest way to achieve that. The need to pay off your business school debt may put you on a corporate treadmill that you may soon begin to hate.

First, create value

Kaufman's section on "value creation" is quite basic, but suffice it to say that every successful business must produce something of value that people want, at the right price for them and that makes it worthwhile financially to keep the business going.

Every successful product or service caters to one of the core human drives, such as the desire for social status, to bond, to learn, to feel defended. A business must take full account of human psychology, being very clear on the end result that people are buying (rather than the product itself). What people will pay a premium for is to have some hassle removed: things which require too much time, or are too complex or confusing, or require some prior level of experience or knowledge, or specialized resources they don't have. "If you're looking for a new business idea, start looking for hassles. Where there's hassle, there's opportunity," Kaufman writes. Lots of "massive markets" in the creator's eye don't actually exist. He mentions the Segway: it was interesting technology, but at $5,000 way too expensive to draw people away from simply walking or riding a bike. The Segway has found buyers, but niche ones only.

Kaufman emphasizes the iterative approach to building value, that is, being faithful to a cycle of development, feedback, and change to get your product right. If this feels like a lot of work, it is. Great business plans and product ideas often don't survive their first contact with real customers. Don't just try out products on friends and family, you have to try them on people who may actually be willing to pay for something, and be willing to hear what they say. The more iterative work you do, the better the end product; you get to know the market a lot better, learning exactly what people will pay for. If there's no demand, you can quickly move on to another idea.

Creating a Minimum Viable Offer, that is, something which seems to be valuable to people and which you think you can make a business out of, can mean launching before you feel ready. Yet as LinkedIn founder Reid Hoffman put it, "If you're not embarrassed by the first version of your product, you've launched too late." Once it's out there, you can make many frequent adjustments to the core offering, adding things and taking some things away. "Pick three key attributes or features, get those things very, very right, and then forget about everything else," said Paul Buccheit, who created Google's Gmail and AdSense. "By focusing on only a few core features in the first version, you are forced to find the true essence and value of the product."

Then sell the thing

All marketing, Kaufman suggests, is about focusing on the "End Result," that is whether people believe they will feel sophisticated, intelligent, powerful, healthy, happy, or prosperous after using your product. Efforts to sell something must involve as much sensory stimuli as possible about your product or service so that people can easily visualize themselves using it. And it helps to have some hook or tag line that focuses not on the features of the product, but on its benefits. Apple's slogan for its first iPod, "1,000 songs in your pocket," was a lot more alluring than a statement about the wonders of MP3 technology.

Remember that most of the marketing work with any product or service is done while it is being created. "Advertising is the tax you pay for being unremarkable," as Robert Stephens put it. If your offering is a commodity much like your competitors', massive resources will have to go into sales and marketing to twist people's arm. You may create a business this way, but it is not a long-term basis for success.

Business books constantly talk about "branding," but in Kaufman's mind a brand is simply a reputation. Reputations arise spontaneously, and so you are never really in control of them. The only thing you can do is work to improve your service constantly, so that people start talking about it. Word of mouth, and trust, are always the best kinds of marketing. When you do engage in advertising, PR, and marketing, the only rule is not to be boring. There is no harm in generating some controversy if it leads to people wanting more information on what you are doing.

Finally, remember that "Your customers want to be heroes." Tell stories about the devoted customers you already have, in order to attract more. "The more vivid, clear, and emotionally compelling the story, the more prospects you'll attract."

Financial nuts and bolts

Every business involves five elements, Kaufman notes: value creation, marketing, sales, value delivery, and finance. If you have little knowledge on the latter, the book is quite useful, covering terms you will have heard of but were never quite clear on:

Discounted cash flow/net present value   Working out what an asset is worth now, taking into account the cash it will generate over several years.

Cash flow statement   A financial snapshot of a company within a certain period of time that will clearly record what is being spent on operations, investments in future production, and financing costs.

Balance sheet   This shows the company's assets and liabilities (not just cash) at any one time, indicating its net worth, or the "owner's equity." Balance sheets can involve various assumptions, such as the worth of a brand name or reputation, or estimates of the value of the company's inventory.

Free cash flow   How much cash is coming in, minus money needed for the capital equipment and assets needed to keep the company running. The more free cash flow you have the better, as it can be used instead of debt to keep generating production and business.

Profit margin   Profit expressed as a percentage, calculated on the difference between your revenue and what you have spent to gain it.

Accrual accounting   In which revenue for a sale or a service is immediately matched up with the expenses used to make the sale, giving a much more accurate picture of ongoing profit margins.

Income statement   A picture of profit within a certain period of time; crucial for seeing what is really working in your business and so helping decisions on where to invest.

Financial ratios   They are many but they include profit margin, return on investment (ROI), debt to equity (too much leverage isn't usually a good thing), interest coverage (how much of the business's profit has to be spent on paying interest on debt), and liquidity (whether a company is about to go bankrupt, or conversely is sitting on a cash mountain).

Amortization   Spreading the cost of some capital asset you've bought over time. If you've bought some software for $500 and will gain revenue from the use of it over the next five years, you could account for the purchase as $100 each year. Amortization can make capital purchases seem more justifiable.

Receivables   Promises of payment from others, which can be used in some forms of accounting.

Purchasing power   Cash in the bank combined with available credit you can access. The amount of purchasing power you have can be decisive for your business's survival.

The last half of *The Personal MBA* includes sections on "The Human

Mind," "Working With Yourself," and "Working With Others." These cover thinking biases in the Daniel Kahneman mold, how to manage your energy, and negotiation strategies, but won't be anything new if you've read a few popular psychology and personal development books. The book ends with sections on understanding, analyzing, and improving systems.

Final comments

In a review of the book, *Management Today* noted an almost "theological divide" between people who believe in the value of MBAs, and those who side with Jeffrey Pfeffer that the more ubiquitous the degree has become, the lower its value. But can reading a book really replace the projects and group work you do in an intense MBA, not to mention the contacts you make? Can you really "own" the concepts in the book without doing your own case studies in a classroom environment with skilled teachers?

The question of whether or not to do an MBA will depend on your circumstances, but the wisest approach is not to ask what the degree can "do" for you, but what you want to learn. For instance, someone from an engineering or a non-profit background could really increase their career chances in the long term through a deeply immersive, quality MBA program that gives them an awareness of business theory and strategy. The ability to apply analytical models to business situations, or in seeing possible new markets, could separate them from their peers. On the other hand, for someone who has worked in business for years, and simply wants to burnish their credentials, it could be a waste of time and money.

At one extreme is Kaufman's book, which is little more than a business education starter; at the other, the expensive, time-consuming in-house MBA. Another alternative is the profusion of MBA equivalents online. Most of the top business schools, including Wharton, Chicago Booth, Stanford, and MIT, run free or low cost programs with lectures by leading academics, either on their own or through platforms such as Coursera.

Josh Kaufman

Kaufman grew up in a farming town in northern Ohio, with a librarian mother and teacher father. "Books were a major part of my life, but business was not," he recalls. After the University of Cincinnati, in 2005 he began a three-year stint at Procter & Gamble with roles in product development, production, marketing, and major retailer distribution. Frustrated with turf battles and the slow pace of change, he left P & G to become a full-time business educator.

His other book is The First 20 Hours: How to Learn Anything . . . Fast *(2014).*

The Art of the Start

*"The best reason to start an organization is to make meaning—
to create a product or service that makes the world a better
place. So your first task is to decide how you can make
meaning."*

*"BE SPECIFIC. The more precisely you can describe your
customer, the better. Many entrepreneurs are afraid of being
'niched' to death and then not achieving ubiquity. However,
most successful companies started off targeting specific markets
and grew (often unexpectedly) to great size by addressing
other segments. Few started off with grandiose goals and
achieved them."*

In a nutshell

**Before anything else, the fundamental purpose in starting any new
enterprise is to create meaning.**

In a similar vein

Richard Branson *Losing my Virginity*
Ben Horowitz *The Hard Thing About Hard Things*
Eric Ries *The Lean Startup*
Howard Schultz *Pour Your Heart Into It*
Simon Sinek *Start With Why*

CHAPTER 18

Guy Kawasaki

When he sat down to write *The Art of the Start*, software company founder, venture capitalist, and former chief "evangelist" (promoter) for Apple Computer, Guy Kawasaki, made the assumption that anyone wanting to start a new enterprise does not want to get bogged down in theory—they want to change the world. His aim was to "cut the crap," providing only really useful information. One of his first insights is that being an entrepreneur is more a state of mind than a job title, and he covers the psychological and spiritual side of being one as well as revealing vital practical strategies.

He wrote the book, he notes, not just for Silicon Valley types, but for anyone wanting to create a great organization. This includes people within existing companies who want to bring great new products or services to market, and even "saints" wanting to start schools, churches, and not-for-profit bodies. Organizations may or may not be set up in order to make money, but what they must all have is a meaningful reason for being.

Meaning and mantra

The best reason for starting anything new, Kawasaki says, is to *make meaning*. "Meaning" can include simply trying to make the world a better place, but can also mean righting a wrong or saving something good from ending. When he joined Apple, the company got its meaning from the mission to replace IBM's typewriters with its Macintosh computers. Later, it was driven by the wish to overtake Microsoft and its Windows operating system. His point is that you need to have a reason for being that will make you want to go to work in the morning, a great challenge separate to money or perks.

The world is full of boring corporate "mission statements," but who remembers them or believes in them? Much better, Kawasaki says, to have a *mantra* (a "sacred verbal formula" or incantation that involves power and emotion) that encapsulates the meaning of your organization. It will be short enough for everyone to know it and believe in it, and it doesn't even have to be written down. Coca-Cola's mission statement, for instance, is "The Coca-Cola company exists to benefit and refresh everyone it touches." But its mantra, if it had one, Kawasaki says, would be a simple and powerful

Refresh the world. There is a difference between mantras (which are really for the employees) and tag lines, which are for customers. Nike's tag line is "Just do it," but its mantra is *Authentic athletic performance*.

Kawasaki provides many tips for recruiting and choosing the right people for your organization, but the main one is to hire people who believe in your meaning or vision, even if they lack qualifications or experience. Through these "soul mates" great organizations are built, not—as myth suggests—through a single individual. Many have a driving force or a figurehead, but dig a bit deeper and you discover they had business soul mates who made the dream a reality.

What you do, how you do it

Kawasaki points out that good business models (often overlooked in the dot. com world) are fundamental to success. You can have endless innovation in other areas, but your business model (or how you reliably make your money) must be down to earth—chances are, yours will be a variation on one that already exists. You should be able to sum it up in ten words or less. Kawasaki's unusual tip is to first run your business model concept by women. He has found through experience that women are much more realistic and savvy about the real economic chances of an idea.

You may be afraid of creating too small a niche for your product, but he points out that all large, successful companies initially grew from very specific products aimed at small markets. These segments grew, revealing other, usually unexpected markets. Even Microsoft started off with a "sliver" of a market (a particular programming language, BASIC, for a particular operating system), which expanded and revealed further potential customers and products. This is the real way to success, he says, not in having grandiose goals.

He suggests weaving a "MAT"—of milestones, assumptions, and tasks—for your organization. You need to have clear goals you want to reach, you need to know the assumptions that are part of your business model, and you need to know what tasks have to be fulfilled to create a great organization.

Pitches and plans

In the era of the "elevator pitch" and groveling to possible financiers, Kawasaki makes a radical suggestion, presaging Eric Ries: don't focus on pitches and plans and actually start making and selling your product first. Get customers almost before you start your business. Business plans for start-up enterprises have limited use, since they are all based on unknowns. You cannot predict the future of something with no track record. It is implementation and execution that matters. Although business plans can be a good exercise for the people involved to clarify aims, and investors do require them, in fact a plan is unlikely to sway an investor one way or the other. They will probably have already made up their minds earlier, and the plan just provides confirmation of their position.

Whenever you do give a pitch or presentation, he writes, imagine a little man sitting on your shoulder who, every time you say something, says "So what?" This will prevent you from assuming that what you are saying is self-evident, awe-inspiring, or even interesting. Instead, whenever you make a general statement, back it up with an example. People want to know how something works *in practice*.

Bootstrapping

The alternative to receiving a cushion of money from venture capitalists or other investors for your enterprise is bootstrapping—starting with very little and keeping costs skeletal.

The primary consideration for a bootstrapped business, Kawasaki writes, is not establishing market share, growth, or paper profits, but cash flow. At least in the early stages, you need to have regular cash coming in even at the expense of longer term, more profitable sales. This means getting your product to the market as soon as possible, even if it is not perfect. If you would let your own parents use your product in its current state, Kawasaki says, then ship it. Even if you only sell it to a limited market, you are getting cash revenues coming in plus real world feedback. This allows you to put out a better version sooner. The downside is you risk your reputation. However, perhaps it is better to have a reputation to risk than no business at all.

Such things make your enterprise into a lean machine focused on results and execution. If you start with a lot of venture capital behind you, he says, it can be like steroids: they can give you an initial boost, but could also kill you. Fund your business from cash, and it will be a strong one from the beginning.

Rules of marketing

To sell a lot of whatever you are making, the product itself has to be effective, simple, and focused. In the words of Peter Drucker, "It should do only one thing, otherwise, it confuses. If it is not simple, it won't work."

In launching it, the key word is "contagion." That is, once people hear about it or use it, they can't stop telling others about it, and buzz is created.

But to reach your largest potential market, you must lower the barriers to entry (make it cheaper or easier to use) so that more people use it and know about it. These people create excitement, which attracts the press, who will write about you, providing free, credible advertising.

People make the mistake of taking their company too seriously. Kawasaki advises to "achieve humanness" in your marketing. This could include featuring users of your product in your marketing materials, making fun of yourself in your advertising, targeting the young, or diverting some of your resources to the needy. He also counsels to "Make friends before you need them—and even before they can help you." In his role at Apple, he assisted journalists from sources no one had ever heard of, not just the *New York Times* or *Forbes*. Later, many of these journalists had moved to larger media organizations, and they remembered.

Kawasaki also gives these tips on naming your enterprise:

- The name should start with a letter early in the alphabet, so you are always at the top of any list
- Don't have numbers in the name
- Have a name with verb potential (e.g. "Xerox it," "Google her")
- Avoid trendiness (e.g. lower-case letters)

"The art of being a mensch"

Mensch is a Yiddish word meaning someone who does what's right and helps people. If you want to build a great company, Kawasaki says, you must have high moral and ethical standards, to set the example for others. For instance, observe the spirit of agreements and always pay for what you receive, whether charged for it or not.

The right thing is not always the easiest thing to do, but you have to create good karma. Helping people who have no way of returning the favor is a way of thanking the universe for the many gifts you have received, including family and friends, good health and economic success.

Final comments

Wealth and prosperity always begin with an idea, but ideas alone are not worth much. As Kawasaki points out, the art of getting an enterprise off to a good start combines both the practical and the psychological. Not many books of this type exhort the reader to focus on "creating meaning" and "being a mensch," while at the same time making sure you have a reliable business model and good cash flow. Yet to overlook either aspect will ensure a business dies or is less than it might have been. To prosper long term, you must have both meaning and nobility of intention, *and* business smarts about the practical things. This holistic view is what makes *The Art of the Start* a worthwhile read.

Despite the book's strong technology industry focus, most of its lessons can be applied to the establishment of anything new, and indeed its subtitle makes the claim, *The time-tested, battle-hardened guide for anyone starting anything*. This includes having children, no less, and Kawasaki notes in his dedication, "A child is the ultimate startup. I have three. This makes me rich." Just as the decision to have a child should not be taken casually, requiring years of loving attention and hard work, so starting a business should not be entered into without sufficient motivation. This is why "making meaning" is of primary importance. If you have a "why" (a powerful reason to do what you are doing), you will be able to cope with, and see beyond, any kind of "how" (obstacles, difficulties) that life throws your way.

Guy Kawasaki

Kawasaki was born in 1954 in Honolulu, Hawaii. After leaving school he went to Stanford University, graduating in 1976 with a major in psychology. He attended law school briefly before doing an MBA at the University of California, Los Angeles. While still a student he began working in the jewelry business. His success in sales, plus a growing interest in software, led to his hiring at Apple.

Kawasaki founded Garage Technology Ventures, a venture capital firm. He is presently "chief evangelist" for Canva, the online graphics tool, and is an Executive Fellow at the Haast School of Business at the University of California, Berkeley. In 2015–16 he was on the board of the Wikimedia Foundation, and is involved with Jimmy Wales's WikiTribune news project.

A noted speaker, his other books include Rules for Revolutionaries *(1999),* Enchantment: The Art of Changing Hearts, Minds, and Actions *(2012),* The Art of Social Media *(2014,) and* Word of Mouth Marketing *(2015).* The Art of the Start 2.0 *(2015) is a revised version of the original book.*

Obliquity

"High-level objectives—living a fulfilling life, creating a successful business, producing a distinguished work of art, glorifying God—are almost always too imprecise for us to have any clear idea how to achieve them. That doesn't imply that these goals lack meaning or the capacity for realisation. We understand their meaning and realise them by translating them into intermediate goals and actions; we interpret and reinterpret them as we gain knowledge about the environment in which we operate. That is why successful approaches are oblique rather than direct."

"Happiness is not achieved through the pursuit of happiness. The most profitable businesses are not the most profit-oriented. The wealthiest people are not those most assertive in the pursuit of wealth. The greatest paintings are not the most accurate representations of their subjects, the forests most resistant to fires are not the ones whose foresters are most successful in extinguishing fires. Soviet planners managed the economy far less successfully than the adaptive, disorganised processes in market economies."

In a nutshell

To fulfill their potential, people and organizations need higher-level goals that go beyond their own gain or profit.

In a similar vein

Jim Collins *Great by Choice*
Guy Kawasaki *The Art of the Start*
Douglas McGregor *The Human Side of Enterprise*
Simon Sinek *Start With Why*

CHAPTER 19

John Kay

The word "obliquity" comes from Sir James Black, the British chemist who won a Nobel Prize and whose research led to billions of dollars' worth of prescription drug profits while working at ICI, then SmithKline and Glaxo. Black was never interested in the profit side, only the research. He often told his colleagues that the path to profits was *not* through research. But in later admitting how wrong he was, Black arrived at the principle of obliquity, that "goals are often best achieved without intending them."

This chimed with what John Kay, a British economist, had observed in successful companies and economies. In *Obliquity: Why Our Goals Are Best Achieved Indirectly*, he argues that we kid ourselves that our deft planning and control will lead to our intended outcomes. The world is too complex for that. Given that rational control is hubris, is it not better to have qualitative rather than quantitative goals?

The oblique path to business success

When chemicals giant ICI's mission statement was "to serve customers internationally through the responsible application of chemistry," it was highly successful. Then it was changed to this: "to be the industry leader in creating value for customers and shareholders through market leadership, technological edge and a world competitive cost base." The application of chemistry to the improvement of life created a lot more value, ironically, than "creating value for shareholders" through a "world competitive cost base."

During Bill Allen's time as head of Boeing from 1945 to 1968 it developed the 737, the most successful airliner in history. When it began development of the 747, which would define commercial aviation for decades, a non-executive director of the firm sought information on projected "return on investment." He was brushed off, because those running the company were on the side of the engineers, not the accountants. "Boeing created the most commercially successful aircraft company, not through love of profit," Kay writes, "but through love of planes. The oblique approach to profitability delivered spectacular results." Boeing lost its way when new CEO Phil Condit forged an emphasis on unit cost reduction and shareholder value, and moved the executive headquarters from Seattle to Chicago, to be closer to

Washington. The result was a share price that climbed at first, then stagnated, and the company was accused of corrupt practices with politicians.

"Maximizing shareholder value," General Electric head Jack Welch once said, "is not a strategy that helps you know what to do when you come to work every day." Indeed. Kay notes that "people who work in a business generally know its nature well enough to see instrumentality at work." By "instrumentality" he means the feeling of being used. Marks & Spencer did so well through the decades because staff knew the company cared about them, beyond concerns for the bottom line. For Simon Marks it was simply about the sort of company he wanted to build. This created remarkable loyalty amongst its staff. They knew that the company's welfare policy was "adopted as a statement of values, not from a calculation of consequences."

Let's remember why we do this

In *Built to Last: Successful Habits of Visionary Companies* (1994), Jim Collins and Jerry Porras looked at pharmaceutical company Merck. They quoted its founder George Merck: "We never try to forget that medicine is for the people. It is not for the profits. The profits follow, and if we have remembered that, they have never failed to appear. The better we have remembered that, the larger they have been."

Fifteen years later, in *How the Mighty Fall*, Collins and Porras revisited the Merck story, noting that CEO Ray Kilmartin had implemented a new company mission: "being a top-tier growth company." This apparently innocuous aim resulted in overvigorous marketing of products like Vioxx, which caused heart complaints in some people and led to extensive payouts through litigation. Compare this to Johnson & Johnson's credo, written by Robert Johnson in 1943, which begins "We believe our first responsibility is to the doctors, nurses and patients, to mothers and fathers and all others who use our products and services." Only in the last line of the J&J mission statement do we find "when we operate according to these principles, the stockholders should realise a fair return."

After comparing similar-sized companies in the same industries, Collins and Porras happened on the counterintuitive fact that, "the company that put more emphasis on profit in its declaration of objectives was the less profitable in its financial statements." The list of companies who put money alone ahead of all else, Kay notes, with the top people paying themselves huge amounts, is long. While Lehman Brothers when bankrupt in 2008, rather than taking responsibility, CEO Dick Fuld kept trying to justify his $300 million remuneration. As Kay wryly puts it, "A corporate culture that extols greed is, in the end, unable to protect itself against its own employees."

Companies that succeed in the long term value teamwork and love the business they are in; it is not all about the outcomes.

The myth of rational decisiveness

Political Scientist Charles Lindblom is known for his decision-making theory of "muddling through." Kay argues that muddling through is actually a more effective way to run a company's decision-making processes over the long term than a single, rational evaluation of the options in the light of defined objectives. Lindblom's approach is doing what seems best in the moment from a few limited alternatives, based on a consensus of people, even if there is no clear rationale for doing it.

This sounds fuzzy, but Kay gives the example of the early days of Walmart, when it was still a family business. Sam Walton did not look at the whole of the USA and make a rational decision about where to open his first store, based on market information. He opened in Bentonville because it was where he lived, and opened the second (also in a smaller town) because his wife didn't want to move to a big city.

Lindblom's muddling through is not simply an intuitive, disorganized process. It is disciplined and ordered to the extent that one makes a decision only in the light of current information; there must be willingness to change course quickly if need be. This realist path does not seem as attractive as a top-down solution that aims to clear away the confusion. Yet such solutions inevitably fail because they don't take full account of the ever-changing environment, and the need to change our objectives according to it, to achieve our larger aim. Napoleon thought that his victories were the result of his intention and planning. Tolstoy saw it differently: great battles involving many thousands of men took their own course. As Kay puts it, "Outcomes arise through complex processes whose totality no one fully grasps." If that is the case, our decision-making processes should be a lot more modest.

Kay discusses the architect Corbusier's wish to start everything from scratch, throwing away the old models of his profession. He conceived houses as "machines for living in." Yet there is a difference between a house and a home, which emerges over time and is the result of people's experiences, views, and emotions. "An oblique approach recognises that what we want from a home, or a community, has many elements," Kay writes. "We will never succeed in specifying fully what they are, and to the extent that we do, we discover that they are often incompatible and inconsistent." Notre-Dame in Paris, he notes, was built by thousands of hands over several centuries.

The "sweeping aside history" school of thought includes Pol Pot, the French revolutionaries, and Lenin, but its spirit lives on in the business literature, Kay notes, in books such as *Reengineering the Corporation* (Michael Hammer and James Champy). Companies that are struggling yearn for a quick fix, but in oversimplifying a problem, error quickly creeps in. In contrast, by accepting complexity, prescriptions are more likely to be realistic and actually work. It may be that the best prescription for an ailing company is simply to return to its core values and treat its people well.

Final comments

Kay ran an economics consultancy for 10 years, and realized that the models he was selling to clients weren't really being used, or at least not in the way he intended. Companies bought economic modeling programs, he noticed, simply to justify decisions they had already made. And yet, there was nothing wrong with this. A good subjective decision-making process works much better than a weak qualitative one. Our knowledge of the social, commercial, and natural environment will only ever be imperfect and partial, therefore our best hope for achieving anything substantial and lasting is greater openness to complexity and difference. This sounds ethereal, but is rooted in economic fact. As Adam Smith observed, a complex system such as a free-market economy works even though no single person has knowledge of the whole, yet it still allows for an efficient allocation of resources. Compare this to the failure of socialist planned economies.

Oblique approaches are less muscular and seem more unsatisfying at the time, but often end up being more successful because they take full account of reality and human irrationality. More importantly, they allow organizations to have missions or goals that cannot be quantified, and indeed pursue things that often make no sense—at least in the short term—in respect of the bottom line. As Sir James Black observed, it's only in pursuing higher-level objectives that you can create an organization that is motivated to outperform. Profit can only come as a result of the greater meaning and value that you provide the world and the people that work for you.

John Kay

Born in 1948 in Edinburgh, Kay studied at Oxford University and taught economics there in the 1970s. He was research director and director at London's Institute for Fiscal Studies for several years before becoming, in 1986, a professor at the London Business School. He was the first head of Oxford University's Saïd Business School in the late 1990s, and has been a columnist for the Financial Times *since 1995.*

Kay has advised the British government on the effectiveness of the City of London's equity markets, and was an adviser to the First Minister of Scotland from 2007 to 2011. He received the CBE award in 2014 for services to economics.

His other books include Foundations of Corporate Success *(1993),* The Long and the Short of it: Finance and Investment for Normally Intelligent People who are Not in the Industry *(2009, 2016), and* Other People's Money: The Real Business of Finance *(2015).*

Penguin and the Lane Brothers

"Switched-on, progressive, accessible. Reader-focused, reader-engaged, reader-respecting. With its low-price, mass-distribution model, and a flourishing list encompassing literature, science, politics, journalism, education, children's books, classics, cooking, maps, music, games, art, architecture, history, sociology, humour and sex, Penguin became a vast 'poor man's university,' and a prototype internet made from paper and ink."

"Small, legible typefaces, paper covers, the 'ideal' rectangular format, low prices, good design, ornithological branding, colour coding, mass printing, mass distribution—the Lanes did not invent any of the elements that came together in the making of Penguin; all were freely available in the public domain, and several had been there for centuries. But the Lanes melded and branded and delivered a compelling combination of the parts."

In a nutshell

There is always a huge market for things that people want that, with a sudden drop in price, they can now afford.

In a similar vein

W. Chan Kim & Renée Mauborgne *Blue Ocean Strategy*
Richard Koch & Greg Lockwood *Simplify*

CHAPTER 20

Stuart Kells

They are so much a part of modern life that it is easy to take them for granted. Yet starting in the 1930s, Penguin paperbacks revolutionized publishing by bringing high-grade fiction authors and knowledge to the masses. With its cheap but highly attractive titles covering fiction and non-fiction—a "poor man's university"—the Penguin brand became so hot that its 1961 share offering was oversubscribed by 15,000 percent. The public face of the company, Allen Lane, was feted in a way that Facebook's Mark Zuckerberg is today.

There are existing biographies of Allen Lane, "the eldest, craftiest and most thrusting" of the Lane brothers who founded Penguin, but Stuart Kells, an Australian antiquarian book expert and writer, believed it was time that Lane's two brothers, Richard and John, got more credit. Kells argues that it was the creative opposition between the three brothers that drove Penguin forward, and for the first seven years of the publisher's existence they ran it together as a triumvirate. John Lane's death in World War Two ended the partnership, and thereafter Allen and Richard were more rivals than friends, but the Penguin concept was so powerful that it became "one of the first truly global media businesses," Kells notes. Penguin's merger with Random House in 2013 created a £2.4 billion enterprise.

For the business reader, *Penguin and the Lane Brothers: The Untold Story of a Publishing Revolution* comes with perhaps too much information on the lives of its founders, but it conveys something of the excitement of book publishing in its heyday, and more importantly, shows how innovation can suddenly shake up a tradition-bound industry.

Little penguins

Allen Williams was born in 1902, followed by Richard in 1905, John in 1908, and a sister, Nora, in 1911. The children enjoyed an idyllic childhood in Bristol and its west of England rural surrounds, and the boys left school early without the requisites for university.

Allen was all set for an agricultural life when a distant uncle of the boys' mother, John Lane, owner of famous publishing house The Bodley Head (after the book-loving philanthropist Thomas Bodley), offered Allen a job with the firm in London, with a view to eventually inheriting it (Lane had no children of his own). After a family meeting it was agreed that Allen would take the job, but it came with a condition. He (and his siblings) had to change his surname to Lane.

The Bodley Head was the cutting-edge publisher of Oscar Wilde and the art of Aubrey Beardsley, and had led book marketing with window displays and advertising. Allen was suddenly thrown from the provinces into the headiness of London literary life. During his apprenticeship with John Lane he traveled to Paris to meet Anatole France and André Maurois, had tea with Thomas Hardy at the Dorchester in London, and became friends with Agatha Christie, another Bodley Head author. As the scion of a respected publishing house, Lane began to enjoy a playboy existence.

While Allen was living the life in London, younger brother Richard endured a horrible three-year experience as an indentured farm laborer in South Australia and New South Wales under the (later discredited) Barwell Boys scheme. Living in rundown shacks with no books, he became determined to carve out a literary life back in England. When he eventually made it back, Richard first worked in a bookshop, then became the secretary of the First Edition Club, which published high-quality books in handsome bindings for a price. He starting reading manuscripts for The Bodley Head, then was formally brought into the fold as a traveling sales rep for the company. Later he became the key contact for dealing with authors and literary agents, and more than Allen was a genuine bibliophile. Meantime, younger brother John had also moved to London. He worked in the City of London for a time and was good at actuarial tables, but was after a long trip abroad put in charge of foreign sales at The Bodley Head.

Cut adrift

Everything changed for the brothers in 1925. Uncle John died suddenly, followed by his wife, the exotic and independently wealthy Annie, in 1927. She left her sizable fortune to the Lane children, and along with cash, Allen Lane now had the majority shareholding in The Bodley Head.

Yet the years following John Lane's death were more of a slide downward than a new dawn for the company. Editorially, The Bodley Head was no longer cutting-edge, the brothers found it hard to get the price–product combination right, and during the Great Depression they had to fight off insolvency. Ultimately, Kells notes, publishing is a business involving a trade-off between costs (commissioning a book from authors, and having them printed), and expected demand (which means investing in production and a certain print run). It is easy to underestimate costs and overestimate demand, or charge too much or too little for a book, leading to losses. Allen Lane frequently made rash decisions of this type, which the more hard-headed Richard would have to countermand.

With the firm commercially adrift and its editorial and business model seemingly broken, the brothers were desperate to experiment with new kinds of books and new publishing models. Yet they did not own the whole firm, and were accountable to other shareholders. They arrived at an unusual solution. The firm's board agreed to let them do their experimenting, on the agreement that it would be undertaken separately to the normal financial affairs of the company, and was personally underwritten by the brothers; they would bear any losses—and gain any profits.

The first enterprise of this "firm within a firm" was Peter Arno's *Parade*, with its racy cartoons, which sold well and gave them some confidence. Their next success was the British publication of James Joyce's *Ulysses*, which had been banned for years, and whose ban had only recently been lifted in the United States. The Lanes got around further prosecution by issuing the book as a limited run in a luxury binding.

Their tight fraternal unit was made even tighter by the fact that the brothers lived together in a London flat. Eccentrically, they spent a lot of time hanging out in its newly refurbished bathroom, which became the firm's "de facto boardroom, control center and innovation shop."

Alternatives: this might just work

Despite some success with small-run, high-end publishing, the Depression got the brothers thinking in the other direction: large runs of well-known fiction reprints at a low price. In the 1930s, Kells notes, the average new hardback book cost 7 shillings, which made it a luxury for most people. In the pages of *The Bookseller*, George Bernard Shaw called for cheaper books for the average person, while on the other side of the argument, Sir Stanley Unwin warned that more affordable editions would cannibalize sales of hardbacks, reducing margins for publishers.

These arguments assumed a trade-off between quality and cost. People could get their cheaper editions, but as costs would have to be cut to the bone, the books would look and feel cheap, compared to nice hardbacks. Yet Richard Lane began to think, why couldn't books "sell for peanuts *and* be well made"?

The story of Penguin's birth goes that, one day, Allen Lane was waiting on a train platform and couldn't find anything good to read in the station newsstand. The only fiction available was dull, small, cheap editions, such as the Reader's Library. There and then, Lane resolved to bring out a line of top fiction books with nice covers at an affordable price. Unfortunately, Kells says, the evidence suggests that the story was a fabrication, a "garage myth" like the founding stories of great tech companies, that purposely leaves out the many other collaborators and factors involved. For instance, a young bookkeeper at The Bodley Head, H. A. W. Arnold, had proposed to Allen Lane that the firm could sell cheap paperbacks for only sixpence (around two to three dollars in today's money) by using titles that were out of copyright, undercutting Everyman's Library editions. Meanwhile a European publisher, Albatross Verlag, was selling a range of colorful, low-cost paperbacks on the Continent. Albatross had proposed a tie-up with The Bodley Head that would involve sharing print costs, allowing it to sell a similar range to the English-speaking market.

While rejecting the partnership, the Lane brothers started planning a British "Albatross." But they had to come up with a name. Dolphins and phoenixes had already been used as emblems by other publishers, but the penguin—with its sharp black and white coloring—would lend itself well to printing in black ink, and seemed to be in the popular imagination at the time, with a new penguin enclosure at London Zoo.

In business case terms, to reach its desired price point of sixpence for the Penguin series, authors would need to be paid a very low royalty, and print runs would have to be very large to make any money. The idea of cheaper books for the masses was nothing new, Kells notes, but it had become suddenly more possible because of book world innovations including: machine typesetting, which meant precise and economical printing; a new ability to print covers in bright colors; and new kinds of paper stock that looked and felt better. Another big factor that favored the idea of the "Penguin" series was the fact that literacy was now almost universal in rich countries, and with a growing population the reading market had never been bigger.

The brothers planned the covers for the first batches of Penguin books. Novels would be orange, crime titles would be green, and biographies blue. The first group of ten authors published included Agatha Christie, Ernest Hemingway, Compton Mackenzie, André Maurois, and Dorothy L. Sayers. They would need to sell 17,000 copies of each, Richard Lane worked out, just to break even. This was a big ask, given that all the books had been published in some form before, either by The Bodley Head or other publishers, and at a time when books rarely sold more than a few thousand copies.

Success: march of the penguins

The series had to received orders of 200,000 to recoup its costs, but by the time of the release date, in August 1935, the brothers had only secured 70,000. The bold move now seemed like hubris, a certain failure.

Yet the bright orange covers lent themselves well to window displays. In the grayness of Depression Britain, Penguins looked different and rather wonderful, and people started buying them, if only to collect. When discount store Woolworths made an order for 60,000 copies, the brothers began to think they had a success on their hands. Unusual distribution channels such as Woolworths, going beyond regular bookshops, would be key to the high volumes that Penguin needed to succeed.

Now, the main problem was not getting orders, but fulfilling them. The brothers leased the airless, windowless crypt of Holy Trinity Church on London's Euston Road as their warehouse, and began working night and day to get copies shipped. With printing after printing, within four months the Penguin series had sold a million copies, and within a year, an astonishing 3 million. At the start of 1936 the brothers formed a new company, Penguin Books Limited, and in the same year, the ailing Bodley Head was wound up.

Penguin expanded quickly in the late 1930s. Pelican, a successful non-fiction offshoot with distinctive light blue colors, kicked off with George Bernard Shaw's *The Intelligent Woman's Guide to Socialism and Capitalism*, followed by an Apsley Cherry-Garrard book on the polar explorer Scott. Working with the war authorities, Penguin launched the Forces Book Club, providing tens of thousands of copies of each title to serving soldiers. That Penguin was able to do this at a time of paper rationing says something about deepening links between it and the British state. Over the course of the war, the publisher became a national cultural institution not unlike the BBC, albeit privately owned. Its ubiquitousness included the issue of 600 titles (new or reprints), starting a children's imprint, Puffin, and even launching an art journal, *Modern Painters*.

Maturity and legacy

John Lane's death while serving on a British ship during World War Two changed the dynamic between the remaining two brothers. The flamboyant Allen cultivated the perception that Penguin and he were one and the same, but it was Richard, the down-to-earth book lover, who continued to drive the literary output of Penguin, whose postwar successes included sales of Graham Green and Virginia Woolf in large numbers. Also in the postwar period, the brothers worked on cementing Penguin's presence in America; some of the people they employed took the idea of cheap-but-good paperback publishing and formed new houses, including Bantam and Signet. Richard and Allen also spent time in Australia, helping to turn Penguin into a major publisher there. In time, Australia would account for a quarter of Penguin's worldwide sales.

Penguin's 1959 publication of D. H. Lawrence's racy *Lady Chatterley's Lover* after a celebrated court case brought it further fame and cash. Selling hundreds of thousands of copies, its pretax profit tripled, paving the way for a stock market flotation, or at the very least its sale to any number of suitors. One of them was *The Economist*, which had been an early supporter of what Penguin was doing, and lauded its effort "to bring serious, well printed books and genuine literature to homes where ephemeral trash has been the staple diet."

As a business, Penguin's mass-production, low-margin model of publishing had given it a mixed record in terms of profitability, but it had a lot of assets and land, including a new headquarters at Harmondsworth, then on the edge of London. Yet a big part of its valuation was the Penguin brand itself. By 1960, Penguin was selling 17 million books a year. By the time of its public flotation the following year, 250 million Penguin books had been sold across 3,250 titles. The Penguin offices were deluged with sacks of mail containing begging letters from people who wanted to buy shares in the company. When it actually listed, there was £100 million of money chasing only £450,000 worth of shares. With such a massive oversubscription, the share price jumped 50 percent on the first day of trading.

Allen Lane and other shareholders were delighted, less so Richard, who under pressure from Allen had agreed to sell his 25 percent stake in the company prior to listing. He was still a well-off man, but had lost out on gaining from the public's judgment on the firm he had done so much to create. As Kells has it, Penguin's cheery ethos and purpose of cutting through the snootiness of publishing to deliver great literature to the widest possible audience, was primarily Richard Lane's doing. Having spent his formative years in Australia, he took on some of that country's unpretentious, egalitarian outlook and applied it to tradition-bound British publishing.

Final comments

The Lane brothers felt themselves to be outsiders within the book industry, but sometimes knowing less can be better than knowing more. Old publishing hands like Basil Blackwell and Stanley Unwin presumed that the Penguin concept would fail, and when it succeeded that it would ruin their own markets for quality hardbacks. George Orwell was worried for authors, warning darkly that much cheaper books would mean people would simply spend their money on other things once their demand for books was satisfied. But as with many other products or services that can suddenly be sold for a much cheaper price, demand exploded.

Penguin paperbacks ushered in one of those rare revolutions in which everyone wins: authors (big new audiences); publishers (bigger markets); and the public (greater literary enjoyment for a fraction of the price). Suddenly, people on low incomes could afford to buy books for the first time, instead of borrowing them from libraries. In an analysis of its business model, Richard Koch & Greg Lockwood contend that Penguin achieved a "virtuous trade-off" (see Chapter 23). That is, the Lanes "avoided the traditional trade-off between price and quality by redefining quality in terms of the *contents* of the book, not the cover's material." Penguin's success was a reminder that "books are software, not hardware." Koch and Lockwood note, "A price that is a fraction of the previous price for a desirable item will always create a vast new market. Moreover, the size of that market is greatly underestimated." What Penguin stood for, though, more than cheap books as such, was a general lifting up of the population. For this service, it remains a much loved brand.

Stuart Kells
Born in 1972, Kells was educated at the University of Melbourne, taking honors and master's degrees in economics, and has a Ph.D. in law from Monash University. His other books are Rare: A Life Among Antiquarian Books *(2011), and* The Library: A Catalogue of Wonders *(2017).*

Blue Ocean Strategy

"Executives are paralyzed by the muddle. Few employees deep down in the company even know what the strategy is. And a closer look reveals that most plans don't contain a strategy at all but rather a smorgasbord of tactics that individually make sense but collectively don't add up to a unified, clear direction that sets a company apart—let alone makes the competition irrelevant. Does this sound like the strategic plans in your company?"

"Value innovation places equal emphasis on value and innovation. Value without innovation tends to focus on value creation on an incremental scale, something that improves value but is not sufficient to make you stand out in the marketplace. Innovation without value tends to be technology-driven, market pioneering, or futuristic, often shooting beyond what buyers are ready to accept and pay for. In this sense, it is important to distinguish between value innovation as opposed to technology innovation and market pioneering."

In a nutshell

Companies make the mistake of focusing on the competition when they should be focused on creating big leaps in value for the customer.

In a similar vein

Richard Koch & Greg Lockwood *Simplify*
Geoffrey A. Moore *Crossing the Chasm*
Peter Thiel *Zero To One*

CHAPTER 21

W. Chan Kim & Renée Mauborgne

When Chan Kim and Renée Mauborgne looked at the field of business strategy, they found that it was all wrong. Conventionally, a company begins by looking at its industry, then matches its capabilities with the opportunities in the market—that is, works out how it can compete. The market is seen as a zero-sum game in which one player wins at the other's expense. In actual fact, new industries, product categories, and markets are being created all the time through new thinking, new discoveries, even new approaches to apparently declining markets. Just as Joseph Schumpeter said, economies are perpetually being remade by the new sweeping away the old, or what the authors call the smashing of "cognitive boundaries." Capitalism is powered not so much by competition, but by the wish to avoid it totally. It seems logical to want to outperform your peers in your industry, but to be great you must make the competition *irrelevant*.

In *Blue Ocean Strategy: How to Create Uncontested Market Space and Make the Competition Irrelevant,* business theorists Kim and Mauborgne (from the French business school INSEAD) wrote for anyone running a company or organization who "finds themselves up against an ocean of bloody competition and wants to get out," who wants to do something so singular that combat and compromise are no longer necessary. Instead of a red ocean filled with competitors thrashing about in bloody combat, they imagined a blue ocean of unlimited demand and high profit.

This powerful imagery helped make the original 2005 book an unexpected hit, selling 3.5 million copies and making strategy, if it was not already, the most sexy area of business studies. The book's inspiring message comes close to personal development, and indeed in the original preface the authors wrote, "These ideas are not for those whose ambition in life is to get by or merely survive . . . If you can be satisfied with that, do not read on."

The expanded 2015 edition incorporates the authors' observations and examples of how people and organizations have put their ideas into practice in the ensuing decade, and has new examples and sections on how companies can better align their staff, their systems, and their partners with the blue ocean strategies they have embarked on.

Not cheaper, not better, *different*

The book begins with a case study: the US wine industry. Until 2000, the industry had an elite image, and the market was not growing much. Wineries competed on perceived complexity and sophistication, and there was a huge range of wines covering many grape varieties. In the public's mind, though, there wasn't a lot of differentiation in the wines being offered. There were a lot of competing premium wines and a lot of competing low-cost wines, catering to different markets, but they were "all different in the same way." When you have an industry like this, the authors note, you won't stand out simply by offering a little more quality for a lower price. You need to provide a completely *different* value offering—that is, stop looking at existing customers and imagine entirely new ones (what Kim and Mauborgne call the "non-customer") who haven't even seen a reason (until now) to buy what is on the market.

American winemakers had invested a lot in being seen to overdeliver on prestige and quality at a certain price point, since the industry (including wine judges and winemakers) thought that complexity was the be-all and end-all of winemaking. Casella Wines, an Australian winemaker, could see that complexity and prestige were actually a turn-off for many potential wine drinkers. They saw that a non-complex wine, with a fun image, may be what most people really want. Wine could be reimagined as a "social drink accessible to everyone: beer drinkers, cocktail drinkers, and traditional drinkers of wine."

In only a couple of years, Casella's Yellow Tail brand, with its simple, attractive taste that did not require aging or oak barrels, and available only in red (a Shiraz) or white (a Chardonnay), swept the US market, and all with little promotion or advertising. Today, it is sold in over 50 countries, and the brand is a symbol of sunny Australian approachability. The crucial point: Casella did not steal the market from competitors, but created its own, making wine drinkers out of non-wine drinkers. In the face of overwhelming choice, their buying decisions on wine were now made simple: either Yellow Tail, or some other non-wine drink. It even made Yellow Tail drinkers of more expensive wine drinkers, who had had enough of the pretentiousness of the wine industry.

By dispensing with the perceived need for aging or craftsmanship in production, and reducing their entire output to one red and one white,

Casella found that they needed less capital investment to produce consistent, high-quality wine; even as a mid-priced wine, it achieved a bigger profit margin compared to other winemakers' products. Yellow Tail was not just clever marketing, but was different from the ground up, and this gave it a different cost structure compared to others.

The authors don't beat around the bush when they write: "When a company's value curve lacks focus, its cost structure will tend to be high and its business model complex in implementation and execution. When it lacks divergence, a company's strategy is a me-too, with no reason to stand apart in the marketplace. When it lacks a compelling tagline that speaks to buyers, it is likely to be internally driven or a classic example of innovation for innovation's sake with no great commercial potential and no natural take-off capability."

It *is* possible for companies to grow fast without having a distinctive value offering, but it is only due to luck, that is finding themselves in a fast-growing industry.

Four crucial questions

In strategy terms, what did Casella do that created a blue ocean of demand in a highly competitive industry? The business literature is full of exhortations to executives to be brave, entrepreneurial, and risk-taking, but a better path to success is using analysis and analytics to work out where the blue oceans lie for your organization or business. The authors provide a Four Actions Framework to guide thinking in your business or industry, which involves asking:

- What factors that the industry thinks are important should be *eliminated* altogether?
- What factors should be reduced *well below* the industry standard?
- Which factors should be *created* and built into the product that the industry does not currently offer?
- Which factors should be *raised well above* the industry standard?

Many products and services have been overdesigned to stand out, making other players in the industry feel they have to offer these features too. This happens often without customers needing or wanting the increased sophistication. Therefore, a company that strips a product or service back to make it simple may create a new market. And by eliminating or reducing complexity and features, you can in one go reduce your costs and give people what they want but at a much lower price.

Or, you can go the other way, the authors note. In the 1980s, Cirque du

Soleil changed the circus world by pushing it upmarket. A tired industry aimed at children suddenly had a high-paying adult audience.

The customer doesn't know

Extensive customer research is often a dead end, the authors argue, since buyers often have little idea of what would be a transformative offering until it is actually placed before them. People, like companies, tend to think in terms of existing product or service categories, but blue oceans of demand are created when those categories are ignored or obviated.

As companies compete in markets, they start to offer finer segmentation in order to "win" segments of it, but this leads to winning smaller and smaller markets. To get blue oceans of demand, you have to reverse this and go for *de*segmentation, finding or developing a product that caters to untapped demand.

Kim and Mauborgne use the word "noncustomer" to describe the people who are not well served by an existing industry, and who would be perfectly willing to jump ship if there was a more compelling offering. Example: A lot of people were turned off playing golf because of one thing: the difficulty of driving the ball off the tee. Putting and chipping were doable, but the small size of the driver head made a successful drive a real skill. Seeing this, Callaway Golf came up with the "Big Bertha" driver, whose bigger head made driving a lot easier. It got more people playing golf, and made Callaway a fortune.

When the British healthy fast-food chain Pret A Manger started in 1986, city professionals routinely dined in restaurants for lunch, but they weren't always happy with the length of time these sit-down lunches took, their expense, and the heaviness of the food. Pret's concept was high-quality, very fresh, moderately priced food that could be chosen and taken to the counter to be paid for, then eaten in comfortable surroundings. You could be in and out of a Pret in 20 minutes, not the hour plus that it took for a meal in a proper restaurant. Pret found legions of "noncustomers" who were ready for something else, but didn't know what that was until they saw it. Today, Pret has over 300 stores in Britain with a turnover of $800 million.

JCDecaux upended the world of street advertising through its brilliant idea to finance and build street furniture like bus stops for municipalities, in return for being able to sell advertising on the furniture. By solving a problem for local governments who often couldn't afford new furniture, JCDecaux created an ocean of revenue through long-term, 10–25-year contracts to supply the bus stops, the cost of which was easily outstripped by advertising revenue. Many advertisers had refused to pay for billboard advertising, but they could see the benefits of bus stop ads, which were more visible to more people, waiting for buses, and could be replaced more frequently.

It is wise, Kim and Mauborgne say, to look for the reasons that customers are currently refusing to use the products or services that your industry currently offers, because "The greatest blocks to utility often represent the greatest and most pressing opportunities to unlock exceptional value." Once you can identify the issues they have, there is the opportunity to provide an alternative that caters to the untapped demand. As Samuel "Roxy" Rothapfel, creator of the luxurious "picture palace" movie theaters that replaced traditional cheap and basic nickelodeons, said: "Giving the people what they want is fundamentally and disastrously wrong. The people don't know what they want . . . [Give] them something better."

A blue ocean organization

But what's to stop another company simply copying your blue ocean strategy?

The authors address this issue. To start, people don't like imitators, and prefer to stick with the original creator of a blue ocean product or service. There is a massive branding advantage with blue ocean products that can last for decades. Secondly, copying another firm's blue ocean strategy would invalidate a lot of a firm's existing offerings and strategies, or require too much organizational change. Many blue ocean creations are an expression of a singular organizational DNA.

Many blue ocean ideas or concepts are easily imitated and not patentable. For this reason, it is very important that you price your blue ocean service or product in such a way that, although others can imitate it, it will not really be worth their while doing so. If you combine exceptional utility with reasonable price, the chances of being imitated are lessened.

Yet blue oceans of demand for something never last forever, and organizations must develop a culture of constant reinvention, sometimes involving the cannibalization of their existing products, if they are to avoid red oceans of competition. Consider the multiple blue oceans created by Apple: the Apple II, the iMac, the iPod, the iTunes music platform, the iPhone, and the iPad all created vast new demand by combining existing technologies to create exponentially greater user value. Each time its products began to be imitated, Apple was moving ahead with new ones. Compare this to Microsoft, the authors say, whose deep dependence on the cash cows of the MS Office software suite and Window operating system saw it take its eye off the ball of innovation.

Final comments

Venture capitalist Ben Horowitz has said there are times in a manager's or CEO's life when there are no "silver bullets" in terms of doing something radically different to create a new market, or going upmarket or downmarket; you just have to face your competitors head on and engage in bloody battle. Maybe so, but such situations only arise if a firm has not staked out a market that is truly its own in the first place.

"If we attack those positions which the enemy has not defended, we invariably take them."

This principle of Sun Tzu's from the *Art of War*, of "taking the enemy where it is not"—or better still, seizing territory where there is simply no opposition to begin with—is a classic blue ocean strategy. The Sun Tzu way, in battle and in life, is to find opportunities where, taking account of your resources, you will have the most impact. Only sometimes will this involve going at the enemy head on. More often it requires thorough calculations that will insure you identify the ground on which you will be strongest. When Sun Tzu warns, "to besiege [the enemy's] citadel is the worst expedient," we are reminded that the principles in *Blue Ocean Strategy* are ageless. "Strategy, after all," Kim and Mauborgne say, "is not just for business. It is for everyone— the arts, nonprofits, the public sector, even countries."

W. Chan Kim & Renée Mauborgne

Kim was born in South Korea in 1952, and was educated at the University of Michigan, where he also began his career as a business professor. He moved to France and became professor of strategy and international management at the Institut Européen d'Administration des Affaires (INSEAD) at Fontainebleau outside Paris. A fellow of the World Economic Forum, he sits on several global company boards, and has consulted to nations on business strategy matters.

Mauborgne is a professor of strategy at INSEAD and with Kim directs its Blue Ocean Strategy Institute. A fellow of the World Economic Forum, he sat on President Barack Obama's Board of Advisors on Historically Black Colleges and Universities for his two terms.

Shoe Dog

"It seems wrong to call it all 'business.' It seems wrong to throw all those hectic days and sleepless nights, all those magnificent triumphs and desperate struggles, under that bland, generic banner: business. What we were doing felt like so much more . . . For some, I realize, business is the all-out pursuit of profits, period, full stop, but for us business was no more about making money than being human is about making blood . . . We wanted, as all great businesses do, to create, to contribute, and we dared to say so out loud. When you make something, when you improve something, when you deliver something, when you add some new thing or service to the lives of strangers, making them happier, or healthier, or safer, or better, and when you do it all crisply and efficiently, smartly, the way everything should be done but so seldom is—you're participating more fully in the whole grand human drama. More than simply being alive, you're helping others to live more fully, and if that's business, all right, call me a businessman."

In a nutshell

Going into a line of business solely to make money is rarely a good idea. Be motivated by the wish to make things better for people in some concrete way.

In a similar vein

Conrad Hilton *Be My Guest*
Ben Horowitz *The Hard Thing About Hard Things*
Walter Isaacson *Steve Jobs*

CHAPTER 22

Phil Knight

When a brand is so big, so well known, we assume we know something about the company behind it, because we know its products. In fact, most big firms don't want us to know the years of struggle and mishap that made them what they are; we are asked to believe only the illusion of effortless perfection.

Phil Knight wrote *Shoe Dog: A Memoir by the Creator of Nike*, because the company had been the subject of many business school studies, but in his mind they may have captured some of the facts, but none of the spirit, of the early days of the company—or focused on the spirit but left out important facts. Many gloss over the hundreds of bad decisions Knight admits he made, which threatened the company's existence or led to the laying off of hundreds of people.

Knight is more thoughtful than your average CEO, and the book is probably not like most business books you've read. At times he is philosophical, even metaphysical. The drama of the Nike story comes alive, and the writing itself is well crafted. Most of the book was written in 2007, but it wasn't published until 2016. Family events got in the way of publication, and it seems he worked on it on and off for years.

Shoe Dog is organized in chronological format, starting in 1962 and ending in 1980, the year Nike went public. This was the right approach. Companies are most fascinating in their early days, when a few key people are fired by a mission and create a culture. Indeed, though Knight was fixated on Nike becoming a success, he loved the *process* of it too, and if nothing else wanted to share with the reader, "the ups and downs, so that some young man or woman, somewhere, going through the same trials and ordeals, might be inspired or comforted. Or warned."

It is worth recalling some of Nike's rise in detail to show the difficulties that plagued the company in its early years and its precariousness as a business even up to the successful listing as a public company in 1980. What kept Knight going was his feeling that he was not just building a business, but following a calling.

Crazy idea

In 1962, at the age of 24, Phil "Buck" Knight was back living with his parents in Oregon. He was a virgin, had never broken a rule, never rebelled. He had gone from institution to institution: the University of Oregon, Stanford business school, then a year out in the US Army. Knight had always wanted to be a great athlete, and had been in the track team at Oregon under legendary coach Bill Bowerman. His talents did not take him any further than this, but he wondered if it would be possible to spend his life in the same buzz of sporting contest, to be "at play" all the time.

While at Stanford, Knight had taken a class in entrepreneurship, and obsessively researched a paper on the idea that Japanese running shoes might one day dominate the American running shoe market, just as Japanese cameras had invaded the camera market. On a run one day through the Oregon woods, he had a kind of epiphany and began to entertain it more seriously, hatching the idea to visit Japan and meet shoemakers. He persuaded his father, a respectable but far from wealthy publisher, to help fund the trip. His dad was not impressed by the business idea, but liked the thought of his son seeing the world—the pyramids, the Himalayas, the Dead Sea, the big cities. In the early 1960s, 90 percent of American had still not been on an airplane, and many had never left their state; traveling around the world was "Something beatniks and hipsters did," Knight notes.

In September 1962 he left, with a college mate, for Honolulu, and after working there for a few months selling encyclopedias (poorly) and securities (better), got to Japan. There he visited shrines, got fascinated by Zen teachings, and finally met executives of the Onitsuka company, maker of Tiger athletic shoes. Knight claimed to be the representative of a US shoe importer, "Blue Ribbon" (a name he pulled out of the air) and arranged for samples to be sent to his business address (his parent's house).

On the way back to America, Knight traveled through Asia and Europe. In Athens he visited the Parthenon and saw the Temple of Athena, the goddess cast as the bringer of victory, or "nike." As he was leaving he noticed the frieze on the temple, which had Athena bending down to adjust the strap of her shoe.

Growth or death

Home from his odyssey, Knight started work full-time at an accountancy firm, and in his spare time was selling Tiger shoes from the trunk of his car at athletic meets. He soon sold out of his first shipment from Onitsuka of 300 pairs, and ordered another 900, taking out a bank loan to buy them for

$3,000. Sporting goods stores were not interested in his shoes, so he became a fixture at track events all over the Pacific Northwest. Though he didn't feel he was a good salesman, shoes were different: "I *believed* in running. I believed that if people got out and ran a few miles every day, the world would be a better place, and I believed these shoes would be better to run in." In 1964, "jogging" hadn't been invented. Going out for three-mile runs in the rain was something weirdos did; runners were often yelled at by motorists or had soft drink sprayed over them.

Knight felt a camaraderie with the runners, and with the enlistment of college friends to become Tiger salesmen, the business started to grow fast. Yet Knight came up against reality in the form of banks, which at that time were obsessed with having "positive cash balances." They resented any new request for capital, and there was no venture capital business back then that put a high value on fast growth. In 1966, Knight's first employee, the bookish Jeff Johnson, opened Blue Ribbon's first retail store, in Santa Monica, devoted to the cult of running. The same year, lying to Onitsuka executives that he had an office on the east coast, Knight negotiated exclusive distribution rights for the whole of the United States, ordering another 5,000 pairs.

Knight's business partner from the start was Bill Bowerman, whom he describes as the "Da Vinci" of athletics shoe design. After Bowerman got Onitsuka to reengineer their track shoes for the bigger, heavier American foot, US sales of Tiger shoes continued to grow. 1967 was a good year, with revenue of $84,000. But still it was not enough to pay a full-time salary for Knight. At 29, he left his job to teach accounting at Portland State. The hours were fewer, so he could spend all his spare time running Blue Ribbon. The university job had another benefit: it yielded a pretty young bookkeeper for the business, Penelope Parks. They married in Portland in 1968. When the following year Penny got pregnant, Knight wondered if he should go back to a stable job. After mulling it over, he decided: "Life is growth. You grow or you die."

Growing pains

Sales kept doubling every year, but Knight was still getting short shrift from his bankers. Liquidity was such a problem that he began approaching friends, acquaintances, and family for money. Knight had hired Bob Woodell, a star athlete who after a tragic accident was now in a wheelchair. Woodell's parents lent Knight $8,000, their total savings. Such acts of loyalty would be rewarded in time, but at the end of 1971, even with sales of $1.3 million, Blue Ribbon was on "life support" as its bank, First National, refused to keep providing lines of credit.

At the same time, Onitsuka was actively looking for a new US distributor to replace Blue Ribbon. To keep the company alive, Knight organized on the sly to import 3,000 pairs of soccer shoes from a factory in Mexico that was producing Adidas shoes. But they needed a name. Knight had asked an art student, Carolyn Davidson, to come up with a logo for the shoes. Davidson eventually created the famous "swoosh" symbol, but a name was a lot harder. "Falcon" was an early favorite, and Knight himself pushed for "Dimension Six." Then, Jeff Johnson excitedly told of a dream he had had in which appeared a strange word, "NIKE." Knight remembered it as the Greek goddess of victory from his time at the Parthenon, but it was not until the last minute, when he hovered over the telex machine, that he told the factory in Mexico what the name would be. Even as he was sending the telex, he wasn't sure about it. He remembers Woodell saying, "Maybe it'll grow on us."

Fast growth

At the National Sporting Goods Association Show in 1972, the Nike brand was introduced to the world. If the public—and the sales reps—didn't like the shoes, it would be the end of Blue Ribbon. When Knight opened the crates of shoes to be displayed, his heart sank. The quality was terrible. Then, a surprise: the salesmen *loved* the swoosh symbol, and even liked the Nike name. Big orders were placed, and by the time shoes were shipped, this time from a new manufacturer in Japan, Nippon Rubber, the quality was fine.

Then, a setback: Onitsuka heard about this new 'Nike' brand, which was now in direct competition with its Tiger shoes, and promptly cut off supply, stating its intention to sue Blue Ribbon for breach of contract. In Knight's mind it seemed like the end times: economy tanking, Nixon, Vietnam, now this. He pretended he was confident about the future and said to his people: this is our big opportunity, to create our own brand and not just be a seller of someone else's. Everyone in America, but particularly in Oregon, was inspired by a young runner, Steve Prefontaine, who was breaking all the records, and who gave his heart and soul to every race, even if strategically it was not important. "I told myself that there was much to be learned from such a display of passion," Knight writes, "whether you were running a mile or a company . . . in our coming battles . . . we'd be like Pre. We'd compete as if our lives depended on it. Because they did."

As the 1970s progressed, Nike seemed to go from strength to strength. Bowerman's "waffle" rubber sole, with its polygonal studs, invented with the use of his wife's waffle iron, was popular. The Cortez was the first running shoe to take pressure off the Achilles tendon, making it the first choice of many runners. Nike even started having success with sports stars wearing its shoes, and at year end 1973 it had knocked up $4.8 million in sales. In

1974 Blue Ribbon won a draining court case against Onitsuka, and was awarded damages. With this out of the way, Knight felt free to press on and dream of becoming as big as Adidas or Puma.

Yet reality impinged, with every month a titanic struggle to pay off First National and other creditors. When the bank cut off Blue Ribbon—accounts frozen, no more credit—it told the FBI that Blue Ribbon was worth investigating for accounting fraud. For Knight, this was the lowest point of his life. Racked by regret at the decisions he had made which now endangered his family, it was hard to go on. Luckily, he had begun a relationship with a Japanese trading company, Nissho, that now agreed to finance Blue Ribbon's imports on a rolling basis. Nissho paid off the company's debts to First National, and suddenly Blue Ribbon was solvent again, with the FBI called off the chase.

Finally, some stability

By the end of 1976, Blue Ribbon—now called Nike, Inc.—had sales of $14 million, helped by athletes at the 1976 Montreal Olympics wearing Nikes. Knight toyed with the idea of going public, because it would bring the big infusion of cash that was so desperately needed. But Nike would be beholden to others, and this would change its culture.

What was that culture? The management level consisted of the "Buttfaces"— an odd bunch of obsessive, hard-drinking, slightly unhinged young men, all ferociously tribal about the company, and brutal with each other. One in a wheelchair, two or three obese (a great look for an athletics shoe company), others with some setback or chip on their shoulder, and mostly from Oregon, with its small place, "prove itself to the world" mentality. Yet because they were all losers in some way, Knight observes, they were all desperate to be part of something winning.

And winning Nike was. It was seen as the only shoemaker really innovating, and also becoming the "in" shoe for actors; they were seen on *Starsky & Hutch*, *The Six Million Dollar Man*, *The Incredible Hulk*. When Farrah Fawcett in *Charlie's Angels* wore Senorita Cortezes, the shoes sold out across America the next day.

Then, another setback. A letter landed on Knight's desk from US Customs with a demand for *$25 million* for customs duties stemming from an archaic law that made imported nylon shoes 40 percent more expensive than locally made ones. As $25 million had been Nike's entire sales revenue for the previous year, paying it would destroy the company. The demand saw Knight approaching burnout after years of high stress. Despite having to open bigger offices and warehouses each year to cope with demand, and the Nike brand becoming famous, it felt like "it could all disappear tomorrow." Nike started a PR campaign to position itself as a great American company fighting for liberty and free enterprise, and started an antitrust action against the other shoe companies who had schemed to get Nike landed with the customs bill. After a protracted legal and lobbying campaign, Nike eventually got the figure down, settling with the US government for $9 million. Without settling, it was impossible for Nike to go public, and despite almost doubling its sales year after year (by 1979, $140 million)—it needed big cash injections to expand.

Nike's 1980 public offering on Wall Street was divided into class A shares for insiders and management, which would allow it to retain control, and class B shares for the public. Eighteen years after he had first flown to Japan to do a deal with Onitsuka, Knight had Nike floated on the New York Stock Exchange, the same week that Apple Computer also went public. Knight's colleagues Bowerman, Woodell, and Johnson became multimillionaires; Woodell's parents' $8,000 loan was now worth $1.6 million; and Knight himself, with 46 percent of the company, was now super rich, with stock worth $178 million. But the morning after the listing, his feeling wasn't elation, more regret that this first, enthralling, chapter of Nike's life was over. Money was never the driver, although lack of it had brought the company to its knees on too many occasions he cared to remember. He and his team had created something from nothing, and the public listing made that achievement more likely to be a lasting one.

Fast forward

Knight would spend a total of 40 years as CEO of Nike. In the year prior to his retirement in 2007, sales had been $16 billion, easily outdoing Adidas, with sales of $10 billion. He himself was now a multibillionaire. Today, Nike is still based in Portland, on a 200-acre woodland campus with 5,000 employees.

At the end of the book Knight addresses the Nike "sweatshop" controversy (conditions in overseas factories), which hurt the company badly. An effigy of him was burned outside the flagship store in Portland, and Nike became a symbol of corporate greed. Initially Knight was enraged, because he felt that the press never reported on the improvements in conditions that Nike had overseen in its factories over the years, its creation of jobs, and its role in the modernization of host countries. He notes the agreement of most economists that poor countries advance through the creation of lots of entry-level jobs, such that Nike creates.

Even so, Nike rebuilt all its factories, brought in the best possible conditions, and has tried to be a model that others follow. Knight proudly notes that the firm developed a water-based bonding agent that eliminated the toxic, cancer-causing fumes created from the agent bonding upper and lower soles, and gave the intellectual property to all its competitors. His focus today is philanthropy. He and Penny give away $100 million a year to various causes, and support The Girl Effect—Nike's program run with the UN, NGOs, and other companies that pours resources into the education and advance of girls around the world.

Final comments

Knight's last bit of advice for the aspiring entrepreneur is simple: don't stop. Stopping is the easiest thing to do in the face of obstacles, but he only succeeded, he says, by keeping on going even when it seemed all was lost.

Knight alludes to a missing link in success, luck or karma or God, that all of us are instinctively aware of, but not many admit: "Athletes get lucky, poets get lucky, businesses get lucky. Hard work is critical, a good team is essential, brains and determination are invaluable, but luck may decide the outcome. Some people might not call it luck. They might call it Tao, or Logos, or Jñana, or Dharma. Or Spirit. Or God." His final thought: "Have faith in yourself but also have faith in faith."

Simplify

"Simplifying has been an invisible red thread running through business history in our lifetime, and that of our parents and grandparents."

"A price that is a fraction of the previous price for a desirable item will always create a vast new market. Moreover, the size of that market is always greatly underestimated."

"Successful simplifiers always come up with a new key, or keys, to unlock and transform a market. These keys are almost never based on market research. Instead, they come from insight— often a sudden epiphany or a bolt from the blue that nearly always arrives away from the office. But one of our aims in this book is to simplify and systematize insight."

In a nutshell

It is the simplifiers, not the innovators, who take the really big prizes in business.

In a similar vein

Clayton Christensen *The Innovator's Dilemma*
Walter Isaacson *Steve Jobs*
Theodore Levitt *Marketing Myopia*
Brad Stone *The Everything Store*

CHAPTER 23

Richard Koch & Greg Lockwood

"As to methods," Ralph Waldo Emerson said, "there may be a million and then some, but principles are few. The man who grasps principles can successfully select his own methods. The man who tries methods, ignoring principles, is sure to have trouble."

Are there any timeless principles, as opposed to methods or tactics, in business? Serial investor Richard Koch has spent his life trying to identify some. He became well known for promulgating the 80/20 Principle, the idea that most significant results come from only a small proportion of effort. But he became rich, he says, through applying another: the Star Principle— that is, investing only in "stars," the largest businesses in fast-growth markets.

Yet Koch realized that the best businesses were not just the ones that were dominant in a fast-growing market, but also those that were the most *simple*. When Koch and venture capitalist Greg Lockwood began researching *Simplify: How the Best Businesses in the World Succeed*, it was clear that all the great business success stories of the last hundred years involved radical simplification, and most of the great businesspeople, from Ingvar Kamprad (IKEA) to Herb Kelleher (FedEx) to Allen Lane (Penguin books) were simplifiers. While it is natural to laud the deep thinkers and innovators and inventors, it is the simplifiers "who deliver the most economic benefit to humanity," bringing "the fruits of invention and discovery to mass markets." The crucial formula in business, the authors argue, is *Benefit x People Affected*. The world really changes not when a lucky few get to enjoy a new product or service, but when it becomes available to millions.

The path of simplicity

There are two ways or strategies of simplifying, by price and by proposition. The worst position for a company to find itself in is to be neither a leader in its products in terms of what they do, nor a leader in terms of price. Inevitably, it will find itself overtaken and outgunned by firms that focus on one or the other. A company has to be very clear on its strategy: product, or price.

Price simplifying   This involves drastically cutting the price of a good or service, by half or more. It does *not* mean radically reducing the quality of the good, but rather reorganizing its provision toward much higher volume and greater efficiency, which means much lower costs. When a product's price is halved, a funny thing happens, the authors note: demand does not merely double, as you might expect, but often increases by "fivefold, tenfold, a hundredfold, a thousandfold or more." The fourth part of the book presents data showing the astonishing returns on investment from companies that have been able to pull the price-halving feat.

Proposition simplifying   With proposition simplifying, the priority is "to make the product or service not just a little better, but a whole order of magnitude better, so that it is recognizably different from anything else on the market." Not just easy to use, or a lot more useful, but in its sheer simplicity possessing an element of "art" that makes people love using it. Examples: Apple's iPad, the Google search engine, the Uber taxi app. These kinds of products usually create a whole new market, because they embody pent-up demand that was not satisfied due to previous complexity or difficulty.

If the players within an industry all provide very different propositions, then there is room for many players within that industry, Koch and Lockwood note, since each is catering to different segments. But in an industry in which the companies all offer roughly similar propositions, a price-simplifying company can come along and crush all the others by undercutting them, and a proposition-simplifying one that makes a much better product must be ready for a stampede to their door. The only real defense against extinction is to develop a unique proposition: either you do things much better than anyone else, or you provide things much more cheaply.

Whereas price simplifiers tend to create a *mass* market, the natural reward of proposition simplifiers is a *premium* market. The latter will be a smaller market, but more profitable, so the return on investment for each proposition can end up being about the same. Sometimes a premium product can go mass market, such as with Apple's iPhone, but this is rare.

Ford's price-simplifying genius

At 45, Henry Ford was a relatively successful automobile maker, but he admitted in his autobiography, *My Life and Work* (see *50 Success Classics*), that his cars were not radically different to others, and the way they were made followed the standard of the industry. That standard was extremely low rates of production. Ford's company, in the first years of the twentieth century, was making only *five* cars a day; the market was well-off motoring enthusiasts.

But Ford had the unfashionable idea that cars should not just be a pleasure, but could become a necessity for the masses, making the lives of millions a whole lot easier and more productive. In 1905/6 he was selling two models, one for $1,000 and another for $2,000. Total sales for the year: 1,599 cars. However, the following year he simplified both models and dropped their prices to $600 and $750. The move, you would expect, might have doubled sales. In fact, Ford sold 8,423 cars, *five times* what he had at the more expensive prices. This seemed like astounding success, but Ford had just begun with price simplification. He decided to start selling a single model, in 1909, that was the essence of simplicity in its engineering and design: the Model T.

Cheaper did not mean inferior, however. To make the Model T both lighter and stronger, Ford pioneered the use of vanadium steel in car chassis. It turned out that this sort of steel was cheaper to make than normal steel. A lighter car meant less fuel consumption, which delighted drivers. Then, from 1913, Ford revolutionized automobile making with the continuously moving assembly line. Not only did it greatly speed up production, so that by 1914 the Highland Park plant in Detroit was turning out 250,000 cars a year, but quality also increased. Instead of craftsmen working away putting together cars in batches, employees with minimal training were put on a single task, practiced to perfection. All this meant that, by 1917, the price of a Model T had plummeted to $360.

As Koch and Lockwood note, even Ford was surprised by how much demand increased as the price dropped: the 40 percent drop in price from the $600–$750 models, to the single model selling at $360, increased demand by *700 times*. As well as being much cheaper than other cars, the Model T was also very simple to operate compared to others at the time. Ford wanted to sell a car that anyone could operate. The very simplicity of the car meant it was cheaper to make, yet every component was proven and tested. This combination of ease of use, reliability, and price was unbeatable.

The exponential response to big price reduction is "one of the most powerful economic forces in the universe," the authors say, creating a virtuous circle in which high sales volume further decreases costs and prices, leading to even greater sales. Ford's radical simplification and democratization of car use created a huge global market, creating spin-off industries and new jobs, and shaping the twentieth century. This is one of Koch and Lockwood's key points: that radical price simplification not only leads to massive profits and a long-lasting company for the simplifier (for modern examples, look at Walmart and Amazon), but the benefits spread through society. As Thomas Edison put it, "We will make electricity so cheap that only the rich will burn candles."

Easy and artful = greater use

Firms that proposition simplify can dramatically enlarge the market they are in by making people want to use their service *a lot more* because it is so easy to use, fun to use, or has an element of art to it. The apps and websites of proposition simplifiers Uber, Spotify, and Airbnb fit this bill. Instead of downloading individual tracks for a dollar, as you do with iTunes, Spotify's genius was to create a subscription service that lets you listen to as many tracks as you want for a low set fee (if you don't want to pay, you can still listen for free but have to put up with ads). The inclusive offer, and Spotify's simple and elegant app and site, has meant that people using it consume more music. Finding a place to stay using Airbnb is dead simple, and you get a more authentic experience wherever you stay, compared to a hotel. The property owner gets to make some money from rooms in their house which may otherwise be lying idle. As the price of Airbnb rooms are often considerably less than a hotel room, the platform has encouraged more travel.

Steve Jobs wanted his early computer, the Macintosh, to "look friendly." Later, with the iPod, iMac, iPad, and iPhone, he said, "We're really shooting for Museum of Modern Art quality." Even the boxes the products came in had to be beautiful and tactile. Of course, the beauty of Apple devices hid incredible complexity and the bringing together of an array of technologies. And that is precisely the point. The authors quote Oliver Wendell Holmes: "I would give my right arm for the simplicity on the far side of complexity." People will often pay a huge premium for some product that makes their life simpler, easier, or more beautiful. The point about "art" in products is that it creates *an emotional connection* with the user—which in an environment of competing wares can be priceless.

When Steve Jobs returned to Apple in 1997 with his product-simplifying and range-simplifying mission, the company was worth a bit over $2 billion. In 2015 it was worth over $700 billion—*330 times* more. That's the power of simplifying. How many more industries are ripe for radical simplifying involving much greater usability, much greater usefulness, or much more esthetic pleasure?

Virtuous trade-offs

If you decide to go for the price-simplified mass market, you can offer people interesting trade-offs. Koch and Lockwood talk about "virtuous trade-offs" in which a company *seems* to be giving away things for nothing, when in fact there is a double benefit. The cheap, nice food and children's play areas in IKEA stores are not a "loss" for the company, but encourage people to spend an afternoon on the premises—and spend more. Kamprad was able to sell great design at an affordable price by making people drive to get the furniture themselves and then erect it. For many people, it was a happy trade-off.

In the 1930s, British publisher Allen Lane wanted to bring top-quality writing to the masses, and realized the only way to do so was to put books by top modern authors into cheap paperback form. Readers had to forego having nice hardbacks, but were more than happy to do so for the low price and iconic design of the Penguin series (see Chapter 20).

As companies mature, so their products naturally seem to get more sophisticated and complex, often moving beyond what the market wants. Big markets are there for the taking by firms that go in the opposite direction: *subtracting* features from the product. Koch and Lockwood note the work of Clayton Christensen (see Chapter 6), who observed that bigger companies are so tied to the idea that they must be on the leading edge of their industry that they fail to see the market for cheaper, simpler versions of things that people actually want.

Final comments

"The most effective and successful price-simplifiers," Koch and Lockwood write, "think of what they do as a mission, a crusade to bring at least some of the good life to people who have not been able to afford it before." Henry Ford did it with his cars, Michael Marks and Tom Spencer did it by providing quality clothing at prices working-class people could afford, and Ingvar Kamprad did it with inexpensive furniture that looked good.

But how do you come up with an industry-changing or industry-creating concept such as these? An obvious path is to "Look for a simplifying system that already exists on a tiny scale but could be made into a universal product and rolled out around the globe." This is the Ray Kroc/McDonald's model. Another way is to take an existing process and automate it. Uber automated ordering a taxi; Tinder automated finding a partner; Betfair automated making a bet; Vanguard automated investing by creating stock market index tracking funds, which eliminated the need for human fund analysts, drastically cutting fees in the process.

It is easy to be overawed by the way things are currently done in your industry. Who are you to question it? Yet "The ordinary way of doing business is not the best way," as Ford found out after he had questioned everything to do with automobile manufacturing and marketing. People within an industry like to paint it as complex or at least complicated, but the biggest gains have always gone to outsiders who feel frustration themselves and wish that things could be simpler, a *lot* simpler.

Richard Koch & Greg Lockwood

Born in 1950 in London, Koch took a degree in modern history at Oxford University before doing an MBA at the Wharton School at the University of Pennsylvania. He began a career in management consulting, first with the Boston Consulting Group, then Bain & Company, where he became a partner. In 1983 he set up his own consulting firm, the LEK Partnership, and seven years later retired in order to invest privately and write. He is on the Sunday Times *"Rich List" thanks to investments that have included Filofax organizers, Belgo restaurants, Plymouth Gin, and the online betting exchange Betfair. His books include* The 80/20 Principle *(1997),* Living the 80/20 Way *(2004),* Superconnect: The Power of Networks and the Strength of Weak Links *(2010),* The Star Principle: How It Can Make You Rich *(2010), and* The 80/20 Manager *(2013).*

Lockwood is a director of Piton Capital, a London venture capital firm which makes investments in companies that possess network advantages. He previously worked in the telecoms field, in corporate finance and in classified media publishing. He has a Masters in Management from the Kellogg Graduate School of Management.

Management in Ten Words

"Some of what follows may strike you as simple and obvious. Yet as I have met and worked with people from different cultures worldwide, I have been struck by how basic, simple truths about life—not just business—have been forgotten or are dismissed as 'too obvious to matter' by clever people who mistake 'simple' for 'simplistic.' We have allowed ourselves to think that, because the world in which we live is complicated, the solutions to problems must be complicated as well."

"The whole experience served to confirm my conviction that if you listen to customers, and act on the truth they tell you, you will be amazed at what can happen."

"Paradoxically, the more successful a business becomes, the easier it is to justify not seeking out the truth and taking difficult decisions."

In a nutshell

It is one thing to survey customers about what they want, but quite another to actually be on their side.

In a similar vein

John Kay *Obliquity*
Richard Koch & Greg Lockwood *Simplify*
Simon Sinek *Start With Why*
Brad Stone *The Everything Store*

CHAPTER 24

Terry Leahy

When Terry Leahy joined Tesco in 1979, it was considered a poor cousin in the British retailing family. Though it grew quickly in the 1980s, it was still dwarfed by Sainsbury's and Marks & Spencer. When he left Tesco in 2011, after 14 years as chief executive, it was six times larger than both those companies, and the third largest retailer in the world, having transcended its UK origins. Though it pulled out of its American operations in 2012, and had a bad spell in the five years after Leahy left, in 2017 it had a turnover of £55 billion across 6,500 stores, employing 475,000 people across a dozen countries.

What is the secret of Tesco's success, particularly its fast growth phase under Leahy, in which he increased the retailer's market share in British supermarkets from 20 to 30 percent?

The world is complicated, Leahy argues in *Management in Ten Words*, but success can be surprisingly simple. We tend to reach for the most advanced solutions, when often the most basic strategy (and sticking to it) will achieve the goal. The trick, of course, is being able to see what this simple strategy or solution is. To get to it, you first must get to the truth about where the business currently stands; to maintain its preeminence, there must be strong values which include loyalty and gratitude to the customer.

"Truth," "Loyalty," "Simple," "Values": each of the book's ten chapters is headed by one of ten words. We look at some of the more useful below.

Truth

In 1992, when Leahy got the job of marketing director at Tesco, marketing was a discrete "silo" in the company, and "customer satisfaction" was also a separate department, ranked alongside process and logistics in importance. Leahy set about making the customer and their wants the center of Tesco's business. That sounds obvious now, but at the time most companies did not actually do much customer research beyond a few focus groups. Leahy launched a full-scale program of research into what customers *really* thought of Tesco, which was often uncomfortable to hear. Instead of running rigid focus groups with specific questions, Leahy presided over free-flowing meetings in which customers could talk about anything, not just their shopping experience but their *lives*. The process allowed Tesco to confirm its *raison d'être*: to be classless, providing value and interesting choices for people on all incomes. It sought to create loyalty among all customers, not just those who could spend the most.

Many companies say they listen to customers, but very few genuinely want to know what they think and feel. Finding and accepting the truth, Leahy says, was the basis of Tesco's big expansion. If it had not been willing to take an honest view of itself, it could never have made the changes that were necessary to lift it from British middle-ranking chain to juggernaut.

The company went so far as to let customers decide the redesign and remodeling of stores; what they thought was important was often different to what designers or managers thought was good. Feedback from parents saw Tesco pioneer sections devoted to special dietary needs; and although it was mainly to enable families to shop for everyone under one roof, instead of going to specialty shops, this act of goodwill became unexpectedly profitable.

A fan of military history, throughout the book Leahy mentions the British general Viscount Slim. Slim taught that every organization "must have a great and noble objective." For Tesco, this meant having goals that went beyond a short-term profit motive. If you deliver benefit first, that is likely to lead to loyalty and long-term healthy sales. An emotional bond is created that keeps people coming back.

Loyalty

All businesses have competing objectives—sales, market share, profits, satisfied staff, investor returns, reputation. But Leahy says it is "vital to have a single objective that overarches all others, giving everyone a compass to guide them." For him, the best objective any organization can have is winning and keeping loyalty. Any time it faces a choice or a decision on which way to go, it should ask itself: "Will it make people more loyal to us or not?"

It makes complete sense to have loyalty as your number one objective, because in the last 30 years there has been an explosion in choice and information for consumers. In 1980, Leahy notes, there were about eight jeans brands. Today there are 800. Given all the choice and information, only companies that form an attachment to people will succeed. You must be the default choice to buy from, invest in, get information from. "The difference between loyal and disloyal customer behavior is not marginal in terms of profit," Leahy writes, "loyalty is the biggest driver of profitability. If you keep customers for longer, you do not have to spend money trying to replace them so often." When a company has loyal customers, it will grow faster because it is losing existing customers much slower than it is gaining new ones. Loyal customers also spend more with you. In fact, Leahy found, the more a customer spends with you, the more they trust you. And when they trust you, they are more willing to try your new products or services.

Central to this outlook was Tesco's Clubcard scheme. Launched in 1995, Clubcard gave a 1 percent discount off all shopping as a reward, and in return the company gained huge amounts of valuable data on shoppers and their habits. An issue at the time was the expense of computer storage; the more data the company gained and sifted through, the more it would cost. But Leahy was desperate for information on customers. If the company didn't really know who they were, how could it serve them properly? Sainsbury's dismissed the new scheme, but Leahy felt it should have admitted Tesco was doing something good: "it is always better to look for the strengths in a competitor's innovation than the weaknesses. You may feel better attacking a competitor, but in the long run it is wise to learn from them."

Key to the scheme was that everyone got the same rate of discount, whether you spent a lot or a little. It was not a ruse to "drum up more business," but a simple thank you—and people knew this and appreciated it. Leahy writes:

"Clubcard taught me a simple truth: people like to be thanked, and if they are thanked, you begin to earn their loyalty. This may be a simple truth but its power, as our competitors found to their costs, can be profound."

As the first supermarket loyalty card in Britain, Clubcard engendered real goodwill. "By proving that we were motivated by their needs more than simply to make money," Leahy notes, "customers started to think about their relationship with Tesco differently."

Loyalty in *employees* also saves a company a huge amount of money and time, and gives it an *esprit de corps*. This comes from a sense of ownership, and Leahy took this literally. By the time he left Tesco, the company had the UK's highest number of employee shareholders.

Courage

Leahy describes himself as naturally shy and cautious, and only embarks on a path when he has weighed up all the risks and consequences, including what may go wrong.

While waiting to catch a plane to Ireland, he had a "moment of clarity" about what Tesco should set out to achieve. This was just a few months before he was made chief executive. When he unveiled his plans to other executives, he remembers, there was "stunned disbelief":

- To be the number one retailer in the UK. At this point Tesco had overtaken Sainsbury's, but was still dwarfed by M&S.
- To be as strong in non-food products as it was in food. At the time, its non-food sales were only 3 percent of its total.
- To develop a profitable services division (e.g. finance, mobile phones). In 1996, this did not exist in Tesco.
- To be as strong overseas as it was in the UK. At the time, less than 1 percent of the company was international.

Echoing Jim Collins' idea of "big, hairy, audacious goals," (from his book *Good To Great*) Leahy insists that "good strategies need to be bold and daring." People need to be stretched, and goals have to cause excitement, "and perhaps just a little fear." But most of all, bold strategies have to create a choice: to seize the moment and go for something larger, or tread water. Make a difference to people's lives, or not. Leahy was inspired by Akio Morita at Sony, who knew that for the company to move ahead it had to conquer markets outside Japan. Leahy could not countenance Tesco resting on its laurels, and knew that "doing nothing is often the greatest risk of all."

Act

Tesco was the first UK supermarket chain to provide an online service. It had no background in online sales, so started in a very simple way. While US dot.com darling Webvan was raising $375 million and building a massive fulfillment center, Tesco simply took orders via phone, fax, and computer, picked stock from its existing shelves and delivered them to a few trial areas. "There was no great invention in that," Leahy remembers, "but at least we were under way. We had a service and we were operating. More importantly, we had the beginnings of a process. We were starting to learn all the things we would have to do, and all the improvements we would have to make for this enterprise to be profitable."

Weighed down by its massive start-up costs, Webvan went bust. Tesco's low-key approach, with extreme focus on the details, proved successful. "When projects fail," Leahy notes, "they generally do so because those commissioning them have not thought through what they want the new system to do, nor have they written down a clear process." Successful implementation has five elements: a clear initial decision; a simple process; clearly defined roles; systems that work; and discipline. In business, process and implementation are sometimes considered boring or second-drawer next to strategy, yet they are crucial for success.

Leahy's comments echo von Clausewitz's remark, which Winston Churchill took to heart in winning World War Two: "Amateurs focus on strategy, experts on logistics."

Values

Tesco was started in 1919 by Jack Cohen, a market trader in the East End of London, and when Leahy joined the company it still had a scrappy street-trading ethos. There were lots of shouting matches and it was very competitive, with little respect for seniority or qualifications. The culture matured over time, but Tesco's egalitarian ethos remained. It is still very much a meritocracy, and its organizational structure is relatively flat, with only six layers between someone on the checkout and the chief executive. This means good ideas can be heard whoever comes up with them.

Reflecting on his upbringing and Catholic education, Leahy says it gave him "a deep wish to help give everyone, no matter their background, a better life." This outlook turned out to be a perfect fit with Tesco's classless "everyone is welcome" outlook, and its focus on value.

People respond to things more out of emotion than reason, Leahy notes. They will buy from someone for more than simple utilitarian reasons; they also need to share your values—to like what you stand for. Tesco could easily have focused on "market share" or "shareholder value," but it knew that a relentless attention to customer value was its reason for being. If it lost sight of that, it was lost.

Final comments

Leahy does not shy away from the long list of mistakes and dead ends the company saw under his watch, including the failed foray into US food retailing with its "Fresh & Easy" chain. In its defense, Leahy says that half of the problem was timing: it launched just as the Great Recession began, and "people don't try new things in tough times."

Tesco's massive expansion and triumph over its rivals would never have happened if it thought the same way as them. "Only if you think big, and plan bigger still, do you stand a chance of seeing real change," Leahy reflects. He includes a quote from the American architect Daniel Burnham: "Make no little plans. They have no magic to stir men's blood and probably will not themselves be realized." The long-term view was also part of Leahy's recipe for success. It "ran like a thread through many decisions we took. For example, starting in a new country takes ten years to build the store network and probably another ten years to create a leading consumer brand." Big thinking goes nowhere without its cousin, thinking long.

Leahy ends the book by reflecting on the role of organizations through human history. Many brought great benefits, but plenty of others were malign. While admitting that Tesco is "just a tiny dot on history's canvas," he felt that its success held lessons beyond retailing. This wish for larger benefit is what lifts *Management in Ten Words* above the pack of self-glorifying business autobiographies. Leahy comes across as humble, and as business writers from Jim Collins to Peter Drucker have pointed out, humility is a key trait of the most successful managers.

Terry Leahy

Leahy was born in Liverpool in 1956, to Irish parents. His father had intended to emigrate to America but came to Liverpool instead, where he worked as a carpenter in the merchant navy before becoming a greyhound trainer and bookmaker. His mother, a nurse, looked after their four sons, Terry being the third. The family lived in a prefab house on a Liverpool council estate.

Leahy's teachers at a local Catholic primary school marked him out as bright, and he won a scholarship to St Edward's, considered the best school in the city. One summer he traveled down to London and got a job stacking shelves of a Tesco store in Wandsworth. On leaving St Edward's his grades were not good enough to study his favored architecture or law, so he moved to Manchester to study management.

On graduating, he got a job with the Co-Op supermarket chain, traveling around Britain selling cold meat and cheese to Co-Op trading societies. In 1979 he was offered a marketing job at Tesco, and in 1992 became marketing director before rising to chief executive in 1997, at the age of 40. He became Sir Terry Leahy in 2002.

After retiring from Tesco he advised start-up companies and also played a role in the redevelopment of Liverpool's waterfront area and the massive Liverpool One shopping precinct. The project, says Leahy, "shows that you should never let your future be a prisoner of your past. Its revival has lessons for everyone about bold plans, timing, risk, and, above all, courage."

The Five Dysfunctions of a Team

"Not finance. Not strategy. Not technology. It is teamwork that remains the ultimate competitive advantage, both because it is so powerful and because it is so rare."

It is also ironic that so many people avoid conflict in the name of efficiency, because healthy conflict is actually a time saver . . . those that avoid conflict actually doom themselves to revisiting issues again and again without resolution."

"Great teams also pride themselves on being able to unite behind decisions and commit to clear courses of action even when there is little assurance about whether a decision is correct. That's because they understand the old military axiom that a decision is better than no decision. They also realize that it is better to make a decision boldly and be wrong—and then change direction with equal boldness—than it is to waffle."

In a nutshell

Organizations increasingly find that they rise or fall depending on the quality of their teams.

In a similar vein

Roger Fisher, William Ury & Bruce Patton *Getting To Yes*
Stanley McChrystal *Team of Teams*
Tom Rath & Barry Conchie *Strengths Based Leadership*
Peter Senge *The Fifth Discipline*
Robert Townsend *Up the Organization*

CHAPTER 25

Patrick Lencioni

"If you could get all the people in an organization rowing in the same direction, you could dominate any industry, in any market, against any competition, at any time."

This remark was made to Patrick Lencioni by a friend who had started a billion-dollar company. The owner instinctively knew that it was not finance, technology, or strategy that ultimately creates corporate success, but what happens in the team of executives running the show.

Across a working life, chances are you will find yourself employed in an organization that is low in morale, overpoliticized, and which saps your energy. You may also be lucky enough to work in a place with *esprit de corps*, in which personal aims are subsumed in the whole. There is a chasm between the two, and the bridge that links them is the quality of teams.

And yet, Lencioni notes, "The fact remains that teams, because they are made up of imperfect human beings, are inherently dysfunctional." The way to a great team isn't complicated, but like anything worth doing, it is hard. As with many business books, *The Five Dysfunctions of a Team* employs fable to make things slightly easier. Lencioni tells the tale of a fictional Californian tech company, DecisionTech, trying to regain its shine.

A corporate fable

Only a couple of years previously, DecisionTech was a Silicon Valley start-up star, with the best engineers and a lot of support funding from top venture capital firms. Yet as deadlines are not met, morale and horizons drop. Shanley, the CEO and founder, is shunted out of the top job, and stays on as business development manager only so he can get a big payout if the company ever goes public.

In his place, the board appoints Kathryn Petersen. At 57, she is "ancient by Silicon Valley standards." Kathryn had only started her business career at 40, after being in the military, bringing up three boys, and working as a schoolteacher. She had spent the previous few years in low-tech manufacturing industries, and had made a local Japanese–American car plant a success. To DecisionTech employees, Petersen seemed like an old school blue-collar industry executive, way too different to their suitless, freewheeling ways. Why had the chairman overrode the rest of the board in wanting to hire her? The chair observed that, although she had no history in high tech, Petersen had demonstrated a great ability in building teams.

In the first couple of months after Kathryn was hired, it seemed to be a poor decision. She did very little managing, and even took two precious days out of staff routines to make the executive team attend retreats in the Napa Valley. Though she knew next to nothing about software or programming, she wasn't fazed by their lack of confidence in her. After all, she reasoned, GE's Jack Welch had not been an expert on turbines or toaster manufacturing, and Southwest Airlines' Herb Kelleher didn't have to be a great pilot to build his company. What both had was an understanding of the power of teamwork.

Kathryn's first big moment comes when she has to overrule the chief technologist and head of sales, Martin, who had made a sales appointment that clashed with the company retreat. Martin asserts that a big sales opportunity is clearly more important than an off-site, internal team-building event, but Kathryn sets him straight, noting that a big sale might be a temporary boost, but long-term decline is inevitable if the executive team is working poorly together.

On the morning of the first day of the retreat, there is relief when Martin comes through the door—at one minute to nine.

The dysfunctions

The retreat begins with some simple exercises. Each member of the executive team is asked to answer five simple questions about themselves, such as home town, number of kids in the family, childhood hobbies and challenges, and first job. Kathryn's idea is that people who work together each day often know little about each other, so these little bits of information help to build intimacy and trust—and lighten the atmosphere.

Kathryn also gets the team to take the Myers–Briggs test, designed to show behavioral tendencies such as introversion and extroversion and how these affect dealing with colleagues. No one is better or worse than anyone else, just different, and every team member must first acknowledge the various minds and outlooks that make up a team.

The contrast between these sessions and the average working day at DecisionTech couldn't be greater. Meetings had become glum affairs without debate and the airing of views. It suffered from the first dysfunction of a team: *absence of trust*. If people trust each other, Kathryn notes, they don't hold back in speaking their mind, and they are not afraid to call people out if required and challenge each other. The enemy of trust is the desire to feel invulnerable. Members of great teams, in contrast, are willing to be called out wrong for the good of the organization.

The big problem with lack of trust, Kathryn explains to the group, is fear of conflict: "If we don't trust one another, then we aren't going to engage in open, constructive, ideological conflict. And we'll just continue to preserve a sense of artificial harmony." This dysfunction, *fear of conflict*, manifests as artificial harmony. When conflict is pushed underground you get orderly meetings which seem good on the surface, but nothing important is discussed or decided, and the workplace becomes politicized. Kathryn defines "politics" as "when people choose their words and actions based on how they want others to react rather than based on what they really think." When something does seem to have been decided, there is a *lack of commitment*. This failure to "buy in" to decisions amongst key people has predictable results: an organization floating on a sea of ambiguity.

Lack of commitment is tightly linked to another dysfunction: *avoidance of accountability*. A good team holds each member accountable for the course they all agreed on, and does so even if it means some interpersonal discomfort. One of Kathryn's team protests that while it is relatively easy to confront a report or subordinate with not meeting some standard or target, doing the same with peers is pretty hard. Why? Because if you are in a band of equals, it feels wrong to tell someone else how to do their job. *But,* if everyone is totally on board with the chosen direction, and the goals are as clear as day, there should be little personal discomfort when pointing out that someone is not measuring up to them . . . because it should be as clear to them as to me that this is the case. If no one is willing to call out another, standards gradually slip. A great team feels responsibility not just for their own silo or division, but for the organization as a whole.

Closely related to avoidance of accountability, Kathryn notes, is the dysfunction of *inattention to results*. What happens is that people routinely pursue their own "numbers" or glory at the expense of the results of the whole team or company. There is nothing wrong with ego, Kathryn says, as long as it's a collective ego. If the focus is on group results, then individual egos will naturally be kept in check. Kathryn's husband Ken coaches a school basketball team that always does well because it plays *as* a team. Any showboating individual players are put on the bench, and the team plays better for it. Applied to the context of a company, it means that everyone is responsible for sales, everyone is responsible for marketing, everyone is responsible for product development, everyone is responsible for customer service, everyone is responsible for what happens in finance. Results must be measured monthly, in clear categories (e.g. revenue, expenses, new customer acquisition, current customer satisfaction, employee retention, public relations, product quality) and everyone must do what they can to reach them, no matter whether the goal seems to be "outside their area." When it becomes crystal clear what results everyone is aiming for, Kathryn points out, there will be no possibility of individual egos sabotaging things, either in taking credit or in blame.

By the end of the first day of the retreat, the DecisionTech team is starting to see just how much "soft" factors can dramatically help or harm their company. It becomes clear how the five dysfunctions—absence of trust, fear of conflict, lack of commitment, avoidance of accountability, and inattention to results—had created a firm which, despite significant advantages, was quickly losing out to more cohesive competitors.

Unison

In the final session of the retreat, Kathryn looks at the chief arena for conflict in organizations: meetings. We hate them because they are boring, but *why* are they boring? Because, she says, there is nothing big at stake and therefore no enthusiasm or conflict. She encourages the team to engage in spirited, passionate debate on the *issues* facing the company, without casting personal aspersions or sarcasm. Not only do teams that are OK with conflict have lively, interesting meetings, she notes, but the intensity of the meetings and the full airing of views, tapping into the collective wisdom of the team, means that issues tend to be solved *quickly*.

In the last hour, the team have a go at formulating a single overarching goal that everyone would agree on. Market share? They don't even know the size of the market, or where the industry is headed. Cost reduction? If there is no product to sell, costs are irrelevant. Product quality? The company's product was already arguably better than its competitors. The team argue away, and narrow it down to "more revenue" or "key customers" (that is, well-known companies) as the most important measures of success. They finally agree on the following: "new customer acquisition," because this would give the media something to write about; give employees confidence; provide the best feedback for the engineers; and provide the reference points to get even more new customers (and follow-on sales). The team settle on a precise number—18 new customers by the end of the year—then define what each executive would have to do within their domains to achieve the number.

Back in the office, Kathryn soon finds the new unity evaporating. "The team seemed as though they were embarrassed by having exposed themselves," she reflects, "and were pretending that it had never happened at all." It comes to her attention that some executives are more loyal to their departments than they seem to be to the organization as a whole. But she insists that their *first* loyalty had to be to the team sitting around the table—the executive team.

Kathryn comes to a big decision on the makeup of the executive team. As head of marketing, Mikey is very productive and respected, and would seem to be an asset to the company moving forward. Yet she brings the other executives down with her sarcastic remarks, unwillingness to listen or help, and conviction that she is the best. None of these things help with building the team, in fact they undermine it. Kathryn decides to fire her, which shocks the rest of the team, but they start to see how serious she is about building a group of people who can think and act *as one*.

Late in the story, a competitor firm makes an offer for the company, and the board leaves it up to the executive team to decide what to do. Their rejection of the offer galvanizes them further into a tight unit.

Committing to decisions

Having told the fable, Lencioni makes a surprising contention: team decisions made *without* masses of analysis or research often turn out to be good ones. This isn't to say that research is unimportant, only that it is a mark of dysfunctional teams that they are endlessly collecting facts and analysis before acting. Yet the hedging of bets only brings paralysis and lack of confidence. Teams, he says, must "resist the allure of consensus and certainty." An organization may never get perfect consensus for acting, and rarely have all the facts needed.

It may seem paradoxical or wrong that a member of a team who has doubts about a certain decision is expected to get behind it 100 percent, but Lencioni's point is that without commitment to decisions, an organization will start to feel like a ship that has lost its bearings. Though he does not refer to it, the British system of cabinet government is a good example of what he means. The goings-on of cabinet meetings are kept secret, and there is usually lively and robust argument on issues. However once a decision is made, it is the government as a whole that speaks. If any minister strongly disagrees with a decision, he or she is expected to resign to preserve the unity of cabinet and government.

Lencioni provides a practical tip for ensuring unity. As a meeting comes to a conclusion, make sure those present know very clearly what has been decided, and what will be communicated to the wider organization. This is a very good way of clearing up any differences in understanding or interpretation between those present, leaving no "wiggle room" to go back on what's been decided.

Final comments

Lencioni's placing of teams at the center of what makes a good company or institution is supported by management philosopher Peter Senge, who in *The Fifth Discipline* described teams as "the fundamental learning units in an organization" (see Chapter 38).

The Five Dysfunctions of a Team is over 15 years old, and the book's fictional characters now seem a bit outdated (among the eight executives, there are six white Americans and two Hispanics—no Indians or Chinese, which must make it an unusual company in Silicon Valley). Still, it remains one of the best and easiest ways to understand the transformative power of good teams.

Patrick Lencioni

Born in 1965, Lencioni grew up in Bakersfield, California, and as a child remembers his father talking about the dysfunctions of the company where he worked. He attended Claremont McKenna College, majoring in economics, before working as a management consultant for Bain & Company. He was a human resources executive at Oracle and was vice president of organizational development at Sybase. In 1997 he founded the Table Group as a consultancy to firms which have included Southwest Airlines, Google, and the San Diego Chargers. He is on the board of directors of the Make-A-Wish Foundation.

Other books include The Five Temptations of a CEO (1998), The Four Obsessions of an Extraordinary Executive (2000), Death by Meeting (2004), The Advantage: Why Organizational Health Trumps Everything Else in Business (2012), The Truth About Employee Engagement (2015), and The Ideal Team Player (2016).

The Box

"Before the container, transporting goods was expensive—so expensive that it did not pay to ship many things halfway across the country, much less halfway around the world . . . The container made shipping cheap, and by doing so changed the shape of the world economy."

"In 1956, the word was full of small manufacturers selling locally; by the end of the twentieth century, purely local markets for goods of any sort were few and far between."

"In 1961, before the container was in international use, ocean freight costs alone accounted for 12 percent of the value of US exports and 10 percent of the value of US imports."

In a nutshell

Great innovations seem simple and obvious in hindsight.

In a similar vein

Alfred Chandler *The Visible Hand*
Richard Koch & Greg Lockwood *Simplify*
Theodore Levitt *Marketing Myopia*
James P. Womack, Daniel T. Jones & Daniel Roos *The Machine that Changed the World*

CHAPTER 26

Marc Levinson

"**W**hy would anyone want to write a book about a boring metal box?" When writing up the story of container shipping, journalist and economic historian Marc Levinson got so tired of this kind of negative reaction that he almost abandoned the project.

But he persevered, and when *The Box: How the Shipping Container Made the World Smaller and the World Economy Bigger* received a great response, he was taken by surprise. It seemed that someone had to put a spotlight on such an apparently mundane innovation before it could be truly appreciated. As it happened, Levinson had good timing, as shipping containers were becoming trendy, used as temporary art galleries, accommodation, and generally as a symbol of urban industrial chic.

Levinson's history reminded us that globalization is not simply about the world getting smaller through online platforms and international call centers, but is very much a *physical* phenomenon involving the ability to move stuff from one country to the next. Containerization, bringing drastically cheaper shipping, made it happen.

The Box is also a semi-biography of Malcom McLean (McLean always spelt his first name without the second "l"), its inventor. McLean's real insight, Levinson says, was managerial. He could see that shipping, rail, and truck companies were not in the ship, train, or truck business as such, but in the *freight movement* business, and containerization was a logical step for them. The advent of containers caused big job losses in dockworker communities, the sidelining of once prosperous ports, and allowed for the incorporation of Asia into world trade. Like every disruptive technology, it changed the world in unexpected ways. No one, Levinson writes in a new 2016 edition of the book, not in government and not in business, foresaw just how much containerization would increase long-distance trade. Today, entirely computerized and automated megaports, super container ships, and the widening of canals continue the revolution.

A problem with no solution

Before containers, things were moved from ship to shore in boxes, barrels, crates, and casks, hoisted by men with hooks, and with cables and hoists operated by other men. Bars of copper, bunches of bananas, bags of coffee, logs of wood, and sacks of cement all had to be handled differently, and in any given year one of every two longshoremen or dockworkers were injured on the job, hit by moving cables or loads. Even though the injury rate was several times that of construction work or manufacturing, there were hardly any health and safety measures.

Jobs on the waterfront were tightly controlled by local families, and often you could only get work by paying a foreman a kickback. In 1951, there were 50,000 men in New York and 50,000 in London working on the docks, but hardly any had full-time jobs. Hiring was by the day, and that was how it had always been. Around the world, in cities such as London, Marseilles, Antwerp, Portland, Fremantle, and Liverpool, lived tight-knit communities all within a mile or so of the docks. Despite higher than normal wages, dockworkers were looked down on socially, and perhaps for good reason. A lot of theft and pilfering went on, and there was plenty of stuff to choose from. A big merchant ship might have 200,000 separate items, from cases to drums to crates, carrying a large variety of things, from wine to clothing to radios.

Sending a truckload of goods from the US to Europe involved freight and port costs equal to 20 to 25 percent of the product's value. The main cost was not shipping itself, but getting the goods from land on to ships, and at the other end having to manhandle it from the ship on to waiting trains or trucks. Everyone seemed to recognize that shipping was inefficient and costly, not least because of powerful unions protecting the conditions of dockworkers and longshoremen. From the 1920s there were various efforts to introduce containers, and after World War Two there were thousands of metal or wood containers being used. But they were not the containers we know today—much smaller, and usually with no lid, just a canvas covering that did little to make loading and unloading easier or cheaper.

A revolution begins

McLean's flash of inspiration about container shipping came while waiting in a traffic jam to load goods from his truck on to a ship. Surely, he wondered, there was a better way?

By 1954, McLean had built a large trucking company with over 600 trucks. With increasing congestion on the roads, he thought it made more sense to ship goods up and down the east coast of the United States. But trucking companies ran trucks, and shipping companies ran ships. His plan was for an integrated system where his firm's trucks would drive up a ramp and detach their trailers on to a company-owned ship. Trucks would hook up to the trailer at the other end. As coastal shipping was in decline, the Port Authority of New York loved McLean's idea and funded a new terminal in Newark, New Jersey. Because there were federal laws forbidding a trucking company to own a shipping company, he sold out of trucking and invested everything in an existing shipping line, Pan-Atlantic.

He soon realized that even this new mode of shipping freight was wasteful, with a lot of the room in the hold taken up by the truck trailer decks and their wheels. He bought ex-government tanker trucks and had the tanks separated from the truck chassis, so that they could be stacked one on top of another. This was the genesis of container shipping. It took a long time for McLean to perfect the system, including reinforced docks and a new kind of shipboard crane to handle the loading and unloading of containers, plus regulatory approvals from the Interstate Commerce Commission and the Coast Guard. But the cost savings were astonishing. In 1956, as McLean got his "Sea-Land service" under way, loading cargo on to a medium-sized ship cost $5.83 per ton. The same job could now be done for *less than 20 cents* a ton.

Seeing the benefits

Like most big innovations, it took time for containerization to be embraced, and for the benefits to be clearly demonstrated. It took time for firms and factories the world over to change their ways to take advantage of the opportunities offered by containerization. Crucial to the conversion would be uniformity.

By the late 1950s there was a growing number of shipping containers, but they came in lots of shapes and sizes. With every shipping company investing in its own system that was not compatible with others, there would be little savings in costs and time. Fortunately, a small government agency, the United States Maritime Administration along with the American Standards Association settled on a "family" of container sizes of 10-foot, 20-foot, and 40-foot lengths, each size being 8-foot high and 8-foot wide. Henceforth, only shippers using these sizes would get Federal Maritime Board subsidies for ship construction. The International Standards Organization followed suit with the aim of achieving worldwide standardization and interchangeability of containers.

Slowly, the promise of standardization was realized. You could fill a container in Kansas City, Levinson notes, in the confidence that just about all trucks, trains, ports, and ships could handle it all the way to Kuala Lumpur. Yet even by 1963, the majority of freight was still being handled the old way, and executives of the steamship companies believed that containers would never handle more than 10 percent of the foreign shipping trade. Surprisingly, containerization only really took off when it was adopted domestically, when big companies like Eastman Kodak and General Electric realized they could save money by sending large volumes of goods across country by putting it on new train-container services, instead of sending smaller amounts by truck.

By the end of the 1960s, overseas container shipping gathered pace, getting a further push thanks to the Vietnam War. Levinson argues that the American military's ability to fight a war on the other side of the world would have been limited if it did not have the ability to ship large volumes of material to Vietnam via container ships. The war had another effect: empty merchant ships returning from Vietnam were rerouted via Japan, and filled with Japanese consumer goods. The Japan–West Coast route became a foundation of modern world trade, the precursor of massive container ships that would in our day bring cheap Chinese products to western shores.

Because the cost of shipping goods "dropped like a stone," poor countries could aspire to selling their wares to rich nations, and small companies could dream of becoming huge ones through exporting. Once, manufacturers had to build factories near their suppliers, because bringing parts and materials from overseas was too expensive. That changed quickly. Now, even with the costs of shipping an item of clothing around the world, a shirt-maker in Malaysia could outcompete local American shirt-makers who worked around the corner from the big department stores that had until now bought their clothes. "In 1956," Levinson writes, "the world was full of small manufacturers selling locally; by the end of the twentieth century, purely local markets for goods of any sort were few and far between." Consumers had a vastly greater choice of goods, and most of them were much cheaper than before.

Since loading and unloading became a predictable, uniform exercise, suppliers and receivers of goods around the world could calculate with more accuracy how much inventory they needed. It was only containerization, Levinson says, that allowed just-in-time manufacturing, with its near zero inventories, to happen, and the long global supply chains that characterize today's economies, in which the parts of a Barbie doll or an iPhone or a Mini car are made in half-a-dozen countries and shipped to a final assembly plant.

. . . and the costs

Containerization brought uniformity, which had social costs. A container port, wherever it was, looked much like any other, and the armies of wharf-workers and their tight communities became a distant memory. Places such as Liverpool that were once bustling maritime centers got sidelined by the revolution in world trade, because their docks and location were no longer suited to container shipping. By the early 1970s, nearly all of London's famous Thames docks had closed, and the flight of port-related manufacturing from Liverpool left the city economically devastated.

Old shipping firms became extinct when they couldn't afford the massive investment needed to convert to containers, and shipping would be drawn to an increasingly small number of huge ports, such as Felixstowe in Britain, Rotterdam in the Netherlands, Hamburg in Germany, and Le Havre in France. In the US, Seattle, Oakland, Los Angeles, and Long Beach saw the creation of new ports that took business away from old ones such as San Francisco and Portland. Riddled with corruption and subject to frequent strikes, the piers of Manhattan and Brooklyn became a shipping backwater compared to the Newark and Elizabeth ports in New Jersey built to handle containers. The change decimated manufacturing in New York, and thousands were made unemployed. The businesses and jobs moved to New Jersey, other parts of New York State, and Connecticut.

In 1976 the *Financial Times* wrote, "the revolutionary impact of containerization, the biggest advance in freight movement in generations, has largely worked itself out." But the real revolution was to come. Through the 1970s worldwide container shipping capacity was increasing at 15–20 percent a year, and the ships themselves got bigger and bigger. "Panamax" vessels, so named because they were built to the maximum size possible to still get through the Panama Canal, could carry up to 3,500 containers. The bigger the ship, the cheaper the fuel and port costs per container. "If ever there was a business in which economies of scale mattered," Levinson observes, "container shipping was it." In the late 1980s "post-Panamax" vessels started to be built, which although too big for the Panama Canal could go back and forth between the world's biggest ports such as Hong Kong, Los Angeles, Singapore, and Rotterdam.

Since the book was written, a new class of container ships has been launched that can carry an astonishing 15,000 containers and have capacity for up to 18,000 if they don't contain heavy things.

Final comments

Economists have traditionally underestimated the role of transport costs, but Levinson notes that in the decade following the worldwide adoption of containers, 1966–76, the volume of international trade in manufactures grew twice as fast as global production of manufactures. Despite a slowdown in world economic growth and oil shocks in that decade, much cheaper shipping costs put a rocket behind trade. (The fact that transport costs still matter a lot is nowhere better exemplified than in Africa, where growth is held back by very poor transport links between nations. It is much cheaper to send goods to another country overseas from Africa, than to send it across land across the continent.)

Containerization, by highlighting the cost to the taxpayer of tariffs on imports, helped drive the intellectual case for free trade and lower protection. This had unforeseen consequences: in the past, it did not matter to a worker in Kansas how much factory workers earned per hour in other countries. Suddenly, thanks to the cheapness of shipping, American jobs could effectively be "exported" to low labor cost countries like China. Thus it can be argued that containerization was an important factor in the rise of anti-globalization, anti-free trade, and nationalist movements. Levinson's book reminds us that although technological innovation can reduce the barriers between countries, such progress can always be reversed by politics.

Marc Levinson

Levinson began his career as a journalist at Time *magazine and with the* Journal of Commerce, *before becoming a writer and editor for* Newsweek. *He has been a finance and economics editor for* The Economist, *a research analyst for JPMorgan Chase, an adviser to Congress on transportation and industry matters, and senior fellow on international business at the Council on Foreign Relations. He has master's degrees from Georgia State University and Princeton University's Woodrow Wilson School, and a Ph.D. from the City University of New York.*

Other books include The Economist Guide to Financial Markets *(1999),* The Great A&P and the Struggle for Small Business in America *(2011), about the largest retailer of its time, and* An Extraordinary Time *(2016), an economic perspective of the 1970s decade.*

Marketing Myopia

"Every major industry was once a growth industry. But some that are now riding a wave of growth enthusiasm are very much in the shadow of decline. Others that are thought of as seasoned growth industries have actually stopped growing. In every case, the reason growth is threatened, slowed, or stopped is not because the market is saturated. It is because there has been a failure of management."

"The view that an industry is a customer-satisfying process, not a goods-producing process, is vital for all businesspeople to understand. An industry begins with the customers and his or her needs, not with a patent, a raw material, or a selling skill."

In a nutshell

Companies stop growing because they fail to correctly understand what business they are in.

In a similar vein

Clayton Christensen *The Innovator's Dilemma*
W. Chan Kim & Renée Mauborgne *Blue Ocean Strategy*
Richard Koch & Greg Lockwood *Simplify*
Al Ries & Jack Trout *Positioning*
Simon Sinek *Start With Why*

CHAPTER 27

Theodore Levitt

Once upon a time, oil companies called themselves oil companies. Today they are "providers of energy." Bus companies used to be bus companies, now they are "transport providers."

Such expansiveness can be traced back to an influential article that appeared in the *Harvard Business Review* in 1960 by Harvard business professor Theodore Levitt. In "Marketing Myopia," he argued that companies and indeed whole industries could fail simply by misunderstanding the business they were in.

His famous example is the railroad industry. The great railroad companies declined not because the market for passenger and freight transportation decreased—it grew substantially. The problem was that these companies saw themselves as being in the railroad business. If they had seen themselves in the *transportation* business, some of them could have kept going as players in the automobile, truck, or aviation fields. They were focused on their product—rail transport—not their customer, that is, people and their need to transport themselves and their goods.

A similar thing happened with the big American film studios. Clearly, they were in the movie business, but if they had seen themselves as being in *entertainment*, they may have become players in the new world of television. In fact, they did the opposite, Levitt writes: "Hollywood scorned and rejected TV when it should have welcomed it as an opportunity—an opportunity to expand the entertainment business."

Companies wither not because their market or industry is saturated (too little demand, too much competition), but because management is not clear on the firm's purpose; it is narrowly focused on the product or service it currently provides, not on what people are actually needing or wanting.

Beware no-substitute markets

In the early twentieth century there was a Boston millionaire who stipulated in his will that all his money be invested in electric streetcars, because "there will always be a big demand for efficient urban transportation." The man sentenced his heirs to penury, Levitt notes, because he failed to see that streetcars were just a passing means of urban transportation. People assume that what is an exciting growth industry today will always be so. When Levitt was writing, electronics and chemicals were seen as the future (recall the advice given to Dustin Hoffman in the 1960s film *The Graduate* that he should "get into plastics"). Today, these are humdrum industries.

Every industry, Levitt notes, is at first seen as a growth industry, because there seems to be "no substitute" for the product or service that it provides. Even industries as prosaic as dry cleaning once seemed fast-growth, because—hooray!—wool clothing could now be cleaned easily and quickly. Dry cleaners thought they had a bright future . . . until clothing and styles changed, with much more use of cotton and synthetics, reducing the need for dry cleaning.

Any investment in an industry that has "no competition" is doomed to fail. Invest in an electric utility, for example, because it has a monopoly on supplying the grid with energy, and you may find some other source (wind, solar, nuclear) reduces your returns in time. Industries can seem a good bet for years, even decades, until alternatives become suddenly viable. Recall that kerosene lanterns were once a good business to be in—until Edison's light bulb came along. "To survive," Levitt writes, any company "will have to plot the obsolescence of what now produces their livelihood." In other words, to develop products that will cannibalize their existing ones. This is the only way to be at the leading edge of *new* markets.

Once, people bought most of their groceries from corner stores that were part of larger grocery chains. When supermarkets started appearing, the chains did not believe that people would drive for miles just to save a little money, losing out on friendly, personalized service. This rigid belief in the supremacy of their model made them feel better . . . until their customers disappeared. The new titans of grocery shopping were dedicated supermarket companies who best met customers' needs.

Beware the "expanding market"

Levitt argues that there are no growth industries, only growth companies. Any firm believing that it is on some "automatic growth escalator" simply because it is in the right field, will soon see decline. It is *ideas* and *management* that will keep it relevant, not some inherent quality of its industry, or demographic dynamism. Companies and investors assume, Levitt notes, that they have planted a money tree just because they have a product or service in a growing population that is becoming more affluent. And manufacturers make the mistake of thinking that, just because economies of scale mean they can make things more cheaply, there will be a market for what they make. In fact, as soon as people gain some wealth, they don't want more of what is currently available, at any price, but demand new products or services that do things differently and better. What an expanding market does, Levitt says, is make companies lazy thinkers. After all, if people seem to be buying their stuff, it must be good, right?

When the big Detroit automobile manufacturers eventually started making smaller cars, and selling a lot of them, they naturally saw it as an example of their marketing savvy. In fact, the success of smaller cars showed that the big Detroit firms had not been catering to the market they seemed to know so well, but rather had been leaving the market to other manufacturers. They had been spending millions of dollars on market research, but not truly asking what people really wanted, only showing them what was already planned and asking them to choose between iterations. Levitt's intuition about Detroit was prescient—in the ensuing 20 years it progressively lost market share to foreign carmakers who had a much better idea of what Americans needed and wanted than American automobile executives themselves did.

Industry laziness and groupthink

Oil, Levitt writes, seems a good example of an industry for which there seems no substitute, *and* which is an expanding market. The big oil firms make outsize profits by dividing up a seemingly captive market, given the billions of cars on the world's roads. There is no real need to create *new* demand; it is there already, and the companies' focus is on increasing efficiency and reducing their costs to ensure higher profits.

Yet such is the creative/destructive nature of capitalism that indispensability rarely lasts for long. Incentives push entrepreneurs or scientists to come up with cheaper or better alternatives. Writing in 1960, Levitt observed that sooner or later, some outsider will upend the oil industry, either making it less relevant or creating some new demand for oil of which the big firms are not party to. The oil industry was extremely lucky, Levitt notes, in that the automobile came along when it did. After all, light bulbs took away the market for kerosene lamps, and coal-burning domestic central heating took away the need for oil-burning space heaters. The gasoline that began powering cars was the oil industry's savior, later joined by the need for aviation fuel. All these developments came from *outside* the industry, but its big companies were in a lucky position to capitalize. Yet they were so myopically focused on oil that they did not even establish themselves in the new natural gas industry, preferring to pooh-pooh its prospects. Not only gas, but new developments in fuel cells, electric storage batteries, solar and wind power would all come from outside the industry, which contented itself with "watching developments."

Levitt notes that people generally hate having to refuel their cars every week or so, stopping at gas stations to buy a product they can't even see, only smell. Whoever made a car that obviated the need to do this (or that made it possible to refuel at home, as you can do with electric cars), would sweep the market.

What real marketing is

Marketing is not finding out what customers think of the current way you do things, or how they feel about your existing products and services, Levitt points out. Real marketing is tapping into people's basic wants and needs. Look at any industry journal, and it is mostly self-congratulatory thinking about how well the industry is doing, or about marginal improvements in efficiency. The basic modus operandi of the industry is never questioned. Long-term alternatives to the industry's products or services, or how it might be blindsided by external developments, are not considered. Yet it is such things that determine the fate of industries and companies.

The irony is that many companies, while being scientific about "R & D," show little interest in identifying their true purpose, or what potential customers might really want, using testable hypotheses. This is admittedly hard work, but as long as marketing remains the "stepchild" of business, industries will be surprised when they decline, and companies shocked when people no long want what they are making.

At the turn of the twentieth century the railroads reigned supreme: they were the best investment, and represented the future. But just thirty years later, after the advent of trucks and automobiles, they were on their knees, surviving by government subsidies. To avoid such fates, Levitt writes, the company of today must be "a customer-creating and customer-satisfying organism." Managers must see themselves not as the makers of products but as *the creators of value*. The chief executive has a particularly important role in this, because making the whole organization more imaginative, creative, and thoughtful requires that employees and public are inspired by a vision of what the company could be and do. Not just a big factory and office churning out things, but a specifically human place that is finely attuned to human needs and wants.

Final comments

Levitt might have nodded sagely at today's big conventional carmakers, who look like being overtaken by upstarts or firms outside the motor industry (Tesla, Google) in electric and driverless cars. If Ford or GM had seen themselves in the personal transport industry, not the internal combustion car industry, they might be valued a lot higher than they are today.

However, it can be argued, as Al Ries has done ("Marketing Myopia Revisited," *AdAge*, 2013), that Levitt's article hindered rather than helped many companies by encouraging them to extend their reach beyond their specialization into areas where they had no history and were bound to fail. IBM, for instance, got into trouble when it moved from being number one in mainframe computers into all sorts of other products. And some train companies survived and prospered not by becoming "transport companies" but by doubling down and specializing in their regions. In 2009, Warren Buffett's Berkshire Hathaway bought out Burlington Northern Santa Fe, whose network covers the western United States, for $26 billion; the corporation remains profitable because it focuses on what it does best: moving freight.

Still, Levitt's article did make companies think more deeply about purpose and strategy, and every company is different. Often, a balancing act is needed to serve today's customers well through focus and specialization, and at the same time position the firm to take advantage of, or even create, future markets.

Conventional wisdom says that an industry begins with an invention, a process, a discovery. But an industry is at heart a "customer-satisfying process," Levitt said. It starts with the needs of a customer, then must work backwards.

Theodore Levitt

Levitt was born in Vollmerz, Germany, in 1925. At the age of 10 his Jewish family emigrated to the United States and he grew up in Dayton, Ohio. After war service he took a degree at Antioch College, then got a Ph.D. in economics from Ohio State University. Following a stint at the University of North Dakota, and several years working as a consultant in the oil industry, in 1959 he joined the faculty of Harvard Business School. He was editor of the Harvard Business Review *from 1985 to 1990. His 1983 HBR article, "The Globalization of Markets," in which he argued that national differences were on the wane, popularized the use of the word "globalization."*

On Levitt's death in 2006, the HBR said that it had sold over 850,000 reprints of "Marketing Myopia." Other books include The Marketing Imagination *(1983) and* Thinking About Management *(1990).*

Team of Teams

"Interconnectedness and the ability to transmit information instantly can endow small groups with unprecedented influence: the garage band, the dorm-room start-up, the viral blogger, and the terrorist cell. The twenty-first century is a fundamentally different operating environment from the twentieth, and Zarqawi had arrived at just the right time. It was more than just chat rooms and YouTube: AQI's very structure—networked and nonhierarchical—embodied this new world. In some ways, we had more in common with the plight of a Fortune 500 company trying to fight off a swarm of start-ups than we did with the Allied command battling Nazi Germany in World War II."

"There's likely a place in paradise for people who tried hard, but what really matters is succeeding. If that requires you to change, that's your mission."

In a nutshell

Widely shared information and devolution of power can make an organization unified and powerful.

In a similar vein

Patrick Lencioni *The Five Dysfunctions of a Team*
Douglas McGregor *The Human Side of Enterprise*
Frederick Winslow Taylor *The Principles of Scientific Management*

CHAPTER 28

Stanley McChrystal

I n 2003 the US military entered Iraq to topple Saddam Hussein in the wake of 9/11. It used conventional methods of warfare, but soon realized it was up against a different kind of enemy in the form of insurgent Sunni groups (the minority Sunnis, who had run Iraq, had been stripped of power by Saddam's fall) united under shadowy jihadist Abu Musab al-Zarqawi.

US General Stanley McChrystal's Joint Special Operations Command—called the Task Force—was "lavishly resourced and exquisitely trained," yet was no match for the constantly changing environment. "For a soldier trained at West Point as an engineer," he writes, "the idea that a problem has different solutions on different days was fundamentally disturbing."

Team of Teams: New Rules of Engagement for a Complex World is about the transformation of the Task Force (originally set up as a response to the failed attempt to rescue Americans in the Iranian hostage crisis), from an organization built on conventional lines into something reflecting twenty-first-century realities.

Yet it was not a strategic effort, but happened in the face of necessity. Only later was it possible to think about it abstractly and study it in terms of management theory and practice. McChrystal and his coauthors, two young Navy Seals and a graduate student from a Yale leadership seminar McChrystal was teaching, realized that the model they had developed, involving "empowered execution" combined with "shared consciousness," could be applicable to organizations everywhere. This model is really just a contemporary version of Douglas McGregor's "Theory Y" organization, yet the authors tell their story with aplomb, adding some corporate examples to the military.

An enemy that's hard to see

In 2005 alone, 8,500 people were killed in terrorist attacks in Iraq. The fear this caused meant people were afraid to leave their homes, shops shut, and utility plants were closed. The book begins with a gala opening of a sewage plant, an event which normally heralds civic advance and pride, turning into a bloodbath as insurgents drive cars filled with explosives into the crowd, killing 35 children, 10 Americans, and wounding 140 Iraqis.

Such chaos was just what Zarqawi wanted, along with a sectarian war between Sunnis and Shias. By destroying the state, it would open the way for an Islamist caliphate and the removal of the American invaders. Zarqawi had sworn allegiance to Osama Bin Laden, and his insurgents became known as Al-Qaeda Iraq (AQI). Insurgency is as old as the hills. What made things different in Iraq was that the insurgents had mobile phones and the internet, and could operate with devastating effect without appearing to have any kind of central command.

The absence of a standard hierarchy in AQI meant that every time the Americans thought they had cut off the head of the organization, it grew another. McChrystal came to a simple realization: You can't understand if an organization is any good until it is seen within its environment, and whether or not it wins in that environment. Despite their overwhelming resources, the Americans were losing.

On his daily runs around the US base, McChrystal would listen to Roy Adkin's *Nelson's Trafagar: The Battle that Changed the World*, which told the story of England's unlikely victory against the Franco-Spanish fleet in 1805. Despite being outnumbered, Nelson captured 19 of the enemy's ships and lost none of his own. His strategy of attack involved leaving the details of engagement up to each ship's commander, which was in total contrast to Napoleon's fleet, managed by strict orders from on high. Each commander in the English fleet was an "entrepreneur of battle," whom Nelson had spent years nurturing so that in the heat of war they could make good decisions on their own. What Nelson did, it seemed to McChrystal, could work in Iraq.

With military efficiency

McChrystal discusses at length the role of Frederick Winslow Taylor and his "scientific management" in the making of the modern world. Inevitably, Taylorian thinking became expressed in the increasing efficiency and specialization in armies. Without Taylorian efficiency, Peter Drucker argued, the Americans would not have been able to mobilize in a short space of time in the 1940s and defeat the Nazis.

Today's US military may be an "awesome machine," McChrystal notes, but that doesn't mean it will win. Incredible surveillance technology and firepower mean it should easily dominate every theater of war, but because scrappy enemy outfits can be empowered like never before, technology makes the world more complex, unstable, and unpredictable, not less. Who would have predicted that the self-immolation of a Tunisian market seller in a protest against the government, and the videos of it that were widely circulated online, would end up helping to remove Middle Eastern governments, including that of Egypt's Hosni Mubarak? Even with the enormous ability to track its citizens, governments today seem powerless to prevent uprisings, such is the power of instant communication and social media. McChrystal recalls how online AQI networks would mean that a terrorist act in one city could have a lightning copycat effect in other places, inspiring a cell that was not even known to exist, or leading to a recruitment surge or sectarian reprisal.

The world that Taylor applied himself to involved visible factors and determinants. It was complicated, but not *complex*. Complexity is when you don't even know what all the factors are, or if you do, how they will play out. The US military was built to handle the very complicated, but didn't know what to do about AQI, which was "a network that, unlike the structure of our command, could squeeze itself down, spread itself out, and ooze into any necessary shape." McChrystal's Task Force started using a phrase: "It takes a network to defeat a network." Instead of efficiency, adaptability. An example: the media had said that the crash of a Black Hawk helicopter almost derailed the attack on Osama Bin Laden's compound in Abbottabad. In fact, the SEAL team that carried it out was so tight, and knew each other so well, that they quickly adopted another infiltration route. They knew that raids always have at least one element that doesn't go according to plan, but this doesn't affect the overall mission. "Their structure—not their plan—was their strategy."

Shared consciousness

What McChrystal was observing in AQI was "the connectivity of small teams, scaled to the size of a full enterprise." The key to success for the Task Force was to instill "teamlike oneness across an organization of thousands." The first part of this was to bring in radical information-sharing. He set up a daily Operations & Intelligence meeting that was beamed live to hundreds of units, not just in Iraq but in Washington and around the world, and not only the US Army but other security-cleared bodies that could contribute. The data collected in every raid was immediately disseminated to relevant units and agencies so that it could be made use of, instead of lying unlooked-at in black plastic evidence bags.

The "need to know" restrictions of the US military had led to no one knowing what other parts of the intelligence community knew; 9/11 happened, McChrystal notes, because information was not properly shared in real time. Yes, you can get incidents like Edward Snowden's and Bradley Manning's leaks, but the benefits of information sharing are greater than the risks. Instead of people just following orders within their organizational silo, with radical information sharing you start to get a holistic awareness. If people are let in on what is happening in the big picture, and with other units, they can make better decisions in their own areas of concern.

NASA, McChrystal says, put a man on the moon in seven years because it transformed itself into an organization based on the sharing of information. He was determined to change the Task Force in the same way. This did not mean turning everyone into a generalist, but rather fusing "generalized awareness with specialized expertise." In place of "need to know," the goal became *shared consciousness*.

Empowered execution

Technology means that people on the ground can now make good decisions, but the chain of command in the US military still necessitated approval for significant moves, such as a strike on a senior AQI commander. McChrystal would be woken in the night to get his official permission, or decisions had to go back to Washington for approval. Because these things could take hours, often opportunities were lost. And yet, McChrystal admits that rarely did he add any insight to the process, and just went along with what was recommended.

When he started letting teams on the front line decide, something changed. "I found that, by . . . containing my desire to micromanage, I flipped a switch in my subordinates: they had always taken things seriously, but now they acquired a gravitas that they had not had before." With responsibility in their hands, they would do everything to ensure that their decisions were thought through and evidence-based. The result, McChrystal writes, was surprising: decisions were not only made more quickly, decisions were *better*. They had worked on the basis that, for the sake of speed, it was worth getting a 70 percent solution instead of waiting to make things 90 percent perfect. The opposite happened: "we were getting the 90 percent solution today instead of the 70 percent solution tomorrow." This outcome, he observes "upended a lot of conventional assumptions about the superior wisdom of those at the top."

As long as subordinates kept McChrystal in a constant loop of information about what they were doing, and why, he was happy to give them free reign. Technology allowed him to be "eyes on" with every operation, watching or hearing it in real time, but he maintained a position of "hands off," letting the ground commanders act in the way they thought was right. This was the total opposite of conventional management thinking, when "organizations have implemented as much control over subordinates as technology physically allowed."

The new paradigm of "empowered execution," however, raised a question: "If leaders were no longer needed to make the right call on important tasks or missions, what *were* they for?"

What a leader is for

In conventional management theory, the CEO or head of an organization is paid to take in masses of information and, from their unique perspective at the top of the organizational chart and awareness of wider contexts, come to judgments or decisions that will affect the business for years to come. Alas, in an era of increasingly shared information, CEOs don't necessarily have access to any more crucial information than subordinates do, and even if they did, are not superhuman enough to process all the information. The age of the all-knowing leader is dead, McChrystal says. The process of transforming the Task Force left him in no doubt that "The role of the senior leader was no longer that of controlling puppet master, but rather that of an empathetic crafter of culture." AQI could not have come into being and been so successful, he argues, were it not for the figurehead of Zarqawi. He did not micromanage the organization, but was the philosophical force behind it, the crafter of its deadly culture.

McChrystal's time at West Point, and his earlier military career, had trained him to act like a chess master, a strategic overseer who took in information and came up with smart decisions. Holding back and letting others decide would have made him seem weak. But in Iraq, the chess master analogy didn't work. His role was more that of a gardener—creating the conditions in which people could grow in their positions, fostering the teamwork that brought results (to create a "team of teams"), and fashioning a culture of shared consciousness and devolved power. McChrystal contends, in the last lines of the book, that "As the world becomes more complex, the importance of leaders will only increase." No matter how advanced artificial intelligence gets, people will look to some *person*—usually the official leader—to guide in terms of moral courage, compassion, and mission.

Through the shifts in thinking and acting outlined above, the Task Force became "not a well-oiled machine, but an adaptable, complex organism, constantly twisting, turning, and learning to overwhelm our protean adversary," McChrystal writes. As well as breaking AQI's advance, it led to the tracking and identification of Zarqawi, and his death, in 2006.

Final comments

As *Team of Teams* was being written, Islamic State of Iraq and Syria (ISIS) had captured Mosul and was threatening Baghdad. It seemed to be a rerun of everything that had happened a decade before. McChrystal had to face the question: "Was the Task Force's success with Al Qaeda an illusion, if a different form of extremism could suddenly do so well?"

On reflection, he felt that it only emphasized the fact that any organization, to be successful in an environment of constant change and complexity, must be constantly innovating and iterating. There are two responses to failure, he notes: blame external factors; or double down on what has worked before. Both are too easy, and neither likely to work. We can justify ourselves on the basis that we "tried hard," but this is a cop-out. The only goal—in war and in business—must be to win, and if that requires radically changing our models of reality, this is what we must do.

Stanley McChrystal

Born in 1954, McChrystal graduated from West Point in 1976. After rising up through the ranks, by 2003, at the start of the Iraq War, he sat on the Joint Chiefs of Staff advising the US president, and gave nationally televised briefings on the progress of the war. He was put in charge of JSOC in October 2003; in December it captured Saddam Hussein. After five years in Iraq, he became the head of the Joint Staff in 2008, and in 2009, after being promoted to four-star general, took charge of NATO forces in Afghanistan. However, following a Rolling Stone article in which he was critical of President Obama's national security team, he tendered his resignation before retiring from the US Army.

McChrystal sits on several corporate boards. His McChrystal Group advises companies and organizations along the lines of the ideas in Team of Teams. A memoir, My Share of the Task, was published in 2013.

The coauthors of Team of Teams are: Tantum Collins, a scholar on global affairs; David Silverman, a former Navy SEAL and now CEO of CrossLead, a consultancy set up with McChrystal; and Chris Fussell, McChrystal's former aide-de-camp and now a partner at McChrystal Group and head of its Leadership Institute.

1960

The Human Side of Enterprise

"We recognize readily enough that a man suffering from a severe dietary deficiency is sick. The deprivation of physiological needs has behavioral consequences. The same is true, although less well recognized, of the deprivation of higher-level needs. The man whose needs for safety, association, independence, or status is thwarted is sick, just as surely as is he who has rickets. And his sickness will have behavioral consequences. We will be mistaken if we attribute his resultant passivity, or his hostility, or his refusal to accept responsibility to his inherent 'human nature.' These forms of behavior are symptoms of illness—of deprivation of his social and egoistic needs."

"Under the conditions of modern industrial life, the intellectual potentialities of the average human being are only partially utilized."

In a nutshell

People will naturally want to do their best for an organization if they feel that their need for personal development is being met.

In a similar vein

Peter Drucker *The Effective Executive*
Stanley McChrystal *Team of Teams*
Peter Senge *The Fifth Discipline*
Alfred P. Sloan *My Years at General Motors*
Frederick Winslow Taylor *The Principles of Scientific Management*

CHAPTER 29

Douglas McGregor

*T*he Human Side of Enterprise was Douglas McGregor's only book, but it is one of the most cited in the social sciences. The leadership scholar Warren Bennis, a student of McGregor at Massachusetts Institute of Technology, argues in a preface to the work that, much as all economists in one way or another pay their dues to Keynes, so all management and organization thinkers must doff their hat to McGregor.

At the time *The Human Side of Enterprise* was written, the dominant model was "Organization Man"; people were expected to subsume their personality in order to fit in to the corporate world. Presaging 1960s counterculture, McGregor instead emphasized human potential and growth, and indeed was strongly influenced by the self-actualizing psychology of Abraham Maslow (see *50 Self-Help Classics*).

McGregor also ushered in a new theory of power involving less hierarchical relations between managers and employees, and a method of working based more on achieving progress through frank discussion of ideas and influence rather than coercion. The book was an affront to people who had been raised to believe in command-and-control management, and who felt McGregor's style was too permissive or weak. What were leaders for, if not giving orders?

McGregor's other contribution was to reject Frederick Winslow Taylor's assumption that people work only because of threats of what will happen if they do not, and believed that the day was already here when people were motivated to work for personal psychic reasons other than just money or status. Modern books such as Daniel Pink's *Drive: The Surprising Truth About What Motivates Us* (2009) owe a lot to theories of workplace motivation by the likes of McGregor, Frederick Herzberg (*The Motivation to Work*, 1959), and David McClelland (*The Achieving Society*, 1961).

Management: applied models of human nature

So many of our actions, McGregor writes, not just in business but in life, are shaped by unexamined theories and assumptions about human behavior. We make predictions, and we seek to control situations, based on these unscientific theories. Every manager has beliefs or rules of thumb, such as

"People need to learn to take responsibility" or "Those closer to the situation can make the best decisions." But the manager often contradicts these, by arranging for a constant flow of information on how subordinates are doing, which suggests other beliefs, such as "People can't be trusted."

Management is not a science, McGregor says, but it can use current social science to shape better practice. Neither is it an art. Those who say it is, do so to justify their intuitive decisions without recourse to systematic knowledge. An example is pay. Pay scales were established to compensate people for work done, assuming that people only work for money. But if this assumption is not true, incentive plans that carry the expectation that work or productivity will improve if compensation increases, will not work. No matter how great the incentive, if people are not satisfied or happy with the work or the workplace or the ethics of the organization, they will not be motivated to do their best. In fact, they will feel justified in extracting maximum dollars or benefits from the organization as a payback for enduring the misery of spending their time in a place which is beneath their dignity. In such a workplace, McGregor notes, the costs involved in checking if people are earning their wages and/or their incentives are often so high that they outweigh potential increases in productivity.

If an organization fails in its objectives, it rarely sees the problem in how it measures and rewards output, but rather blames the workers for being lazy or uncooperative or stupid. Management will only ever achieve its objectives if it can see how its assumptions about how people are, and why they act the way they do, are joined with reality.

The paradigm: Theory X

The idea that there are "universal principles" of management evolved from observations of how two institutions, the military and the Catholic Church, were run. In the military, obedience has been enforced via court-martial, which in extreme cases could involve the death penalty. The Church's ultimate means of control was the threat of excommunication. In both cases, people are kept in line, and the organization achieves its goals, by dire threat.

The same thinking was adopted for commercial organizations, in which the threat of being fired, with all its awful implications for survival, was considered a sufficient deterrent for people to work hard and according to direction. The harshness of such a threat was, in rich countries, lessened by the advent of unemployment compensation, and laws against arbitrary firing.

Still, the belief persisted that the average person "has an inherent dislike of work and will avoid it if he can," McGregor writes, and therefore they, "must be coerced, controlled, directed, threatened with punishment to get them to put forth adequate effort toward the achievement of organizational objectives." This thinking was complemented by the notion that most people don't like responsibility, have little ambition, and desire security above all else. In the 1960s, he notes, this set of beliefs and assumptions about human nature, which he dubbed "Theory X," were not expressed openly, but still informed how organizations were run.

Theory X would not have survived so long, McGregor admits, unless there was quite a lot of truth in its assumptions. Yet its inconsistencies had become very apparent. For one thing, Theory X assumed that people were happy when they got their basic physical needs (food, clothing, shelter, rest, exercise) satisfied, and the obvious way to acquire them was through working for a living. But a satisfied need does not *motivate*, McGregor notes, because once you have food, or a roof over your head, you start looking for other wants to be satisfied, including a sense of belonging, social recognition, the desire to give and receive, and love. Above these social needs are the egoistic needs, which take two forms. Firstly, self-esteem: self-respect, autonomy, a sense of achievement, the desire for knowledge. Secondly, reputation: status, recognition, appreciation by one's peers.

The big problem, as McGregor saw it, was that modern capitalism, with its mass-production system, seemed expressly designed to dismiss people's egoistic needs, particularly if they worked at the lower levels. Taylor's "scientific management" saw the human side of enterprise as something to control, suppress, or channel. Only a few people at the top were allowed to think. Workplaces were treating people as if they were children, so it was no surprise that they would act like children, trying to get what they needed in sly ways.

The alternative: Theory Y

One of the anomalies in Theory X was that companies were offering good wages, safe conditions, security and fringe benefits, and yet, as studies at the time from Ohio State University showed, workers were not being correspondingly more productive. Yet to McGregor this made sense: if all the company was doing is providing for the basic needs, it's no surprise that people are unmotivated. Their social and egoistic needs were being ignored.

In such organizations, employees feel that they are only be able to enjoy the rewards of their labor when they are *not* in the workplace, when they are "free" to enjoy themselves pursuing the things they *really* like. But this assumption is a total waste of people who could be much more engaged and productive if the work itself was made to be rewarding, if the organization supported social grouping and community feeling, and if the egoistic needs for knowledge and advancement were catered for through further training and personal development. If an employer can set up an environment which allows for the higher needs to be met, pay and benefits will become only one factor motivating people to stay and do their job well.

McGregor's new paradigm, which he called "Theory Y," involved a different set of assumptions:

- The desire to work is as natural as the desire to rest or play. When people believe in the aims of a group or organization, they are naturally self-directed and motivated and will use imagination and ingenuity to help it achieve its aims.
- People don't just accept responsibility, but actually seek it out. They want their potential to be realized.

In short, it is rarely that people are the problem if an organization is not doing well, but management's failure to let its people flourish. For instance, in Theory X, promotions (and the possibility of being promoted) are the main means of gaining the commitment of staff to the goals of the organization. But for everyone who is not promoted, the lack of responsibility and self-direction will be a drag on the organization, since these people will see only a gap between what the organization wants and what they as individuals need to function optimally. The idea that people's personal goals are as important as the aims of the company is far-fetched to Theory X management. What would result? Anarchy? No: it means that the employee "will continuously be encouraged to develop and utilize voluntarily his capacities, his knowledge, his skill, his ingenuity in ways which contribute to the success of the enterprise." Theory Y is simply about the integration of individual and organizational goals.

McGregor acknowledges Peter Drucker's "management by objectives" as the big theory in his time, but observes that its application meant little more than companies changing tactics while staying within the direction-and-control paradigm. He is in agreement with W. Edwards Deming that when things go wrong in an organization, it is the system or management that is at fault, not the workers. Together with Deming, McGregor was very anti-performance appraisals, for the simple reason that "any individual's performance is, to a considerable extent, a function of how he is managed." It seems common sense that when a superior points out poor performance, the subordinate will be motivated to change it. In fact, most of the time it just creates defensiveness and resentment. Much better is when an employee appraises themselves based on previously set goals and targets.

Culture matters

Today's emphasis on "culture" in organizations has its origins in McGregor's thinking. It doesn't matter what the formal policies or mission statements of the company are, McGregor said, but rather the "quality of daily interactions." It is these that create the company "climate."

Neither is it enough to have programs to look for the "best talent" and recruit or promote them. Organizations have to create a culture of potential and growth within the organization. Until McGregor's time, a lot of research had gone into identifying "leadership material," but McGregor believed that there were no inborn traits or personalities that made a leader. He argued that organizations shouldn't just have a narrow executive leadership program, but develop heterogeneous leaders across the organization. All this presaged the more "distributed leadership" ideas that guide organizations today, in which every employee is expected to lead in some capacity.

McGregor was in favor of "Scanlon plans," in which employee participation and organizational achievement were preferred to incentive plans which focused on the gains and achievements of individual workers. These were consistent with Theory Y, McGregor felt, in that internal competition would evaporate in favor of the organization as a whole achieving its goals.

Horizontal over vertical

It may seem ironic that the research and time needed to write *The Human Side of Enterprise* was funded by Alfred P. Sloan's foundation, Sloan being, of course, head of General Motors in its prime and the author of *Concept of the Corporation*, which delineated traditional forms of management including the corporate divisional structure and its chains of command.

Yet McGregor's ideas were not about building an anything-goes culture, rather one in which people were expected to think for themselves and solve things—participative, not permissive. "It is probable," he writes, "that one day we shall begin to draw organization charts as a series linked groups rather than as a hierarchical structure of individual 'reporting' relationships."

McGregor believed that the value of really good teamwork was only just beginning to be appreciated. Management and technology fads came and went, but a truly collaborative enterprise would be a powerful thing with many economic (for the firm) and psychological (for the workers) advantages.

This is exactly what came to pass in more advanced organizations. For instance, Steve Jobs, after he came back to head Apple, changed its organization into a network of teams that talked to each other constantly, rather than having silos or divisions, in order to have the whole company move forward as one. Even in the notoriously hierarchical US military, the power of teams has in many cases replaced the emphasis on vertical command in dealing with insurgency groups, when effectiveness and indeed survival depends on thinking quickly on the ground (see Chapter 28).

Final comments

Despite McGregor's influence, Theory X thinking is surprisingly persistent. It would be hard to argue, for instance, that firms including Samsung or Walmart operate in the spirit of Theory Y. Company cultures can be traced back to their founders and their views on human nature—which either involve trust or mistrust. McGregor hated the idea of organizations imposing participative practices under the banner of personal growth—that is, mimicking Theory Y ideas in order to increase the bottom line. As such cynical use of his ideas is now common, it seems that every generation has to discover McGregor's ideas anew.

He was writing at a time when jobs were more stable and secure, wages were growing, and automation was not the threat to paid work it is today. In an uncertain world in which many consider themselves lucky to have a job at all, Theory X workplaces could make a comeback. After all, the company could use a machine, or it could employ you. There is no clear necessity for the development of human potential. McGregor's central question—whether people are the key sources of value in an organization, or a cost to cut wherever possible—remains very relevant.

Douglas McGregor

McGregor was born in Detroit in 1906. In his twenties he gained an MA and Ph.D. in social psychology from Harvard University, and began teaching at Harvard in 1935. At MIT he set up a department of industrial relations and became a professor in its Sloan School of Management. In 1948 he became president of Antioch College, where he stayed for six years before returning to MIT. McGregor died from a heart attack in 1964.

Crossing the Chasm

"Every truly innovative high-tech product starts out as a fad—something with no known market value or purpose but with great properties that generate a lot of enthusiasm within an 'in crowd' of early adopters. That's the early market. Then comes a period during which the rest of the world watches to see if anything can be made out of this; that is the chasm."

In a nutshell

There is a distinct pattern to the acceptance of new products in the marketplace, ignorance of which dooms many start-ups.

In a similar vein

Clayton Christensen *The Innovator's Dilemma*
Jim Collins *Great by Choice*
Ben Horowitz *The Hard Thing About Hard Things*
Al Ries & Jack Trout *Positioning*
Peter Thiel *Zero To One*

CHAPTER 30

Geoffrey A. Moore

How can it be, Geoffrey Moore asks, that the product that becomes number one in its field often has fewer features than its competitors, and sometimes is clearly not "the best"? When this happens, the people in the also-ran company who developed the product look for someone to blame. Just as LinkedIn outmarketed Plaxo, and Salesforce outmarketed RightNow, they think, its clearly *marketing's* fault.

Actually, Moore argues in the million-selling *Crossing the Chasm: Marketing and Selling Disruptive Products to Mainstream Customers*, there is usually something more fundamental going on in such failures: a misunderstanding of the way products or services transition from a small, initial market, to a large, mainstream one. In between the two lies a chasm so fearful and deep that it has claimed, and continues to claim, thousands of unknowing start-ups. "A successful crossing is how high-tech fortunes are made," Moore writes. "Failure in the attempt is how they are lost."

The book is the result of hundreds of consulting assignments to tech companies. Moore's field is marketing within the high-tech world, but he says its lessons can be generalized to other fields. There have been two revised editions, the most recent in 2014. This is the one to get, as the contemporary examples make the principles come alive. Moore has a Ph.D. in English literature and worked as an English professor before moving to Silicon Valley. Apart from the useful content, his writing is crisp and often amusing, making the book stand out from most other books on strategy and marketing.

The map

Consider a product built on a new technology: the all-electric Tesla Model S. Assuming it is cleaner, quieter, and better for the environment, the interesting question from a marketer's point of view is not whether the car is desirable, but *when* a consumer might consider buying one.

If you want to be one of the first in your neighborhood to own a Tesla, and you are entranced by the firm's technology, under what's known as the Technology Adoption Life Cycle you are an "innovator or early adopter." However, if you are waiting until there is just enough charging stations on the roads before you get one, you will be classed as an "early majority" buyer. If you feel you may get an electric car, but only when they start to dominate the roads, you are termed one of the "late majority." And if you are so resistant to the new that you can't ever see yourself moving on from the petrol engine, but admit that you might transition one day, you are a very "late adopter," or "laggard."

The early majority want to wait and see if a technology is a fad or will start to become mainstream. When they make the judgment that it will, a massive new market starts to form. If a company is first on to the market with a technology, and has the means to roll it out as a working product, it has the chance of enjoying a virtual monopoly, or at least 50 percent of the market. In Silicon Valley, examples include Microsoft in software, Oracle in relational databases, Cisco in routers and switches, and Google in search advertising. This is where the big fortunes are made.

The terrain

The thinking behind the Technology Adoption Life Cycle is that your new product makes a series of smooth transitions in appeal from the early adopters to the laggards. An example is Apple's iPad tablet computer, launched in 2009, which was taken up with passion by early Mac enthusiasts, quickly found its way on to the desks of executives and salespeople, and then, because it was the first computer that didn't even look like a computer, and could do amazing things, was taken up by everyone from toddlers to grandpas.

Unfortunately, such products are a rarity, Moore says. The Technology Adoption Life Cycle rarely maps reality, because there is in fact no natural flow from one stage of users to another. The experience of anyone who has lost money on a new company that promises to create a whole new market and yet does not, tells us that there is a big gap—in fact, a chasm—between the smallish market for something new that is taken up by early adopters, and the emerging mainstream market of the early majority.

The chasm is only crossed when a company develops a product that is not just slightly more, but *massively* more easy to use that what currently exists, appealing to the non-technologist. Just because a community of tech enthusiasts raves about a product, it doesn't mean that the rest of the population is interested. They will only buy if people like them (the majority) start to recommend.

Companies often misinterpret an early spike in sales for their innovative product as an early point in a continuously upward sloping curve into the mainstream market. Actually, these early sales are more often a blip. Sometimes, a new technology product is promoted as being able to change life for the majority, but in the end, like the Segway, it stays more of a recreational thing, or is just used in some industrial settings. It turned out that the Segway's wide use was stopped by something as simple as stairs.

Crossing the business-to-business chasm

In the B2B tech world, visionaries or early adopters of a new product are looking for a *breakthrough* in productivity or customer service for their company. For example, when Reed Hastings of Netflix decided to put his entire business on Amazon's cloud, or when Harry McMahon at Merrill Lynch committed to putting the whole sales system on the as-yet-proven Salesforce cloud platform.

Unfortunately for the purveyors of unproven products, these kinds of customers are in a minority. Most businesses are not looking for a breakthrough, but rather to preserve and enhance their existing systems. This is the mainstream market, and if you want to sell to these pragmatists, you have to put yourself in their minds, know what issues they have to deal with, attend their industry conferences. "You need to have earned a reputation for quality and service," Moore advises, be "the obvious supplier of choice."

Beyond the pragmatists in an industry are the conservatives, who "when they find something that works for them, like to stick with it." The way to market your company's offering to conservatives is to make it so compelling it doesn't make sense to say no. For instance, offer a simple, bundled package of services at a very discounted price, and make sure the product works seamlessly with other systems they have. Put everything into creating a "whole solution."

Finally, a step beyond the conservatives are the skeptics, who actively mistrust vendors and look for the gaps between what is claimed for a product and the value it actually provides. Instead of being defensive and dismissing this group, listening to the skeptics can bring great gains. After all, if there is a gap between marketing and performance, it will come back to haunt you. But if even the skeptics can be made happy, you know that your market is solid and long term.

To cross a chasm, secure a beachhead

The biggest mistake companies make, Moore says, is that they believe they can only prosper in the early days by going after any kind of sale that seems to add to their momentum. Yet Moore's experience is that the ones who succeed are very focused on winning and dominating a tight niche, that is, first securing a small beachhead in a big market. If they can do that, they will have little or no competition when and if their product goes mainstream.

In the D-Day analogy that he uses, you have to secure Normandy before you can even think of taking Paris.

Doing this means the development of a "whole product," a complete suite of products and services focused on achieving a single benefit for the user. If you find that you get customers from doing this, you have a clear reference point for getting more. If you experiment with too many products or services, your efforts will be wasted. The reason it works like this is word of mouth. If you focus on a tight niche, the people in that field or industry will, if they like your product, talk to each other about it, and soon a momentum will build toward support of what you are doing. But if you take the sales-driven approach of doing some kind of business across different areas, the customer base will be too diffuse and word of mouth will not develop.

A stark truth for new tech companies is that the pragmatists in their industry only want to buy from the market leader, who usually provides a complete "whole product" solution. Given this, the only hope you have as an emergent company is to have a "big fish, small pond" strategy, to own your segment from the start. Customers may complain about the limitations of your product, but in another sense they will be happy to be "owned" because it simplifies things for them, and they know what they are working with.

When Apple targeted, with its Macintosh, the graphic arts departments of large companies, the fact that it was a smallish market was actually a good thing, as Apple was able to establish its proprietary standard within corporations, despite the fact that IT departments favored IBM PCs. But having established a beachhead, Apple started selling its computers to marketing and sales teams within those companies, and then to the advertising and creative agencies who worked with them.

Generally, "The more serious the problem, the faster the target niche will pull you out of the chasm," Moore observes. "Once out, your opportunities to expand into other niches are immensely increased because now, having one set of pragmatic customers solidly behind you, you are much less risky for others to back as a new vendor."

Final comments

This is the essence of *Crossing the Chasm*, but Moore also includes several chapters consistent with his D-Day analogy—"Target the Point of Attack," "Assemble the Invasion Force," "Define the Battle," and "Launch the Invasion"—which provide the nuts-and-bolts tips and tactics to get that vital beachhead in a mainstream market. Again, although all his examples are from the tech world, the ideas are relevant to any industry.

Perhaps Moore's key point is that a pre-chasm company has an entirely different purpose to a post-chasm one. In a company's early days, its aim is to demonstrate to investors that it has built something with a proven customer base. For example, the chief concern of online social media firms (think Facebook, Twitter, and Instagram in their early days) is to establish their platform as the dominant one in their segment with a growing user base. They may start to create revenue streams, but profitability as such is not expected. With online retailers, the principle is the same. Amazon went for years without turning a profit, but all the while it was investing hugely in the technology and infrastructure needed to cement its dominant position. Only when these things are achieved should investors, and the company itself, work to systematically make money. At this point it inevitably becomes a different company, with proper management, and its R & D focus shifts from creating the initial product to furnishing the "whole product" with associated services and support.

This is all difficult, grown-up stuff, and it will prompt some of the company's original visionaries to want to leave. This is unfortunate, Moore says, but is the price of an enterprise fulfilling its potential.

Geoffrey A. Moore

Moore was born in 1946. After his career in academia he moved to California and began as a corporate trainer in the tech industry, then as a sales and marketing executive. After working for tech marketing guru Regis McKenna he started his own consultancy firm, Geoffrey Moore Consulting, which became the Chasm Group. He also founded the Chasm Institute, a training firm, and is a partner in venture capital firms Mohr Davidow Ventures and Wildcat Venture Partners.

His other books on tech industry marketing and positioning include Inside the Tornado *(1995),* Escape Velocity *(2011), and* Zone to Win *(2015).*

Strengths Based Leadership

"*Organizations are quick to look for leaders who are great communicators, visionary thinkers, and who can also get things done and follow through. All of these attributes are desirable and necessary for an organization to succeed. But of all the leaders we have studied, we have yet to find one who has world-class strength in all of these areas. Sure, many leaders can get by or are above average in several domains. But paradoxically, those who strive to be competent in all areas become the least effective leaders overall.*"

"*Unfortunately, few people have discovered the place in life where they have most potential for growth.*"

In a nutshell

We waste too much energy trying to fix our weaknesses. Successful people single-mindedly work to amplify their strengths.

In a similar vein

Peter Drucker *The Effective Executive*
Patrick Lencioni *The Five Dysfunctions of a Team*
Eric Schmidt & Jonathan Rosenberg *How Google Works*

CHAPTER 31

Tom Rath & Barry Conchie

The French priest/philosopher Teilhard de Chardin talked of "the incom-municable singularity of being that each of us possesses." For Teilhard, our uniqueness was something to be celebrated, not ironed out. He would have appreciated today's focus on "strengths," which says that our singularity will never be expressed if we are doggedly giving most of our energies to our weak spots, instead of joyfully getting better at what we are good at anyway.

Strengths Based Leadership: Great Leaders, Teams, and Why People Follow seeks to explode the myth of the "well-rounded" leader, arguing that "those who strive to be competent in all areas become the least effective leaders overall." The book presents the outcome of decades of research by the Gallup organization, drawing on the insights of Donald O. Clifton (who died in 2003). Clifton conducted 20,000 interviews with leaders of all descriptions, from corporations to non-profits to countries; Tom Rath and Barry Conchie built on this with their own research of 10,000 *followers*.

Not dissimilar to Abraham Maslow, who went against the Freudian grain in the 1960s by deciding to study evolved people and peak experiences, Clifton asked, "What would happen if we studied what is *right* with people?" What were people capable of if they spent most of their effort building on their talents, as opposed to correcting their weaknesses? He defined talents as "naturally occurring patterns thought, feeling, or behavior that can be productively applied," characterized by "yearnings, rapid learning, satisfac-tions, and timelessness." When you go beyond your natural attraction to acting or doing in a certain way, and apply those talents or affinities along with skills, knowledge, and experience, you have a strength. Clifton's belief that talents could be studied and articulated led to the Clifton StrengthsFinder, a survey designed to measure talents, which could then be turned into strengths.

A leader is by definition unique

Rath and Conchie start the book with a little story of an employee, Sarah, and her boss, Bob. Every few months, Bob will return from a seminar with the latest leadership fad that he wants to implement in the organization. Bob likes studying great leaders from history, and from each of them he draws some "answer" about how leaders should be, whether it is empathetic, creative, disciplined, strategic, humble, decisive, or a great communicator. But Sarah knows, and Bob fails to see, that no great leader combines all these qualities; indeed, his time would be better spent identifying his singular strengths.

The only thing that great leaders have in common, the authors note, is that they are very aware of what they are good at, and what they are not, and they have spent their careers fully exploiting their edge so that it becomes even sharper. There can be no definitive list of traits of good leaders, for the simple reason that every person is different, and every remarkable achievement is a case of that person taking their characteristics and making them even more powerfully unique. Paradoxically, when people try to emulate others too much, they take themselves away from the one or two traits that could really make them successful. Moreover, different kinds of leadership is good for different situations. As Rath and Conchie note, Churchill's combative nature was just the thing for standing up to the Nazis, while in India's struggle for independence, Gandhi's calm yet stubborn approach in the face of British power worked precisely because he did not try to copy the kind of domineering leader seen throughout history.

In 2008, Tim Judge of the University of Florida published the results of a longitudinal study of over 7,000 men and women. Those who tested high on self-confidence when they were teenagers and young adults, 25 years later had significantly more career success, higher education levels and better health, than those measured with lower self-confidence. The study backed up Rath and Conchie's own data that a big part of self-confidence is being aware of what you are good at, and leveraging it. If you do this, you are naturally more likely to get better paid for the work you enjoy, and be motivated to remain healthy to enjoy this sense of well-being and power. Focusing on your strengths, it turns out, is not a luxury but a foundation of a good life.

Rath and Conchie include profiles of four individuals who achieved remarkable success by leveraging their dominant strengths. The first is Wendy Kopp, who just out of college founded Teach For America, which hires the best new graduates to go in and work at subpar inner-city schools. Within 12 months Kopp was able to raise $2.5 million to start the project, in order to employ her targeted minimum of 500 teachers. What started as "one of the most successful start-ups of the past century" is now an institution, but it only happened because Kopp knew she was very good at organizing and executing, and put these strengths in the service of another trait, a well-developed social conscience. Today, thousands of graduates forsake top careers at banks or management consultancies to be part of Teach For America. The success of institutions like this, the authors say, shows what happens when an individual gives free rein to their strengths.

Strong individuals = strong teams

Smart organizations know that trying to fix people's weaknesses only reduces their confidence, whereas getting them to identify and express their strengths makes them feel valued and engaged. This engaged feeling is good for the employee, naturally, and makes the organization effective.

When they studied executive teams, the authors found that most members had been hired for their knowledge or competence. This sounds logical, but it means that the best salesperson becomes the sales manager (even if she is only good at selling, not at managing people) and the smartest accounting person becomes the Chief Financial Officer (even if he is no good at the big picture or strategy). As a result, you get frequent mismatches between person and job. Instead of recruiting according to the function of a job, it is better to look first at the strengths of people and then work out how they can contribute. Sometimes, because of their unique view of the world, they will know this better than the organization does.

Rath and Conchie's broad point is that, "While the best leaders are not well-rounded, the best teams are." Together, the members of a team must cover four domains of leadership strength, which they identify as Executing (people who can just get things done), Influencing (the ones who can sell the firm's message to the public, press, or industry), Building Relationships (those with a particular skill at bringing people together and uniting the organization), and Strategic Thinking (the individuals who are looking ahead to what the organization can become). The authors go as far as saying that the people who make up your teams should be "wildly different" to each other.

Consider Abraham Lincoln's "team of rivals," his cabinet of diverse characters who were powerful in their own right, and were allowed to express their strengths under Lincoln's overarching vision. At a corporate level, recall the team that Ray Kroc built around him in the early days of McDonald's. You could not have picked a more motley bunch of people, and Kroc's genius was to give them a relatively free reign while he remained the inspirational figurehead.

Many organizations make the mistake of hiring people for strengths that merely mimic or buttress the ones that the CEO already has. You get an organization built in the leader's image. For a time this may seem to give it power, but at the first real change in market conditions the lack of strength diversity in the team is revealed, and they are unable to adapt. As Israeli president Shimon Peres put it in a Gallup interview, "Most leaders prefer loyalty over brilliance; they're afraid that they're going to be undercut." In contrast, good organizations respect diversity of age, gender, and race, Rath and Conchie argue, because they know that teams of people who think the same way, have the same backgrounds and experiences, are not a recipe for success in a diverse, fast-changing world.

Why people follow

Why do we spend so much time studying leaders, the authors wondered, without bothering to ask followers what makes for good leadership? You are, after all, only a leader if others are willing to follow you. Don't ask a president if she is doing well in the job, ask the people who voted her in. The authors' research identified "four basic needs" of followers:

Trust   Trusting the organization and its management is crucial for increasing employee engagement. If you trust the leadership, you will be motivated. Trust also increases speed and efficiency, because you don't have to establish each relationship each time. Successful teams don't talk much about trust because it is just *there*. It is only in unsuccessful teams that it is an issue.

Compassion   People really want to know that their boss cares about them as a person. If they feel this, they are much more likely to work hard for the organization and stay long term.

Stability   People want to feel that the organization is stable, that its core values don't change, in addition to feeling that it has a secure financial future. The authors profile Simon Cooper, who ran the Ritz-Carlton company. He was acutely aware that many of his employees supported a whole extended family with their wages from the company. Making their positions stable was as important to him as the need to find paying guests.

Hope   If employees feel enthusiastic about the future, they will be more engaged and productive. One of the key roles of a leader is to create a sense of optimism, but Rath and Conchie found that most leaders they interviewed were not doing this, rather spending their time reacting to events. Leaders don't just respond, they initiate. It is easier to get kudos for handling an event, or be efficient at cleaning out your in-box, but the true meaning of leadership resides in being able to *shape the future*.

The most extraordinary leaders, Rath and Conchie note, "do not see personal success as an end in itself." Rather, they want their activity and vision to continue after they have gone, expressed in the lives of their followers or in an institution that embodies them. "Perhaps the ultimate test of a leader is not what you are able to do in the here and now," they write, "but instead what continues to grow long after you're gone."

Final comments

People tend to take for granted what they are good at. Precisely because we can't see ourselves properly, it is worthwhile doing tests such as the StrengthsFinder (the book includes a code for a free online test) so it is all brought to the surface and articulated. My half-dozen strengths, for example, are Futuristic (imagining what could be); Ideation (coming up with new ideas); Leading with Input (collating and providing information); Leading with Intellection (discussion of ideas); Leading with Learner (learning for its own sake); and Strategic (seeing the alternative paths to take). Being clear about such things means that you don't have to beat yourself up about not being a Relator, Harmonizer or Includer, or something else which just isn't you.

While there is certainly a case for school education, and even the first years of university, being designed to open us up to as many disciplines and experiences as possible, adult life is about concentrating one's energies. This does not mean becoming a savant in one area to the extent that we cannot keep learning or making connections between things. It does mean becoming clear on how we can have the most impact, simply by being a greater version of what we already are.

Tom Rath & Barry Conchie

Born in 1975, Rath has degrees in psychology from the University of Michigan and the University of Pennsylvania. After college he began working for Gallup, where he remains a consultant and adviser. His other books include How Full Is Your Bucket? Positive Strategies for Work and Life *(2004, with Donald O. Clifton) and* Eat Move Sleep: How Small Choices Lead to Big Changes *(2013).*

Conchie is a consultant in the areas of corporate leadership, team diagnostics, and succession planning. He worked in the UK civil service before joining Gallup in London, and is based in its Washington DC office.

Positioning

"Even today, companies are focused on building products rather than brands. A product is something made in a factory. A brand is something made in the mind. To be successful today, you have to build brands, not products."

"Heinz is the bigger company with the bigger name, but Vlasic outsells Heinz in pickles and Gerber outsells Heinz in baby food. A big company with a big reputation usually cannot compete successfully with a smaller company with a well-defined position. Size doesn't matter. Positioning does."

In a nutshell

It's senseless trying to go head to head with an established leader of a product or category. Instead, develop a new product or service that you can be first in.

In a similar vein

Clayton Christensen *The Innovator's Dilemma*
W. Chan Kim & Renée Mauborgne *Blue Ocean Strategy*
Richard Koch & Greg Lockwood *Simplify*
Theodore Levitt *Marketing Myopia*

CHAPTER 32

Al Ries & Jack Trout

Many feel that *Positioning: The Battle for Your Mind* is the simplest and best book on marketing ever written, showing readers how to position a product or service so that it "owns" a particular mental space in people's minds.

The positioning concept created a revolution in the advertising and marketing fields. Before positioning, advertising and marketing was all about being the "first," "best," or "finest" (just look at old labels). After positioning, firms often felt comfortable promoting themselves by admitting what they were *not*. For example, Avis's famous campaign admitted it was number two to Hertz in car rental, but asked people to try them because "We try damned hard. (When you're not the biggest, you have to.)"

The book's success that it forced a career change on the authors, Al Ries and Jack Trout. They had been in advertising, but discovered that what companies really prized was marketing strategy based on their positioning concept, so marketing strategists they became. The positioning idea is powerful, they suggest, because it makes sense not just in business, but in life. Most people progress not through competition, but through differentiation.

Positioning was written at a time when Pan Am was still around, Xerox and IBM ruled the roost in technology, and O. J. Simpson was starring in ads for Hertz. Even the 2001 edition, which included updates on the original text in the margins, seems pretty dated. That said, the positioning concept itself is timeless, and it is easy to think of new examples and iterations as you are reading.

Standing for something, anything

Positioning is simply the way you differentiate yourself in the mind of the prospect—what in their eyes you stand for. In an age when we experience a torrent of information and advertising every day, the authors write, being seen to stand for anything at all is an achievement.

You can't be "creative" and try to win one over the customer with crafty advertising, since they will already have a firm view of what your product or service is about. And once they have that view, it's extremely hard to change it, even if you throw potloads of money at a campaign. The only way through the mass of communications bombarding people is to position a product or service so clearly that it doesn't even need advertising, so that it becomes a space in people's mind (e.g. Volvo = safety; FedEx = overnight; BMW = driving). The human mind only has so much attention and bandwidth. Given this "overcommunicated" world, with massive and increasing advertising budgets, people's only defense is to simplify, to cut back to what they trust and are clear about, filtering out all the rest.

From a marketing point of view, you have to work out what message has the best chance of sticking or getting through. "You concentrate on the perceptions of the product, not the reality of the product." In advertising, politics, in fact in all walks of life, it is perception that matters. Given that advertising, despite vast expenditure, so frequently fails to achieve its aims, it's not surprising that public relations, or working to create or shape perceptions of a person, product, or service, has raced ahead as an industry.

The original and the best

Everyone remembers the name of the first man to step on to the moon (Neil Armstrong). Not many can recall the second. Everyone can name the highest mountain on earth (Mount Everest). Not many can name the second highest. In selling products or services, it doesn't matter so much whether yours is the best or not, but whether it is the *first* in people's minds. IBM didn't invent the computer (Sperry-Rand did, with the Univac), but was the first big computer company—and there it remains in many people's minds, decades later. Coca-Cola *was* the first cola, and still is. Hertz *was* the first rent-a-car company, and is still number one. Yes, it's possible to be second or third in something, and still be successful. But it's much easier to be the first.

The numbers show that the first brand that becomes well known in a category will get twice the market share of the second, and the second will get twice as much as the number three. Consider brands like Campbell's soup, Coca-Cola, Colgate toothpaste, Gillette razors, Goodyear tires, Kellogg's cereals, Lipton teas, Wrigley's chewing gum—the list goes on. McDonald's will always outsell Burger King, Goodyear will always outsell Firestone, Harvard will always be more famous than Yale. And yet, the authors say, "Leadership should always be communicated with a certain amount of humility." It is always better to remind people of your authenticity instead, which doesn't require bragging. Coca-Cola's best ever tag line was "The real thing." Simple and true, because whatever brand is the first to fill a category, people *naturally* perceive it as the real thing. Think Heinz in ketchup, Zippo in lighters, Xerox in copiers. Any product that comes after it will be perceived as an imitation.

If you can't be first, admit it and make the most of it. After Avis kept getting bigger, it ditched the We Try Harder campaign for one saying "Avis is going to be number one." This was just unpleasant braggadocio, betraying people's liking for the underdog that was part of the old campaign. People think of Avis as number two, and it should be happy to have that position in their minds. 7UP tried to do something similar with its campaign "America is turning 7UP," suggesting that people were switching from Coke and Pepsi. But everyone just thought, "No it's not." A waste of tons of advertising dollars.

Nothing lasts forever, and there are plenty of big brands that have been slowly and inadvertently killed off by their owners. Xerox, of course, lost focus and declined because it tried to get into computers. Kodak did the same by trying to be a player in a host of areas that had nothing to do with photography. Whatever they did, it failed, because in the public's mind Kodak meant one thing only: photography.

Look for the hole

Most companies are not OK with being successful also-rans. They want to be leaders. But the way to do so is not to go head to head with an established brand, but to create a winning new one.

As an industry follower, the best strategy for finding some kind of dominance is to "look for the hole." In other words, whatever the industry as a whole is doing, try to do the opposite. For years the motor industry was obsessed with making cars longer, lower, and sleeker. Then came the Volkswagen Beetle: short, fat, and ugly—and a hit. Its slogan for the American car market, which is famous for big machines: "Think small."

Another way to carve out a position with a product is to charge a lot more for it. In a throw-away society, people are willing to pay more for things that are designed to last, like a Mercedes-Benz. Chivas Regal became a top Scotch brand by being quite open about how expensive it was. "The price (high or low) is as much a feature of the product as anything else," the authors note.

The contrarian approach can work in advertising, without changing the product at all. For years, all cigarettes ads had pretty women in them, because most smokers were male. Then Philip Morris decided to sell his Marlboro cigarettes by showing men—*real* men: cowboys. How could you advertise your product that is different to the way everyone else does?

Another way to become number one is to attack or reposition the existing number one. When reports emerged that aspirin could irritate the stomach lining in some people and cause allergic reactions, Tylenol wasn't slow to write ads about it, attacking the Bayer aspirin brand and ending with the words, "Fortunately, there is Tylenol." Tylenol is today the number one painkiller brand in the United States.

Emphasizing authenticity is a proven way to come out on top. Once upon a time, three American-made vodkas had most of the US market. The advertising firm behind another brand, Stolichnaya, decided to position it by making much of the fact that it was made in Leningrad, Russia, whereas the others, with fake Russian names like Samovar and Smirnoff, were made in Pennsylvania and Connecticut. Sales soared. "People like to see the high and mighty exposed," Ries and Trout note. "They like to see bubbles burst." After Russia invaded Afghanistan, Stolichnaya's distributor Pepsico got cold feet about the Russian origins, and changed its ads. Absolut was then launched and took the top spot instead. In the authors' minds, Stolichnaya should have weathered the storm and not disowned its Russian origins. Political events come and go, after all. The important thing is to create and maintain a long-term position in people's minds.

Tempted to extend

The dumbest marketing strategy, the authors argue, is line extension, or using the name of an established product to launch a new one. For instance, Life Savers candy, Life Savers chewing gum; Kleenex tissue, Kleenex towels. While logic and intuition seems to favor line extension—acceptance by the trade, consumer acceptance, lower advertising costs—in reality it is nearly always a failure.

Tanqueray, the gin brand, tried to launch Tanqueray Sterling vodka. A mistake, because in everyone's mind Tanqueray means gin. The Levi-Strauss company thought that people would want to buy tailored slacks if they knew they were made by Levi-Strauss. Its "Levi's Tailored Classics" line duly failed. But when it launched the same product under the name "Dockers," it carved out a big global market.

After decades of brand extension failures, big companies still don't get it. The latest thing is, after a big company has bought a brand, to put next to it in smaller font, "A GE company" or (in bottled water, for instance) "A Coca-Cola Company." But does the public ever care who owns a company? People only care about the product. Corporate egos can't bear the thought that, after the firm has acquired a brand, people won't know it. The hard truth: Brands matter to people, companies don't.

"People suffer from the same disease as products," Ries and Trout write. "They try to be all things to all people." Cadillac once meant large luxury American car in the public's mind. Then came the smaller Cadillac Seville.

It led to a burst of sales for Cadillac, but weakened the Cadillac name. The problem is, executives and investors always get in the way, wanting bigger product lines. This brings short-term revenue and profit boosts, but often kills the brand in the long run. It's a simple fact of life, Ries and Trout say, that "strong positions in the prospect's mind are built on major achievements. Not on broad product lines." Don't try to make your brand everything.

The power of a name

But how do you carve out a perception of *yourself* in people's minds? Become known for some great quest or goal or interest that you are devoting your life to, the authors suggest. This makes people want to help you, rather than just seeing you as out for yourself. Become known as the person who attempts a lot, even if you fail more than half of the time. One of the greatest jockeys of all time, Eddie Arcaro, lost 250 races before he rode his first winner.

Another strategy to make a name is simply to *change* your name. Would Ralph Lauren have become Ralph Lauren if he had stayed Ralph Lifshitz? Would Marion Morrison have become huge if he had not changed his name to John Wayne? What if Kirk Douglas had remained Issur Danielovitch? "There is only negative equity in a bad name," the authors argue. "When the name is bad, things tend to get worse. When the name is good, things tend to get better." If your name is too similar to other people, change it. Liza Minelli may never have become so big if she had taken her mother Judy Garland's name and just been "Liza Garland." You have to differentiate to be noticed. Procter & Gamble didn't call its new detergent Ivory, the name of its successful soap. It called it Tide. Toyota didn't try to create a "Super Toyota" or a "Toyota Ultra," it launched the Lexus.

When you come up with a name for your company or your new product, say it out loud before you write it down, and see if people can say it easily and like it. "The mind works by ear, not by the eye." A contemporary example: Jeff Bezos changed the name of his company from "Cadabra" because to an early employee it sounded like "cadaver." Amazon, the name Bezos settled on, sounded good and conjured up an image of width and abundance.

In products and in people, never ever underestimate the power of a name.

Final comments

Ries and Trout's "Law of Two" states that there is usually one dominant brand in a category, and an also-ran with significant market share. Coke and Pepsi, Hertz and Avis. The other players in the category, who have little name recognition, scramble for a diminishing share. Even when *Positioning* was written, this seemed a little unbalanced, but the dynamic is now more evident than ever. The winner-takes-all nature of today's online arena, with its network effects in which the more a platform is used, the stronger it gets, means that the Law of One is more apt. In the United States at least, there is no real competitor to Facebook in social media, Amazon dominates online retailing, and despite the efforts of Microsoft with Bing, there is no real competitor to Google. As Ries and Trout said, you rarely succeed by going head to head with the number one, but rather must position yourself as something different, even if that position is smaller. Instagram can't be Facebook, but it can dominate online image sharing. Twitter can't be Facebook, but it can be number one in, well, tweeting. In a media-saturated world, firms should feel lucky that their brands are known for something, even if they would like to be something else. It is the temptation to mess with people's perceptions that has undone many great brands, just as much as the failure to keep ahead of technology or innovate.

Al Ries & Jack Trout

Ries, now 91, runs a marketing strategy consultancy, Ries & Ries, with his daughter Laura Ries. After graduating from DePauw University in 1950 he worked for General Electric in its advertising section before, in 1963, starting his own advertising agency in New York City. It evolved into the marketing strategy firm Ries & Trout. In 2016 the American Marketing Association added Ries to its Hall of Fame. His books include: Focus: The Future of Your Company Depends On It *(1996) and, with Laura Ries,* The 22 Immutable Laws of Branding *(1998),* The Fall of Advertising and the Rise of PR *(2002), and* The Origin of Brands *(2004).*

Trout worked with Ries at General Electric before joining his firm and eventually becoming partner in it. The duo's other key book is The 22 Immutable Laws of Marketing *(1993). Trout also wrote (with Steve Rivkin)* Differentiate or Die *(2000) and* Repositioning *(2009). Later with his own firm, Trout & Partners, he was an adviser to the US State Department, worked with David Axelrod, President Obama's adviser, and set up offices in China and India. He shifted his emphasis from positioning to repositioning, or highlighting the defects in your competitors so your product or service can stand out. Trout died in 2017.*

The Lean Startup

"Because we lack a coherent management paradigm for new innovative ventures . . . for every success there are far too many failures: products pulled from shelves mere weeks after being launched, high-profile startups lauded in the press and forgotten a few months later, and new products that wind up being used by nobody. What makes these failures particularly painful is not just the economic damage done to individual employees, companies, and investors; they are also a colossal waste of our civilization's most precious resource: the time, passion, and skill of its people. The Lean Startup movement is dedicated to preventing these failures."

In a nutshell

If you believe in your idea so much, be willing to be proven wrong on it by relentless testing and iteration. Whatever survives of the process you will know has a market.

In a similar vein

Ben Horowitz *The Hard Thing About Hard Things*
Guy Kawasaki *The Art of the Start*
Peter Senge *The Fifth Discipline*
Frederick Winslow Taylor *Principles of Scientific Management*
James P. Womack, Daniel T. Jones & Daniel Roos *The Machine that Changed the World*

CHAPTER 33

Eric Ries

As a computer programmer, Eric Ries was at his wit's end. "Throughout my career," he recalls, "I kept having the experience of working incredibly hard on products that ultimately failed in the marketplace." Each time an enterprise didn't work out, he believed it was because of an insufficient technical solution or wrong market timing. He never questioned the conventional wisdom about how to build and launch a product, which usually meant: coming up with a great business plan that would wow investors; building the product in secret; and launching it upon an eager public. It was only when things repeatedly failed to take off that he became desperate for any kind of solution, the more radical the better.

At IMVU, a start-up trying to build an online universe of avatars, Ries was advised by an investor to make marketing and the customer as important as IT engineering right from the start. In practice, this meant launching products way before they seemed ready, constantly testing variants and features on early customers, and a super-fast product cycle. For an engineer trained to get rid of all bugs before launching, and to make it as perfect as possible, this approach just seemed wrong. And yet, IMVU's eventual success only happened, Ries says, thanks to this radical iteration.

A blog that Ries started writing on the new "lean" start-up philosophy became popular, and he began promulgating its tenets around the world to entrepreneurs hungry to succeed more quickly. The result was *The Lean Startup: How Today's Entrepreneurs Use Continuous Innovation to Create Radically Successful Businesses*.

"My hope all along," Ries writes, "was to find ways to eliminate the tremendous waste I saw all around me: startups that built products nobody wanted, new products pulled from the shelves, countless dreams unrealized."

Unlikely friends: entrepreneurship and management
Like many in the world of technology start-ups, Ries was inspired by the legends of garage entrepreneurs whose little companies became big corporations. A lot of the stories covered the going-public phase when the protagonists became multimillionaires overnight. How they actually built the business, how they made crucial decisions, what systems they used, were

reduced to a few scenes. All this "boring" stuff, it seemed, was less interesting than the tale of creative genius, perseverance, and hard work.

But what if, Ries wondered, success was less heroic than that? What if entrepreneurship was more of a process than an art, that anyone with reasonable intelligence could follow to their advantage? His experience at IMVU told him that successful entrepreneurship was about *management*. That is, not simply coming up with a great product (the engineer's focus), but being focused on the market from the very start (the manager's or founder's responsibility). And yet, conventional management, with its planning, strategizing, and market research, was just not applicable to the start-up company. How *could* it be, when the start-up is not even clear on who their customer is yet, or where their market will be? "Planning and forecasting are only accurate when based on a long, stable operating history and a relatively static environment," Ries writes. "Startups have neither."

Lean start-up thinking, Ries hopes, is about bringing the emphasis on systematic innovation together with the very human and individualistic talent for dreaming up new things. In calling for more scientific thoroughness about what aspects of a business are the most valuable or are a drag on resources, and watching the business in action with forensic attention, Ries was inspired by Frederick Winslow Taylor (see Chapter 44).

A new approach to infant enterprise

Ries defines a start-up as "a human institution designed to create new products and services under conditions of extreme uncertainty." The words are carefully chosen. The phrase "human institution" reminds us that a new business venture is not simply about the product, but the people and processes involved in creating a sustainable enterprise. It also refers to the fact that entrepreneurs can be found in a unit of a large corporation, a government department, or a non-profit enterprise as much as in a garage in Silicon Valley. The essence of a start-up is innovation, not the structure or organization in which it is housed. The other crucial difference between start-ups and other enterprises is their inherent uncertainty. It is only start-ups (and their investors) that admit and accept this raw uncertainty that have a real chance of success, because they are not tied to following through on some plan that will chew through money.

In the early days of IMVU, the revenue coming in was embarrassingly low. At first, the monthly target was only $300–500, and it took a while for this to ramp up. Ries's team could have gone in for splashy ads, marketing gimmicks, or PR campaigns to get a spurt of revenue to please the early investors. But these "vanity metrics" or "success theater" antics would have only covered up the true state of things, distracting the team from their focus on steady upwards progress with demonstrated metrics.

Ries talks of the "audacity of zero" common to start-ups. It is too easy for them to have bravado about the great future ahead, as shown in their wonderful (yet untested) business plans, when there is as yet zero revenue. It takes courage to say to employees, investors, even spouses, "These are our numbers," even when they are so modest as to make people wonder why you are bothering. But the shiny audacity of zero often carries along with it massive waste, as the people involved in the start-up, and the investors, spend time and money getting behind something that no one, in their enthusiasm about the great idea, actually bothered to test. Great examples are dot.com-era failures Webvan and Pets.com, which set up huge infra-structures before realizing that the market just wasn't there for what they were offering. The other way, putting out a "minimum viable product," can go against everything the entrepreneur has had drummed into them about "putting your best foot forward." Many entrepreneurs are perfectionists, which makes it hard to release something that is far from perfect. Yet early adopters in the market take into account that something is new and untried, and are usually willing to forgive shortcomings in the service for being part of something new.

If the conventional planning approach of Webvan and Pets.com is at one end of the spectrum, at the other end is what Ries calls the "let's ship and see what happens" ethos. The first has too much discipline, the second too little. Neither are scientific ways of starting a business. The scientific method is to have a hypothesis, and then to constantly test it so that you know, empirically, what aspects of your offering are working and which are not. Of course, it is possible to just get a product out there and see it meet with success, but without testing you will never know for sure what people like about it, or the things they don't like, which, if subtracted from the product, could build an even bigger market.

Lean and learning: elements of start-up success

In his desire to do and see things differently, Ries sought out ideas from other industries. He discovered lean manufacturing (see Chapter 50 on Womack et al.'s *The Machine that Changed the World*) and Toyota's famed production process, which was all about the shrinking of batch sizes in order to offer more customized goods to customers, just-in-time production to eliminate waste and excess inventory, and fast product cycles to incorporate lots of small improvements to the process and product.

By applying the lean ethos to start-up culture, Ries arrived at three tightly related concepts: "Validated learning"—start-ups don't exist to make certain products or services per se, but to learn how to create a sustainable business by constant experiments to see what people find useful or valuable; "Build–measure–learn"—by seeing exactly how customers respond, you can either pivot away from an idea or feature or persevere with it; and "Innovation accounting"—this is the "boring stuff" involving "how to measure progress, how to set up milestones, and how to prioritize work," focused on the process of development and iteration.

If the traditional way of running a company is *efficiency* at the production end of a product or service, the focus of a lean start-up is on *learning*: that is, building a company that never rests in finding out what people really want or need. The paradox is that you can combine a big vision for your company with frequent iterations and changes in what you actually create and sell. The size of your ambition means you are more open as to the best means of achieving it. Conventional learning is often very expensive and painful. You "learn" something when your start-up collapses, leaving investors in the red and people out of a job. Validated learning means the discovery of empirical facts about the start-up's offering which can be applied *now* to make a better product, use an alternative, or abandon the product altogether. The conventional way is to follow through on a business plan despite mounting evidence that it isn't working. Ries tells of how he spent thousands of hours building an add-on to bring people's preferred instant messaging service into the AVMU platform, only to find out (through interviews and observation of people using the site) that they didn't want this. They preferred the idea of a messaging service that was unique to the site so that they could make new friends and chat with random avatars. This was expensive learning. He could have found out much earlier whether his system was the one people wanted, or not, by testing it at the start.

What a start-up does is innovate in some way, and this can just as easily happen inside a big company if there is the will. Intuit became a significant company through its TurboTax software for completing tax returns. Every year Intuit would release a new version of the product with some new feature it hoped would make it sell again. But after embracing the lean start-up philosophy, its TurboTax team started doing hundreds of tests of new innovations to the software, releasing the changes each weekend. The following week the data that came in would guide it to the features it would keep, or abandon. The entrepreneurs within the organization loved doing this because it involved constant learning. It was the middle managers and leaders who had a problem with it, Intuit founder Scott Cook told Ries, because they had got to where they were by being good analysts, not empirical testers.

Whereas under the traditional model Intuit had taken an average of five and a half years to develop a new product that might generate $50 million in revenue, now they were bringing in the same amount with products that had been developed in six months, and creating a much bigger range of products than before. Success came from "killing things that don't make sense fast and doubling down on the ones that do."

Final comments

The lean start-up philosophy is not a fad, and has been influential, because it is an application of the scientific method to business. As Karl Popper argued in *The Logic of Scientific Discovery* (see *50 Philosophy Classics*), a theory is not a theory until it can be falsified. Science (and business) proceeds out of a constant seesaw of hypothesis followed by experiment and testing. If you are not constantly testing your business concept, products, features, and marketing campaigns in the real world, it is probably only a matter of time before you fail or lose market share. It's a well-observed truth that few great businesses are based on their original business model anyway. Due to poor sales or investor pressure or both, they are forced to change tack and discover something that is genuinely popular—the "unexpected success" that Peter Drucker talks of in *Innovation and Entrepreneurship*.

The Lean Startup is over 7 years old, and although the principles are timeless it has plenty of examples (Groupon, Dropbox, Zappos) that seem a bit too familiar now. *The Startup Way* (2017) tells of Ries's subsequent experiences helping established companies stay entrepreneurial and keep growing.

Eric Ries

Born in 1978, Ries was at Yale University when he started his first company, Catalyst Recruiting, which hosted student profiles to match up with potential employers. The company folded in the dot.com bust and Ries moved to Silicon Valley, working as a developer for There.com, an online virtual reality world. After its failure in 2004 he co-founded IMVU. He resigned as chief technology officer in 2008 and joined venture capital firm Kleiner Perkins as an adviser. He has been an entrepreneur-in-residence at Harvard University, and gives frequent talks.

Lean In

"For decades, we have focused on giving women the choice to work inside or outside the home. We have celebrated the fact that women have the right to make this decision, and rightly so. But we have to ask ourselves if we have become so focused on supporting personal choices that we're failing to encourage women to aspire to leadership. It is time to cheer on girls and women who want to sit at the table, seek challenges, and lean in to their careers."

"Sometimes I wonder what it would be like to go through life without being labeled by my gender. I don't wake up thinking, What am I going to do today as Facebook's female COO? but that's often how I'm referred to by others. When people talk about a female pilot, a female engineer, or a female race car driver, the word 'female' implies a bit of surprise. Men in the professional world are rarely seen through this same gender lens. A Google search for 'Facebook's male CEO' returns this message: 'No results found.'"

In a nutshell

More women at the top is not just good for its own sake; companies will only succeed if they are properly representative of half of their market.

In a similar vein

Peter Drucker *The Effective Executive*
Eric Schmidt & Jonathan Rosenberg *How Google Works*

CHAPTER 34

Sheryl Sandberg

Addressing a conference in Saudi Arabia, Bill Gates was asked his best tip for business success. For a start, he said, you will never achieve your economic potential if one-half of the population, with all its brains, talent, and different points of view, is cut out of the workforce.

Things are obviously totally different in the West, but what struck Sheryl Sandberg, Facebook's chief operating officer, as she rose up through corporate ranks, is that the female work revolution still has a long way to go. In historical terms, equality in the workplace is a pretty recent concept, but even so Sandberg wanted to explore the reasons why women have not reached the equality that her parent's generation expected to come about. It is customary to focus on the institutional reasons, but there must be other factors at play, Sandberg reasoned. When she was growing up, she heard a lot about "society" holding women back, but virtually nothing about the role that women's own attitudes might play. Women can be their own worst enemy in the working world, she says, therefore we need to do battle on both fronts—the institutional *and* the psychological. There is no point putting in place rules or quotas for female contribution if there are unaddressed and subtle incentives or pressures at play that make women reluctant to go for the top jobs, sit at the main table, or generally "lean in."

She is quick to admit that many women are not interested in careers or power, that their contribution is simply pursuing their desires, whatever they are, or raising a family. Also, that simply being able to make choices is a privilege that millions of women do not have, both in America and around the world. She notes the criticism that it is easier for her to "lean in," since her wealth allows her to pay for nannies and cleaners and other help. But the advice she offers, she says, would have been useful to her "long before I had heard of Google or Facebook" and that it applies to working women anywhere.

Lean In: Women, Work, and the Will to Lead, written with Nell Scovell, is smart reading for anyone in business, male or female, because it shows what a difference women-friendly and family-friendly policies can make in your organization. If you do not recognize and value a significant chunk of the population and their differences, you might get a one-dimensional workplace that is not fit to create products and services that cater to your whole potential market.

Women and work: vision and reality

When Sandberg went to college in the late 1980s, there was no difference in either abilities or expectations between her male and female classmates. She assumed this would continue into working life, but 20 years later she could see that most people in executive positions were men, and that many college-educated women were staying at home or doing lower-level full-time work. The situation was self-fulfilling, in that companies and organizations invested more in men since they were likely to stay and return the investment. The years in which women could have made the most headway professionally were also the years in which their bodies told them it was time to have children, and it was hard to do both.

Women are increasingly better educated than men, but something happens when they enter the workforce. As careers progress, the skills needed to get a degree prove not to be the ones needed to get ahead at the upper levels of organizations, which involves a fair degree of self-promotion and risk-taking. A 2012 study showed that women were half as likely to men to aspire to the executive suite. It may simply be that jobs which involve power, responsibility, and are very challenging simply appeal more to men. There are signs that young millennial women are as ambitious as men, but men have a particular way of prizing top jobs, and so are more likely to get them. "Aggressive and hard-charging women violate unwritten rules about acceptable social conduct," Sandberg writes. "Men are continually applauded for being ambitious and powerful and successful, but women who display these same traits often pay a social penalty." Given these deep cultural expectations, it is hardly surprising that progress has been less than expected.

Admitting the differences

Sandberg admits that there are biological differences between the sexes, such as women being more nurturing and men being more assertive, but society reinforces any differences and shapes people's expectations of what they might do and how they might behave. It still seems a taboo for girls to be domineering or bossy, for instance, but boys who organize others about are just seen as forthright and focused. Boys and men get positive reinforcement for vigorously pursuing their goals throughout their life. Girls and women are used to being taken down a peg or two whenever they show the same drive and determination. They are described as "difficult," "too aggressive," "not well liked."

Because women are traditionally seen as more communal, sensitive, and giving, this carries into the workplace. The "gender discount" problem involves women feeling that they have to act in certain ways, but in doing so they put themselves at a professional disadvantage. For instance, no one expects a man to go out of his way to help with a colleague, and so he is not penalized when he does not, but if women don't offer help they are seen as hard or selfish, and run the risk of being isolated. Whether they wish to be or not, women have to be "relentlessly pleasant," combining niceness with insistence.

Sandberg is far from happy with this kind of stereotyping, but rather than try to act as if it doesn't exist, she suggests that women need—to a certain extent—to act according to expectations, but turn this into a strength. By focusing on the common good and objective fairness, a woman can become valuable to the company and outshine men. In negotiating pay, she should avoid talking only in terms of "I" want this or that, but saying that "I am negotiating on behalf of my team," or of all women in a similar position. From being considered a weakness, women can turn communality into an advantage that benefits themselves, the company, and women generally.

Impostor syndrome

When *Forbes* put Sandberg at number five on its "Most powerful women" list, ahead of Michelle Obama, she felt "embarrassed and exposed." She told everyone that the list was ridiculous and unscientific, and got colleagues to take their posts of it on Facebook down. Then her executive assistant took her aside and told her to stop trying to disown the piece and just say "Thank you." After all, what man would have acted the way she did? Even as the second most senior person at Facebook, she says:

> *"I still face situations that I fear are beyond my capabilities. I still have days when I feel like a fraud. And I still sometimes find myself spoken over and discounted while men sitting next to me are not. But now I know how to take a deep breath and keep my hand up. I have learned to sit at the table."*

She is not alone; many studies have shown that women often feel like an impostor in their roles, and are an unfairly harsh judge of their own performance, while men tend to do the opposite, judging their performance as better than it in fact is. And while women commonly ascribe their success to luck or good connections or mentors, men naturally put it down to themselves. Women seem to hate having the word "power" or "powerful" ascribed to them. Yet to do anything, to break new ground, you can be sure that you will not be liked by everyone. In her first performance review with Facebook CEO Mark Zuckerberg, he told her that there was one thing that might hold her back: the desire to be liked by everyone. After she let this unconscious desire go, it emboldened her not just within Facebook, but led her to put her head above the parapet and speak out on issues to do with women and work. "Writing this book is not just me encouraging others to lean in," she says, "This is me leaning in. Writing this book is what I would do if I weren't afraid."

Workplaces can be intense, and there is a lot at stake. Simply recognizing the emotional side of work can make you a better boss, Sandberg says. It's OK to cry occasionally at work, or at least let yourself well up. After all, if women never allowed themselves a few tears it would be admitting that the workplace should be run according to male rules and expectations. Her mission is not to see women "fit in," but that by having the courage to be themselves women change the culture of businesses and organizations—for the better.

Sandberg no longer believes in "two selves," the work self and the home self. People should bring all of themselves to work, including the private motivations that affect the career decisions that are before them. The best leaders are never perfect, they are *authentic*, which means being willing to express emotion. People should see you are passionate about things and want the best. This is not weakness, but a sign of commitment.

Men leaning in

You won't hear this in any feminist tome, but Sandberg states boldly that "the single most important career decision that a woman makes is whether she will have a life partner and who that partner is." There is an idea that only unmarried women can make it to the top, given the demands of time and energy that it takes, yet virtually all women who she knows in senior leadership positions have a fully supportive partner—not just supportive in terms of their goals, but with the nuts-and-bolts of helping with the children, the housework, and being willing to move state or even country.

The management guru Elisabeth Moss Kanter was once asked: "What is the best thing men can do to help women's leadership?" "The laundry," she replied. Sandberg's husband Dave Goldberg, who died suddenly in 2015, was a successful player in the tech field, working for a Yahoo company and then becoming CEO of SurveyMonkey. But he limited his hours in order to be a hands-on father, so that his wife could properly take on the demanding Facebook role. Traditionalists might say that such moves emasculate the husband, but Sandberg points to evidence that more equal relationships in terms of jobs and chores and child rearing are happier *because* they are more equal. And her experience is that "couples who share domestic responsibilities have more sex. It may be counterintuitive, but the best way for a man to make a pass at his wife might be to do the dishes."

At times, Sandberg felt horribly guilty about not being at some of her children's events, and having to be away for work, yet she is comforted by the evidence from an exhaustive 2006 report which found that "children who were cared for exclusively by their mothers did not develop differently than those who were also cared for by others." Kids who didn't always have their mother around did not lose out in terms of cognitive skills, social competence, or the ability to form good relationships. More important in child development was having responsive and positive fathers, mothers who encouraged their children to do things and learn on their own, and having parents who were emotionally intimate with each other. This line from the report was the clincher for Sandberg: "Exclusive maternal care was not related to better or worse outcomes for children. There is, thus, no reason for mothers to feel as though they are harming their children if they decide to work."

Indeed, perhaps what will change things the most is boys seeing their mothers build successful careers while sustaining a loving family at the same time. And crucially, that boys see fathers who are just as ambitious about what they want their family and home life to be as they are for their working lives. It's a revolution, Sandberg says, that can only happen "one family at a time."

Taking time out

Depending on the country where you live and its laws, combining work and motherhood can carry significant penalties for a career. Sandberg notes that, in the United States at least, "women's average annual earnings decrease by 20 percent if they are out of the workforce for just one year. Average annual earnings decline by 30 percent after two to three years, which is the average amount of time that professional women off-ramp from the workforce."

Some women want very much to be full-time mothers for the first couple of years of their child's life, while others fall out of the workforce on a more permanent basis simply because the cost of child care makes going back to work seem uneconomic. Sandberg argues that this is the wrong way to see it. Even though expensive, child care is an investment in your family's future, since you are likely to earn a lot more in the future by having stayed in work compared to taking many years off. Sandberg's talks of her decision when she was at Google and Facebook to return to work relatively soon after having her children. Yes, it often seemed hard, yet she also loved the people she worked with and believed deeply in both organizations' mission, so to cut herself off from that for months or years would have also seemed wrong. There are no easy choices when it comes to choosing between work or looking after children, but you have to make a decision that seems right to you. She recalls that the storm of criticism over Yahoo CEO Marissa Meyer's decision to work through her maternity leave "came almost entirely from other women." Above all, women must reserve judgment and support other women in their decisions, rather than being holier-than-thou. Nothing hurts more, even if it is patently not true, than being told you are a negligent or bad mother; and the last person you want to hear it from is another woman.

Final comments

Books such as *Lean Out: The Struggle for Gender Equality in Tech and Start-up Culture* (Elissa Shevinsky) have criticized Sandberg for trying to make women bend too far to be like men in tech companies, and lambast their very male cultures. The very sizable gap between what these corporations claim to be about, and the reality, was demonstrated in the "Google letter" episode in 2017, in which a male Google software engineer penned an anonymous commentary tearing into what he believed was the company's misguided, politically correct attempt to hire more women. Women were very underrepresented in tech companies, he believed, simply because they were inherently less suited to the work.

The controversy made people recall the long list of women who had made real contributions to the computer industry, from Grace Hopper (Univac) to Deborah Estrin (the internet of things), to the scores of women making big contributions at companies such as Amazon and Google. It seems that perceptions take time to shift. "Real change will come," Sandberg writes, "when powerful women are less of an exception." It is easy to criticize people for their gender or race when they are in the minority, because they stand out. Yet "If women held 50 percent of the top jobs," she notes "it would just not be possible to dislike that many people." Whatever seems normal, is accepted.

Sheryl Sandberg

Born in 1969 in Washington DC, Sandberg grew up in North Miami Beach, Florida. She has a degree in economics from Harvard College, and won a prize for top graduating student. She worked for a year at the World Bank under mentor Larry Summers before doing an MBA at Harvard Business School. After a year at McKinsey, the management consultancy, she worked again for Larry Summers at the US Treasury during the Asian Financial Crisis.

In 2001 Sandberg became head of online sales and operations at Google, where she stayed until 2008. As Chief Operating Officer at Facebook she is in charge of all its business operations, including advertising sales and marketing, but also human resources and public policy. As well as Facebook's, she is on the board of the Walt Disney Corporation, Women for Women International, and the Center for Global Development.

In May 2015, Sandberg's husband Dave Goldberg died suddenly of heart arrhythmia. In Option B: Facing Adversity, Building Resilience and Finding *(2017), written with psychologist Adam Grant, she writes about the impact of his death on her family.*

How Google Works

"The famous Google mantra of 'Don't be evil' is not entirely what it seems. Yes, it genuinely expresses a company value and aspiration that is deeply felt by employees. But 'Don't be evil' is mainly another way to empower employees . . . When the engineer in Eric's meeting called the proposed new feature 'evil,' he was pulling the cord to stop production, forcing everyone to assess the proposed feature and determine if it was consistent with the company's values. Every company needs a 'Don't be evil,' a cultural lodestar that shines over all management layers, product plans, and office politics."

"To innovate, you must learn to fail well . . . Any failed project should yield valuable technical, user, and market insights that can help inform the next effort. Morph ideas, don't kill them: Most of the world's great innovations started out with entirely different applications, so when you end a project, look carefully at its components to see how they might be reapplied elsewhere."

In a nutshell

Only by creating a culture of learning and innovation will you attract the right people to your enterprise.

In a similar vein

Martin Ford *Rise of the Robots*
Walter Isaacson *Steve Jobs*
Douglas McGregor *The Human Side of Enterprise*
Alfred P. Sloan *My Years with General Motors*
Brad Stone *The Everything Store*

CHAPTER 35

Eric Schmidt & Jonathan Rosenberg

That Google has changed modern life goes without saying. Most people above the age of 25 will recall their first try of its search engine, which seemed to provide just the information we were after in an intelligent, almost magical way.

The idea for radically better search came to Larry Page when we woke up one night from a dream. Would it be possible, he thought, to crawl and rank every single page on the World Wide Web so that any search term would yield exactly the right information? After doing the math, he realized it was.

As a company, Google would be built on the insight that if you put science and mathematics first they can yield surprising answers to things that had previously seemed insolvable or in the realms of fantasy. Google's modus operandi has been the opposite of most companies'. Instead of starting with a business model and then working backwards to find the product that can fulfill it, it first looks for "a set of technical insights" that are fascinating in their own right. Only then do its engineers start to experiment with uses and applications.

When Page and Sergey Brin started Google in 1998 while still at Stanford University, they wished to create a company that felt like they had never left university. That is, filled with very smart people who would have plenty of leeway to research and develop things, and a collegial organizational structure that made ideas, not bureaucracy, king. The irony is that this varsity vibe created a firm that was fantastically profitable. Google's domination of internet search led to AdWords, which allows companies' products and services to be featured in searches. The better it got, the more Google search became a river of money that could be spent on developing new products and making acquisitions.

For the first crucial decade or so, Google was run as a triumvirate between Page, Brin, and CEO Eric Schmidt, hired from Novell. It worked because the founders were free of the operational aspects of running a big organization, yet still had the last say. By the time Schmidt sat down to write *How*

Google Works, with head of products Jonathan Rosenberg, the firm had 45,000 employees with $50 billion in annual revenues (it is now 60,000 and $75 billion).

Google to Alphabet

Between the time of the original book's release, and a revised edition in 2017, changes at Mountain View, Google's Silicon Valley headquarters, prompted the authors to add a new chapter, "How Alphabet Works."

Larry Page's restructuring of Google Inc. into Alphabet Inc. in 2015 was designed to avoid the big-company mentality in which highly creative people get thwarted by bureaucracy and stale thinking. By breaking it up into many component parts and companies—from Google itself (including Google Maps and Gmail) to units such as Waymo (self-driving cars), Fiber (high-speed internet service provision), DeepMind (artificial intelligence), biotech companies Calico and Verily, "smart home" facilitator Nest, and of course YouTube, which it acquired in 2006—each with their own financial and market pressures, the idea was that the company would stay "nimble, uncomfortable, and relevant" for the people working there.

Yet Schmidt and Rosenberg's book is not a description of what Google/Alphabet is, but of how it thinks and acts. Their purpose was to show that "the art and science of management has changed in the twenty-first century." Empowered by new technology, individuals and small teams can have a bigger impact than whole divisions once did. There are lessons in Google's success, they felt, for all companies.

Be conscious about culture

From the start, Google was dominated by engineers, not managers. Brin and Page tried to stop Sheryl Sandberg (see Chapter 34) joining the firm because she was not an engineer. In the event she did, and stayed six years, but even now the rule of thumb is that at least half of the company must be engineers. When Schmidt was hired as the "grown up" to run the company, it was on the basis that he had been a Unix expert and had helped develop the Java programming language. Rosenberg was brought in not because he had an MBA, but because of his product development success at Apple and Excite@ Home. The founders' aversion to traditional business expertise or management credentials formed the ethos of the company, which has never accepted "the way things were done" in terms of managing and organizing.

A lot of the book is about the steps that Schmidt and Rosenberg discovered were useful in motivating "smart creatives," and how they helped foster a culture that made them comfortable. For many people, the culture of the place they work in is one of only many factors they consider in deciding to work somewhere. Echoing Douglas McGregor's theories, Schmidt & Rosenberg say that for smart creatives, culture is the *number one* factor. They only want to work somewhere that is in areas they are passionate about, and where they will be given freedom to express their talents. As part of the 2004 public offering of Google stock, Page and Brin fought for the right to include a statement of the company's values, to wit: put the user first, think long term, and try to make the world a better place—don't be evil.

They tried to build a real meritocracy, from the raucous Friday meetings with the whole company in which staff were invited to question anything, to a "don't listen to the HIPPOs" (that is, the "highest paid person's opinion") ethos. Dissent at Google is "an obligation, not an option," the authors say. In organizations where the managers don't have as much data or expertise as the employees, there is a tendency for "Because I said so" management to happen. But when everyone has the same access to data, just because you are an executive or the CEO doesn't mean your argument should hold sway. Schmidt found that anything he wanted to happen, he had to prove the case for empirically.

One way that Alphabet has kept nimble is to keep people working for it who would normally have got the itch to start their own companies. Keeping entrepreneurs in-house and maintaining a start-up culture inside a sprawling enterprise has been key to the company's success. "Do the best thing for the person," the authors say, "and make the organization adjust."

Not being "competitive"

In the early 2000s Google was a minnow compared to Microsoft, which the company codenamed 'Finland' in memos. Microsoft could see how lucrative being number one in internet search would be in terms of advertising revenue, and its various attempts in MSN Search, Windows Live, and then Bing reputedly cost it around $12 billion. Google knew the only way it could fend off Finland was to constantly improve its search capability, and over time added images, books, maps, and languages. It worked to improve its infrastructure to keep search fast even as the amount of data exploded, and put a lot into effective search advertising systems for customers. It launched a browser, Chrome, that outperformed and overtook Microsoft's Explorer.

Competition is good when it fires you up to improve your product, Schmidt & Rosenberg note, but at the same time it is a mistake to obsess over the competition, which leads to a "never-ending spiral into mediocrity." Larry Page asked, "How exciting is it to come to work if the best you can do is trounce some other company that does roughly the same thing?"

Following the competition will stop you from doing anything really innovative. In business, the big wins go not to those with a big range of products designed to cater to everyone (as Motorola tried to do), but to those putting everything into making a few products (think Apple's iPhone) that are so brilliant people won't think of going elsewhere.

Innovating the 70/20/10 way

Everyone talks about innovation, and some companies try to become innovative by appointing a "Chief Innovation Officer." But innovation must be in a company's DNA, infusing everything it does. Larry Page pushes Google engineers by telling them, "You aren't thinking big enough." Take the basic science in an area, he says, and imagine what uses could be made of it, not just now but 5, 10, 25 years hence. The company's mantra-like question, "What could be true in 5 years?" forces it to constantly look at its current products and services to see how they could be impacted by emerging technologies and trends, and spurs it to imagine the products of the future. For instance, the authors note how machine learning—that is, machines that are not simply programmed to do something, but learn as they go and get better—has advanced a huge amount since the 2014 edition of the book. In Google's own products, it has led to big improvements in the machine recognition of images (Google photos), the understanding of speech (Google's Alexa device) language translation (Google translate), routing your traffic journey (Google Maps) and detecting spam mail (Gmail).

Sergey Brin has a "70/20/10" rule for allocating Google's resources: "70 percent to the core business, 20 percent on emerging, and 10 percent on new." This is close to the observation of Bill Gates (taken on as a maxim by Schmidt) to "spend 80 percent of your time on 80 percent of your revenue." Indeed, the main rationale for the company's 2015 reorganization was making sure that the firm's cash cow, search advertising, was fully supported without being distracted by more speculative "moonshot" ventures.

Google's principle to "make things 10 times better, not just 10 percent better", fired its work with self-driving cars, contact lenses that measured diabetics' insulin levels, and airborne kites that generate lots of wind energy, but by 2017 the company had realized that often more progress can be made through purposeful and constant iteration. Within this reemphasized "roofshot" outlook sit the 500 improvements made to Google's search engine every year, the big increases in efficiency of Google's data centers, and the massive uptick in viewing hours logged on YouTube within a three-year period, from 100 million to 1 billion a day, due to advances in the algorithms that suggest what videos users should watch. The fact is, only a tiny percentage of Google's employees work on "moonshots" and "10x" projects; the rest are focused on bringing major improvements to products it already has.

Google's famous "20 percent time" rule, which allows staff to work on their own projects or emerging but unproven areas for the equivalent of one day a week, has led to many concrete innovations including Google Suggest (auto-complete for search phrases, making it easier and quicker), and Google News (which aggregates news stories for users based on their interests). However, the reality is that 20 percent time is more like 120 percent time, since Googlers end up working on projects precious to them at nights and weekends after they have done their main job – but the point is that Google as a company fully encourages it and even expects it.

"Ten percent" projects are ones that have only a small chance of succeeding, but which would bring a big payoff if they do. The problem with investing too much in chancy or marginal products, the authors note, is that confirmation bias creeps in. The more money you have poured into something, the more you will start to believe that it is good (even if it isn't) because the costs of pulling out, mentally and financially, seem too high. The ten percent rule works because "creativity loves constraints." Things get better when small resources of time and money force ingenuity. Pictures have frames for a reason, and sonnets work because they are only 14 lines.

In 2002, Larry Page wondered if it would be possible to make every page of every book published searchable online. Instead of giving millions of dollars to a unit to work on the idea, he set up a camera on a tripod in his office and started taking pictures of the pages of a book, seeing how long it took. From this simple experiment he concluded that it was worth taking further, and Google Books was born. Sergey Brin did a similar thing when assessing the idea of Google Street View. He began by driving around taking photos of all the streets around Mountain View. Millions of miles mapped later, Street View is one of Google's most popular and transformative products, allowing visual travel in detail through most of the world's towns and cities. The best way to approach innovation is via simple, cheap tests.

The power of one

The authors argue that product innovation is more important today than it was in the twentieth century, when distribution, brand, and advertising power were the drivers of how big a company could be. Today, any tiny firm that can solve big human problems can become huge—both because the resources it needs to grow, like computing power, are very cheap, and because it can reach the intended market easily through the internet. All this means that individual employees can be incredibly important; any one person can come up with an innovation that can transform the company's prospects. Hence Google's obsessive attention to hiring the best people they can find, keeping the bar so high that the really good, smart people will see it like an exclusive club they want to join. "While A's tend to hire A's, B's hire not just B's, but C's and D's too," Schmidt and Rosenberg observe, "So if you compromise standards or make a mistake and hire a B, pretty soon you'll have B's, C's, and even D's in your company."

The authors' tips for hiring include:

- Don't leave recruiting up to recruiters or the HR department. Have as many people as possible involved, but particularly those who will be actually be working with the candidate.
- Don't hire people for their specialization. In the tech world, being a specialist is likely to make you obsolete before long, as platforms and programs and products constantly change. Hire smart generalists instead, who don't have fixed ideas and so are "free to survey the wide range of solutions and gravitate to the best one."
- Interviews shouldn't be a stressful experience, but should have the feel of "intellectual discussions between friends". Questions should be open-ended to draw out the thinking and character of the candidate. Ones like "How did you pay for college?" and "If I looked at the history section on your browser, what would I learn about you?" will separate the "good CV" people from the ones you actually want in your organization.
- Hire people who are *interesting* as well as competent. Do the "LAX test": if you were stuck in Los Angeles airport with this candidate for several hours, would you enjoy the time and learn something, or would it make you retreat into your tablet? Look for people with a "growth mindset," that is, someone who is perennially hungry for knowledge and who wants to see it applied to make the world better in some way.

Final comments

In 2006 Google launched its search engine in China, against warnings from Sergey Brin, whose family had fled Russian communism. After a series of hacker attacks originating from China, including attempts to get into the Gmail accounts of Chinese political dissidents, Larry Page and Schmidt also began to wonder if persevering in China might go against the firm's "Don't be evil" ethos. Even so, the commercial implications for pulling out were enormous. If it did, the company would give up any chance of a presence in China for the rest of the century.

In the event, Google's executive met and decided, in January 2010, to publicize the attacks, and the fact that the firm would no longer censor any of its results to please the Chinese authorities. Knowing that the site would be shut down, Google did it themselves, directing all Google.cn traffic to its Hong Kong site. Search in China is now dominated by Baidu.

As a company grows, there is a temptation to expand and dominate in every possible market, but in doing so something of its character and values are lost. How a company "works" is not just management or innovation practices, but the higher values that guide them. Google's decision, made carefully and openly, got a thunderous positive reception from its own people, who felt it was just the right thing to do. After all, if an institution loses its founding ethos, what is actually left?

Eric Schmidt & Jonathan Rosenberg

Born in 1955, Schmidt grew up in Virginia. He studied electrical engineering at Princeton University, staying on for an M.S. and Ph.D. in computer science. After stints in research and development at Bell Labs and the Xerox PARC labs, in 1983 he began managing software products for Sun Microsystems. From 1997 to 2001 he was the CEO of Novell, and in 2001 became CEO of Google. He stepped down to become executive chairman in 2011, and remains in that position.

Schmidt was a friend of Steve Jobs, and on the Apple board between 2006 and 2009, but legal fights between Google and Apple about the differences between the iOS and Android operating systems strained the relationship. Schmidt is on the boards of Princeton University, the Khan Academy, and The Economist, *and has been a technology adviser to and supporter of Barack Obama and Hillary Clinton. His stock in Alphabet is worth around $12 billion. The Schmidt Family Foundation, run with his wife Wendy, supports sustainability causes and the use of renewable energy.*

Born in 1961, Rosenberg has an economics degree from Claremont McKenna College and an MBA from the University of Chicago. After roles at Apple and Excite@Home, he joined Google in 2002. He was in charge of products, overseeing the development of Google search, AdSense and Adwords, Gmail, Android, Chrome, Google Books, and Google Maps. He resigned in 2011 when Larry Page became CEO.

The Snowball: Warren Buffett and the Business of Life

"The timing was stupendous. Capital from the insurance companies was pouring into Berkshire at the same time that the market was collapsing, the environment that Buffett liked best. While he had not yet decided exactly what to do with the collective enterprise he had built since the end of 1974, of two things he was certain. One was the business model's power, and the other was his skill in using it. Above all, he had confidence in himself.
'Always,' he says. 'Always.'"

"In the midst of all the chaos of the spring of 2008, there sat Buffett, whose thinking about value and risk had not changed in the nearly sixty years of his career. There are always people who say that the rules have changed. But it only looks that way, he said, if the time horizon is too short."

In a nutshell

Time, discipline, and focus are the most important ingredients in building a fortune.

In a similar vein

Walter Isaacson *Steve Jobs*

CHAPTER 36

Alice Schroeder

I n 1999, prices for "new economy" tech stocks had gone through the roof, with valuations that had nothing to do with the underlying worth of the companies, and that were very far removed from the actual rate of growth in the economy. In the short term, Warren Buffett told a small conference that year, the market is a voting machine. In the long run, it's a weighing machine. The stock market, when it shoots far ahead of the actual economy, is simply a reflection of interest rates being very low, and so people are greedy for higher returns. It doesn't say anything about the real value of the stocks they are buying. The result, he said, was that the next 17 years might not be that different to the period 1964 to 1981, when stock markets barely grew.

Buffett had famously avoided investing in tech companies because they were outside his "circle of competence," but many at the conference—and in the press—thought he had missed the biggest boat of their time.

But the "Sage of Omaha," of course, was right. A few months later the stock market swooned and dropped precipitously, wiping the value off tech stocks. It would take another decade and a half before they become hot again, while Buffett's own Berkshire Hathaway company zoomed ahead by investing in proven, not just potential, value.

Buffett describes Berkshire Hathaway as his "Sistine Chapel," not only a work of art but, as Alice Schroeder puts it, an "illustrated text of his beliefs." For his business partner and longtime friend Charlie Munger, the company is not just a business but Buffett's way of teaching how the world works.

Schroeder got to know Buffett while an insurance analyst covering Berkshire Hathaway and specifically its acquisition of General Re, and as the subtitle of her 900-page biography, *Warren Buffett and the Business of Life*, indicates, it goes beyond being a mere chronicle of events, delving into Buffett's relationships with his wife Suzie, partner Astrid Menks, children, and friends. The book was five years in the making, and needs to be consumed slowly for the details.

Looking for systems, personal and monetary

Born in 1930 in Omaha, Nebraska, as a boy Buffett was entranced by numbers and money. His favorite book was *One Thousand Ways to Make $1,000* and he set a goal of retiring as a millionaire by the time he was 35.

In high school in Washington DC (where his family had moved while his father Howard fulfilled a term as a Congressman) he was a businessman, running paper rounds, selling golf balls, and managing pinball machines. Howard's regular job was as a stockbroker, and he did not discourage his son from dabbling in stocks early on. Early mistakes taught Warren not to worry too much about the price he had paid for a security. The only thing that mattered was not to sell too soon, in order to make a small profit, when by hanging on he could make a much bigger one.

The teenage Warren devoured biographies of industrialists and financiers, and in an effort to get people to like him, in junior high school read Dale Carnegie's *How to Win Friends and Influence People*. Carnegie's witty book electrified him, providing the rules he had been looking for to achieve success, not just with money but in the world, with people. Chief among them was "Never criticize, condemn, or complain." Because people's pride is easily wounded, and they lash back at any criticism, it is nearly always wiser to get people to do things by praising them or admiring them. Buffett, who had hitherto been a sharp-tongued, if insecure, smarty pants, experimented with Carnegie's methods and found that they worked. But unlike most people who read the book and then forgot about it, Buffett kept applying its rules "with unusual concentration," Schroeder notes. He slowly turned himself into the positive, folksy, avuncular figure we know today.

As Buffett's school years came to an end he discovered Benjamin Graham's *The Intelligent Investor* (1949), which provided an alternative model to mere speculation on stocks. The book stunned him as Carnegie's had done, because it provided a rational, mathematical system for evaluating securities separate to the froth and changeability of today's prices.

Looking for value: cigar butts and "great" companies

After taking a degree in finance at the University of Pennsylvania, Buffett applied and failed to get into a graduate program at Harvard. A better option appeared: Benjamin Graham lectured in finance at Columbia University, and Buffett pleaded with the dean of admissions, David Dodd (who also happened to be Graham's business partner and the coauthor of their classic, *Security Analysis*) to let him join the program.

What Buffett got from Graham was an understanding of investing psychology, that there was a difference between the intrinsic value of a stock, taking account of its fundamentals like earnings and cash balance, and the value imputed to the stock by the market. He also learned about the "margin of safety," which came from buying things for a lot less than they were worth, and not buying them using debt.

Buffett began immersing himself in the study of companies that seemed undervalued, and focused on one in particular, GEICO, or Government Employees Insurance Company, selling most of his stock in other firms to buy 350 shares. GEICO was growing fast in a saturated industry, insurance, and had a lower price–earnings ratio than bigger firms. He felt it would double in value within five years. Despite his worship of Graham, GEICO did not meet Graham's criteria for investing, and Buffett slowly began to develop his own investing framework.

After working for a time as a broker and analyst in New York, Buffett tired of the city and decided, in 1956, to move back to Omaha and start his own partnership. The city, though historically important as a rail hub, was a financial backwater. As Schroeder notes, "for a college graduate to become self-employed, to work at home, to work alone, was strikingly unusual in the 1950s." The normal way to get ahead was to join a large corporation and climb up the ladder. But Buffett had always been precious about his time and how he spent his days, and a private investing fund (soon to be several funds) would allow him freedom. For the next few years he made money for his small group of investors, including many friends and family, hand over fist.

Going against the voices of his cautious father and Benjamin Graham, Buffett was very optimistic about the future of American business. Influenced by his partner Charlie Munger's interest in the "great" companies, he started moving away from cigar-butt stocks and investing in firms that had enormous intangible value in their brand names, goodwill, and trustworthiness. For instance, the Buffett Partnership, now attracting a lot of capital, started buying as much American Express stock as it could get its hands on, plowing $3 million into it by 1964 and $13 million by 1966. Buffett told his partners that while other funds were focused on "diversification" of holdings (and indeed, this had been Graham's way), he was so confident in his assessments that the fund might at any one time have 40 percent of its value invested in a single stock.

Buffett's point was that anyone could come to a profitable conclusion about whether a company's stock was worth buying, based on quantitative measures. The real challenge, he thought, was making an assessment based on the qualitative ones. It was here, he believed, that "the big money" was to be made. It is what later attracted him to Coca-Cola, with its fantastic brand, General Re, a reinsurer of some integrity in a shady business, and more recently, in Apple.

But Buffett was also attracted to smaller firms if their value was strongly discounted compared to their assets, and he was intrigued by a textile manufacturer in Massachusetts called Berkshire Hathaway. It would prove to be one of his worst investments, but the name would remain as the holding company for Buffett's investments.

Reaching maturity

By 1966, the Buffett family had a net worth of around $9 million. Suzie thought she and Warren had an understanding that once they reached a certain level of wealth he would stop working. But it was not money driving him, rather a voracious appetite for acquiring stocks and undervalued private companies. Although in the 1960s tech companies such as Xerox and Polaroid were capturing people's imaginations, Buffett insisted that he would not go into businesses he did not understand completely. Nor would he invest in anything "where major human problems appear to have a substantial chance of developing." That is, he preferred companies that were well managed by solid people, and often in businesses that were simple or even boring, such as paint or bricks, insurance or candy.

His "Desert Island Challenge" was asking the question: "If you were stuck on a desert island for ten years and could only buy one stock, what would it be?" "The trick," Schroeder writes, "was to find a company with the strongest franchise, one least subject to the corroding forces of competition and time." Such a business would need to have a "moat" around it which other companies would find difficult to ever breach. After a failed investment in a department store, Hochschild-Kohn, he was very wary of investing in retail, for instance, because the dominant retailer one decade is often not so the next.

Buffett learned the hard way that "Time is the friend of the wonderful business, the enemy of the mediocre." Learning from Charlie Munger's interest in great, quality companies, he came to the view that "It's far better to buy a wonderful company at a fair price than a fair company at a wonderful price." For example, he had to pay full asking price for See's Candy, a Californian confectioner, but was willing to do so because of the huge affection for the brand and its future growth potential. He was attracted to invest in *The Washington Post* because Kay Graham (who became one of his closest friends) had kept raising the quality and profile of the newspaper. Indeed, despite his penny-pinching personal ways, with his direct investments Buffett preferred to invest in ones where he knows and likes the people, even if the returns are a bit less than with more rapacious firms. He kept his investments in the textile industry, for instance, long after he'd realized it wasn't a good business, because "I like the textile-operating people."

Outlier and learning machine

Though personally shy and insecure, as his wife knew, as an investor Buffett always had supreme confidence in his judgment.

Over the decades of his investing life, Buffett seems to have single-handedly disproved the Efficient Markets Hypothesis (EMH), the idea that no individual could ever beat the market over time. One of its proponents, Burton Malkiel (*A Random Walk Down Wall Street*) argued that Buffett had simply been like a monkey throwing darts at the *Wall Street Journal* stock listings. He had been lucky, but time would inevitably see his performance revert to the mean. For adherents of the EMH, the price of a stock at any one time was right, factoring in all possible pieces of information. It was therefore fruitless to try to uncover unseen value. But Buffett and Munger thought that the mathematical models of the EMH people were witchcraft. Their followers had made billions betting on small movements in the price of securities, in other words, on short-term volatility. Buffett's investing style was about making long-term bets on companies which made volatility immaterial. For him, betting on short-term micro-movements was not investing at all.

Buffett, Schroeder writes, "never stopped thinking about business: what made a good business, what made a bad business, how they competed, what made customers loyal to one another." Munger described his partner as "a learning machine." It was the desire to teach his understanding of the world that led him to spend hundreds of hours writing his annual shareholder letters.

Focus: money and people

Buffett had a habit of latching himself on to people in order to vacuum up their wisdom. He had done it with Kay Graham, and later it was Bill Gates. Despite their decades' age difference, Buffett soaked up Gates' knowledge on the tech industry, and also his business prowess. The first time they met, at an island retreat owned by a friend of Kay Graham's, Gates' father posed a question at dinner: "What factor did people feel was the most important in getting to where they'd gotten in life?"

Buffett replied, "Focus." "And Bill said the same thing," Buffett recalls. He sometimes talked of the "Institutional Imperative," which meant, as Schroeder puts it, "the tendency for companies to engage in activity for its own sake and to copy their peers instead of trying to stay ahead of them." It was never easy for a company to stick to what it did best, while at the same time keeping an eye on the future.

Buffett's laser-like focus on company prospects meant that, by 1993, shares in Berkshire Hathaway were worth $18,000 a piece, and Buffett himself had a fortune of over $8 billion. The original partners in his first investment trust, if they had put in $1,000, would now have $6 million. The Buffett family still lived in the capacious but modest home for which Buffett had paid $31,500, and where Suzie had devoted her life to ensuring that all Warren's needs were met so he could work all hours undistracted. But her selflessness eventually led to a feeling of unfulfilled desires and ambitions, and the pair increasingly led two lives. She would attend all Berkshire events, including the fabled annual shareholder's meetings, and join the family on holidays. But Suzie arranged for a friend, Astrid Menks, to become Buffett's regular partner while she went off to pursue her singing career and enjoy a large network of friends. It was an unusual arrangement, but Buffett remained devoted to his wife until her death in 2004.

Final comments

When Schroeder was writing, Buffett was worth $30 billion. In 2017 the value of his chunk of Berkshire Hathaway, if he sold it, would net close to $80 billion. Through the value of compounding, his "snowball" of wealth could potentially double again before he gives most of it away to the Bill and Melinda Gates Foundation, which he believes has much greater expertise than he does in doing good.

For the average investor, Buffett maintains, "Stocks are the thing to own over time. Productivity will increase and stocks will increase with it." Best to put your money in a very low cost index fund that tracks the whole stock market and reaps its collective gains over time. In 2007 he made a $1 million bet (winnings will go to charity) with a hedge fund supremo that the money invested in a S&P 500 index fund would outperform the same invested in a composite fund of hedge funds. Even with its much higher fees, Buffett in 2017 won the bet easily, his $1 million doubling in value, while the hedge fund investment had only added $250,000. Commenting on the bet in his annual shareholder letter, Buffett noted how rich people think they have some right to buy better performance, but often the best returns are got cheaply through common investing vehicles with very low fees. Greedily seeking higher returns usually ends in tears; better to trust in the fact that companies generally get more productive, and economies grow. Trust not in your own smarts or guile, but in national prosperity.

Alice Schroeder

Born in 1956, Schroeder has a degree in finance and an MBA from McCoombs School of Business at the University of Texas, Austin. After qualifying as an accountant she worked for the Financial Accounting Standards Board. In the mid 2000s she quit her job as a managing director at Morgan Stanley bank and moved to Omaha to research and write The Snowball. The book received a $7 million advance and was a New York Times bestseller. Schroeder is a columnist for Bloomberg News and a non-executive director for Bank of America Merrill Lynch.

Pour Your Heart Into It

"I believe in destiny. In Yiddish, they call it bashert. *At that moment, flying 35,000 feet above the earth, I could feel the tug of Starbucks. There was something magic about it, a passion and authenticity I had never experienced in business."*

"It's also about how a company can be built in a different way. It's about a company completely unlike the ones my father worked for. It's living proof that a company can lead with its heart and nurture its soul and still make money."

"If you want to build a great enterprise, you have to have the courage to dream great dreams. If you dream small dreams, you may succeed in building something small. For many people, that is enough. But if you want to achieve widespread impact and lasting value, be bold."

In a nutshell

Huge enterprises can be built by giving people a small moment of joy in their day.

In a similar vein

Richard Branson *Losing My Virginity*
Conrad Hilton *Be My Guest*
Phil Knight *Shoe Dog*
Douglas McGregor *The Human Side of Enterprise*

CHAPTER 37

Howard Schultz

As Starbucks has become the McDonald's of the beverage world—seemingly everywhere— it would be easy to dismiss the company as yet another American corporate symbol bent on profit and world domination. The true story is more complex and interesting.

To begin with, Starbucks existed as a ground coffee merchant for a decade before it began serving coffee as a drink. Its founders were genuine coffee lovers who were more interested in educating people about the joys of real coffee than they were in making money. Not dissimilar to the way Ray Kroc discovered the McDonald brothers and their remarkable burger operation in San Bernardino, California, Howard Schultz, then a marketer of kitchen goods and housewares, had an epiphany when he first visited the original Starbucks stores in Seattle in the early 1980s. Used to the "swill" of American filter coffee, he fell in love with the real thing, and knew instantly he wanted to work for this offbeat and passionate company.

Pour Your Heart Into: How Starbucks Built a Company One Cup at a Time tells the story of Schultz's role in turning the coffee chain into a major brand, which alone would have made it an interesting read. It is also an autobiographical account of how the author's relationship with his father unexpectedly shaped the ethos of the company. If you patronize Starbucks, but know little about its origins, you will find the history of the company fascinating. And if you have entrepreneurial aspirations yourself, this is a book to study.

Falling in love

Schultz grew up in subsidized high-rise housing blocks in a poor part of Brooklyn, New York. Even when newly built they carried a social stigma. His father had never finished school and throughout his life worked in unskilled jobs for exploitative employers. Particularly as a teenager, Schultz judged his father harshly for his underachievement.

With this background, when Howard was accepted into college—for his football, rather than academic skills—it was a major event for the family. They had never left New York before, and drove a thousand miles to the campus of North Michigan University. He majored in communications and also took classes in public speaking, interpersonal communications, and business.

After graduating, with no real idea of what he wanted to do, Schultz took a job selling word processors for Xerox, making fifty cold calls per day. This he did for three years, paying off his college loans, before joining a Swedish company called Perstorp. In time, he became the US manager of its stylish kitchen and homeware brand, Hammarplast, a job paying $75,000 a year with a car and expense account, and managing 20 sales reps. He and his new wife Sheri, an interior designer, revelled in the Manhattan lifestyle and bought a loft apartment.

While working for Hammarplast, Schultz was intrigued by the large orders for a certain type of drip coffeemaker coming from a small company in Seattle. He went out to investigate and discovered Starbucks, a small chain of ground coffee retailers whose customers appreciated a good appliance for making their brews. He met the founders, Jerry Baldwin and Gordon Bowker, two cultured men who catered to a small niche market of learned coffee drinkers. Along with the coffee, Schultz was intrigued by the heritage and ethos of the company.

Baldwin and Bowker were literature lovers, and before they opened their first Seattle store in 1971 they had to think of a name. Starbuck was the first mate on the *Pequod*, the vessel in Herman Melville's *Moby Dick*, a name they felt evoked the seafaring tradition of the early coffee traders. Their logo, a siren with flowing hair encircled by "Starbucks Coffee, Tea and Spice," was inspired by a Norse woodcut found in an old book. From the beginning, walking into a Starbucks store was meant to take a person out of the mundane world, the aroma of its dark roasted coffee combined with its wood furnishings evoking exotic, distant places.

Leaps of faith

Despite its perks, Schultz had been growing restless in his job. "I sensed that something was missing. I wanted to be in charge of my own destiny." In 1982, to the dismay of his parents, he left his position and joined Starbucks, having persuaded the founders to hire him as its marketing director.

In his first few months he was sent to a coffee trade fair in Milan. He loved Italy's crowded, atmospheric cafés, seemingly on every corner, and suddenly realized that the key to Starbucks' future was not just roasting and selling coffee, but serving it. On this trip he had his first café latte, a mixture of espresso and warm, frothy milk that at the time was almost unheard of in America.

Returning home, Schultz's idea to open Starbucks cafés was dismissed as the whim of an overexcited marketing manager. He was eventually allowed to open a small café bar in the corner of a store, but despite brisk sales the founders still did not want to expand the idea. They were resolutely "not in the restaurant business"; cafés went against the whole idea of the company. Torn between his love for Starbucks and a vision of opening Italian-style cafés across America, Schultz realized that his vision might only happen if he left the company to start his own. This would be an even bigger leap of faith than joining Starbucks in the first place.

Selling a vision

Schultz tramped the streets of Seattle for a year giving presentations to investors. Out of 242 people he approached, 217 gave him an outright "No." He was told many times that coffee was not a growth industry, that consumption in America had been declining since the mid 1960s, overtaken by soft drinks, and that the real money was to be made in technology start-ups.

Eventually, he rounded up enough money open "Il Giornale" in the business district of Seattle. The café was a success, and Schultz began opening other branches. However, in 1987 came some interesting news: the Starbucks founders wanted to sell their business. His love for the company had not waned, and he was desperate to buy it. It had been difficult enough raising the $1.25 million for Il Giornale. How would he come up with $4 million for Starbucks? On a promise to investors of opening over a hundred stores around America within a five-year time frame (which seemed like an outlandish projection at the time), he got the money. Il Giornale and Starbucks were melded into one.

"A people business serving coffee"

In ten years, Starbucks became a company with over 1,300 stores and 25,000 employees. Though in the first three years it lost money, thereafter its growth of 50 percent per year turned it into a very valuable business. On going public in 1992 it became a darling of the stock market, usually exceeding profit expectations thanks to the opening of a new store almost every business day. Yet for Schultz, the Starbucks phenomenon was not simply about "growth" and "success" in a business sense. He wanted to create a company that nurtured its staff and treated them with respect. Though the customer was important, it was even more important for the long-term health of the business, he believed, to make sure the baristas and other staff were happy.

Starbucks became the first company to provide comprehensive healthcare for all employees, including part-timers working as little as 20 hours per week, and devised a stock option scheme designed to enrich the average employee, not just the executives. Starbucks became "a living legacy of my dad," Schultz notes, with an ethos and work practices that his father had never enjoyed. His view was: "If you treat your employees as interchangeable cogs in a wheel, they will view you with the same affection." The company also subsidizes employees who wish to get a college degree.

Starbucks's largesse paid off not just in terms of high morale and dedication, but in staff turnover rates, which were much lower than the industry norm. Clearly, long-term business prosperity rested on treating staff not just as "hires" but as *partners*, a term the company still uses.

Romance in the mundane

Schultz ponders the key to Starbucks' success. Was it just the coffee, or something else?

If given a vital new twist, he notes, even mundane things can be turned into gold. In the same way that Nike took a commodity, running shoes, and made them into something special, so Starbucks changed the way people drank coffee: for a dollar or two more, they could have a real sensory experience. His aim was to "blend coffee with romance," creating a warm and enjoyable environment where along with a coffee you could listen to a bit of jazz or ponder life's questions. A trip to Starbucks became an affordable luxury in an otherwise mundane day, providing a "third place" that was not work and not home, providing people with something they didn't know they had wanted. As the first in a new category, it became its leader and attracted many competitors, but Schultz also talks at length about the company's research and development lab, which he believes will help it retain its edge in the future.

Final comments

At times, *Pour Your Heart Into It* reads like a motivational book. Schultz never expected to achieve what he did, so part of his aim is to tell others what is possible when you dare. When you see things others don't see, but you believe strongly in them, he observes, you have to throw caution to the wind. There will be plenty of naysayers, but act anyway. His rule is: "If it captures your imagination, it will captivate others."

Schultz is politically liberal, and his support of gay marriage and gun control has led to various boycotts of Starbucks outlets. He comes across as surprisingly sensitive, forever worrying about his company becoming too faceless and corporate.

At the time the book was written, Starbucks had only a handful of overseas stores. Now, it is in dozens of countries, and its total number of outlets (self-operated and licensed) is over 24,000. In 2008 Schultz returned to the company as CEO, after eight years away from the job. He was worried it had lost its way, had expanded too fast. His second book, *Onward: How Starbucks Fought for its Life Without Losing its Soul* (2011), details his successful efforts to return the company to profitability despite a recessionary economy, while at the same time preserving core values.

The Fifth Discipline

"When was the last time someone was rewarded in your organization for raising difficult questions about the company's current policies rather than solving urgent problems? Even if we feel uncertain or ignorant, we learn to protect ourselves from the pain of appearing uncertain or ignorant. That very process blocks out any new understandings which might threaten us. The consequence is . . . teams full of people who are incredibly proficient at keeping themselves from learning."

"We begin to see that all of us are trapped in structures, structures embedded both in our ways of thinking and in the interpersonal and social milieus in which we live. Our knee-jerk tendencies to find fault with one another gradually fade, leaving a much deeper appreciation of the forces within which we all operate."

In a nutshell

Great companies are communities in which there is a genuine commitment to every member's potential being realized.

In a similar vein

W. Edwards Deming *Out of the Crisis*
Patrick Lencioni *The Five Dysfunctions of a Team*
Stanley McChrystal *Team of Teams*
Douglas McGregor *The Human Side of Enterprise*

CHAPTER 38

Peter Senge

I t is fashionable today for big companies to talk of themselves as "learning organizations," empowering their employees to remain useful. Yet the original meaning of the term went well beyond the updating of skills and knowledge, and was part of a larger philosophy developed by management professor Peter Senge and colleagues at MIT's Sloan School of Management.

The Fifth Discipline: The Art and Practice of the Learning Organization, whose first edition sold over 2.5 million copies, was Senge's breakthrough book. Its thesis was that companies would never reach their potential as long as they were run like schools, with teachers/bosses telling students/workers what to do. The result would be: employees giving "right" answers, not genuinely making things better; a focus on solving technical problems, while systemic flaws are ignored; conflicts being brushed aside in favor of superficial agreement; managing being equated with control; and an atmosphere of competition among staff that was damaging to genuine innovation. In such an opportunistic organization, Senge notes, people are reduced to making "opportunistic grabs at individual power and wealth." In contrast, his learning organization would be based on shared goals, not fear, and curiosity, not trying to please the boss. In short, learning rather than controlling.

Senge's holistic view of business was strongly influenced by physicist David Bohm and his idea of "wholeness" (see *50 Philosophy Classics*). "The tools and ideas presented in this book," he writes, "are for destroying the illusion that the world is created of separate, unrelated forces." When this illusion is let go, it leads to organizations in which collective purpose is genuine, and in which "people are continually learning how to learn together." The organizations of the future will not have a "grand strategist" at the top in the manner of a Henry Ford, Alfred Sloan, Thomas Watson, or Bill Gates, Senge argues, but rather resemble a kind of organic machine, growing and adapting. Only this would give a company true longevity. The book was updated in a 2006 edition that gives more recent examples of the learning organization in action.

What is a learning organization?

Marking the difference between learning organizations and traditional ones based on command and control are certain *disciplines*, Senge says. These include:

Personal mastery   Every organization must be committed to the development of every person within it. If they don't, they fail to capture that person's energy and potential.

Mental models   Seeing the assumptions we make in our understanding of the world, or our picture of how the world works, that we are frequently not even aware of.

Building shared vision   Rather than an organization built around the charisma of a leader, or a response to a crisis, great companies require a lofty goal that is voluntarily bought into by all.

Team learning   The individuals in a team learn faster together than they would if alone. A learning organization arises only through teams engaging in non-defensive dialogue, deep reflection and radical openness—a world away from the "discussion" that characterizes most organizations, in which the dominant get their way.

Systems thinking   An understanding that everything is related to everything else.

Systems thinking is the fifth and most important discipline, Senge says, because it acknowledges that all the disciplines are interdependent and part of a coherent whole. Senge studied systems dynamics at MIT, and came to the view that most of the tough problems facing the planet were related to the inability to grasp their sheer complexity and interconnectedness. The result was government trying to fix things like the environment or inequality or public deficits by intervening to "do something" about the symptoms, without identifying the causes—which were very often erroneous mental models. Therefore, openness to admitting complexity, and willingness to see things as a system rather than a succession of events, was the most important step in creating powerful organizations. Admitting complexity and interconnectedness did not mean you were a mere subject of your environment, but rather seeing that you could become a shaper of that environment. A learning organization is one that is "continually expanding its capacity to create its future," Senge says.

That the conventional meaning of learning as "taking in information," Senge notes, makes it seem dull and lifeless. What learning really is, is recreating ourselves though undergoing *shifts of mind*. Just as learning disabilities often are tragically not detected in children, the same is true for companies. Learning disabilities include: only doing your job, not thinking about the whole organization; believing the enemy is "out there," when the problem is always at least half internal; aggressive action to defeat competitors or complainants, when real success will come from self-examination; and a fixation on particular events, when usually it is some longer-term trend or pattern that is shaping your industry or market.

Companies feel pleased with themselves when they identify a particular structure or practice that has caused a problem, and then proceed to root it out or change it. But this is never enough, Senge says. A true learning organization is focused not just on the problematic structure or system, but on *the thinking that created it in the first place*. It is constantly looking at its thinking models to check if it is making false assumptions which could jeopardize its future.

Mental models

For years, the United States automotive industry operated on articles of faith, such as that cars are primarily status symbols, so styling is more important than quality, and that the American car market was isolated from the rest of the world. Such beliefs reflected reality for quite some time, but only for that time. The carmakers didn't think these beliefs were "mental models," they took them to be truth. Senge asked: "If mental models can freeze companies in practices and views that no longer work, why can't *good* mental models have the opposite effect, allowing them to have breakthroughs and develop?"

In the 1970s the planning team at Royal Dutch Shell noticed that the period of smooth growth in the production of oil, and in its consumption, was coming to an end. For a variety of reasons the world's main oil producers would not be able to pump as much, so it would become a "seller's market." The Shell team did not foresee the OPEC cartel and oil shocks that would rock the world, only the broad outline of the future, but even so Shell's managers didn't want to know; this forecasted future contradicted all of their experience. To have their work taken into account, the planning team tried another tack: they forced the top executives to see how many of their assumptions would have to be true if their imagined trouble-free future would actually come to pass. After sitting down and seeing how unlikely this rosy future was, they had to change their mental models. The result? When the oil crisis came, Shell responded differently to its competitors, for instance quickly speeding up oil field development outside OPEC countries. Shell went from being the weakest of the big seven oil companies to being number two to Exxon by the end of the 1970s. By the early 1980s, scenario planning and mental model examination was part of its culture.

Personal mastery

Learning, as Senge understands it, "does not mean acquiring more information, but expanding the ability to produce the results we truly want in life." People with a high level of personal mastery are "committed to continually seeing reality more and more accurately." They are acutely aware of all the things they don't know, yet paradoxically are more self-confident and assured than people who consider their learning done.

Bill O'Brien, the CEO of Hanover Insurance, brought in Senge and colleagues to help transform his company. During the 1980s it rose from being an industry laggard to one of its smartest and best-run firms. O'Brien was open to Senge's message because he believed that "emotional development offers the greatest degree of leverage in attaining our full potential . . . The total development of our people is essential to achieving our goal of corporate excellence." Managers had to give up the idea of controlling and organizing their staff, and instead provide "the enabling conditions for people to lead the most enriching lives they can." For this to work, a company must have a clear purpose, an inspiring reason for existing, instead of just having a goal of profitability or market share. This purpose usually involves the enlightenment or liberation of people—both staff and customers—in some way: helping them become more independent, more creative, or their lives better or easier.

Senge distinguishes between vision and purpose. A vision is concrete, for example, "Putting a man on Mars by 2030." Purpose is more abstract, for example, "Advancing man's capacity to explore the heavens." Commitment to something larger than ourselves, to the whole, is always very powerful: "The sense of connectedness and compassion characteristic of individuals with high levels of personal mastery naturally leads to a broader vision. Without it, all the subconscious visualizing in the world is deeply self-centered—simply a way to get what I want."

A big part of personal mastery is commitment to the truth: that is, the willingness of people to identify their own patterns, rackets, games, or blind spots that have been obstacles to fulfilling their potential. Senge observes that just as you can't force a person to engage in personal development, so you can't force an organization to become focused on self-mastery and learning. There have even been lawsuits by employees against companies who feel they have been forced to take part in personal development training that went against their religious beliefs. What companies can and should do is create an organization in which "it is safe for people to create visions, where inquiry and commitment to the truth are the norm, and where challenging the status quo is expected." The best thing to create a learning organization is for the leaders and managers to be the model, demonstrating a personal quest for self-mastery that naturally involves the organization in that quest. Only such inspiring examples will chip away at the understanding of organizations as coercive systems. In fact, it is possible for them to be the opposite: a vehicle for personal advance and liberation.

Common vision

Visions can't be imposed by someone at the top, and as a result most employees merely comply with a vision—they are not committed. To be meaningful and powerful, visions must be shared by all in the organization. As Abraham Maslow put it, "the task and the self become the same."

What shared visions do is generate courage, because people do what they have do to ensure that the vision is realized. Visions take time to evolve. As they become clearer, it is easier to get behind them, and what you get is a "reinforcing spiral of communication and excitement." Many companies claim to be driven by a vision when in fact they are just constantly reacting to events. People begin to wonder what it stands for, if it is always changing to follow some new trend or not bothering to stick with its stated vision. "In the absence of a great dream," Senge writes, "pettiness prevails."

His emphasis on looking within for the source of problems, observing that it is the state of our minds that creates reality, is very Buddhist. Indeed, much of Senge's thinking takes a while to accept because it goes against western ideas of having a "line of attack," taking swift action, apportioning blame, and striving to compete and dominate. A truly common vision, because it allows creativity and uniqueness to flourish, would in its very nature transcend the need for such a compartmentalized and aggressive approach.

Final comments

Senge's ideas seemed radical in 1990, but were arguably just a logical further expression of the ideas of Douglas McGregor. Regardless, many companies now aspire to using Sengian dialogue, radical openness, and mental model examination to set themselves apart. It is partly to make them more interesting and enjoyable places to work, with less chance of burnout, but is also driven by the desire to stay around, shaping the market while others are destroyed by shortsightedness.

Management thinker Peter Drucker once said, "Making money for a company is like oxygen for a person; if you don't have enough of it you're out of the game." Senge retorts that "Companies who take profit as their purpose are like people who think life is about breathing. They're missing something." If a company is focused only on the bottom line, employees and potential employees soon see that the company stands for nothing other than material gain. If a firm has no commitment to anything other than its own advance, it is hard for it to establish spirit or loyalty. The result is people working without passion, ready to leave if they can. In contrast, as Shell's Arie de Geus noted in his study of longevity in companies (*The Living Company*, 1997), those with the longest lives saw themselves more as *communities* than institutions.

"The Japanese believe building a great organization is like growing a great tree," Senge reminds us, "it takes twenty-five to fifty years." Such a company, which must constantly evolve by responding to the present, while at the same time imagining a future in which it is not only relevant but a leader, would by nature need to be a learning organization.

Peter Senge

Senge was born in Stanford, California, in 1947, and studied aerospace engineering and philosophy at Stanford University. He obtained a subsequent master's degree in systems modeling from MIT, and then did a Ph.D. in management at its Sloan School of Management. In 1997 he set up the Society for Organizational Learning at MIT.

He has worked with corporations including Ford, Chrysler, Shell and AT&T on organizational development. He is a regular meditator and his philosophy has been influenced by Zen Buddhist practice.

Other books include The Fifth Discipline Fieldbook *(1994),* Presence: An Exploration of Profound Change in People, Organizations, and Society *(2005), and* The Necessary Revolution: How Individuals and Organizations are Working Together to Create a Sustainable World *(2010).*

2009

Start With Why

"People don't buy what you do, they buy why you do it."

"There are very few leaders who choose to inspire rather than manipulate in order to motivate people."

"All great leaders have charisma because all great leaders have clarity of WHY; an undying belief in a purpose or cause bigger than themselves . . . Energy can excite, but only charisma can inspire. Charisma demands loyalty. Energy does not."

In a nutshell

A person or organization only really succeeds in a big way when they arrive at a crystal clear awareness of their purpose—what they are doing to advance others and the world.

In a similar vein

Richard Koch & Greg Lockwood *Simplify*
Al Ries & Jack Trout *Positioning*
Peter Senge *The Fifth Discipline*

CHAPTER 39

Simon Sinek

I n the early 2000s, Simon Sinek was desperate to be an entrepreneur, and so was elated during the first couple of years of running his own market positioning and strategy consultancy. However, by 2005 he was only just getting by, and was terrified the business would go under. "I started having desperate thoughts," he recalls, "thoughts that for an entrepreneur are almost worse than suicide: I thought about getting a job."

What had gone wrong? It dawned on Sinek that he had become wrapped up in the idea of his personal and professional success, and meantime potential clients didn't really know what he and his company stood for. As a result, there wasn't a lot of business. The crisis got him thinking about motivation—not the temporary boost that we might get at a self-help seminar, but the fundamental reasons we act, our "Why."

His dark night of the soul, and subsequent illumination over the importance of clear purpose, led to him giving talks and the writing of *Start With Why*. The pool of examples in the book is small (Apple, Microsoft, and Southwest Airlines feature heavily), and it is repetitive (many points are made two or even three times). However, the best business books are often very simple, and don't need to be backed by copious references or research to achieve their goal of inspiring people to *act*. Sinek's book does this in full measure, and can help you bring about the revolution your life or business needs.

The Golden Circle

Every company knows *what* it does—the products or services it sells. Most companies understand *how* they do it—a unique proposition, a proprietary process, or how they do something better or different to the competition. But very few firms really understand and articulate *why* they exist—the goal or mission that inspires their employees to get out of bed in the morning.

For instance, in its sales pitch, a computer firm starts with a What ("We make great computers"), describes its How ("They're beautifully designed, simple to use"), then delivers its Why, or more like, a Why Not ("Wanna buy one?"). Why does "Why" come last? The reason is that the "What" is clear and concrete, but the "Why" is fuzzy and difficult. Imagine three concentric rings, with "What" at the center, "How" as the middle ring, and "Why" as the outer ring. By simply reversing the order, Sinek says, you create a "Golden Circle" which can transform your company. His example is Apple, whose circles are the complete opposite of the average computer firm. Its Golden Circle might be characterized thus:

- Why: We always go against the status quo, thinking differently
- How: We do this by making beautiful, simple, and user-friendly products
- What: Would you like to buy one of our computers?

People don't buy what you do, Sinek says, they buy *why* you do it. In Apple's case, "their products give life to their cause."

We forget now, but when Apple came out with its first computers, most companies believed the future was in big machines that supported businesses and organizations. Apple said "No, we want to give a person in their living room the same power as a company." Later, they would publicize the iPod not by describing *what* it was (Creative, the Singapore company who invented the technology, had sold their product as a "5gb mp3 player"), but rather by telling us *why* it was worth having: "1,000 songs in your pocket."

The problem with being a "What" company is that people identify the products you make with who or what you are. For instance, Dell is identified with computers, so has always had a hard time shifting other kinds of products. But if you are a company like Apple that is identified with a "Why"—an ethos that drives the company, above and beyond any particular product or service—then you will have little problem branching out into areas that you are not historically associated with, be it watches or cars. What you are buying is Apple. With Dell, you are buying their product; you don't really care about Dell.

Inspired by a purpose, not sold on a feature

The goal of any company is for people to make decisions about buying their products or services based on the heart. If they have to do a cost benefit analysis based on empirical data about whether to buy from you, then you haven't made a lasting connection that can last years or even decades. You want people to be loyal to you because your purpose and products make them feel good about using them. You want people to turn to you as a gut feeling.

TiVo's marketing to potential buyers was based on its obvious benefits: a device that pauses and rewinds live TV, skips commercials, and records shows you like on your behalf. But TiVo never matched up to expectations as a company, Sinek believes, because it only ever sold the rational benefits its product provided—*what* it did—and most people didn't believe they needed these benefits.

What the TiVo founders should have done, Sinek says, is convey to people what they *believed*, why they invented the product to begin with, and their vision of how it would make people's lives better or easier, giving them total control over their viewing. The actual features of the product are just supporting the basic *purpose* of the product. "To TiVo" became a verb phrase to record something from television, but unfortunately for TiVo, people just as often use the record feature provided by a cable or satellite provider. They were never motivated enough to get *the* TiVo recorder, because there was no philosophy behind the product to buy in to, just a set of features.

The reason people prefer to work at Apple rather than Dell, or Tesla instead of Ford, is that in both cases they want to feel like they are part of something bigger, that they are helping to invent the future. For the customer, buying a Macbook or a Tesla Model S makes you feel like you are on the cutting edge. It's not that you love Apple or Tesla the companies, which after all have a corporate structure similar to other firms, but how the things these companies produce makes *me* feel, and what these things say about *me*.

The opposite of a company that is successful because it inspires, is one that is the market leader only because it offers the lowest prices. Isn't Walmart massively successful because of its emphasis on price? Actually, Sinek says, a low price strategy always has costs; most of the scandals Walmart has been involved in have revolved around driving too hard a bargain, either with wages or suppliers, to get the price down. As companies get bigger, they know what they produce to bring in the money, but it is easy to lose track of why they exist. Walmart founder Sam Walton's motivation for his company was one that truly served the community by increasing its living standards through genuinely lower prices, allowing people to shop locally instead of having to drive to urban centers, and contributing to community initiatives. After he died, this "Why" was somehow lost and Walmart only became about lower prices and the bottom line. As a result, it got hit by multiple lawsuits over how it treated employees and suppliers, and people happily desert if they can get the same product cheaper down the road.

Trust and success

In the early 1970s, only 15 percent of Americans traveled by air. Herb Kelleher and partner Rollin King wanted to change that, to be champions of the common man, making it much cheaper to fly between cities in Texas (where they began). Southwest Airline's first tag line was, "You are now free to move about the country." With only two tiers of pricing, flying was now cheap, fun, and simple.

Years later, United Airlines tried to copy Southwest with their budget offshoot Ted, and Delta did the same with Song. Both failed within four years. Why, when they were offering the same thing as Southwest, and with much greater resources? Ultimately, the choices people make are not based just on price, quality, or features. We gravitate to what we know, Sinek writes, what is simple and clear, and what provokes some positive feeling in us, say of trust or loyalty. Why were Ted and Song created? For all we know, they were desperate moves to save an airline behemoth, or to maintain market share. Yet as consumers we somehow have the feeling that Southwest Airlines, even if their prices are not always the cheapest, is always thinking about making things better for *us*, the customer.

The best customers are simply the ones who believe what you believe, just as the best spouse is one who shares your values. The best employees are not the ones which match the skills you need, but the ones who believe in what you are trying to do as a company. Sinek recounts the Antarctic expedition of Ernest Shackleton. It was a failure in the sense that they never got close to the goal of crossing the Antarctic land mass, but a triumph in other ways. Despite being marooned on ice for months with little hope of survival, all came back alive. Leadership experts put this down to the fact that Shackleton created a team of people who were of the same mind. His famous ad in *The Times* to recruit for the expedition did not ask for particular skills, qualifications, or experience, but instead said:

"Men wanted for Hazardous journey. Small wages, bitter cold, long months of complete darkness, constant danger, safe return doubtful. Honour and recognition in case of success."

Don't just hire "passionate people," Sinek says, make sure they are passionate about the same things you are. Lots of companies employ "star" salespeople or managers, but fewer take the time and effort to produce a *culture* that evolves out of two things: (1) a very clear mission that all share; and (2) a climate of trust. Great organizations are ones where people feel protected and valued, and therefore will go the extra mile. Herb Kelleher went against the conventional wisdom by putting employees first, customers second, and shareholders third. His way ended up generating wealth and security, while the rest of the airline industry seemed to exist in a different world of cut-throat competition with tiny margins and high staff turnover.

Final comments

A primary reason for creating a "Why" organization is that it makes decisions a lot simpler, since you are very clear on what you should or should not get involved in, and who you should and should not work with. Sinek used to annoy his business partner by turning away business from people who didn't "feel" right. The reason they didn't feel right was because their outlook or ethos didn't chime with his. After all, he reasoned, if people want to work with him who are not interested in inspiring people (which he feels is his mission), it is very clear that it won't do to work with them. Clarity of purpose not only inspires and energizes, it saves a lot of wasted time and effort dealing with the wrong people and pursuing the wrong projects. Instead, imagine a world in which everyone had a clear "Why," and their life and work was an expression of this purpose. That would be a world in which potential, in life and business, was fulfilled as a matter of course.

Simon Sinek

Sinek was born in London in 1973, and spent his childhood in Johannesburg, London, and the United States. After high school in Demarest, New Jersey, he enrolled at Brandeis University, majoring in anthropology, and for a time studied law at City University in London.

His TED talk, "How Great Leaders Inspire Action," based on Start With Why, *has been viewed 29 million times. His other books are* Leaders Eat Last: Why Some Teams Pull Together and Others Don't *(2014),* Together Is Better: A Little Book of Inspiration *(2016), and* Find Your Why: A Practical Guide to Discovering Purpose for You and Your Team *(2017).*

Mythbreaker: Kiran Mazumdar-Shaw and the Story of Indian Biotech

"He marvelled at how, in her entrepreneurial journey, she has managed to break the kind of myths that abound in the Indian scenario—a tech start-up seeded nearly four decades ago in life sciences and not information technology, by a woman who was not an engineer and who did not come from a business family."

"Kiran Mazumdar-Shaw managed multiple risks to build business within business, consistently ratcheting her company's scientific capability and, no less importantly, her own public profile . . . Over time she became a brand ambassador, not just of a fledgling industry but of innovation-led business in general. By interacting with the funding and regulatory agencies and the political system, she gave a face to the industry."

In a nutshell

The first rule of business is to create a real business that can be constantly ratcheted up and used to fund future growth.

In a similar vein

Duncan Clark *Alibaba: The House That Jack Ma Built*
Jim Collins *Great by Choice*
Sheryl Sandberg *Lean In*

CHAPTER 40

Seema Singh

Everyone knows about the rise of India's tech industry over the past 20 years, with companies such as Infosys becoming major corporations at home and abroad. Fewer are aware of India's efforts to create biotech and pharmaceutical industries. While not nearly as big as its IT sector, India's biotech sector has attracted back many expats working for American biotech firms like Genentech and Amgen. There have admittedly been various scandals about fudged research, production quality, and the abuse of intellectual property, but India's pharma companies have earned increasing respectability and are making healthcare more affordable through lower costs. A company called Biocon stands out, not just because it is one of the oldest and largest, but because of its star cofounder, Kiran Mazumdar.

In *Mythbreaker: Kiran Mazumdar-Shaw and the Story of Indian Biotech,* science and technology writer Seema Singh shows how it is possible, with enough guts and will, to build an industry and a company from scratch in a developing country. Mazumdar shattered the myth that India was not capable of advanced science, and into the bargain showed that it could be done by a woman. In fact, Mazumdar is one of many female entrepreneurs to have emerged in Asia over the past 15 years, such as Cher Wang (cofounder of HTC) and Zhou Qunfei (touchscreens) in China, Park Sung-Kyung (fashion and retail) in Korea, and Eva Yi-Hwa Chen (Trend Micro) in Japan.

Singh's book traces Mazumdar's trajectory from "accidental entrepreneur" (as she has described herself) to billionaire, taking her company from being a maker of "boring" enzymes to a big pharma player tackling modern-world ills including diabetes and cancer, now sadly of increasing prevalence in India.

Aussie platform

In 1978, Kiran Mazumdar was keen to enter the workforce after having gained a degree in brewing from the University of Ballarat in Australia. She would continue in the footsteps of her father, who had been chief brewer at United Breweries in Bengaluru (Bangalore). But when it became clear that Indian breweries did not want to employ a woman in a senior technical post, she instead arranged a job working for a malting company in Scotland.

But before leaving, Mazumdar got a call from Les Auchinloss, the founder of Biocon Biochemicals in Ireland, a maker of industrial enzymes. He was keen to set up an Indian branch of the company, and asked her to take on the role. "You must be joking," the 24-year-old replied. He convinced her to turn down the Scotland post and instead come to Ireland to learn processes for turning two of India's abundant raw materials, fish bladders and papaya, into the compounds isinglass and papain, used in brewing. Auchinloss gave her $3,000 to set up a company, to be based in Bengaluru. Why her? He had heard about Mazumdar from the head of Biocon Australia, who had been on the same Ballarat brewing course. She was the only woman in the class, he noted, and was at the same time very demanding and had lots of integrity—just what Auchinloss wanted. The Australian experience, Singh says, gave Mazumdar confidence: she discovered that she was smarter than her classmates, and acquired the western idea that anything was possible.

Start me up

Biocon India was incorporated in 1978, with Biocon Ireland owning 30 percent of the company, and Mazumdar and the banks the rest. At the time, the Indian government was very wary of foreign ownership and had strict investment rules.

After hiring workers and finding a premises of sorts—an old shed—she focused on marketing and business development. From the start, the company was assured of revenues as Biocon Ireland would buy some of its enzymes. Thanks to her father's brewery connections, she got her foot in the door in many Indian breweries, and began to sell them enzymes for brewing. In 1979 the company made its first sale to America, becoming the first Indian enzyme maker to do so. With steady sales, Mazumdar built a factory, hired a core team, and even created a research and development lab. The latter was important to Mazumdar personally, and would be crucial to the company's success.

The firm started developing pectinases, a kind of enzyme used in the extraction of fruit juice from puree and in brewing, which had been dominated by Japanese makers. Ocean Spray, the American firm that was the largest producer of cranberry juice in the world, began using pectinases made at Biocon's new plant in Bengaluru, which used solid state fermentation technology (an advance on wet enzyme production). Biocon also got into making products for baking.

Corporation games

In 1989, Auchinloss sold Biocon, now a company with operations in many countries, to Quest, a firm owned by Unilever. The deal included Biocon

India, but Mazumdar and her team didn't like the idea of being told what to do by Unilever, chafing at what they saw as a contrast between their very entrepreneurial spirit and the ethos of a large corporation. Mazumdar attempted to raise money for a management buyout, but couldn't come up with the £35 million needed. For their part, Unilever executives tried to get her to dilute her stake in Biocon and take control. Amid the tension they visited Bengaluru, and Mazumdar gave a presentation outlining her theory of "three types of companies":

- Ones that make things happen
- Ones that watch things happen
- Ones which wonder what happened

Biocon India was of the first type, she told everyone in the room, and Unilever was of the third.

Mazumdar was hell-bent on expansion and selling into overseas markets, given the company's great cost advantages compared to similar firms in rich countries, and Quest/Unilever provided funds for the opening of a new factory in 1995, not least because Biocon was providing food enzymes to Unilever's sprawling food empire. The Indian firm was now "strategically important" to Unilever, and it wanted control more than ever.

Breaking free

By the mid 1990s Biocon India had moved into the production of yeast, fungi, and bacteria for a variety of uses, and was keen to move into pharmaceuticals, as it was a faster-growing market than enzymes. But Unilever thought it was too much of a risk, and so Mazumdar and her key executives started their own greenfield company, Helix (later absorbed into Biocon itself), to make pharma products. It took years to develop products, but they started with a fungus-derived immunosuppressant that had been approved by the US Food and Drug Administration.

Unilever ended up selling its stake in Biocon India to the British bulk chemicals business ICI, which again Mazumdar wasn't happy about. Her team considered it an affront to be controlled by a mere "paint company." But help arrived in a surprising way. She had become close to John Shaw, a Scot living in India who had run a clothing company. To help fund Biocon's buyout of ICI, Shaw sold his London home and became Mazumdar's partner, in life and in business. They were married in 1998.

Becoming a pharma

In 1993 the people at Biocon invested in a new venture, Syngene, which would do molecular biology testing on contract for other firms. By 2000, big pharma firms were contracting out a quarter of their R & D work, and Bristol Myers Squibb gave Syngene a lot of work. The start-up would prove to be important to Biocon's success in that it helped to develop its pharma research and manufacturing capabilities while being cofunded by pharma titans including BMS and Pfizer.

Mazumdar had focused in on statins—the class of molecules used to lower cholesterol and so reduce the risk of heart disease—as an area in which Biocon could compete. The company set about making lovastatin, a statin that Merck had developed but whose patent had expired in 2001. Biocon did a deal with Canadian firm Genpharm to sell it into Canada and the US, and got US FDA approval. Mazumdar went out on a limb and built a huge plant to make the statins, and started to become a player in their worldwide production. From the late 1990s into the 2000s the firm grew fast, doubling revenue in some years.

In 2004, Biocon listed on the Indian stock exchange. The offering was oversubscribed 33 times. The company was now valued at $1.1 billion, and Mazumdar and Shaw owned 70 percent of it. The media focused on her new fortune, but she kept telling them that Biocon was about "intellectual wealth creation, not personal wealth." The core team around her were now also multimillionaires.

Post-flotation

In 2007, Biocon sold the enzymes business to a Danish company, Novozymes, for $115 million; Novozymes wanted Biocon's Indian market share. The year before it had launched its Biomab antibody for treating head and neck cancer. This is a major cancer in India because of the popularity of tobacco chewing. Thus, the company completed its transition from enzyme producer to proper pharmaceutical company, competing not only with other Indian pharma companies but with US and European corporations.

In an alliance with an Indian pharma company, Mylan, Biocon moved into the "biosimilar" market, that is making and selling pharmaceuticals that were losing patent protection. In 2010, Pfizer paid Biocon $200 million to license and sell four of its insulin products worldwide. The partnership was called off, but Mazumdar used the money to set up a plant in Malaysia, where the government wanted to kickstart a biomanufacturing cluster.

Biocon India remains at the heart of a growing Bengaluru biotech cluster, with a well-established R & D operation and a pipeline of products. It makes over a third of the world's statins, and is a significant maker of human insulin to treat diabetes.

Final comments

After 30 years at the helm, in 2014 Mazumdar-Shaw stepped down as chief executive of Biocon, making way for Arun Chandavarkar. The move was seen as a replacement of charisma with competence, but Singh suggests that Biocon will lose something as a result, since "Kiran is the only one who can make gutsy bets, show a certain blindness to the odds that is necessary to drive innovation." Tim Cook may be good for Apple, she notes, but he will never be Steve Jobs.

On the other hand, given its very successful public listing in 2004, Biocon has not fulfilled expectations that it would increase 10 or 20 times in value as some middle-sized Indian pharma companies have done, such as Lupin. Its progress has been more constant and steady, an example, Singh argues, of Jim Collins's "flywheel effect" in which a company makes steady gains year after year, continuously improving and upgrading in order to build strong momentum. By Collins's "good to great" scenario, Biocon under Mazumdar-Shaw went from being a strong if unglamorous maker of enzymes, to a company that is playing a part in India's advance as a techno-logically sophisticated country, taking care of its people while being an example of affordable healthcare for the rest of the world. With reference to Collins's book *Great by Choice* (see Chapter 8), Biocon consciously chooses not to grow at ridiculous rates, because this creates its own prob-lems and is never sustainable. Better to climb slowly, and still be around in 40 or 50 years' time.

Seema Singh

Singh is a cofounder of The Ken, *an online technology magazine based in Bengaluru. Before writing* Mythbreaker *she headed* Forbes India's *Bengaluru bureau, and has written for* New Scientist, Cell, Red Herring, Newsweek *and* The Times of India. *In 2000/1 she was a Knight Science Journalism Fellow at Massachusetts Institute of Technology.*

My Years with General Motors

"I have always believed in planning big, and I have always discovered after the fact that, if anything, we didn't plan big enough."

"I always tried to run General Motors by a policy of conciliation rather than coercion; and when a majority was opposed to my thinking, I was often disposed to give way . . . the top officers of General Motors . . . were men of unusual talents and strong convictions, and as president I felt I should respect their judgements."

"We knew that the product had a great potential, but I can hardly say that any of us, at the beginning, realized the extent to which the automobile would transform the United States and the world, reshape the entire economy, call new industries into being, and alter the pace and style of everyday life."

In a nutshell

A big company does not have to be bloated. With good management it can react quickly to changing market conditions.

In a similar vein

Alfred Chandler *The Visible Hand*
Walter Isaacson *Steve Jobs*
Douglas McGregor *The Human Side of Enterprise*
Brad Stone *The Everything Store*
Ashlee Vance *Elon Musk*

CHAPTER 41

Alfred P. Sloan

I f ever there was a work that justifies the title, "business classic," it is *My Years with General Motors*. It was praised by all and sundry when it was published, and became a set text in management schools.

In a 1995 article for *Fortune*, Bill Gates described it as "probably the best book to read if you want to read only one book about business." Sloan's tips on organization, keeping executives happy, and dealing with the competition Gates found inspiring and valuable in heading his own corporate behemoth, Microsoft. Today's average reader, however, may wonder why the book got such a rapturous reception, and why it was such a bestseller. We forget, though, that the automobile industry was once very sexy, on the cutting edge of technology and management techniques. In terms of public esteem and fascination, General Motors, Ford, and Chrysler were something akin to the Apples, Googles, and Amazons of today. In the 1950s however, great titans of industry did not write books at the drop of a hat, as is common today.

Sloan's book bears little resemblance to today's business bestsellers. Despite the intriguing subject matter, it is pretty drily written. Sloan and ghostwriter John McDonald, a *Fortune* journalist, somehow thought it would be interesting for the reader to include entire corporate memos, position papers, and organizational charts, and we get little more glimpse into the character of Sloan, who had the upright demeanor of a Victorian gentleman, than we would reading a GM annual report. There are useful principles to be gleaned, but as a reader you have to earn them, paying close attention through 24 chapters, which cover the company's history from the earliest Durant days, competition with Ford, the depressions of 1920 and 1929, GM's role in the war effort, overseas operations, labor relations, and the evolution of the automobile in both styling and engineering.

My Years with General Motors was almost not published. GM tried to suppress the work because there were parts of it which could have been used as evidence in a Justice Department antimonopoly lawsuit. It was alleged that GM had gone too far in its pursuit of market share, and there was a threat the company could be broken up. Sloan reluctantly went along with GM, but McDonald, who had worked on the book for five long years and stood to lose professionally and financially, sued GM. The corporation gave in, and the book finally appeared in stores in January 1964, when Sloan was nearing 90. The authors seemed to be a funny pairing—McDonald, who had spent time with Trotsky in Mexico and had long supported radical leftist causes, and the former head of the world's greatest capitalist enterprise. Yet McDonald had grown up in Detroit so the emergence of the automobile industry was of real interest to him. He had also written on game theory and strategy, and so was intrigued about the strategies GM had used to become the industry's biggest player. A young Alfred Chandler, before he went on to acclaim as a business historian and management theorist, was enlisted as a researcher.

The auto industry and Sloan rise together

In 1900 there were 8,000 registered motor vehicles in America. The motor car was considered the sport of gentlemen and bankers; they were mechanically unreliable, and there were few good roads. By 1930, there would be *27 million* cars. Deliveries of goods and services became much easier, and workers and farmers saved time in getting to work. Cars enabled a suburban real estate boom and the rise of a middle-class consumer culture. As Sloan's quote above suggests, no one really foresaw just how great the demand for cars would be, and how they would drive America's economy and transform its culture.

The automobile industry in 1908 had consisted of a large number of independent, small carmakers. William Durant was keen to consolidate the industry, yet after pulling together several car brands including Buick, Olds, Oakland, Cadillac, and parts suppliers under one holding company, the General Motors Company, he was still only producing 8,000 cars a year. When the flamboyant Durant forecast that the day would come when a million cars were sold a year, he was not believed. He lost control of the company in 1910 to banks when it fell into financial difficulties, and soon after started the Chevrolet Motor Company. It was so successful that Durant used its stock to exchange it with General Motors stock, in an effort to regain control of the company, which he did in 1916.

Alfred Sloan began his working life with the Hyatt Roller Bearing Company of New Jersey. When it fell into financial difficulty, his father put up some money to keep it going, and Sloan became general manager. He made it a success, and was able to capitalize on the demand for bearings in the emerging automobile industry. Ford was his biggest customer, General Motors second. In 1915, when Durant bought Hyatt for $13.5 million, Sloan and his father received a significant amount of stock in Durant's new United

Motors Corporation of auto parts makers. Sloan became president of United Motors, and after it was acquired by General Motors in 1918, without ever intending to, Sloan became an auto industry executive.

Master of management

With most of his personal wealth tied up in General Motors, Sloan became increasingly anxious about the direction of the company under Durant. In his mid forties he took a month-long vacation and almost decided to leave the company. But Durant's departure from GM under a cloud (stock market speculation gone wrong) created an opening for Sloan.

He drafted a 28-page "General Motors Organization Study" document, which was widely circulated in the company. When GM's then president, Pierre du Pont, adopted the plan in 1920 as the basis of GM's structure, Sloan became the de facto chief executive. Although remaining a vice president, by 1921 he was in charge of all operations.

Sloan promulgated a decentralized model of organization with divisional heads given discretion on strategy, backed up by bonuses for performance and shareholding plans. This "happy medium" between decentralized power and central control would allow a level of entrepreneurship to thrive even in a big company. Sloan contrasted this model with that of the Ford company, whose domination by Henry Ford meant centralized management and a rigid model offering. Today we take decentralization and stock options to motivate managers for granted, but in Sloan's time it was something new.

Even Sloan admitted that the blend of decentralized management and central control was a paradox, but it was in reality the only way to successfully run a company GM's size. As a manager, Sloan emphasized the power of motivation and influence, not command and control. He preferred to run GM by persuading others of his ideas, rather than by edict. "Our decentralized organization and our tradition of selling ideas rather than simply giving orders," he writes, "impose the need upon all levels of management to make a good case for what they propose." He also found that consensus decisions on the whole were better than ones made on the hunch of executives, however brilliant they seemed.

Sloan introduced a very clear separation between policy and administration. He created policy groups covering Engineering, Distribution, Overseas, Research, Personnel, and Public Relations—all guiding the direction of the corporation as a whole, separate to the functional day-to-day operations of each division. These policy groups were the glue that bound all the divisions together and produced a sense of one company. Such organization models are taken for granted today, but Sloan was ahead of the curve in working out how a giant corporation could give managers leeway yet retain a sense of corporate unity and direction. He writes:

"From decentralization we get initiative, responsibility, development of personnel, decisions close to the facts, flexibility—in short, all the qualities necessary for an organization to adapt to new conditions. From coordination we get efficiencies and economies."

He introduced centralization of cash control and finance, with 100 bank accounts across America depositing sales revenues into a General Motors Corporation account, instead of hanging onto it for their own purposes. GM's financial control system became a model for other big companies, and the centralization of purchasing and procurement saved the firm a lot of money. Left too much to their own devices, he noted, the divisions got out of control, but with a rationalization of statistics gathering and accounting there was a steady flow of operating data to central administration. This data meant that a course could be set that worked for the whole corporation.

Under Sloan, General Motors was the largest company in the world, making around half of all cars and trucks in North America, and producing vehicles through its overseas subsidiaries Opel in Germany, Vauxhall in Britain, and Holden in Australia. Despite unproven allegations of monopolistic behavior by the US government, Sloan remained a believer in "Big Business"—not in order to monopolize a market, but to achieve efficiencies and greater coordination of resources.

Yet size itself was never his aim, he says, but simply *growth*. Decentralization and coordination allowed for growth while preventing the firm from falling into "one-man rule." A great company should be run rationally, aided by an excellent structure, rather than being the plaything of personalities. Indeed, Sloan's book aimed to show it was possible to run a company with 600,000 employees and yet somehow make it nimble and adaptive to change.

Master strategist

When he took over at GM, the company was strong at the upper end of the market, with its higher-priced Buick and Cadillac brands, but not competitive at the bottom, where the Ford Model T reigned supreme; in the middle, it offered a confusing mix of Olds, Oaklands, Sheridans, and Scripps-Booth cars. GM was selling 400,000 cars to Ford's million plus (comprised of the low-price, high-volume model T and the high-price, low-volume Lincoln), and accounted for 12 percent of the total automobile market.

Sloan resolved to rid the company of car models that made little sense. It would become a corporation first and foremost focused on *making money*, not on making cars per se. To achieve this, GM would have to provide a high production volume model for each segment of the market, with no overlap between its models. One model per segment, priced accordingly from cheap Chevrolets to expensive Cadillacs. It was during his time that the concept of upgrading was developed, by which a person, as their income rose, would graduate from a Chevrolet to an Oldsmobile to a Buick to a Cadillac over the course of their lifetime, while staying within the GM "family." In this way, GM could cater to the whole population, not just the wealthy, giving rise to the slogan, "a car for every purse and purpose." Yet by using many interchangeable parts across the whole GM product line, the company achieved economies of scale and saved a lot on production costs.

Sloan's insight was that companies don't just compete in actual products or models, but in *policies*, that is, how they imagine and understand their industry. By adopting a "car for every segment" outlook, GM was clearly differentiating itself from Ford, with its very limited model range. GM management resolved that it was not absolutely necessary for any of their cars to be "the best" in their category, as long as the multiple-segment strategy worked and the company was making money.

Slowly, the concept of the "annual model" was introduced, in which a new variant of each model was brought out each year to help it sell. This consumer-driven approach, which naturally pleased the forecourt dealers, could not have been more different to Ford's more static, producer-driven model.

In the mid 1920s car sales really took off, thanks to the advent of installment selling, which meant the average person could afford the expense of a car, and the annual model. Ford, sticking to old models, lost ground to General Motors. When the Great Depression hit, GM sales fell by a third initially, then plummeted further. Production dropped by two-thirds, and its big 1920s profits evaporated. But amazingly, the company escaped going into the red, and it proved to be a chance to reexamine the corporation's ways and change again.

With Sloan at the helm, GM grew faster than the rest of the industry and became the number one producer, overtaking Ford. By the mid 1940s it was making over 2 million cars and trucks a year, and through the 1950s, when everyone predicted recession in the wake of the war, it financed a big expansion of production, reinvesting a lot of profits despite paying a healthy dividend to shareholders. The firm had to retool due to new innovations such as automatic transmissions, power steering, power brakes, and V8 engines, and in 1955 it raised a record $355 million in a stock offering on public markets. GM developed "Duco," a new form of automobile paint that allowed for a much greater variety of colors and less curing time in the factory. It also pioneered independent suspension in the United States to improve ride and handling, and hydraulic brakes. GM was the first to build dedicated "proving grounds" for car testing in all conditions, and invested heavily in design, setting up an "Art and Color" unit which became the Styling division, producing the iconic "finned" cars of the 1950s and 1960s. When it was unheard of, this division even employed women designers. Sloan commissioned the Saarinen brothers to design the famous Technical Center in Flint, Michigan, a modernist masterpiece which, on opening in 1956, expressed the optimism of the car industry.

Of course, in such a booming economy, any automobile company might have done well, but GM increased its market share and profitability. Its success seemed inevitable, but it wasn't. Sloan had to manage a delicate balancing act, pleasing shareholders and the public yet being mindful of responsibilities to employees, dealers, and suppliers.

Final comments

In hindsight, the publication of *My Years with General Motors* was a high point in the history of the company. It is ironic that Sloan attributed much of GM's success to the spur of competition, because too much competition led car manufacturing to become a relatively low-margin business, with all the financial risks that entails. In the financial crisis of 2007–8 GM's structural problems were exposed and it had to file for bankruptcy. Only a massive bailout by the US government, in 2009, allowed it to restructure, saving thousands of jobs in the process.

Today, it is notable that neither GM nor Ford is at the forefront of electric or hybrid car technology. Toyota and Elon Musk's Tesla have led the way, and firms such as Google are at the leading edge of driverless technology. General Motors still sells millions of cars and trucks each year, but its lack of investment in the future has seen it pay a price. Even in the 1950s, Sloan knew that it was not enough to have a viable business today. One had to continually come up with strategies to be the leader tomorrow.

Aside from its historical importance, Sloan's book is a great reminder that technology and engineering are the source of future profits. At the same time, it takes good management and effective strategies to realize their potential in the marketplace. Sloan was a master at both.

Alfred P. Sloan

Sloan was born in 1875 in Connecticut, but from the age of 10 grew up in Brooklyn, New York. His father owned a wholesale tea, coffee, and cigar business. In 1895 he graduated from the Massachusetts Institute of Technology with a degree in electrical engineering before going to work for the Hyatt Roller Bearing Company.

After his retirement as president of General Motors Sloan remained influential in the corporation as chairman of the board, and sat on policy committees, but on the death of his wife Irene in 1956 he resigned.

The couple had no children, but as Sloan was very rich from his ownership of 1 percent of GM, his fortune was poured into the philanthropic Sloan Foundation (current endowment over $1.8 billion, focusing on science, technology, and economics), the Sloan-Kettering Cancer Center in New York, the MIT School of Industrial Management (now the Sloan School of Management), and the Sloan Fellows, which sponsors studies at the Stanford Graduate School of Business and London Business School.

The Everything Store: Jeff Bezos and the Age of Amazon

"Amazon may be the most beguiling company that ever existed, and it is just getting started. It is both missionary and mercenary, and throughout the history of business and other human affairs, that has always been a potent combination."

"Amazon's culture has been engineered to cater obsessively to its customers. The company's loyal patrons enjoy the fruits of that focus every time they interact with it. Suppliers who view Amazon as a bully are perfectly free to sell their wares elsewhere. Employees who feel marginalized or mistreated can leave at any time and many do, sometimes after their first taste of the relentless corporate culture. Yet with so many other retailers in retreat, or tailoring their own operations to get as lean and efficient as Amazon, both suppliers and employees may find their opportunities elsewhere are increasingly limited. Like it or not, they are living in the age of Amazon."

In a nutshell

Even when it loses you money in the short term, a radical desire to please the customer builds loyalty that makes for long-term success.

In a similar vein

Duncan Clark *Alibaba: The House That Jack Ma Built*
Walter Isaacson *Steve Jobs*
Eric Schmidt & Jonathan Rosenberg *How Google Works*
Howard Schultz *Pour Your Heart Into It*
Ashlee Vance *Elon Musk*

CHAPTER 42

Brad Stone

B uying things online has become so much a part of our lives that it's taken for granted. Amazon.com, the world's largest online retailer, has an astonishing 300 million registered users, and sales of $136 billion. Yet for something so ubiquitous, most of us know very little about how the tech titan developed behind the scenes: its origins, struggles, and successes, whose trademarks of radical customer-centrism, very long-term view, and a constant desire to invent are now widely emulated.

Journalist Brad Stone's account of Amazon's first 18 years is a compelling read, showing how an opportunity seized at the right moment began one of the remarkable business stories of our time. Prior to writing the book, Stone had written on Amazon for *Newsweek*, the *New York Times*, and *Bloomberg*. He did 300 interviews with Amazon executives and employees, friends and family of founder Jeff Bezos, and more than a dozen interviews with Bezos himself. Stone seems to have retained his objectivity, however, revealing just how much the company has been driven by the Bezos's relentless ambition (in fact, Relentless was originally going to be the company name and relentless.com still redirects to Amazon). Despite a famous laugh and sunnier image compared to Steve Jobs or Bill Gates, he was only able to achieve his aims through tireless innovation, fierce negotiation, and driving his staff to exhaustion. Despite MacKenzie Bezos (Jeff's wife) famously damning and dismissing the book in an Amazon.com review, *The Everything Store: Jeff Bezos and the Age of Amazon* provides tremendous insight into the company.

Should I stay or should I go

Bezos was born Jeffrey Preston Jorgensen in 1963 in Albuquerque, New Mexico. His mother Jackie was only 16, his father Ted Jorgensen a bit older. The couple broke up, and Jackie began seeing Miguel Bezos, a young Cuban who had moved to the US to escape the Castro regime. Miguel, an engineer, would work his way up to become an executive with the Exxon corporation. Jeff, a highly driven and intelligent child, only discovered that his stepfather was not his real father when he was 10 years old.

In the early 1990s, Princeton-educated Bezos was working on Wall Street at D. E. Shaw & Co, a hedge fund set up to exploit tiny differences in prices of stocks and other securities on global markets. By 29, Bezos had become a vice president in the firm, and in 1994 was put in charge of its efforts to capitalize on the explosive growth of the emerging internet. He developed an online shopping concept with the working title, "the everything store." The idea wasn't taken further, but his research got him interested in the possibilities for selling books online.

In 1994 there were already a few online bookshops, but service was poor and many were just an adjunct to bricks-and-mortar stores. Gripped by the thought of a truly customer-centric online-only bookstore, Bezos told his mentor David Shaw he wanted to do it—but on his own, not under the aegis of the company. Shaw famously took Bezos on a walk around Central Park to talk him out of it, but didn't press him to stay.

Trying to work out what to do—after all, if he left mid-year he would forsake a hefty bonus—Bezos set up in his mind what he called a "regret minimization framework." He imagined himself at 80 looking back on his life, a bit like the butler in one of his favorite books, Kazuo Ishiguro's *Remains of the Day*. Would he regret having left D. E. Shaw, giving up the chance to become wealthy on Wall Street? No. Would he regret not getting involved in the internet? Yes. His parents thought it was a bit rash to leave his job, with his mother suggesting he start the company on the weekends or work on it at nights. Bezos's response: this was the dawn of the internet age; things were moving so quickly, he had to throw himself into it fully—and fast.

Abracadabra! Amazon born

To keep the price of books down, Bezos reasoned that his start-up would need to be based in a low-population state, because sales taxes only needed to be collected in states where a firm had a physical base. He chose Seattle because Microsoft had succeeded from there, it had lots of computer science graduates, and the book distributor Ingram wasn't far away in Oregon. Bezos was 31, his new wife MacKenzie, 24. They drove from Texas (where Bezos had grown up) across the West, stopping at the Grand Canyon on the way.

The couple set up a makeshift office in their Seattle garage, making the first desks out of cheap doors Jeff had bought at Home Depot. His parents put $100,000 into the fledgling outfit, even though he warned them there was a good chance they could lose it all. MacKenzie, an aspiring novelist, handled the finances and helped make the first hires. In November 1994, Bezos had an epiphany when, looking through the A section of a dictionary, he saw "Amazon." Not only the world's biggest river but its biggest by far, it was the perfect name for a bookstore that might, with luck, become many times bigger than any other. In these early days, Bezos and his team would go to a nearby Barnes & Noble café for meetings and coffee. As the firm grew, the irony was not lost on them.

The beta Amazon.com website, launched in March the following year, was primitive: it was mostly text and not very attractive, but had a shopping basket and a basic search engine. A key feature was reader reviews, which Bezos rightly thought could make the site different. Some publishing executives at the time thought negative book reviews on Amazon were doing the industry a disservice, but Bezos knew that the company's real value was not simply in selling things, but in helping people to make objective buying decisions.

Amazon had strong orders from the start, and all staff helped in the warehouse into the night to ship them. When Yahoo began listing Amazon on its directory pages, the pace only got quicker. Yet the company was using up all its cash and needed more. Bezos told potential investors in Seattle that it might reach sales of $114 million by the year 2000, which seemed fantastic, as did the valuation of $6 million. But through 1996, Amazon grew at an incredible 30–40 percent a month, helped by a front-page *Wall Street Journal* article on the company, which was now outgrowing its premises every few months.

Growing up fast

When John Doerr at Silicon Valley venture capital firm Kleiner Perkins invested $8 million for a 13 percent stake, the vote of confidence turbocharged Bezos' ambitions. He hired aggressively, and began imagining Amazon as among the first internet giants that could last decades.

In terms of a business model, the thinking was that by getting big fast, the company could offer lower prices, and so get bigger again. Bezos insisted on hiring the smartest people possible, filtering out any who talked about a "work/life balance." He wanted total commitment, and anyone who did not share his "low regard for the way things were done" did not last long.

Bezos was worried about Barnes & Noble's stated plans to "crush" Amazon by launching its own site. He told his employees that the only thing they could do was double down on customer service to make shopping at Amazon a great experience. Barnes & Noble's site was, in the end, never as attractive or efficient as Amazon's; the firm was too focused on its physical stores, which yielded a much higher profit per book than selling online. Despite its sales being a tiny fraction of Barnes & Noble's and its competitor Borders at this time, Amazon's stock market flotation in 1997 raised $54 million. Bezos's parents, brother, and sister became instant multimillionaires.

The go-go years 1998 to 2000 saw Amazon raise a further $2 billion in three corporate bond offerings. Yet even those with internet fever were not as expansive as Bezos in his predictions of how far Amazon would go in changing retailing. Right from the start, his letters to shareholders took a very long-term view, eschewing profit for market leadership and revenue growth, and crucially, repeat buying and customer loyalty.

Bezos focused on building new distribution infrastructure, including many new warehouses, not just in the US but in the UK and Germany, and making multiple acquisitions, most of which would fail. He had begun poaching Walmart executives to manage the expansion, and Walmart sued Amazon for "stealing trade secrets." Bezos was actually a devotee of Walmart founder Sam Walton, and had studied his autobiography *Made in America* (see *50 Success Classics*). He copied Walton's extreme frugality when it came to staff expenses, Walmart's "bias for action" (experimenting all the time to see what works), and Walton's belief in copying the best features of other companies. The cool new internet star was happy to take inspiration from a giant of traditional retailing.

Breakthrough features

In 1998, Amazon introduced two of its defining features. Sales rank gave a sales ranking to every book and product it sold, which changed each time there was a sale. Bezos knew that authors and publishers would become addicted to watching the rise and fall of book sales ranks in real time, and so it proved to be. It is hard to appreciate how new and fascinating sales rank—which tracked everything from number one bestsellers to titles languishing in the 2 millions—was at the time, when bestseller lists only ran to 20, 50, or 100 titles.

Also in 1998, Amazon introduced "1-click ordering," which it had patented. At a time when people were wary of giving their credit card details to online firms, this was novel. The ease of successful repeat orders would only increase the trust in the company.

Yet eBay threatened to overshadow Amazon's aim to be the "everything store." It seemed better suited to the internet age; it was after all simply a platform for buyers and sellers without having to build expensive distribution centers. Perhaps fixed prices were old hat, to be replaced by eBay-style auctions? Bezos launched Amazon Auctions in 1999, but it was a failure. eBay already had a huge mass of sellers that were used to its system, and regular Amazon purchasers weren't interested in bidding for things. zShops, whereby third-party sellers could sell items via Amazon for fixes prices, also failed. A move into toys and electronics proved a challenge, as Amazon had to beg and plead established makers like Hasbro and Sony to become an "established supplier." Whatever stock they were allocated, they had to sell it or they were stuck with it, often in vast quantities. In 1999, for example, Amazon had to swallow a $39 million inventory of unsold toys.

That year, Bezos was named *Time* "Person of the Year," yet 2000 and 2001 were a fall from grace for Amazon. In the dot.com bust the firm's stock price plummeted into the single digits. People who had joined the company saw their stock options become almost worthless, and Bezos became obsessed with debunking the reports of investment analyst Ravi Suria, which forecast that the company was headed for insolvency.

Yet Stone notes that Bezos was never diverted from his characteristically long-term view of e-commerce and Amazon's role in it, and kept reminding staff that if they doubled down on great customer experience, the company would continue to grow. An example of his obsession with the customer: when the fourth Harry Potter book was coming out, Amazon offered it at a 40 percent discount and with expedited shipping. It lost a few dollars on every one of the 250,000 copies sold, which unnerved executives and Wall Street, but Bezos believed that it was only by going the extra mile with customers that you would get long-term loyalty.

Constant innovation

In 2002, Amazon began experimenting with free shipping, initially offering it with orders over $100. To get to that figure, it seemed that people would fill their baskets with a range of things. This pleased Bezos, who wanted to turn the site into a one-stop place to shop. In time, the threshold for free shipping would drop from $100 to $25 and be the seed of today's Amazon Prime service. Prime was a leap in the dark, because customers who bought a lot of goods within the span of a year would soon be costing Amazon money in foregone shipping fees. It could be a colossally expensive mistake. In fact, Stone notes, Prime turned people into "Amazon addicts," loving the fact that they were offered special bonuses (including, to come later, free Prime films and television) and that whatever they ordered would appear extremely quickly. Amazon also opened up its expedited service to Marketplace sellers (third-party sellers who were allowed to use the Amazon platform), who could now get their wares fulfilled by Amazon. In the warehouses, grouping similar kinds of orders together through algorithms allowed Amazon to reduce its costs. It was reinventing fulfillment and distribution. Bezos was relentlessly pushing Amazon staffers to innovate, and in 2003 had championed another new feature, "Search inside the book," which many thought was crazy, as it might stop people buying (in fact, the amount of content you could read was limited).

Even with these innovations, when Amazon held a gala event in 2005 to celebrate its tenth anniversary, Stone notes, it was still a media "afterthought" next to the big story of the time: Google. Amazon's tiny profit margins were compared unfavorably to online money-making machines like Google, which despite being a year old had a market capitalization four times Amazon's. To rub it in, Amazon was having to pay for millions of ads on Google to bring people to its site, and Google's Seattle office began attracting dozens of Amazon people with its many perks and less combative culture. Bezos had always wanted Amazon to be seen as a technology pioneer, but Wall Street, the press, and the public increasingly saw it as just an online retailer.

Bezos reminded his top executives that as institutions grow there is a natural resistance to bold and risky bets, yet the only way to escape the firm's predicament and fulfill its long-term potential was to "invent our way out." One bet that seemed to be paying off was Amazon Web Services. AWS was a pioneer of cloud computing, providing cheap server space to thousands of small firms and start-ups who needed powerful computing without having to lay out large amounts for their own servers. AWS was years in the making, with Bezos driving two separate teams to come up with a service that was infinitely scalable. It now generates billions of dollars in revenue from companies such as Netflix and Pinterest, and US government agencies including NASA. AWS, Stone writes, "completely outflanked" the big hardware behemoths like Sun Microsystems; Google's Eric Schmidt also took his hat off to the "book guys" reinventing themselves as the kings of cloud computing.

Built to last

Amazon managed to produce another success in the mid 2000s. In 2004 e-books were available in Microsoft and Adobe formats, but did not sell well. They were tricky to download, and most were read on desktop computers. Amazon had zero experience in hardware, but Bezos launched a left-field idea, against a lot of internal opposition, of the firm producing its own dedicated e-book reader. Unlike existing e-book reading devices like the Sony Reader and Palm's Treo, Bezos wanted the device to be incredibly easy to use, and to let users download books via regular cellular phone networks. The device would effectively be a phone that could download books.

In advance of the "Kindle" launch in November 2007, Bezos's people bullied and coerced publishers into getting ready e-editions of all their books. The first version had a choice of 100,000 to buy, and could hold 200 titles. The most controversial feature was the flat price for e-books: $9.99. Publishers felt hoodwinked by the move, which would mean lower margins and increasing market power for Amazon, along with more pressure on physical bookshops. Amazon took an increasingly aggressive approach to publishers (Bezos' favorite line: "Amazon isn't happening to the book business. The future is happening to the book business") forcing them to reduce their margins against the threat of being dropped down in search rankings. The big publishers rebelled, colluding with Apple to try to sideline Amazon; it hit back, deleting the Buy buttons for these publishers' e-books on its site, and only selling their physical books through third-party sellers. The conflict was resolved eventually, but Amazon's "we win, you lose" approach to publishers and suppliers went against the values of many employees, and quite a few left.

Amazon was also sustaining bad press for having avoided paying US sales taxes for years, compared to offline retail giants like Walmart and Costco who did, and was having to make convoluted arrangements to prevent taxes making its goods more expensive. In Europe it avoided national taxes by funneling all revenues to low-tax Luxembourg. Bezos's response to the criticism was always one of "bemused perplexity," Stone notes. People didn't understand that Amazon was not a mercenary company, but a *missionary* one, who would not be stopped in its religious zeal for pleasing the customer. The more dominant it was, the greater facility it would have to achieve this.

Against the barrage of criticisms that it was killing main street retailing, Bezos began thinking about ways in which Amazon could become a "loved" company like Nike or Disney or Whole Foods, and not be seen as merely exploitative like Goldman Sachs or Exxon. To do this, it had to be seen as an inventor and pioneer. If this was the public's image of the company, he believed, everything else could be justified.

Final comments

The rapacity of firms such as Amazon, with their hard-driving founders, raises interesting questions over whether, if consumers get a much better deal in terms of lower prices, bigger range, and innovative products, "the end justifies the means." Go behind the scenes at any big tech company, and you will find burnouts and heartbreaks that seem to be the by-product of executing on almost impossible missions and targets. Stone interviews one long-time executive of the book division, Erik Goss, who had post-traumatic stress disorder over the course of a year after he left Amazon.

In the company's very early days, when Bezos was not at all certain his idea would succeed, the firm had a laidback culture, but as it did, and massively, success emboldened him. Joy Covey, Amazon's first chief financial officer, justified Bezos's behavior but noting that you can't create revolutions while "being too accommodating of others."

In 2017, Amazon's stock price hit new heights after its $13.7 billion acquisition of Whole Foods, the upscale supermarket chain, while the stock prices of traditional retailers dropped. It plans to alter the landscape of grocery buying as it has done with virtually everything else it has touched. The company is now worth $500 billion, which is twice that of Walmart and roughly the same as Facebook. Apple, Google, and Microsoft are worth more, but perhaps not forever. Such fantastic wealth has allowed Bezos to indulge his pet interests, including journalism (he acquired *The Washington Post* with his own money) and space (Blue Origin aims to revolutionize commercial space travel in the way Amazon has for technology and retailing).

If one could only take two lessons from the Bezos/Amazon story, the first would have to be "think long." As long-time Bezos friend, the inventor Danny Hillis, noted to Stone, "If you look at why Amazon is so different than almost any other company that started early on the internet, it's because Jeff approached it from the very beginning with that long-term vision . . . It was a multidecade project. The notion that he can accomplish a huge amount with a larger time frame, if he is steady about it, is fundamentally his philosophy." The other lesson may be taken from one of the firm's 14 leadership principles:

Think Big: Thinking small is a self-fulfilling prophecy. Leaders create and communicate a bold direction that inspires results. They think differently and look around corners for ways to serve customers.

Shel Kaphan, the company's first employee, today gives this advice to anyone involved in a start-up: Always assume that it could end up being much bigger than you imagine.

Brad Stone

Born in 1971, Stone is a technology journalist working in Bloomberg's San Francisco office, covering the major tech companies. The Everything Store *won the* Financial Times *and Goldman Sachs Business Book of the Year Award in 2013, while Stone's research for the book led to the revelation, in the eleventh chapter, that Ted Jorgensen is Bezos's biological father. Even in 2012, Jorgensen, who was running a bicycle shop in Phoenix, Arizona, had no idea who his son was: he had abided by Jeff's mother's wish to stay out of Jeff's life, and assumed he would never hear about his son again.*

Stone is also the author of The Upstarts: How Uber, Airbnb, and the Killer Companies of the New Silicon Valley Are Changing the World *(2017).*

Black Box Thinking

"We cover up mistakes, not only to protect ourselves from others, but to protect us from ourselves. Experiments have demonstrated that we all have a sophisticated ability to delete failures from memory, like editors cutting gaffes from a film reel . . . Far from learning from our mistakes, we edit them out of the official biographies we all keep in our own heads."

"Success is always the tip of an iceberg. We learn vogue theories, we fly astonishingly safe aircraft, we marvel at the virtuosity of true experts. But beneath the surface of success—outside our view, often outside our awareness—is a mountain of necessary failure."

"Failure is rich in learning opportunities for a simple reason: in many of its guises, it represents violation of expectation. It is showing us that the world is in some sense different than the way we imagined it to be."

In a nutshell

Willingness to fail frequently, while absorbing the lessons of failure and making constant adjustments, is the only real path to success.

In a similar vein

Jim Collins *Great by Choice*
Eric Ries *The Lean Startup*
Peter Senge *The Fifth Discipline*

CHAPTER 43

Matthew Syed

I n little more than a hundred years, flight went from being a dream, to something dangerous, to something so safe we take it for granted. Today, the rate of accidents in the airline industry is one per *2.4 million flights*, making it easily the safest form of transportation. There are still accidents, but they are very rare. We are fortunate, too, to live in a time of advanced medicine and healthcare, in which fatal mistakes are mostly a thing of the past. If only this were true.

Matthew Syed's book begins with a horrible story. In 2005 a 37-year-old British mother of two, Elaine Bromiley, went in for a routine, low-risk sinus operation under anesthetic. As the anesthetic stops the normal system of breathing, it is necessary to have a tracheal tube inserted down the throat so that the patient has oxygen. In this instance, the doctor in charge, despite repeated efforts, was unable to get the tube in. As the minutes ticked by, Bromiley was fast losing all oxygen to her brain. The doctor's attention narrowed so much he forgot about the emergency measure, a tracheostomy, in which a hole is cut in the neck and a supply of oxygen is provided directly into the windpipe. This relatively simple procedure would have saved her life. As it happened, she fell into a coma and died a few days later.

Your chances of dying in even a routine operation are much, much higher than taking a commercial flight. Not because the technology is less advanced, or because doctors and nurses care less than pilots about human life, but because the systems for noticing failure and incorporating its lessons into practice have not been nearly as thorough as that seen in aviation.

In *Black Box Thinking: Marginal Gains and the Secrets of High Performance*, Syed's thesis is that "the explanation for success hinges, in powerful and often counter-intuitive ways, on how we react to failure." This has important implications for business, too. "Black box thinking," Syed says, is simply an extreme focus on the detail of processes—what actually happens in the moments you are doing something—that either lead to failure or success.

Covering up

In an investigation undertaken in 1999, "To Err is Human," the American Institute of Medicine found that 50,000–100,000 people were dying unnecessarily each year through preventable medical errors. In 2013 a study by the *Journal of Patient Safety* put the number at 400,000—akin to two passenger jets crashing every 24 hours. In rich countries, preventable medical error is the third biggest cause of death after cancer and heart disease. And the number doesn't even take into account complications from poor diagnosis and treatment.

Syed is quick to note that preventable deaths are not caused by malign or even bored doctors, but when doctors are working diligently. So why do so many deaths happen? One reason is complexity. There are thousands of conditions and diseases, and they are easily misdiagnosed and treated. The other involves resources. Doctors are often overworked, and have little time to ponder their decisions. But more important than these is the fact that errors often happen in *predictable* patterns that occur within *cultures* that allow them to happen. In the operating theater, you can kill a patient not because you are not focused, but because you are *too* focused. In the case mentioned above, the doctors didn't realize they had spent eight minutes trying to get air through the patient's mouth, time in which they could have saved her life by performing a tracheostomy. A nurse tried to make suggestions to perform this procedure, but she wasn't listened to. The problem with mistakes is, of course, having to admit them. This is difficult for all of us, but particularly so for people like doctors who are looked up to as great experts with many years' training.

Syed tells the remarkable story of Peter Pronovost, whose father died at the age of 50 because he was wrongly diagnosed with leukemia when he actually had lymphoma, and didn't get the bone marrow treatment that would have prolonged his life. Pronovost, now a professor at Johns Hopkins University School of Medicine, vowed to get processes in hospitals changed. His investigation of tens of thousands of deaths through infections caused by catheters being placed in large veins to administer drugs, led to much greater awareness of the need for sterility around the procedure. His five-point patient safety checklist saved 1,500 lives over a year and a half period in one state alone, Michigan, and was later copied around America, saving thousands more.

Built on errors

In 1978, United Airlines Flight 173 was some distance out of its destination airport, Portland, when something alarming happened. The light indicating whether the landing gear was down, was not on. The pilot in charge, Captain McBroom, got so fixated on the issue that he lost all sense of time, and the plane literally ran out of fuel, miles before Portland airport's runway. McBroom's skill meant that the plane came down in a wooded urban area, and many survived the impact, including McBroom himself. He later told investigators that the fuel tanks had emptied "incredibly quickly," even suggesting there was a leak in the tanks. In an echo of the doctors involved in the Bromiley case, he did not consider the fact that his sense of time was affected by the landing gear emergency.

Flight 173 was a watershed in aviation safety, showing that "Attention . . . is a scarce resource; if you focus on one thing, you will lose awareness of other things." Time just flies by when you are in an emergency, making you forget about crucial things like how much fuel you have left. The report on Flight 173 led to measures to make crews more communicative, assertive, and willing to challenge chief pilots. It is all too easy to cast pilots and surgeons as willfully culpable, but Flight 173 showed how catastrophic human errors arise from poorly designed systems and cultures. As with the Bromiley case, the pecking order stopped subordinates from more forcefully calling for the action that would have saved life.

Syed contends that Jeffrey Sullenberger's famous landing of his passenger plane in the Hudson River in 2008 was not the act of individualistic heroism that was portrayed in the press. He was able to land on the water with no fatalities for many reasons, including great communication with his copilot until the moment of impact, and Airbus's autopilot system, which allowed the wings of the plane to be perfectly level when the plane glided onto the water. Sullenberger himself said in an interview: "Everything we know in aviation, every rule in the rule book, every procedure we have, we know because someone somewhere died."

Luckily, aviation has a system, flight recording of data (it is stored in "black boxes," which are actually orange to aid visibility in the event of a crash), so that investigators can piece together what happened, and once their conclusions are published (which is a legal requirement), the whole world of aviation can learn from it. When pilots have near misses, if they file a report within 10 days there is immunity from prosecution. The reporting of such "small errors" means that catastrophic ones can be avoided.

Elaine Bromiley's husband Martin didn't want her death to be forgotten, and for lessons to be learned from it. There was resistance by the hospital to investigating what happened, but he was a pilot by profession and had lectured on system safety. He started to sense that what had occurred carried a "signature," a pattern of action that if not analyzed and changed would happen again, to someone else. His efforts, and those of other medical safety campaigners, have led to the increased use of checklists in medical procedures, systems for junior doctors and nurses to raise an alarm if they believe a patient is in peril from wrong practice, and even dedicated staff to keep track of time—which is so easily lost sight of when things go wrong.

In the face of failure we tell stories

The first court of criminal appeal was established in England in the nineteenth century, after a hard-fought campaign against judges, who believed their decisions had to be final. Miscarriages of justice were seen as one-offs, rather than part of any systemic fault in the justice system. Then in 1984, when British scientist Alec Jeffreys stumbled on a way of extracting DNA signatures from blood, it became clear just how easy it was to convict people wrongfully from the evidence at crime scenes. After 1989, when DNA testing in crime became established, there was a spree of exonerations of men who had spent years on prison, some for 10 or 15 years. There are now hundreds of people who have had convictions overturned.

Even when DNA evidence was conclusive, police and prosecutors often fought back to try to keep people behind bars. Rather than accepting the evidence and trying to reform their systems, they tried to protect their integrity. This, in a way, makes sense: admitting you are wrong can call into question not just your skills or job, but your very vocation. When a prosecutor, who spent years at law school and climbed his way up the legal system, is exposed as presenting a case with huge holes in it, or convicted the wrong person who has spent years in jail, he may feel as if his whole career is a sham. No wonder evidence will be rejected, no matter how powerful or insurmountable. For a prosecutor, convicting the wrong person, as social psychologist Richard Ofshe puts it, is "one of the worst professional mistakes you can make—like a physician amputating the wrong arm." As Syed writes, "DNA evidence is indeed strong, but not as strong as the desire to protect one's self-esteem."

Psychologist Leon Festinger coined the term "cognitive dissonance," to mean the tension we feel when reality doesn't match our expectations or beliefs. When this happens we can either accept that we were wrong, which makes us feel less than who we thought we were; or deny, reframe, spin, or ignore the evidence altogether. When you have so much of yourself invested in something, the chances of the latter happening are high.

Syed includes a section on British prime minister Tony Blair's continued justification of the decision to go to war in Iraq, despite evidence that there were no Weapons of Mass Destruction in the country (the stated pretext for the invasion). When Syed interviewed Blair's former head of communications, Alasdair Campbell, and asked him about the Iraq decision, Campbell replied, "Tony is a rational and strong-minded guy, but I don't think he would be able to admit that Iraq was a mistake. It would be too devastating, even for him."

Even apparently scientific domains such as economics are subject to the "narrative fallacy," the human tendency to weave convincing stories of why things turned out the way they did, after they've happened. If a team won, it's because of x-y-z. If they lost, it's because of the same x-y-z. In 2010 a group of eminent economists signed a public letter warning against the practice of central bank quantitative easing, saying it would wreck the economy and cause inflation. None of this happened, but four years later, when invited to reflect on their prediction, none would admit they were wrong; many provided convenient fudges concerning how they would be shown to be correct in the long run. Syed notes that the economics profession is split on almost religious grounds between Keynesians and monetarists. A study found that less than 10 percent of economists change their fundamental view during their careers; a Muslim is more likely to become a Christian, or vice versa. "This is surely a warning sign that instead of learning from data," he says, "some economists are spinning it. It hints at the suspicion that the intellectual energy of some of the world's most formidable thinkers is directed, not at creating new, richer, more explanatory theories, but at coming up with ever-more tortuous rationalisations as to why they were right all along."

Business is the processing of failure

It is ironic that economists are so tribal, and so unwilling to change their views in the face of new evidence, particularly given that their subject—capitalism—is built on the processing of failure. Joseph Schumpeter coined the term "creative destruction" to describe the churn of businesses and industries as new products and processes show their worth and old ones die. This can only happen, Syed notes, because "free market systems mimic the process of biological change," that is, the process of natural selection. A successful product is simply one that is perfectly adapted to its environment.

The business highway is littered with the corpses of products that were brilliantly planned and perfectly executed, but which nobody wanted. Such humbling experiences led to today's "test early, adapt rapidly" outlook, in which master plans are replaced by "rapid interaction with the world"—in short, failing more often.

Syed spent time with the Mercedes Formula 1 team, whose success has been the result of intense, constant iteration based on millions of points of data. It created an initial basic engine, then refined it through thousands of little failures and adaptations. These "marginal gains" happen, says Paddy

Lowe, who runs the Mercedes technical operation, when intelligent people work together in order to win, spurring very rapid innovation. "Things from just two years ago seem antique. Standing still is tantamount to extinction."

People still have the misguided idea that success is about "coming up with a great idea," but Syed points to evidence that the most innovative companies, the ones with the most patents, aren't usually the most successful. It's one thing to come up with amazing new technologies and ideas, quite another to employ the discipline to make a saleable product, setting up the supply chains and marketing and sales systems to make it a success. James Dyson was not the first person to think of a cyclonic vacuum cleaner, but he was the first to have the determination through trial and error to make it into a product that worked. He told Syed, "The original idea is only 2 percent of the journey. You mustn't neglect the rest." If creativity is about increasing variation, that is, considering every kind of possibility, which involves implementing a culture of dissent, actual production is about eliminating variation, that is, making something that is exactly the same, every time it comes off the line:

"Creativity not guided by a feedback mechanism is little more than white noise. Success is a complex interplay between creativity and measurement, the two operating together, the two sides of the optimisation loop . . . Every error, every flaw, every failure, however small, is a marginal gain in disguise. This information is regarded not as a threat but as an opportunity."

Syed notes the debate about whether you should be trying to transform the world (vocal promoters of this view include Peter Thiel and Elon Musk) or tweak it, putting out a "minimum viable product" (see Eric Ries, Chapter 33) that then gets iterated into something people want to own or use. The reality, he says, is that you have do both in today's world. Breakthrough concepts that upend industries are what every business dreams of, but to be able to actually dominate the new market you must have a product or service that has been put through the fires of relentless testing and refinement—that is, failing often.

Final comments

Syed's thinking is influenced by that of philosopher of science Karl Popper (see *50 Philosophy Classics*), who showed the extent to which science only progresses through recognizing its failures to accurately describe the world. Only if theories survive active attempts of falsification are they added to the mountain of knowledge.

In life and in business, the natural wish is to shield ourselves from the possibility of failure, because failure hurts. What we do instead is make our goals so vague that no one can hold us accountable for not meeting them, and find face-saving excuses for not acting. Yet it is only by changing our relationship to failure, Syed says, that real success becomes possible, as individuals, in organizations, as a society. Look closely at any high achiever, or any business that is doing well, and you will find an outlook of learning and an almost pathological desire to examine what happened when things didn't work. Syed recalls Michael Jordan's famous Nike commercial: "I've missed more than nine thousand shots. I've lost almost three hundred games. Twenty-six times I've been trusted to take the game-winning shot and missed." Footballer David Beckham was famous for his relentless training, and for his prowess at converting free kicks into goals. He told Syed, "But when I think about free kicks I think about all those failures. It took tons of misses before I got it right."

Matthew Syed

Born in 1970, Syed grew up in Reading, UK. He studied philosophy, politics, and economics at Oxford University before becoming a sports journalist, and is a regular sports and cultural commentator for the BBC and The Times. *He was England's top-ranked table tennis player for a decade, and represented Great Britain in the men's table tennis singles at the 1992 and 2000 Olympics.*

His other books are Bounce: Mozart, Federer, Picasso, Beckham, and the Science of Success *(2011) and* The Greatest: What Sport Teaches Us About Achieving Success *(2017).*

The Principles of Scientific Management

"We can see our forests vanishing, our water-powers going to waste, our soil being carried by floods into the sea; and the end of our coal and our iron is in sight . . . Awkward, inefficient, or ill-directed movements of men, however, leave nothing visible or tangible behind them . . . even though our daily loss from this source is greater than from our waste of material things, the one has stirred us deeply, while the other has moved us but little."

"Those who are afraid that a large increase in the productivity of each workman will throw other men out of work, should realize that the one element more than any other which differentiates civilized from uncivilized countries—prosperous from poverty-stricken peoples—is that the average man in the one is five or six times as productive as the other."

In a nutshell

Increased efficiency allows workers as well as managers and owners to prosper.

In a similar vein

Martin Ford *Rise of the Robots*
Douglas McGregor *The Human Side of Enterprise*
James P. Womack, Daniel T. Jones & Daniel Roos *The Machine that Changed the World*

CHAPTER 44

Frederick Winslow Taylor

I n the early twentieth century, Frederick Taylor noted, people were already complaining of the loss of the planet's physical resources, or at least their inefficient utilization. But for Taylor, one of the first management gurus, this concern only obscured the loss of *human* resources through great inefficiency in working practices.

The goal of management, Taylor said, was simple: "maximum prosperity for the employer, coupled with maximum prosperity for the employee." You would not know this, he observed, by looking at the industrial unrest that was happening at the time he was writing, which seemed to put capital and labor at loggerheads. Yet if the whole enterprise could become more efficient at what it did, he believed, it was possible to have both higher wages and successful businesses at the same time.

Management thinker Peter Drucker put Taylor up there with Darwin and Freud as one of the minds that created the modern world—that is, a world focused on productivity and time-keeping—and considered Taylor's *Principles of Scientific Management* "the most powerful as well as the most lasting contribution America has made to western thought since the Federalist Papers." ("The Rise of the Knowledge Society", *Wilson Quarterly,* Spring 1993) Fine praise, but it is true that most of today's drives for efficiency and productivity, from Total Quality Management to Six Sigma, and from lean production to automation, can be traced back to Taylor's thinking.

What Taylor essentially did was elevate management above labor, or the system above the individual worker. "In the past the man has been first," he writes, "in the future the system must be first." This philosophy entailed the end of the "craftsman" ethic in production, replaced by human beings as units of efficiency.

Rule of management, not thumb
Taylor explains how manufacturing had developed along craft lines. That is, each apprentice learned how to do things by watching his master, with the

result that for every task there may have been twenty or thirty ways of doing it, using different implements. And yet, scientific observation and measuring of any task (through a study of motion and time) revealed that "there is always one method and one implement which is quicker and better than any of the rest."

In place of the "rule of thumb" approach to making things, in which the owner or foreman had to trust that the craftsman was doing things the best way, there was now science. The scientific approach meant a much greater role for management in determining what was efficient. This knowledge would no longer be possessed by the worker himself, since it was often too advanced for his level of education. Taylor describes this new relationship as close, friendly cooperation to ensure that the enterprise reaches its full potential and can be sustainable. It obviates the need for, on the one hand, the hard-driving boss whipping his men into activity, and on the other the go-slow antics of workers. By cooperating, both can prosper. He notes that, in his time, enterprises using the system of scientific management were prospering, and their men were being better paid, compared to the factories and shops run along old lines.

The fruits of productivity

Taylor talks at length about "soldiering," or putting in half as much effort as you are being paid for, which he says is the "greatest evil with which the working-people of both England and America are now afflicted." At a time when organized labor was agitating to appropriate more of the profits of enterprise, Taylor insists that this could never happen while slow working was accepted. It was founded upon the false belief that if people worked harder, fewer workers would be needed and they would be thrown out of a job.

This view was blind to the fact, he says, that if the company is growing and finding new markets, it will need more people even if efficiency increases. Efficiency means lower costs of manufacture, and it is an iron law of commerce that "The cheapening of any article in common use almost immediately results in a largely increased demand for that article." Taylor's example is shoes, which were once so expensive because they all had to be made by hand. As a result, many people wore the same pair for several years, or simply went barefoot. With the advent of machinery to make shoemaking easier (and cheaper), many more people were employed in the industry than before. Taylor notes the bad press given to "sweatshop conditions" and people being overworked, while hardly any attention is given to intentional *under*-work, which perpetuates inefficiency and low wages.

He uses the term "efficiency" throughout, but what he is really talking about is productivity, writing "unless your men and your machines are daily turning out more work than others around you, it is clear that competition will prevent your paying higher wages to your workmen than are paid to those of your competitor." Taylor's focus is the domestic US economy, but his thinking could have been applied to international markets. If a nation's businesses are productive, in terms of getting more and more output per worker, their costs will be lower and so their goods will be competitive on world markets. This is the only route to national prosperity.

Breaking it down

Taylor came from a well-off family, but instead of taking the usual career route of his peers, such as banking or law, he was attracted to engineering. After doing an apprenticeship as a pattern-maker and machinist, in his early twenties he worked at the Midvale Steel Works in Philadelphia, first working a lathe himself and then being put in charge of a gang of men on lathes. He was promoted because he continually sought to increase the rate of work. Some of his friends in the shop told him his life was at risk because he wasn't going along with the way things were done, which sometimes included breaking machines on purpose to keep the work rate down. But because Taylor was of a different social class (his family were friends with the owners of Midvale) he didn't fear being ostracized. He persuaded the owner of Midvale that it was worthwhile doing careful studies of how work was done, to improve efficiency.

This led to his famous study of men carrying loads of pig iron. He found that, if the loads of pig iron being carried around were reduced to a certain weight, a strong man could carry on working all day without getting tired. If there were frequent rest periods so that the man's arms could recover their strength, giving his blood a chance to renew his muscle tissues, he could work all day, carrying 47 tons of pig iron instead of the standard 12 tons. For this extra productivity, the company could afford to pay the man $1.85 a day instead of the standard $1.15. Taylor's conclusion: you don't have to rely on a person's conscience or initiative to do good work, all you have to do is break the work into pieces and make each piece more efficient, telling the worker how things now had to be done.

At Bethlehem Steel Company, Taylor had found that only one man in the eight-man team being studied could carry 47 tons in a day, and that was simply because of his sheer physical strength. He was unusual—but not that unusual, and Taylor had no difficulty finding men of similar strength from the surrounding locality. Under the old system of management, he asks, what were the chances that the gang of eight men would get rid of seven of them, in order to become much more efficient? Zero. Yet it meant that the men who were pushed out of the pig iron handling jobs were quickly found other kinds of work within Bethlehem for which they were much better suited, and where they could earn higher wages. Scientific selection of workers doesn't just greatly improve efficiency, he argues, it leads to happier workers.

Of shovels and ball bearings

There was even a science of shoveling, Taylor found. As a consultant at Bethlehem, he instituted many different kinds of shovel to handle different loads and materials. For instance, a small shovel should be used for shoveling heavy ore, while a large one could be used to handle lighter ash. The result, as with pig iron, was to even out the energy needed for a worker across the day, and so they could process more material. In a company of Bethlehem's size that employed 600 shovelers in a two-mile long yard, this could mean a massive difference to the firm's costs and output. Before, men were organized in gangs under the command of a foreman; now each individual worker was being analyzed each day by a team of clerks for the amount of work they were doing, and given feedback so that they could see if they were measuring up to a certain standard, and plan their day's work in advance. Even with the additional wages of clerks and time-study men to analyze and track the workers, Taylor notes, the cost of handling a ton of steel in the works was cut in half. At the same time, the workers appreciated the extra order in the plant, and their higher wages, and the relations between management and labor was good. He noticed that when men are organized into gangs, their efficiency and motivation falls to the level of the worst member of the gang. But when men are treated as individuals, and given feedback on their work, they are a lot more motivated to improve. When asked to work a bit more for higher wages, he saw other effects: "they live rather better, begin to save money, become more sober, and work more steadily."

Taylor refers to a study by Frank Gilbreth into bricklaying. Gilbreth was able to reduce the number of actions involved in laying bricks from 18 to 5, which led to an increase in the number of bricks laid per hour from 120 to 350. This never would have been achieved by bricklayers organizing themselves to become more efficient, Taylor notes. It only occurred through an outsider analyzing the work objectively, and seeing how it could be improved from a scientific standpoint. When Taylor and his team were asked to reorganize a factory making ball bearings for bicycles, he did something unheard of: reduced the working day of the women tasked with inspecting the balls from 10.5 to 8.5 hours. Their output remained the same with the shorter hours, but only after a careful selection of workers. The most efficient women were not necessarily the most intelligent, trustworthy, or hard-working, simply the ones with the quickest eye to spot imperfections. Those who tested high on quick eye acuity were kept on in the job, while the others were let go. The lesson: in many jobs it is very particular aptitudes that matter, not general qualities. In fact, the problem with the trustworthy women was that they over-inspected, thus wasting time. Such studies led to the "differential rate piece work" system, in which "the pay of each girl was increased in proportion to the quantity of her output and also still more in proportion to the accuracy of her work." The system led to big gains in the quantity and quality of work done.

Taylor's legacy

Scientific management made production costs much cheaper, which meant cheaper goods, while standardized production meant more uniform quality. The incredible advances in productivity, in which one person can today perform the work of 50 or 100 a century ago, is the result of Taylorist thinking.

Yet a result of Taylor's managerial revolution, despite the good intentions he expresses in the book about management and labor coming together, was an inevitable dehumanization of many jobs. Pride of individual craftsmanship was replaced with a robotic "one best way" of doing things, and if you didn't agree with that way you were quickly out of a job. Taylor's thinking reached its apotheosis in Henry Ford's car plants. Arguably it was not the production line itself that led to Ford's massive productivity, which enabled him to reduce the price of a car, but the fact that every task and process had been refined to the hilt for maximum efficiency. They may have been paid a handsome $5 a day, but for workers the trade-off was mind-numbing monotony. Taylor claimed a bright new world for workers, but the speeding up of work that resulted from scientific management just meant that at the end of the day workers were exhausted. His time-and-motion studies were ridiculed, with *Life* publishing a cartoon about the fifteen unnecessary motions of a kiss.

Scientific management's detractors have included labor unions the world over, who tried to protect the old craft system. Anarchist Emma Goldman and philosopher Antonio Gramsci were both appalled by its effects on the worker. In the 1960s, Douglas McGregor took aim at Taylorism in *The Human Side of Enterprise*, which he believed grew out of its progenitor's fundamental mistrust of human motives. For Taylor, workers were fundamentally lazy and worked only for money, and so had to be watched like a hawk. McGregor's more expansive view of human beings as having higher-order motives like pride in work, responsibility, and even creativity, established an alternative paradigm. The result is that, today, most companies put the McGregor view at the center of their professed vision of workplace culture, while at the same time running the business on Taylorist lines of ruthless efficiency.

Final comments

Taylorism is never dead, just expressed in different forms. Any kind of "business process reengineering" by management consultants, or the use of behavioral science to screen job candidates or those already in their job, or the use of surveillance to see how much time workers are spending on social media, are all measures Taylor would have approved of. If the endgame of scientific management was to increase productivity and lower costs on an ongoing basis, surely the age of automation and algorithms, which steadily take humans out of the equation altogether, is the Taylorist dream come true. From a Marxist perspective, Taylorism can be seen as a tool of capital to reduce the power of labor under the guise of making cheaper goods that all can afford.

One of Taylor's legacies was inspiring the study of business as a discipline in its own right, separate to economics and political economy. After he was invited to give a series of lectures at Harvard, in 1908 the Harvard Business School was opened. Its promoter, economics professor Edwin Gay said, "I am convinced that there is a scientific method involved in and underlying the art of business." Some now rue the development (see Matthew Stewart's *The Management Myth: Debunking Modern Business Philosophy*), seeing business as common sense rather than science, and arguing that a liberal arts education is just as likely to help a person succeed in commerce as an MBA.

There is also a literary legacy of *The Principles of Scientific Management*. Easy to read and understand, with interesting examples, it was a bestseller in its day and for years after, and so laid the foundation of the modern business book genre.

Frederick Winslow Taylor

Taylor was born in the Germantown area of Philadelphia in 1856, to a Quaker family descended from the Mayflower Pilgrims. His father was a lawyer and his mother was involved in social causes including the abolition of slavery.

After being schooled by his mother and at Philips Exeter Academy, Taylor was set to go to Harvard but pulled out because of poor eyesight. He did an apprenticeship instead at a pump-manufacturing plant before moving to Midvale Steel, and while there completed an engineering degree via correspondence. After three years as a plant manager at a paper mill in Maine, in 1892 Taylor went into business as a consultant engineer. In 1895 he published his influential paper on the piece-rate system.

While a consultant to Bethlehem Steel he developed several patents for new processes for cutting steel, the proceeds of which made him well-off. In the following years he developed a lucrative business advising companies, his profile greatly helped by the Eastern Rate Case, in which prosecutor Louis Brandeis claimed that, instead of raising freight rates, the railroads could save $1 million a day just by becoming more efficient. It was actually Brandeis, a Taylor acolyte, who coined the term "scientific management."

Taylor was president of the American Society of Mechanical Engineers in 1906–7. However, after a row with the society over its refusal to publish The Principles of Scientific Management, *he had it published himself. Late in his career he became a professor in the Tusk business school at Dartmouth College. He died of pneumonia in 1915.*

A champion tennis player and golfer in his younger years, he won (with Clarence Clark, whose family were part owners of Midvale Steel) the first US doubles championship and finished fourth in golf in the 1900 Olympics.

Zero To One

"Every moment in business happens only once. The next Bill Gates will not build an operating system. The next Larry Page or Sergey Brin won't make a search engine. And the next Mark Zuckerberg won't create a social network. If you are copying these guys, you aren't learning from them."

"In the real world outside economic theory, every business is successful exactly to the extent that it does something others cannot. Monopoly is therefore not a pathology or an exception. Monopoly is the condition of every successful business."

"The competitive ecosystem pushes people towards ruthlessness or death. A monopoly like Google is different. Since it doesn't have to worry about competing with anyone, it has wider latitude to care about its workers, its products, and its impact on the wider world . . . Only one thing can allow a business to transcend the daily brute struggle for survival: monopoly profits."

In a nutshell

Competition is overrated. The most successful businesses are those which create a natural monopoly through the brilliance of their product.

In a similar vein

Ron Chernow *Titan: The Life of John D. Rockefeller Snr.*
Clayton Christensen *The Innovator's Dilemma*
Ben Horowitz *The Hard Thing About Hard Things*
W. Chan Kim & Renée Mauborgne *Blue Ocean Strategy*
Richard Koch & Greg Lockwood *Simplify*
Ashlee Vance *Elon Musk*

CHAPTER 45

Peter Thiel

I n March 2000 the NASDAQ composite technology stock index went to over 5,000 points. By October 2002 it was down to 1,114.

Many became disillusioned with the tech industry, and there was a new favoring of globalization over technology as a means to increase prosperity. For investors, there was a shift toward conventional businesses—"from clicks to bricks"—and the dot.com crash led to the "lean" revolution, in which start-up companies avoided the need for big capital investment by moving away from "world-changing" boasts to simply trying to fill market niches while proceeding cautiously, step by step, testing products and services in real-time markets.

In *Zero To One: Notes on Startups, or How to Build the Future*, PayPal founder and venture capitalist Peter Thiel bemoans this shift toward incrementalism. There were indeed many companies founded on hot air in the dot.com mania, he admits, but many others simply had outsized aims to change an industry or create a new one. Surely it is better, he writes, "to risk boldness than triviality." Much of what happens in the world of business is copying or incremental ("1 to n"), but the creation of something genuinely new, something "fresh and strange," he says, is about going "from 0 to 1."

Thiel sees two big modes of progress: technology, which he defines as "any new and better way of doing things"; and globalization, which is essentially the spread of already successful practices and technologies around the world. There has been rapid technological development but little globalization, or vice versa, at various times in history, but Thiel believes that globalization is ultimately not as important as technology as the driver of progress, because globalization simply uses existing technologies (such as coal plants or cars) that end up causing a lot of damage and are self-defeating. The world only really changes, and living standards rise, by *transformative* technologies.

The key to all technological progress, Thiel argues, is the new venture, or start-up, in which "small groups of people bound together by a sense of mission have changed the world for the better." It is hard to launch anything on your own, but equally, most big new things don't come out of large, existing companies.

Zero To One grew out of a class on start-ups that Thiel gave at Stanford University. One keen student, Blake Masters, took detailed notes that people started circulating beyond the university, so Thiel decided to turn the notes into a book. Where so many business books simply mouth the dominant thinking of the day, Thiel's contrarian wisdom makes *Zero To One* stand out.

The ideology of competition vs. the beauty of monopoly

In 2012 America's airlines made on average 37 cents per passenger for each flight, despite the industry's revenue of $160 billion. In the same year, Google had revenues of $50 billion, of which *21 percent* was pure profit. As a result, Google is worth more than all the airlines put together. The difference between the airlines and Google is that the airlines are in stiff competition with each other, but Google reigns supreme in online search and advertising.

Economics tells us that competition is good, as it results in an equilibrium between goods produced and prices charged. Yet such perfect competition, Thiel notes, results in tiny profits for the players involved, or no profit at all. In total contrast to this kind of competition is monopoly. He is not interested in monopolies brought about by corruption or cronyism, rather those companies which dominate because they have a product that no one else can touch. "Americans mythologize competition and credit it with saving us from socialist breadlines," Thiel writes, "Actually, capitalism and competition are opposites."

Businesses often look similar, but look closer and they are starkly different. Monopolists are so much more successful than companies having to engage in competition that they will go to some lengths to hide the fact of their success, fearing more regulation or public outcry. It is only monopoly companies that can afford to have non-commercial aims and look after their workers. Recalling Tolstoy's famous truth about happy families all being alike, Thiel contends that all happy companies are different, in that "each earns a monopoly by solving a unique problem." In contrast, "All failed companies are the same: they failed to escape competition." Contrary to conventional wisdom, good monopolies—like John D. Rockefeller's Standard Oil, in the early twentieth century, which dramatically improved the quality and safety of lighting, then allowed for standardized lubrication of car engines—can genuinely contribute to the progress and well-being of society. You could argue that Google is another.

The only reason that we cling to the idea of competition as a generator of growth and well-being is that it is an *ideology*. Thiel is not just talking about competition in business, but in life. People scramble to get into the best universities, fight hard to get the best grades, then fight again to be recruited by the best banks, law firms, or management consultancies. If they do, they are "made." Thiel was also once on this track. He was devastated when he failed to get a clerkship with a Supreme Court judge, yet in hindsight it was the best thing that happened. If he had spent his life in such spirit-sapping competitions, he would never have created anything new, such as PayPal. There are times when you need to compete and to try to destroy the competitor (or merge with them, as Thiel did when he and Elon Musk joined forces on PayPal), but most of the time direct competition is a waste of energy. It's much, much better to create a monopoly.

What are the characteristics of durable advantage or monopoly? They include proprietorial technology that is at least *ten times* better than anyone else's (for example, Google's search was ten times better than anyone else's; Amazon offered ten times as many books as a physical store; and Apple's iPad was so much better than tablet computers produced by Microsoft and Nokia)—and economies of scale. A feature of monopoly businesses is that they get stronger as they get bigger; for instance, there is no limit to how big Facebook, Google, or Twitter could be, whereas plenty of other businesses run into problems when they try to scale up.

Thiel notes a frequent mistake of start-ups: believing that they will succeed by getting "1 percent of a $100 billion market." That market will already be saturated with competition. It's better to pioneer a new market by providing something to a small group of particular people. Amazon's Jeff Bezos wanted to dominate online retailing but started with books, which were uniform and easy to ship. eBay started out catering to small-time obsessive hobbyists. And of course "universal" Facebook began as a service on a single university campus. "Always err on the side of starting too small," Thiel writes. "The reason is simple: it's easier to dominate a small market than a large one. If you think your initial market might be too big, it almost certainly is." Thiel and his colleagues at PayPal first made headway with a very specific group, eBay "power sellers," by making it easy for them to process a lot of transactions, rather than aiming for the general public.

There is too much talk of "disruption" in business today, Thiel says. Start-up founders seem focused on "battling the enemy" of some large, dark corporation or industry instead of starting something genuinely new. But thinking about the enemy too much will thwart creativity. Disruption has a bad connotation—it's destructive, not creative. The start-up founder's task is to avoid competition, not incite it.

Where are the definite optimists?

Thiel considers himself a libertarian, but he salutes grand efforts of the past involving government that put a man on the moon or built an atomic bomb within a few years. Today, he laments, government is more focused on social insurance than it is about creating progress. Neither the left-liberal egalitarians nor the libertarian individualists have any definite plans. One focuses on fairness and equal distribution, the other on personal freedom, but no one seems to be making big, concrete plans for the future. In the corporate sector, companies "are letting cash pile up on their balance sheets without investing in new projects because they don't have any concrete plans for the future." Thiel makes a distinction between "indefinite" optimists, those who believe things are getting better but who offer no blueprint or definite ambitions, and "definite" optimists who believe that the future can be designed and built.

What about Darwin's theory that progress happens without anyone actually intending it? This has led to a start-up culture in which it is believed that "nothing can be known in advance," Thiel notes. We are told to make only a "minimum viable product," and "iterate our way to success." Yet at a philosophical level, if something is not going to produce a major step forward, Thiel asks, what is the point in doing it?

Thiel argues that the real secret to Apple's success was not simply its great products, but its *planning*. It had a schedule of new product releases years into the future, and these products didn't arise out of focus group discussions or copying others. "A business with a good definite plan," Thiel writes, "will always be underrated in a world where people see the future as random." In 2006, Yahoo offered $1 billion for Facebook, but Mark Zuckerberg dismissed it because he had big plans for his company. He was right; the bigger the plan, the longer the time frame needed to see it through. The best technology companies are not valued on the cash they are generating today, but on the number of users ten or fifteen years from now, when their plan says they will be the dominant platform in their niche. Big, definite plans to create or transform a market translate into big valuations.

A killer team

One of Thiel's laws is, "a startup messed up at its foundation cannot be fixed." Apart from the new product or service you are launching, the most important decision you will make as a founder is who you partner with. Of course, complementary skills matter, but much more crucial is whether the people who start a company already have a track record of working together successfully. Just as you wouldn't marry the first person you meet at a party, so it would be mad to start a company with someone you just met at a networking event.

With new hires, you want to find out whether they will actually want to spend their days with you and your colleagues, whether it is a good fit. The main thing you should offer people is "the opportunity to do irreplaceable work on a unique problem alongside great people." You want to offer an environment that was like the Google of 1999 or the PayPal of 2001. In the early days of PayPal, the team was incredibly tight-knit and spent their work and social lives together. Thiel made sure they were as personally alike as possible, or as he puts it, "we were all the same kind of nerd"—obsessed with science fiction, capitalism and creating a new digital currency to replace government currencies including the US dollar. The most successful start-ups look almost like cults to outsiders, except that in place of a fanatical death wish like the Jim Jones cult, they have a dogmatic fixation on a positive mission. "People at a successful startup are fanatically *right* about something those outside it have missed," Thiel writes. "They have a Secret that will change things."

The "PayPal Mafia" included Elon Musk (who would go on to form Tesla Motors and SpaceX), Reid Hoffman (LinkedIn), and Steve Chen, Chad Hurley, and Jawed Karim (YouTube). PayPal was sold to eBay in 2002 for $1.5 billion.

Eggs in one basket

Venture capital is all about trying to capture the exponential growth of new companies in their early stages. These companies provide returns many, many times that of all the rest. Thiel explains that even though less than 1 percent of new companies in the United States receive VC funding, the ones that succeed have a massive effect on the economy at large. VC-backed companies create 11 percent of all new private sector jobs, and generate revenue of 21 percent of GDP. The biggest 12 tech companies, now worth over $2 trillion, were all backed by venture capital.

Even professional investors, Thiel says, regularly underestimate the degree of difference between a successful company and the rest. Assuming that the distribution of returns across the companies they invest in is quite even (e.g., out of a portfolio of six, two will fail, two will break even, and two make returns of two times or four times investment), investors believe in diversi-fication, on the basis that the winners will balance out the losers. But this approach often simply leads to a basket of flops. All you need is a single success story, and that success (Theil's Founders Fund invested in Facebook, for instance) will way outstrip any other investments, even if they run to 20 or 30. This results in the "scary" rule that VC investors should only put money into start-ups which could return the value of every company in the portfolio combined, that is, to "succeed on a vast scale." If you just put $250,000 into hundreds of start-ups, you will quickly go broke. At any one time, Thiel's fund only invests in half a dozen companies that it believes could become massive monopolies, based on fundamentals.

As in business, as in life: the more you dabble, diversify and hedge your bets, Thiel says, the more you are saying to yourself that you are not confident in your future, and that you believe in uncertain outcomes: "life is not a portfolio; not for a startup founder, and not for any individual."

Surprisingly, Thiel argues that you should think twice before starting your own company. It may be wiser to join an already fast-growing company. For example, you may want to be the sole owner of your company, but if it fails you have nothing. If you had joined Google in the early days, in contrast, with a stake of only 0.01 percent, you would now be worth $35 million.

Final comments

There is no formula for success, Thiel says, and entrepreneurship can be taught only to a certain extent; the creation of new and valuable things is still a bit of a mystery. Yet he has observed a powerful pattern in that "successful people find value in unexpected places." Many people think they can start a great enterprise by building a new operating system or social media platform, but as Thiel notes, "Every moment in business happens only once." The business stars of the future are creating things no one at the moment even believes there is a need for. His question, "What valuable company is nobody building?", should be at the forefront of every entrepreneur's mind.

Thiel ends the book speculating on the techno-utopian idea of the "Singularity," in which technologies converge to produce a great advance in living standards. Whether or not this actually happens, what matters, he says, is that we as individuals do the singular, that is making the most of our own potential to bring something into being which can "create the new things that will make the future not just different, but better." And the best vehicle for such "beyond incremental" advances is still the start-up company.

Peter Thiel

Thiel was born in 1967 in Frankfurt, Germany. His parents emigrated to the United States when he was a year old and settled in Cleveland, Ohio. His father, a chemical engineer, moved the family to South Africa and Namibia for work, before returning to live in Foster City, California, near the emerging Silicon Valley. He was a keen reader of science fiction, Tolkien, and Ayn Rand, was ranked seventh nationally in chess, and on graduating from school won a place to study philosophy at nearby Stanford University. He became involved in campus politics, and in 1987 set up The Stanford Review to oppose political correctness and a perceived liberal bias on campus. His ideas on competition were strongly influenced by the philosopher René Girard.

After graduating from Stanford Law School in 1992, Thiel spent an unhappy period in New York as a lawyer and then a derivatives trader, then returned to California and, with investments from friends and family, set up a venture capital fund, Thiel Capital. With Max Levchin he launched PayPal in 1999, and after its sale to eBay in 2002 formed two investment funds, Clarium and Mithril. In 2004, Thiel provided $500,000 seed money for Facebook, which gave him a 10 percent stake in the company and a seat on its board. In the same year he formed Palantir, a data analytics company whose antifraud and criminal-catching technology is used by US intelligence agencies. Thiel's Founders Fund, started in 2005, has included investments in Airbnb, Lyft, and Spotify. More recent investments are in longevity technology, marijuana, and the building of cities at sea.

The philanthropic Thiel Foundation provides $100,000 fellowships for students who wish to leave college and pursue a promising business idea. Thiel has been a strong critic of the cost and benefits of college education.

In 2016 he bankrolled wrestler Hulk Hogan in a privacy case against the celebrity news website Gawker. Hogan's victory effectively bankrupted Gawker, which had outed Thiel as being gay. Thiel donated $1.25 million to the Trump campaign for president, and spoke at the Republican Convention in 2016.

Up the Organization

"In the average company the boys in the mailroom, the president, the vice-presidents, and the girls in the steno pool have three things in common: they are docile, they are bored, and they are dull. Trapped in pigeonholes of organizational charts, they've been made slaves to the rules of public and private hierarchies that run mindlessly on and on because nobody can change them."

"When the vast majority of big companies are in agreement on some practice or policy, you can be fairly certain that it's out of date. Ask yourself, "What's the opposite of this conventional wisdom?" And then work back to what makes sense."

"You don't have to abandon or compromise your principles in order to succeed in organizations. The reason for this is that everybody else is so busy selling out, or has sold out so often, that when you come along and don't sell out or compromise, you stand out immediately."

In a nutshell

The key to great corporate performance is not employing great people, as conventional wisdom says, but letting your existing people flower.

In a similar vein

Peter Drucker *The Effective Executive*
Patrick Lencioni *The Five Dysfunctions of a Team*
Douglas McGregor *The Human Side of Enterprise*
Al Ries & Jack Trout *Positioning*

CHAPTER 46

Robert Townsend

Robert Townsend worked for 14 years (1948–62) at American Express, a company that he notes "was rich enough to do almost everything wrong." The experience taught him to consider the value of doing the opposite to the conventional wisdom. *Up the Organization: How to Stop the Company Stifling People and Strangling Profits* was a sort of protest against giant organizations that seemed to be taking over in the 1960s, from General Motors to the US Defense Department. Townsend noticed that friends of his in small companies were imitating big-company ways ("if Time Inc. puts its executives in fancy offices, that must be the way to be big"), and was horrified. Instead, he offered a manifesto for building a company that operated "as if people were human," and in this was influenced by Douglas McGregor's classic *The Human Side of Enterprise* (see Chapter 29).

Up the Organization was written at a time when the memo and the Xerox machine ruled, when employees had to fill out a requisition form to make a long-distance call, and when the only women seen in high corporate circles were ambitious wives. It may seem like an artefact from the *Mad Men* era (indeed, the fictional television series covers the period 1960 to 1970, when the book was published), but in fact there is more timeless good sense in Townsend's short, alphabetically ordered chapters than a stack of mediocre contemporary business books.

Most of us are the descendants of rapacious, greedy, and treacherous people who "would make Genghis Khan look like Mahatma Gandhi," Townsend writes. Our first option is to accept this truth and live a corporate life in which we extract what cash, benefits, and leisure we can; the second is "nonviolent guerrilla warfare" in which we continually fight against laziness in our organization, so it can come back to life and serve its original purpose. With our heritage of ballsy aggression, we can at least create companies in which people don't shy away from conflict, and which are charged with purpose and optimism about creating a new market or changing an industry.

This is exactly what Townsend did when, as the CEO of Avis, he helped the rental car firm double its sales, become an innovator, and make a profit for the first time. It was under Townsend that the famous "We Try Harder" motto was launched. His book is a stream-of-consciousness take on what was wrong, and right, about modern business, arranged in pithy, wise, and often funny chunks of advice in alphabetical order.

Advertising

One of Townsend's first pieces of advice is to fire your existing ad agency and find the hottest new one in town, one that is fired up and truly creative—and then give them free reign to produce the ads they want.

Normally, the original ad made by an agency is watered down when it is seen by management, but Townsend decided to give its main Avis account to now legendary ad man Bill Bernbach, on the understanding that his agency could do what it wanted. Bernbach's team did a lot of research on Avis, and came back with the blunt conclusion that "the only honest things they could say were that the company was second largest and that the people were trying harder." This wasn't much basis for an advertising campaign, but Townsend had made an agreement and stuck to it. The rest was history. The "We Try Harder" line (introduced in 1963) was phenomenally successful and is still used by the company today.

The moral? "Don't hire a master to paint you a masterpiece," Townsend writes, "and then assign a roomful of schoolboy-artists to look over his shoulders and suggest improvements."

Computers and their priests

Townsend is damning of IT people, whom he calls "complicators, not simplifiers." Their jargon serves to prevent you from knowing what they are doing and building a mystique or priesthood around themselves. Never forget that computers and IT people are in the service of the organization. When hiring one, Townsend suggests, make it a condition that he spends two to four weeks a year in a service or sales position. Such an indignity will separate the IT people that are truly behind the organization, and those who see it as a vehicle for their skills and advancement.

Townsend warns us never to shift a manual function to an automated one without a long transition period. No company has ever failed taking automation very slowly, but plenty have bit the dust by computerizing the factory or the office prematurely. All decisions on IT should be made at the highest level, and with total understanding of what's involved. Don't let computer nerds use your company as their playpen for new ideas they've developed without rigorous testing and challenge.

Financial control

"Man is a complicating animal. He only simplifies under pressure. Put him under some financial pressure. He'll scream in anguish. Then he'll come up with a plan which, to his own private amazement, is not only less expensive, but also faster and better than his original proposal."

Job descriptions

Another of Townsend's radical suggestions is to do away with job descriptions. All they do is "freeze the job as the writer understood it at a particular instant in the past." Any higher paid, non-repetitive job is constantly changing, and is a chance for a person to be genuinely creative in their work. Being judged according to some fixed job description saps morale. It should be clear to see what someone has achieved, irrespective of what they were meant to do according to a description written by Personnel.

Kill bureaucracy

Appoint a zealot to go around the organization calling out wasteful form-filling and report-writing, who must yell out "Horseshit!" whenever he finds an example of institutionalization.

Hiring

When hiring, avoid expensive outsiders and promote people inside the firm who have proved to be successful. With their knowledge foundation in the company, what they don't know can be quickly learned within a few months. The top-rated outsider may flail around for years getting to grips with the company and industry. Don't hire graduates of Harvard Business School, who are trained to expect they will become Captains of Industry but generally lack what every good organization needs: humility, respect for people on the front line, industry, loyalty, judgment, fairness, and honesty.

Real leadership

Leaders come in all shapes and sizes, but the common denominator is that the people under them turn in superior performances. The best leaders, as Lao Tzu said, are barely noticed because they are totally focused on supporting their staff, not looking to shine themselves. A good manager should be without pride, being willing to do menial things if it means serving the team. As in the military, the good leader eats last.

When you see a corporate leader who is focused only on the price of the company stock, is invisible to the rank and file, doesn't like honest criticism, and who thinks he is God, it is time for him to go.

Marketing
Keep this function the preserve of the key executive team, who once or twice a year must go into a huddle and define what the company is selling, why, and to whom at what price. Don't leave marketing up to someone with "Head of Marketing" written on their door.

Be a Martian
Avis was forced into relocating from Boston because their building was going to be knocked down to build a turnpike. They asked, "Where would a Martian locate the HQ of a company dedicated to renting vehicles?" The answer: not in Manhattan, where its competitors were based, but near the airports of JFK and LaGuardia, so line managers could see HQ managers quickly. Avis's headquarters is still in New Jersey today.

Meetings
Keep meetings to a minimum, and do not allow your company's parts to wage war against each other by memo. Most things that are said in memos should be said face to face, or not at all.

Mistakes
Townsend admits that two out of every three decisions he made at Avis were wrong, but as there was no stigma for failure, the mistakes were discussed openly and corrected. "Admit your mistakes openly, maybe even joyfully," he says, and get the rest of your company to act the same way. Only a work culture in which failure has no stigma can create something great (see Chapter 43).

Objectives
It took Avis six months to come up with its single objective: to become "the fastest growing and most profitable car rental business." It was worth being so focused, because ideas for acquiring hotels, airlines, and travel agencies could be quickly knocked on the head as a diversion.

He quotes Peter Drucker: "Concentration is the key to economic results . . . no other principle of effectiveness is violated as constantly . . . Our motto today seems to be: 'Let's do a little bit of everything.'" Townsend kept a sign on his wall that read, "Is what I'm doing or about to do getting us closer to our objective?" It saved him a lot of time on useless trips, lunches, conferences, junkets, and meetings.

Cato boiled Rome's mission down to three words: "*Delenda est Carthago*" ("Carthage must be destroyed"). Keep narrowing yours down, say it again and again, and you will see the effects.

People

Many organizations are still patterned on the Catholic Church or the Roman legions. This may have made sense when workers were "uneducated peasants," but today we employ people for their brains. Townsend advocates people being able to decide on their own office hours and when they take vacations, because "Everybody will have a different system of building up steam and releasing it."

Companies lure workers on the promise of higher wages, medical schemes, vacations, pensions, profit sharing, bowling nights, and baseball teams, but as Townsend notes, none of these can be enjoyed during the working day. Such perks tell the potential worker that they won't like working, but as Douglas McGregor showed, people can be motivated by the work itself to an extent that the day flies by (see Chapter 29).

When Townsend became chief executive he did not cull the management team, but simply allowed it to be much more effective by giving people free rein. The key to great corporate performance is not employing great people, as conventional wisdom says, but letting your existing people flower. Of course some won't be able to change, but plenty of others will jump at the chance to fully use their brains and commitment.

Get rid of personnel departments, because they treat people as if they are units. Just have one person to do the basics for people getting paid, and focus on providing the right *environment*: "Provide the climate and proper nourishment and let the people grow themselves. They'll amaze you."

Organization charts

Don't use them. People hate seeing their names in little boxes underneath other people's bigger boxes. List people by function, or alphabetically. The best organizations see themselves more like a circle than a tree, chart, or anything vertical or rectangular.

Organization charts tend to set an organization in stone, but a good one is constantly changing in the pursuit of its goal. Therefore, Townsend says, never formalize how the organization works, but if you have to do a diagram, do it in pencil and don't have it circulated.

Secretaries

Don't have a secretary. Secretaries become gatekeepers who have favorites. Townsend found he got much closer to the people who reported to him without having this buffer. People are annoyed at not being able to get through to you direct, and they are impressed when you pick up the phone or reply in handwritten notes.

If he could design the company building, Townsend would make the executive area "look like the cubicles of a Trappist monastery," while making the office support area a bright, luxurious place in which to work. After all, these are the people who are the first point of contact with the public. They should feel comfortable and enthused in doing that job.

Work socializing
Don't socialize with people who report to you; it will lead to accusations of favoritism. Have social relations only with peers.

Final comments
Organizations, Townsend says, are full of phonies, self-promoters, and hangers-on who care only for their own advance. Yet "Every success I've ever had," Townsend writes, "came about because I was trying to help other people . . . Every promotion I got came about when I was up to my ears helping my associates be as effective as possible while having as much fun as possible. On the other hand, every time I had a really clever idea for making *me* a lot of money or for getting *me* into some interesting job, it turned out to be an utter failure."

In a later edition of the book he added a section on women in the workplace. In addition to the advice of being yourself and not try to act like a man, he advises women to make all decisions in the light of the question, "How would I do this job if I owned the company?" This focus on the greater good will set you apart from the men, who are generally Machiavellian self-promoters. If the organization's interests are your interest, it will be a meaningful place to work, worth your time and effort. Don't seek to be great, but to be part of something great.

Robert Townsend

Born in Washington DC in 1920, Townsend spent his childhood in Great Neck on Long Island, New York, before doing a degree at Princeton University. After graduating in 1942 he served in the US Navy in World War Two. In 1948 he was hired by American Express, and spent the next 14 years rising to a senior vice president position. He was lured to be CEO of Avis by André Meyer at the bank Lazard Frères, which had bought the ailing rental car firm in 1962. Townsend would head Avis from 1962 to 1965.

Other books include Further up the Organization *(1984), an updated version of* Up the Organization, *and* The B2 Chronicles: Uncommon Wisdom for Un-corporate America *(1995). Townsend died while on vacation in Anguilla in 1998.*

1987

The Art of the Deal

"I have an almost perverse attraction to complicated deals, partly because they tend to be more interesting, but also because it is more likely you can get a good price on a difficult deal."

"I don't do it for the money. I've got enough, much more than I'll ever need. I do it to do it. Deals are my art form. Other people paint beautifully on canvas or write wonderful poetry. I like making deals, preferably big deals. That's how I get my kicks."

"I like thinking big. I always have. To me it's very simple: if you're going to be thinking anyway, you might as well think big. Most people think small, because most people are afraid of success, afraid of making decisions, afraid of winning. And that gives people like me a great advantage."

In a nutshell

To succeed in business, balance boldness and promotion with patience, caution, and flexibility.

In a similar vein

P. T. Barnum *The Art of Money Getting*
Conrad Hilton *Be My Guest*

CHAPTER 47

Donald Trump

Thanks to his self-promotion, extravagant lifestyle, and big deals, Donald J. Trump was already famous when *The Art of the Deal* was published; a symbol of capitalism, New York City, and the flash 1980s all rolled into one.

Yet the book had lucky timing, coming out just ahead of the troubles that beset Trump in the late 1980s and early 1990s which brought him dangerously close to ruin. Much to his enemies' chagrin, he sorted himself out and came back bigger than ever. When F. Scott Fitzgerald said, "there are no second chances in American life," he did not count on the power of a brand, and like the great showman P. T. Barnum a century before, a large part of Trump's fortune comes down to his name.

When producers approached Trump to be the focus of a new reality television series based on entrepreneurship, he saw an opportunity to cement his fame with a new generation. Yet despite the array of Trump books that were published to capitalize on the success of *The Apprentice*, *The Art of the Deal* (written with Tony Schwartz) remains the best insight into Trump the businessman. Though now 30 years old, it outlines the essential philosophies and ways of working that The Donald used over several decades. The scale of his operations may have grown, but the Trump of the 1980s is largely the same one of today. Here we look at some of the deals, beliefs, and strategies that have seen him thrive and prosper even in tough times. (Not covered are the achievements in a job which required his relocation to Washington DC, of which history will be the judge.)

Think big

Trump's father, Fred, was a developer of rent-controlled housing in the New York boroughs. Despite it being a low-margin and unglamorous form of developing, his tenacity ensured his success. Though the young Donald spent a lot of his boyhood following his dad around on sites, he always dreamed of Manhattan and creating landmark projects that made a statement.

His first project in Manhattan was the Commodore, a huge, rundown hotel in a low-rent district. At the time, he notes, "I was only twenty-seven years old, and I'd hardly slept in a hotel," but he embarked on building a 1,400-room monster, the biggest in New York for 25 years.

Promote, promote

It's a myth, Trump observes, that location is everything in real estate. It *is* important, but to make the most of any property (particularly apartments) what you need is to create a sense of worth or mystique that will make people want to buy. He remarks:

"People may not always think big themselves, but they can still get very excited by those who do. That's why a little hyperbole never hurts. People want to believe that something is the biggest and the greatest and the most spectacular."

To get your project noticed you must be different, even outrageous, and being so increases your chances of becoming a story in the media. Trump claims not to court publicity for publicity's sake, however, a small article in the *New York Times*, he notes, will be worth much more than a full-page advertisement costing $100,000—even if the slant is negative.

Have patience, then be ready to swoop

Despite his flashy image, a major element in Trump's success is being prepared to wait. For example, for years he prized the Bonwit Teller site that would become Trump Tower, repeatedly writing to its owners to state his interest. He kept up his efforts, he notes, "because much more often than you'd think, sheer persistence is the difference between success and failure." When the site fell into the hands of new owners who were in a poor financial position, it was to Trump they turned to sell.

On another occasion, he read about a company in dire straits whose executives had been living high, flying around in a corporate Boeing 727. At the time this plane cost $30 million new. Trump offered a measly $5 million, and in the end paid $8 million—still a hefty discount. If you can make seemingly outrageous demands while keeping a straight face, he notes, you will get bargains.

Many of his successes came from offering to buy assets before they were on the market. To many sellers, a bird in the hand is worth two in the bush. "The worst thing you can possibly do in a deal," he writes, "is seem desperate to make it." You need leverage; find out what the seller needs or wants and give them this something extra in addition to the purchase price.

Secrets of the deal maker

In New York City, big-time real estate development is a complex matter. The city has strict and Byzantine planning and zoning laws which mean that most development proposals, particularly larger ones, are knocked back. Trump's building of the famous Trump Tower on 5th Avenue and 57th Street (with its marble waterfall lobby, luxury stores, and apartments owned by stars and billionaires) turned out to be a great success, but to get it built he had to wrangle with the city authorities about its height, its esthetics (given its land-mark position), and how much public amenity it would provide. Long and often fragile negotiations were required to buy the lease for the existing building (then housing Bonwit Teller), for the land that the building sat on, for the air rights above the Tiffany store next door, and for a small pocket of land required to have a rear yard (another city requirement). He had to raise the money for the project, yet the banks were not willing to provide it until everything was settled. It was only the success of his previous project, the Commodore/Hyatt hotel, that enabled him to finally get a mortgage.

A key to understanding Trump's success is that he actually *likes* handling complexity. What to others look like big problems, to him appear as massive opportunities that draw on his creative powers. All his deals are a case of juggling many balls in the air at once, and this is even before the first bricks are laid. The more complex the deal, he notes, the fewer developers will be interested in the first place—but this means greater potential rewards if it does come off. While most people do not have a stomach for such uncertainties, Trump has thrived.

Though one of his trademarks is hubristic confidence, in fact he always goes into any deal looking at what could possibly go wrong. "Protect the downside," he notes, "and the upside will take care of itself"—every deal must have a fallback position. If he buys a site or a building, for instance, he has to be ready for his plans to be rejected. An intended tower block of apartments can be changed into office accommodation or a hotel if necessary. The deal maker must be willing to let go of personal preferences to ensure a profitable outcome.

The way of The Donald

Other things we learn about Trump in the book include:

- In college, while his friends were reading comics and the sports pages, he was poring over listings of property foreclosures;
- His first abode in Manhattan was a rented studio apartment that looked onto a courtyard;

- He is not keen on parties or small talk, and goes to bed early;
- He doesn't like to schedule too many meetings, preferring to see how the day unfolds. He routinely makes 50–100 phone calls;
- He's a stickler for cleanliness and makes sure all his properties sparkle;
- He trusts his intuition, calling off deals that "don't feel right" even if they look great on paper. On the other hand, he has often gone ahead with deals against the opposition of his advisers (such as his purchase of the Hilton casino in Atlantic City, which was a success);
- He got interested in the gambling business when he discovered that the Hilton corporation owned 150 hotels around the world, but its two casinos in Las Vegas provided 40 percent of its profits;
- He takes a lot of stands on principle: "I fight when I feel I'm getting screwed, even if it's costly and difficult and highly risky";
- His love of glamour, he says, was inherited from his mother, and his hard work ethic from his father;
- He likes to hire women for many of his top jobs;
- His favorite place is Mar-a-Lago, the spectacular Florida property built in the 1920s by the heiress to the Post cereal fortune (now a private club), which he got for a bargain price;
- He is proud of his reconstruction of Wollman Ice Rink in Central Park, completed in four months after years of delays by the city authorities.

Final comments

Who is the real Donald Trump? Though famously fond of exaggeration and self-promotion, underneath there is a businessman who loves his work. In his biography *No Such Thing As Over-Exposure*, Robert Slater notes that (despite the famous "You're fired" line from *The Apprentice*) few people are ever let go in the Trump organization, and generally he is more forgiving than his image suggests. He is also loyal, with trusted financial and legal people who have been advising him for years. As Trump himself notes, "In my life, there are two things I've found I'm very good at: overcoming obstacles and motivating good people to do their best work."

In its current renaissance, it is easy to forget that for much of the 1970s and 1980s New York City was in a mess, close to bankruptcy and ridden with crime. But Trump clearly loved his city and thought it the center of the universe, and as a reward for that confidence was able to pick up valuable properties for low prices. He is often painted as vainglorious, but the other side of the coin is strong self-belief. Without it, he would have been no more than a small to medium property developer.

Toward the end of the book, Trump gets philosophical, wondering what, ultimately, is the meaning of all his empire-building. His honest answer: he doesn't know, except that he loves doing the deals themselves, irrespective of how much money he now has. Life is fragile, he notes, so whatever you do you must have fun doing it.

Littered with interesting mentions of the great and the good of New York in the 1980s, including novelist Judith Krantz, TV personality David Letterman, financiers Michael Milken and Ivan Boesky, Ian Schrager of Studio 54 fame, mayor Ed Koch, Calvin Klein, and the Cardinal of St Patrick's Cathedral, *The Art of the Deal* is an enjoyable read as well as offering valuable lessons. Trump fans should also get the sequel, *The Art of the Comeback*, written ten years later, and *Think Big: Make It Happen in Business and Life* (2008).

Donald Trump

Born in Queens, New York, in 1946, Trump was the fourth of five children. His mother Mary was a Scottish immigrant from the Isle of Lewis, and his father the son of German immigrants (originally named "Drumpf") who ran a hotel in British Columbia.

As a boy, he was assertive and aggressive. At 13 he went to New York Military Academy in upstate New York, where he stayed until his senior year. After graduating he considered going to film school in California, but instead enrolled in Fordham University in the Bronx because he preferred to stay close to home. He attended the University of Pennsylvania's Wharton School of Finance (arguably America's best business school for entrepreneurs), graduating in 1968. In 1971 he began working for his father's company, the Trump Organization, before starting out on his own.

In 1977 he married Czech model and skier Ivana Zelníčková, who for several years worked as a manager in Trump hotels. They had three children, Donald Jr., Ivanka, and Eric, but divorced in 1992 after Donald's affair with model Marla Maples, whom he married in 1993, producing a daughter, Tiffany. In 2004 Trump married Slovenian model Melania Knauss. With their son Barron (named after Barron Hilton) they live in Trump Tower in a penthouse valued at over $30 million, or in their other home at 1600 Pennsylvania Avenue, Washington DC.

Trump became President of the United States on 20 January 2017, after defeating Hillary Clinton for the office.

The Forbes *Rich List of 2017 estimated Trump's fortune at $3.5 billion, making him the world's 544th richest person.*

Elon Musk

"What Musk has developed that so many of the entrepreneurs in Silicon Valley lack is a meaningful worldview . . . Where Mark Zuckerberg wants to help you share baby photos, Musk wants to . . . well . . . save the human race from self-imposed or accidental annihilation."

"He's set about building something that has the potential to be much grander than anything Hughes or Jobs produced. Musk has taken industries like aerospace and automotive that America seemed to have given up on and recast them as something new and fantastic. At the heart of this transformation are Musk's skills as a software maker and his ability to apply them to machines. He's merged atoms and bits in ways that few people thought possible, and the results have been spectacular."

"If Tesla actually can deliver an affordable car with 500 miles of range, it will have built what many people in the auto industry insisted for years was impossible. To do that while also constructing a worldwide network of free charging stations, revamping the way cars are sold, and revolutionizing automotive technology would be an exceptional feat in the history of capitalism."

In a nutshell

The visionary entrepreneur is not content to create a business, but must shape the future.

In a similar vein

Ron Chernow *Titan: The Life of John D. Rockefeller Sr.*
Walter Isaacson *Steve Jobs*
Peter Thiel *Zero To One*

CHAPTER 48

Ashlee Vance

When online payments firm PayPal was sold to eBay in 2002 for $1.5 billion, cofounder and major shareholder Elon Musk became a newly minted internet millionaire. Like others who had done well out of the online world, he might have been expected to keep investing in Silicon Valley start-ups, sit on a couple of boards, buy a garage of cars, and play a lot of golf.

As it happened, the bounty from PayPal ($180 million) proved to be just the seed of Musk's uber-ambitious plans, and was soon thrown toward the three areas he had long believed would change the world: electric cars, rockets, and solar power. Electric cars and solar power, because carbon-based fuel had become toxic politically and environmentally; and rockets, because humanity needed to become an "interplanetary species"—colonization of Mars was not a luxury but a necessary insurance policy against anything catastrophic happening to Earth.

As Ashlee Vance, a Silicon Valley tech writer, notes at the start of his compelling biography, *Elon Musk: Tesla, SpaceX, and the Quest for a Fantastic Future*, following the dot.com bust people went from believing they were inventing the future to pursuing incremental solutions to problems, seeking to entertain people or produce clever apps. Where was the real innovation? Into the breach steps Elon Musk, the Howard Hughes of our time who wants to make *things* that can solve the world's problems. "I think there are probably too many smart people pursuing Internet stuff, finance, and law," Musk told Vance. "That is part of the reason why we haven't seen as much innovation."

Here we trace Musk's rise from geek to industrialist, on the way considering the personal and managerial qualities that have powered his vision.

Boy story
Born in 1971, Musk grew up in a wealthy suburb of Pretoria, South Africa, during apartheid. He was a geeky, reserved kid who had a photographic memory and read compulsively—everything from *Lord of the Rings* to the *Encyclopaedia Britannica*. He got his first computer at 10, and from an early age had an interest in rockets and electric cars. He dreamed of escaping intellectually suffocating Pretoria and living in America.

At 17, after five months at the University of Pretoria studying physics and engineering, he left for Canada (his mother Maye had Canadian citizenship, so he was able to get a Canadian passport). He spent a year traveling around Canada doing odd jobs, before, in 1989, enrolling at Queen's University in Ontario to study business, economics, and psychology. Two years later he transferred to the Wharton School at the University of Pennsylvania on a scholarship, getting an economics and then a physics degree. In the summers he would intern at Silicon Valley start-ups, getting a feel for the Valley's culture, and take road trips with his brother Kimbal. With the nascent internet, in 1995 they decided to start Zip2, "a primitive Google Maps meets Yelp," and slept in the office to save money.

As internet fever began to grow, computer giant Compaq made an offer for Zip2 for $307 million. As a significant shareholder, Musk made $22 million from the deal. Having been a Canadian backpacker only a few years before, he was now a young darling of Silicon Valley. He bought an apartment and took delivery of a $1 million McLaren F1 supercar, which he drove around the Valley as if it was a Ford Focus, until wrecking it (he was uninsured).

In Canada, Musk had worked as an intern at the Bank of Nova Scotia, and came out of the experience thinking that bankers were "rich and dumb." He decided that banking was ripe for a revolution, and began setting up an online bank with the X.com domain name, pouring $12 million of his own money into the venture. After getting the OK from federal banking regulators, X.com went live at Thanksgiving 1999. It aimed to make moving money around quickly and easily, in contrast to the behemoths of American corporate banking. Within a couple of months, 200,000 people had signed up. But Musk's bank soon had a competitor in the form of Confinity, a fintech start-up set up by Peter Thiel and Max Levchin. Confinity originally rented office space from X.com, but the rivalry meant they had to move down the road. As the real prize for both enterprises was the market for internet payments, they ended up combining forces as X.com. The merger was riven by ideological and management battles, and Musk was replaced in a coup by Thiel, who would rebrand the company as PayPal.

Rather than being embittered, Musk kept upping his stake in PayPal so that he was the majority shareholder, and even supported Thiel. In 2002 eBay bought out PayPal for $1.5 billion, and though Musk came out of the deal with $180 million after taxes, it was Thiel whose management style was praised, while Musk was painted by the press as an egomaniac with poor judgment. History has been kinder to Musk, who was clearly as responsible for PayPal's success as Thiel was, Vance argues, but Musk succeeded despite being, as Vance puts it, a "confrontational know-it-all."

SpaceX

After being forced out of PayPal, Musk became enamoured of Los Angeles, and moved his young family (wife Justine and their sons) there. The other reason was LA's history in the aeronautics and space industry. His mind was turning to the future of space travel; he wanted to do "something meaningful" beyond internet services, to reinspire the public to believe in science and progress. NASA didn't seem to have any concrete plan for going to Mars, for instance.

Musk made two trips to Russia to try to buy a couple of old ICBM missiles which could be converted into rockets, before working out that he could build his own, filling a gap in the market for taking small satellites and research payloads into space. He now had a new mission: to make space journeys radically cheaper.

With space expert Tom Mueller in charge of the science and engineering, in 2002 SpaceX was launched with the aim of becoming "the Southwest Airlines of Space," with frequent, reliable, low-cost space launches—a total contrast to the bloated federal space bureaucracy and corporate space outfits like Boeing, TRW, and Lockheed Martin.

By 2008 Musk had poured $100 million of his own money into SpaceX, but was seeing one failed launch after another. To make matters worse, his marriage was falling apart. Finally, in September 2008 the fourth SpaceX launch was successful, becoming the first privately made rocket to ever leave the Earth's atmosphere. NASA decided to give it a contract for $1.6 billion for a dozen flights to the International Space Station. After a rocky start, SpaceX was on its way.

Tesla

SpaceX would have been enough of a challenge and headache for anyone, but all the while Musk was ramping up his plan to turn the world toward electric cars.

General Motors had come out with the EV1, and of course there was the Toyota Prius, but they were seen as earnest, dull vehicles with an uncertain commercial future. Meanwhile, Stanford University geek J. B. Straubel was talking up the capacity of lithium ion batteries—normally used to power laptops—to produce electric cars that could be potentially very fast. Musk heard about Straubel and gave him some seed funding to develop a battery pack that could power a fast car and have good range, appealing to upmarket car buyers. But Musk's real involvement with the electric car business came after he had met Martin Eberhard and Marc

Tarpenning, who in 2003 had incorporated a start-up called Tesla Motors (after the electric motor pioneer Nikola Tesla). It turned out to be a perfect meeting of minds. The trio dreamed of ending America's addiction to oil and producing a mass-market electric car where all others had failed. Musk provided $6.5 million in funding, and the new firm soon had Straubel under its employ. By 2006 Tesla had 100 employees. Musk, along with Google's Larry Page and Sergey Brin and venture capital investors, was pouring more cash into the company. At the press event to launch its first car, the Tesla Roadster, Musk said, "Until today, all electric cars have sucked." The Roadster cost $90k and had a 250-mile range, but overheated quickly and was not ready to go into full production. As the launch date for the Roadster moved back again and again, with supply chain and manufacturing problems, and the press having a field day with Tesla's problems, the CEO installed by investors to sort things out thought that Tesla's best chance of success would be to sell the intellectual capital to a major auto maker. But Musk wasn't willing to let his vision for the company die and dug in his heels, talking up a four-door luxury sedan car—the "Model S"—that would go into production after the Roadster.

Tesla ended up selling 2,500 Roadsters, but it was a long way from this to building a proper factory with hundreds of millions of dollars of investment. Help came in the way of a $50 million investment from Mercedes-Benz, to take 10 percent of the company, who were massively impressed with Tesla's battery packs and motors, which they thought they could use in their own cars. A bigger step toward becoming a major automotive player was a Department of Energy loan of $465 million. However, this still fell short of the $1 billion needed to build and launch a mass-market car. The Great Recession came to the rescue. In 1984, General Motors and Toyota had built a high-tech plant in Fremont, California, to build cheaper, higher-quality cars for the US market, but when GM fell into near bankruptcy in 2008, the plant was put up for sale. Tesla came to a deal with Toyota to take over the factory for a knockdown price of $42 million (while also giving Toyota a 2.5 percent stake in Tesla). The final funds to build the Tesla S came from a 2010 flotation of the company on the stock market, raising $226 million. It was the first IPO of an American carmaker since 1956.

Musk inputted on every detail of the building of the Tesla S. For instance, as he now had five boys himself, he insisted that it provide seven seats, while at the same time looking and feeling like a performance car. The door handles on the Model S were designed to pop out when the driver gets near, which had never been done. Despite its technical innovation, at the start of the production the factory was producing a risible ten cars a week, and speculators were shorting Tesla stock. A lot of orders were canceled, and presidential candidate Mitt Romney dismissed Tesla as a "loser" among other green companies that had taken federal money. Even amid this pessimism, Musk was talking up Tesla as becoming "the most profitable car company in the world," and setting up a network of totally free charging stations across America for Tesla drivers, powered by solar energy. Even if there was "some kind of Zombie apocalypse," Musk told the press, a Tesla driver could drive across America without any need for fuel.

The early Model S cars had reliability problems and were not up to the standard of options, fit, and finish of other cars costing $100,000. In 2013 word of mouth on the car "sucked," Musk admits, and unless he could convert people with deposits to actual sales, the firm faced bankruptcy. He began talking to Google's Larry Page about Google purchasing the company. Then a miracle happened. Musk had ordered around 500 people who worked at Tesla to hit the phones and become salespeople (whatever their title) and convert depositors to buyers. The company was suddenly flooded with cash, even making a profit of $11 million in 2013, and delivering 4,900 cars in the financial year. The deal with Google was called off.

Today, Tesla has a suite of cars planned, including its mass-market Model 3, which aims to finally turn electric cars mainstream. Buying an internal combustion car now, Vance suggests, would be "like paying for the past." The public and investors agree. Despite its comparatively tiny output so far, Tesla Inc. is currently valued at $61 billion, more than Ford and GM.

Back to space

SpaceX Falcon 9 rockets now blast off once a month, putting satellites into space that help run the internet, weather forecasting, entertainment, radio, and navigation systems, and carrying supplies to the International Space Station, vastly undercutting what the established players would charge. As satellites are ever more crucial to modern life, SpaceX's business has a certain future. It is building its own satellites, making more and cheaper launches, and developing the Dragon V2 module, a reusable rocket that can blast off and return safely anywhere on Earth. It looks much like the interior of spacecraft in science fiction movies, not like the cramped quarters of NASA craft.

A launch of the Falcon Heavy, which is designed to be able to take over 50 tons of materials to Mars, is planned for 2018. The first rocket to Mars is planned for 2022, creating a cargo route in advance of settling people on the planet in the late 2020s. NASA is planning another Mars mission in parallel, but is looking at the mid 2030s.

Fulfilling Musk's solar energy ambitions, in 2016 Tesla Inc. absorbed SolarCity, which had been started by his cousins Peter and Lyndon Rive in 2006. SolarCity is at the forefront of solar power generation, and Musk is chairman of the company.

Final comments

The events above are related to show that there was nothing inevitable about Musk's success. His paths with SpaceX and Tesla were littered with technical failures and near bankruptcies. His ex-wife Justine noted to Vance, "People didn't always get the sacrifice he made in order to be where he was." The lesson of figures such as Howard Hughes, Steve Jobs, and Elon Musk is that being very flawed on a personal level does not prevent that person doing things that change the world for the better. Extreme innovation seems to go hand in hand with extreme personality.

In an industry dominated by governments, SpaceX could well end up being the dominant business of the future, with Musk as the real-life Tony Stark from *X-Men*. Some of his other plans include a hyperloop system, connecting cities around the US, starting with LA to San Francisco, a space-based internet system, giving the entire world high-speed satellite bandwidth, and battery systems for home use that allow people to live off the grid. "I'm not an investor," Musk told Vance, "I like to make technologies real that I think are important for the future and useful in some sort of way."

What makes Musk different, his friend Larry Page notes, is that he pushes the limits of what is possible on the engineering side, but is also a master at business, leadership, and governmental matters. This mix of blue sky thinking and willingness to work in the mud is what makes an entrepreneur. In words that could have been spoken by Musk, Page comments, "Good ideas are always crazy until they're not."

Ashlee Vance

Vance was born in South Africa in 1977, grew up in Houston, Texas, and has a degree from Pomona College in California. For five years until 2008 he wrote for the online technology website The Register, and has also worked as a feature writer for Bloomberg Businessweek *covering major tech companies. His "Hello World" video series for Bloomberg looks at the tech cultures and latest developments in various countries. His first book was* Geek Silicon Valley *(2007), a guide to the area.*

Jack: Straight From the Gut

"There's no straight line to anyone's vision or dream. I'm living proof of that. This is the story of a lucky man, an unscripted, uncorporate type who managed to stumble and still move forward, to survive and even thrive in one of the world's most celebrated corporations. Yet it's also a small-town American success story. I've never stopped being aware of my roots even as my eyes opened to a world I never knew existed."

"We build great people, who then build great products and services."

In a nutshell

Never underestimate how far you can go by just being yourself.

In a similar vein

Alfred P. Sloan *My Years with General Motors*

CHAPTER 49

Jack Welch

J ack Welch was inspired to write this memoir after receiving hundreds of letters from people. All their working lives they had felt the pressure to conform to be successful, but in him they found a successful non-conformist, a person who had shaped the company he worked for instead of letting it shape him.

Hired by General Electric in 1960 to join a team developing a new type of plastic, from the beginning Welch was determined to fight bureaucracy and be himself, even if it meant getting sacked. His first year was so awful, he says, he almost left, and notes that his career had followed the celebrated 1960s movie *The Graduate*, in which a young Dustin Hoffman is told he should "get into plastics."

Despite blowing up a factory and building another one only to discover the product had major flaws and was not ready to go to market, Welch rose through the ranks. Managing to more than double GE's embryonic plastics business in three years, eight years after joining GE he was general manager of the division. In 1981 he was made CEO of GE, staying in the job until 2001.

Rise of a maverick

In 1970s American corporate life, command and control was the way to manage and no one talked about "passion" or "fun." Welch took a different approach: "I tried to create the informality of a corner neighborhood grocery store in the soul of a big company." His philosophy of informality included riotous celebrations whenever even small milestones were reached. "In those days, I was throwing hand grenades, trying to blow up traditions and rituals that I felt held us back."

But it was his results that really got him noticed. Chairman Reg Jones, who had the tag "most admired businessman in America," installed him in a new job at GE headquarters as chief of consumer goods, which accounted for 20 percent of GE's revenues.

Welch now found himself in the race for the succession of GE's top job. His self-confidence had always made him believe he was CEO material; now it was getting serious. After a highly charged lead-up period and against a number of more obvious candidates, in April 1981 he got the top job. He had little experience with the media, Washington, or Wall Street, and the *Wall Street Journal* described his succession to head one of America's industrial juggernauts as the replacement of "a legend with a livewire." Hardly a vote of confidence.

"People first, strategy and everything else second"

Welch admits he did not have detailed plans for where he wanted the company to go, only that he knew how he wanted it to "feel." Creating a new culture among 400,000 employees and 25,000 managers with layers of bureaucracy was always going to be a hard task. It would end up taking two decades.

For Welch, it was all about people. By hiring the best, you got the best ideas, and if those ideas could freely circulate in a "boundaryless" environment (a term he invented), it would be one of the best places in the world to work. In his first years he spent a lot of time in staff reviews, trying to cut out the dead wood and identify the stars. Intense locked-door sessions involving brutal personal scrutiny resulted in many staff leaving.

Welch pioneered the system of managers having to annually remove 10 percent of their staff. Most found this difficult and painful, but rather than creating a climate of fear it allowed people to know where they stood, in stark contrast to what Welch describes as the "false kindness" of personnel reviews of the past, which betrayed both the person involved and the organization. GE employee surveys actually showed that most employees wanted the system to become more, not less, performance driven. People work better to operating targets, and even better to big goals that may be only just attainable. The GE system undermined the conventional wisdom that promoting people for performance, and doing the opposite for bad performers, is bad for morale. We are graded all through school and college, Welch argues, why should it stop when we go to work? And if players in baseball teams can get wildly different pay packages, yet still play well as a team, why can't this apply to the workplace? "Rigorous differentiation," he says, "delivers real stars—and stars build great businesses."

By the mid 1980s Welch had reduced the GE workforce by around 25 percent, earning him the nickname "Neutron Jack" (the people get blown away but the buildings are left standing). At the same time he spent $75 million on a new fitness and conference center at headquarters and did a major upgrade of the firm's Crotonville management development center. The backlash was immediate: how could he lay off so many while lavishing money on such luxuries? If GE was going to move ahead, he was telling everyone, it had to spend more money on fewer people.

Strategies to motivate 300,000 people

Welch's signature business strategy for the multitude of GE's businesses was that each of them would have to become either number one or number two in their field, or they would be sold off. The strategy struck fear into some of GE's underperformers, but was easily understood and created a focus. If they were not number one or two, why, exactly, were they in the business?

Another strategy was to make every business pretend it had only 10 percent market share and thereby have to find ways to create rapid growth. One outcome of this strategy was that GE began to move into services to support its manufacturing. It developed the concept of "market definition," which calculated the total size of the market including all services related to the product (e.g. for jet engines, everything from fuel to finance). By these measures, their potential market was much larger; instead of just "making and selling products," they were selling management.

Other initiatives developed under Welch include: "Six Sigma" quality control (requiring only 3.4 defects/million in production operations; the norm was 35,000); globalization—not simply acquiring more businesses around the world but developing local talent; and e-business—Welch couldn't even type or use the internet in 1997, but a couple of years later had GE aggressively facing up to any possible challenges from start-ups.

Despite some failures (a disastrous acquisition of investment firm Kidder, Peabody and the collapse of a takeover of Honeywell International, thanks to EU regulators), GE grew six times larger under Welch, becoming a player in everything from CT scanners to finance to television, through the acquisition of the NBC network.

In his final year (2000), earnings jumped to a record $12.7 billion on revenues of $130 billion. In the previous six years, GE had more than doubled its revenues, attracting the title "most valuable company in the world."

A GE in Jack's image

Born in 1935, John F. Welch Jr. grew up in the working-class part of Salem, Massachusetts. His father was an Irish-American railroad conductor, and neither parent had graduated from high school. He credits his strong-willed mother for much of his success. Over card games she taught him how to compete ferociously, and told him that his stutter was simply a case of his brain being too fast for his mouth. His "hugs and kicks" way of dealing with GE staff was taken directly from Grace Welch, as was his trademark self-confidence. Yet in the book he makes a distinction: "Arrogance is a killer, and wearing ambition on one's sleeve can have the same effect . . .

Self-confident people aren't afraid to have their views challenged. They relish the intellectual combat that enriches ideas." This attitude of brash openness would become part of GE's culture.

Toward the end of the book he talks about "sick" companies and the drain they are on communities. Only a healthy firm generating profits can boost a town or a city, with the ability to spend money on environmental measures and generally be a good corporate citizen.

Welch's mother cried the day Franklin Delano Roosevelt died, such was her faith in government. Reflecting his own era's mistrust of government, Welch imparts the belief that if anything is going to save the world, it is successful companies.

Power of thinking long

Japanese companies are well-known for their long-time horizons, but it is worth recalling that GE, begun when Thomas Edison needed a corporate vehicle to sell his newly invented light bulbs, is now over 135 years old, with its capitalization dwarfing many states. Yet within its long history, *Fortune* magazine noted, the company has had fewer leaders than the Vatican has had popes. Indeed, Welch observes that the maneuvering to choose its CEO is not that different from the tortuous process that goes towards choosing a new pontiff.

Welch's successor, Jeffrey Immelt, put it this way: "I run a company that is 125 years old. There's going to be someone after me, just as there was someone else before me." Immelt's father Joseph worked in GE's Cincinatti plant all his life, rising to manage an aircraft engines division. When Immelt took over from Welch in 2001, he commissioned a study into the best-performing companies around the world. One of the findings was that these firms value "deep domain expertise." That is, they tend not to bring in outside managers to "shake things up" or "extract value," but instead place great store by the deep knowledge and expertise of people who have worked in their companies for years and who have been groomed to be top managers.

Organizations only become like this through having clarity of purpose and giving themselves a longer time frame in which to achieve this purpose. In business, as in life, seeing further ahead makes all the difference; despite his larger than life personality, Welch exemplified the focus and power of thinking long that GE is known for.

Final comments

There is a lot of talk now about being an entrepreneur and an innovator, with the suggestion that if you don't start your own company you are somehow missing out. The fact is, most people still work for companies, and this book's message is that you can still have a very satisfying working life if you can find a firm that is as interested in generating new ideas as it is in making money.

Jack is a classic not simply because of Welch's success, but because it is a fine record of American big business in the last decades of the twentieth century. It gives the reader a good feel for what it must be like to be the CEO of one of the world's biggest firms (playing golf with famous people seems to be one of the perks) and the author's descriptions of acquisitions and the fight for the leadership are gripping.

With the help of *Businessweek* writer John A. Byrne, *Jack* was written during Welch's last year in office, and conveys the buzz of those final days. GE has grown during Immelt's time, but nothing like it did during the Welch era. Even in giant corporations, individuals can make a big difference.

The Machine that Changed the World

"Lean production is 'lean' because it uses less of everything compared with mass production—half the human effort in the factory, half the manufacturing space, half the investment in tools, half the engineering hours to develop a product in half the time. Also, it requires keeping far less than half the needed inventory on site, results in many fewer defects, and produces a greater and ever growing variety of products."

"In old-fashioned production plants, managers jealously guard information about conditions in the plant, thinking this knowledge is the key to their power. In a lean plant . . . all information—daily production targets, cars produced so far that day, equipment breakdowns, personnel shortages, overtime requirements, and so forth—are displayed on andon *boards (lighted electronic displays) that are visible from every work station. Every time anything goes wrong anywhere in the plant, any employee who knows how to help runs to lend a hand."*

In a nutshell

New practices in manufacturing and management have saved vast resources and brought higher-quality goods.

In a similar vein

W. Edwards Deming *Out of the Crisis*
Martin Ford *Rise of the Robots*
Alfred P. Sloan *My Years with General Motors*
Frederick Winslow Taylor *The Principles of Scientific Management*
Ashlee Vance *Elon Musk*

CHAPTER 50

James P. Womack, Daniel T. Jones & Daniel Roos

You may think you know all about lean production and the famous "Toyota Production System," but it is worth being reminded of the spectacular success of the Japanese automobile industry. In 1955, Japan had less than 1 percent of world auto production; by 1990, when *The Machine that Changed the World* was published, Toyota had become half as big as General Motors, and was catching up to Ford in output. Today it vies with Volkswagen to be the biggest single vehicle producer.

Henry Ford famously wrote the entry for "mass production" in the 1926 edition of *Encyclopaedia Britannica*, but it was Toyota that wrote the rule book for a new kind of production system, based on "lean" principles, that dramatically increased quality while reducing waste and costs. James Womack, Daniel Jones, and Daniel Roos cast lean production as nothing less than a "machine" that changed manufacturing, and therefore the world.

Their book, which became a staple of business school curricula, was written in a time of angst about trade relations between America and Japan, when Japanese cars were taking increasing market share in the United States thanks to their quality, affordability, and fuel efficiency. Though it seems comical now, some western manufacturers believed that Japan's efficiency in carmaking came from its building of smaller vehicles. It was also thought that the new production methods coming out of Japan were a unique outcome of Japanese culture and political economy, and so were not applicable in the US, UK, or elsewhere. Womack et al. set the record straight: "just in time," lean manufacturing processes were successful not because they were the creation of the Japanese, but because they could be copied universally, and across all kinds of manufacturing.

The Machine that Changed the World was the outcome of a five-year global research effort (the International Motor Vehicle Program, coordinated by MIT) funded by carmakers and parts suppliers who wanted objective information on how to transform their own systems. It was updated in 2007, and after another decade still provides a good background to the revolutions in manufacturing that have taken place over the past 100 years.

The beauty and flaws of American mass production

The salient feature of mass production was not, as most people think, a moving production line, but rather *interchangeability of parts*. This was in total contrast to the craftsman-made automobiles that came before Ford opened his famous Highland Park plant, in which no two parts, because they were hand-tooled, were exactly the same. Complete interchangeability of parts meant that cars could be put together much quicker, saving huge labor costs. Instead of one fitter spending a day putting together all the pieces of one car, he moved around the workshop performing a single specialized task, often taking just minutes. With every part fitting well, and put in place by a fitter who knew his task inside out, productivity soared. The process got even quicker when Ford installed a moving assembly line, which forced a pace on workers and ended their wasting time by having to walk around the factory. These reductions in production costs allowed Ford to continually reduce the price of the Model T car. The more he could make, the cheaper they got.

Ford's system, however brilliant, ran up against economic and logistic realities. Inventory became a perennial problem (as it did with its big competitor, General Motors), given the costs of warehousing parts and cars. The other issue was too much production capacity. A plant may be set up to produce 2,000 vehicles a day, but what if a recession caused a slowdown in demand? The Ford and GM model was inherently flawed, the authors point out, because it begot "too many managers, too many workers, too many plants."

The mass-production system also had a worker problem. The system is set up so that professionals design products to be made in great numbers by unskilled or semiskilled workers, to achieve economies of scale. The result is that consumers get cheap goods, but "at the expense of variety and by means of work methods that most employees find boring and dispiriting," the authors note. The wages of Ford's early workers were high for the industry, but operatives were seen as disposable. From the production line employee's point of view, the work could be crushingly monotonous because there was little new learning and no career progression. The mass-production model meant a shift from "craftsman's pride" to human-robot labor.

In Japan, necessity breeds invention

In the wake of World War Two the Japanese government banned foreign direct investment in the motor industry and put up high tariff barriers. This spurred on domestic manufacturers to enter the industry, and they competed vigorously across the same vehicle classes. Yet they did not adopt the Detroit mass-production model, not least because there was no pool of immigrant workers, as in America. Unions were strong in Japan, and managed to get lifetime employment instituted. Toyota had to find ways to get the most out of their employees over an average 40-year working life. Instead of the interchangeability of American mass production's parts and humans, in Japan it made more sense to keep workers learning so they could add value.

Toyota could not afford the massive die presses that General Motors and Ford had, that could stamp out thousands of fenders or hoods, so came up with its own system of rapid die changes to produce body parts just in time for needs. The result was much less inventory needing to be stored (inventory would now be counted in minutes, not days) and quicker noticing of faults. Checking quality was not the job of some inspector, but the task of people actually on the floor. Instead of becoming a mindless automaton doing one task repetitively, groups of men were required to do many tasks, and to take responsibility for the quality of their work through *kaizen*, or continuous, incremental improvement. There would be no "rework," as in western production lines, in which mistakes were fixed by someone else down the assembly line.

Toyota also gave suppliers a much more active role in the design and engineering of parts. Instead of full vertical integration (that is, the owning of suppliers to ensure supply), the company simply took small stakes in each supplier, and often gave them loans. A *kanban* or "just in time" system developed in which Toyota and its suppliers worked as one big machine, the parts being brought to the factory as they were required. By eliminating inventories, the system put huge risks on production, because a whole assembly line could be stopped if a single part wasn't on hand. Yet Toyota's chief engineer, Taiichi Ohno, saw this as a good thing: it meant that every member of the system had to anticipate any problems beforehand. Without safety nets, they had to up their game.

Leaning in: a manufacturing revolution

This tight supply chain took years to get right, and the whole "lean" production system was two decades in the perfecting—but the world began to notice. What people prize above all in the car they buy is reliability, and

Toyota's system began to produce cars that were more reliable even than expensive German or British saloons. The European makers were still stuck in a craftsman mindset of fixing problems before a car was sent away from the factory, which ensured that their cars were expensive without necessarily being reliable; "craftsmanship" really meant waste. When Toyota released its luxury brand Lexus in 1989 it took the automotive world by storm because of its unparalleled build quality. Sales of Mercedes, BMW, Cadillac, and Lincoln suffered in its wake. The Honda Accord would have similar success: US models were built at the company's Marysville, Ohio plant along lean production lines, and the Accord became the biggest selling car model in the US, where previously it had always been a GM or Ford.

At GM, Alfred Sloan had pioneered the "yearly model," which offered trim and minor engine upgrades each year, but the mass-production system was in fact restricted to slow product development because of huge fixed costs in machinery and plant, which had to be amortized. Plants based on lean production, in contrast, were built for flexibility, allowing shorter model runs and greater variation within the model line. The lean system also encompassed sales. Instead of the factory churning out cars which it hoped dealers could sell, dealers became part of the production system. Toyota began making cars to order that could be delivered to customers in only two or three weeks, and Toyota salespeople even started making house calls to make the process of buying a car easier. Repeat buyer loyalty over a life-time was highly prized.

In sum, lean auto producers found they could combine the best of craft manufacturing and mass production: the same number of goods could be produced at low cost, but using the combination of more skilled workers and technology could produce things at greater variety, and make it a more interesting place to work into the bargain—if with more responsibility. In a lean factory, information and data is not hoarded by managers but available to all. The effect is that workers know how the factory is doing as a whole in real time, and whether it is meeting its production and quality targets. When something isn't right, everyone has an interest in finding out what went wrong and making sure it isn't repeated. Imagine the sense of owner-ship this provides, and the effect on quality and morale.

Just as Ford and GM's mass-production techniques encountered resistance when they were first transplanted outside America, because they disrupted existing ways of manufacture, so lean production, pioneered in Japan, met opposition in America and Europe because it challenged existing structures and institutions which had arisen around conventional mass production. If a new mode of production is brought in from another country, Womack and his coauthors note, it "tends quickly to let loose a nationalistic reaction." Their point is that you can't assume new production techniques will be automatically adopted in different places around the world just because they are more efficient. There are domestic political, social, and cultural factors that may end up weighing in favor of tradition and against efficiency. In America in the 1980s and 1990s, rather than trying to reform existing plants or shift to lean production, US carmarkers simply closed existing plants and opened new ones. It was better to start from scratch than try to fix outdated management or poor labor–company relations in an existing plant.

Final comments

In 1990, Womack, Jones, and Roos made a bold prediction that assembly line labor would mostly disappear by the end of the decade. In the afterword to the 2007 edition they admit their mistake, noting that automation has increased incrementally rather than taken over in factories. Why? "While robots are flexible and reprogrammable in theory," they point out, "well-trained production associates are more flexible and reprogrammable in practice," adding that Toyota "never automates unless absolutely necessary."

The biggest change since the book was written is the rise of China as a vehicle manufacturer. It has been the world's biggest producer for the last decade. In 2015, total world motor vehicle production was 90 million units, and 24 million were made in China (21 million cars, 3.4 million commercial vehicles). In the same year, US vehicle production was half that of China, followed by Japan at 9 million, Germany at 6 million, and then South Korea, India, and Mexico. Chinese makers include government-owned SAIC, which builds local versions of Volkswagen and GM cars under license, Dongfeng, which does the same for Honda, Nissan, and Peugeot, and Geely, and independent maker. These companies are focused on serving a massive, fast-growing market and providing it with autos at an affordable price. Add into the mix low labor costs, and lean production has not been a priority. However, with buyers becoming more discerning in terms of quality and variety, and wages increasing, the need to eliminate waste will change Chinese auto-making. Given cultural and political tensions between the two countries, China is loath to be seen to be copying anything "Japanese"—a resistance very reminiscent of American carmakers' reluctance to adopt in full lean thinking in the 1980s and 1990s. But market forces may eventually force China's makers to adopt lean systems, albeit "with Chinese characteristics."

James P. Womack, Daniel T. Jones & Daniel Roos
Womack was the research director of MIT's International Motor Vehicle Program, which coined the term "lean production." In 1997 he founded the MIT Lean Enterprise Institute, which he headed until 2010. His academic qualifications include a Ph.D. in political science from MIT and a master's degree in transportation systems from Harvard. With Jones he coauthored Lean Thinking: Banish Waste and Create Wealth in Your Organization *(2003).*

Jones, who has a B.A. in economics from the University of Sussex, was European Director of MIT's Future of the Automobile and International Motor Vehicle Programs. He founded Britain's Lean Enterprise Academy, which advances lean practices across various sectors of the UK economy including manufacturing, healthcare, construction, and retailing.

Roos was a director of the MIT Center for Transportation Studies, and a founding director of its International Motor Vehicle Program. He remains on its advisory board.

50 More Business Classics

By no means exhaustive, here are some other business titles, old and newer, that you may find inspiring, interesting or useful. At the end is a handful of good books on the future as it may affect business.

Entrepreneurship & Innovation

1. **Chris Anderson *The Long Tail* (2008)**
   Seminal title by a Silicon Valley entrepreneur which showed how the internet changed buying habits and the economy forever. Recently updated with new examples.

2. **Peter Drucker *Innovation and Entrepreneurship* (1985)**
   Innovation and entrepreneurship should be pursued systematically as a discipline, not as a whim. See commentary in *50 Economics Classics*.

3. **Katherine Graham *Personal History* (1998)**
   Born into privilege, Graham's life was turned upside down when her husband Phil committed suicide while at the helm of the *Washington Post*. With little business experience she took it to new heights. Played by Meryl Streep, Graham is immortalized in Steven Spielberg's *The Post* (2017).

4. **Tony Hsieh *Delivering Happiness* (2013)**
   Hsieh's online shoe business Zappos became successful through putting employee happiness first, and a desire to radically please the customer.

5. **Salim Ismail *Exponential Organizations* (2014)**
   We live in an era when new companies can harness technology to grow much faster than established peers, scaling up quickly by leveraging assets such as community, big data, and algorithms.

6. **Ingvar Kamprad *A Testament of a Furniture Dealer* (1976)**
   The IKEA founder's 16-page manifesto that calls for the elimination of waste and keeping costs to the bone so as to provide great design at a low price.

7. **Tracy Kidder *The Soul of a New Machine* (1981)**
   Pulitzer-winning account of a minicomputer company's work culture

of 100-hour weeks and the race to release a product. The technology has changed but manic tech industry practices have not.

8. **Ray Kroc** *Grinding It Out* **(1977**
   The story of Kroc's discovery of the McDonald brothers' burger place in California, and how he replicated the system across America. See *50 Success Classics* (2nd edition).

9. **David McClelland** *The Achieving Society* **(1961)**
   To understand entrepreneurship, you need to understand the psychological drive for achievement, argued Harvard professor David McClelland. Much of his research was in developing countries where he believed achievement motivation could be instilled.

10. **Sam Walton** *Made In America* **(1992)**
    The early days of Walmart and the principles that drove its massive expansion.

11. **Thomas Watson Jnr** *A Business And Its Beliefs* **(1963)**
    IBM's founder ascribes the company's success to culture and values rather than technology itself.

Management & Leadership

12. **Chester Barnard** *The Functions of the Executive* **(1938)**
    Before Peter Drucker and Jim Collins there was Chester Barnard, an AT&T executive and later public servant. He broke away from formal models of organization to describe what managers actually did and how they could become more effective.

13. **Warren Bennis** *On Becoming a Leader* **(1989)**
    Leadership is not "managing people," but self-expression, that is, taking on roles that allow you to be who you are in the most powerful way.

14. **Kenneth Blanchard and Spencer Johnson** *The One Minute Manager* **(1981)**
    Clarity about goals saves a lot of energy that can be deployed in other areas. See commentary in *50 Success Classics* (2nd edition).

15. **John Brooks** *Business Adventures* **(1959-69)**
    Tales from the American corporate and financial world that have lessons for today. Bill Gates and Warren Buffett both marked it as their favorite business book.

16. **Bryan Burrough & John Helyar** *Barbarians at the Gate* **(1989)**
    Two *Wall Street Journal* reporters' racy account of the battle for biscuit giant RJR Nabisco, the biggest takeover in history. Great insight into leveraged buyouts, junk bonds, and corporate greed.

17. **Jan Carlzon** *Moments of Truth* **(1987)**
    Carlzon turned around Scandinavian Airlines by introducing an extreme customer focus and flatter organizational structures. Every interaction between an employee and a customer is a "moment of truth" that adds up to success or failure for an enterprise.
18. **Ed Catmull** *Creativity Inc.* **(2014)**
    Over three decades at the helm of Pixar, Catmull emerged as a Disney of his time. He shows how to remove the barriers to creativity and great teams, with important lessons for all entrepreneurs and businesses.
19. **Jim Collins** *Built To Last: Successful Habits of Visionary Companies* **(1994)**
    Despite criticism by Daniel Kahneman of its "hindsight bias" and "halo effect," the 18 "visionary" companies featured in *Built To Last* are mostly still household names. Many of their competitors have not fared so well. Collins's *Good To Great* is covered in *50 Success Classics* (2nd edition).
20. **Peter Drucker** *The Practice of Management* **(1954)**
    The greatest tribute to Drucker is that much of what he argues for in this book, from creating objectives to good decision making, is now standard practice in organizations. Yet his easy style makes it an engaging read still.
21. **Henri Fayol** *General and Industrial Management* **(1916)**
    The first real theory of management, accepted wisdom for decades.
22. **Ari de Geus** *The Living Company* **(1999)**
    Organizations that last a long time and withstand crises have an organic approach to growth and put learning and people above profits.
23. **Elihu Goldratt** *The Goal* **(1984)**
    Now in its third edition, Goldratt's fable is a surprising page-turner expressing principles of organizational change. In short, have a single focus or aim for the enterprise, and identify all constraints or bottlenecks that get in its way. Eliminate them, and it will be hard not to be successful.
24. **Marshall Goldsmith** *What Got You Here Won't Get You There* **(2007)**
    Whether you reach the peaks of corporate life or not often comes down to eliminating character flaws and getting better at interpersonal relations. An antidote to *The Peter Principle*.
25. **Robert Greenleaf** *Servant Leadership* **(1977)**
    Leaders worth their salt are servants to some higher goal or other

people first, and lifted up to higher positions due to their contribution. A rather metaphysical approach to leadership, but influential.

26. **Andy Grove** *High Output Management* **(1995)**
   Lauded by Mark Zuckerberg and Ben Horowitz, the Intel supremo's book shows how to manage teams and performance in order to create things of value within certain time frames.

27. **Michael Hammer & James Champy** *Reengineering the Corporation* **(1993)**
   In one of the biggest selling business books of the 1990s, the authors called on businesses to examine all their processes and make them fit for the twenty-first century. The hard work required for "reengineering" separated the book from most management fads.

28. **Charles Handy** *The Age of Unreason* **(1989)**
   Constant change in an "age of unreason" can put us in a tailspin, but only individuals and organizations who are constantly learning will have the chance to create their futures, not just react to events.

29. **Frances Hesselbein** *My Life In Leadership* **(2011)**
   Hesselbein's 14-year term heading the Girl Scouts of America breathed new life into it, setting a great example of non-profit leadership. At 101 she heads a Leadership Forum in her name at the University of Pittsburgh.

30. **Frederick Herzberg, Bernard Mausner & Barbara Snyderman** *The Motivation to Work* **(1959)**
   Seminal research showing that people work for things other than simply money: recognition, responsibility, achievement, personal growth.

31. **Chalmers Johnson** *Miti and the Japanese Miracle* **(1982)**
   Johnson coined the term "developmental state" to describe countries like postwar Japan and Korea which combined capitalism with strong state guidance and support.

32. **John P. Kotter** *Leading Change* **(1996)**
   The Harvard professor's bible of change management, still core reading in leadership and organizational development programs and in companies seeking to instill an ethic of constant improvement.

33. **Bethany McLean & Peter Elkind** *The Smartest Guys in the Room* **(2003)**
   The rise and fall of Enron, a lesson in corporate egoism gone mad.

34. **David Marquet** *Turn the Ship Around* **(2013)**
   Written by a US submarine commander, this book provides inspiring lessons on cooperative leadership that are applicable in less dramatic work situations.

35. Richard Nelson & Sydney Winter *An Evolutionary Theory of Economic Change* (1982)
Orthodox economic theories of the firm as rational are wrong. Firms are more organic and irrational than we like to believe, driven by habits, routines, and culture.

36. Taiichi Ohno *Toyota Production System* (1978)
The Japanese engineer's articulation of his famed "lean thinking" and "just in time" practices that revolutionized manufacturing.

37. Rosabeth Moss Kanter *Supercorp* (2009)
The veteran Harvard management thinker tackles corporate social responsibility, showing how companies with a social conscience can prosper more than the average firm.

38. Laurence Peter & Raymond Hull *The Peter Principle* (1969)
People tend to get promoted to the level of their incompetence. For example, Donald Trump may have been good at business, but should he have been made president of a country?

39. Tom Peters & Robert Waterman *In Search of Excellence* (1982)
McKinsey consultants Peters & Waterman looked at 43 successful American companies which displayed eight common themes, from a "bias for action" to closeness to the customer. While some of the companies crashed and burned, leading many to question the methodology, many of their "exemplars" (a select group of 14 companies) are still going strong. This surprise bestseller democratized business thinking—it was no longer just for bosses, anyone could get interested about how enterprises succeed.

40. Jeffrey Pfeffer *Power: Why Some People Have It—And Others Don't* (2010)
Despite the trend to flatter organizations and collaborative work styles, Stanford business theorist Pfeffer argues that understanding power is still crucial to success in the workplace, and clear hierarchy is needed to get things done, as it always was.

41. Edgar Schein *Organizational Culture and Leadership* (1985)
Schein shows how to transform the abstract concept of culture into a practical tool that managers and students can use to understand the dynamics of organizations and change. Now in its 5th edition with updated case studies, Schein's book is used in leadership and business courses.

42. **Herbert Simon** *Administrative Behavior* (1947)
A polymath economist, Simon's theory of decision making took account of the "bounded rationality" of human beings and outlined practices to improve decisions within organizations.

43. **Matthew Stewart** *The Management Myth* (2010)
A former management consultant takes aim at his industry and its scientific pretensions, from Frederick Taylor to Tom Peters.

44. **Gillian Tett** *The Silo Effect* (2015)
Humans tend to hive themselves off into groups, but organizations only prosper and innovate when their divisional structures—silos—are broken down.

45. **James Surowiecki** *The Wisdom of Crowds* (2004)
Crowd platforms such as Wikipedia and Kickstarter have proven the wisdom that multiple perspectives can lead to dramatically better results. With great examples, Surowiecki's book heralded this paradigm shift and reminds business readers of the power of bottom-up decision-making and knowledge sharing in all enterprises.

Strategy & Marketing

46. **Seth Godin** *Purple Cow* (2003)
As people respond much less to advertising now, the only way you will stand out is by making a product or service that people talk about to their friends.

47. **Gary Hamel & C. K. Prahalad** *Competing for the Future* (1994)
The purpose of business is to shape the future of the market and industry, not just compete in it.

48. **Philip Kotler** *Marketing Management* (1967)
Marketing was once bolted on to the more "important" work of production. Kotler put it at the center of business, shifting the emphasis away from price and distribution to meeting customers' needs. The 14th edition (2011) is updated with new case histories and covers new trends and strategies.

49. **Michael Porter** *Competitive Advantage* (1985)
While Porter's *Competitive Strategy* (1980) provided a solid theory of business strategy, this title was about achieving results in practice, against multiple threats and competitors and with limited resources.

50. **Richard Rumelt** *Good Strategy, Bad Strategy* (2011)
Much of what passes as strategy is poorly formulated "strategic plans," or mushy "vision." Good strategy involves a diagnosis of the challenges facing the business and coherent action to make things right.

Further reading: The future
Erik Brynjolfsson & Andrew McAfee *Machine, Platform, Crowd* **(2017)**
Snapshot of an emerging world in which machine learning replaces much of the work of human minds, platforms become the new crossroads for the production and consumption of goods and services, and the world online "crowd" takes on many of the functions of companies.

Peter Diamandis & Steven Kotler *Abundance: The Future Is Better Than You Think* **(2012)**
Bestselling antidote to Armageddon scenarios which shows how an array of rising technologies in energy, food production, and medicine can plausibly eliminate scarcity within thirty years.

Alec Ross *The Industries of the Future* **(2016)**
Genetic code will become more important than computer code. Human data is the raw material of the information age as oil was to the industrial.

Klaus Schwab *The Fourth Industrial Revolution* **(2017)**
World Economic Forum founder ranges over the technologies shaping our world over the next 20 years, and the risks of society not keeping pace.

Final note
For commentaries on personal development/business crossover books such as Stephen Covey's *The 7 Habits of Highly Effective People*, Dale Carnegie's *How To Win Friends and Influence People*, Charles Duhigg's *The Power of Habit*, and Daniel Goleman's *Emotional Intelligence*, see *50 Self-Help Classics* (2nd edition) and *50 Success Classics* (2nd edition).

Credits

The following editions were used in researching the book:

Barnum, P. T. (2005) *The Art of Money Getting or Golden Rules for Making Money*, Project Gutenberg, http://www.gutenberg.org/ebooks/8581

Branson, R. (2005) *Losing My Virginity: The Autobiography*, London: Virgin Books.

Carnegie, A. (2006) *The "Gospel of Wealth" Essays and Other Writings*, edited and with an Introduction by David Nasaw, New York: Penguin.

Chandler, A. D., Jr. (1977) *The Visible Hand: The Managerial Revolution in American Business*, Cambridge, Mass.: Belknap Press.

Chernow, R. (1999) *Titan: The Life of John D. Rockefeller, Sr.*, New York: Vintage.

Christensen, C. M. (1997) *The Innovator's Dilemma: When New Technologies Cause Great Firms to Fail*, Boston, Mass.: Harvard Business School Press.

Clark, D. (2016) *Alibaba: The House That Jack Ma Built*, EPub edition, Ecco/HarperCollins.

Collins, J. & Hansen, M. T. (2011) *Great by Choice: Uncertainty, Chaos, and Luck—Why Some Thrive Despite Them All*, New York: Harper Business.

Deming, W. E. (2000) *Out of the Crisis*, Cambridge, Mass., and London: MIT Press.

Drucker, P. F. (1988) *The Effective Executive*, London: Heinemann.

Fisher, R., Ury, W. & Patton, B. (2012) *Getting To Yes: Negotiating an Agreement Without Giving In*, London: Random House Business.

Ford, M. (2015) *Rise of the Robots: Technology and the Threat of Mass Unemployment*, London: Oneworld.

Gerber, M. E. (1995) *The E-Myth Revisited: Why Most Small Businesses Don't Work and What to Do About It*, New York: Harper Business.

Hilton, C. (1957) *Be My Guest*, New York: Fireside.

Horowitz, B. (2014) *The Hard Thing About Hard Things: Building a Business When There Are No Easy Answers*, EPub edition, New York: Harper Business.

Isaacson, W. (2011) *Steve Jobs*, London: Little Brown.

Kaufman, J. (2012) *The Personal MBA: A World-class Business Education in a Single Volume*, London: Portfolio Penguin.

Kawasaki, G. (2004) *The Art of the Start: The Time-tested, Battle-hardened Guide for Anyone Starting Anything*, London: Portfolio.

Kay, J. (2011) *Obliquity: Why Our Goals Are Best Achieved Indirectly*, London: Profile.

Kells, S. (2015) *Penguin and the Lane Brothers: The Untold Story of a Publishing Revolution*, ebook edition, Melbourne: Black Inc./Schwartz Publishing.

Kim, W. C. & Mauborgne, R. (2015) *Blue Ocean Strategy: How to Create Uncontested Market Space and Make the Competition Irrelevant*, expanded edition, Boston, Mass.: Harvard Business School.

Knight, P. (2016) *Shoe Dog: A Memoir by the Creator of Nike*, London: Simon & Schuster.

Koch, R. & Lockwood, G. (2016) *Simplify: How the Best Businesses in the World Succeed*, London: Piatkus.

Leahy, T. (2012) *Management in Ten Words*, London: Random House Business.

Lencioni, P. (2002) *The Five Dysfunctions of a Team: A Leadership Fable*, San Francisco: Jossey-Bass/Wiley.

Levinson, M. (2016) *The Box: How the Shipping Container Made the World Smaller and the World Economy Bigger*, 2nd edition, Princeton, New Jersey: Princeton University Press.

Levitt, T. (2008) *Marketing Myopia*, Boston, Mass.: Harvard Business School Press.

McChrystal, S. with Collins, T., Silverman, D., & Fussell, C. (2015) *Team of Teams: New Rules of Engagement for a Complex World*, ebook edition, London: Portfolio Penguin.

McGregor, D. (2006) *The Human Side of Enterprise*, annotated edition, New York and London: McGraw-Hill.

Moore, G. (2014) *Crossing the Chasm: Marketing and Selling Disruptive Products to Mainstream Customers*, 3rd edition, New York: Harper Business.

Rath, T. & Conchie, B. (2008) *Strengths Based Leadership: Great Leaders, Teams, and Why People Follow*, New York: Gallup Press.

Ries, A. & Trout, J. (2001) *Positioning: The Battle for Your Mind*, New York: McGraw-Hill.

Ries, E. (2011) *The Lean Startup: How Relentless Change Creates Radically Successful Businesses*, ebook edition, London: Portfolio Penguin.

Sandberg, S. (2013) *Lean In: Women, Work, and the Will to Lead*, EPub edition, London: WH Allen/Random House.

Schmidt, E. & Rosenberg, J. (2017) *How Google Works*, ebook edition, London: John Murray.

Schroeder, A. (2008) *The Snowball: Warren Buffett and the Business of Life*, London: Bloomsbury.

Schultz, H. & Yang, D. J. (1997) *Pour Your Heart Into It: How Starbucks Built a Company One Cup at a Time*, New York: Hyperion.

Senge, Peter M. (2006) *The Fifth Discipline: The Art and Practice of the Learning Organization*, revised and updated edition, London: Random House Business.

Sinek, S. (2009) *Start With Why: How Great Leaders Inspire Everyone to Take Action*, London: Portfolio Penguin.

Singh, S. (2016) *Mythbreaker: Kiran Mazumdar-Shaw and the Story of Indian Biotech*, Noida, Uttar Pradesh: HarperCollins India.

Sloan, A. P., edited by McDonald, J., with Stevens, C. (1965) *My Years with General Motors*, New York: McFadden Books.

Stone, B. (2013) *The Everything Store: Jeff Bezos and the Age of Amazon*, EPub edition, London: Transworld.

Syed, M. (2015) *Black Box Thinking: Marginal Gains and the Secrets of High Performance*, London: John Murray.

Taylor, F. (2011) *Principles of Scientific Management*, Project Gutenberg, http://www.gutenberg.org/cache/epub/6435

Thiel, P., with Masters, B. (2014) *Zero To One: Notes on Startups, or How To Build The Future*, London: Virgin Books.

Townsend, R. (1970) *Up the Organization: How to Stop the Company Stifling People and Strangling Profits*, London: Coronet.

Trump, D. with Schwartz, T. (1987) *The Art of the Deal*, New York: Ballantine.

Vance, A. (2015) *Elon Musk: How the Billionaire CEO of SpaceX and Tesla is Shaping our Future*, London: Penguin Random House.

Welch, J., with Byrne, J.A. (2001) *Jack: Straight From the Gut*, London: Headline.

Womack, J. P., Jones, D. T. & Roos, D. (2007) *The Machine that Changed the World*, London: Simon & Schuster.

Acknowledgments

Gratitude to:

The key people at Nicholas Brealey Publishing in London, Holly Bennion, Ben Slight, and Louise Richardson, and to Giuliana Caranante and Melissa Carl in the Boston office, who help edit, market, and sell my books.

The Hachette Rights team in London, Joanna Kaliszewska, Grace McCrum, Nathaniel Alcaraz-Stapleton, and Flora McMichael, who ensure my work gets into other languages, is serialized, and goes into audio format.

The Hachette offices around the world, particularly in India, Australia, and Singapore, who get the *50 Classics* books widely distributed.

Thanks also to: Cherry, who put up with my working weekends and pushed me on to write the best book possible; Sacha, who offered a welcome respite from the writing on our usual great holiday in Burgundy; Oxford sangha friends, who give me a mental and spiritual refuge and a good laugh each week; and Tuanne, who discussed business ideas with me and was an inspiration as the book came together.

Finally, a thank you to all the living authors represented here for your valuable contributions to entrepreneurship, innovation, management, strategy, and marketing.

About the Author

The author of eight books including *50 Economics Classics* (2017), *50 Psychology Classics* (2017, 2nd edition), and *50 Success Classics* (2017, 2nd edition), Tom Butler-Bowdon is known for bringing important ideas to a wider audience. His *50 Classics* series has sold over 350,000 copies and is in 23 languages.

Tom is a graduate of the London School of Economics (International Political Economy) and the University of Sydney (Government and History). He lives in Oxford, UK.

Visit his website www.Butler-Bowdon.com